American Economic Growth and Standards of Living before the Civil War

A National Bureau
of Economic Research
Conference Report

American Economic Growth and Standards of Living before the Civil War

Edited by   Robert E. Gallman and
John Joseph Wallis

 The University of Chicago Press

Chicago and London

ROBERT E. GALLMAN is the Kenan Professor of Economics and History at the University of North Carolina, Chapel Hill. JOHN JOSEPH WALLIS is associate professor of economics at the University of Maryland, College Park. Both editors are research associates of the National Bureau of Economic Research.

The University of Chicago Press, Chicago 60637
The University of Chicago Press, Ltd., London
©1992 by the National Bureau of Economic Research
All rights reserved. Published 1992
Printed in the United States of America

01 00 99 98 97 96 95 94 93 92   1 2 3 4 5 6

ISBN (cloth): 0–226–27945–6

Library of Congress Cataloging-in-Publication Data

American economic growth and standards of living before the Civil War
    /edited by Robert E. Gallman and John Joseph Wallis.
        p.   cm.—(National Bureau of Economic Research conference
    report)
    Includes bibliographical references and index.
    1. United States—Economic conditions—To 1865—Congresses.
    2. Cost and standard of living—United States—History—19th
    century—Congresses.   I. Gallman, Robert E.   II. Wallis, John
    Joseph.   III. Series: Conference report (National Bureau of
    Economic Research)
    HC105.A64   1992
    339.4′7′0973—dc20   92-27972
                                                                        CIP

Contents

Acknowledgments

This volume contains the papers given at a conference held at the Cambridge Hilton in Cambridge, Massachusetts, on 20–22 July 1990. The conference was part of the Development of the American Economy program of the National Bureau of Economic Research. We are grateful to Martin Feldstein and Geoffrey Carliner for their support of the conference, and to Robert Fogel and Claudia Goldin for their encouragement and guidance.

We want to give an extra measure of thanks to Kirsten Foss Davis and the NBER conference department for their help with conference arrangements, which were spectacular. As editors we thank Ann Brown of the NBER and Julie McCarthy of the University of Chicago Press for their patient assistance with the editorial process.

Introduction

Robert E. Gallman and John Joseph Wallis

The Industrial Revolution and the Standard of Living:
What Are the Questions?

Scholarly concern with the early stages of modernization, and particularly with the effects of developments during the industrial revolution on standards of living, has had a long history. The European literature on the subject has been much more extensive than the American, and British experience has drawn particular attention. The debate over the standard of living during the British industrial revolution has been extended, complex, and acrimonious. The acrimony has proceeded in part from ideological differences between disputants, but also in part from misunderstandings arising out of the complexity of the problem and the variety of ways in which it can be approached. How should the topic be defined? Should the focus of discussion be on the strictly material, measurable aspects of development and the standard of living? Or should the effects of modernization on social organizations—the nature and functioning of the family, for example, or changing degrees of personal freedom—enter into it? If the focus is restricted to the material side of the question, how should one deal with such issues as changes in the length of the

Robert E. Gallman is Kenan Professor of Economics and History at the University of North Carolina, Chapel Hill. John Joseph Wallis is associate professor of economics at the University of Maryland, College Park. Both are research associates of the National Bureau of Economic Research.

This introduction has been reviewed by all of the participants in the conference from which this volume is derived. Particularly helpful comments were received from Stanley Engerman, Claudia Goldin, Thomas Weiss, and Jeffrey Williamson. The manuscript was also reviewed by Karin Gleiter, the Carolina Population Center, and Barry Popkin, Department of Nutrition and the Carolina Population Center, the University of North Carolina, Chapel Hill. Both provided helpful suggestions. The usual caveat applies.

work year, or the intensity of work, or externalities—positive and negative—surrounding industrialization? How should one distinguish events that are associated in time, but by chance, from those associated through causal links? And if we are to consider causal links, don't we have to work out a grand counterfactual, a comprehensive model that will show the consequences of a failure to industrialize, as well as the impacts of industrialization? All of these topics have been discussed in connection with the British case. Considerable ingenuity has been expended to obtain answers to a number of these questions, but it would be fair to say that the answers so far obtained are not accepted by all students of the subject.[1]

If we ignore noneconomic issues, externalities, changes in work intensity, and so forth, and consider only the standard measurements, the British debate suggests that there is still much room for disagreement. Real per capita national product measures can tell us about the opportunities for improved material well-being that have (or have not) emerged in the early stages of modernization. In the British case, these measures have been subject to frequent revision, and new interpretations persistently appear. Even if the fundamental series are finally settled on, and if they show improvements in per capita real income across the relevant period—which they seem to do—there remain questions as to how widespread the benefits of modernization were. If there were gains, were they used chiefly to expand the capital stock, or did consumption also go up? Were they absorbed by capitalists, or did labor share in the largess? Economic change involves shifts in the structure of the economy, with winners and losers. Who were the winners and who were the losers? one may ask. What happened to the size distributions of income and wealth? Were there shifts in the structure of wages? Furthermore, even if we look at a brief period—say two decades of intense change—the cast of economic actors will have changed significantly between the beginning of the period and its end. In what sense can we then speak of winners and losers? That X is better or worse off than his father (her mother) does not mean that X has gained or lost anything.

All of these topics have been treated at great length in the literature on the

---

1. There are two bodies of literature that are relevant, each too extensive to be fully cited here. A few references will have to suffice. The first body of literature has to do with national accounting concepts that have been designed with the object of producing measures useful in the study of economic growth. Simon Kuznets's two essays "National Income and Industrial Structure" and "National Income and Economic Welfare," chapters 6 and 7 of Kuznets (1953), raise all of the important issues. Kuznets (1952) contains an interesting effort to incorporate the value of leisure in the national product. The volumes produced by the NBER for the Conference on Research in Income and Wealth, especially in the early years of the conference but also more recently, contain much useful material; see, for example, Nordhaus and Tobin (1973). See also Usher (1980). The literature specifically on the standard of living during the industrial revolution is extensive and complex. For recent treatments, see Crafts, Mokyr, and Williamson (all 1987). A brief but comprehensive and thoughtful discussion is contained in Floud, Wachter, and Gregory (1990, chaps 7, 8). Finally, there is the insightful review and extension of the literature recently prepared by Stanley L. Engerman (1990).

British industrial revolution. The American discussion has so far been much less comprehensive, and fewer issues have been thrashed out. Various lines of work have been conducted, however, and the time is propitious to bring them all together and to see how coherent an account can be made. The essays in this volume do not take up all of the possible subjects described above. They treat economic development rather fully, including changes in aggregate inputs and outputs; they also take up the distribution of the rewards of development, and, at least indirectly, externalities. Some of these essays introduce new evidence, while others range over a field of research and pull things together for the first time. The volume opens up the topic and sets an agenda for research.

Conventional Indexes of Economic Development: Inputs, Outputs, Structural Changes, Income, Consumption, Wages, and Distribution

The story of the economic development of the United States in the six or eight decades before the Civil War that emerges from the pages of this volume is quite clear, certainly clearer than the comparable British story.[2] The supplies of inputs to the productive process rose very rapidly. Before 1800 the labor force and the capital stock sometimes grew faster than population, and sometimes a little more slowly. After 1800, however, the supplies of inputs typically grew at higher rates than did population; the rate of change of per capita supplies accelerated, and especially large gains were achieved in the last two decades before the Civil War (Weiss, Gallman).[3] The distribution of inputs among industrial sectors, regions, and types of economic activity steadily shifted in the direction of the more rewarding opportunities. For example, the highly productive industrial and commercial elements of the economy laid claim to larger shares of the labor force and the capital stock as time passed (Weiss, Gallman); workers gravitated to the West, where real wage rates exceeded those in the East, and the adjustment led to a convergence of regional wage rates (Margo); farmers changed the mix of their output in response to the promptings of the market (Rothenberg). These developments are reflected in the course of change of aggregate total factor productivity, which increased persistently (Gallman).

Productivity improved within northern agriculture and manufacturing, and in manufacturing, at least, productivity growth accelerated (Rothenberg, Sokoloff). The forms of innovation changed. Early in the period they were predominantly organizational adjustments that took advantage of the opportunities afforded by widening markets. Later, in the 1840s and 1850s, inno-

---

2. In what follows we focus on trends and virtually ignore cycles and long swings. Most of the papers follow the same plan, although a few (e.g., the one by Margo) take account of major short-term shocks to the economy.

3. All references that are not accompanied by a date refer to papers in this volume.

vations typically called for mechanization and capital deepening (Rothenberg, Sokoloff). In both instances, innovative activity—as measured by patent applications—closely followed the opening of markets (Sokoloff). There is the strong suggestion that profit opportunities encouraged innovative activity. Tools and machinery came to play much more important roles in production and in innovation (Sokoloff, Gallman). Between 1800 and 1860 the fraction of the real capital stock accounted for by land clearing and breaking fell by half, while the share represented by tools, machines, and other equipment doubled (Gallman).

These developments generated important and ever-growing increases in per capita income (Weiss). Americans were well off, by the standards of the day, as early as the late eighteenth century (Weiss, Steckel). Thomas Weiss shows that they were even better off than had previously been supposed. The rate of growth of real per capita income was somewhat lower than earlier studies had suggested, but it at least matched the rate recorded by the leading industrial nation of the period, Great Britain. That means that the American performance must have been one of the very best—perhaps the best—to be recorded during the six decades before the Civil War. Furthermore, the rate of gain persistently and markedly accelerated, so that in the last two decades before the war Americans enjoyed dramatic improvements in real income.[4] The aggregate economy was growing faster than any large economy had ever grown before.

Two features of Weiss's new series deserve special mention. First, as Claudia Goldin, the discussant for Weiss's paper, makes clear, the new income estimates are firmly based. These estimates will endure. Second, Weiss has worked with two alternate concepts of national product. One is the conventional concept, useful for making measurements that can be compared with standard estimates for other countries. The second incorporates elements of economic activity that are generally omitted from the national accounts. These elements consist of the value of home manufactures and the value of land clearing and breaking by the farm sector. As most of the papers in this volume show, the six decades before the Civil War encompassed the beginnings of the process of American economic and social modernization. For such a period it is important to have national product estimates of Weiss's second type. During this period new activities were arising and old ones were being displaced. Unless the declining activities—such as home manufacturing—are allowed to influence the measured rate of growth of the economy, an inaccurate account of the changing material circumstances of the society will be rendered.

The gains in income described by Weiss were widely shared. Real wage

4. There were also gains in real consumption per head in this period, according to the national income measurements. Compare the data on the real value of consumption goods flowing to consumers in Gallman (1966, 27), with data on the population of the United States in, for example, U.S. Bureau of the Census (1975).

rates rose throughout the nation, and free laborers everywhere participated in the economic improvement (Margo); slave laborers, however, may not have done so. Lee Soltow's work indicates that wealth and income distributions—arranged by size of holding or of income flow—changed little between 1798 and 1870. Soltow has given direct consideration to the lot of the very poorest free persons. The data are indirect, but his ingenious efforts squeeze useful matter from recalcitrant sources. He turns up no strong evidence of general deterioration in the lot of the poor. The process of industrialization generates forces that can lead to a widening of the distributions of wealth and income, and previous scholarship suggested that this was the American experience during the period here under discussion (Williamson and Lindert 1980). Soltow's findings contradict this position; according to Soltow, the benefits of growth were widely distributed, and income and wealth size distributions were fundamentally stable.

American diet improved in variety and quality, at least until the 1830s, and at least for the rich and those of middling status (Walsh). Evidence for the poor is too weak to permit firm conclusions, according to Lorena S. Walsh, but she believes the poor (free and slave) at least held their own. Since Americans were already extremely well-fed at the end of the eighteenth century, no marked increased in the volume of food (as distinct from its quality and variety) consumed per capita could be expected (Walsh, Steckel).

The sources on consumption for the years after the 1830s have not been well exploited as yet, but production data suggest that supplies of food were as generous in those years as before. For example, Walsh points out that the literature on widows' allowances has widows receiving 13–23 bushels of grain per year, in the years 1750–1830. She goes on to say that some of this supply must have been used in trade, since "the higher grain allowances include more than anyone was likely to have consumed." Data on grain production in the years from 1839 onward are abundant; they are to be found in the state and federal censuses and in the Patent Office Reports. This evidence indicates that grain production generally kept pace with population growth in the years 1839–79, and that per capita levels were as high as they had been in the years 1750–1830 (see tables 1–3).[5] The caloric content of grain supplies per capita was very high, especially when one recalls that Americans also consumed substantial amounts of meat and vegetables (Walsh).

Walsh believes, however, that distribution problems may have led to at least mildly deteriorating circumstances for the free poor, after the 1830s. In view of the extremely high levels of per capita net supplies of food in the United States in this period, it is difficult to imagine that the diet of the poor could have worsened by much. To suppose otherwise requires us to believe that

5. The widows' allowances refer to food for adults, whereas the data in table 1 have to do with net output per man, woman, and child.

Table 1   U.S. Outputs of Grains, Field Peas, and Potatoes, Net of Seed and Feed Allowances and Exports, per Member of the Population, Crop Years 1839–79

	Bushels	Daily Calorie Equivalents[a]
1839	16.3	1,843–2,539
1844	16.8	1,919–2,703
1849	15.0	1,698–2,463
1854	15.4	1,775–2,651
1859	16.5	1,953–2,784
1869	15.1	1,755–2,507
1874	16.1	1,882–2,891
1879	17.5	1,840–2,989

Sources: Population: U.S. Bureau of the Census (1975), ser. A-7, 1840, 1845, 1850, 1855, 1860, 1870, 1875, 1880. Outputs and calorie equivalents: see table 2.
Note: Excludes rice.
[a]Excluding milling wastes. See table 2.

substantial amounts of grain were wasted or somehow lost in the distribution network. No doubt the distribution system increased waste of certain types, but improvements in distribution surely reduced the waste that comes when trading connections between potential buyers and potential sellers are weak.

The volume and variety of household equipment owned by the middle and upper classes improved significantly. These improvements probably underlay changes in cookery, diet, and the exploitation of household space (Walsh). They brought with them higher standards of comfort and some economies. For example, the production of heating stoves increased dramatically; heating stoves made for much more comfortable living quarters, and much lower fuel costs.

Sources of Evidence

The conclusions described above are drawn from an exceptionally wide array of data types. At one extreme, Robert E. Gallman's estimates are constructed chiefly from aggregates that refer to major components of the economy and rest mainly on evidence drawn from sources such as the federal census and the federal direct tax of 1798. Lee Soltow employs the same types of sources but uses them to study distributions, rather than totals or averages. He is interested in observations for individuals and families, how they were arrayed in the cross section, and how the cross-section measurements changed as time passed. Thomas Weiss has made his labor force estimates on the basis of a meticulous analysis of census data, but at the state level, not the national or individual level.

Winifred B. Rothenberg employs community tax lists to work out information on the changing structure and productivity of the agriculture of various

Table 2   **U.S. Outputs of Grains, Field Peas, and Potatoes, Crop Years 1839–79**

	1839	1844	1849	1854	1859	1869	1874	1879
Panel A: Outputs, Net of Seed and Feed Allowances (millions of bushels)								
Wheat	72	84	87	104	151	241	310	399
Corn	70	99	115	162	158	146	249	404
Oats	37	45	44	47	52	85	82	125
Barley	4	4	4	7	12	20	24	25
Rye	14	11	11	9	16	13	13	15
Buckwheat	5	7	6	5	12	7	7	8
Peas & beans	4	5	6	6	9	3	8	6
Potatoes	52	58	55	60	92	120	108	146
Sweet potatoes	34	34	35	36	38	21	27	31
Total	292	347	363	436	540	653	828	1,159
Panel B: Outputs, Net of Feed and Seed Allowances, Exports[a] and Milling Wastes, Expressed in Daily Calorie Equivalents per Member of the U.S. Population								
Wheat	920	975	868	895	1,082	1,194	1,336	1,107
Corn	894	1,073	1,030	1,247	1,088	804	1,084	1,351
Oats	148	153	130	118	113	146	125	171
Barley	23	23	21	31	43	58	59	57
Rye	151	98	85	65	94	63	54	55
Buckwheat	35	42	32	24	47	22	18	19
Peas and beans	59	60	59	57	72	21	43	29
Potatoes	161	153	126	116	155	160	127	154
Sweet potatoes	148	126	112	98	90	39	45	46
Total	2,539	2,703	2,463	2,651	2,784	2,507	2,891	2,989

Sources: **Panel A:** Data underlying table A-2 in Gallman (1960, 46–48). **Panel B:** Estimates of the numbers of pounds of processed products that could be made from the bushels of output recorded in panel A were constructed. The conversion coefficients were taken from U.S. Department of Agriculture (1952, 39–42). In the cases of peas and beans, potatoes, and sweet potatoes, the products were unprocessed. The number of pounds of unprocessed products contained in a bushel, in each of these cases, was taken from the same source (33 [soybeans], 71). (The peas and beans reported in panel A are not soybeans but are likely to have been of a similar weight: 60 pounds per bushel.) The processed products chosen were wheat meal and wheat flour; cornmeal and dry hominy; oat flour; pearled barley; rye flour; and buckwheat flour.

The figures in panel B are based on wheat meal and cornmeal, and they underlie the upper-bound estimates in table 1. The milling loss rates for wheat flour and dry hominy are much greater; the conversion rates for these products underlie the lower-bound estimates in table 1.

The caloric contents of foods were taken from Nutrition Research, Inc. (1979, 200, 202, 204, 226, 230, 232): dry wheat meal, all-purpose sifted wheat flour, cornmeal, corn flour, oat flakes, light dry, pearled barley, light sifted rye flour, dark sifted rye flour, light sifted buckwheat flour, dark sifted buckwheat flour, potatoes baked in skin, and baked sweet potatoes.

Use of USDA coefficients (*Composition of Foods,* 1984, 1989), in place of the Nutrition Research figures, would have led to slightly higher estimates of the caloric value of the foods listed in this table. The export figures are from U.S. Department of the Interior, Census Office (1883, 5–7).

[a]Wheat flour, corn, and cornmeal.

Table 3   U.S. Outputs of Major Grains, Crop Years 1839–49

	1839	1841	1842	1843	1844	1845	1847	1848	1849
Panel A: Total Outputs (millions of bushesl)									
Wheat	85	92	102	100	96	107	114	126	101
Corn	378	387	442	495	422	418	539	588	592
Oats	123	131	151	146	172	163	168	186	147
Rye	19	19	23	24	27	27	29	33	14
Barley	4	5	4	3	4	5	6	6	5
Buckwheat	7	8	10	8	9	12	13	10	
Total	616	642	732	776	730	730	868	952	869
Panel B: Total Outputs per Member of the U.S. Population, (bushels)									
	36	35	39	40	36	35	39	42	37

Source: U.S. Patent Office data underlying Gallman (1963).
Note: For caveats, see Gallman (1963).

Massachusetts communities, and to understand the diverse reactions to the broadening of markets registered by different communities—reactions of both an economic and a political nature. Kenneth L. Sokoloff, making use of the federal censuses and the McLane Report, assembles evidence on manufacturing at the level of the firm. He also produces an index of innovative activity based on the numbers of applications made to the Patent Office. Robert A. Margo reports on wage rate data collected from an underexploited source, the pay lists of civilians working for the army at various posts around the country. The regional coverage of this data set is exceptionally wide, and this makes it an unusually valuable source.

Whereas the Weiss, Margo, Rothenberg, Sokoloff, and Gallman studies look chiefly at the resources available to Americans and the productive results they achieved from them, Lorena S. Walsh is concerned with the disposition of the final product. Her sources are extraordinarily diverse and revealing. The lines of work she synthesizes make use of probate records, widows' allowances, business and household accounts, cookbooks, and the proceeds of archaeological digs. Each of these sources provides a somewhat different perspective on the standard of life. Soltow employs an equally wide array of types of evidence to try to understand the circumstances of the free poor.

Unconventional Approaches to the Measurement of the Standard of Living

All of the papers that deal with economic growth yield very similar results: growth was going forward at a rapid and accelerating pace, and the distribution of income among income classes seems to have changed little. But Walsh points out that economic growth may very well have interfered with the access of the poor to adequate diet, the results of the income distribution studies to the contrary notwithstanding. With growth, natural sources of food derived from hunting and gathering (sources missed by the income studies) may have been reduced. She does not believe this was at all a serious loss in the nineteenth century—these sources had dwindled long before the beginning of the period under review. But systems of distribution depending on kinship may have deteriorated, with the expansion of market-directed activities, particularly after the 1830s, and the poor may have suffered thereby.

Unfortunately, according to Walsh, the period 1840–60 is one for which work on consumption is quite thin. Consequently, while we may know that nonmarket forms of distribution were attenuated during this period, we do not know the extent of the impact of this development on the poor. It is not simply a question of the importance of the kinship distribution networks and the extent to which they were destroyed by the market. There are also questions of the exact roles these networks played and the ease with which they could be replaced by other institutions. For example, networks that distributed fresh meat seem to have arisen in a setting in which fresh meat could not be stored for long and in which market outlets were inadequate. Under these circumstances, the Smith family might slaughter an ox and share the meat with the Joneses and the Browns, in the expectation that these families would reciprocate when it came their turn to kill a beast (Walsh). Or Smith might share with Jones and Brown, on the agreement that they would help Smith with his harvest, or provide him with firewood, or engage in some other trade. Smith might also use the slaughter of an animal as the occasion for dispensing charity to a poor relation, or giving a newly launched couple—say a son and his wife—a helping hand. With the opening of markets in fresh meat, Smith might find it simpler to sell off his excess production and handle his obligations to his kin and his need for labor by paying out cash. Did he remain as generous as before? Or did he become less generous? Or did his cash income lead to larger real disbursements? Did he tend to the needs of his poor relations? How far did the state supplant him in the charitable field? If the full impact of the rise of the market on the poor is to be understood, these are important questions to address.

Population gravitated to regions and economic sectors where incomes were high, and these movements raised average incomes. There were probably some associated costs. For example, did the shift from agricultural to industrial work change the length of the work year, or the intensity of the work, or the security of the work, or the extent to which the work was interesting? The literature of American economic history is filled with suggestions that the answers to these questions are that the industrial work year was longer, more intense, more insecure, and more boring. If, in fact, these assertions are correct—and if there were no fully compensating advantages—then the income and wage data overstate the true welfare gains achieved by economic growth in the decades before 1860. But whether they are correct has not been established. Here is an area in which additional scholarly work is called for, although the research problems are extraordinarily difficult.

For example, a very substantial part of the industrial labor force created in this period consisted of immigrants. It therefore makes little sense to compare industrial and agricultural work conditions in the United States alone, to gauge the income gains of industrialization, net of all costs of industrialization. The proper comparison would consider the lot of the immigrants in their home countries before immigration and their situations after their arrival in the United States, taking account not only of the work conditions of these people in these two sets of circumstances, but also their incomes before and after immigration. That is, a new kind of national income series is called for, one that is a hybrid of the incomes earned in the United States and the incomes earned abroad by those immigrants who entered the United States before 1860. Constructing such a series would be a daunting task. We mention the point mainly to indicate the scale of the difficulties involved when one attempts to work out the net income gains achieved by structural change. It should be clear, however, that the measured gains from structural change would probably be greater if the condition of immigrants before immigration were taken into account, than if it were not.

Immigrants affected the standard of living in the United States in other respects. The flood of immigrants in the 1850s apparently weakened labor markets, such that the real wage rate of the native-born stopped rising toward the middle of the decade (Margo). Immigrants were associated with the rapid expansion of American cities. Housing facilities were crowded, and the problems of managing water supplies and wastes outran the ability of political organizations to cope with them (Steckel). There were costs in terms of illness and discomfort that are not taken into account in the income statistics. It is not entirely clear whether we should view the costs resulting from diseases borne by immigrants as exogenous changes in the standard of living, having little to do with economic development, or endogenous changes, flowing from it. The choice between these two positions turns on our view of the motives of the immigrants. If they simply fled intolerable conditions at home—for example, the Irish famine—and fetched up in America as the only practicable haven, the former interpretation should be adopted: diseases were exogenous. If they were drawn by American industrial opportunities, however, the latter is the appropriate view of things: diseases were occasioned by modernization. But the distinction is, in a sense, an artificial one, similar to the distinction sometimes made in migration studies between push and pull forces. (See Gould 1978, especially 628–34.) In any case, regardless of the position adopted with respect to the causal links (if any) between development and the deterioration of the disease environment, some allowance for deteriorating city conditions should be made in assessing changes in the standard of life during this period. This assessment should be made in the context of the equilibrating changes in wage rates, as Jeffrey Williamson has suggested (Williamson 1981, 1987).

The standard of living was surely affected by the incidence of disease, and there is some evidence that problems of morbidity increased in this period (Steckel). Population growth, to the extent that it led to higher population densities, encouraged the spread of epidemics; overcrowded cities became breeding grounds for germs (Steckel). The great cholera epidemics, beginning in 1833, were brought to North America by immigrants. The yellow fever epidemic of 1853 similarly came from abroad. Furthermore, students of malaria in the United States believe that there was an efflorescence of the disease (especially in the West) in the antebellum years, which carried forward into the seventies. It came about, some scholars believe, because of the enhanced movement of people associated with economic development, the Civil War, and in particular, the westward movement (Steckel).

Certainly malaria was a common western disease. Mark Twain probably had it in mind when, in describing life in Hannibal, he said: "Bear Creek . . . was a famous breeder of chills and fevers in its day. I remember one summer when everybody in town had the disease at once" (Twain 1901, 211). In 1861 Anthony Trollope visited the United States and described the typical westerner: "Visit him, and you will find him . . . too often bearing on his lantern jaw the signs of ague and sickness" (1862, 128): "their thin faces, their pale skins, their unenergetic temperament" (133). "He will sit for hours over a stove . . . chewing the cud of reflection" (135). Western women "are generally hard, dry, and melancholy" (135). Then a telling comparison: Americans from the Northeast "are talkative, intelligent, inclined to be social . . . almost invariably companionable. . . . In the West I found men gloomy and silent" (394).[6]

Although the paper-givers and discussants—especially Steckel, Walsh, Main, Shammas, and Soltow—draw attention to these aspects of American life, they have not assembled direct measurements of the significance of each for the standard of living, measurements comparable, for example, to the income and real wage indexes. Nor have they attempted to judge the elements of gain from modernization that the income statistics ignore.[7] That is, we are not now in a position to compute the real American national product per capita, exclusive of the costs and inclusive of the benefits that are left out of account when scholars study economic change; we do not have a nineteenth-century Nordhaus-Tobin index. Steckel, however, reports on a measurement

6. A colleague, Karin Gleiter, tells us that Charles Dickens mentions what was clearly midwestern malaria in his novel *Martin Chuzzlewit.*

7. The benefits are often ignored. City housing for the poor was cramped, but on the whole city dwellers could more easily find anonymity and privacy than could people living in small villages, or even on isolated family farms. A greater choice of companionship, new forms of entertainment, and more abundant supplies of information were also available in cities. For centuries country living has been characterized as innocent but vulgar and brutal; city life, sophisticated but wicked. In the discussion of the effects of the transition to urban life during the early stages of modernization, frequently the adjectives *vulgar, brutal,* and *sophisticated* drop out, and we are left with innocent country folk braving the wickedness of the city.

device that captures some of the effects of these developments, although it does not show the sources of individual costs, nor can it be combined with the national income–style measurements.

New Indexes of Well-being: Height and the Concept of Net Nutrition

Steckel argues that measurements of human size—height and weight—are sensitive indicators of nutritional status. For example, the distribution of heights of adult males of a given cohort in a large population is a genetic phenomenon, but the average height will reflect the nutritional status of the cohort during the years in which it went through its important growth spurts, one in infancy, the other during adolescence. The changes in well-being of a given population may be studied, then, by observing the average heights of succeeding cohorts of men or women. The level of well-being may be judged by comparing the average height achieved by a population with the one that would have been achieved under ideal circumstances. (In practice, comparisons are made with heights of modern populations.)

There remain, however, important dating problems. The growth spurts of a cohort are separated by about fifteen years. If, for example, a cohort born in the late 1830s is shorter than the previous cohorts, the events that produced this result may have occurred as early as the late 1830s or as late as the mid-1850s. Although there is no published documentation on the topic as yet, biologists believe that losses in infancy might be made up in adolescence.[8] The second growth spurt period is therefore probably the more important for determining whether or not there will be stunting. If a cohort is stunted, then, we should examine the period when this cohort was in its midteen years, to find the source of stunting.

Nutritional status is a net concept; it takes into account both gross nutrition and the claims against nutrition exerted by the activities of the individual (for example, work) and by illness. For example, a cohort may exhibit relatively short heights if the gross nutrition of its members was relatively low during childhood, or if the claims against gross nutrition occasioned by work or disease were relatively high. If a nation's population experiences a decline in average height, the causes may be sought in a deterioration in diet, an increase in energy expended in work or other activities, or an increase in the incidence or virulence of disease. Height can be affected only if net nutrition is altered during the crucial phases of childhood growth, and if the deprivation is not made good before the end of the adolescent growth spurt. The growth spurt may be delayed by deprivation; if it is put off too long, the individual will be stunted.

It will be obvious, then, that not all of the cost factors discussed on the

8. Personal communication from Barry Popkin, Department of Nutrition, University of North Carolina, Chapel Hill. Popkin has in mind documentation based on longitudinal evidence. Steckel's cross-sectional study strongly suggests teenage catch-up among antebellum slaves.

previous pages will be reflected in height changes. For example, an adult who has achieved his final height and then undertakes work of an intensity that depletes his nutritional reserves may get sick, but he will not grow shorter. Nor will a child be stunted if he experiences an insult to his nutritional status (through illness or through a change in work regime) that is on a modest scale or is subsequently corrected by good nutrition. Height changes, therefore, reflect important, uncompensated (or incompletely compensated) shifts in nutritional status during childhood.

Height is a useful general indicator of well-being, and a valuable one because, unlike national income statistics, sources of evidence on heights are fairly widespread in time and space, and measurements are relatively easily made (Steckel). Nonetheless, height indexes are not substitutes for national income statistics; they report only on nutritional status, not on any other aspect of human life. Heights can fall while income and consumption per capita are rising, and vice versa.

American history provides several sources of evidence on height. Steckel reports on measurements drawn from two: military records and coastwise shipping manifests; the latter contain data on slave heights. According to these records, Americans achieved nearly modern heights by the late eighteenth century. They were then taller, on average, than Europeans, and the cohorts of free whites born in each decade down to the 1830s were all tall by modern standards. In the case of slaves, adult males were shorter than free males throughout, and the heights of cohorts born late in the eighteenth century actually declined. But that development was reversed, and the cohort of the late 1820s was within one or two centimeters of the heights of free white males. Heights of both free and slave males then began to decline, very moderately at first, and then more dramatically. The drop was especially sharp for the cohort born during the 1860s, but the decline continued thereafter, until late in the century (Steckel).

Steckel's results, then, represent an important qualification on the conclusions drawn by most of the other papers in this volume. The other papers describe a period of successful economic growth, during which the standard of living was probably rising. Steckel's paper suggests that in net nutrition, at least, there were some losses. His findings tend to be confirmed by the results Clayne L. Pope has obtained with respect to mortality (Pope 1992). Pope's sample shows that mortality rates cycled in the nineteenth century and, in particular, that period life expectation dropped importantly in the 1840s, 1850s, and 1860s. Period measures—measures of the life expectation of all cohorts alive in a given interval—pick up more clearly the impacts of the peculiar experiences of a short historical period than do cohort measures. Pope's work supports Steckel's findings that all was not well in the two decades before the Civil War.

This does not necessarily mean that people became worse off, on balance. Walsh describes poor Americans at the turn of the century sitting on the floor and eating their meals with their hands, straight from the pot. A cohort might gladly sacrifice, on average, a centimeter or so in height for a table, chairs, plates, knives, and forks. At the turn of the century, most people used fireplaces to heat their homes and cook (Walsh). By 1860, the total number of heating and cooking stoves produced in the United States in the previous thirty years was probably well in excess of twice the number of free American families.[9] Heating and cooking conditions must have improved enormously. These might be regarded as fair recompense for slightly shorter heights—if shorter heights and improved amenities were causally related; whether they would have been regarded as worth the three or four years of life that Pope finds were lost, on average, in the 1840s and 1850s is another matter.

How does one account for the decline in height that Steckel has reported? Steckel considers the possibility that gross nutrition fell but finds little reason to believe that happened. (See also tables 1–3, which indicate that nutritional levels remained high from 1839 through 1879.) A second possibility is that the urban crowding and environmental degradation that went hand in hand with industrialization led to a deterioration in the disease environment, with unfavorable results for net nutrition (Steckel). Easterners were typically shorter than southerners and westerners. The initial concentration of industrialization in the East might help to account for this phenomenon. Immigrants also were concentrated in the Northeast, and they no doubt made the pool of disease germs a richer brew. They also brought with them dietary practices based on conditions in the home country. They were themselves shorter than native Americans, and their children, raised on a traditional diet, may also have been shorter.[10] These are important considerations. There is one puzzle remaining, however. The effects of pollution, crowding, and disease must have fallen with particular force on the poor. If that is so, class differences in heights should have widened and the shape of the distribution of heights should have changed. In fact it apparently did not (Soltow).

No doubt other reasons could be elicited to explain the decline in heights in the East, particularly the urban East, but Steckel also found that western and southern cohorts were becoming shorter. The best explanation for this phenomenon seems at present to be that the disease environment became worse.[11] For example, cholera struck in 1833, 1849, and 1866 and quickly spread all over the country; in 1853 yellow fever killed one-tenth of the population of New Orleans. The timing is plausible; that is, these diseases hit the United

9. Inferred from Depew (1895, 2:361).

10. The entry of married women into the northeastern industrial labor force could have led to earlier weaning of children, with unfavorable consequences for net nutrition. But the number of married women in the industrial work force was so small that this practice—if it existed at all—probably did not have a detectable effect on average height.

11. This discussion of the disease environment depends on Ackerknecht (1945, 1965), Bilson (1980), Boyd (1941), Drake (1964), Duffy (1966), Rosenberg (1962), Toner (1873), and Wickes (1953).

States in the periods in which cohorts were apparently suffering deprivation. But cholera and yellow fever should probably not be implicated in the stunting of the population. They were too destructive for that. Death rates of the infected population ran from 50 percent to 90 percent. Infants and adolescents were not stunted, they were killed outright. In any case, victims of these diseases who recover usually do so in a relatively short period of time, so that even these people are unlikely to suffer stunting.

Malaria is a likelier villain, but not so clearly guilty as to warrant conviction. It is a recurring disease that can debilitate a population and can readily be associated with stunting. The problem is one of timing. The height data show that stunting began after the cohorts of the 1830s or 1840s and ended late in the century. But the disease was widespread very much earlier than this—for example, it was well-established in Illinois by 1760—and apparently became endemic in the West by the 1840s and 1850s. The movement of population during the Civil War may have given the epidemic form of the disease new life, but the disease seems to have stabilized again before the end of the period of stunting. The puzzle remains unsolved.

One of the most interesting features of Steckel's findings is that they follow very closely the results obtained by Floud, Wachter, and Gregory with respect to England (1990, chaps. 7, 8). That is, the English data show that heights peaked with the cohorts born in the 1820s and then fell from the 1830s to the early 1850s. The timing is not identical with the American pattern, but it is close enough to demand attention. Both countries were in the process of modernization in this period, but modernization had begun much earlier in England than in the United States and was much farther advanced in the years in which cohort heights were falling. The coincidence of height declines in the two countries suggests that the forces at work were international in their effects, and perhaps not closely tied to industrialization per se. There is the record of the international diffusion of catastrophic disease, and it is also well known that, in the period in which heights were declining, migration from Britain to the United States was increasing, ultimately to achieve very high levels.

It should be said, however, that Floud, Wachter, and Gregory do not take this position. They attribute the decline in heights in Britain to urbanization: in the early stages of industrialization, they say, real incomes rose enough to have a favorable effect on net nutrition and average height. It was only after the early stages had passed that the burdens imposed on the population by urbanization had clearly visible results.

Such an account will not serve for the United States, however, as we have seen. The declines in height took place in the countryside as well as the cities, and urbanization directly affected a much smaller fraction of the population in the United States than in Britain. It is possible, of course, that the British experience is to be explained by disease, occasioned by rapid urbanization, and that the British pattern was then transmitted to the United States by British emigrants. If that is the case, however, what were the diseases that played the central roles in this drama?

Conclusions

We began this introduction by saying that the story of development told in these papers is quite clear: Americans at the end of the eighteenth century were well off by the standards of the day—indeed, quite well off by modern standards, as well. Their incomes were high, and they were so well-nourished that they had almost attained modern heights. Economic development was under way, and it went forward at an accelerating pace. Income per capita rose faster and faster, and the structure of the economy shifted. The United States was in the process of converting its economy from one that was predominantly agricultural and commercial to one that would become predominantly industrial.

Associated with development, there was a pronounced and quite persistent improvement in certain aspects of the standard of living, interrupted occasionally, perhaps, by major shocks to the economy, such as the impact of the Crimean War on the prices of grains. These long-term changes were negotiated without producing major shifts in the size distribution of income and wealth. The gains from growth were widely shared. But there were also some costs and benefits to development that are not incorporated in the standard income, consumption, and real wage estimates. We do not as yet have measurements of them, and clearly a major task for future scholarship is to attempt to produce such estimates. In particular, we need to know more about the effects of structural changes on patterns of work, morbidity and mortality, and nonmarket networks for the distribution of output. The sources on patterns of consumption for the last two decades of the period before the Civil War are as yet underutilized. Walsh's paper describes many of them, sources that have been much more effectively researched for the years before 1840. Additionally, the federal and state censuses provide detailed information on the output of consumer goods, and the reports of the Secretary of the Treasury provide similarly detailed information on imports. We need more work along these lines.

The measurements of height yield a kind of incomplete gross index of the costs of development. Here also there are tasks for future scholarship. Specifically, can we be sure that it was development, per se, that produced the results that Steckel reports in this volume? If so, which aspects of development were responsible and how far was each responsible? Where did the burdens of development fall with particular weight? If development was not at fault, what did cause the unfavorable turn of events with respect to morbidity and mortality in the two or three decades before the Civil War? These are the questions that future scholarship must answer. The essays here have settled important issues and have set the stage for the next round of research.

References

Ackerknecht, Erwin H. 1945. *Malaria in the upper Mississippi valley, 1760–1900.* Baltimore: Johns Hopkins University Press.

———. 1965. Diseases in the middle west. In *Essays in the history of medicine in honor of David J. Davis.* Chicago: Davis Lecture Committee.

Bilson, Geoffrey. 1980. *A darkened house: Cholera in nineteenth-century Canada.* Toronto: University of Toronto Press.

Boyd, Mark F. 1941. An historical sketch of the prevalence of malaria in North America. *American Journal of Tropical Medicine* 21: 223–44.

Crafts, N. F. R. 1987. British economic growth, 1700–1850: Some difficulties of interpretation. *Explorations in Economic History* 24, no. 3: 245–68.

Depew, Chauncey M. 1895. *One hundred years of American commerce.* Vol. 2. New York: D. O. Haynes and Company.

Drake, Daniel. 1964. *Malaria in the interior valley of North America.* A selection by Norman D. Levine. Urbana: University of Illinois Press.

Duffy, John. 1966. *Sword of pestilence: The New Orleans yellow fever epidemic of 1853.* Baton Rouge: Louisiana State University Press.

Engerman, Stanley L. 1990. Reflections on the "standard of living debate": New arguments and new evidence. Paper presented at the Conference on Capitalism and Social Progress, University of Virginia, October.

Floud, Roderick, Kenneth Wachter, and Annabel Gregory. 1990. *Height, health, and history: Nutritional status in the United Kingdom, 1750–1980.* Cambridge: Cambridge University Press.

Gallman, Robert E. 1960. Commodity output, 1839–1899. In *Trends in the American economy in the nineteenth century,* ed. William N. Parker. NBER Studies in Income and Wealth, 24. Princeton: Princeton University Press.

———. 1963. A note on the Patent Office crop estimates, 1841–1848. *Journal of Economic History* 33, no. 2: 185–95.

———. 1966. Gross national product in the United States, 1834–1909. In *Output, employment, and productivity in the United States after 1800,* ed. Dorothy S. Brady. NBER Studies in Income and Wealth, 30. New York: Columbia University Press.

Gould, J. D. 1978. European inter-continental migration 1815–1914: Patterns and causes. *Journal of European Economic History* 8, no. 3: 593–680.

Kuznets, Simon. 1952. Long-term changes in the national income of the United States of America since 1870. In *Income and wealth of the United States: Trends and Structure,* ed. Simon Kuznets. Income and Wealth Series, 2. Cambridge: Bowes and Bowes.

———. 1953. *Economic change: Selected essays in business cycles, national income, and economic growth.* New York: W. W. Norton.

Mokyr, Joel. 1987. Has the industrial revolution been crowded out? Some reflections on Crafts and Williamson. *Explorations in Economic History* 24, no. 3: 293–319.

Nordhaus, William, and James Tobin. 1973. Is growth obsolete? In *The measurement of economic and social performance,* ed. Milton Moss. NBER Studies in Income and Wealth, 38. New York: National Bureau of Economic Research.

Nutrition Research, Inc. 1979. *Nutrition almanac.* Revised edition. New York: McGraw-Hill.

Pope, Clayne L. 1992. Adult mortality in America before 1990: A view from family histories. In *Strategic factors in nineteenth century American economic history: A volume to honor Robert W. Fogel,* ed. Claudia Goldin and Hugh Rockoff. Chicago: University of Chicago Press.

Rosenberg, Charles E. 1962. *The cholera years: The United States in 1832, 1849, and 1866*. Chicago: University of Chicago Press.

Toner, J. M. 1873. The natural history and distribution of yellow fever in the United States, from A.D. 1668 to A.D. 1874. In *Contributions to the study of yellow fever*, reprinted from the *Annual Report of the Supervising Surgeon, U.S. Marine Hospital Service* (1873).

Trollope, Anthony. 1862. *North America*. New York: Harper and Brothers.

Twain, Mark. 1901. *Life on the Mississippi*. New York and London: Harper and Brothers.

U.S. Bureau of the Census. 1975. *Historical statistics of the United States, colonial times to 1970: Bicentennial edition: Parts 1 and 2*. Washington, D.C.: GPO.

U.S. Department of Agriculture. Human Nutrition Information Service. 1984. *Composition of foods: Vegetables and vegetable products, raw, processed, prepared*. Agriculture Handbook no. 8–16. Washington, D.C.: GPO.

———. 1989. *Composition of foods: Cereal grains and pasta, raw, processed, prepared*. Agriculture Handbook no. 8–20. Washington, D.C.: GPO, October.

U.S. Department of Agriculture. Production and Marketing Administration. 1952. *Conversion factors and weights and measures for agricultural commodities and their products*. Washington, D.C.: GPO, May.

U.S. Department of the Interior. Census Office. 1883. *Report on the productions of agriculture. Report on the cereal production of the United States*. Washington, D.C.: GPO.

Usher, Dan. 1980. *The measurement of economic growth*. Oxford: Blackwell.

Wickes, Jan G. 1953. A history of infant feeding, parts III and IV. *Archives of diseases in childhood* 28: 332–40, 416–50.

Williamson, Jeffrey G. 1981. Urban disamenities, dark satanic mills, and the British standard of living debate. *Journal of Economic History* 41, no. 1: 75–83.

———. 1987. Debating the British industrial revolution. *Explorations in Economic History* 24, no. 3: 269–92.

Williamson, Jeffrey G., and Peter H. Lindert. 1980. *American inequality: A macroeconomic history*. New York: Academic Press.

1   U.S. Labor Force Estimates and Economic Growth, 1800–1860

Thomas Weiss

The level and trend of prosperity in the period before the Civil War has been of long-standing interest. Contemporaries were of course concerned about their economic status and its uncertainty, as well as the path that lay ahead. Because the period was crucial to the long-term development of the United States, many scholars have examined it, some hoping to uncover the determinants of the economic transformation, others wishing simply to better understand the country's past.

According to some scholars, America began the nineteenth century as a poor country, and the prospects did not appear bright. "The man who in the year 1800 ventured to hope for a new era in the coming century, could lay his hand on no statistics that silenced doubt" (Adams 1955, 12). By 1840, on the other hand, a contemporary visitor could report that "in no country, probably, in the world is the external condition of man so high as in the American Union. . . . Labourers [in America] are rich compared with the individuals in the same class in Europe."[1]

While there are several dimensions to that "external condition," or in more modern parlance the standard of living, a key indicator is output per capita. With that quantitative evidence the nation's economic status could be as-

Thomas Weiss is professor of economics at the University of Kansas and a research associate of the National Bureau of Economic Research.

This paper has benefited from the comments of Lou Cain, Stan Engerman, Peter Fearon, Claudia Goldin, John McCusker, Kerry Odell, Joshua Rosenbloom, and the editors of the volume. The work was financed in part by the National Science Foundation (No. SES 8308569). This research is part of the NBER's program, Development of the American Economy. Any opinions expressed are mine and not those of the NBER.

1. By external condition was meant material well-being or wealth, as opposed to the internal nature of the human mind. The latter was the chief interest of the author, phrenologist George Combe. (The quotation comes from his 1841 work, *Notes on the United States of North America during a Phrenological Visit*, reprinted in Bode 1967, 294.)

sessed, its progress charted. There have been many attempts to do so, including the notable early efforts of Ezra Seaman, who generated national income estimates covering 1840, 1850, and 1860.[2] Those contemporary efforts, however, did not provide evidence about the changes that occurred before 1840. Seaman's works are consistent enough that we can roughly gauge the path of change over the years he examined, but we have little before that.

More systematic quantitative analysis of the period began in 1939 with Robert Martin's estimates of national income, which presented a controversial picture of change from 1799 to 1840. In his view, the American economy was no better off in 1840 than it had been near the end of the eighteenth century. During the intervening years the country had experienced substantial prosperity, but subsequently lost it. While he gave the first fairly complete statistical picture of the economy, he did not describe adequately how he constructed that particular course of events, and his estimates have been the target of much criticism and his conclusions the subject of much debate.

Simon Kuznets (1952) staked out the first opposing view, arguing that Martin's figures were implausible in light of the economy's shift out of agriculture and its westward movement. Given these reallocations of resources to more productive uses, the economy must have experienced growth. While Kuznets did not provide alternative estimates, his view was that per capita income must have risen by at least 19 percent between 1800 and 1840.[3] William Parker and Franklee Whartenby (1960) raised doubts about both Martin's and Kuznet's calculations. Their argument was that agricultural productivity may have declined, which would have outweighed the other favorable effects pushing up per capita income. Douglass North (1961) questioned the Parker-Whartenby point about agricultural productivity, but still concluded that there was little growth before 1840. He argued that the economy moved with the fortunes of international trade; there were fluctuations and periods of substantial growth, especially before 1807, but overall per capita income in 1840 was probably lower than it had been in 1799. George Taylor took a longer perspective, describing change from 1607 to 1860. For this critical period he concluded that "output per capita over the years 1775 to 1840 improved slowly if at all. . . . the average for 1836–1840 was at best not much higher than that for the prosperous years around the beginning of the century" (1964, 427, 440).

The matter is still not settled despite continued efforts to fill in the blanks of the empirical record, and the years before 1840 are referred to repeatedly as a "statistical dark age." One of the more imaginative attempts to enlighten the

2. Seaman's (1852, 1868) estimates are not completely in accord with more modern definitions of national output and appear to underestimate the level of the nation's output. See Gallman (1961) for an assessment of Seaman's work, as well as that of Tucker and Burke.

3. This increase reflects just the rise in the participation rate and the shift of the work force from agricultural to nonagricultural industries. Kuznets also argued that per worker productivity probably increased so the rise in per capita income would have been even larger (1952, 221–39).

picture is that of Paul David, who produced what he termed controlled conjectures or conjectural estimates of growth.[4] His conjectures rest heavily on two underlying series, the Towne and Rasmussen series on farm gross product and the Lebergott estimates of the labor force and its sectoral distribution.[5] The output series in turn rests on the key assumption that in the years before 1840 much of agricultural output increased at the same rate as population.[6] That is, output per person remained constant. While there are good reasons to challenge this, it has served as a useful approximation, and can continue to until enough new evidence on the relationships between height, nutrition, and diet is amassed.[7] The estimates of gross domestic product per capita presented later in this paper rely on this farm output series.[8]

The other pillar of the controlled conjectures, the labor force series, has been revised with important implications for our understanding of the American past. The chief purpose of this paper is to present these new figures, although the bulk of that description is contained in the appendix. The body of the paper focuses on the substantive consequences of these revisions on agricultural productivity change and on the conjectural estimates of economic growth in the years before 1840.

A comparison of the Lebergott series and the new one is presented in table 1.1. The total labor force figures have been changed very little, but the composition has been altered substantially. The new farm figures are higher than the previous ones in the later decades of the period by a fairly uniform per-

4. Diane Lindstrom constructed a different set of hypothetical figures based on the likely values of the elasticity of demand. She first estimated growth in the Philadelphia area, and subsequently extended the procedure to the nation, making use of Poulson's data on commodity output. She found that growth between 1810 and 1840 "probably occurred at the higher end of the .53 to 1.01 percent per annum range" (1983, 689). Her work also contains useful discussions of the various estimates for the period.

5. For ease of exposition I shall refer to the Lebergott series. Lebergott (1966) developed the estimation procedures and produced the initial estimates, while David (1967) revised some of the figures, especially those for 1800. There is now very little difference between the two series. The biggest discrepancy was in the estimate for 1800, but Lebergott now accepts David's revision (Lebergott 1984, 66). David had adjusted Lebergott's slave labor estimate in 1820, 1840, and 1860, but subsequent investigation indicated the correction was unnecessary (Weiss 1986b).

6. Approximately 90 percent of the estimate of farm gross product for the years 1800 to 1830 rests on this premise. Towne and Rasmussen were dissatisfied with having to make this assumption because it implied stagnant agricultural technology and productivity. At the same time, they believed that productivity did not advance much before 1840, and so the assumption may not have done great injustice to the true trend. They did, however, caution that "small variations in the estimates of gross farm product per worker from decade to decade during 1800–40 should not be considered significant" (1960, 257).

7. That evidence so far indicates a decline in stature among those born between 1835 and 1870, suggesting that those cohorts suffered nutritional deficiencies. This implies that, among other things, food output and consumption per capita may have declined after 1835 (Fogel 1986; Komlos 1987). The exact timing of this decline, its consequences for consumption and output, and the relationship of those declines to the census year's figures have yet to be established.

8. Since David's conjectural estimates rest on this series, its use here highlights the impact of the new labor force figures. As indicated in the notes to table 1, however, I have made some minor adjustments to the Towne and Rasmussen figures.

Table 1.1   **Estimates of the Total and Farm Labor Force, United States, 1800 to 1860**

Year	Total Labor Force (thousands of workers)		Farm Labor Force (thousands of workers)		Farm Shares (%)	
	Lebergott	Weiss	Lebergott	Weiss	Lebergott	Weiss
1800	1,680	1,712	1,400	1,274	83.3	74.4
1810	2,330	2,337	1,950	1,690	83.7	72.3
1820	3,135	3,150	2,470	2,249	78.8	71.4
1830	4,200	4,272	2,965	2,982	70.6	69.8
1840	5,660	5,778	3,570	3,882	63.1	67.2
1850	8,250	8,192	4,520	4,889	54.8	59.7
1860	11,110	11,290	5,880	6,299	52.9	55.8
	Average Annualized Rates of Growth					
1800–1810	3.32	3.16	3.37	2.87	0.05	−0.29
1810–20	3.01	3.04	2.39	2.90	−0.60	−0.13
1820–30	2.97	3.09	1.84	2.86	−1.09	−0.22
1830–40	3.03	3.07	1.87	2.67	−1.12	−0.38
1840–50	3.84	3.55	2.39	2.33	−1.40	−1.18
1850–60	3.02	3.26	2.67	2.57	−0.35	−0.67
1800–1820	3.17	3.10	2.88	2.88	−0.28	−0.21
1820–40	3.00	3.08	1.86	2.77	−1.10	−0.30
1840–60	3.43	3.41	2.53	2.45	−0.88	−0.92
1800–1840	3.08	3.09	2.37	2.82	−0.69	−0.26
1800–1860	3.20	3.19	2.42	2.70	−0.75	−0.48

Sources: Lebergott (1966, table 1; 1984, 66); and the Appendix below.

Note: David's estimates are identical with Lebergott's in the years 1810, 1830, and 1850. In other years, the differences between the David and Lebergott figures are small. David's total labor force estimates (in thousands) are 1,700 in 1800, 3,165 in 1820, 5,707 in 1840, and 11,180 in 1860; the farm figures in those respective years are 1,406, 2,500, 3,617, and 5,950 (David 1967, appendix table 1).

centage; 7 percent in 1840, 8 in 1850, and 6 in 1860. While the levels of the two series differ, they show roughly the same growth over the period, as well as over each of the two decades. In sharp contrast, the revised estimates for the opening decades of the century are below the previous figures by approximately 10 percent in 1800 and 1820 and 15 percent in 1810. In spite of these disparities, the two series show very similar changes over the earliest twenty-year period—the farm labor force increased at 2.88 percent per year.[9] The most striking difference shows up in the years 1820 to 1840, over which time the new series increased at a rate of 2.77 percent per year, in contrast to the

9. There is, however, a noticeable difference in the growth over each of the decades. The Lebergott figure increases quite rapidly in the first decade and then much slower; my estimate shows about the same percentage increase in each of the two decades. The Lebergott series shows a small increase in the farm share of the labor force in the first decade of the century.

1.86 percent rate in the old series. The changes by decade during this subperiod are equally disparate.

An overall assessment of the two alternative series, based on comparisons between the rates of decline of the farm labor force share and of the rural population share, suggests that the new series is the more plausible.[10] As can be seen in table 1.1, the farm share declined at about the same rate in each series over two of the twenty-year subperiods, 1800 to 1820 and 1840 to 1860. During those intervals the rural share of the population declined at annual rates of 0.06 and 0.57 respectively, somewhat slower than the farm shares in both periods. In the period 1820 to 1840, however, the comparative results diverge noticeably. The rural population share declined by 0.20 percent per year, and while the Weiss series declined slightly faster at 0.30 percent per year, the Lebergott farm share declined by 1.10 percent per year. This greater conformity between changes in the rural population and the farm labor force in my series provides some confidence in the new figures.[11]

The erratic pattern of growth in Lebergott's farm labor force produces its corollary in the growth of labor productivity. A striking feature of that series is that output per worker in agriculture grew at its fastest rates of the century between 1820 and 1840.[12] Over the antebellum period, output per worker increased by 47 percent, or about $70 (in 1840 prices), with two-thirds of the increase occurring during this twenty-year stretch.[13] With the new labor force figures, agricultural productivity showed a healthy advance over this period, but not a record-setting performance.[14] Of the $43 increase in output per worker that took place between 1800 and 1860, only about one-third ($15) occurred during the middle twenty years.[15]

10. Gallman was suspicious of the Lebergott series because it showed changes in the farm labor force that seemed inconsistent with the changes in the rural population. The disparity seemed greater in the antebellum period, when the farm share of the labor force declined by substantially more percentage points than the rural population share. Gallman focused on the changes between 1800 and 1850, noting that "the agricultural share of the work force fell by 28 percentage points between 1800 and 1850, at a time when the share of the rural population in total population was declining by only 9 points" (1975, 38).

11. Over the entire century the new series shows a much higher correlation between the change in the farm share and in the rural population share on a decade-to-decade basis. The correlation coefficient using the new series is .91, while with the Lebergott figures the coefficient is only .24.

12. The average rate of productivity advance between 1820 and 1840 depends on the definition of farm output. Using the revised figures for farm gross product, narrowly defined, the rate was 1.33 percent per year, the highest of any twenty-year period, or any decade, in the century. Using the original Towne and Rasmussen figures the rate of advance was 1.54 percent, also the highest of the century.

13. These calculations are based on the revised farm gross product series, narrowly defined (see Weiss 1990). With the original Towne and Rasmussen figures, output per worker increased by 52 percent, or $75 dollars, with 70 percent of the increase occurring between 1820 and 1840.

14. Using the revised figures for farm gross product, narrowly defined, the rate was 0.44 percent per year, one of the highest rates for the antebellum period, but below that of the postbellum decades. Using the original Towne and Rasmussen figures the rate of advance was 0.65 percent.

15. These calculations are based on the revised farm gross product series, narrowly defined (see Weiss 1990). With the original Towne and Rasmussen figures, output per worker increased by 30 percent, or $48 dollars, with 45 percent of the increase occurring between 1820 and 1840.

Productivity increases in agriculture are an important determinant of the conjectural estimates of per capita income, and thus shape our view of changes in the standard of living before the Civil War. As will be seen, the two productivity series generate noticeably different income paths. In turn, the farm labor force is key to our understanding of the period before 1840, and it is thus worthwhile to examine these new figures. The appendix describes the figures in great detail, but a few aspects of the estimates must be highlighted here.

1.1   The Labor Force Estimates

My estimation followed Lebergott's approach but was executed at the state and regional level. In concept and coverage the new total and farm labor force estimates are similar to his. The total labor force is the sum of the workers in five population components; free males aged 16 and over, free females aged 16 and over, free males aged 10 to 15, free females aged 10 to 15, and slaves aged 10 and over. Each estimate of the number of workers is the product of the group's population and its specific participation rate. The levels and changes in the total labor force are nearly identical in the two series, with the figures differing by 2 percent or less in every year (see table 1.1).[16] The more noticeable differences in the two series show up in the distribution of workers between the farm and nonfarm industries. These differences are not always in the same direction; the new figures are above the old ones in the later decades of the period but below them in the opening decades of the century. Three things account for most of the differences.

In all years the new estimates incorporate a smaller number of slaves in farming. Lebergott estimated the number of slaves engaged in farming by assuming that 95 percent of the slave population aged 10 and over lived in rural areas, 87 to 90 percent of which were engaged in farming.[17] I used the county-level data on employment and population for 1820 and 1840 to estimate that roughly 75 percent of the rural slave population aged ten and over was engaged in farming. These shares were assumed to hold for the other antebellum years as well.[18] The differences are substantial; in 1850 for example, my figure is smaller than Lebergott's by 329,000.[19]

16. These minor differences arise from the use of slightly different participation rates for certain demographic components, and because I used state-specific participation rates for each group. As the relative size of the various states' populations changed over time, the national average participation rate for each age-sex group fluctuated and diverged slightly from the constant national figure used by Lebergott.

17. Lebergott indicated that he intended to allocate only 87 percent of the rural adult slaves to farming, but in the execution the 90 percent figure was used. In 1860, he used a different figure altogether, namely, the participation rate for free males aged 15 and over.

18. The 1840 share was estimated to be .741, that for 1820 was .769. The 1840 figure was used to estimate the slave farm workers in 1850 and 1860; the 1820 figure was used in other years.

19. The differences in our estimates of the number of slaves engaged in farming amounts to about 7 percent of Lebergott's farm labor force, except in 1800 and 1860 when the figures are 3.8 and 5.1 percent (see Weiss 1991 for details).

The revised figures accord better with other evidence about the nonfarm activities in which slaves were engaged.[20] With the smaller share engaged in farming, nearly a fifth of the *rural* slave labor force worked at nonfarm activities. This is in stark contrast to Lebergott's estimate that virtually no rural slaves worked at nonfarm occupations, a figure much too low, given all the other activities that took place on the plantation and in rural areas more generally.[21]

In 1850 and 1860 this downward bias is more than offset by the addition to farming of workers who had reported their occupation as "laborer, not otherwise specified." Researchers have long recognized that in the postbellum period this census category included many workers who were engaged in farming, but previous estimates for the antebellum period had placed all of them in nonfarm industries, apparently because the large numbers of slaves in farming masked the problem at the national level. A careful examination of the state data, and the location of many of these workers in rural areas, argues for the assignment of many of them to farming. In particular, when one looks at just the free states, where slavery could not distort the picture, it is evident that some of these laborers must have been employed in farming (Weiss 1987c).

My allocation of some of these workers to farming raises that sector's labor force by 630,000 workers in 1850 and 582,000 in 1860. These are not trivial amounts—making up 13 percent of the farm labor force in 1850 and 9 percent in 1860—but seem clearly called for. Without such laborers, the ratio of the farm work force to the rural population in the *free states* was .15 in 1850 and .16 in 1860, substantially below the average of .192 in the years 1870 through 1910. With the addition of these workers, the 1850 and 1860 ratios are .196 and .189, respectively, very much in line with the behavior of the ratio in the postbellum years.

The third major reason the new estimates differ from the older ones is because of varying judgments about how to correct deficiencies in the census counts for 1820 and 1840. I assessed those censuses in order to determine which industries were covered, which age and sex portions of the population were included in the counts of workers, and which state figures were in need of revision (Weiss 1987a, 1988). Neither census covered all industries, but both reported figures for agriculture and for certain other commodity-producing industries. There appears, however, to be some difference in age and sex coverage. While both censuses tried to report on all workers aged ten and over, including slaves, they did so imperfectly, and the accuracy and com-

---

20. Blodget's estimates for 1805 imply that only 75 percent of the slaves were engaged in farming, with 300,000 being "slaves to planters" and 100,000 being "variously employed" (1806, 89).

21. A useful collection of pertinent articles can be found in James Newton and Ronald Lewis (1978). See also Robert Starobin (1970) and John Olson (1983). Olson's sample data from plantation and probate records indicate that between 11 and 27 percent of the rural slaves were engaged in nonfarm activities. The figure derived from the county-level data falls securely in this range.

pleteness of the counts varied by county and state.[22] In principle, however, they provide a count of the entire farm work force in 1840, and the bulk of it in 1820. In both years, the worst anomalies in the census figures could be identified and corrected.[23]

The revisions were carried out by examining the county and subdivision data in much the same manner as had been done by Lebergott (1966). The census statistics included many slave workers, but not all, so the farm worker totals in most slave states had to be revised. Fortunately, the reported figures in a large number of southern counties were accurate and could be used to revise those in other counties (Weiss 1987a). The corrections and additions to the census counts of farm workers amounted to 206,000 in 1820 and 160,000 in 1840, increases of 11.2 percent and 4.4 percent, respectively.[24]

1.2   Substantive Results

We can now turn to the substantive issues about the standard of living in the United States before 1860. The effect of the labor force revisions on the conjectural estimates of growth in the years before 1840 can be seen in table 1.2.[25] The old series is presented there along with several new versions. The figures in variant A were constructed to show the consequences of only the labor force revisions on the conjectural view of the economy's performance. The variant B estimates were refined in several ways, but still rest heavily on the productivity advances emanating from a conventional, narrowly defined agricultural output series. Variant B, however, drops the assumption that nonfarm productivity change grew at the same rate as farm productivity, and makes use of some minor adjustments to the Towne and Rasmussen estimates of farm gross product in the years 1800 to 1830.[26] The final variant incorporates an addi-

22. In both years the statistics in the slave states were flawed, and in 1820 the enumerations of male workers aged 10 to 15 were low in many states. It appears that males aged 10 to 15 were included in the 1820 census figures of the New England states but were not always counted elsewhere.

23. The 1820 census statistics were supplemented by estimates of the missing components, females aged 16 and over and free males aged 10 to 15 years. No estimate of female farm workers aged 10 to 15 was made for 1820 or for any other antebellum year. Some of these workers may be included in the 1840 and 1860 census counts, but the number must be very small. The available evidence for the postbellum period shows very few such workers.

24. My assessment of the 1840 census indicated that the reported labor force in the covered industries was low by about 300,000 workers. My adjustment procedures, however, produced a correction of only 206,000 workers, 160,000 of which were in farming. By comparison, Lebergott reduced the census count of farm employment by 148,000. Richard Easterlin, in his original examination of the 1840 census, revised the count of farm workers upward by 104,000, although in some states in the Northeast he reduced it (1960, 127). In a subsequent work he accepted Lebergott's farm totals, and thus implicitly the notion that the census figure was too high, but gave no reasons for his change of mind (1975, 110).

My adjustments reported here for 1820 and 1840 include the additions of male workers aged 10 to 15 and females aged 16, and corrections for errors of addition in the census totals.

25. The details of these conjectural estimates are presented in Weiss (1989).

26. In particular, I have revised the value of hog and cattle production in the years 1800 to 1830. For the period 1800 to 1840 or 1800 to 1860 this adjustment lowers the rate of growth of output

Table 1.2   **Estimates of Gross Domestic Product per Capita (valued in 1840 prices)**

		Weiss		
Year	David Narrow GDP	Variant A Narrow GDP	Variant B Narrow GDP	Variant C Broad GDP
1800	$ 58	$ 73	$ 66	$ 78
1810	56	75	69	82
1820	61	77	72	84
1830	77	83	79	90
1840	91	91	91	101
1850	100	100	100	111
1860	125	125	125	135
Average Annualized Rates of Growth				
1800–1820	0.27	0.28	0.41	0.46
1820–40	1.96	0.84	1.19	0.93
1840–60	1.60	1.60	1.60	1.44
1800–1840	1.13	0.56	0.80	0.69
1800–1860	1.29	0.90	1.06	0.94

Sources: David (1967, table 8); Gallman (1971, table 1); Weiss (1989, tables 4, 6); Weiss (1990).

Note: The conjectural estimating equation is

$$O/P = (LF/P)[S_a(O/LF)_a + S_n(O/LF)_n]$$

Output per capita (O/P) in any year equals the participation rate (LF/P) times the weighted average output per worker, which equals output per worker in agriculture (a) and nonagriculture (n) weighted by each sector's share of the labor force. This equation yields an index of output per capita in each decennial year 1800 through 1840, which is used to extrapolate the 1840 dollar value of per capita output to each of the other years.

In David's and my variant A series this equation was estimated by assuming that $(O/LF)_n = k(O/LF)_a$, where k is the ratio of the sectoral output per workers in the base year. The Weiss variant A series uses the new labor force estimates.

Variant B includes several modifications: I have relaxed the assumption that nonfarm productivity advanced at the same rate as that of farming; I have made some minor revisions to the Towne and Rasmussen farm gross product figures used to derive the agricultural output per worker series; and the annual value of shelter is estimated independently of the conjectural growth equation (see Weiss 1989, 1990).

The rate of nonfarm productivity advance is a weighted average of the rate for manufacturing and for all other nonagricultural industries. The manufacturing rate for 1820 to 1840 (2.3 percent per year) comes from Sokoloff (1986, table 13.6); the manufacturing rate for 1800 to 1820 and that for all other nonfarm industries for 1800 to 1840 is assumed to be the same as that in agriculture. For 1840 to 1860 the figures come from the direct estimates of nonfarm output divided by the new labor force estimates.

The per capita value of shelter for 1840 through 1860 comes from Gallman and Weiss (1969). Those figures yield a ratio of the annual flow of shelter to the stock of dwellings of roughly 20 percent. For earlier years the shelter figures were estimated as the product of that ratio times Gallman's estimates of the stock of residential dwellings (for 1800, 1805, and 1815) and by interpolation (for 1810, 1820, and 1830).

Variant C is the same as variant B except that it makes use of a broader, unconventional measure of agricultural output and gross domestic output (see table 1.3).

Poulson examined commodity production for 1809 and 1839 and estimated that commodity output per capita advanced at only 4 percent per decade (1975, 140).

Lindstrom formulated an alternative way of constructing per capita income estimates that incorporated information about the income elasticity of demand for agricultural products. She developed her method to derive growth estimates for Philadelphia. When applied to the United States, the procedure yielded growth rates ranging from 0.53 to 1.01 percent per year between 1809 and 1839 (1983, 688).

tional major refinement, the use of a less conventional, more comprehensive measure of farm output and gross domestic product that includes the value of farm improvements and home manufacturing.[27]

In the most direct comparison, David's figures versus variant A, the levels of per capita product in the revised conjectures are higher in each year 1800 through 1830, roughly 25 percent at each of the first three benchmarks.[28] The two series offer different perspectives on the course of growth in the antebellum period. In the new series, growth was slower overall and exhibited more gradual acceleration over the period. According to David's estimates, the nation had reached its modern rate of growth long before the Civil War; from 1820 onward the antebellum record was nearly identical to the postbellum, doubling every forty years. In the new series there is a greater distinction between the ante- and postbellum records. In that former era the rate in each twenty-year period exceeded that of the preceding two decades, indicating clearly that the United States experienced a gradual acceleration in the growth of per capita output rather than a sharp, sudden increase.

While the two series tell dissimilar stories about the entire antebellum period, the difference rests entirely on the subperiod 1820 to 1840. There is no difference between the two series regarding the growth of per capita output between 1840 and 1860 because both series are based on Gallman's direct measures of output. Very similar results prevail for the earliest twenty years as well; the levels of output per capita differ, but the rates of growth are equal and low.

The discrepancy in the middle twenty years reflects the revisions to the underlying labor force series. The new series shows a more rapid growth of the farm labor force over this period, which results in a much slower rate of

---

by very little, only 0.08 percent per year in the first instance and 0.06 in the second. The growth during the 1830s, however, is reduced more noticeably from 3.57 to 3.25 percent per year. These adjustments are explained in Weiss (1990).

27. In order to obtain this more comprehensive measure I estimated the value of farm improvements and home manufacturing by extending back to 1800 Gallman's estimates of those components for the years after 1839. These adjustments have very little effect on the growth of farm gross product over the entire antebellum period, but do reduce growth by about 0.2 percent per year between 1820 and 1840. As will be seen, this adjustment is dwarfed by the impact of the labor force revisions.

Gallman's estimate of home manufacturing is more comprehensive than that of Towne and Rasmussen, and includes home baked goods, home production of textiles and clothing, and the value of home butchering (Gallman 1966, 35, 71–76). The Towne and Rasmussen figures include only the value of home textile production.

28. The higher levels pass Gallman's test of the reasonableness of the implicit flow of nonperishable consumption and investment spending (1971, table 4), and the changes in the new residuals imply an income elasticity of demand for nonperishables that is more consistent with other evidence for the nineteenth century. The new nonperishable figures yield elasticities of 1.7 for the period 1800 to 1820, and 1.8 for the years 1820 to 1840. David's figures give elasticities of 2.4 and 2.5 for those same periods. The new figures are somewhat higher than that implied by the direct income figures for 1840 to 1860 (1.31) and fall in the upper range of those for the late nineteenth century, but they are nonetheless much closer than David's.

agricultural productivity advance and a smaller shift in the composition of the work force toward the more productive nonagricultural sectors. The underlying difference in agricultural productivity growth is so great that even when nonfarm productivity is allowed to grow much faster than farm in the years 1820 to 1840, as is shown in variant B, the new income figures still show a slower rate of advance than did David's conjectures. The standard of living in this case falls between the David and variant A versions, the per capita figures being 12 to 21 percent above David's in the years 1800 through 1820, and approximately 10 percent below my variant A estimates. While lower than the variant A figures, they nonetheless seem high enough to pass Gallman's test of the reasonableness of the implicit flow of nonperishable consumption and investment spending.[29]

The chief alterations resulting from the relaxation of the assumption of equal productivity advance are, by construction, concentrated in the middle twenty years. The David series showed an annual growth of per capita income of only 0.27 percent between 1800 and 1820, then a much more substantial increase of 1.96 percent over the subsequent twenty-year period, followed by a slightly slower rise of 1.60 percent over the years 1840 to 1860. In the variant A case, which shows only the effect of using the new labor force estimates, the conjectural growth was also very small in the opening twenty years and then picked up in each of the subsequent twenty-year periods. In the variant B series the pattern of acceleration still prevails, but with a noticeable quickening of the rate after 1820.[30] Still, the revised pace of 1.19 percent per year is well below David's figure, the rate in each twenty-year period exceeds that of the preceding two decades, and there is still a greater distinction between the ante- and postbellum records than was revealed in David's series.

The broadening of the output measure (variant C) adds considerably to the average per capita output, raising it by $10 to $12 in each year. As these amounts are slightly larger in the earliest years and are larger fractions of the output, the rate of growth is altered as well. The effect on growth, however, is not too substantial, lowering the rate for the longer periods, 1800 to 1840 or 1800 to 1860, by about 0.1 percent.

Even at these slower rates, the standard of living advanced noticeably during the period, especially after 1830. And, as with the other variants, the rate of advance accelerated in each succeeding twenty-year period, proceeding smoothly from a modest rate of 0.46 percent per year in the opening twenty years of the century to 1.44 for the closing twenty years.

29. Gallman has estimated that the flow of perishable consumption per capita was quite steady over the course of the nineteenth century, changing primarily because of changes in the composition of the population (1971, 71–79; 1972, 197). His estimates showed a very mild rise from $42 in 1800 to $45 in 1840. When these perishable consumption estimates were subtracted from the per capita income figures implied by David's conjectural growth rates, the residuals were quite small, implausibly so in Gallman's view (1971, 81). The residuals implied by the variant B figures are not as large as in variant A, but are well above David's.

The components of this comprehensive estimate of gross domestic product are presented in table 1.3. As can be seen, the increase in per capita output from 1820 to 1840 gets a boost from the rise in the value of shelter, which increased by $3.40 over the twenty years, or at an annual rate of 2.18 percent. This could be the result strictly of the estimating procedures, but even without that increase, per capita output rose by nearly $14, or at a rate of 0.82 percent.

More telling, perhaps, is the increase in the residual, the portion of output beyond the apparent basic necessities. In 1800 the value of that residual was only $19. While Henry Adams did not know the exact figure, he made a perceptive comment about the precarious size and nature of the overall output level. "Not only were these slender resources, but they were also of a kind not easily converted to the ready uses required for rapid development" (Adams 1955, 28). That critical component, however, increased by $17 between 1800 and 1840, and another $23 in the subsequent twenty years. It increased at a rate in excess of 1 percent per year in each twenty-year period, and each decade except the second. Over the longer term this residual increased at 1.6 percent per year in the first forty years and 1.9 percent for the entire antebellum period. As Adams hinted, this was the output needed for industrialization, and of course provided as well the discretionary items that are the fruits of economic progress. In this light, Americans were advancing in style.

When combined with other evidence about economic performance between the Revolution and the Embargo of 1807, it appears that the young nation was reasonably well-off for some time, and showed improvement after 1793. Goldin and Lewis (1980) have estimated rates of growth for the period 1793 to 1807, and Jones (1980) has provided an estimate of per capita output for 1774.[31] Goldin and Lewis produced four variants but felt there was "some empirical basis for accepting the upper bound estimates," and so I have focused on just that one.[32] I have produced a narrow and a broad measure of

30. The acceleration in the variant B series reflects a different pattern of labor productivity growth. The growth of total output per worker between 1820 and 1840 is now faster than that underlying the variant A series, but still slower than David's. While the pattern of acceleration now seems more like his, the source of it is fundamentally different. In David's series the acceleration of total output per worker required a sharp rise in agricultural productivity growth, from virtually zero to 1.35 percent per year, and a substantial effect from the shift of labor toward the more productive nonfarm industries. Now the overall acceleration is accomplished with only a mild increase in the rate of agricultural productivity advance and rests more on the speeding up of productivity advance in manufacturing.

31. Gallman has produced an estimate for 1774 as well, by invoking some reasonable judgments about the minimum productivity change that occurred between 1774 and 1840. He argued that with no increase in productivity, per capita income in 1840 would have been 22 percent higher than it was in 1774, and with only modest productivity gains, per capita output would have increased by 35 to 40 percent (Gallman 1972, 23–24). He placed the 1774 value between $60 and $70 (in 1840 prices). Jones used Gallman's range to confirm the reasonableness of her estimates.

32. Goldin and Lewis showed fairly rapid growth between 1793 and 1807, with per capita income advancing at an annual rate of between 0.86 and 1.33 percent. These rates are below the 1.6 found for the late antebellum years, but are higher than the rate of advance over the longer period of 1800 to 1840. Most of the growth in their series occurred very early, before 1800 and

Table 1.3   **Per Capita Values of Gross Domestic Product and Components (1840 prices)**

| | GDP Variant C | Perishable Output | Nonperishable Output | | | |
			Shelter	Home Manufacturing	Farm Improvements	Residual
1800	77.61	42.00	5.50	8.55	2.45	19.10
1810	81.70	43.00	5.80	8.53	2.93	21.45
1820	83.90	43.00	6.30	8.52	2.75	23.33
1830	90.16	44.00	7.80	8.38	2.49	27.49
1840	101.03	45.00	9.70	8.00	2.32	36.01
1850	110.84	47.00	9.00	8.35	2.51	43.98
1860	134.61	55.00	9.90	8.01	2.03	59.67
		Average Annualized Rates of Growth				
1800–1810	0.52	0.24	0.53	−0.03	1.80	1.16
1810–20	0.27	0.00	0.83	−0.01	−0.63	0.85
1820–30	0.72	0.23	2.16	−0.16	−1.01	1.65
1830–40	1.15	0.22	2.20	−0.46	−0.70	2.74
1840–50	0.93	0.44	−0.75	0.42	0.81	2.02
1850–60	1.96	1.58	0.96	−0.41	−2.12	3.10
1800–1820	0.39	0.12	0.68	−0.02	0.58	1.01
1810–30	0.49	0.12	1.49	−0.09	−0.82	1.25
1820–40	0.93	0.23	2.18	−0.31	−0.85	2.19
1830–50	1.04	0.33	0.72	−0.02	0.06	2.38
1840–60	1.45	1.01	0.10	0.01	−0.66	2.56
1800–1840	0.66	0.17	1.43	−0.17	−0.14	1.60
1800–1860	0.92	0.45	0.98	−0.11	−0.31	1.92

Sources: See the notes to table 1.2 for the derivation of the per capita values of GDP and shelter. The values of home manufacturing and farm improvements come from Weiss (1990). The perishable figures come from Gallman (1971, table 4). The residual is obtained by subtracting these four other figures from GDP. The sum of perishable output, shelter, and the residual equals the variant B measure of GDP per capita shown in table 1.2.

GDP, the difference being the inclusion of the value of home manufacturing and farm improvements in the broader variant (see table 1.4). I have assumed that the rates of growth of the two series were the same from 1774 to 1800, just as they were from 1800 to 1820.[33] The levels of output, however, differed by nearly 20 percent.

For the last quarter of the eighteenth century, per capita output increased at

---

especially between 1793 and 1796. I have used just one of the upper-bound estimates, that with the higher values of the elasticity of export supply and import demand. The differences in their series using lower elasticities are concentrated in the years 1793 to 1798. See Goldin and Lewis (1980, 20, table 7).

33. After 1820 or so the value of farm improvements and home manufacturing grew more slowly than the rest of gross national product.

Table 1.4   Estimates of Gross Domestic Product and Per Capita Gross Domestic
                   Product, 1774 to 1810 (valued in 1840 prices)

	Population (thousands)	Narrow Definition		Broad Definition	
		Per Capita	Total	Per Capita	Total
1774	2,419	$ 60	$ 144	$ 70	$ 170
1793	4,332	59	257	70	302
1800	5,297	66	348	78	411
1807	6,644	71	473	84	558
1810	7,224	69	500	82	590
Average Annualized Rates of Growth					
1774–93	3.11	−0.03	3.08	−0.04	3.08
1793–1800	2.91	1.51	4.47	1.52	4.47
1800–1807	3.29	1.15	4.48	1.16	4.48
1793–1807	3.10	1.34	4.47	1.34	4.48
1793–1810	3.05	0.93	4.01	0.93	4.01
1774–1800	3.06	0.38	3.45	0.37	3.45
1774–1810	3.09	0.42	3.52	0.42	3.51

Sources: The 1774 population was calculated by assuming that population grew at the same rate between 1770 and 1774 as it had in the preceding decade (U.S. Bureau of the Census, 1975, ser. A-7).

The narrow 1774 per capita output figure comes from Jones (1980). She derived per capita income figures in pounds sterling by dividing her wealth estimates by assumed wealth-income ratios. I used the higher of her two estimates (12.7 pounds) because she argued that her wealth estimates may be too low, and Gallman has argued that an even lower wealth-income ratio would be appropriate. I converted her figure to dollars at the par value of exchange ($4.44 per pound) and deflated by the David-Solar price index to value it in 1840 prices.

The broader value was obtained by multiplying the narrow figure by the ratio of broad to narrow GDP (1.18) that prevailed in the years 1800 and 1810.

The total GDP figures are equal to the population times the estimated per capita figures, and are in millions of dollars.

The 1800 and 1810 per capita figures come from table 1.3.

The 1793 and 1807 figures were derived by assuming that the rates of growth estimated by Goldin and Lewis prevailed between those dates and 1800. I used the rates derived from their upper-bound estimates (1980, 20, variant 4 in table 7).

The rates of growth reported here were calculated from the unrounded figures.

an annual rate of 0.38 percent per year.[34] This is barely slower than that for the first two decades of the nineteenth century, but noticeably below the rates that prevailed thereafter. All of this early growth, however, was concentrated in the period after 1793. The economy suffered a setback during the Revolution and in the years immediately thereafter, but it was apparently quite mild.[35]

34. For the entire thirty-six–year period, per capita output grew at 0.42 percent per year, and gross domestic product increased at the healthy rate of 3.5 percent per year.

35. If Gallman's higher estimate ($70) were the true figure for 1774, then the turmoil was much more serious. Jones's lower figure ($51) implies that the economy experienced a healthy advance during the period. (See McCusker 1978 for a discussion of the problems of converting colonial values to dollar figures.)

Following that disruption came a particularly strong expansionary performance. From 1793 to 1807 per capita output grew at 1.34 percent per year,
faster than any twenty-year period in the first half of the nineteenth century.[36]
Some of this ebullient performance from 1793 to 1807 may reflect business-
cycle recovery or long swing expansion and perhaps exaggerates the long-
term trend rate of growth. While the cyclical location of 1793 is not known
for certain, 1807 is usually thought of as a peak.[37] A true appreciation of that
period's performance must await a clearer picture of the cyclical and long
swing behavior for the entire antebellum period.[38]

There was a noticeable difference within this expansionary phase. The first
half of the period had the better performance, increasing at 1.51 percent per
year, and much of this increase was concentrated in the shorter period 1793–
96. In the second subperiod, from 1800 to the Embargo of 1807, per capita
output still grew quite rapidly (1.15 percent), but noticeably slower than the
preceding seven-year period. The combination of evidence reveals that in
spite of this early surge the opening decade of the nineteenth century showed
one of the slowest rates of advance in the antebellum period. After 1807 the
economy again faltered, with per capita output showing a small absolute decline (about $1.50) between 1807 and 1810, resulting in a noticeable slowing
of the rate of growth for the entire decade to just 0.5 percent per year. This
setback is, of course, consistent with the well-known effects of the embargo.
What is worth noting, however, is that the decline was small, the level of per
capita output remained fairly stable during the period of disruption, and it
subsequently recovered quite nicely.

One of the more striking features of the American economic performance
that emerges from this combined series is the similarity to the British record
as reconstructed by N. F. R. Crafts.[39] Over the long period from 1774 to 1831
Crafts's evidence indicates that British per capita output grew at 0.40 percent
per year, extremely close to the U.S. figure for that same period—0.38 percent using the broad measure of output, 0.43 using the narrow.[40] Within that

36. Only the late antebellum period, 1840 to 1860, had a better record, and even then only the
narrowly defined measure showed clearly superior results. The broadly defined series advanced at
1.44 percent per year over those twenty years, barely faster than the performance between 1793
to 1807.

37. See Engerman and Gallman (1983, 17) for a discussion of the cyclicality in this period.

38. The conjectural benchmark estimates for 1800 through 1840 are not influenced by those
economic fluctuations because a big chunk of output was derived by assuming a constant per
capita value of farm products. The economy's fluctuations are masked, but the underlying trend is
more evident.

39. Some of his figures have been challenged by others, such as Mokyr (1987) and Williamson
(1987). More recently, Hoppit, in a generally critical essay about producing quantitative estimates
of national product before 1831, nevertheless allows that "Crafts's estimates are generally preferable to those of Deane and Cole" (1990, 176). See also Harley (1990) for a recent discussion of
the state of the debate.

40. For the slightly longer period 1774 to 1840 (1841 in the British case), the rates are 0.50 for
Britain and 0.55 for the broad U.S. measure, 0.64 for the narrow.

time span the performances are amazingly alike. From 1780 to 1801 the British per capita figure advanced at 0.35 percent per year, virtually identical to the U.S. rate of 0.38 from 1774 to 1800.[41] From 1801 to 1831 the British figure of 0.52 percent per year is again nearly identical to the growth in the broad measure of U.S. output per capita (0.50 percent per year) that took place between 1800 and 1830, but slightly less than the advance in the more narrowly defined series (0.61 percent per year).[42]

Given these comparative growth rates, the per capita figures remained in roughly the same proportion over the period. British output per capita was close to 30 percent above the narrowly defined U.S. figure through 1820, the margin narrowing thereafter to 22 percent in 1830 and 18 percent in 1840.[43] Using the broad measure of U.S. output, the advantage is narrowed considerably to around 10 percent for the entire period, but again showing convergence after 1820.[44]

The Deane and Cole estimates show much more rapid growth and a much different relative standing. Using the narrow measure of output, the American figure exceeded the British in 1774 by about 14 percent (about $8 in 1840 prices). With the much more rapid British growth underlying the Deane and Cole series, the income levels were brought to rough equality by 1793 and remained in that relative position until 1810, with the British subsequently moving ahead by 7 percent in 1820 and about 20 percent in 1830 and 1840. With the broader measure, however, the U.S. figure exceeded the British up through 1820, then slipped below by 5 percent in 1830 and 1840.

It is well to realize that these similar rates of growth in the per capita figures mean much higher rates of growth of aggregate output in America, where the economy had to provide for a much faster growing population. The American economy was advancing at a rate near to or above 3.0 percent per year from 1774 on, and probably from some earlier date as well. According to Crafts the British "it seems clear did not reach a 3 percent per year growth in real output

---

41. Taking into account the very slow growth or decline that occurred between 1774 and 1780, the U.S. record after 1780 would have surpassed the British.

42. Both performances, of course, differ from the record revealed in the Deane and Cole figures; growth of 1.11 percent between 1774 and 1831, 1.08 in the last two decades of the eighteenth century, and 1.32 percent between 1801 and 1831 (Deane and Cole 1962, 282).

43. The ratio peaked in 1793 with the British figure being 36 percent above the American. I have converted the British figures to dollars using the official exchange value of $4.44 per British pound. Davis and Hughes (1960, 55) argue that the true par value for the period 1834 to 1874 was $4.87.

44. In the broad measure as well there were slight variations in the relative positions, with a peak in 1793 when the British figure was 16 percent above the U.S.

It is not clear whether the British figure represents the narrow or broad measure of output. Neither Crafts nor Deane and Cole make obvious whether their GDP statistics include the value of farm improvements or home manufacturing. It appears from the sources used that they are excluded, so the proper comparison is with the narrow U.S. figure. On the other hand, these items were of lesser importance in Great Britain, so there was a much smaller difference between the narrow and broad measures there, and thus comparisons with the broad U.S. figure seem pertinent as well.

before 1830" (1985, 47). The Deane and Cole figures, on the other hand, show that they did so in the 1820s, as well as for the longer period 1800 to 1831.[45]

McCloskey has praised the British economy for showing "substantial growth of income per head in the face of a sharp rise in the number of heads" (1981, 117). He based this observation on the growth implicit in the Deane and Cole figures, and on the relatively slow growth of British population, and so would be less impressed by the slower growth shown in Crafts's estimates. The U.S. experience, on the other hand, merits that earlier awe, generating growth of per capita output equal to that of the most advanced nation in the face of a sharply faster increase in the number of people producing and consuming that burgeoning output.

1.3 Conclusions

This paper has set out new estimates of the American labor force for the antebellum period, and considered their consequences for our understanding of economic growth and the standard of living at the time. The alterations to the labor force series have a noticeable impact on that record, largely because the revisions are concentrated in the agricultural sector, raising the size of that sector's labor force in the later years of the period and lowering it in the opening decades of the century. These changes affect the rate and pattern of agricultural productivity advance and by assumption the pace and pattern of advance in nonagricultural industries too. The relaxation of certain operating assumptions underlying the conjectural figures gives a boost to output per capita and its growth after 1820, while broadening the measure of output to include the value of home manufacturing and farm improvements raises the level of output, but slows the growth slightly.

Overall the revised picture of growth is more modest than was revealed in the earlier conjectural estimates, but the growth was still a notable accomplishment. In the broadest measure of output, growth over the entire antebellum period was close to 1 percent per year; for the period 1800 to 1840 it was slightly lower (0.7 percent per year). Even with this modest increase the economy of 1840 had clearly surpassed the achievements at the turn of the century, or that just prior to the Revolution. It was not quite the suddenly buoyant performance revealed in the conjectures of Paul David, but it was better than pictured by earlier writers. George Taylor and Douglass North, along with Robert Martin, had clearly underestimated the economy's long-term performance and its ability to deal with misfortune and to recover from it. Even Kuznets's suggestion that per capita output had increased by at least 19 percent between 1800 and 1840 was a bit pessimistic.

45. According to Crafts, national product estimated by Deane and Cole increased at 3.06 percent per year between 1801 and 1831 (1985, 45).

The focus here has been on the dollar figures of output, which is just one aspect of the living standard. They mask the low, and perhaps declining, life expectancy, ignore the trauma of public outbreaks of disease, and fail to capture the impact of the possibly declining dietary standards. The figures also overlook the lack of privacy afforded by crowded housing, the monotony of life, the lack of variety, and the long hours required to obtain this average output. Still, it appears that the average American with a per capita output of nearly $80 at the turn of the century could have been quite comfortable. With the subsequent increases the average person could indeed have measured up to George Combe's calculation that "reckoning the whole property, and the whole population of the Union, and dividing the value of the one by the sum of the other, my impression is that the product would shew [*sic*] a larger amount of wealth for each individual in the United States, than exists in any other country in the world, Great Britain alone probably excepted" (Bode 1967, 295).

Appendix

The Total Labor Force

The total labor force is the sum of estimates of the number of workers in five population groups; free males aged 16 and over, free females aged 16 and over, free males aged 10 to 15, free females aged 10 to 15, and slaves aged 10 and over. The number of workers in each group was estimated as the product of the population and the group's specific participation rate. This is the same method used by Lebergott (1966) to derive estimates of the national labor force. My calculations, however, were made at the state level, and the national total was built up from the individual state estimates (see table 1A.1).[46]

The participation rates assumed to prevail in the antebellum years for each group were estimated from the available census statistics. Data on certain groups, primarily adult males, were collected by the census in some antebellum years, but for the most part the evidence pertained to the postbellum period. For each state, a participation rate was estimated for each of the four free population groups, using primarily the census evidence for 1870 through 1920. For slaves aged 10 and over, I used the participation rate postulated by Lebergott and subsequently used by David (1967).

Examination of the individual state data for each age-sex group indicated that a trend was evident only in the participation rate of females aged 16 and over. For the others, the postbellum means were assumed to have held in the antebellum years as well. These figures gave an unadjusted level of the ante-

---

46. The census population figures were reorganized in certain years in order to obtain the age breakdowns desired. It was also necessary to estimate the sex distribution of slaves in 1800 and 1810. For details of this estimation see Weiss (1987b).

Table 1A.1 **Estimates of the U.S. Labor Force, 1800 to 1860 (hundreds of workers aged 10 and over)**

	1800	1810	1820	1830	1840	1850	1860
Alabama			521	1,261	2,551	3,425	4,481
Arkansas			48	103	348	764	1,637
California						780	2,036
Colorado							295
Connecticut	694	744	813	940	1,029	1,294	1,621
Dakotas							10
Delaware	191	207	214	225	235	274	359
District of Columbia	32	56	84	105	108	165	250
Florida				155	265	390	619
Georgia	666	1,060	474	2,169	2,883	3,903	4,765
Illinois		33	150	389	1,319	2,360	5,167
Indiana	16	59	352	803	1,705	2,699	3,795
Iowa					132	535	1,922
Kansas							323
Kentucky	672	1,270	1,846	2,348	2,724	3,474	4,124
Louisiana		435	747	1,093	1,752	2,561	3,509
Maine	361	554	756	1,080	1,410	1,821	2,081
Maryland	1,273	1,409	1,493	1,627	1,665	2,104	2,385
Massachusetts	1,229	1,425	1,636	2,037	2,632	3,681	4,544
Michigan		17	36	106	640	1,219	2,386
Minnesota						25	538
Mississippi	38	182	334	620	1,761	2,798	3,968
Missouri			215	435	1,213	2,210	3,771
Nebraska							103
Nevada							57
New Hampshire	486	581	698	817	920	1,138	1,178
New Jersey	592	698	808	943	1,118	1,492	2,156
New Mexico						194	261
New York	1,628	2,610	3,863	5,604	7,591	10,363	13,471
North Carolina	1,724	2,054	2,410	2,842	2,913	3,480	4,180
Ohio	113	550	1,440	2,386	4,088	5,831	6,907
Oregon						49	185
Pennsylvania	1,606	2,140	2,835	3,806	4,956	7,170	9,166
Rhode Island	214	248	271	335	395	565	685
South Carolina	1,498	1,873	2,287	2,761	2,847	3,307	3,564
Tennessee	294	778	1,277	2,147	2,677	3,450	4,024
Texas						833	2,431
Utah						33	94
Vermont	371	532	636	780	851	1,019	1,010
Virginia	3,426	3,860	4,257	4,802	4,939	5,632	6,427
Washington							61
Wisconsin					123	891	2,356
United States	17,125	23,374	31,499	42,718	57,781	81,925	112,901

Source: See the text for details.

bellum participation rates that pertained to the entire population in the age-sex category. They were adjusted to reflect the fact that the antebellum work force was almost entirely white, and that the foreign-born share of the white population was lower in the years before 1860 than in the postbellum period.

Additional evidence existed for some of the antebellum years, specifically 1820, 1840, 1850, and 1860. The evidence for the first two years did not permit useful disaggregation by age and sex. The latter two, however, did provide valuable information, especially on the numerically largest group, males aged 16 and over. With some adjustments, this evidence enabled me to obtain the adult male work force in 1850 and 1860. The implied participation rates were combined with the postbellum data to give additional observations on this important group. Perhaps most noteworthily, these antebellum rates confirmed that there was no trend in the adult male participation rate, and indicated as well that the changing share of the foreign-born had virtually no effect on the particular group's participation rate.[47]

Males Aged 16 and Over

The antebellum participation rates for males aged 16 and over were derived in two categories. The first comprises the rates derived from the census data for 1850 and 1860. The census reported some labor force figures in each of those years, and for almost all states the rates implicit in the reported evidence seem reliable. An adjustment was made to the original census figures of several states, as explained below, but for the most part the individual state rates in these two census years were obtained from the reported statistics. In the other category, rates for 1800 through 1840, the value for each state was assumed to equal the mean of the rate for the years 1850 through 1920. As already indicated, the postbellum evidence did not reveal a trend in the adult male participation rate, so it seemed reasonable to assume there was none in the antebellum period either. The evidence for 1850 and 1860 confirmed the absence of any trend for part of the antebellum period, which enhances our confidence in the assumption for the other years.

The census evidence for 1850 and 1860 had to be adjusted in order to obtain the specific age coverage desired, and in a few states the figures were corrected for enumeration errors.[48] The number of 15-year-old workers was deducted in order to obtain a count of free workers aged 16 and over. The deduction was made by multiplying the estimated population 15 years of age by the participation rate of 15-year-olds reported for 1900. The 15-year-old popula-

---

47. Of course the changing importance of the foreign-born had an impact on the overall participation rate through its effects on the age-sex composition of the population.

48. The assessments of the 1850 and 1860 census data were based on the behavior of the labor force statistics relative to the population, and proceeded on the assumption that the census counts of population are accurate, or at least equally reliable at the various census dates. There is evidence that the census underenumerated the population in some locations in some antebellum years, but it is not known whether the entire census in any year was in error (see Steckel 1988).

tion was estimated as a fraction of those aged 10 to 14 years, the fraction being the average for each state for the years 1870 to 1920.

The revised rates in both years are very close to each state's mean for the years 1870 through 1920, with the consequence that the inclusion or exclusion of these antebellum values has little effect on the overall mean (see table 1A.2). The participation rates assumed for the years 1800 to 1840 are the means based on all eight census years 1850 through 1920; the larger number of observations being presumed to increase the reliability of the estimates.

The adjustments made to the 1850 and 1860 figures were straightforward, and for 1850 quite small.[49] The 1850 census covered free males aged 15 and over and was adjusted primarily to obtain a figure covering only those aged 16 and above. Beyond this the figures were examined for possible deficiencies, and necessary corrections were made in eleven states, changing the U.S. labor force figure by a little less than 17,000 workers, or less than 1 percent. This small revision for the nation reflects offsetting changes in some states, so the adjustments at the state and regional levels were larger (see table 1A.3).

The 1860 census reported a combined figure for free male and female workers aged 15 and over, and required greater adjustment. In addition to converting from a coverage of those 15 and over to those 16 and over, the census counts of adult male workers in some states had to be adjusted for obvious deficiencies. Samples of evidence taken from the manuscript schedules suggest that the published figures include a fairly reliable count of female workers, implying participation rates that were approximately equal to those of the postbellum period. It seems certain that the rates were low in all years, but at least there was consistency over time. The male participation rates in some states, however, were low in comparison with the postbellum figures, indicating an undercount of workers. My corrections of the 1860 figures amounted to 3.4 percent. The number of adult male workers implicit in the census count, my adjustments, and the revised figures are shown in table 1A.4.

The mean participation rates calculated from the observations for 1850 through 1920 pertain to the entire free male work force aged 16 and over, and make no distinction between blacks and whites, or native and foreign-born. The reason is simply that the limited evidence available does not indicate any differences in the participation rates of these groups for males aged 16 and over. In 1890 and 1900, when comparative data are available, the participation rate for white males aged 16 and over was virtually identical to that for whites and blacks together.[50] This was true not only at the national or regional level, but in each state as well (see table 1A.5). Thus, even though the free work

49. Additional details of the assessment of and adjustments to the 1850 and 1860 census data can be found in Weiss (1986a).

50. The 1900 figures are reported by state in table 1A.5. For 1890 only national figures are available. The white rate for males aged 15 and over was 0.882 in 1890, very close to the 0.887 rate for all males that age. An allowance for those 15 years of age would push the rates even closer (U.S. Bureau of the Census 1890, part 2, cxxii.)

Table 1A.2   Participation Rates of Free Males Aged 16 and Over

| | Mean 1850 to 1920 | | | Revised Rates | |
	Including 1860	Excluding 1860	Mean 1870 to 1920	1850	1860
Alabama	.921	.920	.931	.853	.931
Arkansas	.901	.904	.904	.904	.883
California	.906	.907	.901	.944	.900
Colorado	.919	.919	.919		.919
Connecticut	.902	.904	.908	.885	.881
Dakotas	.899	.899	.899		.899
Delaware	.907	.906	.912	.872	.912
District of Columbia	.887	.887	.892	.853	.892
Florida	.904	.909	.914	.881	.871
Georgia	.919	.917	.926	.868	.926
Illinois	.890	.889	.892	.875	.892
Indiana	.893	.893	.889	.918	.889
Iowa	.884	.883	.876	.926	.895
Kansas	.883	.889	.889		.845
Kentucky	.900	.903	.908	.872	.884
Louisiana	.913	.912	.922	.853	.922
Maine	.891	.887	.886	.899	.918
Maryland	.907	.911	.913	.904	.875
Massachusetts	.909	.911	.913	.900	.895
Michigan	.902	.905	.906	.900	.881
Minnesota	.896	.893	.890	.911	.919
Mississippi	.916	.915	.922	.872	.922
Missouri	.893	.897	.898	.890	.869
Nebraska	.892	.892	.892		.892
Nevada	.927	.920	.920		.968
New Hampshire	.900	.903	.901	.912	.885
New Jersey	.904	.906	.912	.869	.889
New Mexico	.910	.910	.908	.925	.908
New York	.907	.904	.905	.897	.933
North Carolina	.910	.907	.911	.878	.936
Ohio	.899	.900	.895	.927	.895
Oregon	.897	.894	.897	.880	.915
Pennsylvania	.905	.902	.899	.921	.927
Rhode Island	.920	.920	.922	.908	.922
South Carolina	.913	.912	.922	.851	.920
Tennessee	.880	.882	.888	.846	.860
Texas	.901	.900	.903	.886	.903
Utah	.893	.893	.892	.902	.892
Vermont	.884	.887	.885	.902	.859
Virginia	.901	.900	.908	.853	.908
Washington	.918	.921	.921		.902
Wisconsin	.912	.909	.920	.842	.928
United States	.902	.903	.903	.894	.905

Sources: The mean rates for 1870 to 1920 come from Miller and Brainerd (1957, table L-3). I corrected their 1910 figures to account for the census overcount (see Weiss 1985). The means for 1850 to 1920 use the 1870–1920 figures plus the rates implicit in the census labor force counts for 1850 and 1860 (see tables 1A.3, 1A.4). The revised figures come from tables 1A.3 and 1A.4.

Table 1A.3   **Estimates of Male Workers Aged 16 and Over, 1850**

	Participation Rates			Gainful Workers	
	Original Census		Revised	Adjustment	Revised
	15+	16+	16+	to Census	Count
Alabama	.824	.830	.853	2,637	97,534
Arkansas	.892	.904	.904		39,283
California	.943	.944	.944		77,567
Connecticut	.774	.781	.885	12,531	106,251
Delaware	.836	.850	.872	542	21,712
District of Columbia	.805	.825	.853	373	11,283
Florida	.866	.881	.881		12,793
Georgia	.855	.868	.868		117,578
Illinois	.857	.875	.875		209,754
Indiana	.894	.918	.918		242,656
Iowa	.904	.926	.926		48,252
Kentucky	.859	.872	.872		184,099
Louisiana	.802	.812	.853	3,840	79,307
Maine	.878	.899	.899		159,738
Maryland	.836	.850	.904	7,729	129,110
Massachusetts	.887	.900	.900		288,274
Michigan	.882	.900	.900		106,628
Minnesota	.899	.911	.911		2,315
Mississippi	.861	.872	.872		70,785
Missouri	.722	.732	.890	26,597	150,127
New Hampshire	.895	.912	.912		92,342
New Jersey	.858	.869	.869		124,796
New Mexico	.908	.925	.925		17,214
New York	.884	.897	.897		869,533
North Carolina	.870	.878	.878		132,938
Ohio	.906	.927	.927		517,629
Oregon	.700	.710	.880	915	4,750
Pennsylvania	.980	.996	.921	−50,042	613,606
Rhode Island	.899	.908	.908		42,123
South Carolina	.841	.851	.851		64,689
Tennessee	.813	.823	.846	4,493	165,255
Texas	.871	.886	.886		41,743
Utah	.881	.902	.902		3,099
Vermont	.886	.902	.902		89,740
Virginia	.829	.842	.853	2,872	221,278
Wisconsin	.785	.796	.842	4,372	80,768
United States	.877	.891	.894	16,859	5,236,550

Sources: U.S. Bureau of the Census 1850, 1860, 1900b; Miller and Brainerd 1957.

Notes: Column 1 figures are based on the original census data.

Column 2 figures are based on the original census data minus an estimate of the 15-year-old males in the labor force and population. The population estimates were made using the mean ratios of 15-year-olds to those aged 10–14 years that prevailed in each state in the period 1870 to 1920. The worker estimates were obtained by applying to these population estimates the participation rate for 15-year-olds obtained from the 1900 census. For the South, the participation rate

(continued)

Table 1A.3   (notes, continued)

for all 15-year-olds was adjusted to a white-only basis using the ratio of the white to total participation rates for those 10–15 years old.

Column 3 figures, the revised participation rates, are the original census values (excluding 15-year-old workers) except in twelve states. Where the original rate was judged too low, the revised figure was set equal to the lower of two values, either the 1850 regional mean (Alabama, District of Columbia, Louisiana, and Virginia) or the lowest rate observed for that state in the 1870–1920 period (Connecticut, Delaware, Maryland, Missouri, Oregon, Tennessee, and Wisconsin). In Pennsylvania, the one state where the original figure was too high, the revised rate was set equal to the highest rate observed in the period 1870–1920.

The revised count (col. 5) is the product of the revised participation rate and the population base of males 16 and over.

The adjustment (col. 4) is the difference between the original and revised census count.

force in the antebellum years was almost entirely white, there is no reason to adjust the postbellum figure from its basis in the total work force to one covering only white workers.

Likewise there seems little reason to make any adjustment for the declining importance of the foreign-born in the antebellum period. The evidence for 1890 and 1900 does show some small differences between the participation rates of native and foreign-born males, the largest being a 5-percentage-point difference in Massachusetts (see table 1A.5). The more relevant differences, however, those between native whites and all whites, were much smaller. In the Northeast these differences were roughly 1 percentage point, with the largest being 2 percentage points in Massachusetts. Outside the Northeast the differences were less than 1 percentage point everywhere except Michigan and Minnesota, two states of little importance in the antebellum period. Moreover, the foreign-born share of the population remained roughly constant back until 1860, but was smaller in earlier years. In the Northeast, where the foreign-born were of greatest importance, their share of the population in 1850 was only 22 percent compared to 31 percent in 1900. Yet, even though the foreign-born share was substantially less in 1850 than in the postbellum years, the participation rates were very close to the postbellum statistics. This suggests that, in the absence of the foreign-born, native men had a higher participation rate. Given the closeness of the total and native white rates in 1890 and 1900, and the likelihood that the native rate would have adjusted somewhat in the absence of foreign-born workers, I used the mean participation rate for all male workers aged 16 and over, making no adjustment for the changing importance of the foreign-born population.

Females Aged 16 and Over

The postbellum evidence indicated that there was a trend in the adult female participation rate, best captured by an equation of the following form:

$$\ln PR_i = a_i + b_i t$$

Table 1A.4   **Estimates of Male Workers Aged 16 and Over, 1860**

	Implicit Figures		Revised Participation Rate	Gainful Workers	
	Workers	Participation Rate		Adjustment to Census	Revised Count
Alabama	114,352	0.799	.931	18,910	133,262
Arkansas	77,721	0.883	.883		77,721
California	212,653	0.972	.900	− 15,836	196,817
Colorado	26,724	0.835	.919	2,704	29,428
Connecticut	130,540	0.881	.881		130,540
Dakotas	1,481	1.421	.899	− 544	937
Delaware	32,004	1.003	.912	− 2,900	29,104
District of Columbia	19,970	0.970	.892	− 1,597	18,373
Florida	19,787	0.871	.871		19,787
Georgia	131,396	0.821	.926	16,852	148,248
Illinois	348,575	0.677	.892	111,019	459,594
Indiana	307,114	0.804	.889	32,328	339,442
Iowa	172,373	0.895	.895		172,373
Kansas	29,677	0.845	.845		29,677
Kentucky	230,879	0.884	.884		230,879
Louisiana	93,307	0.783	.922	16,546	109,853
Maine	180,296	0.918	.918		180,296
Maryland	150,730	0.875	.875		150,730
Massachusetts	347,113	0.895	.895		347,113
Michigan	207,614	0.881	.881		207,614
Minnesota	48,906	0.919	.919		48,906
Mississippi	77,556	0.763	.922	16,155	93,711
Missouri	273,380	0.869	.869		273,380
Nebraska	11,060	1.018	.892	− 1,373	9,687
Nevada	5,638	0.968	.968		5,638
New Hampshire	93,585	0.885	.885		93,585
New Jersey	178,747	0.889	.889		178,747
New Mexico	26,998	1.061	.908	− 3,901	23,097
New York	1,112,524	0.933	.933		1,112,524
North Carolina	166,768	0.936	.936		166,768
Ohio	569,800	0.844	.895	34,713	604,513
Oregon	17,880	0.915	.915		17,880
Pennsylvania	773,766	0.927	.927		773,766
Rhode Island	46,041	0.849	.922	3,978	50,019
South Carolina	60,994	0.733	.920	15,590	76,584
Tennessee	196,450	0.860	.860		196,450
Texas	95,443	0.752	.903	19,134	114,577
Utah	7,903	0.824	.892	655	8,558
Vermont	87,260	0.859	.859		87,260
Virginia	258,717	0.846	.908	18,951	277,668
Washington	6,000	0.902	.902		6,000
Wisconsin	211,599	0.928	.928		211,599
United States	7,161,322	0.871	.905	281,384	7,442,705

Sources: U.S. Bureau of the Census 1860, 1900a, 1900b; Bateman and Foust 1973.

Notes: The implicit count of male workers aged 16 and over is the residual number of workers left in the original census figure after deducting an estimate of the number of workers 15 years

(continued)

Table 1A.4   (notes, continued)

of age and female workers aged 16 and over. The implicit participation rate is based on that residual count of workers.

The revised participation rates are the implicit values (col. 2) unless that figure deviated noticeably from the mean value for the years 1850 and 1870 through 1920, the 1850 rate having been revised as explained in table 1A.3. Where the implicit figure is highly deviant, as in Alabama, the revised participation rate is the 1870–1920 mean.

where PR is the participation rate of females aged 16 and over, t is the time trend variable, and i is the state.

This equation was used to derive a set of participation rates for the antebellum years, 1800 through 1860. This basic rate was then adjusted to a white-only basis, to better reflect the demographic makeup of the antebellum free work force. This adjustment was made on an individual-state basis using the ratio of the white to total participation rate that prevailed in 1900. Adjustments were made only in the South, plus Delaware, the District of Columbia, Maryland, and Missouri. In the rest of the country the two participation rates were so close, due to the small numbers of free blacks in the populations of those states, that they were treated as identical. The various 1900 participation rates are presented in table 1A.6.

I made no adjustment for the lesser importance of the foreign-born in the populations of the antebellum years. The limited evidence available, that for 1900, shows that the participation rates for native white, foreign-born, and all white females were close though not identical (see table 1A.6). Thus even though the foreign-born share declined from 29.2 percent in the Northeast in 1900 to 19.8 in 1850, and was yet smaller in earlier years, the change would have virtually no effect on the participation rate.[51]

The estimates of the participation rates for free females aged 16 and over are presented in table 1A.7. As can be seen, my estimates show a slow and steady rise from 0.076 in 1800 to 0.113 in 1860.[52] This trend was continued in the postbellum period when the rate for those 16 and over increased from 0.147 in 1870 to 0.206 in 1910 (U.S. Bureau of the Census 1910, 1870).

Males and Females Aged 10 to 15 Years

The estimates of the participation rates for males and females aged 10–15 years were derived in similar ways. The procedure consisted of estimating the total participation rate in each state, and then adjusting it in some states to

51. For 1840 and earlier years I estimated the share to be around 11 percent. Gemery (1990) shows different values, but nonetheless lower than that for 1850.

52. Lebergott included an independent estimate of adult female workers in each year, which showed that their participation rate varied slightly from year to year rather than rising steadily. It is unclear whether his data pertain to those 16 and over or 10 and over, but the latter seems more likely. Their participation rates implied by Lebergott's estimates are .044 in 1800, .076 in 1810, .06 in 1820, .065 in 1830, .08 in 1840, .097 in 1850, and .096 in 1860.

Table 1A.5   **Participation Rates of Males Aged 16 and Over, 1900**

	Total	White	Ratio White to Total	Native Whites	Foreign-Born	Foreign-Born Share
Northeastern states						
Connecticut	.909	.908	1.000	.891	.938	.366
Delaware	.908	.909	1.000	.906	.925	.135
District of Columbia	.884	.874	0.988	.887	.794	.146
Maine	.886	.886	1.000	.881	.909	.173
Maryland	.903	.900	0.997	.900	.901	.145
Massachusetts	.898	.898	1.000	.876	.930	.395
New Hampshire	.903	.903	1.000	.891	.935	.264
New Jersey	.919	.919	1.000	.909	.939	.343
New York	.910	.910	0.999	.899	.929	.363
Pennsylvania	.914	.913	1.000	.907	.932	.254
Rhode Island	.919	.919	0.999	.904	.940	.414
Vermont	.887	.887	1.000	.881	.914	.183
Midwestern states						
Illinois	.896	.896	1.000	.888	.913	.310
Indiana	.893	.892	1.000	.893	.883	.092
Iowa	.879	.879	1.000	.879	.880	.223
Kansas	.878	.879	1.001	.877	.890	.147
Michigan	.902	.902	1.000	.889	.929	.338
Minnesota	.900	.900	1.001	.883	.920	.471
Missouri	.901	.901	1.000	.901	.906	.121
Ohio	.896	.896	1.000	.896	.896	.172
Wisconsin	.886	.887	1.000	.884	.891	.406
Southern states						
Alabama	.938	.929	0.991	.929	.935	.030
Arkansas	.930	.925	0.995	.924	.938	.031
Florida	.915	.902	0.986	.901	.915	.112
Georgia	.922	.908	0.985	.907	.923	.020
Kentucky	.905	.905	1.000	.906	.887	.046
Louisiana	.922	.909	0.985	.907	.917	.124
Mississippi	.928	.906	0.976	.906	.932	.026
North Carolina	.920	.916	0.996	.916	.911	.007
South Carolina	.925	.905	0.979	.905	.916	.019
Tennessee	.914	.911	0.997	.911	.916	.022
Texas	.910	.908	0.998	.905	.927	.126
Virginia	.900	.891	0.990	.894	.819	.032
Western states						
California	.899	.893	0.994	.882	.916	.339
Colorado	.899	.900	1.001	.883	.947	.262
Dakotas	.887	.902	1.017	.881	.926	.463
Nevada	.892	.901	1.010	.888	.924	.365
New Mexico	.892	.899	1.008	.892	.940	.130
Oregon	.903	.900	0.996	.890	.935	.218
Utah	.883	.886	1.004	.869	.923	.324
Washington	.919	.918	0.999	.904	.949	.313
United States	.905	.902	0.997	.897	.920	.236

(continued)

Table 1A.5   (notes, continued)

Source: U.S. Bureau of the Census, 1990a.

Notes: The foreign-born share (col. 6) is the share of the white population.

The national figures for 1890 indicate a participation rate of .887 for all males *aged 15* and over and .882 for whites, for a ratio of 0.997. The native white rate was .864 and that for foreign-born was .938 (U.S. Bureau of the Census 1890, cxxii). The census reported the figures for those aged 15 and over, and a crude adjustment for those 15 years of age pushes the rates slightly closer. By assuming that the participation rate for 15-year-olds was the same as that for the group aged 15 to 19 years of age, one can obtain an upwardly biased estimate of 15-year-olds in the labor force. Deducting that figure from the census total gives the following rates for males aged 16 and over: all males .896, whites .893, native whites .877, and foreign-born .939.

reflect the different demographic composition of the antebellum population, the components of which exhibited different participation rates.

The basic estimates, the state-specific participation rates for all males or females in this age group, are the means for the years 1870 through 1910. The evidence for 1900 (U.S. Bureau of the Census 1900b) indicated that in some states the participation rates for whites differed noticeably from that for blacks and whites combined, especially in the South. The mean rate for the years 1870 to 1920 was adjusted to a white basis by multiplying it by the 1900 ratio of the white to total participation rate. This adjustment had a noticeable effect only in the South, Delaware, the District of Columbia, and Maryland.

The 1900 evidence also indicated that there were substantial differences between the native and foreign-born white participation rates, the latter being approximately twice the former in the northern regions where the foreign-born population was of greater importance. Thus a further adjustment was made in the northern states to reflect the fact that the foreign-born were a smaller component of the population in the antebellum years. This was done by calculating a weighted average of the native and foreign-born rates, the weights being each group's share in the white population.

The participation rates used to estimate the antebellum work force for these age groups are presented in table 1A.8.

Slaves

The participation rate for slaves aged 10 and over was assumed to be 90 percent. It was further assumed that those under the age of 10 did not work. Lebergott (1966) made the case for the constant 90 percent figure, although the description of his procedures suggested that he had used 90 percent in some years (1810, 1830, and 1850) and 87 percent in others. In fact, he used 90 percent in all years except 1860, in which he used the 1850 rate for free white males in the South (approximately 86 percent). Since that rate was not judged appropriate for 1850, it seemed inconsistent to use it for 1860, so I used the 90 percent figure in all years.

Table 1A.6   **Participation Rates of Females Aged 16 and Over, 1900**

	Total	White	Ratio White to Total	Native Whites	Foreign Born	Foreign-Born Share
Alabama	.304	.134	.440	.134	.108	.018
Arkansas	.177	.104	.586	.103	.126	.020
California	.188	.186	.991	.191	.173	.268
Colorado	.173	.168	.970	.168	.165	.214
Connecticut	.263	.258	.983	.263	.247	.340
Dakotas	.158	.156	.990	.179	.126	.439
Delaware	.198	.166	.836	.164	.176	.116
District of Columbia	.370	.239	.645	.241	.226	.123
Florida	.228	.118	.517	.114	.163	.085
Georgia	.288	.134	.466	.134	.137	.013
Illinois	.182	.179	.984	.185	.165	.286
Indiana	.138	.133	.963	.135	.113	.078
Iowa	.151	.150	.996	.160	.109	.193
Kansas	.123	.118	.956	.121	.094	.125
Kentucky	.155	.116	.751	.115	.129	.042
Louisiana	.278	.127	.456	.127	.121	.102
Maine	.205	.204	.998	.192	.268	.164
Maryland	.464	.458	.986	.673	.319	.609
Massachusetts	.120	.081	.677	.078	.153	.039
Michigan	.165	.164	.994	.177	.135	.302
Minnesota	.187	.186	.996	.220	.141	.428
Mississippi	.335	.131	.390	.130	.156	.014
Missouri	.154	.141	.912	.140	.141	.105
Nevada	.162	.158	.978	.166	.137	.265
New Hampshire	.266	.266	.998	.236	.353	.256
New Jersey	.224	.213	.950	.214	.211	.316
New Mexico	.102	.101	.989	.102	.095	.091
New York	.250	.245	.980	.244	.248	.349
North Carolina	.233	.155	.663	.155	.147	.004
Ohio	.169	.166	.980	.171	.136	.150
Oregon	.157	.157	.996	.159	.145	.169
Pennsylvania	.195	.189	.967	.195	.165	.204
Rhode Island	.314	.308	.984	.313	.302	.411
South Carolina	.379	.201	.530	.202	.165	.013
Tennessee	.175	.102	.583	.102	.125	.015
Texas	.151	.099	.655	.095	.132	.107
Utah	.137	.136	.994	.139	.129	.332
Vermont	.184	.184	.997	.187	.166	.155
Virginia	.206	.117	.567	.117	.141	.018
Washington	.152	.151	.993	.156	.136	.256
Wisconsin	.174	.174	.998	.210	.111	.365
United States	.206	.178	.864	.175	.191	.212

Source: U.S. Bureau of the Census 1900a.

Table 1A.7   **Participation Rate Estimates, 1800 to 1860 (free females aged 16 and over)**

	1800	1810	1820	1830	1840	1850	1860
Alabama			.107	.109	.111	.113	.116
Arkansas			.030	.035	.041	.047	.054
California						.084	.099
Colorado							.055
Connecticut	.083	.093	.104	.117	.131	.146	.164
Dakotas							.068
Delaware	.046	.053	.060	.068	.077	.087	.099
District of Columbia	.091	.100	.111	.123	.136	.150	.166
Florida				.063	.069	.076	.083
Georgia	.101	.104	.107	.110	.113	.116	.120
Illinois		.027	.033	.041	.050	.062	.076
Indiana	.016	.020	.024	.030	.037	.045	.056
Iowa					.047	.056	.068
Kansas							.057
Kentucky	.040	.045	.049	.055	.061	.068	.075
Louisiana		.114	.115	.117	.118	.119	.121
Maine	.050	.057	.066	.075	.086	.099	.114
Maryland	.064	.071	.079	.088	.098	.109	.121
Massachusetts	.132	.144	.156	.170	.185	.202	.220
Michigan		.076	.083	.091	.099	.108	.118
Minnesota						.072	.086
Mississippi	.116	.117	.118	.119	.120	.121	.122
Missouri		.028	.034	.041	.050	.061
Nebraska							.061
Nevada							.072
New Hampshire	.107	.117	.128	.141	.154	.169	.185
New Jersey	.061	.070	.079	.090	.103	.117	.133
New Mexico						.062	.070
New York	.074	.083	.094	.106	.120	.136	.153
North Carolina	.048	.054	.061	.068	.076	.084	.094
Ohio	.032	.038	.044	.052	.062	.072	.085
Oregon						.022	.032
Pennsylvania	.048	.055	.063	.073	.084	.096	.110
Rhode Island	.154	.166	.178	.191	.206	.221	.237
South Carolina	.152	.156	.160	.164	.168	.172	.176
Tennessee	.021	.025	.029	.033	.039	.045	.052
Texas						.059	.066
Utah						.028	.038
Vermont	.046	.053	.061	.070	.080	.092	.105
Virginia	.062	.066	.071	.077	.082	.089	.095
Washington							.038
Wisconsin					.055	.066	.080
United States	.076	.079	.083	.090	.096	.105	.113

Source: See the text for an explanation of the estimates.

Table 1A.8   Antebellum Participation Rate Estimates

	Males Aged 10–15			Females Aged 10–15		
	1860	1850	1800–1840	1860	1850	1800–1840
Alabama	.534	.534	.534	.155	.155	.155
Arkansas	.414	.414	.414	.076	.076	.076
California	.076	.076	.076	.025	.025	.025
Colorado	.104	.104	.104	.024	.024	.024
Connecticut	.134	.128	.124	.088	.082	.078
Dakotas	.109	.109	.109	.030	.030	.030
Delaware	.231	.230	.228	.081	.080	.079
District of Columbia	.078	.076	.073	.037	.034	.033
Florida	.272	.272	.272	.055	.055	.055
Georgia	.446	.446	.446	.137	.137	137
Illinois	.154	.154	.154	.044	.044	.044
Indiana	.172	.172	.172	.029	.029	.029
Iowa	.154	.154	.154	.025	.025	.025
Kansas	.140	.140	.140	.018	.018	.018
Kentucky	.333	.333	.333	.051	.051	.051
Louisiana	.243	.243	.243	.074	.074	.074
Maine	.092	.092	.087	.037	.036	.032
Maryland	.184	.183	.181	.087	.086	.084
Massachusetts	.120	.117	.112	.077	.073	.067
Michigan	.108	.108	.108	.038	.038	.038
Minnesota	.109	.109	.109	.037	.037	.037
Mississippi	.407	.407	.407	.098	.098	.098
Missouri	.211	.211	.211	.038	.038	.038
Nebraska	.116	.116	.116	.025	.025	.025
Nevada	.062	.062	.062	.014	.014	.014
New Hampshire	.098	.097	.091	.059	.054	.051
New Jersey	.141	.139	.136	.080	.077	.074
New Mexico	.215	.215	.215	.040	.040	.040
New York	.123	.121	.117	.075	.072	.067
North Carolina	.506	.506	.506	.166	.166	.166
Ohio	.144	.144	.144	.039	.039	.039
Oregon	.083	.083	.083	.013	.013	.013
Pennsylvania	.177	.177	.173	.070	.069	.067
Rhode Island	.225	.218	.210	.162	.154	.143
South Carolina	.395	.395	.395	.220	.220	.220
Tennessee	.388	.388	.388	.049	.049	.049
Texas	.290	.290	.290	.073	.073	.073
Utah	.138	.138	.138	.026	.026	.026
Vermont	.112	.112	.109	.046	.046	.044
Virginia	.292	.292	.292	.050	.050	.050
Washington	.066	.066	.066	.017	.017	.017
Wisconsin	.117	.117	.117	.045	.045	.045
United States	.210	.214	.213	.066	.068	.068

Sources: U.S. Bureau of the Census 1870, 1880, 1890, 1900a, 1900b. See the text for details.

Notes: These rates are for white males and females. For each state the estimate was obtained by multiplying the postbellum mean participation rate for whites and blacks in this age group by the 1900 ratio of the white to black participation rate. Since the native white and foreign-born rates differed, the rates in some states varied across time to reflect the changing proportions of the foreign-born in the population.

The national figure varied slightly in the years 1800 to 1840 as the importance of different states' population and labor force changed.

David (1967) revised Lebergott's figures to remove the alleged anomaly of an 87 percent rate in alternate years. Since Lebergott had in fact used 90 percent, the revision had the effect of creating a pattern of variation where there had been none.

The Agricultural Labor Force

The estimates of the antebellum agricultural labor force were based as much as possible on the existing census statistics. The census accounts are not flawless, suffering from ambiguities regarding coverage and classification, and some apparent measurement errors. On the other hand, they were collected at specific dates during the antebellum period, so do represent the contemporary state of affairs and capture some of the economic realities of the time. Moreover, the more egregious errors are quite apparent and can be readily corrected. Following the lead of previous researchers, I examined and assessed the census data for 1820, 1840, 1850, and 1860 and made revisions where called for. Since the assessments and revisions of the earlier censuses made use of the evidence in the later ones, the presentation of my estimates proceeds backward in time. The revised estimates of the agricultural labor force are summarized in table 1A.9.

Estimates for 1850 and 1860

In both 1850 and 1860, the agricultural labor force is the sum of the slave and free farm work force estimates, covering those aged 10 and over. The free farm total is the sum of four components in 1860 and five in 1850. In both years the sum includes the original census count, my revisions to that count, the number of "laborers, not otherwise specified" allocated to farming, and an estimate of males aged 10 to 15 in farming. For 1850, a fifth component, an estimate of the number of female farm workers aged 16 and over was added (see tables 1A.10 and 1A.11).

The original census count in 1860 covered the free population (male and female) aged 15 and over, while the 1850 figure pertained to only males aged 15 and over. In both years, the census figures were adjusted from the coverage of those aged 15 and over to those aged 16 and over. The census counts were also adjusted for flaws found in some states (Weiss 1986a). The net effect was to adjust the census counts of farm workers aged 16 and over downward by 38,000 workers in 1850 and upward by 71,000 in 1860. The reduction in 1850 reflects the net outcome of the removal of 55,000 workers 15 years of age and the addition of 17,000 workers to correct for undercounting in eleven states. Most of the upward adjustment in 1860 was made to correct the Illinois figure. After deducting an estimate of the number of females included in that state's count, the residual implied that only 68 percent of the males aged 16 and over

Table 1A.9 **Revised Estimates of the Farm Labor Force, 1800 to 1860 (hundreds of workers aged 10 and over)**

	1800	1810	1820	1830	1840	1850	1860
Alabama			470	996	1,973	2,619	3,388
Arkansas			40	84	283	637	1,304
California						43	531
Colorado							8
Connecticut	504	493	515	559	570	514	518
Dakotas							8
Delaware	151	161	143	173	160	155	168
District of Columbia	7	10	10	9	10	10	13
Florida				128	200	295	448
Georgia	512	835	1,164	1,687	2,264	2,953	3,484
Illinois		30	124	331	1,054	1,737	3,173
Indiana	15	52	309	725	1,444	2,013	2,596
Iowa					105	392	1,318
Kansas							217
Kentucky	549	1,022	1,462	1,849	2,099	2,555	2,929
Louisiana		289	528	729	1,057	1,568	2,233
Maine	262	391	579	799	976	932	922
Maryland	886	924	888	937	831	975	1,043
Massachusetts	732	725	734	785	879	808	777
Michigan		13	19	83	542	801	1,447
Minnesota						12	333
Mississippi	31	147	267	492	1,436	2,197	3,139
Missouri			160	343	924	1,471	2,484
Nebraska							55
Nevada							7
New Hampshire	364	423	535	93	623	582	509
New Jersey	476	518	477	525	587	640	674
New Mexico						151	169
New York	1,118	1,701	2,560	3,563	4,560	4,371	4,491
North Carolina	1,390	1,656	1,942	2,249	2,315	2,669	3,035
Ohio	97	456	1,111	1,823	2,896	3,574	3,841
Oregon						23	110
Pennsylvania	1,126	1,410	1,649	1,952	2,390	2,963	3,290
Rhode Island	115	119	128	140	143	124	133
South Carolina	1,107	1,392	1,891	2,082	2,138	2,417	2,650
Tennessee	247	652	1,065	1,772	2,223	2,749	3,047
Texas						627	1,830
Utah						23	62
Vermont	304	426	543	662	700	714	622
Virginia	2,740	3,057	3,175	3,748	3,367	4,018	4,484
Washington							27
Wisconsin					70	551	1,470
United States	12,735	16,902	22,489	29,820	38,819	48,885	62,989

Note: See the text for the details of estimation.

Table 1A.10   **Farm Labor Force Estimates, 1860**

		Census Data			Additions to Census		
	Revised Figures	Original Count	Revisions	Laborers n.o.s.	Slaves 10+	Female 16+	Males 10–15
Alabama	338,771	86,339	8,690	9,655	211,960	1,907	22,127
Arkansas	130,374	58,389	−1,866	6,631	55,958	1,106	11,261
California	53,144	38,313	−2,881	17,067	0	688	645
Colorado	815	222	22	550	0	15	20
Connecticut	51,772	42,903	−1,029	7,312	0	810	2,585
Dakotas	766	926	−337	153	0	8	24
Delaware	16,805	11,566	−1,212	3,950	929	180	1,572
District of Columbia	1,292	680	−52	137	504	11	23
Florida	44,832	10,565	−213	2,019	30,813	276	1,649
Georgia	348,446	95,192	7,376	9,271	216,796	2,134	19,812
Illinois	317,316	201,981	50,563	48,782	0	5,593	15,989
Indiana	259,586	200,244	14,607	28,460	0	4,730	16,275
Iowa	131,837	116,230	−2,370	11,157	0	2,261	6,819
Kansas	21,708	19,317	−279	1,748	1	341	921
Kentucky	292,885	149,326	−3,950	20,596	105,768	3,233	21,146
Louisiana	223,331	30,933	4,212	11,242	172,466	1,124	4,478
Maine	92,226	81,164	−1,348	9,062	0	1,139	3,347
Maryland	104,369	42,883	−1,101	14,480	42,972	836	5,135
Massachusetts	77,678	65,299	−1,249	10,303	0	1,210	3,325
Michigan	144,748	125,531	−2,407	16,852	0	2,607	4,772
Minnesota	33,345	28,055	−427	4,731	0	559	986
Mississippi	313,852	61,559	8,968	7,400	224,465	1,272	11,460
Missouri	248,417	165,773	−4,022	19,657	53,084	3,269	13,925
Nebraska	5,489	4,499	−579	1,365	10	97	194
Nevada	733	384	0	345	0	6	5
New Hampshire	50,918	45,860	−829	4,382	0	624	1,505
New Jersey	67,360	50,269	−1,438	14,381	0	970	4,148
New Mexico	16,929	12,003	−1,796	5,541	0	303	1,181
New York	449,128	378,196	−8,736	61,767	0	5,195	17,901
North Carolina	303,454	106,280	−3,626	16,723	158,649	2,763	25,428
Ohio	384,057	302,768	9,337	51,623	0	8,065	20,329
Oregon	10,988	9,240	−80	1,576	0	134	252
Pennsylvania	329,040	253,994	−7,094	57,359	0	4,090	24,781
Rhode Island	13,273	10,959	359	1,088	0	156	867
South Carolina	264,959	46,849	7,469	5,690	196,302	1,195	8,649
Tennessee	304,679	131,918	−3,934	21,397	130,490	3,145	24,807
Texas	182,963	63,640	10,263	89,514	10,743	1,368	8,803
Utah	6,207	4,596	277	1,018	16	118	300
Vermont	62,232	53,113	−1,051	7,918	0	690	2,252
Virginia	448,429	145,517	5,935	38,323	236,436	4,178	22,218
Washington	2,670	1,958	−6	693	0	21	26
Wisconsin	147,037	126,069	−2,935	18,590	0	2,505	5,313
United States	6,298,859	3,381,502	71,233	581,735	1,927,133	70,934	337,257

Note: The revised figures are the sums of the original count, the revisions to the census data, the allocation of laborers not otherwise specified (n.o.s.), and the additions to the census of estimates of those not
included in the original count, slave workers aged 10 and over and males aged 10 to 15. The figure for
females aged 16 and over is an estimate of the number implicit in the original census count. See the text
for details.

Table 1A.11   **Farm Labor Force Estimates, 1850**

		Census Data			Additions to Census		
	Revised Figures	Original Count	Revisions	Laborers n.o.s	Slaves 10+	Female 16+	Males 10–15
Alabama	261,874	70,490	−477	6,365	166,084	1,511	17,901
Arkansas	63,650	29,199	−862	5,440	23,582	539	5,752
California	4,253	2,124	−2	1,979	0	57	95
Colorado	0	0	0	0	0		0
Connecticut	51,371	32,050	3,515	12,541	0	736	2,530
Dakotas	0	0	0	0	0		0
Delaware	15,457	7,895	6	4,939	1,130	149	1,337
District of Columbia	1,040	453	10	90	453	17	17
Florida	29,545	6,111	−102	2,495	19,888	166	987
Georgia	295,257	85,533	−2,404	9,102	182,701	1,874	18,451
Illinois	173,704	141,167	−3,224	23,063	0	2,841	9,857
Indiana	201,341	163,263	−3,246	24,464	0	3,435	13,426
Iowa	39,206	32,778	−662	4,175	0	637	2,278
Kansas	0	0	0	0	0	0	0
Kentucky	255,496	115,393	−3,030	22,897	98,738	2,700	18,798
Louisiana	156,820	20,878	746	8,396	122,836	777	3,187
Maine	93,247	77,163	−1,086	12,692	0	1,027	3,452
Maryland	97,466	29,396	1,218	17,318	43,698	1,464	4,372
Massachusetts	80,796	56,525	−851	20,553	0	1,175	3,394
Michigan	80,098	65,829	−1,163	11,014	0	1,402	3,015
Minnesota	1,210	564	−5	594	0	18	39
Mississippi	219,673	52,623	−1,453	4,900	152,787	998	9,818
Missouri	147,107	65,717	11,942	17,977	40,730	1,858	8,883
Nebraska	0	0	0	0	0	0	0
Nevada	0	0	0	0	0	0	0
New Hampshire	58,156	47,564	−645	8,940	0	630	1,667
New Jersey	64,006	32,971	−767	26,953	0	837	4,012
New Mexico	15,145	7,963	1,814	4,280	0	235	853
New York	437,124	315,487	−5,661	104,854	0	4,726	17,718
North Carolina	266,933	82,983	−2,632	25,857	135,636	2,413	22,676
Ohio	357,418	270,832	−4,883	65,272	0	6,832	19,365
Oregon	2,311	1,706	−26	527	0	34	71
Pennsylvania	296,275	209,044	−19,712	80,919	0	3,498	22,526
Rhode Island	12,358	8,826	−192	2,697	0	155	872
South Carolina	241,727	43,167	−1,213	6,516	183,887	1,088	8,283
Tennessee	274,940	119,633	−2,155	15,778	114,486	2,863	24,335
Texas	62,745	25,652	−163	4,964	28,430	489	3,372
Utah	2,341	1,583	−18	610	13	41	111
Vermont	71,447	48,390	−780	20,757	0	657	2,422
Virginia	401,845	112,178	−1,240	40,651	226,238	3,678	20,340
Washington	0	0	0	0	0	0	0
Wisconsin	55,141	41,003	1,537	9,366	0	1,025	2,209
United States	4,888,524	2,424,133	−37,865	629,935	1,541,315	52,584	278,422

Note: The revised figures are the sums of the figures in the other six columns, including the estimate of females aged 16 and over.

were in the work force. My adjustment of 51,000 farm workers makes up about 23 percent of the revised state figure.

The farm work force was made up primarily of workers with occupations that were readily identified with the industry.[53] In addition to those occupations there were others that were found in more than one industry. The chief such occupation was "laborers, not otherwise specified," for which there were nearly one million workers reported for the United States in 1850 and 1860: 909,786 in 1850 and 969,301 in 1860. I distributed these between farm and nonfarm industries in each state on the basis of the division that existed in a base year (1910) adjusted to reflect the change in urbanization that had occurred over time (see Weiss 1987c). This allocation of laborers raised the census count in farming by 629,935 in 1850 (26 percent) and 581,735 in 1860 (17.2 percent).[54]

The number of males aged 10 to 15 in farming was taken to be the number of males that age in the *rural* labor force, which is equal to the number of males 10 to 15 years in the rural population times the state-specific participation rate for that age-sex group. Since the rural share of the population declined over time, the farm share of these workers also declined, from 96 percent in 1800 to 84 percent in 1860.

For 1850, the number of females aged 16 and over in farming was estimated to be equal to 1.5 percent of the free females of that age in the South and North Central states, and 0.7 percent of those in the Northeast. The percentages were derived from the Bateman-Foust sample of rural northern households in 1860 (Bateman and Foust 1973). Since there was a slight trend in the overall participation rate for females aged 16 and over, the constancy in the percentage engaged in farming means that the share of the adult female labor force in farming declined over time, falling from 12.6 percent in 1800 to 8.1 percent in 1860.[55]

To this free farm work force I added, in both 1850 and 1860, estimates of the number of slaves engaged in agriculture. In both years the slave figures were estimated as 74 percent of the rural slave population aged 10 and over.[56]

---

53. The assignment of occupations to industries was done according to the classification used by Miller and Brainerd (1957, 382), which followed closely that of Edwards (1940).

54. Lebergott chose not to allocate any unclassified laborers to farming in either 1850 or 1860 (1966, 152–53).

55. No estimate of females in farming was necessary for 1860 because they were included in the census count. I estimate that the implicit number of such workers was 70,934.

56. It was necessary to estimate the age distribution of the rural slaves because the census did not provide the breakdowns by residence. The census did provide the age breakdown for all slaves, and since most lived in rural areas, the distribution there must have been very similar. The 1840 age distribution of rural slaves confirms that the total and rural distributions were very close. Whichever distribution is used, the total slave population for the respective years or the 1840 rural distribution, the farm labor force estimates are within 0.4 percent of each other in 1860 and 0.2 percent in 1850.

The percentage was the coefficient obtained from a regression equation fitted to the 1840 data for 488 counties (see the 1840 section, which follows).

Estimates for 1840

The estimates of the agricultural work force for 1840 are based almost entirely on the census statistics. The census of 1840 collected and reported some employment statistics, but unfortunately, the figures did not cover all industries, and the census did not specify which portions of the population were counted in those industries that were included. There is no reason to think that the census intended to neglect any free workers regardless of sex or age, because the census takers were directed to collect the number of persons in each family employed in the covered industries (Wright, 1900, 33, 143). The exact demographic coverage, however, was not spelled out precisely, and whatever the intention of the Census Bureau the report appears to have varied from one census district to another.

The census was also vague about the definitions of the industries that were reported. The Census Bureau published employment statistics for seven industries: mining; agriculture; commerce; manufactures and trades; navigation of the ocean; navigation of canals, lakes, and rivers; and the learned professions and engineers. Which occupations belonged to which industries was apparently left to the discretion of the census marshals. Moreover, the possibility that an industry like manufacturing included fishing and forestry, or that commerce included all professional services, cannot be dismissed.

This double imprecision regarding industrial and demographic coverage made it difficult to decipher exactly which employment statistics were reported. Nonetheless, I think I have been able to determine the age and sex coverage, thereby enhancing the usefulness of the industrial figures that were reported (see Weiss 1987a for details). For the seven industries covered, it appears that the census attempted to count all free workers aged 10 and over and included some, but not all, slaves. Given the incompleteness of the slave enumeration, the reported figures in the South could not be used without adjustment. Outside the South, with some obvious exceptions, the figures appear to be reasonably accurate counts of the number of free workers engaged in the covered industries. While these statistics do not give us the total labor force in each state, they do provide reliable evidence on the bulk of the work force, and especially on the agricultural sector.

In summary, the assessment consisted of adjusting the reported census total to include an estimate of workers employed in those industries that were not covered, primarily personal services, fishing, and forestry. From this revised total I deducted my estimate of the number of female workers aged 16 and over, male and female workers aged 10 to 15, and slave workers aged 10 and over. The residual left after these additions and deductions should be free male workers aged 16 and over. Since there is very good evidence as to the likely participation rates of adult male workers, I used that to judge the reasonableness of the residual figures. There were some states in which this residual was clearly anomalous, most of which were confined to the South and appear due to the difficulties of counting the number of slave workers. Elsewhere the residuals seemed very reasonable in most states. There were a few extreme deviations (Pennsylvania and New Jersey being much too low, and a few New England states being too high), but for most the residuals were very small. For twelve out of the seventeen nonslave states the residual was within 10 percent of the expected value of the adult male participation rate. The implication of this test is that the residuals were close to the expected values because the census counted all workers, at least all free workers, aged 10 and over. To be sure, there were errors and deficiencies that varied across states, but with a few exceptions the reported statistics outside the South are good measures of the number of all free workers employed in the covered industries.

Revisions for the Free States

In those few northern states where the residual was substantially out of line, I made adjustments on a county-by-county basis. After examining the ratios of the reported number of workers to the population aged 10 and over in each county, I corrected any that were noticeably out of line. Where there was no labor force reported, the revised count was derived by multiplying the population by the mean participation rate for those counties in which there was no suspicion of error (the adjusted state mean). In other counties that had low ratios or unusually high ones, I examined the subdivisions to try to locate the source of the county's deviant statistic. Where the ratios were low in every subdivision, the adjusted state mean participation rate was used to produce corrected figures. In the others where the original ratios were too low or very high, some subdivisions appear to have reliable counts, and their ratios were used to correct the figures in the other subdivisions.

Revisions for the Slave States

The assessment and revision of the census figures for the southern states was not as straightforward, due to the presence of slave workers. Since the slave share of the population varied from state to state, and across counties within states, the overall participation rates varied widely. Moreover, the presence of slave workers may have influenced the participation rates for whites. Unfortunately the census reported only the combined number of free and slave workers, so the components could not be assessed independently.

My assessment consisted of estimating a residual figure for the free work force that could be compared to the free population. The ratio of this residual labor force to the population enabled me to identify counties in which the reported figures seemed reliable, and those in which revisions were needed. The reliable data were used to estimate a regression equation in which the reported labor force was a function of the slave and free populations resident in the county. The equation was then used to estimate the work force in those counties that needed to be revised.[57]

For each state whose census employment figure seemed out of line, the county data on rural employment were assessed in several ways.[58] The key assessment statistic was the ratio of a residual estimate of the free work force to the free male population aged 10 and over.[59] The residual was derived by calculating the size of the slave work force, using the county's slave population aged 10 and over and assumptions about their labor force participation rate, and deducting that figure from the census total. The test ratio represents an implicit participation rate for males aged 10 and over. If those ratios fell in line with the expected values of the male participation rates, the census figure from which they were derived must be a reasonable count of the free and slave labor force. If the ratio were out of line, the census statistic is likely in error.

In fact a range of the residual free work force was estimated, and several criteria were used to sort the counties into three categories: those in which the data seemed reliable and were included in the regression sample, those in which the census counts were very deviant and needed to be revised, and those where the counts seemed somewhat high or low and were excluded from the regression sample, but were left unrevised. A minimum residual was derived by assuming that the entire slave work force (90 percent of the slave population aged 10 and over) was included in the industries covered by the 1840 census.[60] An upper bound to the free residual was obtained by assuming that

57. The coefficient on the slave population variable was also used to estimate the slave work force engaged in farming in 1850 and 1860.

58. This procedure dealt with just the rural data; the cities were excluded and treated separately. There were a few counties in which the reported employment exceeded 90 percent of the entire population aged 10 and over. These counties were not used in estimating the regression equation, and their employment figures were revised downward to equal 90 percent of the population.

59. A similar calculation using the free male and female population was also carried out and yielded identical results. The ratios using the male denominator indicated more obvious discontinuities and thus indicated more clearly which sample of counties had reliable employment figures for purposes of estimating the regression equation. Moreover, the male population seemed like the more appropriate base to use since, outside of New England, female workers were small in number in the antebellum period.

60. While it is true that a few slaves under the age of 10 may have been working, and in any particular county the participation rate of those over 10 could have exceeded 90 percent, the use of that figure should yield the maximum number of slaves in the census enumeration in most counties, and thus the minimum free residual. The number of slaves under the age of 10 that were likely employed made up only a small percentage of the population aged 10 and over. For those

only 70 percent of the rural slaves aged 10 and over were in the covered industries.[61]

Where the ratio based on the minimum residual was above the expected value, the county's employment figure must have been too high. Those counties were excluded from the regression sample, but their employment statistics were not revised.[62] The ratio based on the maximum free residual was used to judge whether the census had underenumerated workers. If a ratio biased upward in this fashion fell below the expected value, the census count must have been too low. These counties were excluded from the regression, and their employment figures were revised.[63]

With the exclusion of those counties in which the check ratio was too high or too low, a sample of 488 counties was left in which the ratios seemed reasonable. The reasonableness of the ratios implies that the census must have counted quite accurately the number of free and slave workers in those counties. This sample was used to estimate a regression equation with which I could calculate the "true" employment in those counties that had not passed the ratio test. The following equations were estimated for covered and agricultural employment:[64]

$$\text{CoveredLF} = .380 \text{ FreePop10+} + .771 \text{ SlavePop10+} \qquad R^2 = .97$$
$$\qquad\qquad (.007) \qquad\qquad\qquad (.007)$$

$$\text{AgLF} = .337 \text{ FreePop10+} + .741 \text{ SlavePop10+} \qquad R^2 = .95$$
$$\qquad\qquad (.008) \qquad\qquad\qquad (.008)$$

---

aged 10 and over, the ultimate maximum would be 100 percent, so my estimated maximum can be no more than 10 percent too low. Since some of the rural slaves were employed in industries not included in the census count, namely, as domestic servants, the 90 percent figure is likely the maximum value. Moreover, while the actual figure may have varied from county to county, the 90 percent figure is consistent with the estimator used to derive the total slave labor force.

61. The industries covered by the 1840 census included all commodity production, not just agriculture. The use of the 70 percent figure implies that 22 percent of the rural slave work force was engaged in personal service, the chief industry not covered by the 1840 census. Such a share is roughly twice as large as the percentage of slaves estimated to be engaged in domestic service on plantations (Olson 1983, 55–59). Since 70 percent is the lower bound to the slave work force in the covered industries, after subtracting it from the reported census figure the remainder is an upper bound to the number of free workers included in the count.

62. The expected value was the 1860 ratio of the free labor force aged 16 and over to the free male population aged 16 and over for each state. Since the 1860 data include all industries, and since the ratio based on those 16 and over should be higher than that for those aged 10 and over, this should provide a stringent test and result in the exclusion of only the most deviant counties.

63. The 1860 ratio of free agricultural workers aged 16 and over to free males aged 10 and over served as the expected value. This was deemed a lower bound because the numerator was confined to agriculture (excluding the other commodity-producing industries and trades that were included in the 1840 count), and covers only those aged 16 and over, while the denominator includes the population aged 10 and over. In total, 101 counties were judged to have excessively low counts of employment; 49 had negative residuals, 52 residuals between 0 and 0.42.

64. The equations were estimated using weighted least squares to correct for heteroscedasticity, with the weights being values of the free population aged 10 and over. The CoveredLF measures employment in the industries "covered" by the census report. A number of forms of the estimating

The coefficients are highly significant (the standard errors are in parentheses), and perhaps more important, the values for the free population represent very plausible participation rates, giving confidence to the estimates for the slave population. There were three exceptions to this estimating procedure. For Arkansas, Delaware, and Florida, the expected revisions were so small that I simply examined the counties for obvious omissions. In Delaware, this resulted in no revisions, while the figures were revised by 2,173 in Arkansas and 7,876 in Florida.

The employment data in southern cities were assessed separately and were revised in ten places.[65] The following equation was fit to the data for twenty-two of the remaining cities, and the regression coefficients were used to estimate the revised labor force in the covered industries in the ten cities.[66]

$$\text{LF} = .159 \text{ FreePop10} + + .881 \text{ MaleSlaves10} + \qquad R^2 = .997$$
$$\qquad (.004) \qquad\qquad\qquad (.044)$$

The covered labor force was increased by 8,106 workers, bringing the revised urban count to 77,926. The revisions were distributed among agriculture, manufacturing and trades, commerce, and all other occupations in the same proportion as prevailed in the unadjusted data. In cities where no employment had been reported by the census, the distribution of the sample cities was used to allocate the revised figures.

The adjustments and the revised figures are shown by state in table 1A.12. For the nation, the correction to the census count totaled 202,637 workers (4.2 percent), 160,010 of which were added to agriculture.[67] Most of the additions were in the South, 147,939 in total, 131,231 in agriculture.

Estimates for 1820

The census of 1820 collected and reported some employment statistics, and like the 1840 census did not cover all industries or spell out the exact demographic coverage. Whatever the intention of the census superintendent, the report appears to have varied from one census district to another.

It is possible that the census tried to record the occupations of all workers

---

equations were tried, using different combinations of population components, using log and non-log values, with a constant term included and excluded, and with the dependent variable being the number of workers and the participation rate.

65. Eight of these had very low residual ratios, while one (Hagerstown, Maryland) had an extremely high ratio. Georgetown had a residual ratio that was only slightly low, but reported no employment in commerce, so its count was revised.

66. Three cities were excluded from the regression: Augusta, Georgia; Lexington, Kentucky; and St. Louis, Missouri.

67. This revised count is still slightly lower than might be expected on the basis of the average adult male participation rates. My estimate of the full undercount is around 300,000 workers; the conservative revisions made here remove about two-thirds of that deficiency. See Weiss (1987a) for details.

Table 1A.12   **Revised and Census Counts of Workers, 1840**

	Covered Industries			Agriculture		
	Revised Count	Original Census	Adjustment	Revised Count	Original Census	Adjustment
Alabama	210,688	189,470	21,218	197,330	177,439	19,891
Arkansas	30,300	28,127	2,173	28,300	26,355	1,945
California		0				0
Colorado		0				0
Connecticut	92,751	92,609	142	56,955	56,955	0
Dakotas		0				0
Delaware	21,382	21,382	0	16,015	16,015	0
District of Columbia	4,937	1,790	3,147	1,045	110	935
Florida	22,409	14,533	7,876	19,993	12,117	7,876
Georgia	242,715	222,233	20,482	226,426	209,383	17,043
Illinois	124,494	124,204	290	105,419	105,337	82
Indiana	170,505	175,678	−5,173	144,424	148,806	−4,382
Iowa	13,126	13,126	0	10,469	10,469	0
Kansas		0				0
Kentucky	240,017	228,233	11,784	209,888	197,738	12,150
Louisiana	125,605	98,405	27,200	105,716	79,289	26,427
Maine	132,856	141,040	−8,184	97,591	103,603	−6,012
Maryland	113,043	101,087	11,956	83,075	72,046	11,029
Massachusetts	213,372	212,904	468	87,879	87,837	42
Michigan	64,020	65,273	−1,253	54,232	56,521	−2,289
Minnesota		0				0
Mississippi	150,891	146,831	4,060	143,591	139,724	3,867
Missouri	110,165	110,165	0	92,408	92,408	0
Nebraska		0				0
Nevada		0				0
New Hampshire	84,216	99,457	−15,241	62,328	77,949	−15,621
New Jersey	93,831	90,649	3,182	58,691	56,701	1,990
New Mexico		0				0
New York	692,446	689,302	3,144	456,010	455,954	56
North Carolina	251,289	235,532	15,757	231,461	217,095	14,366
Ohio	380,738	357,947	22,791	289,568	272,579	16,989
Oregon		0				0
Pennsylvania	396,156	345,829	50,327	238,939	207,533	31,406
Rhode Island	34,337	41,673	−7,336	14,304	16,617	−2,313
South Carolina	233,408	212,907	20,501	213,849	198,363	15,486
Tennessee	244,385	250,273	−5,888	222,294	227,739	−5,445
Texas		0				0
Utah		0				0
Vermont	85,892	89,454	−3,562	70,017	73,150	−3,133
Virginia	412,971	390,195	22,776	336,670	319,045	17,625
Washington		0				0
Wisconsin	10,616	10,616	0	7,047	7,047	0
United States	5,003,561	4,800,924	202,637	3,881,934	3,721,924	160,010

Sources: U.S. Bureau of the Census 1840; Weiss 1987a.

Notes: The "covered industries" are those for which the 1840 census reported employment. See the text and Weiss (1987a) for details. The procedures adopted to revise the census figures produced covered totals for Indiana and Michigan that exceeded the independently estimated total labor force. Each of the revised industry figures in those states was reduced proportionally so that their sum equaled the independent total. The adjustments indicated in this table represent the net change to the figures for those two states.

according to the instruction that "assistants may select the column of occupation to which each individual may be set down" (U.S. Bureau of the Census 1979, 11; Wright 1900, 33, 135). The occupational data, however, were recorded after the enumeration of free white persons but before that of slaves and free blacks (U.S. Bureau of the Census 1820), so it is possible that enumerators excluded these latter persons from the occupational count. Moreover, the social mores of the time might have resulted in the enumerators making a complete count of adult males, but being lax about the inclusion of females or youths.[68] Finally, these instructions did not specify any minimum age at which workers were to be counted.

The census was also vague about the definitions of the industries—agriculture, commerce, and manufacturing—that were reported. It is conceivable that the three were to be exhaustive. As noted above, the assistant could select a column in which to put each individual, and the instructions discussed the difficulties of placing people in categories. A major concern, however, was to avoid duplication: "no individual should be placed in more than one of" the occupations (U.S. Bureau of the Census 1979, 11; Wright 1900, 135). Moreover, there was no statement compelling the enumerators to place each individual in at least one, and the three occupational categories were referred to as "the three principal walks of life" (U.S. Bureau of the Census 1979, 11), clearly leaving room for the exclusion of some workers and occupations that belonged to lesser lines of activity.

Census marshals apparently had some discretion in deciding which occupations belonged to which industries. It was believed that there would be little problem with agriculture and commerce. "[Of] those whose occupations are exclusively agricultural or commercial there can seldom arise a question" (U.S. Bureau of the Census 1979, 11). No details of the classification principles or scheme were given, however. On the other hand, manufacturing was to include "all those artificers, handicraftsmen, and mechanics, whose labor is preeminently of the hand, and not upon the field" (Wright 1900, 135). Of course, in order for the list to be exhaustive, "commerce" must have included, in addition to wholesale and retail trade, all professional and personal services, as well as any occupation, such as those in fishing and forestry, that was not obviously placed in the other two great categories.

My assessment of the data is that the industrial coverage was not exhaustive, but for the industries covered, the census attempted to enumerate all free and slave workers aged 10 and over (see Weiss 1988 for details). The counts are incomplete, however, so could not be used without adjustment. While the undercounts were most pronounced in the slave states, the figures for some nonslave states also required revision. It appears, as well, that the extent to which workers aged 10 to 15 were counted varied from county to county, and state to state. Overall, the census appears to have enumerated quite accurately

68. Abel and Folbre (1990) make this point about women. More generally, the enumerators may have simply focused on the head of household, thereby ignoring women and youths.

the number of workers engaged in agriculture (and presumably the other covered industries) in about half the states and in a number of counties in every state.[69] This subset of reliable statistics provided a solid base of evidence, especially for the agricultural sector, with which to adjust the evidence where it appears the census miscounted.

It was impossible to determine for sure which industries (or occupations) were covered and which population groups were included in the 1820 count, given the broad scope of the industrial categories and the ambiguity in their definitions. In order to determine which states' figures were in need of adjustment, I circumvented these definitional problems by examining only the agricultural statistics and focusing on the rural areas. The key statistic used in this assessment was the ratio of the farm labor force to the *rural* population, which remained at least constant, and more likely declined, over time. Thus the 1820 ratios should have been close to or slightly above the 1840 ratio, but in fact were below in almost every state, indicating an undercount. This could have occurred because there was a general undercount or because the census excluded specific population components.[70]

Attempts to correct the census by making a uniform adjustment across all states for the population groups likely to have been excluded—slaves and males aged 10 to 15—improved the count in some states but worsened it in others. It seems that these workers were included to some extent in almost every state, but the accuracy of that count varied by state and region. The assessment indicated that the underenumeration of agricultural workers was concentrated in the South, but some free states' figures seemed low as well. I carried out a more detailed examination of the county data in each state, including the free ones, to determine more precisely where the errors occurred and where the census figures needed to be revised. These more detailed assessments and revisions were carried out separately for free and slave states, and for rural and urban areas.

Revisions for the Free States

For rural counties in the free states the assessment statistic was the ratio of census employment in agriculture, manufacturing, and commerce to the free male population aged 16 and over. These three industries might have been so broadly conceived by the census that they employed virtually all adult male workers. If so, this ratio would be at least equal to the adult male participation

69. This assessment refers to the set of corrected census data, which incorporates various revisions made in later censuses, and correction of other arithmetical errors. The most noteworthy change is a correction to the Indiana count. The original census figures, which appear to have been carried through subsequent censuses, contained a substantial error in addition in the agricultural total. The original figure of 61,315 is nearly double the correct amount of 31,074.

70. It is possible, but unlikely, that the 1840 ratio is too high. In any case the results reported here would be the same if I used the average ratio for the years 1840 to 1860, or either of the years 1850 and 1860.

rate (approximately 0.9). Since the 1820 census was to have counted female workers and males aged 10 to 15, the ratio should be even higher. The 1840 ratio, 1.07 in the rural areas of northern states, indicates that the 1820 figure should in fact have been well above 0.9. The implication of a lower value is that either these other groups were not counted, or they and some adult males were employed in those industries not covered by the census. In urban areas nonfarm employment might have been possible, but in rural areas the alternatives must have been quite limited, so any ratio below 0.9 was suspect.

In some counties this test ratio was extremely low, implying that the census must have undercounted workers generally, and thus missed some free males aged 16 and over, as well as having failed to count properly female workers and males aged 10 to 15. A ratio as low as 0.72, for example, implies that the census failed to count any female or young male workers and that the industries covered by the census employed only 80 percent of the adult male workers. Again, because the labor force figures were to have included some females over 10 and males aged 10 to 15, the ratios, and the implied shares of adult males employed in those industries, should be higher.

The 1840 evidence for rural areas indicates that the three industries employed at least 80 percent of the male workers aged 16 and over. We do not know the age-sex breakdown of each industry, but agriculture, the chief component of the census labor force count, employed 76 percent of the male workers aged 16 and over in rural areas in 1840. If all rural workers in manufacturing and commerce in 1840 were males over 16, then the three industries would have employed 98 percent of the adult male workers. Since adult males made up the bulk of the total labor force, the share engaged in the three industries must have been fairly constant over time in the rural areas. Thus in those counties where the 1820 ratio falls below 0.72, the employment figures must be way too low.

Where the 1820 ratio was extremely low, I increased the county's employment in order to achieve a 0.72 ratio. These additions were taken to be males aged 16 and over. In those counties, as well as those in which the assessment ratio fell between 0.72 and 0.9, I assumed that the census failed to count males aged 10 to 15 and added an estimate of such workers. The estimate was equal to the number of workers that age in the rural labor force in that county. Given that these adjustments were carried out for the rural areas, the added workers were all allocated to agriculture.

The city data were assembled separately and assessed by comparing the 1820 data for each city with that for 1840. I assumed that the urban ratios of agricultural, manufacturing, and commerce workers to the male population aged 16 and over did not change much between 1820 and 1840, and used the 1840 ratios to judge whether the 1820 counts in individual cities were deviant and in need of revision. The evidence indicated that the coverage varied, either industrially or by demographic coverage, but in eighteen cities the counts were unexplainably low. The figures for these cities were revised by increasing the labor force count so that the 1820 ratio of workers in agriculture, manufacturing, and commerce to males 16 and over equaled that for 1840.[71]

Revisions for the Slave States

As was the case for 1840, the assessment and revision of the slave states' figures was not as straightforward due to the presence of slave workers. My assessment consisted of deriving a residual estimate of the free work force, which was compared to the free male population in order to identify counties in which the reported figures seemed reliable, as well as those in which revisions were needed. The calculations were carried out for only the rural population in each county; the cities were excluded and treated separately. Where the county figures were reliable, they were used to estimate a regression equation that was subsequently used to correct the work force in those counties where the census had undercounted workers.

To obtain the free residual I assumed an agricultural participation rate for slaves, used it to estimate the slave work force in each county, and deducted that figure from the reported labor force. In fact a range of the residual free work force was estimated, and several criteria were used to sort the counties into three categories: those for which the data were judged reliable and could be used in the regression estimation, those in which the census counts were very deviant and needed to be revised, and those where the counts seemed somewhat high or low and so were excluded from the regression estimation but were left unrevised. A minimum residual was derived by assuming that the entire slave work force (90 percent of the slave population aged 10 and over) was counted in agriculture in the 1820 census. An upper bound to the free residual was obtained by assuming that only 70 percent of the rural slaves aged 10 and over were in agriculture.[72]

The minimum residual was used to identify counties in which the employment figures were too high. These counties were excluded from the regression sample, and their employment count was reduced to assure a 0.9 ratio of agricultural workers to the male population aged 10 and over.[73]

71. For those cities where the 1840 value is questionable, the 1820 count was revised so that the city ratio equaled the 1840 state average for urban areas.

72. The 70 percent figure implies that 22 percent of the rural slave work force was engaged in industries not covered by the 1820 census, chief of which must have been personal service. Such a share is roughly twice as large as the percentage of slaves estimated to be engaged in domestic service on plantations (Olson 1983, 55–59). Since 70 percent is the lower bound to the slave work force in agriculture, its subtraction from the reported census figure yields an upper bound to the number of free workers in agriculture. The list of deviant counties is not sensitive to the choice of the slave participation rate. If a 60 percent figure were used, the list would be the same.

73. The 0.9 ratio implies that all males aged 10 and over were engaged in agriculture. Since the average participation rate for males aged 16 and over was approximately .9, and that for males aged 10 to 15 was around .4 in the South, the weighted average for males 10 and over had to be below .9. Thus the revised figures in these counties may still be slightly high, or can be thought of as including female farm workers.

On the other hand, the maximum free residual biased upward the test ratio, and where that ratio still fell below the expected value, the census count must have been too low. The expected value was the 1850 ratio of free agricultural workers aged 16 and over to free males aged 16 and over. All counties whose ratios fell below the 1850 figure were excluded from the regression sample. The figures were revised, however, only where the county's ratio fell below one-half the 1850 value.[74]

A number of forms of the estimating equations were tried, with the following giving the best results:[75]

$$CoveredLF = .860 \ FreeMales16+ \ + \ .772 \ SlavePop10+ \qquad R^2 = .97$$
$$(.023) \qquad\qquad (.009)$$

$$AgLF = .727 \ FreeMales16+ \ + \ .769 \ SlavePop10+ \qquad R^2 = .97$$
$$(.023) \qquad\qquad (.008)$$

The R^2 values are high, the coefficients are highly significant (the figures in parentheses are the standard errors), and the coefficients for the free population variables are very plausible estimates of their participation rates. It seems that we can have a great deal of confidence in the estimates for the slave population.

These equations were used to correct the census figures for any undercount of males aged 16 and over and slaves aged 10 and over in the counties identified as highly deviant. The regression results, however, could not be used to correct for any underenumeration of other agricultural workers, so a separate estimate of male workers aged 10 to 15 was made in those counties that appear to have excluded them. The adjustment was set equal to the number of workers of that age estimated to be in the county's *rural* labor force. Since the inclusion of some of these workers in the regression sample counties may have biased upward the estimated coefficients for adult males and slaves, I offset that bias by making no adjustment for the possible exclusion of female farm workers.[76]

74. There were two exceptions, Mobile County in Alabama and New Hanover in North Carolina. Given their more urbanized economies, low ratios of agricultural workers to population could be expected. A residual estimate of the free census labor force gave reasonable ratios of workers to male population aged 16 and over.

A few other counties, those in which the ratio of the minimum residual to males aged 16 and over exceeded 1.0, were deleted from the regression sample because such high ratios indicated the possibility of an overcount.

75. The CoveredLF measured employment in the three industries "covered" by the 1820 census. The sample consisted of 274 counties. The equations were estimated using weighted least squares to correct for heteroscedasticity, with the weights being values of the free male population aged 16 and over. Alternative forms of the equation were tried using different combinations of population components, log and nonlog values, with a constant term included and excluded, and with the dependent variable being the number of workers and the participation rate.

76. Since some other workers were included in the census statistics of some counties, these regression coefficients are upwardly biased estimates of the number of adult male and slave workers. The bias, however, should not be very great, since many of the counties appear not to have enumerated free male agricultural workers aged 10 to 15. This was indicated by the number of

The difference between the revised figure for covered employment and that for agriculture was divided between manufacturing and commerce. In those counties where some employment was reported, the distribution was assumed to be the same as that in the original returns; otherwise the balance was distributed in the same proportion as prevailed in the regression sample counties.[77]

The employment counts in southern cities were revised separately following the same procedure as used for the rural areas, but the specifics differed. The free residual work force used to evaluate each city's figure was derived by deducting an estimate of the covered slave work force equal to 40 percent of the urban male slaves aged 10 and over and 10 percent of the female slaves aged 10 and over. These shares are those found for Charleston in 1848 (see Goldin 1976, table 2, 14–15). These residuals were used to derive ratios of the free work force to free males aged 10 and over, and the reasonableness of the ratios was judged by comparison with the ratios for 1840 for each city.

Virtually every southern city was in need of revision; the census figures were accepted in only three cities. The revisions were based on the 1840 data. Where the 1840 ratio seemed reasonable, it was used to revise the 1820 statistic. If the 1840 figure for a specific city seemed low, the average for the Middle Atlantic cities was used to revise the 1820 census data. The covered labor force was increased by a total of 10,504 workers, bringing the revised urban count to 35,596. The revisions were distributed among agriculture, manufacturing, and commerce in the same proportion as prevailed in the unadjusted data.[78] In cities where there was no employment reported in the original, the distribution of the sample cities was used.

The revised *census* employment figure for each state is the sum of the revised rural and urban counts. The adjustments and the revised labor force figures are presented in table 1A.13.

---

counties in which the ratio of the minimum residual agricultural worker count to male population aged 16 and over fell below the 0.7 cutoff.

77. There were two exceptions to this estimation procedure. Tennessee was assessed and revised in the same fashion as the rest of the slave states, but its counties were not included in the regression sample. For Arkansas, the predicted undercount was too small to justify a detailed examination. Instead, I simply increased the census count by an estimate of the number of agricultural workers aged 10 to 15. That estimate was very nearly equal to the estimated undercount.

78. The census did not report employment data for four cities in North Carolina, so I estimated those figures. The total labor force in each was calculated as the sum of workers in five population groups, where the figure for each group is the product of an age-sex specific participation rate times the relevant population. The total was distributed across industries by assigning the reported county figures for commerce entirely to the cities, and distributing the balance of the urban labor force according to the average distribution for the other southern cities.

For the District of Columbia, in addition to the adjustment of the city's labor force, the rural portion of the labor force was revised by applying the southern regression equations to the rural population.

Table 1A.13   **Revised and Census Count of Workers, 1820**

	Covered Industries			Agriculture		
	Original Count	Revised Census	Adjustment	Original Count	Revised Census	Adjustment
Alabama	37,445	49,677	12,232	35,359	47,019	11,660
Arkansas	3,871	4,282	411	3,613	4,024	411
California						
Colorado						
Connecticut	71,640	72,667	1,027	50,518	51,545	1,027
Dakotas		0			0	
Delaware	16,613	17,627	1,014	13,259	14,273	1,014
District of Columbia	2,109	4,117	2,008	525	1,004	479
Florida		0			0	
Georgia	106,881	122,718	15,837	101,185	116,389	15,204
Illinois	13,635	13,635	0	12,395	12,395	0
Indiana	34,702	34,525	−177	31,074	30,897	−177
Iowa		0			0	
Kansas		0			0	
Kentucky	145,557	159,852	14,295	132,161	146,222	14,061
Louisiana	65,233	64,091	−1,142	53,941	52,793	−1,148
Maine	66,971	69,899	2,928	55,031	57,879	2,848
Maryland	102,546	115,347	12,801	79,135	88,785	9,650
Massachusetts	110,225	121,587	11,362	63,460	73,449	9,989
Michigan	2,056	2,597	541	1,468	1,882	414
Minnesota		0			0	
Mississippi	22,977	27,772	4,795	22,033	26,714	4,681
Missouri	16,694	18,532	1,838	14,247	16,039	1,792
Nebraska		0			0	
Nevada		0			0	
New Hampshire	62,151	63,242	1,091	52,384	53,475	1,091
New Jersey	58,583	65,510	6,927	40,812	47,739	6,927
New Mexico		0			0	
New York	315,801	333,710	17,909	246,650	255,993	9,343
North Carolina	188,591	209,056	20,465	174,196	194,212	20,016
Ohio	131,406	132,501	1,095	110,991	111,084	93
Oregon		0			0	
Pennsylvania	208,099	234,673	26,574	140,801	164,890	24,089
Rhode Island	19,812	20,659	847	12,559	12,849	290
South Carolina	176,138	200,603	24,465	166,707	189,135	22,428
Tennessee	110,661	115,220	4,559	101,919	106,461	4,542
Texas		0			0	
Utah		0			0	
Vermont	60,211	63,566	3,355	50,951	54,306	3,355
Virginia	312,832	357,933	45,101	275,062	317,470	42,408
Washington		0			0	
Wisconsin		0			0	
United States	2,463,440	2,695,598	232,158	2,042,436	2,248,923	206,487

Sources: U.S. Bureau of the Census 1820; Weiss 1988.

Note: The "covered industries" are those for which the 1820 census reported employment. See the text and Weiss (1988) for details.

Estimates for 1800, 1810, and 1830

For the remaining antebellum years, 1800, 1810, and 1830, the farm and nonfarm figures were derived as the sum of separate estimates of the workers in urban and rural areas.

For cities, the farm labor force was estimated directly as a small share of the urban labor force, and the nonfarm figure was the residual. The farm share for each of these years was based on the evidence for 1820 and 1840, which indicated that in most states the share was similar in both years. The chief disparities arose because of changes in the set of cities making up the urban total. For the nation the farm share of the urban labor force was 3.9 percent in 1820 and 5.0 in 1840. For 1800 the share in each state was assumed to equal the higher of its 1820 or 1840 figures. The 1810 value was set equal to the mean of the 1800 estimate just derived and the 1820 figure, and the 1830 figure equaled the mean of the 1820 and 1840 values. The results are U.S. averages of 4.3 percent in 1800, 5.0 in 1810, and 4.9 in 1830.

There were four exceptions to this procedure in 1800. In Maine, New Hampshire, and Rhode Island differences in the sets of cities in 1820 and 1840 caused the latter year's farm share to be much higher than the former's. In these cases, I used the 1820 data for those cities that were in existence in both 1820 and 1800. These were Portland, Maine; Portsmouth, New Hampshire; and Newport and Providence in Rhode Island. For Georgia, there was no reported urban farm labor force in 1820, so I used the 1840 figure.

Five states with urban populations in 1810 had none in 1800, so the 1800–1820 mean could not be calculated. For two of these states, New Jersey and Ohio, I used the 1820 figure. For Kentucky and Louisiana I used the U.S. average for 1820, a figure above that for the South Central region and higher than the reported 1820 figure for either state. For Georgia, I used the 1840 figure.

There were four exceptions in 1830. Because there were no 1820 urban statistics in Alabama, Georgia, and Missouri, I used only the 1840 figure. For North Carolina I used the 1840 figure rather than average it with a suspiciously low share reported for 1820.

Rural Estimates

Different procedures were used to estimate the rural labor force in the free and slave states.[79] In the free states, the nonfarm labor force was estimated directly, and the farm figure was the difference between the total and the nonfarm estimate. For the slave states, just the opposite tack was taken; the farm labor force was estimated directly, and the residual was the nonfarm labor force.

For the free states, the rural nonagricultural labor force was the sum of

79. The slave states include Delaware and Maryland.

estimates for three components: free males 16 years of age and over engaged in four industrial categories—manufacturing and commerce, navigation, fishing and forestry, and mining; free females 16 years of age and over *not* in farming; and free females aged 10 to 15 in the rural labor force.

To obtain the number of rural free males aged 16 and over engaged in each of four categories, I multiplied the number of males of that age in the population by the share engaged in that industry. The estimation shares were derived from the evidence for later census years and are summarized in table 1A.14.

Manufacturing and commerce were the major employers of the free rural nonfarm labor force. Fortunately, the *rural* shares for these two industries could be calculated for each state for both 1820 and 1840. The 1820 shares were below the 1840 ones, and there were regional variations as well as differential changes in the shares over the twenty years. For the nation the 1820 share (17.5) was quite close to and slightly below that for 1840 (18.9).

For each state, the 1800 share was derived by extrapolating an 1820-base-year figure backward on the basis of the percentage change in the *regional* share that had occurred between 1820 and 1840. The appropriate base-year figure was taken to be the mean value for the least industrialized states in each region in 1820. The one exception was the North Central region, where the mean for Illinois and Indiana was used. That region's least industrialized states, Iowa and Wisconsin, had no employment in these industries in 1820. The 1810 value for each state was derived by assuming a constant rate of increase between the estimated 1800 shares and the 1820 figures. The 1830 values were derived in a similar way, assuming a constant rate of increase between 1820 and 1840.

Shares of the male population engaged in navigation in each state could be calculated for the urban and rural labor forces combined in 1860, and separately for 1840. The 1840 evidence indicated that the rural shares were below the statewide figures, by different amounts in the various regions. That evidence also revealed that, outside of New England, inland navigation employed far more men than did ocean navigation. The distinction is important because the 1840 shares of the male population engaged in navigation were higher than the 1860 (2.2 versus 1.4 percent for the nation), suggesting that there may have been a trend that would put the 1800 share above that of 1840. Given that inland navigation was the more important category in 1840, however, the existence of such a trend is unlikely. Except in New England, the figures for 1840 were more likely above those for 1800 because the former include many workers employed on canals and other inland transportation that had not been in operation before 1825.[80] Thus for the years before 1825 the

---

80. Before 1817 "there was not, perhaps, 100 miles of canal work finished in the United States." By 1840 there were some 3,000 miles in operation. Abandonment began in the 1840s, and in the 1850s abandoned mileage exceeded new construction (Goodrich 1961, 7). Moreover, the number and tonnage of steamboats operating on western rivers rose from one (371 tons) in 1811, to 69 (14,208 tons) in 1820, to 494 (82,626 tons) in 1840 (Haites, Mak, Walton 1975, 130–31).

Table 1A.14   Shares of Rural Male Population Aged 16 and Over Engaged in Each Nonagricultural Industry

Year	Manufacturing and Commerce	Navigation	Fishing and Forestry	Mining	Total
1800	.107	.0071	.0017	.0027	.1185
1810	.137	.0071	.0017	.0030	.1488
1820	.175	.0089	.0022	.0034	.1895
1830	.182	.0111	.0029	.0038	.1998
1840	.189	.0137	.0037	.0043	.2107

Sources: U.S. Bureau of the Census 1820, 1840, 1860. See also the text.

Notes: The numerator in each industry in 1840 and in manufacturing and commerce in 1820 is the census count, which covered males 10 years of age and over. I have assumed that none of those reported workers were aged 10 to 15 years.

For navigation, the 1840 national share (rural plus urban) was .0222; the 1860 counterpart was .0137. The 1840 share engaged in fishing and forestry calculated from the industrial census count is .0146. For mining, the 1840 national share (rural plus urban) was .0038, compared to .0048 for 1860.

ocean navigation figures were more appropriate. I assumed that for 1800, 1810, and 1820 the share of males engaged in navigation was equal to the 1840 rural figure for ocean navigation.[81] The 1830 figures were derived by assuming a constant rate of growth in the share between 1820 and 1840, where the latter year's figure includes both ocean and inland navigation.

For fishing and forestry I derived shares based on the statistics for 1840 and 1860. In 1840 the census reported an establishment-based employment figure for fishing and forestry, while the 1860 census reported an occupational count in the census of population. The former shows a much higher share of the population so engaged than does the latter. This could represent the fact that the share of the male population engaged in these activities had been declining over time, in which case the appropriate 1800 figure should be above the 1840. On the other hand, the establishment-based figure could be high relative to the 1860 figure because it includes some workers other than males aged 16 and over and double-counts some workers who were employed by two firms. Moreover, the 1840 establishment statistic probably includes some workers who, in the population census, were reported to be engaged in manufacturing or commerce. Since those workers are included in my work force figures for those industries, I would not want to double-count them in these estimates. The 1860 census figures avoid the problems that plague the 1840 ones, but pertain to the total fishing and forestry labor force, not just the rural.

81. Navigation's share of the labor force changed along with the increased importance of cities because large numbers of urban adult males worked in the industry. According to the 1840 census data, 7.6 percent of urban males aged 16 and over were employed in navigation, with the share being nearly 17 percent in New England cities.

The estimation shares used for 1800 were taken from the 1860 evidence. I first ranked the 1860 statewide shares within regions, and used the mean of the bottom half of the ranking for each region as an approximation of the shares for the *rural* population in 1800. In a few states where the ratio fell below this mean I used the specific state's figure. The values for 1810, 1820, and 1830 were derived by assuming a constant rate of growth in the shares between 1800 and 1840.

Statewide shares for mining (urban plus rural) could be derived for 1840 and 1860, while for 1840 the rural and urban shares could be obtained separately as well. The rural and total shares in 1840 were quite close, and there was a general increase between 1840 and 1860, with the shares being higher in 1860 in every region except the South Atlantic. I presumed that the 1800 rural figures would be below those for 1840. For most states, I obtained the 1800 figure by extrapolating the 1840 rural share backward on the rate of change in the regional value that occurred between 1840 and 1860. For three states in the South Atlantic, where the 1840 shares were higher than in 1860, I assumed that the rate of change between 1800 and 1840 equaled that of the South Central region.

The estimate of females aged 16 and over who were *not* in agriculture is the residual difference between the total number of adult women in the rural labor force minus those in farming. The farm figure was estimated using the share of rural women so engaged in 1860 as calculated from the manuscript census sample data. That figure was a mere 0.7 percent for the northern states. The number of free females aged 10 to 15 engaged in nonfarm activities was set equal to the number estimated to have been in the rural labor force.

The rural farm labor force in the nonslave states was then calculated as the difference between the total rural labor force and the sum of the above nonfarm estimates.

For the *slave* states, the farm labor force is the sum of the estimates of farm workers in four groups. The two largest, slaves aged 10 and over and free males aged 16 and over, were estimated using the regression equation derived from the 1820 county-level data. The equation was used in 1800, 1810, and 1830 to estimate this major portion of the farm labor force in each slave state.[82]

---

82. Maryland posed a special case. The state was less agriculturally oriented than the rest of the slave states, and as a consequence the regional regression equation produces estimates of the farm labor force that are much too high in comparison with years for which census data are available. The regression equations were useful for estimating the farm labor force in 1820 and 1840 in those few counties that were out of line in those census years, but they gave a much higher farm figure for the state as a whole when applied to all counties. Instead, the 1800, 1810, and 1830 Maryland farm labor force was obtained by using the slave coefficient to estimate the number of slave farm workers, but using the 1820 and 1840 shares of the rural male population aged 16 and over engaged in farming to estimate the number of free male farm workers. Those shares were .572 in 1820 and .544 in 1840. I assumed that the average annual rate of decline in the share that occurred between 1820 and 1840 held back to 1800. The interpolated value for 1830 is .557, and the extrapolated figures for 1800 and 1810 are .601 and .586.

Free female farm workers aged 16 and over were estimated as 1.5 percent of the rural population in that age category, the percentage obtained from the 1860 manuscript census sample. Finally, the number of free males aged 10 to 15 in farming was taken to be all those of that age estimated to be in the rural labor force.

For the slave states, the nonagricultural labor force was obtained by subtracting the agricultural estimate from the total rural labor force.

References

Abel, Marjorie, and Nancy Folbre. 1990. A Methodology for Revising Estimates: Female Market Participation in the United States before 1940. *Historical Methods* 23: 167–76.

Adams, Henry. 1955. *The United States in 1800*. Ithaca: Cornell University Press.

Bateman, Fred, and James Foust. 1973. Agricultural and Demographic Records of 21,118 Rural Households. Indiana University. Data tape.

Blodget, Samuel. 1806. *Economica: A Statistical Manual for the United States of America*. Washington, D.C. Reprint. New York: Augustus Kelley, 1964.

Bode, Carl. 1967. *American Life in the 1840s*. New York: Doubleday and Co.

Crafts, N. F. R. 1985. *British Economic Growth during the Industrial Revolution*. Oxford: Oxford University Press.

David, Paul. 1967. The Growth of Real Product in the United States before 1840: New Evidence, Controlled Conjectures. *Journal of Economic History* 27: 151–97.

Davis, Lance, and Jonathan R. T. Hughes. 1960. A Dollar Sterling Exchange, 1803–1895. *Economic History Review* 13: 52–78.

Deane, Phyllis, and W. A. Cole. 1962. *British Economic Growth, 1688–1959*. Cambridge: Cambridge University Press.

Easterlin, Richard. 1960. Interregional Differences in Per Capita Income, Population, and Total Income, 1840–1950. In *Trends in the American Economy in the Nineteenth Century*, ed. William N. Parker. NBER Studies in Income and Wealth, 24. Princeton: Princeton University Press.

———. 1975. Farm Production and Income in Old and New Areas at Mid-century. In *Essays in Nineteenth Century Economic History*, ed. David C. Klingaman and Richard K. Vedder. Athens: Ohio University Press.

Edwards, Alba. 1940. *Comparative Occupation Statistics for the United States, 1870–1940*. Special Report of the Sixteenth Census of the United States. Washington, D.C.: Government Printing Office.

Engerman, Stanley L., and Robert E. Gallman. 1983. Economic Growth, 1783 to 1860. *Research in Economic History* 8: 1–46.

Fabricant, Solomon. 1949. The Changing Industrial Distribution of Gainful Workers: Comments on the Decennial Statistics, 1820–1940. In *Studies in Income and Wealth* 11: 1–49. New York: National Bureau of Economic Research.

Fogel, Robert W. 1986. Nutrition and the Decline in Mortality since 1700: Some Preliminary Findings. In *Long-Term Factors in American Economic Growth*, ed. Stanley L. Engerman and Robert E. Gallman. NBER Studies in Income and Wealth, 51. Chicago: University of Chicago Press.

Gallman, Robert E. 1961. Estimates of American National Product Made before the Civil War. *Economic Development and Cultural Change* 9: 397–412.

————. 1966. Gross National Product in the United States, 1834–1909. In *Output, Employment, and Productivity in the United States after 1800,* ed. Dorothy S. Brady. NBER Studies in Income and Wealth, 30. New York: Columbia University Press.

————. 1971. The Statistical Approach: Fundamental Concepts Applied to History. In *Approaches to American Economic History,* ed. G. R. Taylor and L. F. Ellsworth. Charlottesville: University Press of Virginia.

————. 1972. Changes in Total U.S. Agricultural Factor Productivity in the Nineteenth Century. In *Farming in the New Nation,* ed. D. Kelsey. Washington, D.C.: Agricultural History Society.

————. 1975. The Agricultural Sector and the Pace of Economic Growth: U.S. Experience in the Nineteenth Century. In *Essays in Nineteenth Century Economic History,* ed. David C. Klingaman and Richard K. Vedder. Athens: Ohio University Press.

Gallman, Robert E., and Thomas Weiss. 1969. The Service Industries in the Nineteenth Century. In *Production and Productivity in the Service Industries,* ed. Victor R. Fuchs, 287–381. NBER Studies in Income and Wealth, 34. New York: National Bureau of Economic Research.

Gemery, Henry. 1990. Immigration and Economic Growth in the Early National Period. Colby College. Manuscript.

Goldin, Claudia. 1976. *Urban Slavery in the American South, 1820–1860.* Chicago: University of Chicago Press.

Goldin, Claudia, and Frank Lewis. 1980. The Role of Exports in American Economic Growth during the Napoleonic Wars, 1793 to 1807. *Explorations in Economic History* 17: 6–25.

Goodrich, Carter, ed. 1961. *Canals and American Economic Development.* New York: Columbia University Press.

Haites, Erik, James Mak, and Gary Walton. 1975. *Western River Transportation.* Baltimore: Johns Hopkins University Press.

Harley, C. Knick. 1990. The State of the British Industrial Revolution. University of Western Ontario. Manuscript.

Hoppit, Julian. 1990. Counting the Industrial Revolution. *Economic History Review* 43: 173–93.

Jones, Alice Hanson. 1980. *Wealth of a Nation to Be.* New York: Columbia University Press.

Komlos, John. 1987. The Height and Weight of West Point Cadets: Dietary Change in Antebellum America. *Journal of Economic History* 47, no. 4: 897–927.

Kuznets, Simon. 1952. Current National Income Estimates for the Period prior to 1870. *Review of Income and Wealth* 2: 221–41.

Lebergott, Stanley L. 1964. *Manpower in Economic Growth.* New York: McGraw-Hill.

————. 1966. Labor Force and Employment, 1800–1960. In *Output, Employment, and Productivity in the United States after 1800,* ed. Dorothy S. Brady. NBER Studies in Income and Wealth, 30. New York: Columbia University Press.

————. 1984. *The Americans.* New York: W. W. Norton and Co.

Lindstrom, Diane. 1983. Macroeconomic Growth: The United States in the Nineteenth Century. *Journal of Interdisciplinary History* 12, no. 4: 679–705.

McCloskey, Donald. 1981. The Industrial Revolution 1780–1860: A Survey. In *The Economic History of Britain since 1700,* ed. Roderick Floud and Donald McCloskey. Cambridge: Cambridge University Press.

McCusker, John. 1978. *Money and Exchange in Europe and America, 1600–1775.* Chapel Hill: University of North Carolina Press.

Martin, Robert. 1939. *National Income in the United States, 1799–1938.* New York: National Industrial Conference Board.

Miller, Ann, and Carol Brainerd. 1957. Labor Force Estimates. In *Population Redistribution and Economic Growth,* Everett Lee et al. Philadelphia: American Philosophical Society.

Mokyr, Joel. 1987. Has the Industrial Revolution Been Crowded Out? Some Reflections on Crafts and Williamson. *Explorations in Economic History* 24: 293–325.

Newton, James, and Ronald Lewis, eds. 1978. *The Other Slaves: Mechanics, Artisans, and Craftsmen.* Boston: G. K. Hall.

North, Douglass. 1961. Early National Income Estimates of the U.S. *Economic Development and Cultural Change* 9: 387–96.

Olson, John. 1983. The Occupational Structure of Plantation Slave Labor in the Late Antebellum Era. Ph.D. diss., University of Rochester.

Parker, William, and Franklee Whartenby. 1960. The Growth of Output before 1840. In *Trends in the American Economy in the Nineteenth Century,* ed. William N. Parker. NBER Studies in Income and Wealth, 24. Princeton: Princeton University Press.

Poulson, Barry. 1975. *Value Added in Manufacturing, Mining, and Agriculture in the American Economy from 1809 to 1839.* New York: Arno Press.

Seaman, Ezra. 1852. *Essays on the Progress of Nations.* New York: Charles Scribner.

———. 1868. *Essays on the Progress of Nations.* New York: Charles Scribner and Co.

Sokoloff, Kenneth. 1986. Productivity Growth in Manufacturing during Early Industrialization. In *Long-Term Factors in American Economic Growth,* ed. Stanley L. Engerman and Robert E. Gallman. NBER Studies in Income and Wealth, 51. Chicago: University of Chicago Press.

Starobin, Robert. 1970. *Industrial Slavery in the Old South.* New York: Oxford University Press.

Steckel, Richard. 1988. Census Matching and Migration: A Research Strategy. *Historical Methods* 21: 52–60.

Taylor, George. 1964. American Economic Growth before 1840: An Exploratory Essay. *Journal of Economic History* 24: 427–44.

Towne, Marvin, and Wayne Rasmussen. 1960. Farm Gross Product and Gross Investment in the Nineteenth Century. In *Trends in the American Economy in the Nineteenth Century,* ed. William N. Parker. NBER Studies in Income and Wealth, 24. Princeton: Princeton University Press.

U.S. Bureau of the Census. 1820. *Fourth Census: Population.* Book I. Washington, D.C.: Gales and Seaton, 1821.

———. 1840. *Sixth Census: Enumeration of Inhabitants.* Washington, D.C.: Blair and Rives, 1841.

———. 1850. *Seventh Census: Population.* Washington, D.C.: Robert Armstrong, Public Printer, 1853.

———. 1860. *Eighth Census: Population.* Washington, D.C.: Government Printing Office, 1864.

———. 1870. *Ninth Census: Population.* Vol. 1. Washington, D.C.: Government Printing Office, 1872.

———. 1880. *Tenth Census: Population.* Vol. 1. Washington, D.C.: Government Printing Office, 1883.

———. 1890. *Eleventh Census: Population.* Vol. 1, part 2. Washington, D.C.: Government Printing Office, 1895.

———. 1900a. *Twelfth Census: Population.* Vols. 1, 2. Washington, D.C.: Government Printing Office, 1901.

————. 1900b. *Twelfth Census: Special Report: Occupations.* Washington, D.C.: Government Printing Office, 1904.

————. 1910. *Thirteenth Census. Vol. 4, Occupations.* Washington, D.C.: Government Printing Office, 1914.

————. 1975. *Historical Statistics of the United States.* Washington, D.C.: Government Printing Office.

————. 1979. *Twenty Censuses: Population and Housing Questions, 1790–1980.* Washington, D.C.: Government Printing Office.

Weiss, Thomas. 1985. Adjustments to the Census Counts of Population and Labor Force, 1870, 1890, and 1910. University of Kansas. Manuscript.

————. 1986a. Assessment and Revision of the Antebellum Census Labor Force Statistics: 1850 and 1860. University of Kansas Manuscript.

————. 1986b. Revised Estimates of the United States Workforce, 1800 to 1860. In *Long-Term Factors in American Economic Growth,* ed. Stanley L. Engerman and Robert E. Gallman. NBER Studies in Income and Wealth, 51. Chicago: University of Chicago Press.

————. 1987a. Assessment and Revision of the Antebellum Census Labor Force Statistics: 1840. University of Kansas. Manuscript.

————. 1987b. Demographic Aspects of the Urban Population, 1800 to 1840. In *Quantity and Quiddity: Essays in Honor of Stanley L. Lebergott,* ed. Peter Kilby. Middletown, Conn.: Wesleyan University Press.

————. 1987c. Estimation of the Farm/Nonfarm Distribution of Laborers, Not Otherwise Specified; by State, 1850 to 1900. University of Kansas. Manuscript.

————. 1988. Assessment and Revision of the Antebellum Census Labor Force Statistics: 1820. University of Kansas. Manuscript.

————. 1989. Economic Growth before 1860: Revised Conjectures. Historical Factors in Long-Run Growth Working Paper no. 7. Cambridge, Mass.: National Bureau of Economic Research.

————. 1990. Farm Gross Product, Labor Force, and Output per Worker in the United States, 1800 to 1900. University of Kansas. Manuscript.

————. 1991. Comparison of Farm Labor Force Estimates for the Antebellum United States. University of Kansas. Manuscript.

Whelpton, P. K. 1926. Occupational Groups in the United States, 1820–1920. *Journal of the American Statistical Association* 21: 335–43.

Williamson, Jeffrey G. 1987. Debating the British Industrial Revolution. *Explorations in Economic History* 24: 269–92.

Wright, Carroll. 1900. *The History and Growth of the United States Census.* Washington, D.C.: Government Printing Office.

Comment   Claudia Goldin

Thomas Weiss's estimates of the antebellum labor force suggest a smoother transition from an agricultural to an industrial labor force than that implied by previous research. The Weiss estimates for the proportion of the labor force in

Claudia Goldin is professor of economics at Harvard University, a research associate of the National Bureau of Economic Research, and director of the NBER's program, Development of the American Economy.

agriculture are lower by about 10 to 16 percent for 1800, 1810, and 1820 than are those in the works of Stanley Lebergott and Paul David.[1] The Weiss estimate is virtually identical to the Lebergott-David number for 1830, but it is 5 to 10 percent higher for 1840 to 1860. Thus there is a considerably slower decrease in the agricultural labor force in the Weiss data. Although the Lebergott-David numbers reveal a decline in the proportion of labor employed in agriculture of 29.4 percentage points or 55 percent across the entire 1800 to 1860 period, the Weiss data indicate a decrease of only 18.7 percentage points or 34 percent. Most of the revisions in the Weiss data seem sensible, particularly the inclusion in the agricultural work force of individuals listed as "laborers" in the census who resided in rural counties. My comments, therefore, focus on the implications of Thomas Weiss's estimates.

Because the Weiss estimates place 132,000 fewer workers in agriculture in 1800, 260,000 fewer in 1810, and 251,000 fewer in 1820, and because output per worker was considerably higher outside the agricultural sector than within, one implication is that output per worker was greater than we previously thought. The average worker was now 48 percent more productive in 1800, 34 percent more productive in 1810, and 27 percent more productive in 1820 than in estimates using the Lebergott-David labor force data. And because output per worker rises but participation rates are less affected by the revisions, income per capita also rises.

Income per capita was not just higher given the Weiss revisions, it was substantially higher. All Americans were 26 percent richer in 1800 and 34 percent richer in 1810 than was the case before the Weiss revisions. Because the estimate of income per capita is constrained, using either the Weiss or Lebergott-David numbers, to equal that for 1840 produced by Robert E. Gallman, an income advantage can occur only during the 1800 to 1839 period. Even if the economy had grown at 1 percent average annually, which probably exceeds the rate it did grow at over the period, the increased income implicit in the Weiss labor force revisions amounts to more than twenty-five years' worth of economic growth. It is not surprising, therefore, that the Lebergott-David estimates of the proportion of the labor force in agriculture imply much higher rates of economic growth than do the Weiss revisions. That is, the Weiss labor force estimates imply that America in 1800 was a considerably richer nation (by almost 30 percent) than those based on Lebergott-David, and thus that the rate of economic growth to 1840 must have been less—by one-half for the 1800 to 1840 period.

But is it economic growth that is of importance or is it income per capita? Although pre-1840 America, according to Weiss, was a considerably richer nation, it grew more slowly and its growth accelerated less over the antebellum decades. Because of the extensive debate over the possibility of a "take

1. Paul David, "The Growth of the Real Product in the United States before 1840: New Evidence, Controlled Conjectures," *Journal of Economic History* 27 (June 1967): 151–97.

off," Weiss and others have emphasized the growth of per capita income and not its level. But the Weiss labor force estimates will redirect attention toward the level of per capita income in 1800 and its implications for economic growth in the eighteenth century.

Revisions to the agricultural labor force were undertaken by Weiss because considerable skepticism had been voiced about the Lebergott-David numbers. The most convincing evidence that the agricultural labor force series contained errors was offered by Robert E. Gallman.[2] Gallman noted that the estimated proportion of the labor force working in agriculture did not correlate well over time with known statistics on the proportion of the population living in rural areas. For some years the two series are not positively correlated, and for others change in one series vastly exceeds change in the other. Weiss, therefore, undertook his project to revise the labor force estimates for the antebellum period.

Now that we have the Weiss revisions, it is instructive to assess how different they are from estimates based on the rural labor force statistics, using a procedure suggested by Gallman. The relationship between the proportion of the population that is rural and the percentage of the labor force in agriculture is not a simple linear one. Assume, instead, that the percentage of the labor force in the agricultural sector divided by the percentage of the population that is rural declines over time at a constant rate, possibly because nonagricultural employments arise in rural areas at about that rate. The rate is taken to be 0.01875, which is the approximate pace at which this occurred (by decade) from 1870 to 1900, a period for which we have data on both series. That is,

$$\text{Simulation of } (L_a/L_t)_{\text{year}} = \{0.66 \times (1.01875)^{(1900 - \text{year})/10}\} (P_r/P_t)_{\text{year}}$$

where 0.66 is the approximate ratio $(L_a/L_t)/(P_r/P_t)$ in 1900, L = the labor force, P = population, year = the census year, a = agricultural, r = rural, and t = total. Note that a decline in $(L_a/L_t)/(P_r/P_t)$ implies a decline in $(L_a/P_r)/(L_t/P_t)$. That is, the agricultural labor force as a fraction of the rural population declines relative to the labor force participation rate for the entire nation. Because the aggregate labor force participation rate of the population is relatively constant over this period, most of the movement in the ratio $(L_a/L_t)/(P_r/P_t)$ is coming from change in the fraction of the rural population engaged in agriculture, L_a/P_r. Column 2 of table 1C.1 gives the simulation of L_a/L_t for 1800 to 1900.

The correspondence between the Weiss numbers and the simulation, given by the ratio in column 3, is truly astounding. Only in the case of 1880 is the ratio off by more than 3 percent, and in half of the cases the simple extrapolation is within 1 percent. The Weiss estimates, however, are substantial revi-

---

2. Robert E. Gallman, "The Agricultural Sector and the Pace of Economic Growth," in *Essays in Nineteenth Century Economic History,* ed. David C. Klingaman and Richard K. Vedder (Athens: Ohio University Press, 1975).

Table 1C.1   **Percentage of the Labor Force in the Agricultural Sector**

	Weiss[a] (1)	Simulation (2)	(1)/(2) (3)	(1)/Lebergott-David (4)
1800	74.4	74.6	0.997	0.901
1810	72.3	72.3	1.00	0.864
1820	71.4	71.1	1.00	0.905
1830	69.8	68.6	1.02	0.989
1840	67.2	65.8	1.02	1.06
1850	59.7	61.3	0.973	1.11
1860	55.8	57.0	0.979	1.05
1870	52.5	51.8	1.01	
1880	51.3	49.2	1.04	
1890	42.7	43.5	0.982	
1900	40.2	39.8	1.01	

[a]The data from 1870 to 1900 are from Lebergott.

sions of the Lebergott-David numbers, with the exception of the datum for 1830.

There are two ways to interpret the results of this exercise. First, it points to a far simpler manner of deriving the proportion of the labor force in agriculture from known statistics on the rural population. But had Weiss presented this estimation I would have been extremely skeptical. This leads to the second implication. Because we have the hard evidence of the Weiss data and the simple model that could have produced them, we can speculate about the process that led to the decrease in the proportion of the labor force in rural settings. It was, in part, determined by the proportion of the labor force in agriculture, but it was also tempered by the rise of nonagricultural job opportunities in rural areas, which increased at a constant rate. Note that the parameter value, estimated to be 0.01875 from the 1870 to 1900 data, was not produced by a regression of the Weiss data on the proportion of the population residing in rural areas. Such a regression would have produced a series minimizing the sum of squared residuals and would have resulted in an even closer relationship than that given in column 3.

In sum, Weiss has furnished new estimates of the antebellum labor force and of the proportion of the labor force working in agriculture. These estimates appear to have been well crafted, and almost identical ones can be produced from a simple model of the relationship between the proportion of the population that was rural and the proportion of the labor force employed in agriculture. One implication, therefore, concerns the process that created jobs in rural areas that were nonagricultural. Another implication concerns economic growth and the level of incomes in the antebellum period. America, according to the new Weiss estimates, was considerably richer from 1800 to 1839 than we previously thought—at times by more than 30 percent. Thus growth during the eighteenth century has now become more of a possibility.

2   American Economic Growth before the Civil War: The Testimony of the Capital Stock Estimates

Robert E. Gallman

2.1 Introduction

Robert Giffen, of paradox fame, thought estimates of aggregate wealth have eight uses; the following have immediate relevance:

1. To measure the accumulation of capital in communities at intervals of some length . . .
2. To compare the income of a community, where estimates of income exist, with its property . . .
4. To measure, in conjunction with other factors, such as aggregate income, revenue, and population, the relative strength and resources of different communities.
5. To indicate generally the proportions of the different descriptions of property in a country to the total—how the wealth of a community is composed.
6. To measure the progress of a community from period to period, or the relative progress of two or more communities, in conjunction with the facts as to progress in income, population, and the like; to apply, in fact, historically and in conjunction with No. 1, the measures used under the above heads 2, 3, 4 and 5 for a comparison at a given moment. (1889, 136–37)

Robert E. Gallman is Kenan Professor of Economics and History at the University of North Carolina, Chapel Hill, and research associate of the National Bureau of Economic Research.

The research underlying this paper was funded by the National Bureau of Economic Research, during my tenure as an Olin Fellow, and by the National Science Foundation, to which organizations I express my gratitude. In another form the paper was given to seminars at the California Institute of Technology, the University of Chicago, the University of California at Davis and Los Angeles, and Northwestern University. At all of these seminars I received useful suggestions, especially from Lance Davis, David Galenson, Morgan Kousser, Kenneth Sokoloff, and Sokoloff's graduate class in economic history. The discussant of the paper, Stanley Engerman, was, as always, most helpful.

Simon Kuznets, who made use of the list, said that the distributions alluded to in item 5 should include the size distribution of wealth (Giffen 1889; Kuznets 1958; see Engerman and Gallman 1983 for more on these issues).

The remarks of Giffen and Kuznets provide a justification for this paper, a list of things to include in it, and a set of suggestions as to how it should be related to the other papers prepared for this conference. Particularly attractive is Giffen's notion that many different types of aggregate series, as well as compositional indexes, should figure in the measurement of growth. He would have felt comfortable at the conference at which this paper was given, as the participants approached the questions of economic development and standards of living from various directions, using data on labor force, income, wealth, consumption, wages and prices, productivity, and heights.

Kuznets believed that a perfectly realized index of development would trace out shifts in human material welfare. Such an index could be employed to measure changes in the standard of living—so long as we understand that term to refer to the material aspects of life—without the need to introduce other measurements. But Kuznets was well aware that the indexes of development with which scholars must work are far from ideal and that, therefore, a variety of them may be required. In the spirit of Giffen and Kuznets, then, this paper treats the capital stock series as one that bears on the standard of living, rather than as one that measures it.[1]

Capital stock series have two possible conceptual relationships to economic growth (Gallman 1986). First, such a series may be used to measure the wealth accumulated by a society. The accumulation will be influenced by the economic performance of the economy in the past, by the degree of frugality displayed by its people individually, by the success the society had in its military activities, and by communal saving and investment decisions. The measure is clearly different from income, in that it relates to a stock collected over a period of years, not a flow during one year. Income and capital series are likely to change at different rates, then, at least in the short run. But the two types of series do both bear on the material well-being of the people of the society.[2] In the very long run they are also likely to exhibit roughly the same

1. This is not the first attempt to study the American economy before the Civil War by examining capital stock data. See, for example, Jones (1980); Goldsmith (1952, 1985); Davis, Easterlin, Parker et al. (1972). I think, however, that it is the most serious effort to assure that the various estimates are consistent from one date to the next.

2. One virtue of a capital stock series as an indicator of growth is that the short-term movements of such a series are likely to be much less violent than, for example, the short-term movements of a true income series. If estimates are available only at intermittent years, the rates of growth computed from the former are much less likely to be influenced by transient phenomena than are the rates of growth of the latter. It should be said, however, that this distinction probably does not apply to the income estimates for the years before 1840 that were put together by Thomas Weiss for this volume, since his estimating procedure does not pick up the effects of short-term influences on income, nor is it intended to. Weiss's estimates come close to describing the output capacity of the economy, rather than actual output.

growth rates, so that a capital series can serve in some instances as a proxy for income.

The second approach is to view capital in its capacity as an input into the production process. Whereas the first approach looks chiefly to the past and sees capital as the accumulation created by society, the second looks to the present and the future. It sees the capital stock as one factor influencing current production, as well as production to be expected of the economy in future. Clearly, such a series is particularly useful when combined with estimates of the other inputs.

If the direct relationship between real capital and material well-being is to be examined, the capital stock series should be deflated by a consumers' price index. That is, the stock should be appraised in terms of its equivalent in consumer goods. If, on the other hand, one is concerned with productive potential, proper deflation is in terms of the prices of the components of the capital stock. Both forms of deflation are employed in this paper. That is, the capital stock is treated as an index of both the material well-being of the society and its productive power.

The concept of capital is elastic. Some analysts have included land and investment in humans as elements of the stock. For most purposes, it is best to treat land as land and human capital as a characteristic of labor. In the present instance, the second preference makes a virtue of a necessity: there are no comprehensive estimates of human capital covering the full period of interest here. This paper introduces a set of estimates of the land stock, but they are not treated as part of the supply of capital.[3]

Although land is not included in the capital stock series of this paper, improvements to land are. In this respect the series is unconventional. Most capital estimates include structures but omit other important improvements, such as the clearing and first breaking of land. In this paper a conventional series is presented and is linked with estimates extending well into the twentieth century, for comparative purposes. But the series that is subjected to the most intense examination is one that includes the value of land clearing and breaking. These activities took up a substantial part of the work time of agricultural workers and made an immensely important contribution to the capital stock before the Civil War. They cannot properly be ignored.

3. Should the value of slaves be counted as part of the value of the capital stock? If we are interested, say, in the savings and investment behavior of planters, then the answer is surely yes. This paper is not concerned with that topic. It is concerned with the measurement of long-term economic growth. Slaves are regarded as part of the labor force. They are also treated as part of population, for purposes of computing per capita levels of the capital stock.

While I will present no estimates of the value of human capital, the general pattern of change in this variable across the period under review here is quite clear. Both the fraction of the population of children attending school and the length of the school year increased as time passed, as did the fraction of the work force holding semiskilled and skilled jobs. The rate of increase of human capital is therefore almost certain to have risen as time passed. See Fishlow (1966a, 1966b) and Uselding (1971).

The value of consumer durables is also sometimes incorporated in capital stock estimates, but appears in only one table in this paper, because appropriate figures are only intermittently available. The loss is not great. The value of consumer durables was small, compared with the rest of the capital stock, through most of the period considered in this paper, and the rate of change of the capital stock is approximately the same, regardless of whether or not durables are treated as capital (see table 2.2).

The United States (for convenience, the term will be applied to the colonies of 1774) began life as a debtor nation and gradually shifted to the position of a creditor nation. Ignoring recent experience, the national capital stock—which measures the net capital holdings of Americans—grew very much more rapidly over time than did the domestic capital stock, defined as capital physically located in the United States, regardless of who owned it. Through the rest of the paper, both series will be examined, although most attention will be devoted to the domestic capital stock.

The title refers to the period before the Civil War, but the series introduced will typically cover a much longer stretch of time. The fundamental questions at issue have to do with persistent changes, and these questions can be properly addressed only if data bearing on long periods are available. Some rates

Table 2.1   **Capital and Wealth, 1774 and 1805, Estimates of Jones, Goldsmith, and Gallman (millions of current dollars)**

| | 1774 | | 1805 | |
	Jones	Gallman	Goldsmith	Gallman
All structures			370	352
All land improvements		180		732
All privately owned real estate	250			
Shipping		8	40	80
Other producers' durables	13[a]	15	32	65
Inventories	20	39	100	336
Animals	42	42	60	160
Total domestic capital			602	993
International claims			−80	−57
Total national capital			522	936
Total domestic capital, including the value of clearing and first breaking of farmland		284		
Total private domestic capital, plus land	327			

Sources: Jones (1980, 90, converted to dollars by means of the exchange rate on page 10); Gallman, see text; Goldsmith (1952, 315).

[a]Includes household equipment.

of growth covering relatively short intervals—such as the two decades 1840–60, which have been the focus of much scholarly interest—will be exhibited, but the reader should bear in mind that such rates are influenced by short-term phenomena. They cannot be used as the exclusive means of identifying shifts in trend rates of growth.

Section 2.2 deals briefly with the nature of the data underlying the estimates and the broad rules guiding the estimating procedure. Section 2.3 treats the rates of growth of the real capital stock and the real capital stock per capita, with the purpose of putting growth before the Civil War into historical perspective. Giffen's suggestion that the rates of change of capital and income be compared is taken up.

Economic development involves structural shifts as well as growth in the aggregates. Section 2.4 treats the changing composition of the capital stock and shows its connection to the nature of American economic development. Section 2.5 brings together estimates of all three factor inputs and combines them into several series describing the growth of total factor inputs. Estimates of changes in total factor productivity are presented. Section 2.6 is a summary of conclusions.

The data on which the estimates rest pose many problems. Appendix A takes up several important features of the series and considers a few tests of the most affected components.

2.2 The Estimating Procedures

Estimates were made for the years 1774, 1799, 1805, 1815, and 1840–1900 (at decade intervals) and for various dates in the twentieth century. As Giffen points out, capital series can be used to study economic growth, "regard being always had to the fact that the data and methods employed are sufficiently alike for the special purpose in hand" (1889, 136). The object of this section is to consider whether "the data and methods employed are sufficiently alike for the special purpose at hand." The subject is treated further in appendix A.

The current price capital stock estimates for 1850 and 1860 are based chiefly on census materials, which have been tested in a variety of ways and adjusted to make them consistent from one date to the next and to make them conform to an appropriate concept. The best overall tests that have been conducted so far are checks against perpetual inventory estimates derived from measurements of investment flows. The results of the checks are excellent (Gallman 1986, 1987).

The 1840 figures were similarly derived from census data, augmented in various ways, chiefly by contemporary estimates produced by Ezra Seaman. The census in 1840 was quite different from the ones that followed. It was administered under a different law and asked different questions. For some purposes it is quite good, but it is clearly weaker than the later censuses as a source of material for the estimation of the capital stock, although it has survived testing quite well.

The estimates for these three years and some of the tests that have been run are described in Gallman (1986, 1987). These sources also contain the estimates for the years 1870–1900, which will be used in the present paper to put the experience of the years 1774–1860 in context. Tests of the post–Civil War data by means of perpetual inventory estimates suggest that the 1870, 1880, and 1890 aggregate capital stock figures are unlikely to be perfectly consistent. It appears probable that the 1880 figure is too low. Calculations of the rates of change of the capital stock from this series are therefore likely to understate the true rate of growth for the period 1870 to 1880 and overstate it in the years 1880 to 1890, matters of no great importance for present purposes.

The twentieth-century figures were assembled by splicing the nineteenth-century estimates to Raymond Goldsmith's series, which are based on perpetual inventory procedures (Goldsmith 1982). As indicated above, census-style and perpetual inventory estimates appear to be roughly comparable.

The estimates for the years before 1840 come from a variety of sources quite different from the censuses, which increases the risk that the capital stock estimates based on them may not be consistent, one with the other, and all with the figures for the years 1840 onward. The data that are farthest removed in type from census data are the ones underlying the capital stock figure for 1774. These data were taken chiefly from Alice Jones's (1980) work with probate records. The figures for 1799, 1805, and 1815 rest principally on sources that are more likely to be consistent with census records: the direct taxes of 1799, 1813, and 1815. (I used the data in Blodget [1806] 1964, Pitkin 1835, and Soltow 1984.) The 1805 estimate is based on the work of Samuel Blodget ([1806] 1964) and Raymond Goldsmith's (1952) adjustments of Blodget's work. The principal underlying source is the direct tax of 1799. Blodget apparently carried the 1799 data forward to 1805 at a rate of growth he believed most probable. The 1805 estimate falls out of line with those of 1799 and 1815 and is probably too high. The history of the period leads one to expect a higher rate of growth between 1799 and 1805 than between 1805 and 1815, of course, but not quite so high as the Blodget data suggest. Of course it is possible that the 1805 figure is close to the truth and that the other two are too low, but I do not think that is the case. It is also possible that the bias was introduced by my adjustment of the Blodget data (see table 2.1), but I doubt that is so.

The 1774 through 1815 estimates depend on the sources listed above, augmented and adjusted so that the same concept of capital underlies each final aggregate figure, and so that the same estimating principles are applied in each case. The last point is an important one. While accurate estimates were sought in each instance, it seemed clear that it would be better to have a series for which the general level might be wrong, but which describes the rate of growth in a reasonably accurate way, than to have one for which the individual estimates might be closer to the truth, but which gives a more strongly biased account of the rate of growth. The choice made was always for consistency rather than for perfect accuracy.[4]

Table 2.1 compares some of the details of the new estimates with those provided by Jones and Goldsmith. As will be evident, the adjustments made to the Jones figures were relatively unimportant, so that the new estimates tell very much the same story as do the data taken from Jones. The differences between my estimates and Goldsmith's are greater, and are particularly pronounced with respect to inventories of all kinds. Goldsmith's estimates seem too low to me; for example, imports in 1805 ran around $150 million, and imports represented a relatively small part of total economic activity, even in 1805. Even a very modest estimate of the fraction of imports held, on average, in inventory across the year would leave very little for inventories of domestic goods, were we to accept Goldsmith's figure for total inventories. But the question of the appropriate *level* of inventories in 1805 is perhaps not the important issue. The important point is the one made in the previous paragraph. In building the inventory estimates for all of the years, 1774–1900, I have tried to follow consistent methods and have paid more attention to consistency than to the specific level of any one estimate. Consistency permits appropriate comparisons to be made across time, an important desideratum. Users of capital stock series for the nineteenth century, then, would be well advised to use either Goldsmith's estimates or mine, but not some combination of the two.

All of the capital figures are expressed in market prices or in net reproduc-

---

4. For example, imagine a series that has true values of 100 and 200 in two widely separated years. If the estimates produced for these years are each too large by 10 percent, then the estimated series and the true series will describe the same rate of growth. That would not be the case if the estimates were closer to the truth in each year, but deviated from it by different percentages—say the first estimate amounted to 95 and the second to 210. Obviously, one cannot know with certainty that the first circumstance or the second holds in any given instance. But there are cases in which one has the choice of following a consistent procedure and using consistent data from one date to the next, in full knowledge that the results are unlikely to be exactly correct, or employing different methods and bodies of data, in an effort to come as close as possible in each year to the true value. Where I was presented with these options, I chose consistency. (Emerson, after all, only deplored a foolish consistency.) But consistency at the component level does not guarantee unbiased rates of growth at the aggregate level. Suppose that the level of each component series is biased by a given percentage in each year, but the given percentage varies from one component to the next, by amount, sign, or both. For example, suppose that the figures composing the slow-growing components are biased in an upward direction, while the figures representing the fast-growing components are biased in a downward direction. The rate of growth of the aggregate composed of these elements will be biased in a downward direction. All that can be done in this case is to attempt to judge and to describe the direction and probable importance of the bias in the rate of growth.

The details of the construction of the capital stock estimates for the years 1774–1815 will be provided in a monograph currently under way.

tion costs. The two are virtually identical, where it has been possible to run a test. They are net of retirements and of capital consumption, with one exception, to be discussed further below.

The cost-of-living deflator is the one assembled by Paul David and Peter Solar (1977), the only series that covers the full period. According to Claudia Goldin and Robert Margo (1989), the index rises too little or falls too much in the nineteenth century before the mid-1840s. If they are correct, the rate of growth of the capital stock deflated by this series is too high in the period before the mid-1840s, a point to which we will return. Dorothy Brady's investment goods price indexes from volume 30 of *Studies in Income and Wealth* (1966), extended to the years before 1840 in a variety of ways, were the chief bases for the deflation of the capital stock, viewed as an input. The Brady index numbers refer to census years. They had to be adjusted modestly to make them relevant to the dates to which the capital stock estimates refer (the last day of the census year). Conceptually, these index numbers are exactly what are required. They were augmented in various ways to permit the deflation of inventories and certain types of farm improvements, for which Brady supplied no indexes. The problems of assembling appropriate deflators for the years before 1840 require a paper of their own. They are treated further in appendix A.

2.3   Rates of Growth in Historical Perspective

The concern of this paper is with American economic growth before the Civil War, which means that the measures of central concern to it are real measures, particularly real measures deflated by population. The current price estimates are worth at least a brief inspection, however. On the whole, they are less processed than the real figures and may therefore be a little more reliable. Table 2.2 contains current price estimates of the capital stock, conventionally defined.[5] Three points come through very clearly. The rates of growth are all very high; the capital stock in 1980 was apparently about 40,000 times as large as the stock of 1774, an extraordinary figure. Although most of the rates were computed over considerable stretches of time, and therefore should not be unduly influenced by transient phenomena, they vary quite widely from one period to another. Finally, it is clear that the experience before the Civil War was by no means uniform. In particular, the rates of growth are especially low in the years between the turn of the century and 1840, and especially high from 1840 to 1860. The second period is short, and

---

5. The conventional concepts are the domestic capital stock and the national capital stock. The former includes the value of structures, equipment, and inventories physically located in the country at issue; the latter includes all of these items, but also adjusts for net international claims, so that the measure includes the value of capital owned by nationals of the country at issue. Unconventional estimates may include, additionally, the value of the clearing and first breaking of land, the value of human capital, the value of consumer durables, etc.

Table 2.2   **Indexes and Average Annual Rates of Change of the U.S. Capital Stock, Current Prices, 1774–1980**

	Domestic Capital	Domestic Capital & Consumer Durables	National Capital
Panel A: Indexes			
1774	100	100	100
1799	399		415
1805	581		628
1815	999		1,110
1840	1,573	1,503	1,691
1850	2,579	2,538	2,919
1860	5,298	5,274	6,000
1870	8,620	8,751	9,201
1880	11,795	11,761	12,805
1890	20,526	20,198	22,396
1900	27,386	26,457	30,886
1929	138,592	135,343	170,360
1953	444,239	436,493	541,061
1980	3,761,382	3,665,337	4,560,608
Panel B: Average Annual Rates of Change (%)			
1774–1840	4.3	4.2	4.4
1774–99	5.7		5.9
1799–1840	3.4		3.5
1840–1900	4.9	4.9	5.0
1840–60	6.3	6.5	6.5
1860–1900	4.2	4.1	4.2
1900–1929	5.8	5.8	6.1
1929–53	5.0	5.0	4.9
1953–80	8.2	8.2	8.2
1774–1980	5.2	5.2	5.3

Sources: See text.

the rates of growth computed across it could be influenced by business cycles or long swings. But Abramovitz's (1989) chronology of long swings and protracted depressions suggests that this is probably not a problem.

The record described by table 2.2 is influenced both by real phenomena and price level changes. The price index numbers in table 2.3 allow one to judge how important the latter developments were. Between 1774 and 1900 the long-term trend of the two price indexes appears to be close to zero, but in the short term prices were quite unstable. In the twentieth century there is additionally a pronounced upward trend. Notice, finally, that while the two indexes tend to move together, the consumer index is the more volatile. The plan to deflate by two separate price indexes, then, seems to have substantive, as well as theoretical, merit.

Table 2.3   **Capital Stock Deflators, Base 1860, 1774–1900**

	Domestic Capital Price Index	Consumer Price Index
1774	81	97
1799	111	148
1805	115	141
1815	157	185
1840	91	104
1850	94	94
1860	100	100
1870	127	157
1880	112	123
1890	96	109
1900	90	101
1929	165	205
1953	357	320
1974		589
1980	1,193	

Sources: See text.

The deflated series appear in table 2.4. Four matters of interest strike one immediately: First, deflation does reduce the volatility of the series somewhat; part of the short-term movement observed in table 2.2 is due to price fluctuations. Second, it is clear that the real capital stock has grown more slowly in the present century than it had previously. Third, it is also clear that the rate of growth accelerated between the years before 1840 and the years thereafter. The broad pattern, then, is of an early acceleration, followed by a subsequent retardation. Finally, notice that these findings emerge from all four series, the national and domestic capital stocks, deflated by the consumer price index and by the capital price index. But the detailed pattern of change differs from one series to the other. For example, compare the results obtained for the period 1929–53. The real capital stock, viewed as accumulated consuming power, grew much faster than did the real capital stock, viewed as an input to production: the prices of capital goods increased faster than consumer prices, between these two dates.

More interesting for present purposes is the pattern across the years 1774–1840. Notice (table 2.3) that consumer prices advanced much farther than capital goods prices between 1774 and the turn of the century, and fell much farther between then and 1840. Across the full span, 1774–1840, the two index numbers show roughly similar changes, so that the two capital stock series yield about the same results. But the interpretation of the subperiods before 1840 depends entirely on the system of deflation one chooses to use. And the systems of deflation, recall, view the capital stock in two quite different ways: as the value of the accumulations of the years, expressed in consumer goods, as against the productive power of the capital stock.

Table 2.4   **Indexes and Average Annual Rates of Change of the U.S. Capital Stock, 1860 Prices, 1774–1980**

	Domestic Capital Deflator		National Capital Deflator	
	Capital Price Index	Consumer Price Index	Capital Price Index	Consumer Price Index
Panel A: Indexes				
1774	100	100	100	100
1799	289	262	306	271
1805	409	400	449	431
1815	513	525	571	581
1840	1,401	1,472	1,514	1,571
1850	2,212	2,665	2,497	3,007
1860	4,292	5,148	4,849	5,805
1870	5,486	5,335	5,897	5,669
1880	8,462	9,318	9,157	10,071
1890	17,217	18,295	18,665	19,877
1900	24,552	26,347	27,632	29,584
1929	68,472	66,398	77,681	80,390
1953	102,132	137,182	114,109	163,571
1980	223,632		297,638	
Panel B: Average Annual Rates of Change (%)				
1774–1840	4.1	4.2	4.2	4.3
1774–99	4.3	3.9	4.6	4.1
1799–1840	3.9	4.3	4.0	4.4
1840–1900	4.9	4.9	5.0	5.0
1840–60	5.8	6.5	6.0	6.8
1860–1900	4.5	4.2	4.4	4.2
1900–1980	2.8		3.0	
1900–1929	3.6	3.2	3.6	3.5
1929–53	1.7	3.1	1.6	3.0
1953–80	3.5		3.6	
1774–1980	3.9		4.0	

Sources: See text.

No doubt the contrast is in some measure spurious, however. Items of construction compose an important part of the capital stock throughout (see table 2.8). The deflators for this component in the years before 1840 were constructed in part from data on wage rates. Wage rates tend to be less volatile than prices (see Robert A. Margo's paper in this volume). The capital stock price index numbers for the period before 1840 may therefore understate the fluctuations experienced by the prices of capital goods. It is thus possible that the measured rate of growth of the real capital stock, viewed as an input, is too high across the years 1774–99 and too low between 1799 and 1840. The matter is unlikely to be important with respect to the main point of present concern, however. It seems clear that the rate of growth of the capital stock did accelerate between 1774–1840 and the subsequent years.

The capital stock treated so far ignores a component of investment that was important, particularly in the years before 1840: the activities of land clearing and first breaking which engaged so large a part of the working lives of American farmers (Primack 1962). Table 2.5 contains index numbers describing the change over time in the real value of the domestic capital stock, inclusive of the value of these farm-making activities. The overall rate of growth of this aggregate—3.9 percent, 1774–1900—is very much lower than the one recorded for the less comprehensive capital stock treated in table 2.4—4.5 percent (capital stock deflator in each case). These findings reflect the fact, of course, that farm formation was a very important part of capital, but one that increased over time much more slowly than the other components of the stock, a point to which we will return.

The acceleration picked out by the data of table 2.4 reappears in table 2.5 and in a more marked form. But notice that the pattern is somewhat different. The series deflated by the prices of capital now shows a higher rate of growth across the period 1799–1840 than across the period 1774–1799, in contrast to the results shown by table 2.4. The explanation is that introduction of the farm-making elements of the capital stock necessarily altered the capital price index numbers. Farm making was carried out by farm laborers, and the value of farm making is the value of the time of farm workers. Farm wage rates thus figure in the estimation of the value of land clearing and breaking, as well as in the deflation of these components of the stock. Farm wage rates rose quite pronouncedly between 1774 and 1840, which gives the deflator an upward tilt.

All of the series discussed above refer to the aggregate capital stock. A more interesting variable, however, is the per capita capital stock. Estimates appear in table 2.6. Deflating by population produces two important, if easily anticipated, results. First, the retardation of growth in the twentieth century disappears, while the acceleration between 1774–1840 and 1840–1900 becomes very much more pronounced. The acceleration appears in every variant but is particularly evident in the series describing the most comprehensive measure, deflated by capital stock prices.

The acceleration in the rate of growth of the capital stock reflects in part the increase in the investment rate and the rise in the capital/output ratio, which seems to have begun as early as the turn of the century, at least in the case of the conventional measurements, but which was particularly pronounced from 1840 until 1900 (Davis and Gallman 1978; table 2.7). That does not appear to be the only source, however. The rates of growth of real national product per capita from 1840 onward were higher than the rates of growth of real capital per capita in the period before 1840, regardless of the capital concept adopted and the deflator employed (Davis and Gallman 1978; Gallman 1966). Accepting the rate of change of the capital stock series before 1840 as an upper-

Table 2.5   Indexes and Average Annual Rates of Change of the U.S. Domestic Capital Stock, Including the Value of Clearing and Breaking Farmland, 1860 Prices, 1774–1900

		Deflator	
		Capital Price Index	Consumer Price Index
Panel A: Indexes			
	1774	100	100
	1799	227	245
	1805	290	332
	1815	353	379
	1840	913	1,229
	1850	1,362	2,140
	1860	2,432	3,980
	1870	3,004	3,884
	1880	4,520	6,543
	1890	8,491	12,229
	1900	11,807	17,253
Panel B: Average Annual Rates of Change (%)			
	1774–1840	3.4	3.9
	1774–99	3.3	3.7
	1799–1840	3.5	4.0
	1840–1900	4.4	4.5
	1840–60	5.0	6.1
	1860–1900	4.0	3.7

Sources: See text.

bound estimate of the rate of change of real national product, the evidence suggests quite clearly that the rate of growth of real national product per capita accelerated in the years before the Civil War.

These results are generally consistent with Thomas Weiss's inferences concerning income, which he derived from his labor force series (see table 2.7 and Weiss's paper in this volume). Both Weiss's figures and the capital stock data were assembled from fragmentary evidence and are subject to substantial margins for error. But both series seem to tell about the same story, and that affords greater confidence that the story is a true one.[6]

6. The capital and income (Weiss) data permit a check on an inference advanced by Davis and Gallman, who guessed that the net investment rate averaged between 6.2% and 7.0% in the period 1805–40 (Davis and Gallman 1978, 2). The rates of growth and capital/output ratios in or underlying table 2.7 are consistent with net investment rates, computed against GDP, of between 5 percent and 6.5 percent. The Davis and Gallman figures were computed against NNP, however. If the data in and underlying table 2.7 are adjusted to make them conform more nearly to the concepts Davis and Gallman were employing, the implied investment rates become roughly 5.9 percent and 7.2 percent, reasonably close to the Davis-Gallman figures.

Table 2.6   **Indexes and Average Annual Rates of Change of the U.S. Domestic Capital Stock and Structures, Per Capita, Conventional and Unconventional Concepts, 1860 Prices, 1774–1980**

	Conventional Concept, Deflated by		Including Clearing & Breaking, Deflated by	
	Capital Price Index	Consumer Price Index	Capital Price Index	Consumer Price Index
Panel A: Indexes				
1774	100	100	100	100
1799	132	120	104	112
1805	154	150	109	125
1815	143	147	99	106
1840	193	202	126	169
1850	224	270	138	217
1860	321	384	182	297
1870	323	315	177	229
1880	396	436	212	306
1890	643	683	317	456
1900	759	815	365	534
1929	1,348	1,461		
1953	1,520	2,294		
1980	2,735			
Panel B: Average Annual Rates of Change (%)				
1774–1840	1.0	1.1	0.4	0.8
1774–99	1.1	0.7	0.1	0.4
1799–1840	0.9	1.3	0.5	1.0
1840–1900	2.3	2.3	1.8	1.9
1840–60	2.6	3.3	1.9	2.9
1860–1900	2.2	1.9	1.8	1.5
1900–1929	2.0	1.6		
1929–53	0.5	1.9		
1953–80	2.2			
1774–1900	1.6	1.7		
1900–1980	1.6			
1774–1980	1.6			

Sources: See text.

2.4 Changing Composition of Capital Stock

Rates of change say something about the process of growth and development; data on the structure of the economy tell more. Development consists of structural change.

The conventional measure of domestic capital, in current prices, exhibits two pronounced compositional shifts: the fraction of the capital stock accounted for by animals drops very far, indeed, while the share attributable to

Table 2.7   **Real GDP and Real Domestic Capital per Capita, Conventional and Unconventional Concepts, 1840 Prices, 1800–1860**

	1800	1840	1860
Real GDP per capita ($)			
Conventional, variant A	73	91	125
Conventional, variant B	66	91	125
Unconventional, variant C	78	101	135
Real domestic capital per capita ($)			
Conventional	104	157	262
Unconventional	175	219	316
Capital/output ratios			
Conventional, variant A	1.42	1.73	2.09
Conventional, variant B	1.57	1.73	2.09
Unconventional, variant C	2.24	2.16	2.34

Sources: The real GDP per capita estimates are from Weiss's paper in this volume. For the remaining estimates, see the text.

structures rises, both of these developments occurring chiefly after 1815 (see table 2.8). But current price data are not so useful, in this context, as constant price data, which tell a very interesting story. They show that the structure of the capital stock changed very little, down to 1840. Thereafter, there were accelerating shifts. The share of animals in the total dropped precipitately and inventories dropped mildly, while the share of structures rose a little and the share of equipment rose very much. There is the strong suggestion of an economy shifting in the direction of industrial activity and modern economic growth: away from agriculture and animal power, and toward manufacturing and mechanical power. There is no question that stirrings can be identified well before 1840—Kenneth Sokoloff's work shows clearly that important industrial change can be dated to 1820, at least. (See Sokoloff's paper in this volume.) But these activities could not have carried a very heavy weight in the economy much before 1840, and that is probably what the data in table 2.8 are showing us. Bias in the estimates may overstate the decline in the relative importance of animals after 1870, and may contribute to the finding of stability in the share of structures in the capital stock before 1840 (see appendix A), but these matters are probably not of much importance.

The introduction of the value of farm making into the capital stock produces some expected shifts. Concentrating on the constant price data, the value of land clearing and breaking accounted for over half of the capital stock in 1774 and something under half in 1799. This figure dropped modestly to 1840—when it was a little less than a third—and more dramatically thereafter, reflecting the relative decline of the agricultural sector. In this variant, inventories retained roughly the same share of the capital stock after 1799, while the share of structures experienced a strong upward movement from the same date.

Table 2.8   **Constituents of the Domestic Capital Stock, Expressed as Shares in the Domestic Capital Stock, 1774–1900**

	1774	1799	1805	1815	1840	1850	1860	1870	1880	1890	1900
Panel A: Excluding the Value of Farmland Clearing and Breaking											
Current Prices											
Structures	.39	.33	.35	.41	.45	.47	.54	.54	.55	.61	.60
Equipment	.13	.14	.15	.13	.14	.13	.12	.11	.11	.13	.14
Inventories[a]	.23	.35	.34	.26	.24	.26	.22	.24	.24	.19	.19
Animals	.25	.18	.16	.21	.17	.13	.12	.11	.09	.08	.07
Constant (1860) Prices											
Structures	.40	.34	.40	.41	.43	.46	.54	.55	.50	.49	.46
Equipment	.08	.09	.09	.07	.08	.09	.12	.13	.16	.25	.30
Inventories[a]	.28	.35	.32	.29	.26	.27	.22	.22	.25	.21	.19
Animals	.25	.23	.19	.22	.23	.17	.12	.10	.09	.06	.04
Panel B: Including the Value of Farmland Clearing and Breaking											
Current Prices											
Structures	.24	.21	.26	.33	.33	.35	.42	.44	.47	.55	.55
Equipment	.08	.09	.11	.10	.10	.10	.09	.09	.10	.11	.13
Inventories[a]	.14	.23	.24	.21	.18	.20	.17	.20	.21	.17	.18
Animals	.15	.11	.12	.17	.12	.10	.09	.09	.08	.07	.06
Land clearing & breaking	.40	.36	.28	.19	.28	.25	.22	.17	.14	.10	.08
Constant (1860) Prices											
Structures	.17	.19	.25	.27	.29	.33	.42	.44	.41	.44	.42
Equipment	.04	.05	.05	.05	.06	.07	.09	.11	.13	.22	.28
Inventories[a]	.12	.20	.20	.19	.17	.19	.17	.18	.21	.19	.18
Animals	.11	.13	.12	.14	.15	.12	.09	.08	.07	.05	.04
Land clearing & breaking	.56	.44	.39	.36	.32	.28	.22	.19	.17	.11	.08

Sources: See text.

[a]Excluding animals.

Table 2.9 is another way of considering the same phenomena. It shows indexes of the per capita supply of each of the components of the capital stock. The growing importance of structures and, particularly, equipment comes through powerfully, while the value of the stock of land clearing and first breaking is shown to have fallen well behind the growth of population. There were two elements involved in the production of this result. First, the volume of farmland per capita declined over time, as the population became less and less rural and farm-centered. Since American agriculture was able to feed a growing population and expand its overseas sales, the decline in the value of farm improvements per capita went hand in hand with the growing

Table 2.9   **Indexes of Per Capita Real Magnitudes, 1860 Prices, 1774–1900**

	1774	1799	1805	1815	1840	1850	1860	1870	1880	1890	1900
Structures	100	112	156	150	211	263	438	449	503	793	886
Equipment	100	142	166	133	202	262	479	538	785	1,981	2,867
Inventories[a]	100	166	176	149	178	218	253	258	360	479	526
Animals	100	122	121	130	179	154	154	126	139	148	132
Land clear-ing & breaking	100	81	74	64	73	70	72	62	66	60	55

Sources: See text.

[a]Excluding animals.

productivity of agricultural land. Second, as population moved westward, out of the wooded areas, the cost of preparing land for cultivation fell. Toward the end of the nineteenth century, then, the real value of farm improvements (exclusive of structures) per acre was smaller than it had been in the eighteenth century. The meaning of this change is taken up further in appendix A.

On the whole, the structural evidence supports the conclusions that one might tentatively draw from the aggregate series: the American economy began to experience the process of modern economic growth in the years after the War of 1812; by the 1840s the modern components of the economy were large enough and growing rapidly enough to have an observable impact on the rate of growth and the structure of the economy.

2.5   The Growth of Total Factor Inputs

The measurements of the capital stock, viewed as an input to the productive process, yield information that clearly bears on the speed and nature of American economic growth. Measurements of total factor inputs would be even more useful. The assembly of the additional required inputs is not very difficult. Estimates of the volume of agricultural land (the only land input that could be taken into account) already exist. (Gallman 1972, 201, 202, extended to 1774 in the same manner as the extension to 1800.) Weiss has generated new labor force figures for the years 1800–1900, at ten-year intervals, and they were readily extended to 1774.[7]

7. The estimate is based on Jones (1980, 30) and Weiss's chapter in this volume. According to Jones there were 53,056 indentured servants in 1774 and 480,932 slaves. All indentured servants were in the work force; following Weiss's judgment for 1800, slaves ten and older probably amounted to 65 percent of the population of slaves, and nine-tenths of these people were in the work force. According to Jones, there were 396,158 free adult males, of whom, if we follow Weiss's treatment for the nineteenth century, 87.2 percent were in the work force. The rest of the population—1,034,456—consisted of youths and children, by Jones's account. Assuming half were males (a safe guess) and that they were distributed among the age groups as the white population of 1800 was, then there were about 55,000 males, ten to fourteen years old, of whom 22.1

Table 2.10, panel A, contains statements of the rates of growth of each input and each input per member of the population for various periods between 1774 and 1900. Notice that the labor force grew slightly more slowly than population between 1774 and 1800 and a little faster between 1800 and 1840. Thereafter, with the expansion of immigration, and its effect on the structure of population, the labor force participation rate rose faster than before. On the whole, the patterns of change of the other inputs are similar. The volume of agricultural land per capita actually declined throughout, but the rate of decline was less after 1800 than before, while the quantity of capital increased faster than population, the rate rising persistently over time. The strong suggestion of these data is that the per capita supply of all inputs, taken together, must have grown very slowly, if at all, down to 1800, when it began to increase, the increase becoming more marked as time passed.

This, in fact, is what is shown by panel B of the table, which sets out the rates of change of all three factors combined. The rates of growth of total inputs and inputs per capita accelerated over time, the change in the per capita rates being particularly striking.

There are three series describing rates of change of aggregate inputs. In the first, the underlying labor input is measured by the numbers of workers, without regard to the length of the work year or the differential quality of the workers. In the second and third, very crude efforts have been made to adjust the labor supply for sectoral differences in the work year, trends over time in the work year, and differences among sectors in the "quality" of workers. In series LFQV, the weights by which the rates of change of the three input series are combined (estimated factor income shares) vary from one year to the next; in series LFQF, the weights are fixed at the 1880 levels. The techniques employed to make the estimates are described in appendix B; the adjustments are almost certainly too large. That is, the rates of change represented by LFQV—and possibly LFQF, as well—are probably too large. The three sets of figures, however, may very well establish boundaries within which the rates of change of a properly adjusted labor input series would lie.

In any case, the rates of change of the combined input series do describe the same general pattern: an acceleration in the supply of inputs and, especially, inputs per capita. For the period following 1800, these findings once again parallel Weiss's (table 2.7). Furthermore, there was not only an acceleration in the rate of change of aggregate inputs, but also in total factor productivity: the long-term rate of gain was substantially higher after 1840 than before (table 2.10, panel C).

---

percent were in the work force (following Weiss's judgment for 1800), and there were 53,815 who were fifteen to twenty years old, of whom (again following Weiss) 87.2 percent worked. Adding free females, ten years old and older (497,973, with a participation rate of 7.5 percent, per Weiss), brings the total labor force to 776,241. A check on the total: assuming an overall participation rate of 32.5 percent (typical of the early decades of the nineteenth century, according to Weiss) yields a figure of 765,039, close enough.

Table 2.10   Rates of Growth of Factor Supplies, Factor Supplies per Capita, and Total Factor Productivity, 1774–1900

	1774–1800	1800–1840	1840–1900	1840–60
Panel A				
Labor force (LF)	3.09	3.09	2.72	3.41
LF/population	−0.08	0.11	0.20	0.31
Land	2.26	2.80	2.17	2.87
Land/population	−0.91	−0.18	−0.35	−0.23
Capital (K)	3.39	3.45	4.40	5.17
K/population	0.22	0.48	1.88	2.07
Panel B				
Total factor inputs, LF	3.10	3.18	3.20	3.91
Total factor inputs/population, LF	−0.07	0.20	0.68	0.81
Total factors, inputs, LFQV	3.21	3.44	3.75	4.78
Total factor inputs/population, LFQV	0.04	0.46	1.23	1.69
Total factor inputs, LFQF	3.25	3.47	3.57	4.41
Total factor inputs/population, LFQF	0.08	0.49	1.05	1.31
Panel C				
Total Factor Productivity				
GDP, LF		.46		.82
GNP, LF			.80	.70
GDP, LFQV			.25	−.17
GDP, LFQF			.43	.20

Sources: The real GDP estimates underlying the first set of total factor productivity estimates (panel C) are Weiss's, chapter 1 in this volume (broad concept, variant C). They are expressed in 1840 prices, as are the capital stock estimates (domestic capital) used with them to estimate total factor productivity.

The real GNP estimates (panel C) were derived from those underlying Gallman (1966). They are expressed in 1860 prices and include the value of all land improvements made in the given year and the value of home manufactures. The capital stock estimates used in the analysis involving the GNP refer to the national capital stock.

The labor input series is based on Weiss's labor force figures. *LF* refers to this series in unadjusted form. *LFQV* means that the labor force has been adjusted to take into account differences in work time and labor quality, both among sectors and over time (1840 onward); that is, the sectoral "weights" are variable. *LFQF* means that the labor force figures have been adjusted to take into account differences in time and quality among sectors, but not across time; that is, the sectoral "weights" are fixed. (In fact, the weights employed are those of 1880; only two sectors are distinguished in the fixed weight variant: "agriculture" and "all other.")

The rates of growth of the capital stock, 1840–1900, were computed from the series that incorporates the value of fencing.

The weights assigned to the rates of growth of the individual factors of production are labor, .68; land, .03; and capital, .29. These weights are intended to reflect income shares. (Land improvements, of course, are treated as capital.)

For estimating details, see the text, especially appendix B.

These results are surely not amazing. The years from 1774 through 1815 were years in which the young country engaged twice in major wars; when peace was achieved, American products were frequently prevented from entering their natural markets under reasonably free conditions. There was one period of booming trade, when the Napoleonic Wars created great opportunities for American merchants, opportunities ended by the Embargo of 1807 and then the War of 1812. With the return of peace, the factory system began to spread in earnest, and by 1840 the production of textiles had been virtually completely transferred out of the home and the shop and into the factory. The variety of American manufacturing activities increased markedly in the 1840s and 1850s, and machine building began to assume the central position it was to occupy in American industrialization for the rest of the century. The aggregate statistics are simply the embodiment of these well-known developments. The degree to which the benefits of economic growth were offset by costs unrecorded here and the extent to which the benefits were shared among Americans are matters of considerable importance. But since they are taken up by John Wallis and me in the Introduction and by other authors contributing to this volume, it is reasonable to pass them by here.

2.6   Conclusions

The conclusions of this paper are readily summarized. The capital stock series suggest that the pace of American economic growth accelerated in the decades before the Civil War. The evidence for this statement is to be found in the real per capita capital stock figures, the various estimates of aggregate real inputs per capita, and the changing structure of the capital stock, which describe a process of industrialization. The components that make up the series have their weaknesses, but the review of these components conducted above, and also in appendix A, turned up no compelling reasons to believe that the computed rates of growth and structural changes are importantly biased.

The acceleration of the rate of growth should not be allowed to obscure the progress made before 1840. The series assembled in this paper support Thomas Weiss's finding that per capita GDP increased in the decades between 1800 and 1840. Furthermore, the per capita supply of capital seems to have been increasing since 1774, and the supply of all factors of production, combined, seems to have increased at least as fast as population between the beginning of the Revolution and the turn of the century. There were bad times as well as good ones, and the standard of life surely sometimes declined, perhaps for extended periods. But the trend was mildly favorable between 1774 and 1799/1800, if these series are to be believed, more clearly favorable from the turn of the century until 1840, and even more pronouncedly favorable thereafter. The capital stock figures, however, bear only on the side of life that has to do with the provision of commodities and services. Industrialization may have brought a deterioration of the quality of life for some and may have for a time overwhelmed the capacity of society to deal with problems of public health. Other indexes of the standard of life, stressing health, for example, may yield results at odds with those reported in this paper—certainly this is the suggestion of the work described by Richard H. Steckel in his essay for this volume. The important point to be taken from the results described herein, however, is that the performance of the economy, narrowly conceived, was improving, and at an accelerating pace. The means for dealing with the problems created by the reorganization of society were therefore increasing. Solutions awaited the accumulation of the necessary knowledge and the emergence of a will to act.

Appendix A
Estimating Problems and Tests of Estimates

This appendix takes up a few of the chief problems encountered during the construction of the capital stock estimates, and describes some of the tests that were run to check the estimating decisions that were made.

Land Clearing and Breaking

The largest item in the more unconventional—but more meaningful—of the capital concepts employed in this paper is the value imparted to land by the processes of clearing and first breaking. The estimating procedure was simple. The following variables were established for each year: the number of acres of improved farmland of each relevant type (land originally under forest, land originally under grass) in each state or region; the number of labor hours per acre required to improve land of each type; the cost of farm labor in each state or region (Primack 1962; Lebergott 1964). Simple multiplication and addition produced the final figures. Constant price estimates were obtained by substituting technical coefficients and wage rates relevant to 1860 for those relevant to the current year. For the years 1840–1900—but not earlier—estimates of the value of fencing, drainage, and irrigation works were also made.

Certain characteristics of the series that may be associated with biased rates of change are immediately evident. The weight attributed to the clearing and breaking series is incorrect; it is probably too low, especially for the years before 1840. Since the clearing and breaking series exhibits relatively low rates of change over time, giving it a heavier weight would tend to reduce the rates of growth of the aggregate capital stock series, particularly before 1840. Thus the acceleration of the rate of change described previously in this paper would be enhanced.

The weight attached to the series is too low because the estimates ignore all elements of clearing and breaking cost except labor. Labor was, no doubt, the principal cost, but it was not the only one. Second, the only improved land treated is agricultural land; no account is taken of land under houses, factories, shops, and so forth. Third, for the years before 1840, important elements of improvement—particularly fencing—had to be ignored. If it had been possible to treat all of these phenomena, the improvement series would have had a larger weight.

There are, however, certain offsets. First, the value of fencing may very well have increased faster than the value of clearing, before 1840; it is almost certainly true that the volume of land under houses and so forth increased faster than the volume of improved land in agriculture, at least after 1840. Introducing these elements into the analysis might raise the rate of change of the improvements series, although probably not by much.

Another factor may appear, at first blush, to be more important than any so far discussed: the estimates make allowance for land retirements (land allowed to go back to nature), but not depreciation. The reason depreciation has been ignored is that land improvements, if properly maintained, do not depreciate. Bad farming practices may erode the fertility of the land, and the opening of western farms may reduce the value of eastern farms, but these changes have to do mainly with the value of land, rather than with the value of improvements. Now in a sense this characteristic of improvements is shared with other elements of the capital stock. Properly maintained, houses and ships and even machines can last very long, indeed. The difference is that most of the houses, ships, and machines that existed in, for example, eastern Pennsylvania in 1774 are gone today, while much of the improved land of that period is still improved. A substantial part of it is now under houses and shopping malls and highways, rather than under Indian corn, but it is still improved. Furthermore, in the cases of buildings, machines, and so forth, one can devise reasonable depreciation rates that properly describe the average lifetime experiences of these elements of capital and that are roughly relevant to long reaches of history. That is not possible for land improvements.

The discussion above implicitly introduces another issue. The improvements series consists of reproduction cost estimates. Various tests have shown (see Gallman 1987) that the reproduction cost and the market value of structures and manufactured producers' durables were, on average, about the same in the nineteenth century. Is this also true of land improvements? If not, then how is the analysis affected? The few simple tests that have been run seem to suggest that they are alike. At least two efforts have been made to estimate the market value of clearing and breaking at midcentury: one by Stanley Lebergott for the Midwest, the other by Stanley Engerman and Robert Fogel for the South (Lebergott 1985; Fogel and Engerman 1977). Comparisons are not easily made, and the efforts reported here may be polluted by wishful thinking, but I do not believe that is the case. The results suggest that estimates computed along the lines laid out above are very similar to the ones obtained by Lebergott and Engerman and Fogel. The suggestion then is that the market price and the reproduction cost of land improvements were about the same, on average, at midcentury.

The same may also hold for 1774. At least it is true that when one subtracts from Alice Jones's estimate of the value of real estate, my estimates of the value of land clearing and structures plus a rough allowance for other elements of land improvement (a relatively small part of the total), the remaining value, divided by the number of acres of land privately held (derived from Blodget [1806] 1964), yields an average price of land per acre—exclusive of improvements—that is almost identical with Blodget's estimate of the average value of unimproved land in 1774. The test is very roundabout and places much weight on a residual. Nonetheless, it encourages one to think that market price and reproduction cost may have been about the same, on average, at that date.

There is some evidence to the contrary, however. Specifically, Blodget's estimates of the average value of improved land per acre in 1774, 1799, and 1805 are substantially smaller than my estimates of the cost of improving land per acre. Bear in mind that Blodget's figures include the value of the land itself, while mine do not. The margin is so great that one has the impression that if Blodget's figures are truly market-price figures, and mine truly reproduction cost figures, then farmers of the late eighteenth century and the early nineteenth century were behaving irrationally, improving much more land than could be justified by the market. I do not believe that and therefore think that either Blodget is wrong or I am.

In making my estimates I assumed that all of the land improved at each of these dates had originally been forest land. That is probably not correct, and since forest land cost more to improve than grass land, this assumption probably leads to an overstatement of the value of cleared land at these dates. But the overstatement is tiny and is surely more than offset by the fact that the cost of factors other than labor was left out of account.

I also assumed that the labor hours per acre required for clearing were the same at these early dates as at midcentury. Primack (1962) believed that there were no important improvements in clearing techniques until after the Civil War, and while his interests were confined to the last half of the century, his remark is probably relevant to the early dates treated in this paper as well. In any case, if I am wrong about this matter, I have *understated* the value of improvements at these dates, not *overstated* them.

I also assumed that the treatment of stumps was the same at all dates: specifically, that one-third of the stumps were removed immediately and that the rest were left in the land to rot away on their own. It may be that an even smaller share of the stumps was taken out in the earlier years, but allowing for the removal of no stumps would not bring my estimates and Blodget's very much closer together.[8]

A more promising source of disparity lies in the way in which labor time was valued. I assumed that the opportunity cost of the labor employed in clearing and first breaking could be approximated by the agricultural wage rate. In fact, however, one would suppose that clearing and first breaking would have been conducted by farmers in the off season, when real opportunities may have been restricted to maintenance tasks around the farm, hunting, fishing, and so forth. The wage rate, then, may overstate the opportunity cost of labor. That seems not to have been the case at midcentury, when, as indicated above, reproduction cost and market value of improvements were very similar. It may be that by midcentury clearing and breaking were more commonly hired out (e.g., to prairie sodbusters) than previously and that farmers themselves had better opportunities for off-season work. If that were the case, the estimating technique might work better for the mid-nineteenth century than for the earlier dates. But that would be a relatively unimportant matter. Our concerns are chiefly with the constant price series, which are properly a function of the techniques and wage rates of 1860. The contrast with Blodget refers exclusively to the current price estimates.

In any case, my by no means unbiased guess is that Blodget is simply wrong on the matter of the value of improved land. The check of my work against Jones's estimate of the value of real estate and Blodget's estimate of the value of unimproved land seems reasonably strong. Furthermore, in comparison with Jones's estimate, Blodget's figures on the values of improved land seem very much too low. I therefore incline toward the view that the improvements series—particularly in constant prices—gives a reasonable view of what it purports to describe. At least I cannot make a case for viewing the series as strongly biased in one direction or the other or as generating strongly biased rates of growth.[9]

Structures

The estimates for 1850–1900 rest chiefly on census data; for 1840 on the work of Seaman (1852); for 1815 on the direct tax of 1813–15 and the work

8. The matter of stumps is tricky. What is the reproduction labor cost of ten acres of stumpless cleared land that was formerly under trees? Is it the full labor cost of clearing the land and removing all the stumps? Or is it the labor cost of cutting down the trees, removing the one-third of the stumps that were originally removed, and plowing the land? I decided that the second choice was the correct one, but clearly one could make a case for the first, or perhaps even a third or fourth option.

9. A word should be said about the land series, although there is inadequate space to go through the estimating procedures and tests. The 1850–1900 data come from the census, with some adjustments. The adjustments depend in part on the work of Primack (1962). The 1840 figures are weaker. They come from Seaman (1852) again adjusted and distributed, partly on the basis of the work of Primack. The figures for 1774 through 1805 are from Blodget ([1806] 1964), adjusted in various ways. The 1815 figure is a rough extrapolation from 1805. For a discussion of these matters, see Gallman (1972).

of Pitkin (1835); for 1805 on the work of Blodget ([1806] 1964) and Goldsmith (1952); for 1799 on the direct tax of 1798 and the work of Soltow (1984); and for 1774 on the work of Jones (1980). All of these data have been very heavily processed, frequently with the object of extracting one element from a larger aggregate, or dividing the aggregate among its components. In each case but two, however, there is a quite substantial component of real data that bears directly on the estimating problem. The weakest links are the ones for 1805 and 1840; there are no data expressly relevant to these dates. The underlying sources of evidence are the works of Seaman and Blodget. The latter extrapolated his estimate from an earlier date, for which real evidence *is* available, while the former both extrapolated from an earlier date and blew up partial estimates to encompass the universe. These figures have been tested, of course, but they are less trustworthy than are the rest.

There is not space to deal with all the estimating problems and with all the tests run with respect to the estimates relating to structures. In what follows, the most serious problem, which has to do with deflation for the years before 1850, will be treated.

For the years 1850–1900 there is no serious problem relating to deflation; indeed, the price index number situation is unusually good. For most of these years Dorothy Brady's two sets of deflators—for houses and churches, on the one hand, and factories and office buildings, on the other—are available. These are true price indexes, which makes them quite unusual among construction deflators. Usually it is necessary to make do with cost indexes. Brady's data need modest adjustment to make them expressly apposite to the task of deflating the capital stock, but no heroic efforts are needed to put them in proper condition for this purpose.

The problem appears in the years before 1850, for which Brady's indexes are not available. One possibility for this period is to follow the lead of David and Solar (1977), who linked Brady's housing price index to a construction cost index and then carried it back to the late eighteenth century. Since the relative importance of factories and office buildings before the 1840s was probably slight and since construction techniques in this period may not have varied much between residential construction and commercial buildings (except at the cutting edge of factory design and construction), an extension of the housing price index would be an entirely adequate way to deal with the deflation problem for all kinds of structures. David and Solar, however, did not use Brady's published series; they used the unrevised figures that Brady prepared for the Income and Wealth Conference. It turns out that in most instances the differences between the published and unpublished series are slight—matters of a point or two. There is one exception. In the published conference volume, Brady (1966) dropped her estimate of the price index of housing in 1839.

The Brady unpublished index falls from a level of 128 in 1839, to 94 in 1849, and then rises to 100 in 1859. Available construction cost indexes fall much more modestly and rise more sharply over these two decades, implying that, if the unpublished Brady index is correct, productivity in construction must have been rising quite dramatically. David and Solar believe that the experience reflects chiefly the diffusion of the balloon frame, which was invented in 1833. They therefore suppose that the annual rate of productivity improvement realized in the 1840s was also achieved in the period 1834–39. They construct a building cost index and employ it with the Brady price index to estimate productivity gains, 1839–59, and they then use it, together with their estimate of the rate of productivity improvement, 1839–49, to extrapolate the Brady price index number for 1839 back to 1834. They assume that there were no important productivity improvements before 1833 and extrapolate the 1834 price index number to earlier years in the century on their construction cost index. The productivity improvement for the period 1834 through 1859 implied by their calculations is a little more than 36 percent.

The procedure is ingenious and surely adequate to the purposes of David and Solar. It is not so clear that it is adequate to the purpose of creating a deflator for the most important component of the conventional capital stock series. First there is the matter of Brady's decision to suppress her 1839 estimate. Does this mean that she had had second thoughts about the strength of that estimate? Presumably. Nonetheless there remains evidence that Brady believed that construction prices did fall in the late 1830s and early 1840s. Her price index for factories drops very sharply between 1836 and 1844, for example. But of course this index refers to factories, not residences.[10]

Is it reasonable to suppose that the balloon frame led to a rise in productivity of 36 percent in the first twenty-five years of its existence? Probably not. The balloon frame saved on framing. Framing accounted for about 25 percent of the cost of a building. Consequently, even if the balloon frame eliminated the expense of framing and even if the balloon frame was adopted throughout the industry within this period, the rise in productivity could not have come close to reaching 36 percent. Neither condition was met, of course.[11]

10. One should not infer much about productivity changes from the relative movements of price and cost indexes between 1836 and 1844, however. Between these two dates lay a very sharp contraction. At least part of the decline in prices reflected falling profits, not rising productivity. It is also likely that workers discounted standard wage rates in order to hold their jobs.

11. For example, "although many authorities assert that balloon frame construction had 'almost completely replaced the hewn frame for domestic construction by the time of the Civil War' . . . in North Carolina field surveys demonstrate the prevalence of heavy mortised-and-tenoned house frames until the Civil War" (Bishir, Brown, Lounsbury, and Wood 1990, 457). An architect whose book was published in 1855 writes: "There is no doubt that if the subject received closer attention, a better mode of framing than that generally employed, could be suggested. Timbers are often unnecessarily heavy, but are afterwards so weakened by the mode of framing which is in vogue, and which compels the cutting of mortices and tenons and insertion of one timber into another, that the frame is less substantial than if constructed of lighter stuff differently put together. It is difficult to persuade carpenters of this" (Wheeler 1855, 407). The implication of the last statement is important. The building industry was a conservative, locally organized industry. The architect goes on: "The *New York Tribune* of January 18th, 1855, reported a meeting of the American Institute Farmers' Club, and contained amongst other items some remarks from one of the mem-

The framing of a building called for many workers. Barn-raising parties were organized expressly for this purpose. The balloon frame eventually changed all that. With the new system a man and a boy could frame a house by themselves. Thus the innovation became immensely important to the farming community, particularly for people on the frontier, for reasons that transcended normal cost considerations. It also diffused quickly in new western cities, places under intense demand pressure and without established artisanal power groups. (Chicago and San Francisco were both balloon frame cities.) But it did not immediately spread to the East.

There were, of course, other innovations during this period, so that the rise in productivity that David and Solar identify need not be the result exclusively of the balloon frame. The principal changes that seem to have been taking place involved the transfer of some activities from the building site to mills. For example, it is said that it became more common to use manufactured nails, as well as manufactured windows and doors, which presumably lowered costs. But the census returns of 1810, 1850, and 1860 suggest that manufactured nails were already widely used before the 1830s. Mill-made sash, doors, and blinds do not appear in the census returns—separately, at least—before 1860, when their output amounted to a value of about $9.5 million, in a year in which the total value of conventional construction (exclusive of railroads and canals) ran to about $345 million. Mill-made windows and so forth were therefore by no means negligible by this date, but they did not bulk large enough to suggest that their introduction led to a major improvement in productivity. Furthermore, it may well be that their contribution to productivity actually came after 1849, rather than before. At least the treatment of these lines of production by the census suggests that this was so. David and Solar find most of the productivity change (almost three-quarters of it) occurring before 1849.

The general idea lying behind the David and Solar treatment of construction prices is clearly reasonable, and their execution of it may have solved their problem satisfactorily. The technique is less likely to solve my problem satisfactorily, however. Unfortunately, there is no option that is clearly superior.

---

bers upon a novel mode of constructing cheap wooden dwellings" (408). The "novel method" was the balloon frame.

The extent to which innovations had diffused is relevant because it would have determined the degree to which prices responded to innovations. Prices would have been potentially affected only in localities in which the new framing system had begun to diffuse, and even there, prices need not have fallen immediately, if competition among builders was not severe. If builders commonly used cost plus pricing, of course, prices would have fallen immediately in areas where the balloon frame was put in use.

There is a question as to whether Brady's prices refer to average practice or best practice. I have assumed they refer to average practice. If I am not correct in this assumption, and if builders followed cost plus pricing practices, then the Brady price index numbers exaggerate the true decline in average prices. The course of average relative prices of residences after 1849 suggests that the ambiguity with respect to the meaning of the price indexes is unimportant for these years.

Nonetheless, I decided to accept the Brady indexes for the years 1849 onward. I then adjusted them to fit my needs, and extrapolated the adjusted 1849 (1850) index number to 1840, 1815, 1805, 1799, and 1785 on the Adams (1975) variant B (allowing for input substitutions) construction cost series. The index was extended to 1774 on a construction cost series based on the David and Solar common wage index, a Maryland farm wage rate, taken from Adams (1986, 629–30), and the Bezanson-Gray-Hussey arithmetic average price index for Philadelphia (U.S. Bureau of the Census 1975, ser. E-111). The last two steps need further discussion.

The Adams construction cost index was exceptionally carefully made from good basic data. It is an excellent construction cost index, and the version used allows for factor substitutions due to shifts in relative input prices. For present purposes, however, it has certain potential shortcomings. The ideal index, for present purposes, is a true price index, an index that allows for changes in productivity. The Adams index does not do that, except insofar as productivity changes are associated with shifts in factor proportions. As proxy for a true price index it will exaggerate any long-term price increases and understate any long-term price decreases, so long as productivity improvements are taking place. The capital stock series that it is used to deflate will then exhibit a rate of change that is biased in a downward direction. In the present instance, the bias would exaggerate the observed acceleration in the rate of growth of the capital stock. If the bias were serious enough, it would account fully for the acceleration. That seems highly unlikely, however. The sources of productivity improvement in construction do not appear to have been important before the mid-1830s, and, as I have tried to show, even in the period between the mid-1830s and the beginning of the true price indexes in 1849, the amount of productivity improvement is unlikely to have been very great. In any case, the Adams index has other shortcomings for present purposes, and it turns out that at least one of these may introduce a compensating bias, in direction at least, and perhaps in amount as well.

The Adams index refers exclusively to Philadelphia. How successfully does it represent the United States? Two questions immediately arise. First, housing price levels varied by region, and as time passed, the relative importance of the various regions changed. Did the shifts in regional weights affect the trend in the national average of housing prices? Probably not, and if they did, they tended to *raise* average prices a little. By ignoring the effects of the regional shift I can perhaps compensate slightly for whatever bias is present from the use of a cost index in place of a true price index. These conclusions are based on the results of a test of the following form.

The census of 1840 requested information on the numbers of two types of houses constructed in the census year, those built of brick and stone and those built of wood, as well as the value of both types of houses taken together. I used the state data in a regression analysis to obtain an intercept value and coefficients for each of the two types of houses. These data were then employed to value the houses constructed in each state, and the figures thus obtained were divided through the census returns of the value of houses built to get an index number for each state. The index number compares the value of the houses constructed in the state with the value that would have obtained if prices had been at the level of the national average. Clearly, the index numbers reflect not only variations in building prices—which are required for the proposed analysis—but also differences in average size and quality of new houses, from state to state. Since cost, size, and quality were likely to have varied together—frontier areas having lower building costs, smaller houses, and houses of lower quality than the well-settled areas—the index numbers almost certainly exaggerate the regional variations in building costs, a point to be borne in mind as the analysis unfolds.

The individual state index numbers were then used to deflate the state returns of the value of real estate in 1799, according to the direct tax. The sum of the deflated returns was then divided through the aggregate current price value of real estate in 1799, according to the direct tax. The result was an index number of 0.932, which compares with the 1840 index number of 1.000; that is, according to these calculations, the shifting weights among states tended to raise, very slightly, the true price index of structures between 1799 and 1840.[12] The index numbers almost certainly overstate the true impact of the redistribution of the value of structures among states in this period, because the state index numbers probably overstate (for reasons previously given) the true variation in building costs among states. It appears unnecessary, then, to adjust the Adams cost index to take into account the effects of the shifting real-value-of-structures weights among states. This is particularly the case in view of the fact that the Adams index is a cost index and is likely, therefore, to exaggerate the extent to which the prices of buildings rose or to understate the extent to which they fell during this period. Finally, if the bias is slight between 1799 and 1840, it is almost certainly negligible between 1774 and 1799.

There is another aspect of the regional specificity of the Adams index that must be considered. Do changes in Philadelphia costs properly represent changes in costs in other regions? The strong suggestion that one gets from looking at price and wage indexes from New England and New York (Rothenberg 1988; David and Solar 1977; Warren and Pearson 1933) is that they do not: Adams's cost index moves in step with the Bezanson-Gray-Hussey general price index (Philadelphia—U.S. Bureau of the Census 1975, ser. E-97), while the Rothenberg, David-Solar, and Warren-Pearson indexes also move more or less together, but quite differently from the Philadelphia indexes. (At least these statements apply to the benchmark dates relevant here.) David and

12. The two indexes should ideally be weighted by the state distribution of the real value of houses in the capital stock. These, in fact, are the weights utilized for 1799, but the weights for 1840 are the real values of houses built in the census year.

Solar report that a construction cost index they assembled from materials prices from New York (Warren and Pearson 1933) and common wage rates from Philadelphia (Adams 1975) and the Erie Canal (Smith 1963) exhibits a less pronounced decline between 1809 and 1834 than does the Adams index. I constructed an index from Warren and Pearson materials prices and David-Solar common wages (using Adams's weights and his procedure for allowing for factor substitutions) for all the relevant dates. The Adams index shows a much more pronounced drop over time than does the WP-DS index. There is the strong suggestion that a properly derived national construction cost index would exhibit more pronounced price increases and less pronounced price declines, over the long run, than would a Philadelphia index. The bias imparted to the real capital stock series from using a cost index to proxy a price index is, then, compensated for—in part? in whole? more than compensated for?—by the fact that Philadelphia prices moved differently from national average prices, at least after 1799, and probably from 1774 as well.

There is one final problem with the deflator: it represents the costs of commercial construction in a city. A substantial fraction of the stock of structures in the years 1799 through 1840 must have been built in the countryside by unprofessional labor. The matter may not be very important, however. According to Adams, Philadelphia construction and Maryland farm wage rates moved in roughly similar ways among the dates 1785, 1799, 1805, 1815, and 1840.

One cannot claim great accuracy for the deflator, but on the whole it seems satisfactory.

Animal Inventories

There are at least two problems with the animal inventory estimates. First, they include only farm animals from 1840 onward (animals used in the mines are part of the "equipment" estimates in mining) and probably only farm animals at earlier dates as well, whereas ideally one would like to have all domestic animals throughout. The omissions are not trivial, but neither are they of overwhelming importance. In 1860, just over 12 percent of domestic animals, by value, were located off farms (U.S. Bureau of the Census 1860, cviii, cxxvi, 192); in 1900, the fraction was just under 7 percent (U.S. Bureau of the Census 1900, cxliv). The suggestion is that the total stock of animals increased a little more slowly than did the stock of farm animals, but correcting for this shortcoming would probably not affect very substantially the conclusions previously reached.

The second problem has to do with deflation. The constant price series was made by applying base-year prices (1860) to estimates of the numbers of animals in each year. The assumption is that a pig is a pig. In fact, pigs in 1890 were, without much doubt, superior animals to pigs of 1830. The deflator, then, is biased, and deflation tends to understate the importance of the growth of the stock of animals. Furthermore, the effect is also likely to be to underplay the acceleration in the rate of growth of the per capita capital stock. The reason is that most of the gains in the quality of animals were realized after midcentury. In earlier decades there were probably periods when, on balance, the quality of animal stocks actually deteriorated. Nonetheless, numbers can reasonably proxy real values before 1840 or 1850, whereas they are less able to perform this function thereafter. There are, of course, problems with the evidence on numbers as well, but they seem less pressing and do not deserve a place in this brief treatment of the subject. On the whole, the series, despite these qualifications, is acceptable for the uses to which it has been put.

Other Inventories

The procedure followed is one employed by Kuznets (1946, 228). Inventories were taken as a fixed fraction of the value of imports and the value of outputs of the agricultural, manufacturing, and mining sectors. No allowance was made for changes in the efficiency with which inventories were used, a matter of limited importance, especially before the Civil War. If there were improvements in efficiency, then the estimating procedure tends to exaggerate the acceleration in the rate of change of the real per capita capital stock. The details of how the value of imports and outputs were obtained are best left to another occasion.

Equipment

The data for the years 1840 onward were derived chiefly from the census, were deflated by Dorothy Brady's true price indexes, and were tested—with considerable success—against perpetual inventory estimates (Gallman 1987). For the earlier years, the chief sources were Jones (1980), Blodget ([1806] 1964), Goldsmith (1952), and U.S. Bureau of the Census (1975, for Treasury data on shipping). The series seems adequate for present purposes, but should not be trusted for much more.

Conclusions

It should be obvious that a substantial margin for error must be allowed for all of the estimates discussed in this paper, especially those dated before 1850, and particularly for those at the turn of the century. On the other hand, it is not obvious that the rates of change computed from the series are subject to important biases. The conclusions reached in sections 2.3–2.5 need not be altered—at least not on the basis of the results of the review conducted in this appendix.

Appendix B
*Time-Quality Adjustments to the
Labor Force Estimates*

This appendix describes the time-quality adjustments that were made to the labor force estimates, for purposes of the measurement and analysis of changes in total factor inputs and changes in total factor productivity (table 2.10). The last paragraph takes up the estimation of the elasticities of output with respect to factor inputs that are necessary to make estimates of total factor productivity changes.

The estimates were made in two steps. First, the farm labor force figures were adjusted to take into account changes in the farm work year.[13] Then quality-time weights were devised for the two remaining sectors that could be readily distinguished: mining, manufacturing, and hand trades, and all others. The weights consisted of the ratio of labor income per worker in the relevant sector to labor income per worker in agriculture. Since two of the important factors accounting for sectoral differences in labor income per worker are the relative duration of the labor year in each sector and the relative quality of workers in each sector, one is perhaps justified in referring to these ratios as time-quality weights. Unfortunately, however, other factors—factors irrelevant to the time-quality adjustment—also affect intersectoral differences in labor income per worker. Sectoral labor income deviations arose out of short-term disequilibria in labor markets, as well as from enduring quality differences among workers. Furthermore, some part of the variations in labor income surely reflected regional and urban-rural price differences, rather than real income disparities. It is likely that both of these factors typically operated to widen the gaps between labor incomes in agriculture and the other two sectors identified, each of which enjoyed higher labor incomes per worker than did the agricultural sector. Since the labor forces attached to these two sectors were growing faster than the agricultural labor force, the excessive time-quality weights given these sectors mean that the rates of change of the time-quality adjusted labor series are biased upward. The present status of regional and urban-rural price series does not permit an appropriate deflating of the labor income series, and there is no way of knowing how serious the bias arising out of disequilibria in labor markets is.

There are other difficulties with these measurements.

1. It would be helpful to have detailed breakdowns of the labor force and labor earnings, so that a more fully articulated weighting scheme might be developed, but adequate data simply are not available.

2. Sectoral labor income estimates were developed from value-added data. Value-added estimates involve some double-counting. If the extent of double-counting varied from one sector to another, the labor income estimates would

13. First in principle, but not in fact. The quality adjustments were worked out first.

not be good indexes of the true relative sectoral labor incomes. It is quite unlikely, however, that this problem is, in fact, at all serious.

3. The labor income estimates were taken as residuals, the difference between total sectoral income and sectoral property income. Property income was estimated as the product of the value of capital and land and estimated rates of return. Since the estimates of inventories could not be distributed among sectors, property income was computed against the value of land and fixed capital only. If the relative importance of inventories varied by sector, the sectoral property estimates are biased. Unfortunately, there is no way to be sure that this was not the case, although it is unlikely that we have here a major source of bias.

4. More important, the system of estimating property incomes involved the assumption that the rate of return on property *of a given type* was the same in all sectors. In fact, this is unlikely to have been the case. The work of Bateman and Weiss shows that the returns to property in the antebellum South were much higher in manufacturing than in agriculture (1981, 107, 108, 114).[14] Unfortunately, there is no good basis for producing different sectoral rates of return for all types of property for all sectors in all years. We can be quite sure, however, that the procedure followed to produce labor income estimates has led to an exaggeration of the relative levels of labor income in the "mining, manufacturing, and hand trades" sector, and probably in the "all other" sector as well. This in turn means that the time-quality weights attached to the nonfarm sector labor forces are too high and that, therefore, the rates of change of the adjusted labor series are biased upward.

The sectoral value-added series (current prices) were taken from volumes 24 and 34 of Studies in Income and Wealth (Gallman 1960, 47, 54, 56, 63; Gallman and Weiss 1969, 305), and were adjusted in the following ways. The estimates of farmland improvements were dropped from farm value-added, and new estimates, derived from data in volume 30 of Studies in Income and Wealth (Brady 1966) were substituted for them.[15] Value added by the "all

---

14. The rates of return I have used do vary from one sector to another, as the structure of the capital stock varies; only the rates for individual types of property are constant. But the differences in the average rates that have emerged are small, compared with the ones observed by Bateman and Weiss. For example, the average rates I have obtained in four of the years are

	1840	1860	1880	1900
Agriculture	11.6%	11.0%	9.4%	7.6%
Manufacturing, mining, and hand trades	13.0	12.6	10.9	9.4
All other	13.2	12.5	10.7	8.9

Bateman and Weiss (1981, 116) report rates of return for large manufacturing firms of 17% in 1850, and 21% in 1860.

15. Gallman 1966, 35, variant I. The estimates are available in constant prices only. Current price estimates were made by assuming that the ratio of improvements to farm value added was the same in current and constant prices. The average value of improvements for 1834–43 was taken to correspond to the value of improvements in census year 1839, and so forth. The ratio of the value of improvements to the value of farm value added in 1859 was estimated on the basis of

other" sector was formed by adding to total value added by services (taken from volume 34 of Studies in Income and Wealth), value added by construction (drawn from volume 24 of Studies in Income and Wealth, construction variant A), and then subtracting the value of shelter and value added by the hand trades. The value of shelter was dropped because the production of shelter involves the use of practically no labor and therefore the value of shelter should not figure in the estimation of sectoral labor quality weights. Value added by the hand trades was added to value added by manufacturing and mining, taken from volume 24.

The gross rate of return for each type of property is composed of the net rate plus depreciation (if any). The following depreciation rates were assumed: Land, 0; animals, 0; buildings, fences, irrigation, and drainage works, 2 percent; land clearing and breaking, 0; tools and equipment, 6.67 percent. The net rate of return was taken to be 10 percent in 1860 and was adjusted in the other years on the basis of an index number of the rate of return on New England municipal bonds (Homer 1963, 287–288, linked at 1857–59 to Boston City 5s, 305).

The labor force data were drawn from Weiss's paper in this volume. The division of the nonfarm labor force between the two nonfarm sectors was based on Lebergott (1964).

The adjustment for changes in agricultural work hours was based on data in Gallman (1975, 73), and the David, Lebergott, and Weiss series. From Gallman (1975, 73, inclusive of improvements, variant B), and the David and Lebergott farm labor force series, it was possible to compute an index of the hours worked by farm laborers in 1800, 1850, and 1900. With this index and the Weiss farm labor force in each of these three years, an index of the number of hours worked per worker was computed. Index numbers for the missing intermediate years were interpolated on a straight line. The index for 1774 was assumed to be the same as the index for 1800. The aggregate quality-adjusted labor force series were then adjusted for changes in the number of hours worked by multiplying them by the index of hours worked per worker.

The procedure adopted to make estimates of the elasticities of output with respect to inputs was similar to the one by which labor and property incomes were computed for the three sectors (see above). The only difference was that the calculations were made at the national, not the sectoral, level and that components of capital left out of the sectoral calculations—inventories, the international sector—were here added back in.

---

the ratio of improvements, 1849–58, and farm value added 1854. A similar procedure was followed to obtain the ratio for census year 1869.

References

Abramovitz, Moses. 1989. The nature and significance of Kuznets cycles. In *Thinking about growth and other essays on economic growth and welfare*, 245–75. Cambridge: Cambridge University Press.

Adams, Donald R. 1975. Residential construction industry in the early nineteenth century. *Journal of Economic History* 35: 794–816.

———. 1986. Prices and wages in Maryland, 1750–1850. *Journal of Economic History* 46, no. 3: 625–45.

Batemen, Fred, and Thomas Weiss. 1981. *A deplorable scarcity.* Chapel Hill: University of North Carolina Press.

Bezanson, Anne, Robert D. Gray, and Miriam Hussey. 1936. *Wholesale prices in Philadelphia, 1784–1861: Part I.* Industrial Research Study no. 29. Philadelphia: University of Pennsylvania. Reprinted in U.S. Bureau of the Census, *Historical statistics of the United States*, ser. E-97, E-111. Washington, D.C.: GPO, 1975.

Bishir, Catherine W., Charlotte V. Brown, Carl R. Lounsbury, and Ernest H. Wood, III. 1990. *Architects and builders in North Carolina: A history of the practice of building.* Chapel Hill: University of North Carolina Press.

Blodget, Samuel. [1806] 1964. *Economica: A Statistical manual for the United States of America.* Reprint. New York: Augustus Kelley.

Brady, Dorothy S. 1966. Price deflators for final product estimates. In *Output, employment, and productivity in the United States after 1800*, ed. Dorothy S. Brady, 91–115. NBER Studies in Income and Wealth, 30. New York: Columbia University Press.

David, Paul, and Peter Solar. 1977. A bicentenary contribution to the history of the cost of living in America. *Research in Economic History* 2: 1–80.

Davis, Lance E., Richard A. Easterlin, William N. Parker, et al. 1972. *American economic growth: An economist's history of the United States.* New York: Harper and Row.

Davis, Lance E., and Robert E. Gallman. 1978. Capital formation in the United States during the nineteenth century. In *The Cambridge economic history of Europe*, vol. 7, pt. 2: 1–69, 496–503, 557–61. Cambridge: Cambridge University Press.

Engerman, Stanley L., and Robert E. Gallman. 1983. U.S. economic growth, 1790–1860. *Research in Economic History* 8: 1–46.

Fishlow, Albert. 1966a. The American common school revival: Fact or fancy? In *Industrialization in two systems*, ed. Henry Rosovsky, 40–67. New York: John Wiley and Sons.

———. 1966b. Levels of nineteenth century American investment in education. *Journal of Economic History* 26: 418–36.

Fogel, Robert W., and Stanley L. Engerman. 1977. Explaining the relative efficiency of slave agriculture in the antebellum south. *American Economic Review* 67: 275–96.

Gallman, Robert E. 1960. Commodity output, 1839–1899. In *Trends in the American economy in the nineteenth century*, ed. William N. Parker, 13–67. NBER Studies in Income and Wealth, 24. Princeton: Princeton University Press.

———. 1966. Gross national product in the United States, 1834–1909. In *Output, employment, and productivity in the United States after 1800*, ed. Dorothy S. Brady, 3–76. NBER Studies in Income and Wealth, 30. New York: Columbia University Press.

———. 1972. Changes in total U.S. agricultural factor productivity in the nineteenth century. *Agricultural History* 46: 191–209.

————. 1975. The agricultural sector and the pace of economic growth: U.S. experience in the nineteenth century. In *Essays in nineteenth century economic history,* ed. David C. Klingaman and Richard K. Vedder, 35–76. Athens: Ohio University Press.

————. 1986. The United States capital stock in the nineteenth century. In *Long-term factors in American economic growth,* ed. Stanley L. Engerman and Robert E. Gallman, 165–206. NBER Studies in Income and Wealth, 51. Chicago: University of Chicago Press.

————. 1987. Investment flows and capital stocks: U.S. experience in the nineteenth century. In *Quantity and quiddity: Essays in U.S. economic history in honor of Stanley L. Lebergott,* ed. Peter Kilby, 214–54. Middletown, Conn.: Wesleyan University Press.

Gallman, Robert E., and Thomas Weiss. 1969. The service industries in the nineteenth century. In *Production and productivity in the service industries,* ed. Victor R. Fuchs, 287–381. NBER Studies in Income and Wealth, 34. New York: National Bureau of Economic Research.

Giffen, Robert. 1889. *Growth of capital.* London: George Bell and Sons.

Goldin, Claudia, and Robert A. Margo. 1989. Wages, prices, and labor markets before the civil war. NBER Working Paper no. 3198. Cambridge, Mass.: National Bureau of Economic Research.

Goldsmith, Raymond W. 1952. The growth of the reproducible wealth of the United States of America, 1805 to 1905. In *Income and wealth of the United States: Trends and structure,* ed. Simon Kuznets, 247–328. Income and Wealth Series, 2. Cambridge: Bowes and Bowes.

————. 1982. *The national balance sheet of the United States, 1953–1980.* Chicago: University of Chicago Press.

————. 1985. *Comparative national balance sheets: A study of twenty countries, 1688–1978.* Chicago: University of Chicago Press.

Homer, Sidney. 1963. *A history of interest rates.* New Brunswick, N.J.: Rutgers University Press.

Jones, Alice Hanson. 1980. *Wealth of a nation to be.* New York: Columbia University Press.

Kuznets, Simon. 1938. On the measurement of national wealth. In *Studies in income and wealth, 2,* 3–61. New York: National Bureau of Economic Research.

————. 1946. *National product since 1869.* New York: National Bureau of Economic Research.

Lebergott, Stanley L. 1964. *Manpower in economic growth.* New York: McGraw-Hill.

————. 1985. The demand for land: The United States, 1820–1860. *Journal of Economic History* 65: 181–212.

Pitkin, Timothy. 1835. *A statistical view of the commerce of the United States of America.* Reprint. Greenwich, Conn.: Johnson Reprint Corporation, 1967.

Primack, Martin. 1962. Farm formed capital in American agriculture, 1850 to 1910. Ph.D. diss., University of North Carolina, Chapel Hill.

Rothenberg, Winifred. 1988. The emergence of farm labor markets and the transformation of the rural economy: Massachusetts, 1750–1855. *Journal of Economic History* 48: 537–66.

Seaman, Ezra C. 1852. *Essays on the progress of nations.* New York: Charles Scribner.

Smith, Walter B. 1963. Wage rates on the Erie Canal. *Journal of Economic History* 23, no. 3: 298–311.

Soltow, Lee. 1984. Wealth inequality in the United States in 1798 and 1860. *Review of Economics and Statistics* 66: 444–51.

U.S. Bureau of the Census. 1860. *Agriculture of the United States in 1860*. Washington, D.C.: GPO.

————. 1900. *Agriculture: Part 1: Farms, live stock, and animal products*. Washington, D.C.: GPO.

————. 1975. *Historical statistics of the United States, colonial times to 1870: Bicentennial edition: Parts 1 and 2*. Washington, D.C.: GPO.

Uselding, Paul. 1971. Conjectural estimates of gross human capital inflows to the American economy, 1790–1860. *Explorations in Economic History* 9: 49–62.

Warren, George F., and Frank A. Pearson. 1933. *Prices*. New York: John Wiley and Sons. Reprinted in U.S. Bureau of the Census, *Historical statistics of the United States*, ser. E-52, E-59. Washington, D.C.: GPO, 1975.

Wheeler, Gervase. 1855. *Homes for the people in suburb and country*. New York: Charles Scribner.

Comment   Stanley L. Engerman

Robert Gallman here uses measures of the capital stock to estimate and describe the pattern of economic growth in the United States from the Revolutionary period to the end of the nineteenth century. The measures represent a continuation of his ongoing work, previously published in several places.[1] In these earlier publications he has presented many of the details of calculation for the 1840 to 1900 estimates, as well as described the various concepts and tests going into their preparation. In general, most of these problems are well-known and ably discussed, so there can be little new to say here in regard to the major issues. Following another remark of Giffen's, we can only compliment Gallman for doing the best that can be done with the limited data available, and though the "figures are necessarily rough," they make "a little clear what would otherwise be most dark, and they suggest problems for inquiry which would not otherwise be thought of." For "the figures, though rough, can be reasoned on safely with care."[2]

There is one initial point about the basic concept of capital that Gallman uses that is worth noting. His measures are restricted to variants of physical capital. There are no estimates of human capital, even of the slave population for which market values do exist. But, compared to the familiar constructs of Goldsmith, Gallman's measure is not of all tangible wealth, since he does not

Stanley L. Engerman is John H. Munro Professor of Economics and professor of history at the University of Rochester and a research associate of the National Bureau of Economic Research.

1. Robert E. Gallman, "The United States capital stock in the nineteenth century," in *Long-term factors in American economic growth*, ed. Stanley L. Engerman and Robert E. Gallman, NBER Studies in Income and Wealth, 51 (Chicago: University of Chicago Press, 1986), 165–206; and "Investment flows and capital stocks: U.S. experience in the nineteenth century," in *Quantity and quiddity: Essays in U.S. economic history in honor of Stanley L. Lebergott*, ed. Peter Kilby (Middletown, Conn.: Wesleyan University Press, 1987), 214–54.

2. Robert Giffen, *Growth of capital* (London: George Bell and Sons, 1889), 157.

include all of the value of land, nor is it all reproducible tangible wealth, since he does include some of the value of land.[3] Rather, Gallman's estimates include the value of improvements made to land, approximately equal in some years, it turns out, to the market value of improved land. Although Gallman's measure does omit the value of privately owned unimproved land and the "pure rent" on the acres improved, in most years the value of improved land represents the largest part of the total value of land. Thus the distinction between the Goldsmith and the Gallman treatments of land, while interesting and important, will not seriously distort most long-term comparisons.

Gallman uses the capital stock both as a means of measuring economic growth, for a period of time for which the basis of income measurement is not readily available, and as part of the explanation of the nature of economic growth, using capital stock measures with related input data to describe the patterns of change. There are some points to consider in the use of changes in the capital stock to measure changes in income level, as well as some differences between measures of potential income (which is perhaps the most desired measure of economic growth), observed (measured) income, and capital. There are choices made out of potential income that influence observed income and the observed capital stock. The choices between goods and leisure, and decisions in regard to fertility, clearly influence measured output per capita, as do the effects of intensity avoidance, risk avoidance, and market avoidance upon the product mix and thus potential income forgone. Capital, being based upon the amounts of income not consumed in the past, will have a different growth rate than income if there are changes in the savings rate over time. In addition, in considering the effects of savings upon the capital stock and its measured potential for future growth, it is also necessary to consider the form that these savings and investments take, and the related differences in types of assets and in their longevity. Savings can be used to provide either producer durables or consumer durables (the latter are omitted by Gallman, except for dwellings). It has, for example, been argued that in English history the level of savings was long sufficient to have financed the industrial revolution, but that a change in its structure and composition was needed for long-term growth.[4] Further, as Gallman points out, the longevity of capital will influence the breakdown between gross and net investment, and of the available capital stock. Estimates of asset durability and obsolescence are not, as Gallman notes, independent of the performance of the economy and its rate

3. See, for example, Raymond W. Goldsmith, "The growth of the reproducible wealth of the United States of America, 1805 to 1905," in *Income and wealth of the United States: Trends and structure*, ed. Simon Kuznets, Income and Wealth Series, 2 (Cambridge: Bowes and Bowes, 1952), 247–328; and *The national balance sheet of the United States, 1953–1980* (Chicago: University of Chicago Press, 1982).

4. M. M. Postan, "Recent trends in the accumulation of capital," *Economic History Review* 6 (1935): 1–12.

of technical change. Kuznets suggests that one of the basic shifts from the premodern to the modern era was not in the gross investment rate, but rather reflected an increase in asset longevity, lowering capital consumption, and leading to a larger capital stock from the gross investment.[5]

How good a proxy for the rate of growth of income is the rate of growth of the capital stock? In the long-run, increases in both are part of modern economic growth, and high growth (relative to preindustrial times) of both will come together. In the United States, the capital stock generally grew more rapidly than did GNP throughout the nineteenth century (and, depending on which of the several variants used from table 2.4, possibly after 1774), accounting for the rising capital-output ratio over that period. For shorter intervals, however, there are also differences not only in magnitudes, but even in the comparative ranking of rates of change, and the periods of acceleration or deceleration can differ. Thus the choice between income and capital as a measure of growth can influence examinations of the turning points in the growth process. Nevertheless, since for the period before 1840 it seems more possible to build up capital estimates from probate inventories and tax reports than to generate income data when no census production (or labor force) data are available, clearly these capital stock estimates for the early period must provide an essential set of measurements to be used by economic historians in the quantitative study of economic growth.

Gallman's estimates indicate that the post-1840 years of the nineteenth century had rates of growth of the capital stock per capita more rapid than those in preceding years.[6] In particular, the 1840 to 1860 growth rate exceeded that of the pre-1840 years and, indeed, almost all twenty-year periods since. This is not the same as dating the acceleration of growth in 1840, since the most analyzed data are for 1774, 1805, and 1840 (with 1815 given less attention). Thus it is hard to pinpoint from the data exactly when after 1805 (or 1815) the growth spurt began, but clearly some increase in capital's growth rate occurred in the first half of the nineteenth century (for at least three of the four series shown in table 2.6). For the last quarter of the eighteenth century the capital stock probably also grew at higher rates than did income, particularly for the concept of capital that excludes land clearing. Note, also, that the 1774–1840 rate of increase of the U.S. capital stock was considerably above that for Great Britain in this period.[7]

5. Simon Kuznets, "Capital formation in modern economic growth (and some implications for the past)," in *Third International Conference of Economic History* (Paris: Mouton, 1968).
6. In general, unless otherwise stated, the comparisons will be based on the Gallman capital stock series including land clearing and breaking, with the consumer price index as a deflator. While most comparisons would not differ if any of the other series were used, some would require minor alteration.
7. C. H. Feinstein, "Capital formation in Great Britain," in *The Cambridge economic history of Europe* (Cambridge: Cambridge University Press, 1978), vol. 7, pt. 1.

The growth pattern of the U.S. capital stock was consistent with the general pattern of growth in income, which also had an acceleration in the interval between 1800 and 1840. Compared to Thomas Weiss's (chap. 1 in this volume) newest estimates of national income, and using the estimated capital stock including land clearing, capital grew at a more rapid rate than did income between 1800 and 1840, while both had considerably higher rates of growth after 1840 than before, with the shift upward in the growth of capital being sharper than that in income. Weiss has some acceleration in the growth of per capita income after 1820, consistent with Gallman's post-1815 acceleration in capital stock growth.[8]

Significant structural shifts in the composition of the capital stock occurred, particularly when looking at the measure of capital stock including the value of land improvements. The relative shares of the other four major components of capital changed relatively little prior to 1840, particularly in constant dollar measures. The share of land improvements declined sharply starting with the 1774 estimates, while a quite dramatic decline in the share of animal inventories began in 1840. (There was possibly a smaller reduction in the food obtained from these inventories.) Both declines reflect the relative reduction in the role of the agricultural sector in the economy. There was a sharp rise in the share of equipment in constant dollar estimates (influenced by the fall in the relative price of equipment compared to construction), which starts around 1840 and accelerates after 1870.

As noted, one cause of the shift in the structure of capital was the decline in the share of the agricultural sector in the nineteenth century, a decline that in the Weiss labor force estimates was particularly sharp in the period from 1840 to 1860. There was a considerably greater decline in the capital share in agriculture than in Weiss's labor force estimates for 1800 to 1860, and overall a larger, but smoother, decline after 1840 than that in the Lebergott labor force series. And, if we use equipment as a rough measure of modernization, the fact that in 1840 it accounted for only 6 or 8 percent of the constant dollar capital stock suggests that up to that time increased investment in this component had only a limited potential for influencing the overall measured rate of growth of the economy, a point also indicated by the estimates of the share of the labor force in manufacturing.

It will be useful to place some of the issues raised by Gallman's capital stock estimates in a broader international and intertemporal perspective, particularly in comparisons with the other major developing economy of the late eighteenth and early nineteenth century, Great Britain.

First, the United States had high growth rates in total and per capita capital stock from quite early years, rates of growth not achieved by many other countries until the period after World War II, a finding rather similar to that

8. Note that Margo (chap. 4 in this volume), whose series for real wages begins in 1820, finds a shift upward in real wages in the 1830s or (in his preferred series) the 1840s.

for the growth of income.[9] Indeed, U.S. capital stock, total and per capita, grew much more rapidly than did that for the "first industrial nation," Great Britain, between the late eighteenth century and the end of the nineteenth.

Second, the high U.S. capital stock growth was accomplished with, before 1840, a savings ratio rather low by later standards.[10] The U.S. ratio of savings to income was probably lower than that of the British in the years between 1760 and 1840, the British ratio rising somewhat earlier (between 1760 and 1800) than that of the United States. After 1840 the U.S. ratio rises, sharply after the Civil War, and remains high through the remainder of the nineteenth century. Unlike the United States savings ratio the British ratio remained basically unchanged throughout the nineteenth century. The United States had, by the late nineteenth century, the highest savings rate among developed countries, rates not reached by many countries until after World War II.

Third, while the United States had a slightly higher share of land in total tangible wealth at the start of the nineteenth century than did Great Britain, in subsequent years of the nineteenth century both countries had roughly similar declines in the land share, although there was significant decade-to-decade variability. What might seem noteworthy, given the major differences in geographic expanse, industrial structure, and so forth, is the relative smallness of the intercountry differences in the shares of land in total wealth.

Fourth, the United States had a considerably lower capital-output ratio than did Great Britain (and the rest of the world) in the nineteenth century. Of the twenty countries for which Goldsmith provides data on capital-output ratios for net tangible assets, no country before 1939 had a capital-output ratio as low as that of the United States in 1850, with the exception of India.[11] The United States had, at the onset of growth, probably the lowest average ratio of capital to output of all developing countries; the British ratio of tangible wealth to income in 1800 was several times that of the United States. Post-1840, however, there were sharp rises in the United States in both the rate of savings out of current income and the ratio of capital to output. By the end of the century the U.S. capital-output ratio was among the lower, but was by no means the lowest, among developed countries. For the British, the capital-output ratio fell sharply throughout the century. The relative differences in the movement of output growth per unit of capital growth pose some interesting comparative questions for studies of the sources of growth.

Gallman's basic findings regarding the growth of the capital stock and its acceleration in the first part of the nineteenth century present a pattern similar to that of the growth of income, and all of this seems quite plausible given

9. See Raymond W. Goldsmith, *Comparative national balance sheets: A study of twenty countries, 1688–1978* (Chicago: University of Chicago Press, 1985).

10. See Lance E. Davis and Robert E. Gallman, "Capital formation in the United States during the nineteenth century," in *The Cambridge economic history of Europe* (Cambridge: Cambridge University Press, 1978), vol. 7, pt. 2. Gallman, "United States capital stock."

11. Goldsmith, *Comparative national balance sheets.*

other sources and the present state of knowledge. Thus the consistency is somewhat reassuring.

These capital stock estimates for the early national period pose many familiar historical questions, which Gallman has discussed here and elsewhere.[12] How were they financed? What individual behavior led to this new level of savings and investment? Did this require the formation of new institutions and legal provisions? And, given the role of land clearing and its importance, how much did it cost in terms of forgone output or was it, for the most part, forgone leisure? And, if the latter, was this increase in investment in improvements undertaken due to a taste change in favor of goods or was it due to a shift in the opportunity cost of time? Thus, as Gallman suggests, what seem for some purposes to be interesting questions for measurement are also significant issues for the broad understanding of the historical process.

12. As have Davis and Gallman in "Capital formation in the United States."

3   Inequalities in the Standard of Living in the United States, 1798–1875

Lee Soltow

A presentation of the standard of living for the United States in 1800 or 1860—or even for all intervening years—by using an average value per person of any economic variable yields, at best, a partial quantification of the matter. Ideally, one would also like to study a time series of averages just for the rich and just for the poor. Even better would be tables stating shares for the five quintile ranges, similar to those that have been available for income since 1947.

How wonderful it would be if there were complete distributions of wealth and income for each of the sixty years prior to 1860. One then could make statements about how the poor fared, relative to the rich, with the onset of the industrial revolution. In what sense might the rich have grown richer? Perhaps it was middle groups that gained relative to those above and below them when changes in the industrial and occupational structures occurred, as depicted by other participants in this conference on the standard of living.

This paper is a statement of some scattered and irregular distributions for years for which data are available. I feature tables for wealth and income, and distributions for saving (wealth), house values and rent, food consumption and nutrition (as reflected in heights of males and farm production), and clothing expenditure (as shown by home-woven yardage). I place special emphasis on shares of the poor, on households and individuals below the fortieth percentile for any particular variate. Changes in relative inequality will be emphasized, although this is possible in only three situations.

3.1 Sources and Findings

Very few distributions exist for the United States in the nineteenth century. Most prominent among them are those for wealth in 1798, 1850, 1860, and

Lee Soltow is professor of economics at Ohio University.

1870, as revealed in the censuses of wealth for those years. A strategic frequency classification of real estate values in Ohio in 1835 can serve as an intervening quantification in sketching changes in the hierarchy of values. These five distributions appear presently in chart form. Further perspective will be provided with a chart showing wealth distributions for those of older age in 1850; these are individuals whose fortunes were formed between 1800 and 1850. The central features of the two charts are very similar, and one must generally conclude that wealth inequality among free persons with real and personal estate changed very little in the first three-quarters of the nineteenth century.

The wealth data for the nineteenth century suffer one glaring defect; they tell us nothing about the 40 to 50 percent of adult free males and the 30 to 40 percent of families who possessed no wealth other than clothing, tools, a little furniture, and perhaps some farm animals. It is of fundamental importance to know whether this group expanded or contracted before the Civil War, and whether this group's condition either improved or deteriorated. Unfortunately, there are no time series or any selected points in the period on which one can focus in depicting change for lower groups. In analyzing conditions we must begin somewhere; to this end I will present in various sections of this paper some data concerning the lower 40 percent of people.[1] The most poignant statistics in this respect will be those dealing with persons living in shanties in Ontario in 1851. Some inkling of conditions on marginal farms will be presented for South Carolina in 1850. The extent of deprivation, as it appears in data for education and family formation, will be given for the United States in 1870; these frequency tables do suggest deprivation. Persons without wealth reported both significantly lower marriage rates and fewer children.

The data for wealth suggest that half of adult free males held real estate in 1798, and that this proportion decreased to .41–.43 in the period from 1850 to 1860. Yet one must not make too much of this matter, since surely the long-run trend in the occupational shift from agriculture to manufacturing and services was operative during the century. What we really need is a number of *income* distributions for the total labor force similar to those that are available for years after 1947. To do this demands using statistics, or possibly proxies, for *all* individuals in the country. Two main sources of information comprising certain aspects of such a comprehensive coverage are housing values or rents and heights of army recruits.

I have made an estimate of the distribution of income among families and individuals for 1798 using the splendid information available from the dwelling tax of that year coupled with information on the number of persons in dwellings. This distribution, as pictured in figure 3.1, suggests an important ordering principle: the inequality in wealth or real estate among wealthholders (with a Gini coefficient, G, of about .6) approximates the degree of inequality

---

1. Amartya Sen (1976) stresses the importance of the degree of inequality in the lower tail.

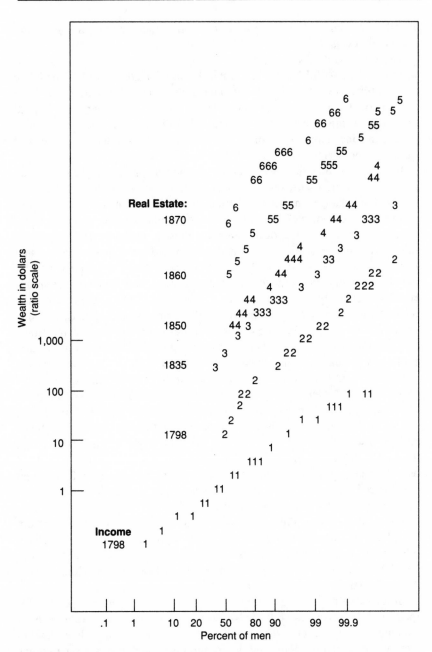

Fig. 3.1   A tier chart of the distribution of real estate among adult free males in the United States in 1798, 1850, 1860, and 1870 (whites), and in Ohio in 1835 (a lognormal probability chart)

Source: See table 3.1.

found in housing and dwelling-derived income among all families and unrelated individuals (G = .6), at least in 1798.

The 1798 wealth-dwelling pattern is suggestive of a similar pattern for 1850 and 1860, one with little change in the shapes of relative distributions in the half-century. Nevertheless, there are no dwelling-value distributions available for the country that can serve as checks until 1980, a date generally beyond the scope of this paper. The 1798 and 1980 distributions strongly point to decreasing inequality of income, but one suspects that the drop occurred largely in the twentieth century.

In New York State there were censuses of housing in 1865 and 1875 as well as in 1798; of necessity, one must turn to these data in order to make statements about changes in income distribution. A small sample from the manuscripts in 1865 indicates very little change—perhaps some lessening in inequality. Fortunately, the distribution of housing values in 1875 has been tabulated. A major section of this paper is devoted to comparing the housing distributions of New York in 1798, 1875, and 1980. The frequency tables clearly show little change before 1875; the housing share of the lowest groups remained relatively constant. Only after that date does this share rise dramatically. I present some further dimensions of housing in later sections, stressing the variability in lower income shares in various regions of the country. Housing data for Boston, Amsterdam, and Antwerp point, in a most rudimentary fashion, to similar shifts in relative inequality in both Boston and Amsterdam.

Heights of all army recruits are available for the periods centering on 1818, 1864, and 1918. One can argue that food consumption and general nutrition affect not only mean height, but also the median, first quartile, first decile, and so forth, values of height distributions at the different dates. I investigate relative distributions and offer Lorenz curves of height for the above dates. Very little change, if any, is found, and perhaps very little change after 1918 as well. Shares of lower groups remained constant. The 1812–63 food-height experience is consistent with that for housing in the nineteenth century but not in the twentieth century. Some might assert that U.S. standards of food consumption always were sufficiently high that one might not be able to discern the effects of differences in consumption by studying relative height. Others might assert that relative heights essentially do not reflect income distribution. Yet differences in relative heights decreased in Scandinavia, Holland, and Amsterdam during the last century.

Historical information is available for distributions of housing, perhaps for food, and for saving (as reflected in wealth). Not so certain are aspects of clothing distribution. One suspects, however, that the shift from household to factory production of cloth (and of clothing) benefited lower-income groups relative to upper groups. Some hints of this process are indicated in data from the New York State censuses of 1825, 1835, and 1845, at least from the standpoint of home production of cloth yardages; I will present a distribution from sample data of household yardage production. In my general summary I consider the consistency in inequality of saving as well as inequalities in expenditures on housing, food, and clothing combined as an income distribution.

What do the distributions for the nineteenth century tell us? One must conclude that relative inequality changed very little before the Civil War. Still to be revealed is the fact that lower-income groups had only a small share of resources in any one year, at least in many respects.

3.2   Wealth Distribution

For the most part, individuals probably had a better understanding of their assets than of their incomes, particularly in a rural setting. In any case, strong emphasis must be placed on the measurements of wealth. Our censuses of real estate, coupled with the censuses of population for various years in the nineteenth century, are truly unique.

3.2.1   Real Estate

The distribution of wealth in real estate among adult free males in the United States in 1798, 1850, 1860, and 1870 appears in figure 3.1, a depiction using lognormal probability paper. An exact lognormal curve plots as a straight line on this convenient chart form; it is desirable since many wealth and income distributions are approximately normal in shape when using logarithms of the variate. The greater the slope of the line (b), the greater the Gini coefficient of inequality (G); there is an exact relationship between b and G for straight lines on this chart.[2]

Calculations of the inequality coefficients and slopes are stated in table 3.1. The G and b estimates for wealth in real estate in 1798 and 1850–70 differ very little, and one reaches the conclusion that there was little or no change in inequality. But what about the intervening half-century between those census dates? The data for Ohio in 1835 prove to be a strategic source in filling this gap. Ohio's wealth in real estate reflected settlement a generation after it achieved statehood. In 1800–1835, its pattern of inheritance reflected in part the inheritance patterns of settlers from Pennsylvania, Virginia, and other states. In his trip to Ohio in 1831 and 1832, Tocqueville (1966) singled out Ohio for its tremendous developmental efforts. In 1840, Ohio's population accounted for 17 percent of the country's population. From the standpoint of real estate ownership, Ohio's distribution was similar to that in the nation as a whole.

Further insight into wealth patterns in 1840, 1830, and earlier can be ob-

---

2. Figure 3.1 is a lognormal chart whose horizontal scale is the standard normal deviate, z, stated here in probability form such as Prob ($z < -1.28$) $= .10$. A straight line on this chart is a lognormal curve, and I used the form $LL = a + bz$, where LL is the value at the lower limit of the class in the case of a frequency table; b is an estimate of the standard deviation using logarithms of the variate.

Table 3.1   **Summary of the Degree of Relative Inequality of the Distributions of Wealth in Real Estate among Free Adult Males in the United States in 1798, 1835, 1850, 1860, and 1870**

	Wealth > 0			Wealth ≥ 0			Straight-Line Model		
	G	Mean	Number (thousands)	G	Mean	Number (thousands)	b	R^2	Points[a]
Real estate									
1870 whites, U.S.	.624	4,150	3,700	.833	1,850	8,300	1.79	.981	24
1860 free, U.S.	.649	3,500	3,000	.845	1,540	6,800	1.77	.995	31
1850 free, U.S.	.643	2,470	2,000	.848	1,046	4,800	1.83	.996	29
1835 Ohio[b]	.637	530	139	.799	294	250	1.73	.993	32
1798 free, U.S.[c]	.632	1,430	433	.818	708	878	1.78	.982	30
Income, dwelling-derived									
1860 free, U.S.				?		?			
1798 free, U.S.[d]				.631	348	878	1.26	.996	26

Sources: 1850–70 distributions are computed from spin samples described in Soltow (1975, 96), samples with sizes of 10,393 in 1850, 13,698 in 1860, and 9,824 in 1870. The 1835 distribution for Ohio includes 164,962 property values derived from the tax duplicates in1835; properties are collated by owner's name within a county to yield 138,785 owners. The 1798 wealth distribution is derived from a disproportionate sample of 46,046 evaluations as described in Soltow (1984; 1989a, chap. 2). The dwelling-derived income distribution stems from a sample of 39,890 dwelling values and nineteenth-century summary tables of ten dwelling-tax classes, as described in Soltow 1987a; 1989a, chap. 3, 42, 263, 264). I am preparing a computer tape of these six distributions and nine others that I will submit to the Inter-University Consortium for Political and Social Research.

Notes: G = Gini coefficient of realtive inequality; b = the slope of the line on lognormal probability paper, shown in figure 3.1. Adult males are twenty-one years and older.

[a]Distributions were partitioned into classes with lower limits generally having a first digit of 1, 2, 5, or (in the lowest range) 1, 2, . . . , 9. These classes or points, when plotted on figure 3.1, usually displayed one or two points at the lowest level that clearly were below the linear shape of all other points. I eliminated these one or two before fitting the linear model.

[b]Owners' names were collated within counties, yielding wealth for 138,785 owners. See Soltow (1987b, 138).

[c]An upward collation adjustment has been made using an elasticity coefficient of 1.11, as suggested from the Kentucky experience. See Soltow (1984, 450).

[d]This is my preferred estimate using an elasticity of dwelling expenditure with respect to income of 1.2. See Soltow (1987a, 184; 1989a, 247, 273).

tained by classifying persons in the 1850 census by *age*. For those 70 and older, 60–69, 50–59, and 40–49, their wealth in the 1850 census to a great extent reflects their activities in previous decades. Plottings of the distributions for each group are given in figure 3.2. Certainly there are neither discontinuities nor serious alterations in the slopes of the lines that would signal discontinuities in relative inequality. The results for 1860 and 1870 are similar; data for total estate (real and personal wealth) appear in the last three columns of table 3.2, but without considering the small number of persons with wealth from $1 to $99, or those with no wealth.

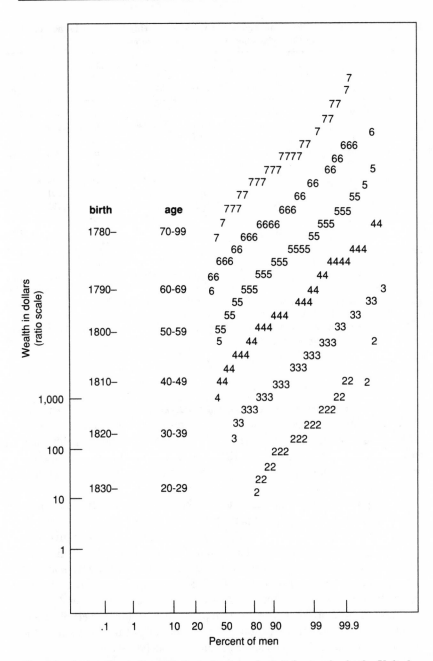

Fig. 3.2   A tier chart of wealth in real estate of adult free males in the United States in 1850, classified by age
Source: See table 3.1.

Table 3.2   Wealth Distribution among White Males Twenty and Older in the United States in 1870, Classified by Five-Year Age Intervals

Age	Number in Sample	Proportion with Wealth ≥ $100	Persons with Wealth ≥ $100				
			Number	Mean ($)	G	R^2	b
20–24	1,756	.26	449	1,590	.66	.974	1.23
25–29	1,381	.56	769	1,630	.63	.972	1.26
30–34	1,147	.65	750	2,730	.68	.984	1.35
35–39	1,105	.73	803	3,370	.66	.984	1.40
40–44	858	.76	653	4,910	.66	.994	1.39
45–49	788	.78	612	5,970	.66	.994	1.40
50–54	705	.83	557	6,090	.71	.991	1.42
55–59	415	.83	370	6,160	.65	.992	1.37
60–64	373	.80	297	5,220	.64	.993	1.35
65–74	426	.86	366	7,060	.72	.992	1.41
20–29	3,137	.39	1,218	1,610	.64	.974	1.25
30–44	3,110	.71	2,206	3,610	.67	.988	1.40
45–64	2,311	.79	1,836	5,920	.67	.994	1.39

Source: A sample of 10,235 males twenty and older, including 9,125 whites. The data are described in Soltow and Stevens (1981, 221 n. 72).

Note: G = Gini coefficient of relative inequality; R^2 = coefficient of determination for the straight-line model with slope b fitted on lognormal paper.

3.2.2   The Poor in a Land of Wealth

The fundamental weakness in the wealth analysis is the absence of perspective concerning those without estates. In this respect, some headway may be made if we can determine the characteristics of those without wealth; such data are revealed particularly in the 1870 census. I choose to describe this year because of information on education, marriage, and number of children, derived from a study I made of literacy.

The proportion owning estates valued at above $100 is the crucial element in understanding the condition of persons who are, in some sense, in the lower half of the wealth distribution. In this connection, the proportions given for five-year age intervals in the second column of table 3.2 are strategic. The pattern that emerges is that the majority had wealth after age twenty-five, and that a strong majority enjoyed at least some wealth after age forty-five. The inequality of wealth only among those above $100 was similar at any age. It is as though those arriving at the bottom of the distribution in their older age appear in an orderly fashion, joining the lognormal distribution as it previously existed without being on some parallel line pitched at a lower level.

The aging process obviously leads to greater shares of wealth and probably of total income of persons below the median (see table 3.3). Part of this increasing equality arises from the enhanced probability of receiving inheri-

Table 3.3

Array of Wealthholders with Wealth ≥ $0	Share of Aggregate Wealth of All, by Age		
	20–29	30–34	45–65
Lowest 50% in array	.00	.0234	.0426
Lowest 40% in array	.00	.0074	.0275
Lowest 30% in array	.00	.0004	.0046
Lowest 20% in array	.00	.0000	.0000

tances as one becomes older (Soltow 1982). And part arises from the ability to share in capital gains once having acquired real estate.

The possibility arises that the above interpretation is misleading. Perhaps those without wealth die at older ages in far greater numbers than do those with wealth. Table 3.2 shows that the maximum number of holders appears in the age group 35–39, and that this number is not much larger than for those 25–29. Admittedly, many confounding factors arise when one compares class frequencies in this fashion; these include immigration and the effects of the Civil War.[3]

Of more direct importance would be the characteristics of poor and rich at any specific age. How much of a handicap arose from not having wealth or income? The census does reveal a few characteristics dealing with economic well-being. The first of these was the ability of the parent to send children to school, an expenditure in some ways as significant as that for food, clothing, and housing. The data of table 3.4 indicate that the children of the rich enjoyed attendance probabilities (SCH) one-third to two-thirds again as large as the probabilities for the poor. Though these are significant differences, to my mind they are relatively small. A system had arisen that gave benefits to the poor in significant numbers. This was not a society of aristocrats, with school attendance probabilities for the rich two or three times those of the poor.

Data from tables 3.2 and 3.4 can be combined for white males aged forty-five to forty-nine. About 22 percent of adult males had no wealth. The majority of their children aged ten to fourteen were in school. The record for those next in line above the poor was no better, while the children of the somewhat rich had school attendance probabilities only somewhat better than those for the children of the poor.

An alternative measure of the differences between poor and rich is derived from counts of marital status and the number of children born to a family.

3. Dr. William Ogle (1887, 650–51) compared death rates at various ages of the old English life table for the years 1838–54, with the Upper Class Experience Table. He found that the percentage surviving after thirty years was 60 in the former group and 70 in the latter for males thirty years of age. See also Humphreys (1887, 277) and Fogel (1986, 467).

Table 3.4   Enrollment Rates in Schools (SCH) of White Children in the United States in 1870, Classified by Age of Child, Occupation of Father, and Wealth of Father

Wealth Class of Father ($)	Age of Farm Children			Age of Nonfarm Children		
	5–9	10–14	15–19	5–9	10–14	15–19
All children						
0–99	.34	.56	.43	.44	.62	.24
100–999	.35	.56	.33	.52	.68	.32
1,000–9,999	.50	.73	.46	.56	.74	.44
10,000 and up	.62	.86	.67	.59	.83	.63
Children with fathers of age 45–49	.					
0–99	.42	.53	.44	.47	.67	.29
100–999	.39	.50	.24	.56	.64	.36
1,000–9,999	.53	.69	.52	.61	.72	.34
10,000 and up	.65	.91	.68	.68	.86	.58

Source: A sample of 19,117 children in 9,125 white families reporting fathers. The above data are for 12,312 children aged 5–19 and, of these, 1,867 with fathers 45–49. Also see Soltow and Stevens (1981, 221 n. 72).

Table 3.5   Marriage Rates and the Average Number of Nuclear Children of White Males in 1870, Classified by Wealth

Age	Proportion Married		Average Number of Children	
	Without Wealth	With Wealth	Without Wealth	With Wealth
20–24	.21	.71	0.12	0.60
25–29	.43	.86	0.57	1.26
30–34	.59	.93	1.06	2.15
35–39	.64	.93	1.81	3.05
40–44	.65	.93	2.13	3.36
45–49	.77	.93	2.55	3.60
50–54	.64	.93	1.69	3.39
60–64	.71	.86	1.61	1.99

Source: A sample of 9,125 white males twenty and older and the 16,828 children of those having children enumerated as living with them. See also tables 3.2 and 3.4, particularly for the number of adult males, fathers and nonfathers, in each age interval; and Soltow (1982).

Surely the economic literature dealing with marriage rates from at least the time of Malthus has stressed that the poor should postpone marriage. Here was a most vital element of the economic well-being of the poor, as contrasted to that of the rich, and I must ask what the differential marriage rates for age-specific groups were, considering the data of table 3.5.

Marriage rates among those with wealth reached a maximum of 93 percent, with remarkable constancy from age thirty to age fifty-nine, as stated in the table. There was a very substantial difference in the marital status among the relative poor and rich, particularly for those in their twenties. The poor obviously were forced to postpone marriage, much as Malthus might have wished. Yet they were also penalized in their fifties when about one-third remained single, as determined by subtracting their marriage rates from the 93 percent upper asymptote of those with wealth. One can argue, of course, that there is an element of tautology in the data. An individual with wealth owned a farm or at least a home. The adult male urgently needed a spouse as a home manager.

Even more questionable are data for the numbers of children born to the poor and to the rich. A child of the poor wasn't necessarily a burden to the family since he might easily have been able to earn his keep after the age of eight. Or the table could be turned around, showing the wealth of the adult male to be greater the more children he had, at least for a certain range. Nevertheless, one can say that those with wealth had almost twice as many children as the poor. By my standards, I choose to interpret this to mean that the poor were living with strong disadvantages. Some of these were related to housing and its distribution, a subject I highlight in this paper.

3.3 Dwelling-Derived Income

Are we willing to believe that relative inequality has remained roughly constant during the last two centuries? Is there other evidence about economic inequality for the entire population? I say yes, and that it appears dramatically in the value placed on living conditions of people, as measured by dwelling values. Surely house values directly represent the inequality of economic well-being in a most dramatic form and may, in a way, be an average measure of the total expenditure on food, clothing, shelter, and medical care, coupled with saving or dissaving.

3.3.1 United States in 1798

My preferred estimate of income distribution in 1798 for all families or individuals appears in figure 3.1 and in table 3.1. It is based on dwelling values and numbers of persons in houses, revealed in the 1798–1800 data sets. The distribution is lognormal in shape and demonstrates very substantial inequality, with a Gini coefficient of .6 or above, considerably more than that found for families and unrelated individuals at the end of the 1980s, when G was less than .5. There was a great range in the standard of living at that early time, as evidenced in the contrast between the home of Elias Haskett Derby, America's first millionaire, and the primitive log huts without windows or chimneys. There was large regional variation and, indeed, variation between townships and counties (see section 3.3.7). The standard of living, from this point of view, revealed extreme inequality, and averages or aggregates shown in national accounts seem far removed from reality for most individuals.

3.3.2   Utah in 1857

If only we had an expression for inequality for 1850 or 1860 that would allow us to see if long-run changes were taking place. One source of income distribution for all persons, or a large portion of the population, not reviewed in this paper derives from the early assessment records of the Mormon church. A study of income distribution among Mormon families in Utah in 1857 shows the share of total income of the lowest 40 percent of families to be 16 percent of aggregate income. This 16 percent portion is obviously larger than the 6 percent share for 1798. Yet it is not immensely larger, considering the fact that Mormon society at the time was relatively homogeneous. The Mormon distribution plots as a rough straight line on log paper and reflects the fact that some people were reported to be sickly or suffering from flooding or droughts.[4] The homogeneity of the Mormon data and the relatively late settlement date are definite limitations. We must turn to housing data for New York State to measure inequality change.

3.3.3   New York in 1798, 1875, and 1980

I will present distributions of dwelling values in New York State for 1798, 1875, and 1980—configurations roughly a century apart from each other—as a test of changing inequality. Admittedly, the data suffer from the fact that more than one family or unrelated individual might have lived in a dwelling, particularly in an urban setting. The fitting or "crowding" of individuals into dwellings is a complex affair. Some adjustments are made for the crowding of individuals by applying an elasticity coefficient to house value, but the issue is far from being resolved. Yet the data for 1798 and 1875 are particularly fruitful since the numbers of dwellings per adult male were similar in those years. Today there are almost as many dwelling units as there are adult males.

Again, I will focus on the shares of lower groups. Did the share of aggregate house value for the lower 40 percent of house values decline in the nineteenth century as lower groups suffered relatively? Or did our economy improve, in some fashion, in terms of the provisions transferred to the relative poor?

---

4. See Soltow and May (1979, 157). More elaborate distributions are presented by Kearl and Pope (1986, 222) and Pope (1989, 162); in a letter to the author, dated 27 March 1990, Pope discusses the problems inherent in the use of Mormon data to establish income distributions.

The 1857 Mormon array is the only complete nineteenth-century income distribution I have at my disposal for testing of lognormality. Its plot at percentiles 10, 20, . . . , 90, 95, 98, and 99 yields an excellent straight line on lognormal paper:

$$\text{log income} = 11.05 + 730Z,$$
$$(.02)\quad (.020)$$

where Z is the standard normal deviate, $R^2 = .992$, and $N = 13$ (standard errors in parentheses).

There is some question about the extent of coverage, and the incomes of at least a few boys are included. Yet there also are comments such as, "been sickly nearly all the time," and "crop destroyed by frost."

The Data

The distributions of table 3.6 for 1798 are derived from the inventory of real estate made in New York and, indeed, in all states in that year. The table data say that the overall Gini coefficient for New York dwelling values was .74 in 1798, .66 in 1875, and .37 in 1980. These values can be amended by using continuity factors, but essentially they tell us that inequality decreased a little during the first century, and much more dramatically in the second.[5] Shares of lower groups rose relative to shares of the rich as the average value of a dwelling climbed, in current value, from $360 in 1798, to $3,500 in 1875, and to $37,000 in 1980, tenfold and then fivefold increases when adjusted with a consumer price index (David and Solar 1977, 16–17).

What did all of this mean to a family or individual at the fortieth percentile? The family's well-being, in housing, was enhanced materially in terms of flooring, ceilings, fireplaces, windows, and doors. The demise of log houses, as dramatic as the edifices seem to us today (and even as they appear in historical or fine arts museums), was a genuine step toward improvement. Log houses were the overwhelming construction type in 1798; the number of log houses recorded in the New York State censuses of 1855, 1865, and 1875 were 33,000, 20,000, and 13,000. These simple dwellings, having values that averaged 5 to 10 percent of the values of framed houses, rapidly disappeared. The family at the fortieth percentile had moved from a log cabin to a framed house.

Such must have been the story for many consumer items. The styles and qualities of clothing became less distinguishable. Homespun and linsey-woolsey disappeared as did log cabins. Stated more positively, our fortieth-percentile family probably owned a watch or clock in 1875, but not in 1798. Changes in transportation would be more difficult to quantify. The family probably was less likely to own a horse; it could, on the other hand, afford to buy a railroad ticket.[6]

The change in the housing situation in New York State is better understood by examining overall changes than by studying separately the changes in its urban and rural sectors. I attempt a classification based on New York and Kings counties, the only areas among the 1798 tax districts I could deem to be essentially urban. Table 3.6 shows little change in dwelling-value inequality in these two counties, but the issue is far from resolved; there simply is insufficient detail above the median in 1875, as presented in the table and in the discussion in its source note.

The dwelling distributions for counties other than New York and Kings

---

5. A case can be made for almost no change in inequality from 1798 to 1875, as stated in the note to table 3.6.

6. For clothing, see Kidwell and Christman (1974); Soltow (1990) includes a table showing that the distributions of timepieces in Scotland and Connecticut in 1798 were similar. Soltow (1981, 206, 210) deals with horse ownership.

Table 3.6   **Distribution of Dwelling Values in North York State, New York and Kings Counties, and the Other Counties in 1798, 1875, and 1980**

Class Limits ($)	All	New York and Kings	Other Counties
	Number of Dwellings in 1798		
30,001 and up	1	1	0
20,001–30,000	4	2	2
15,001–20,000	3	2	1
10,001–15,000	45	42	3
6,001–10,000	340	320	20
3,001–6,000	1,180	1,052	128
1,001–3,000	4,561	3,237	1,324
501–1,000	5,640	2,014	3,626
101–500	21,413	560	20,853
1–100	39,993	24	39,969
Total	73,180	7,254	65,926
Mean ($)	363	2,049	178
Inequality (G)	.737	.406	.626
Lognormal chart			
R^2	.978	.992	.997
Slope (b)	1.337	0.839	1.368
Aggregate value ($ millions)	26.578	14.863	11.714
Males twenty-one and up	118,000	13,910	104,090
	Number of Dwellings in 1875		
10,000 and up	65,373	53,060	12,313
5,000–9,900	60,942	33,272	27,670
2,000–4,999	144,311	23,604	120,707
1,000–1,999	151,310	5,429	145,881
250–999	201,357	2,126	199,231
100–249	66,326	727	65,599
50–99	14,286	116	14,170
10–49	7,134	24	7,110
Total	711,039	118,358	592,681
Mean ($)	3,300	11,720	1,590
Inequality (G)	.66	.38–.44	.59
Lognormal chart			
R^2	.999	—	.997
Slope (b)	1.428	0.71–0.83	1.219
Aggregate value ($ millions)	2,460	1,362	1,097
Males twenty-one and up	1,267,000	410,000	857,000
	Number of Dwellings in 1980		
200,000 and up	24,667	7,085	17,582
100,000–199,999	127,264	10,183	117,081
50,000–99,999	913,233	121,885	791,348
40,000–49,999	557,256	79,920	477,336
30,000–39,999	825,674	159,700	665,974
20,000–29,999	1,333,726	394,124	939,602

Table 3.6   (continued)

Class Limits ($)	All	New York and Kings	Other Counties
	Number of Dwellings in 1980		
10,000–19,999	1,310,429	479,706	830,723
5,000–9,999	259,874	93,714	166,160
2,000–4,999	24,267	8,944	15,323
Total	5,376,390	1,355,261	4,021,129
Mean ($)	36,520	29,080	39,030
Inequality (G)	.373	.371	.364
Lognormal chart			
R^2	.997	.975	.999
Slope (b)	0.69	0.68	0.68
Aggregate value ($ billions)	196	39	157
Males twenty-one and up	5,478,887	1,169,026	4,309,861

Sources: Soltow (1989a, 80); New York (1875, table 47); U.S. Bureau of the Census (1980, part 34, New York, 99, 537–42). Rentals or units were assumed to be 12 percent of dwelling values.

Note: A continuity adjustment factor can be applied within each class of the New York tables. The lognormal linear model can be fitted to the logarithms of the lower- and upper-class limits and their probits for each class; the resulting standard deviation of each class can then be translated into its interval Gini coefficient. These considerations raise the overall Gini coefficient for all, New York and Kings, and the other counties in 1798 from, respectively, .737, .406, and .626 to .769, .407, and .680. The 1875 distributions, adjusted upward by using these procedures, yield results very similar to those in 1798. In fact, one can make the case that housing inequality in New York State was very similar in the years 1798 and 1875.

demonstrate inequality decreases similar to those for the state, but they are less dramatic. In fact, one can argue that the measured drop in inequality for this group is rather small from 1798 to 1875: .626 to .590 for G, and 1.37 to 1.22 for the slope of the chart line. I tentatively conclude that this is my best evidence (aside from the issue of crowding) of change in income inequality in the nineteenth century.

Why did these distributions demonstrate so much inequality in the past? There were very large differences in standards from one county to the next. When this area variation is eliminated from the sixty-three tax districts in 1798, the inequality decreases dramatically.

The Dwelling House Value of the ith Individual in the jth Tax District	*All*	*New York and Kings*	*The Other Counties*
$G(DHV_{i,j})$	.737	.406	.626
$G(DHV_{i,j} \sqrt{DHV_j})$	.574	.372	.592

There simply were large area differences in the quality of housing in the early federal period in New York State.

Crowding

An obvious point of concern in making the comparisons in table 3.6 derives from the fact that there were 1.61 adult males per house in 1798 and that the ratio was 1.73 in 1875, and 1.02 in 1980. If housing values are to represent income distribution properly, then I should squeeze or "crowd" the men into houses in the earlier years to devise a house value per man (or perhaps per family). If 1.6 men were placed in each house or, say ten in every six houses in 1798, and it were assumed that there was equality in effective rental within each house, then relative inequality would remain roughly the same as stated in the table for houses. But what if more persons were squeezed into houses of higher (lower) value? Relative inequality would be thought to be less (more) than it now is for houses.

In the absence of concrete information for New York crowding, I must direct my attention to two most powerful theorems formulated by Aitchison and Brown (1969, theorems 2.6 and 2.3) concerning the jth moment and the reproductive property of a lognormal curve.[7] In reality, the theorems state that a methodical crowding based on dwelling value (V), say V^j or V^{-j}, decreases or increases the Gini coefficient some, but retains the lognormal form if the original distribution is lognormal. In the case of our distribution for 1798, a new class frequency $f_2 = f_1 V^{+.085}$, or $f_2 = f_1 V^{-.085}$, can effectively raise the total frequency about 60 percent; it alters the mean, lowers or raises the slope of the straight line on lognormal probability paper, and lowers or raises the Gini coefficient about 6–7 percent. The theorems state, in effect, that a frequency table with class frequencies and class means (f_i, V_i) ($i = 1, 2, \ldots, n$ classes) and which is lognormal in shape may be transformed into another lognormal curve by methodically squeezing (in a constant elasticity form) people into homes of larger values in a fashion lowering inequality some, but not much. Alternatively, squeezing more people into houses of lower value strengthens inequality. This alteration can be checked roughly by computer. Given the frequency table, with class frequencies and class means (f_i, V_i) for ten classes and its somewhat lognormal shape, one can obtain the new table with $f_2 = fV^{-.085}$, with each person having a value $V_2 = f_2 /(fV^{-.085})$; this raises the Gini coefficient from, say, .600 to .638.

This technical appeal is made to argue that the New York dwelling distribution probably almost represents rental value or income in all three periods. Inequality of rentals within the house can raise dispersion at least a little. Statistical evidence demonstrates that a distribution of dwelling values and its actual rentals had essentially the same relative dispersion.

3.3.4   Summary of Inequality Change

There was very extensive variation in the values of dwelling houses in New York State in the nineteenth century. Consider one spectacular example from

---

7. Theorem 2.6 states, "The jth moment distribution of a $\wedge$-distribution (lognormal) with parameters μ and σ^2 is also a $\wedge$-distribution with parameters $\mu + j\sigma^2$ and σ^2, respectively."

the 1875 census for Buffalo, where the Tenth Ward was a district for the wealthy and the Thirteenth for the poor. In the Tenth, there appeared a house valued at $500,000; it was a palatial mansion built between 1868 and 1870 by William Fargo, president of the American Express Company. The household, to be fair, included Fargo, his wife, daughter, two granddaughters, a second young family, and the butler, cook, parlor maid, chambermaid, nurse, and governor. In the Thirteenth lived John Madigan, laborer, and his family, in a house valued at $50.

Admittedly, these are extremes, so we should look at the share of total value of the lowest 40 percent in the array of dwelling values.[8] This 40 percent group, eliminating New York and Kings counties, accounted for 7 percent of value in 1798, 8 percent in 1875, and 18 percent in 1980; the maximum share for this group would have been 40 percent. One can say that the lower groups rose a little, from 7/40 to 8/40, a slight increase, and then spectacularly, to 18/40 of what might have been achieved with perfect equality.

3.3.5   Rents

All of my housing distributions are subject to the criticism that they do not properly account for the number of families or, say, the number of adult males living in a house. Even if this "crowding" phenomenon is unrelated to the value of the house, some consideration should be given to the shares of different persons in the house. Surely space and room values usually are not shared equally.

What I really would like is a distribution of *rents*, actual and implicit, for different families and unrelated individuals living in houses. The only early distributions I know about in this connection are those for the end of the eighteenth century in Amsterdam and Antwerp. These can be compared to the housing distribution in Boston where at least the number of persons in each house was enumerated. The Amsterdam data also allow us to measure changes in rent inequality from 1809 to 1914, an outside check on the fact that change did occur from the nineteenth to the twentieth century.

A special tax was assessed in Amsterdam in 1805.[9] It demanded not the ordinary inventory of house values as such, but an assessment of value for each person in the house, where the individual was either the major dweller or individual living in a room or in a half or complete cellar. My wife and I drew a sample from this inventory and found, much to my satisfaction, that the distribution of rentals was similar to that for dwelling values.[10]

8. The tabulated distributions for 1875 include at least a few hospitals, orphanages, buildings for religious orders, some large boardinghouses, and even some business or partial business edifices in which people lived. I am currently sampling manuscripts from urban areas in 1875, and have a rough estimate that about 10 percent of value shown for urban areas in 1875 should be eliminated. I do not think that inequality coefficients would decrease very much with this correction.

9. Details of Amsterdam housing data are given in Lievense (n.d., especially 49).

10. Sample drawn from Gemeente Archief, Amsterdam, archive number GAA 5045A, vols. 1–60; missing are vols. 2, 9, 11–13, 22, 23, 25, 27–29, 34, 53, 54. We recorded all units from

Did I know enough about economic distribution to state, before seeing the figures, that Amsterdam's frequency table would demonstrate more or less inequality than was true for Boston or for urban America in 1798? Certainly I thought that European cities in general, with their established hierarchies, should display more inequality. But I was warned by an Amsterdam archivist that there was an absence of hierarchy in his city. There were essentially no titled people, even by Danish or Swedish standards, let alone by those of France or England. There was no nobility, and Holland's government was seated in the Hague. Yet my working hypothesis had to be that there was more inequality in Amsterdam.

The distributions shown in table 3.7 do confirm my hypothesis, but not overwhelmingly, to say the least. Disparities appear more at the top than among the lower groups. Consider the shares of those with rental below the median, the complements of the upper shares stated in the table: Amsterdam, 1805, .132; Antwerp, 1799, .133; Boston, 1798, .160; U.S. urban, 1798, .112. Boston showed less relative deprivation, but some of the differential is due to measurement error. I had to assume equality of rentals among dwellers within housing units in Boston. To have made this equality assumption for Amsterdam would have almost eliminated the differential. Thus the startling conclusion must be that lower shares were very little lower in Amsterdam. This statement surely does not apply to either Copenhagen, Stockholm, or London. And the Amsterdam-Boston results do not include the influence of country estates owned by the rich.

Some mention should be made of the results in table 3.7 that demonstrate that inequality in Amsterdam's distribution of housing in the twentieth century was less than it was in the nineteenth century. These results parallel those found earlier for the distributions in New York State. I have found similar results in another context from a study of housing in Scotland.[11]

3.3.6 Poor in Ontario Shanties

For statistical purposes, how convenient it would be if there had been a census each year in the early part of the nineteenth century, enumerating in detail those poor individuals or families in the lowest decile range, in the

every tenth page of vols. 1, 4, 8, 16, 20, 24, 32, 36, 40, 44, 48, 52, 56, and 60, and all pages from these volumes outside the selected interval from f. 31 to f. 799. The sample was thus from 154 pages to obtain 1,062 units from within the selected interval and 1,487 pages to obtain the 1,884 units outside the interval. These counts exclude the 3.6 percent of units that were not rented. Several dozen dwelling units were in warehouses, piers, and businesses. I eliminated one *grondhuis* with very nominal rent. There were 4,681 pages in all of the extant volumes.

Aggregates of the verponding evaluation in each of the 60 *wijks* (GAA 5045) in 1785–87 show that the *wijks* missing for 1805 represented 22.45 percent of value. This factor and the page-count factors stated above indicate that the 2,946 observations in the sample represented 6.0 percent of the 49,300 units in the city at the time.

11. Soltow (1971). This study was derived from the censuses of housing in Scotland since 1861; these censuses encompass all persons in housings units, not just the rich.

Table 3.7   **The Relative Distribution of Annual Rental Values in Amsterdam in 1805, Antwerp in 1799, Boston and Urban Areas in the United States in 1798, and Amsterdam in 1919**

	A_R, the Proportion of Aggregate Rental Value of the N_R Group				
	Amsterdam 1805	Antwerp 1799	Boston 1798	U.S. Urban Areas 1798	Amsterdam 1919
Proportion of all cases (N_R)					
.01 (top)	.102	.107	.091	.109	.053
.02	.166	.183	.149	.174	.105
.05	.297	.335	.266	.311	.224
.10	.453	.477	.396	.456	.337
.20	.644	.649	.566	.638	.482
.50	.868	.867	.840	.888	.742
.80	.965	.970	.964	.982	.921
.90	.987	.990	.986	.995	.967
1.00	1.000	1.000	1.000	1.000	1.000
Mean	f160	f194	$131	$77	f142
Inequality (G)	.581	.591	.520	.602	.386
Number of units	49,300	13,800	4,245	73,000	141,556
Number in sample	2,946	1,376	2,423	6,780	141,556
Population	200,000	51,000	23,000	320,000	640,000
Units/population	0.25	0.27	0.18	0.23	0.22
Straight-line model plotted on a lognormal chart					
Correlation (R^2)	.976	.981	.994	.994	.953
Slope (b)	0.949	1.047	0.939	1.275	0.567

Source: For Amsterdam in 1805, see Soltow (1987b, table 6). I took a sample of every tenth item from Antwerp (1799), chosen because the listing of rental values within each building was more methodical than in 1796 or 1797; see also De Belder (1977, 3–4); Lis (1986, 71, 76); Reyniers-Defourny (1979). Data for Boston and the United States appear in Soltow (1987a, 1989a). Data for Amsterdam 1919 are from Amsterdam (1923, 19).

lowest quintile range, and below the median and fortieth percentiles. This model census would have stated the average income or other characteristics of individuals in each decile range. Even the magnificent quinquennial censuses of Sweden from 1805 to 1855 tell us only the numbers of those deemed destitute, poor, somewhat rich, and rich. I search for any tallies of lower income subsets in the century that can serve as proxies for any one of these ideal census measures that cover a significant portion of the population—counts covering more than the few percent who were orphans, blind, hospitalized for mental illness, and supported widows.

One possibility is to examine those families or households living in "shanties," as enumerated in the Ontario, or upper Canada, census of 1851. The houses were classified and ordered in such a way that they suggest a skewed, if not a lognormal, distribution, as shown in table 3.8.[12] Values were not stated, but those reported for stone, brick, frame, and log for New York in 1855 coupled with Ontario frequencies provide some insight by suggesting a lognormal curve with a Gini coefficient of about .7 and a shanty value of $5 to $20.

A study by regions shows large variation, given in table 3.9. Those counties with greater development were less likely to have poorer housing. Thus there was an inverse relationship between the proportion of shanties and the proportion of land held that was cultivated, as demonstrated in the county classifications.

What were the characteristics of persons living in shanties? Were they beginning settlers? Were they young, with relatively few children? We can examine some of the demographic characteristics by using the sample of 1,201 dwellings presented in table 3.10. Turning first to families living in shanties, we see that their average age was surprisingly high, being only a year or two less than the overall average. Occupational distribution was decidedly different from that of the total population; household heads living in shanties were more than two-and-one-half times as likely to be farmers or those with "other" occupations. Shanty heads were more likely to be foreign-born than might be expected, leading one to suspect that they may have been in Ontario for shorter portions of their adult lives. Finally, 42 percent were Roman Catholic as opposed to the 20 percent proportion for all heads. Shanty heads tended not to be Methodists or Baptists or members of minor sects.

Evidence from the large minority group of log-house heads reveals surprisingly few differences from the characteristics of all persons. Their ethnic or birth traits were representative; the one exception was that there were relatively fewer among them who were born in the United States. They tended more to be farmers, not laborers or those with other occupations.

A further sample was devised to furnish more suggestions about the demographic characteristics of persons living in shanties. A sample of every tenth dwelling from the principal sample yielded the data in table 3.11 on family composition. Judging from the age of the oldest Canadian-born child and the youngest foreign-born child for twelve shanty families, I find the median length of residence in Ontario to have been eleven years, not two to five years as I had expected. This evidence indicates that shanty families were not in earlier stages of their life cycles. They were much less likely to have been native-born and were more likely to have been Roman Catholics. These data could be developed much more generally. Results for foreign-born could be compared to those of immigrants to Canada in an earlier period, as suggested by Bernard Bailyn (1986, chaps. 6, 10).

12. Aitchison and Brown (1969, 27) suggest that classifications based on some homogeneity principle often are approximately lognormal.

Table 3.8   **Dwelling Types in Ontario in 1851**

Type	Frequency	Proportion	Value (New York, 1855, $)
Stone	4,211	.029	6,900
Brick	5,117	.035	5,500
Frame	53,931	.370	785
Log	65,503	.449	46
Shanty	17,191	.118	5(?)
Total	145,953	1.000	

Source: Canada (1851–52, appendix 15, table 8, 430–31); New York (1855, 249–50).

Table 3.9   **The Proportion of Dwellings That Were Shanties (PSHAN) and Log or Shanty (PLOGSHAN) in Ontario for Forty-two Counties in 1851**

PSHAN	Frequency	PLOGSHAN	Frequency
.40 and up	4	.80 and up	10
.20–.39	4	.60–.19	15
.10–.19	16	.40–.59	12
.05–.09	13	.20–.39	6
.01–.04	4		
Under .01	1		
Total	42		42

Source: Canada (1851–52, 402–29).

3.3.7 Poverty Areas in the United States in 1798

A promising field for the historical investigation of the degree of well-being of persons below median income can be derived from studies of many areas such as townships, counties, states, or larger units. Usually there is large variation in shares of the poor when using these area classifications, but the shares can be related to other economic variables of the localities. Detailed studies of this type demand very large data sets indeed; examples of such are the 165,000 property values in Ohio in 1835 and the distribution of housing within each of 1,200 townships in New York in 1875.

The possibility of a historical study of areas exists for 687 tax districts in the United States in the year 1798 even though data are not as complete as one would like, particularly for southern states. What index can be used as an indicator of relative poverty? The fertility of the land and its relative distance from urban areas or ports can be an element in the ability of an area to provide jobs and land for lower groups. I consider the average value of land per acre (VAC) for each of the 687 to be an expression of these characteristics. I plotted the 687 VAC and colored those where VAC was $5 or more. I optimistically hoped that well-defined contours would in some way tie into Bailyn's

Table 3.10   **Characteristics of a Sample of 1,201 Dwellings in Ontario in 1851, Classified by Type of House**

	Shanty	Log	Frame	Stone, Brick	Other	All	Rural	Urban
Sample size	146	578	403	60	14	1,201	1,140	61
Age, household head	41	43	42	48	41	42.9	43	42
Stories	1.0	1.03	1.2	1.4	1.1	1.123	1.1	1.3

Proportion of Cases

Occupation, household head								
Farmer	.45	.73	.40	.58	.50	.574	.60	.16
Laborer	.32	.10	.10	.05	.07	.126	.12	.15
Other occupation	.17	.12	.44	.37	.43	.251	.23	.62
Female	.05	.03	.04	.00	.00	.033	.03	.07
None, unemployed	.01	.02	.02	.00	.00	.017	.02	.00
Total	1.00	1.00	1.00	1.00	1.00	1.000	1.00	1.00

Birth, household head								
Foreign-born	.88	.75	.68	.73	.79	.742	.74	.84
England	.08	.10	.19	.15	.29	.133	.13	.13
Scotland	.15	.19	.10	.20	.14	.157	.15	.20
Ireland	.62	.33	.21	.18	.29	.316	.31	.48
Germany	.00	.05	.03	.03	.00	.036	.04	.00
United States	.03	.07	.13	.13	.07	.089	.09	.02
Canadian-born	.12	.25	.32	.27	.21	.258	.26	.16
Ontario	.08	.22	.29	.27	.14	.231	.24	.13
Quebec	.03	.03	.01	.00	.00	.019	.02	.02

Religion								
Catholic	.42	.22	.10	.08	.00	.197	.19	.33
Baptist	.02	.04	.04	.05	.00	.037	.04	.02
Church of England	.24	.17	.25	.25	.29	.211	.21	.25
Methodist	.08	.16	.27	.23	.03	.188	.19	.15
Presbyterian	.21	.27	.15	.23	.14	.217	.22	.21
Other	.03	.13	.20	.15	.50	.146	.15	.05
Total	1.00	1.00	1.00	1.00	1.00	1.000	1.00	1.00

Source: Canada (1851–52). I recorded all entries from each of about 330 pages. My procedure considered even-numbered films and every eightieth page from this personal census.

Table 3.11

	Shanties	Nonshanties
Number	15	97
Proportion with wives	.83	.82
Average number of children	3.51	3.54
Average number of sons twenty and older	0.3	0.33
Median number of years in Ontario	11	Not computed

(1986) beautiful immigration maps, but I must candidly admit that this project failed. First, I had difficulty in obtaining precise latitudes and longitudes; even plottings for each of the 359 counties proved difficult because of strong variation in VAC between contiguous counties. Collapsing contiguous areas into 180 plots did demonstrate concentration of fertility areas in the Shenandoah Valley, eastern Pennsylvania, and southern New England. Yet in itself such a map really does not offer much of any explanation of relative inequality among *persons*. Areas in which VAC was under $5 very well may have been those with more acreage per farm. Even the average value of land per adult male tells me little about distribution within each district.

A more direct measure of shares of lower groups in 1798 can be determined from stated or estimated proportions of houses in a district that were under $100 in value. Even here there is doubt, since districts either somewhat or far removed from urban centers had both lower prices and a large majority of houses in this category. It seems better to express dollar dwelling values as a proportion of the mean value in order to consider relative shares. To this end I will focus on the share of aggregate dwelling value below the fortieth percentile, SDHV40. It is the aggregate value of the poorest 40 percent of houses, expressed as a proportion of the overall aggregate value; this measure may vary from .00 to .40.

A background display of the part this measure plays in the distribution of U.S. dwellings derives from a sample of 39,890 items and from stated frequencies (computed by authorities in 1798) for ten frequency classes of dwelling values. This study produces an essentially lognormal distribution both nationally and for each of seven areas, presented in figure 3.3. The regularity of plots adds confidence in stating lower dwelling-value shares in each of the seven districts, as given in table 3.12. In general, the shares of these "poor" houses were quite low—9 to 10 percent of aggregate value. Differences must be treated with caution, particularly those for the South, the region with less complete data. Within the North, shares interestingly were larger for rural areas nearer cities than those further removed either to the West or to the North. The poor in northern urban areas were almost as well-off as in rural areas, and better-off when more than eighty miles removed from the six major East Coast cities. Southern areas seemed to follow the same scheme. Rural southern areas further removed from the East were influenced by values in Tennessee and Kentucky.

Let me now further disentangle these shares by considering areas in finer detail. In general, the relative inequality of an entire large area is greater than the average relative inequality of its counties and greater yet than the average relative inequality of its more numerous tax divisions. The overall Gini coefficient for the rural North within eighty miles of its major cities is larger than the average coefficient for its fifty-one counties, and this, in turn, is larger than the average for its 233 tax districts. The overall coefficient is composed of inequality within districts and that between the means of its districts. The

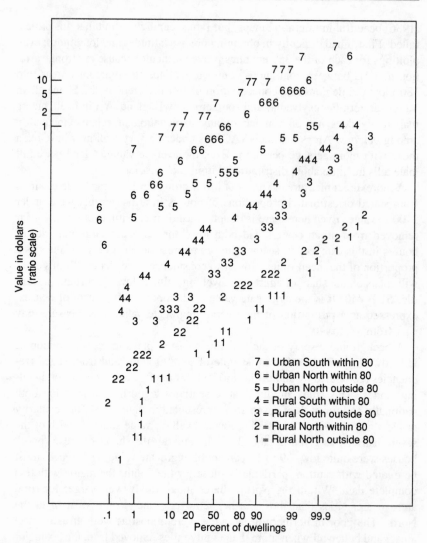

Fig. 3.3   A tier chart of the distribution of values of dwellings in each of seven regions in the United States in 1798
Source: See table 3.12.

shares of the lowest 40 percent presented in two different columns of table 3.12 reflect these considerations. Also, the columns reflect the fact that there was more detail for some regions than for others. Yet it is fruitful to explore this analysis further.

The estimate of SDHV40 for each of the 687 districts in the United States demands some kind of interpolation from among class limits and class frequencies of ten tax-rate classes. I have derived estimates by applying the log-

Table 3.12   **The Proportion of the Aggregate Value of Dwellings Accounted For by Persons below the Fortieth Percentile (SDHV40) in Seven Sections of the United States in 1798**

Seven Regions	Considering All Values within a Region	Considering All Values within Each Tax District	
	SDHV40	Number of Districts	Average SDHV40
Rural north Within 80 miles	.091	233	.101
Outside 80 miles	.069	153	.090
Urban north Within 80 miles	.082	44	.153
Outside 80 miles	.109	2	.135
Rural south Within 80 miles	.064	70	.088
Outside 80 miles	.036	75	.066
Urban south Within 80 miles	.106	4	.141
All	.0916	681	.101

Source: SDHV40 is computed from the seven distributions of housing values derived from a sample of 39,890 dwelling values and stated frequency counts for ten classes, as described in Soltow (1989a, chaps. 2, 3, and appendixes 1, 5). The SDHV40 for each of 681 tax districts was computed from lognormal equations applied to estimates of district Gini coefficients (Soltow 1989a, 80 n. 20). Shares for six districts could not be determined.

Note: Whether the district was within eighty miles was determined by the minimum distance between a district and one of the six major cities: Boston, New York, Philadelphia, Baltimore, Norfolk, or Charleston.

normal considerations used previously within each of the ten in developing 687 Gini coefficients. From each of these I have computed SDHV40 assuming overall lognormality within each district. The shares of the lower 40 percent of houses varies quite substantially from district to district, as shown in table 3.13. The distribution is at least slightly skewed and reminds one in a superficial sense from the standpoint of economics, but in an engaging statistical sense, of the distribution by county of pauper rates for England and Wales in 1803, a distribution with about the same average and relative dispersion.[13] But surely persons living in poorer houses in the United States were enjoying far better economic conditions.

What are the regional variation characteristics of the 40 percent shares? Again, I had hoped to present a map by plotting shares at their respective latitudes and longitudes, but the variation in shares among contiguous tax

13. Great Britain (1805, 13: 714). A clearer analogy could be made by studying the proportion of houses under, say, $33 in rural areas and under $100 in urban areas of the United States in 1798. For a plot of the distribution of pauperism rates, see Yule (1919, 92–93).

Table 3.13   **Value Shares of Poorer Houses (SDHV40) for Each of 681 Tax Districts in the United States in 1798**

SDHV40	Number of Districts
.25 and up	3
.20–.249	9
.15–.199	81
.10–.149	253
.05–.099	236
.02–.049	84
.007–.019	15
Mean	.101
Gini coefficient (*G*) of SDHV40	.254

Source: See table 3.12. Transformation equations giving shares from Gini coefficients are stated in Aitchison and Brown (1969, chap. 2).

Note: Using the terminology of the Statistical Analysis System and the Gini coefficient, *G*, for each district, I have $\sigma = ((2**.5) * \text{PROBIT}(1+G)/2)$, and then, SDHV40 = PROBNORM(PROBIT(.40) $- \sigma$). It proved to be impossible to compute *G* for six districts reporting frequency totals only for the lowest tax class.

districts made such a procedure very cumbersome. Consider instead a few regression equations. There was a tendency for shares to be larger in districts with *higher* dollar land value per adult free male (VALAND21).

$$\text{SDHV40} = .089 + .000020 \text{ VALAND21};$$
$$(.000005)$$

$R^2 = .020$, $N = .681$. This persisted to a certain extent if the minimum number of miles from one of the six major coastal cities (MILES6) is considered.

$$\text{SDHV40} = .123 + .000011 \text{ VALAND21} - .000281 \text{ MILES6};$$
$$(.000005) \qquad\qquad (.000019)$$

$R^2 = .27$, $N = 681$. The proportion of the lower 40 percent tended to rise .011 with each $1,000 increase in per capita wealth in land (excluding houses) and to go down .028 for districts one hundred miles from urban centers.

Another way of stating the pattern is to consider the age of the tax district by considering the formation date of its county. When this variable is added to the above equation, its regression coefficient shows a significantly larger share for the lower group in areas of older age. It is doubtful that all of this pattern could be a shanty effect or a log cabin effect, since the majority of dwellings in rural areas in both the East and the West were log dwellings.[14]

14.   SDHV40 = .599 + .00012 VALAND21 − .00017 MILES6 + .0028 AGE;
          (.00004)   (.00002)   (.0004)
$R^2 = .33$, $N = 681$.

Surely it would be advantageous to have expressions for lower groups for just before the Civil War, or even just after, for the United States or its northern region. The effects of settlement and its changes then could be better understood. The data set just discussed, that of housing in 1798, is probably the most important among the nine sets presented in this paper. It gives detail for the entire country and for its various areas, and gives values for those below the median, something not available for the sets dealing with real estate values, wealth, and census farms. Yet it is inferior to data for stature or for New York housing in the sense that we have no feeling for changes in shares occurring in various regions of the United States over long periods of time.

3.4 Inequality in Height and in Nutrition

Any variable that registers a value for each and every member of a population must be attractive to anyone wishing to study shapes of distributions for economic characteristics of individuals. The height or stature of adult males continues to be a prominent variable that measures, at least in part, the well-being of a large segment of society's labor force. But what statistical procedures should be applied if one wishes to gauge economic changes? Robert Fogel (1986, 456) states that the genetic and environmental components of height are difficult to assay, but "for most well-fed contemporary populations, . . . systematic genetic influences appear to have very little impact on *mean* [my emphasis] heights." Margo and Steckel (1983, 168) assert that "although genes are important . . . physiologists and nutritionists agree that differences in mean height across populations are largely the result of environmental factors." In another article, Steckel (1983, 3) again notes the role of environment in average height differences, but states that "genes are important determinants of the heights of individuals." These men, and others, often employ procedures involving regression analysis where the dependent variable is height, not height below the median, specific quartile, or decile in the array of heights.

Emphasis on means and multiple regression equations can be somewhat tangential in studies of dispersion in heights. This can arise even though investigators are very keenly aware of inferences that can be made about distributions. Thus, John Komlos (1990, 607) begins his most recent article on height with this statement, "The secular trend in the distribution of income and wealth . . . has been a topic of concern . . . [in studies dealing with] the last two centuries." Yet nowhere does he present a distribution of heights, let alone a Lorenz curve of heights of individuals.

There is some silence concerning the shapes of the distributions of heights, an unwillingness to present frequency curves of stature at different dates in a fashion where they can be compared at various percentiles. If we had plottings of Lorenz curves or probit curves of heights in 1812, 1864, 1918, and 1980, then we might judge the changes in the inequality in height itself.[15] Such an analysis could serve as a focus for the significance of measures of stature. If height, income, and nutritional adequacy are positively related to each other in, say, 1812 and again in 1863, then we should focus on the relative changes among the short and the tall in this half-century. This approach could provide insights into changes for both the poor and the rich.

One who is continually interested in the degree of equality or inequality within a society, and how much it might change, becomes frustrated if statements about inequality that appear in the literature of economics cannot be tested. An early example of such was made by Edgar Martin (1942, 57) when he asserted, "Nowhere was there greater contrast between the diet of the rich and that of the poor than in the South." In this respect, what do height data say? One might even blatantly ask if the lowest 40 percent in stature had a smaller proportion of aggregate height in the North as compared to the South.

3.4.1   Height Distributions

I attempt to contrast inequality in height by means of a series of distributions for the United States, as presented in table 3.14, for periods encompassing the War of 1812, the Civil War, and the First World War. To be sure, one can argue that the figures are not comparable from the standpoint of being representative of age, ethnic and nativity mixture, color, or region. Yet the data do represent large samples of recruits, a group that perhaps often included those who soon would be rejected on account of physical defects. I use my sample for 1799–1819 that was originally drawn for a study of illiteracy, since I later will present illiteracy rates and their changes for the short and the tall from 1799 to 1894. In general, the Civil War heights exclude those from the South and thus may tend to understate slightly the degree of inequality. Yet an analysis of height inequality related to specific age, nativity, and residence regions, to be presented shortly, indicates that the matter is not important; data for 1799–1819 and 1918 for the North and South confirm this conclusion. The information for the Civil War definitely includes individuals before rejection and, according to Baxter (1875, 1: vii.), "may be said to represent the adult male population without selection." The height study for 1976–80 is a sample of males in general and is unrelated to the process of army recruitment.

The height distributions for the four periods given in table 3.14 are convenient since they differ in dates by about fifty to sixty years and cover, in a

15. The first rather elegant presentation of height as a normal curve was achieved by Elliott (1863, 41–44, diagram C), using a chart and equations, at the International Statistical Congress in Berlin in 1863. Surely Elliott would have compared his data set with the distribution for a later date had he had access to information such as that obtained by Davenport and Love (1921, 67–74) for the First World War. Van Wieringen (1979, 1986, 318–19) presents a table depicting height percentiles for 1950 to 1978 and 1983 for Dutch draftees; he also gives a chart that depicts cumulative frequencies above specified heights for years after 1850.

Table 3.14   **Nine Distributions of Heights among Army Recruits in the United States in 1799–1819, 1861–65, and 1918, and in a Sample of the General Population in 1976–80**

Height (inches)	1799–1819		Civil War Period			1918		1976–80	
	(1)	(2)	(3)	(4)	(5)	(6)	(7)	(8)	(9)
75 and up	.0099	.0115	.0031 ⎫	0151	.0202	.0056	.0044	.0471	.0506
73–74	.0261	.0300	.0226 ⎬			.0262	.0236	.1344	.1323
71–72	.1110	.1228	.0989	.0645	.0808	.1028	.1003	.2665	.2673
69–70	.2444	.2561	.2306	.1772	.2046	.2291	.2342	.2812	.2789
67–68	.2863	.2830	.3052	.2887	.2993	.2980	.3084	.1801	.1826
65–66	.2145	.1962	.2308	.2636	.2413	.2161	.2154	.0699	.0664
63–64	.0716	.,0672	.0915	.1418	.1172	.0907	.0865	.0160	.0175
61–62	.0218	.0189	.0137	.0416	.0312	.0246	.0208	.0036	.0030
Below 61	.0144	.0143	.0036	.0075	.0054	.0069	.0064	.0012	.0014
Total	1.0000	1.0000	1.0000	1.0000	1.0000	1.0000	1.0000	1.0000	1.0000
Mean	67.8	67.9	67.75	67.30	67.67	67.49	67.60	70.0	70.1
Inequality (G)	.02268	.02270	.021	.02219	.02197	.02236	.02166	.02121	.02129
Lognormal model									
N (classes)	19	19	16	8	8	21	21	17	17
R^2	.979	.980	.998	.999	.999	.996	.994	.987	.987
Slope (b)	0.045	0.045	0.037	0.039	0.039	0.042	0.041	0.041	0.042
G, sixteen classes[a]	.0227	.0227	.0211	.0221	.0219	.0223	.0216	.0216	.0217
Number of men	1,452	1,232	719,438	501,068	315,620	867,755	66,885	2,236	2,236

Sources: Distributions 1 and 2 are derived from a sample of 2,762 army enlistees drawn from Record Group 94 in the National Archives, Washington, D.C., for the years 1799–1894. Further details are given in Soltow and Stevens (1981, 52).

Distribution 3 is derived from sixty-eight distributions involving seventeen age classes for each of four nativity groups; each distribution has thirty height classes. The total number of recruits or enlistees accounted for in these classes is 729,320. See Gould (1979, 96–103). Gould presents a summary table of the distribution of ages of 1,012,273 enlisted volunteers during the Civil War on page 34 of this study; I standardized distributions 1, 2, and 9 so their relative ages from 18–35 or 18–34 reflect Gould's distribution in those age ranges.

Distributions 4 and 5 involve over half a million recruits (and those rejected) during the Civil War. The frequency tables have only eight height classes (59″, 61″, . . . , 73″) (Baxter 1875, 2: 2–81, 166–97).

Distributions 6 and 7 involve draft recruits in 1918, as stated in Davenport and Love (1921, vol. 15, *Statistics,* pt. 1, 109). Disbributions have twenty-one classes for height and twenty-two classes for nativity and ethnicity. I was unable to standardize for ages.

Distributions 8 and 9 are derived from two frequency tables, one for males 18–24 and the other for 25–34; each has twenty-one height classes. I weighted the two distributions so they would reflect Gould frequencies (United States 1987, 24, 35).

Notes: The distribution frequencies are proportion of total cases. The distributions are for a sample of army enlistees, 1799–1819, ages 18–35, age standardized, (1) all color, all nativities, (2) white native-born; recruits and draftees in the Civil War, (3) ages 18–35, birth in northern states and Ireland, (4) all colors, all nativities, age unspecified, (5) native-born white, age unspecified; draft recruits in 1918, (6) all colors, all nativities, (7) agricultural North, native-born whites over 73 percent; general population of males, 1976–80, (8) ages 18–34, (9) Ages 18–34, age adjusted (frequency as a proportion of total cases).

[a]The degree of inequality measured depends on the types of individuals included in the population and is particularly sensitive to age and nativity composition. Frequency tables with, say, eight classes instead of sixteen generally will have a smaller G because no allowance is made for inequality between the lower

Table 3.14   (notes, continued)

and upper class limits of a class. Finally, published tables with or ⸗end classes demand some assumptions about their class means. These and other aspects of measurement mean that the results for both G and b in this table must be treated with caution.

One possible procedure for handling the nine distributions uniformly is to consider the one-inch classes 61, 62, . . . , 74, coupled with two open-end classes below 61 and over 75 with assumed means of 60 and 76. These sixteen classes have been used as my preferred measure of inequality in this table. It was necessary to make interpolations using the lognormal slope to obtain sixteen or seventeen classes from the eight published classes in distributions 4 and 5. This procedure for establishing sixteen classes provides the arrangements used for constructing the Lorenz curves in table 3.15; the 1799–1819 heights 75 inches and taller average 76 inches, but include three men at 88 inches and one at 82 inches.

general sense, most of the last two centuries. They allow us to make statements about changes in inequality of stature over long periods; I shall make inferences about these changes because they may reflect changes in the distributions of income and wealth. To be realistic, one must realize that demographic and genetic influences may be dominant and may swamp economic influences. Changes in marriage pairings, differential fertility rates, and child birth-order patterns impose influences not accounted for in the table. Other factors such as age and nativity can be controlled to a certain extent.

I would like my distributions of army recruits to be representative of the population as a whole if I am to make inferences with respect to general economic conditions. If the foreign-born among adult males was 10 percent of the population in 1812 and 30 percent in 1864, I would like to apply these same proportions to all data for army recruits. Nevertheless, I would like to study dispersion for just white native-born and for specific age ranges, preferably with the same age mixture. Yet from a practical standpoint, these matters may not be of major consequence.

The Baxter data for more than a half million recruits during the Civil War provide a distribution of thirty height classes (from below 61 inches to above 75 inches) for each year of age from sixteen and under, to thirty-five and over, in the case of four nativity classes. These yield the following equation for those eighteen and older:

$$\text{Gini coefficient of height} \times 10^5 =$$

$$2{,}058 - 1.98 \, \text{AGE} + 7.8 \, \text{NB2} + 2.7 \, \text{NB3} - 100.2 \, \text{NB4}$$
$$(.67) \qquad\quad (8.8) \qquad\quad (8.8) \qquad\qquad (8.8)$$

$R^2 = .80$, $N = 60$ cells, where NB1 $= 1$, if born in New England; NB2 $= 1$, if born in New York, New Jersey, and Pennsylvania; NB3 $= 1$, if born in Ohio and Indiana; and NB4 $= 1$, if born in Ireland. Gini coefficients for younger age groups were slightly larger. Inequality varied very little for regional nativity groups in the United States. Surprisingly, inequality among Irish-born was less—about 5 percent less, on the average. The data in table 3.14 for my sampling of 1799–1819 allow age weighting, which forces the same age distribution and average age as in 1861–65, and allows separate representation of native-born.[16]

Each distribution in the table is essentially lognormal in shape. The R^2 coefficients are often greater than .990, but did fall to as low as .980 or lower when detail allowed the plotting of points in the upper and lower tails beyond two or three standard deviations. A tier chart of the nine distributions given in table 3.14 shows essentially nine straight lines parallel to each other (with slopes, b, roughly the same), demonstrating the very surprising fact that relative inequality remained essentially constant for the period of nearly two centuries under consideration. The Gini coefficients are also about the same for each of the distributions and present an alternative verification of the relative constancy of inequality.

To better understand the results of table 3.14, let me consider first the initial distribution. It says that the degree of inequality for 1799–1819 was .02268, as registered by using the Gini coefficient. The distribution plots as an excellent straight line on lognormal probability paper, with

$$\text{ln height} = 4.22 + .040Z,$$
$$(.0001)$$

$R^2 = .98$, fitted to 1,452 sample points (Z is the standard normal deviate). The slope 0.040 is an estimate of the standard deviation of the logarithms of heights. Only one point, that for an individual 82 inches tall, deviates appreciably from the line. These results are conservative estimates of inequality in the sense that heights under 60 inches did not appear, and those of boys under eighteen years have been excluded.

3.4.2 Lorenz Curves of Height

The Gini coefficient of height, $G(H) = .02268$, is quite small, at least relative to that for income distribution of the population as a whole at the time, perhaps as high as .60, as suggested by considerations of dwelling income in 1798 (Soltow 1989a, 247.) A lognormal distribution with $G(X) = .02$ can be transformed to one with $G(X^{33}) = .60$, using the convenient exponent of 33; I propose employing this magnification factor with heights, especially in comparing relative shares used in plotting Lorenz curves.[17] Inequality in the first 1799–1819 distribution becomes $G(H^{33}) = .64$, as determined from a computer run and as stated in table 3.15. Such a procedure conceivably implies, in a dangerous fashion, that a height distribution could be transformed into an income distribution using an elasticity of 33, a most unlikely possibility in the absence of data for other periods for income or height.

16. Age-specific distributions for white and colored native-born recruits in the United States during the Civil War show the former group to have less relative inequality. For men accepted, see Baxter (1875, 2: 199–299).

17. The factor of 33 is derived using theorem 2.1, found in Aitchison and Brown (1969).

Table 3.15   Lorenz Curve Shares of Adjusted Aggregate Height, H^3, of Army Enlistees and Others, for the Nine Frequency Tables from 1799 to 1980 Presented in Table 3.14

	1799–1819		1861–65			1918		1976–80	
$N(H^{33})$, the Top Proportion of All Men	All 18–35, A.S. (1)	Native White 18–35, A.S. (2)	All Irish-Born 18–35 North (3)	All (4)	Native White, A.S. (5)	All (6)	Native White 73% of Agricultural, North (7)	General Population 18–34 (8)	General Population 18–34, A.S. (9)
.01(top)	.188	.173	.136	.159	.164	.158	.149	.069	.067
.02	.260	.260	.197	.227	.234	.226	.212	.137	.134
.05	.385	.385	.325	.363	.367	.357	.341	.331	.336
.10	.508	.508	.468	.503	.508	.495	.479	.470	.477
.20	.668	.667	.642	.670	.671	.665	.650	.639	.644
.30	.779	.780	.754	.777	.779	.771	.758	.754	.757
.40	.855	.851	.832	.851	.849	.846	.836	.828	.830
.50	.903	.901	.890	.900	.898	.900	.892	.886	.888
.60	.939	.939	.929	.938	.939	.936	.931	.931	.933
.70	.966	.966	.960	.966	.965	.965	.962	.960	.961
.80	.984	.983	.981	.984	.983	.984	.982	.981	.981
.90	.995	.996	.994	.995	.995	.995	.994	.994	.994
1.00	1.000	1.000	1.000	1.000	1.000	1.000	1.000	1.000	1.000
$G(H^{33})$	.645	.642	.610	.640	.638	.634	.619	.602	.606

Source: See table 3.14; results must be treated with caution since an extreme height has a significant impact. For an early statement of this problem, see Sheppard (1897).

Note: Adjusting height, H, uses an elasticity coefficient of 33 for the sixteen classes and frequencies stated in table 3.14. A.S. = age standardized.

What is the evidence of height inequality in other periods? Tables 3.14 and 3.15 and the Lorenz curves in figure 3.4 show the surprising general result that inequality in height changed very little in the four periods.[18] Measurement error arising from the choice of lower- and upper-class limits of frequency distributions and midpoint assumptions might alone account for stated differences in Gini coefficients and also in lognormal slopes. The fact that Civil War figures largely exclude those from southern states may reduce the Gini coefficient by 2 to 3 percent.[19] It is particularly true that the drop in the Gini coefficient in this century, shown in table 3.14 to be about 5–10 percent, might be either larger or smaller if, say, Vietnam draftee heights were employed. Perhaps it goes too far afield to discuss changes in height inequalities in other countries such as Sweden, Norway, and Germany. Data for heights of Norwegian army recruits show impressive drops from 1761 to 1899–1903, 1922, and 1960–62.[20]

The Gini coefficients and lognormal slopes for the nine selected distributions of table 3.14 show little difference. One must generally conclude, given the strong possibility of measurement error, that relative inequality changed little. One of the statistical problems apparent in drawing generalizations stems from grouping errors. The first two distributions, derived from my sampling data, must be forced into the mold of the eight to sixteen published classes of the other distributions, a procedure I have performed, as explained in the source note of table 3.14. My preferred comparison is the Gini coefficient derived from sixteen classes shown in the next-to-last line of table 3.14, an arrangement obtained from an endeavor to achieve grouping uniformity. This row shows inequality for native-born in columns 2, 5, 7, and 9, of .0227, .0219, .0216, and .0217. There is slight evidence of decreasing inequality if one singles out these figures. This drop appears in more dramatic form when heights are sensitized, as shown in table 3.15. Yet, a glance at the plottings of the sensitized shares in figure 3.4 must lead one to conclude that any changes in equality of height were really quite minimal, certainly as contrasted to those I show for housing.

My presentation that highlights distribution of height as a normal curve certainly is not very novel. As long ago as 1863, E. B. Elliott plotted a frequency curve of the heights of 764 soldiers in the Army of the Potomac and, on the same chart, he plotted a normal curve fitted to his data. His measure of

18. I choose not to emphasize the fact that the sensitized Gini coefficients in table 3.15 for 1799–1819 are larger than those for the Civil War period. An element of taller men in my sample receives greater relative importance, obviously, in the sensitized version as compared to midpoints in frequency tables.

19. A computer run of data for 1799–1819 has $G(H)$ as .02246 for those of northern birth and .02364 for those of southern birth.

20. See Sweden (1969, pt. 1, population), for quinquenniel distributions from 1877 to 1949; Sandberg and Steckel (1980, 97) show a plot of the standard deviation of height from 1740 to 1880; for Norway, see Kill (1939, 64) and Udjus (1964, 47); for Germany, see Komlos (1990).

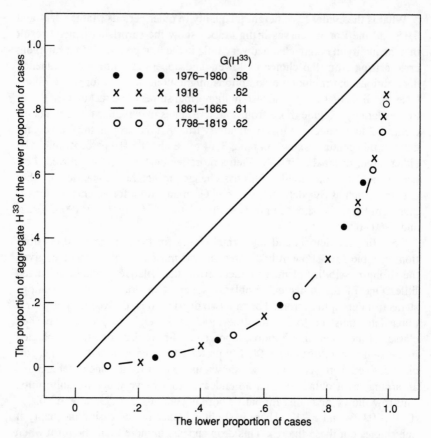

Fig. 3.4   Lorenz curves of the heights (H^{33}) of army recruits and draftees in three periods

Source: See table 3.15 for the four distributions numbered 2, 5, and 7 for native-born whites and 9 for the general population sample in 1976–80.

dispersion was the mean deviation, formulated at a time three decades before the development of the standard deviation. Since the mean deviation and standard deviation have an exact relationship for a normal curve, a reader can compute the coefficient of variation for his 764 cases from the parameters he reported for the 764. His coefficient of variation, .042, is for all practical purposes the same as mine derived from table 3.14 or table 3.15. Really, the only concept Elliott lacked was that of relative dispersion, as presented by Karl Pearson three decades later.[21]

Frankly, I had thought that relative inequality in heights in the United States

21. Elliott (1863, 40–44, diagram A). Pearson's work was cited by Yule (1919, 154, 160).

would have dropped because I suspected that income inequality has decreased since 1918. Perhaps changes in inequality in height, as distinguished from changes in mean height, are a result of a complex interaction of demographic, genetic, and environmental influences. In any case, one cannot readily offer height dispersion as an index of deteriorating income equality in the first half of the nineteenth century.

3.4.3   Literacy and Height

One glimpse of possible change in the characteristics of the short and the tall may be illustrated by using literacy rates. There is evidence that literacy improved more for the short than the tall, as illustrated with the following logistic equations for my sample of army recruits from 1799 to 1894: for 2,320 whites twenty-one and older with height (H) of 60 or more inches, and where ILL $= 1$ if illiterate, and ILL $= 0$ otherwise. 1799–1849:

$$ILL = 6.763 - .1063\ H;$$
$$(.0205)$$

$N = 1,658$, with 641 illiterate, and $P(\chi^2 = 28) < .001$; 1850–94:

$$ILL = -2.023 + .0064\ H;$$
$$(.0474)$$

$N = 662$, with 112 illiterate, and $P(\chi^2 = .02) < .892$. Among these, three occupational groups were distinguished, all showing similar drops in the force of illiteracy. Most impressive, of course, were all those with stated occupations other than farmer or laborer. There were similar findings for the subset of native-born recruits. We can say that at the beginning of the nineteenth century, literacy and height were strongly related. By the second half of the century, there was no advantage for the tall. The evidence is ever so slight that the short in some ways excelled in literacy among tradesmen and artisans if not among farmers or laborers.

3.4.4   The Poor in Farm Censuses

How desirable it would be to have distributions for food consumption, even if it were for adults only, that show inequalities in intakes of calories and nutritional quality for persons of different occupations and stature. Would there have been large variation in individual consumption? Would there have been a deprived group suffering from malnutrition? In the absence of consumption data, we might at least examine some production data at the farm level, particularly for the more marginal farms. The distribution of the number of cows possessed by farmers may be far removed from the inequality of milk consumption, but it does provide some gauge of the degree of sales necessary to achieve equality of intake.

South Carolina, 1850

Can anything be learned about the lower 40 percent from the censuses of agriculture for 1850–70? Do the farms of those with less than, say, twenty acres reveal characteristics of deprivation? Perhaps not. If these small farmers had holdings with little cash value, low crop production, and few cattle and livestock, they may be representative of individuals engaged in a multitude of other activities, including those measured by the value of home manufacturing, but overwhelmingly from income derived from alternative occupations.

I choose agricultural statistics for South Carolina as an example of what can be learned from farm data. In 1850 the state reported 29,967 farms and plantations, predominantly owned and managed by half of its 57,702 white males aged twenty and older. Farms arguably accounted for 52 percent of the white labor force, at best, and not 60 percent or more. Would a larger proportion of the white labor force have wished to possess acreage? Let us examine the lower tail of the acreage distribution for signs of deprivation. Marion Chandler and I drew a systematic sample of 861 farms from the state's agricultural census for investigation. Of these, 759 had improved acreage. The sample distribution of improved acreage plots neatly as a straight line on lognormal paper to ten acres at -1.1 standard deviations; at this point the line plummets rapidly (⟋). The bottom 13 percent of farms, reporting almost no improved acreage, would have averaged about seven acres had the lognormal linearity continued among all cases.[22]

Yet the remarkable fact seems to be that there were so few farms below ten acres. Only 19 percent of farmers had less than twenty acres, and they appear to have been reasonably well equipped, if one considers some of their reported holdings, presented in table 3.16. It is possible that farmers reporting no acres had located on rental properties.

A lognormal plotting of the distribution of improved and unimproved acres shows a pattern similar to that just described for improved acres. This time the discontinuity appears at twenty-five acres, with 18 percent of farms below this level. Cash values were reported for only 733 of the 861 farms; the remaining 128 may have been rental, as distinguished from owner, properties, at least in part. The 733 exhibit an excellent lognormal linearity throughout the entire range. The 128 farms without stated cash value were more marginal, as shown in table 3.16, and appear to have experienced little activity in the economic sense. Yet almost all farmers owned a horse, a cow, and some livestock. Importantly, the 128 had an average of six acres in improved land. These, particularly, may have been occupied by persons with alternative employment. The distributions of cows and horses demonstrate lognormal linearity except for the 7–9 percent of farms reporting neither. The upshot is that the agricultural census yields few clues about income for all persons below the median.

22. Another extrapolation of the lognormal curve to about the level where all white adult males would have owned acreage would mean that the smallest farm would have had about one acre or a little less of improved land.

Table 3.16   Average Holdings of Marginal Farms in South Carolina in 1850

	Improved Acres		Cash Value of Farm	
	Under 20, or Not Stated	20 or More	$0, or Not Stated	$1 and Up
Number of farms	156	705	128	733
Improved acres	10.8	138	5.9	133
Unimproved acres	3.8	379	0	377
Cash value ($)	175	2,740	0	2,060
Cash value of farm implements and machinery ($)	32	131	15	130
Horses	1.2	3.3	1.3	3.2
Milch cows	2.3	6.4	1.9	6.3
Value of livestock ($)	135	494	124	482

Source: A systematic sample from the agricultural census, drawn and processed by Marion Chandler and Lee Soltow. At least part of those with no acreage or no cash value stated may have been rented properties.

Ohio Acreage in 1835

Comprehensive data sets for the production of marginal farmers for years before the census of 1850 are difficult to obtain. We should examine the acreage owned by Ohio farmers in 1835 for their implications concerning persons who were nonowners. We can compare counties with greater and smaller ownership rates and then make some inferences concerning marginal groups.

Stress has been placed on the great *regional* variation in landownership from county to county, township to township, and village to village. If the proportion owning land (LOP) was 80 percent in one township and only 20 percent in another not far away, wouldn't this indicate that land deprivation was not crucial? Otherwise, farm laborers would have migrated, lessening the dispersion in LOP. Some insight into the degree of ownership can be obtained from the set of 164,962 property values reported in Ohio in 1835.

One can obtain the number of property owners in each county by collating property values by the name of the owner. This procedure results in some difficulties because there can be several persons sharing a common name in a more densely populated county. It is impossible to conduct a genealogical study for all persons in Ohio; therefore it is necessary to accept some degree of measurement error in the collation of names. Separate estimates, based on collations at village level, township level, county level, a four-region level, and state level, all indicate general agreement in the patterns of inequality, no matter what level of collation is employed.[23] I choose to focus on the county-level arrangement.

The LOP in an Ohio county in 1835 is calculated by dividing the number of landowners in the county by an estimate of its population of adult males

---

23. This problem and others are discussed in Soltow (1987b).

twenty-one and older. This population is taken to be 25 percent of the geometric mean of the county's total population in 1830 and 1840. The resulting dispersion in this proportion is shown in table 3.17; three-eights of the state's population lived in counties where ownership rates were more than 60 percent. Land in these areas was spread very generously indeed among people. In about 5 percent of counties there was an abundance of property owners, and the vast majority of residents enjoyed ownership. In this paper, perhaps I should highlight the proportion without land if a major focus is to be on persons below median income. To consider those without land (or house ownership) as a deprived group, however, is somewhat tenuous, particularly for those who were artisans or tradesmen who rented.

What can be learned about areas with high ownership rates? One suspects that they would tend to be those counties well endowed, from the standpoint of overall wealth. Consider just one aspect of ongoing research in this area.

$$LOP = .495 + .000256W;$$
$$(.000123)$$

$R^2 = .06, N = 73$ counties, where W is the aggregate value of real estate in the county, divided by its adult male population. Ownership rates did tend to be higher in wealthier counties. Those counties having a larger proportion of their population in agriculture (NAGRIC_T), as measured by the 1840 census, had wider spread in ownership but the relationship was rather weak.

$$LOP = .404 + .20 \text{ NAGRIC\_};$$

$R^2 = .03, N = 72$. This regression equation projects to limits of .40 for counties with no agricultural population and .60 for the entire population in agriculture. If Ohio followed this pattern over time and if it moved from 80 percent in agriculture to 70 percent in a decade, then it would experience a 2 percent drop in the LOP. This certainly does not mean that those just below median income need to have suffered from the standpoint of alternative employment. To a certain extent we can understand the meaning of "marginal" farms, shown by the case of South Carolina in 1850. One final perspective of Ohio in 1835 will be presented by partitioning counties into two groups, based on the LOP and by observing their lognormal configurations.

Table 3.18 distinguishes those forty-three "landless" counties in Ohio from the thirty with wide ownership, where "landless" in this context means the lower 40 percent who owned no land. Plots of the distributions of landed wealth among wealthholders for the two groups reveals no essential differences in slope, b (1.435 and 1.422), or relative inequality, G (.638 and .628), as measured by the Gini coefficient. It is almost as though the more marginal holders who were participating more broadly in the second group merely queued at the bottom of the parade of wealthholders, orderly blending in. It is somewhat tempting to think that if all persons had chosen to own or had been

Table 3.17   The Landowner Proportion (LOP) in the Seventy-three Counties in
                    Ohio in 1835

LOP	Number of Counties	Proportion of Ohio's Population
.80 and up	5	.06
.60–.79	25	.31
.40–.59	36	.53
.29–.39	6	.09
.19 and less	1	.01
Total	73	1.00
Weighted population		
Mean		.56
Gini coefficient		.14
Median		.55

Source: Ohio Tax records (1835); see also Soltow (1987b).

capable of owning land, the relative value distribution would have been log-normal, with a G of a little over .6.

Were persons in those counties with a lower ownership rate suffering in any sense relative to persons in counties with widespread ownership? At this date I am unable to interview those landless, but I can review some significant indicators, as listed at the bottom of table 3.18. In landless counties obviously there were fewer persons in the agricultural sector. They were older counties, as judged by formation dates, and tended to have more investment in manufacturing. Yet they did display more illiteracy and were to remain more illiterate. In these counties, school attendance was appreciably less. Nevertheless, overall average wealth among the rich and poor in succeeding decades was about the same for both groups. It is difficult to generalize about shares of lower groups on the basis of whether or not they owned land.

3.5 Household Clothing Production

Measurements have been made of the degree of inequality in family and individual condition with respect to saving (wealth), housing, and food and nutrition. Can anything be said about clothing? One can dream of a meter's being placed on a sample of persons on a Wednesday or a Sunday that would register the value of the clothing worn by each of them, in any year from 1798 to 1860. Alternatively, what would be the Gini coefficient for clothing expenditures for one year?

I must be content with an admittedly tangential presentation, one dealing with the variation in yards of cloth manufactured in individual households in New York State in 1825. This was a year when household production was very substantial relative to production in factories, more so than is stated in the censuses of 1835 and 1845. The distributions presented in table 3.19 do dem-

Table 3.18   Distribution of Real Estate (RE) among Owners Twenty-one and
                    Older in Ohio in 1835, Classified by Counties with Low and High
                    Landowning Proportions (LOP)

Real Estate Value ($)	43 Counties, Each with LOP <.60	30 Counties, Each with LOP ≥.60
50,000 and up	4	7
20,000–49,999	57	48
10,000–19,999	198	107
5,000–9,999	582	266
2,000–4,999	2,885	1,298
1,000–1,999	6,196	3,571
500–999	12,432	9,081
200–499	22,335	20,320
100–199	14,243	13,982
50–999	7,545	8,040
20–49	4,242	5,481
10–19	1,655	1,691
5–9	944	926
2–4	321	332
1	36	50
Total	73,675	65,110
RE ≥ 1		
Mean ($)	598	462
Inequality (G)	.638	.628
Lognormal chart		
R^2	.999	.994
Slope (b)	1.435	1.422
Number of nonowners	82,249	28,832
Males twenty-one and older	155,924	93,742
RE≥0		
Mean ($)	283	314
Inequality (G)	.829	.744
Lognormal chart		
R^2	.998	.990
Slope (b)	1.625	1.648
Weighted county averages		
Landowner proportion (LOP)	.472	.695
Proportion employed in agriculture, 1840	.694	.779
Proportion illiterate adults, 1840	.064	.040
School attendance per person aged 5–19, 1840	.284	.490
Daily newspapers per adult male, 1840	.039	.006
Proportion illiterate adult males, 1850	.056	.039
Capital investment in manufacturing, adult males, 1840 ($)	65	24
Cash value per acre of farms, 1850 ($)	28	20
Cash value per acre of farms, 1960 ($)	42	34
Total value of real estate, adult males, 1860 ($)	1,820	1,760

Table 3.18   (continued)

Real Estate Value ($)	43 Counties, Each with LOP <.60	30 Counties, Each with LOP ≥.60
Average latitude	39.8°	40.4°
Average longitude	82.8°	82.2°
Average year of county formation	1805	1809

Source: See table 3.17 and Inter-University Consortium for Political and Social Research (n.d.). The parameters for the lognormal chart were obtained from fitting the linear model to thirty-five and forty selected points for 1≤RE≤91,40 for RE≥1; for RE≥0, a sharp discontinuity appears for the ten-or-so points from RE of 1 to 90, and only those points on the chart above 90 were considered in the linear fitting.

Table 3.19   **Home-woven Yardage in New York in 1825: A sample of 1,775 Families and Households and 4,744 Adults in Thirteen Counties**

Total Yards per Household	Number of Households	Total Yards per Adult[a]	Number of Adults
1,000 and up	1		
500–999	2	500 and up	2
200–499	56	200–499	1
100–199	257	100–199	29
50–99	493	50–99	360
20–49	479	20–49	1,699
10–19	143	10–19	1,165
1–9	41	5–9	561
0	303	0.1–4	239
		0	688
Total	1,775		4,744

Inequality Coefficient

	Per Household	Per adult
G for yardage ≥ 0	.518	.487
G for yardage > 0	.418	.400

Source: New York (1825). Approximately every tenth page was sampled from extant records of this census, as available in the L.D.S. Genealogical Library, beginning with microfilm no. 806800 for Broome County.

[a]Adults were males eligible to vote and women sixteen and older. The distribution per adult assumes an equal distribution within each household.

A plotting of the thirteen counties (Broome, Chautauqua, Cortland, Herkimer, Jefferson, Lewis, Oneida, Orange, Steuben, Tioga, Tompkins, Washington, and Yates) among the fifty-five in the state shows a wide scatter of areas. The yardage per adult was 20.1 in the thirteen counties and 20.5 for the other forty-one counties, excluding New York, as reported in summary tables for 1825. Total yards is the simple addition of yards of fulled cloth, flannel, and other woolen cloth not fulled, and yards of linens, cotton, and other thin cloths manufactured "in the domestic way."

onstrate sizable inequality. They suggest that standards of living for clothing consumption may have varied significantly among households to the extent that they depended on this home production.

3.6   Alternative Measures of Inequality

In this paper I have singled out distribution measurements dealing only with wealth, housing expenditures or rents, literacy, schooling, number of children, stature, farm food production, and home-woven yardage. Nothing has been said about inequalities in medical treatment or life expectancy. Surely there must be alternative ways of measuring inequality; some of these can prove to be quite innovative and may yield annual distributions.

One could display distributions of the number of servants in households as a measure of well-being of the rich or possibly the degree of dependency of the poor. A tax on the value of carriages of various types owned by the select few percent of households indicates opulence in the early federal period. Distributions of horses owned indicates facility in transportation. Numbers of seats and differential pricing in theaters, and later on trains, certainly reflect class differences. Frequency tables of the number of watches and clocks convey notions of standards of living for various groups and how these standards changed as better methods of production and resulting lowering of prices were experienced. An extreme is a unique table classifying couples at marriage in five distinct economic classes in Amsterdam for each of some 250 years. It divulges the increased equality in the twentieth century, as opposed to inequalities existing from the seventeenth to the nineteenth centuries. Its *annual* distributions from 1829 to 1860 (and in some respects from 1818 to 1860) highlight rough constancy of relative inequality better than any statistical series I have developed (Soltow 1989b, 1989c).

Alternatively, landownership for persons classified by age indicates the rise in populations relative to land availability in such diverse areas as Connecticut and Norway over the last three or four centuries. Studies in the inequalities in the standard of living may be only beginning.

3.7   Conclusions

This paper has dealt with ten or so data sets depicting the distributions of wealth and income, or proxies for them such as educational level, marriage rates, and number of children, in households with and without wealth. The main emphasis has been on the degree of inequality, the disparity between rich and poor, appearing in these distributions for the United States in the nineteenth century. I also have tried to measure the change in inequality, but this was possible only in three facets: wealth, housing, and height.

Stated differently, the incomes of people have been viewed as the composition of saving (as measured by wealth), rent expenditure (as measured by dwelling values), food expenditure (as measured by height and household farm production), and clothing expenditure (as measured most indirectly by household cloth manufactured). An estimate of the income distribution, made from dwelling values in 1798, has a lognormal shape and a Gini coefficient of inequality (G) of about .6. This income inequality can be viewed as a synthesis of inequalities varying between a G of .8 or higher for saving (wealth) to one of .4 for food expenditure, and one can generate such a synthesis on the computer using lognormal assumptions (Soltow 1989a, 272–73).

An income inequality coefficient of .6 in 1798 means that there were large disparities at the time, substantially larger than today, when the coefficient is rising, but still is less than .5 (U.S. Bureau of the Census 1990, 30; Maxwell 1990). Is this dwelling-derived estimate of income inequality in 1798 too large? I believe the estimate is reasonable, considering the fact that the relative distribution of the sizes of families was substantial at the time, with a G of about .3. There was a strong degree of variation in the average income of counties and smaller area units. Adjustment for this variation decreases G from .60 to .55. Consider also the fact that the economy at that time was dominated by seasonal movement in a rural setting subject to floods, drought, insects, fires, sickness, and the remainder of the disruptions due to war. There were great differences attributable to farm size, land fertility, and land terrain. The effects of inheritance on wealth, dependent on past accumulation, were large. Traces of the influence of primogeniture persisted in several states. And slavery strengthened inequality of income among the free.

Did the relative inequality of income change before the Civil War? Probably not much, if at all, but conclusions must be derived from several different sources with varying degrees of precision. Consider first the distribution of wealth, our most complete time series. Figures 3.1 and 3.2 demonstrate that G's for inequality of wealth in real estate were .6 to .65 from 1798 to 1870 for those possessing estates. Coefficients for real and personal estate in 1860 and 1870, and probably earlier, were roughly the same. It is true that the proportion of adult males owning land decreased from .5 in 1798 to below .45 two generations later.

Wealth distributions are generally silent about the 40 percent of individuals with no wealth. We do know from complete census enumerations that those without wealth were less likely to be married, less likely to have children, and that they had lower literacy rates and children with less schooling. Yet these statistics concerning the poor do not seem particularly disturbing to me. The shanty counts for Ontario in 1851 do impress one with the fact that there were large minority groups who lived in very humble circumstances, at least compared to most lower groups at the present time.

It is from housing data for New York State that we obtain our most authoritative facts about the relative shares of households. The lowest 40 percent of homes (excluding New York and Kings counties) accounted for 7 percent of aggregate housing value in 1798, 8 percent of the value in 1875, and 18 percent of the value in 1980. It is these important quantifications that lead me to conclude that there was little change in inequality in the period of our interest, and that the poor really had very little compared to the middle and top groups in the nineteenth century.

Finally, we must not ignore distributions of heights, in part because they are available for *all* recruits in roughly the years 1812, 1864, and 1918 and for a sample of all adult males for 1976–80. I find that relative inequality in these figures, the Lorenz curves in these years, approximately duplicate each other. There is no evidence of deterioration among lower groups relative to upper groups to the extent that nutrition and food consumption do affect height distributions. The New York dwelling and the height measures both signify little or no inequality change in the nineteenth century. The two sources are inconsistent as they signal inequality change for the twentieth century. Probably food consumption was much less sensitive than was housing to the relative rise in income of lower groups.

There are many ways of measuring inequalities in the standard of living in any one year. Some of these are suggested in this paper as possible areas to be investigated in the future. Surely additional and alternative measurements must be devised. The study of inequalities in the standard of living is only in its infancy. The relative shares available to the rich and the poor in the nineteenth century must be a fundamental part of the documentation measuring economic growth.

References

Aitchison, J., and J. A. C. Brown. 1969. *The lognormal distribution.* Cambridge: Cambridge University Press.

Amsterdam. 1923. *Statistiek der Bevolking van Amsterdam tot 1921.* No. 67. Amsterdam: het Bureau van Statistiek der Gemeente Amsterdam.

Antwerp. 1799. Stadsarchief: Matrice de role d'Anvers, fonciers, ville. Sections 1–4.

Bailyn, B. 1986. *Voyagers to the West.* New York: Alfred A. Knopf.

Baxter, J. 1875. *Statistics, medical and anthropological, of the Provost Marshall General's bureau, derived from records of the examination for military service in the armies of the United States during the late War of the Rebellion of over a million recruits, drafted men, substitutes, and enrolled men.* Vols. 1 and 2. Washington, D.C.: U.S. War Department.

Canada. 1851–52. *Appendix to census of Canada, Upper Canada.* National Archives of Canada. Microfilm C-11, 712, to C-11, 762.

Davenport, C. B., and A. G. Love. 1921. *Statistics: Army anthropology.* Vol. 15, part 1. Washington, D.C.: GPO.

David, P. A., and P. Solar. 1977. A bicentenary contribution to the history of the cost of living in America. *Research in Economic History* 2: 1–80.

De Belder, J. 1977. De behuizing te Antwerpen op het einde van de XVIIIde eeuw. *Belgisch tijdschrift voor niewste geschiedenis* 8: 367–446.

Elliot, E. B. 1863. *On the military statistics of the United States of America.* Berlin: Decker.

Eveleth, P. B., and J. M. Tanner. 1976. *Worldwide variation in human growth*. Cambridge: Cambridge University Press.

Fogel, R. W. 1986. Nutrition and the decline in mortality since 1700: Some preliminary findings. In *Long-term factors in American economic growth*, ed. S. L. Engerman and R. E. Gallman. NBER Studies in Income and Wealth, 51. Chicago: University of Chicago Press.

Gould, B. A. 1979. *Investigations in the military and anthropological statistics of American Soldiers*. New York: Arno Press. Reprint of U.S. Sanitary Commission's memoirs of the War of the Rebellion, vol. 2. New York: Hurd and Houghton, 1869.

Great Britain. 1805. *Parliamentary papers, 1803–1804*. House of Commons, vol. 13.

Humphreys, N. 1887. Class mortality statistics. *Journal of the Royal Statistical Society* 50: 255–85.

Inter-University Consortium for Political and Social Research. N.d. *Historical, demographic, economic, and social data: The United States, 1790–1970*. Ann Arbor, Mich.: Inter-University Consortium for Political and Social Research.

Kearl, J. R., and C. L. Pope. 1986. Choices, rents, and luck: Economic mobility of nineteenth-century Utah households. In *Long-term factors in American economic growth*, ed. S. L. Engerman and R. E. Gallman. NBER Studies in Income and Wealth, 51. Chicago: University of Chicago Press.

Kidwell, C., and M. Christman. 1974. *Suiting everyone: The democratization of clothing in America*. Washington, D.C.: Smithsonian Institution Press.

Kill, V. 1939. *Stature and growth of Norwegian men during the past two hundred years*. Oslo: hos J. Dybwad.

Komlos, J. 1990. Height and social status in eighteenth-century Germany. *Journal of Interdisciplinary History* 20: 607–721.

Lievense, E. N.d. Gronnen en methoden voor het onderzoek in archieven naar de geschiedenis van huizen binnen de singel gracht. Gemeentearchief Amsterdam. GAA call no. SZ.

Lis, C. 1986. *Social change and the labouring poor: Antwerp, 1770–1860*. New Haven: Yale University Press.

Margo, R. A., and R. H. Steckel. 1983. Heights of native-born whites during the antebellum period. *Journal of Economic History* 43: 167–74.

Martin, E. W. 1942. *The standard of living in 1860*. Chicago: University of Chicago Press.

Maxwell, N. L. 1990. *Income inequality in the United States, 1947–1985*. Westport, Conn.: Greenwood Press.

New York. 1825. *State census*. L.D.S. Genealogical Library, Salt Lake City. Microfilm.

New York. Secretary of State. 1855. *Census of the State of New York for 1855*. Albany: C. Van Benthuysen, 1857.

———. Superintendent of the Census. 1875. *Census of the State of New York for 1875*. Albany: Weed, Parsons, and Company, Printers, 1877.

Ogle, W. 1887. Summary of several male life tables. *Journal of the Royal Statistical Society* 50: 648–52.

Ohio. 1835. Ohio Historical Society Archives. Data recorded from tax duplicates by G. Pettey. Ohio State Historical Library, Columbus.

Pope, C. L. 1989. Households on the American frontier: The distribution of income and wealth in Utah, 1850–1900. In *Markets in history*, ed. D. Galenson. Cambridge: Cambridge University Press.

Reyniers-Defourny, R. 1979. *De bevolkingstelling van Antwerp in de France*. Stadsarchief, Antwerp. Mimeo.

Sandberg, L. G., and R. H. Steckel. 1980. Soldier, soldier, what made you grow so tall? *Economy and History* 23: 91–105.

Sen, A. 1976. Poverty: An ordinal approach to measurement. *Econometrica* 44: 219–31.

Sheppard, W. F. 1897. On the calculation of the average square, cube, etc., of a large number of magnitudes. *Journal of the Royal Statistical Society* 60: 698–703.

Soltow, L. 1971. An index of the rich and poor in Scotland. *Scottish Journal of Political Economy* 18: 49–67.

———. 1975. *Men and wealth in the United States, 1850–1870.* New Haven: Yale University Press.

———. 1981. Horse owners in Kentucky in 1800. *Register of the Kentucky Historical Society* 79: 203–10.

———. 1982. Male inheritance expectations in the United States in 1870. *Review of Economics and Statistics* 64: 252–60.

———. 1984. Wealth inequality in the United States in 1798 and 1860. *Review of Economics and Statistics* 66: 444–51.

———. 1987a. Distribution of income in the United States in 1798: Estimates based on the federal housing inventory. *Review of Economics and Statistics* 69: 181–85.

———. 1987b. Tocqueville's view of the Northwest in 1835: Ohio a generation after settlement. In *Essays on the economy of the old Northwest,* ed. D. C. Klingaman and R. K. Vedder. Athens: Ohio University Press.

———. 1989a. *Distribution of wealth and income in the United States in 1798.* Pittsburgh: University of Pittsburgh Press.

———. 1989b. Income and wealth inequality in Amsterdam, 1585–1805. *Economish-en Sociall-historisch Jaarboek* 52: 72–95.

———. 1989c. The rich and destitute in Sweden, 1805–1855: A test of Tocqueville's inequality hypotheses. *Economic History Review,* 2d ser., 42: 43–63.

———. 1990. Inequality of wealth in land in Scotland in the eighteenth century. *Scottish Economic and Social History* 10: 38–60.

Soltow, L., and D. L. May. 1979. The distribution of Mormon wealth and income in 1857. *Explorations in Economic History* 16: 151–62.

Soltow, L., and E. Stevens. 1981. *The rise of literacy and the common school in the United States.* Chicago: University of Chicago Press.

Steckel, R. H. 1983. Height and per capita income. *Historical Methods* 16: 1–70.

Sweden. 1969. *Historical statistics of Sweden.* Part 1, *Population.* Stockholm: Statistical Centralbureau.

Tocqueville, A. de. 1966. *Democracy in America.* Henry Reeve text. New York: Alfred A. Knopf.

Udjus, G. U. 1964. *Anthropometrical changes in Norwegian men in the twentieth century.* Oslo: Universitetsforlaget.

United States. 1987. *Vital and health statistics.* U.S. National Center for Health Statistics, ser. 11, no. 238. Washington, D.C.: GPO, October.

U.S. Bureau of the Census. 1984. *1980 Census of Housing.* Washington, D.C.: GPO.

———. 1990. Money, income, and poverty status in the United States, 1989. In *Current population reports,* ser. P-60, no. 168. Washington, D.C.: GPO, 1991.

Van Wieringen, J. C. 1979. Secular growth changes and environment: An analysis of developments in the Netherlands, 1850–1978. *Collegium Antropologicum* 31: 35–48.

———. 1986. Secular growth changes. In *Human Growth,* 2d edition, ed. F. Falkner and J. M. Tanner, vol. 3. New York: Plenum Press.

Yule, G. U. 1919. *An introduction to the theory of statistics.* London: Charles Griffin and Co.

Comment   Clayne L. Pope

This paper adds to the long list of Lee Soltow's contributions to our knowledge concerning the changing distribution of economic rewards across time and space. Had I (and I suspect there are many others like me) paid Soltow a royalty for every occasion when I have opened *Men and Wealth in the United States* to make a comparison or check a number, he would be in the rich tail of the wealth distribution himself.[1] His contributions to the study of the trends in the distributions of income and wealth, use of the federal census manuscripts, and international comparisons of inequality are well known. He has brought new and useful sources of evidence on inequality, most recently the housing inventory of 1798, to the attention of others.

In this paper he has set a challenging task for himself and his readers— better understanding of the economic conditions or standard of living of the poor. Most of the papers of this volume are directed toward changes in the mean level of living. The focus of this paper is the poorest 40 percent of the population. While he does use the familiar census manuscripts with their estimates of household wealth and real estate, Soltow's search for evidence on this issue leads him from the shanties of Ontario and the tenements of New York, to the marriage arrangements of Amsterdam, and on to the correlation of literacy and heights of military recruits. I interpret this energetic search in disparate sources as evidence of the difficulty in gaining substantive knowledge on either the level of living of the poor or their share of the aggregate consumption or income. In spite of Soltow's clear expertise and his diligence, this paper reinforces the impression that we have a long way to go before we can speak with confidence about the standard of living of the poor or their share of the economic pie. Our most commonly accessible measures of economic status in the past are occupation and wealth. The census and other sources often give occupation while probate inventories, tax rolls, and some census enumerations give wealth. Unfortunately, neither occupation nor wealth tell us much about the relative position of the poor. The very poor have no measured wealth, and they share the occupation of "laborer" with many whose economic status is considerably higher. Soltow's search for the poor through unconventional sources is understandable though not necessarily fully successful.

One methodological point might be useful before consideration of the substance of the paper. Soltow compares the various distributions of economic success to the lognormal distribution. The lognormal is second only to the

Clayne L. Pope is professor of economics at Brigham Young University and a research associate of the National Bureau of Economic Research.

1. Lee Soltow, *Men and Wealth in the United States, 1850–1870* (New Haven: Yale University Press, 1975).

normal distribution in its usefulness.[2] If it may be assumed that a distribution is lognormal, counterfactual statements may be more easily examined because one has a simple two-parameter statistical model for the distribution.

It is possible to test statistically how well a lognormal distribution fits a body of data. The lognormal, a two-parameter distribution, is a special case of a three-parameter generalized gamma distribution which is, in turn, a special case of a four-parameter generalized beta distribution.[3] One could estimate the more general three- or four-parameter distribution and compare the estimated parameters to the restrictions that reduce the more general distributional specification to the two-parameter lognormal distribution.[4] Statistical tests may then be used to compare the nested statistical models to see if the use of a lognormal distribution sacrifices too much precision.[5]

For many issues, the fit of the data to any model distribution is not relevant. That is, we are simply interested in the actual size distribution, the share of the poorest fifth of the population, the computed Gini coefficient, and so on. The model distributions are useful for counterfactual statements, adjustments to the data or estimation of covariates of the distribution. For many of the issues in Soltow's paper, the goodness of fit of the data to the lognormal specification is not particularly germane because we are simply interested in the distribution per se.

The most serious difficulty with application of the lognormal distribution to wealth, or to a much lesser extent income, is the fact that many households report no wealth or income. Wealth distributions always have considerable mass at zero, and the fits to the lognormal distribution exclude zero values, as Soltow is careful to tell us. The zero wealth values present a serious problem

---

2. For discussions of the distribution and its applications see Edwin L. Crow and Kunio Shimizu, *Lognormal Distributions: Theory and Applications* (New York: Marcel Dekker, 1988), and J. Aitchison and J. A. C. Brown, *the Lognormal Distribution* (Cambridge: Cambridge University press, 1966).

3. James McDonald, "Some Generalized Functions for the Size Distribution of Income," *Econometrica* 52, no. 3 (May 1984): 647–63.

4. For example, the generalized gamma

$$f(y; a, \beta, p) = \frac{ay^{ap-1}e^{-(y/\beta)^a}}{\beta^{ap}\Gamma(p)}$$

becomes lognormal if

$$\beta^a = \sigma^2 a^2 \quad \text{and} \quad p = \frac{a\mu + 1}{\beta^a}.$$

5. When my colleague James McDonald applied this approach to grouped data for family income in the United States in 1970, 1975, and 1980, he found some differences between the performance of the four- and three-parameter specifications, with the generalized beta (four-parameter) doing significantly better. He also found that distributions such as the Weibull and the Singh-Maddala fit better than the lognormal. The error in the Gini coefficient implied by use of the lognormal ranged from 8 percent to 17 percent. See McDonald, "Some Generalized Functions." However, the lognormal is convenient. For historical issues, data problems are clearly more pressing than the differences implicit in distributional assumptions.

in most research on the wealthholding of households. The zero values are a mixture of households that truly have no wealth and households with little wealth. Inclusion or exclusion of zero values usually changes the coefficients of regressions explaining wealth and always changes the estimates of the level of inequality. This problem, which I view as a heaping problem, does not have a satisfactory solution as yet. Model distributions may be of some help in solving the problem of reported zeros in the data.

Each of the measures of economic success reviewed in this paper approaches the issue of poverty from a different vantage point. The parable of the blind men and the elephant serves as a warning. Each source may be producing information about a different aspect of poverty. In this discussion, I would like to pose questions or difficulties in the use of three of the data sources—height, housing values, and wealth.

Height

The distribution of heights is the result of a mixture of differences within the population in genetics and nutritional status. Note that the distribution of heights does not correspond closely to a distribution of economic status. That is, height of 77 inches compared to 70 inches is not analogous to an income of $50,000 compared to one of $35,000. To quote Tom Thumb from the musical *Barnum,* "Bigger isn't Better." The link of height and poverty works through the gap between height determined solely by genetic potential and actual height. Some of the individuals in the short tail of the height distribution are close to genetic potential and have not suffered any particular poverty. Others are short because of poor nutritional status that may well be the result of poverty. The point is that height is not a very good predictor of poverty except in the extreme. Knowledge about height inequality does not translate easily into knowledge about economic inequality.

Many height distributions have been compiled from censored or truncated data sets. Most researchers have used the assumption that heights are normally distributed to recover the actual distribution from the censored data. It is hard to see how that procedure would lead to a normal distribution with more dispersion if the right-hand side of the distribution is largely determined by genetics. It may be that height distributions, useful for trends in the mean standard of living, will not be directly useful for the study of the very poor until we have much greater precision in the measurement of the height distribution and its deviation from normality.

The more promising use of heights is likely to continue to be multivariate analysis that is used to identify groups with varying proportions of poverty—urban, rural, geographical regions, or occupational groups. Along this line, Soltow's results on height and literacy are intriguing. However, the nineteenth-century cycle in mean height may be playing a role in the regressions.

Housing

The distribution of housing values represented by the distributions for New York in 1798, 1875, and 1980 are related to an important element of poverty. Certainly, we would be willing to use housing today as a useful indicator of poverty. But there are substantial adjustments to be made in moving from the value of housing to the consumption of housing services. The problem is illustrated in table 3.6. There are virtually no dwellings in New York or Kings counties in the lowest two classes in 1798 or in the lowest three classes in 1875. I would not be ready to conclude that housing services were better in those counties. We know that locational rent in large cities can be substantial. Location certainly confers advantages that raise wages. Unfortunately, the poor are more likely to be unemployed or infirm and unable to capitalize on locational advantages that make their wages and earnings higher to offset the higher cost of their housing services. Thus, the lower level of inequality of housing values in New York and Kings counties compared to the other counties may be illusory.

Wealth

In one sense, wealth is not particularly useful for analysis of poverty because the poor are unlikely to have recorded wealth. In 1860, Soltow found that 38 percent of households owned no wealth.[6] If we could assume that all who have no wealth were poor, the wealth distributions would serve well, but such an assumption is unwarranted. Wealth-income ratios vary systematically over the life cycle. Indeed, part of the life cycle involves the transfer of human capital into nonhuman capital for bequest or later consumption. This omission of human capital from wealth estimates limits the usefulness of wealth distributions for the study of poverty. Even beyond the life cycle, there is also a great deal of unexplained variation in the wealth-income ratio. The connection between wealth and income is probably least firm in urban areas where renting of housing is more common. Urban households with no wealth may well include many households living comfortably beyond poverty.

Wealth distributions are useful, however, for the study of mobility of households out of poverty or at least low wealthholding. If households are linked over several different years of observation, the group that remain with little or no wealth can be identified. For example, there was substantial mobility in nineteenth century Utah with very few of the poorest households in one census year still poor in the succeeding census.[7] We need more evidence on the extent of occupational and wealth mobility for poor households. Unfortunately, the data sets useful for the measurement of mobility are rare and difficult to create.

6. Soltow, *Men and Wealth*, 60.
7. See J. R. Kearl and Clayne L. Pope, "Wealth Mobility: The Missing Element," *Journal of Interdisciplinary History* 8 (Winter 1983): 461–88.

Soltow's paper makes clear how difficult it is to find historical information on the poorest segment of the population. Sources such as relief rolls or orphanage records may yield more information, but we are not likely ever to have much quantitative data on the condition of the very poor. However, the problem may not be as serious as first appearances suggest. Throughout this paper, Soltow reminds us of how little change in inequality has occurred over the past two centuries (with the exception of dwelling values). With rather stable levels of inequality, changes in the level of living for the poor must correspond quite closely to changes in the mean standard of living for the full population. In terms of height and nutrition, it would seem reasonable that the status of the poor increased at the same or a somewhat faster rate than the rate of change of the general mean. Consequently, our attention can, for the most part, be on the trend in the average level because the distribution was changing very slowly if at all.

Once the movement of the mean level of living is established, attention could be shifted to the mobility of the households out of poverty. Our view of poverty will clearly be conditioned on the turnover of the poor or the extent of movement out of the poorest groups of the economy. I applaud Soltow's energy in the collection and analysis of various distributions of economic status. But I believe most of our research should be directed toward better measurement of the average level of living and the mobility of households within the generally stable distributions of economic status.

4 Wages and Prices during the Antebellum Period: A Survey and New Evidence

Robert A. Margo

Data on wages and prices are fundamental to the study of the economy of the United States before the Civil War. Even economic historians who are unwilling to employ a real wage index—the ratio of wages to a weighted average of prices—as a summary statistic of the standard of living or the rate of economic growth (Engerman and Gallman 1983; Fogel 1986) agree that evidence on wages and prices should be compiled and assessed. The extent to which levels and trends in real wages varied across occupations and regions provides valuable information on levels and trends in inequality, and on the spatial integration of labor markets.[1] Evidence on long-run trends in real wages is also useful for cross-country comparisons (see Jeffrey G. Williamson's comment on this paper).

The short-run behavior of wages and prices is also of interest. In the long run, one might expect that real wages are determined by real forces—the demand and supply of labor. In the short run, there may be persistent effects of nominal or real shocks (for example, immigration, technological change) on nominal wages, leading to short-run fluctuations. Whether a wage lag existed prior to the Civil War and, if so, what role the lag played in macroeconomic fluctuations, are unsettled issues. Although economic historians have largely focused on long-run trends, short-run fluctuations have commanded the atten-

Robert A. Margo is professor of economics at Vanderbilt University and a research associate at the National Bureau of Economic Research.

The author is grateful to Donald Adams, Stanley Engerman, Robert Fogel, Jeffrey Williamson, and participants at the NBER-DAE conference on antebellum living standards for helpful comments.

1. Occupational wage differentials are also important to the debate over the labor scarcity hypothesis. According to Habakkuk (1962), skilled labor was relatively more abundant in the United States than in Great Britain, and this alleged relative abundance influenced the choice of technique in American manufacturing. Little evidence has been found, however, to support Habakkuk; see Adams (1968), and Margo and Villaflor (1987). For a contrary view, see Zabler (1972).

tion of social, labor, and political historians (Hirsch 1978; Wilentz 1984; Ross 1985; Fogel 1989, 1990).

This paper surveys recent research on antebellum wages and prices and presents some new evidence on real wages. Section 4.1 briefly discusses some of the problems involved in using real wages as a proxy for living standards. Section 4.2 reviews recent research; it concludes that, while progress has been made in investigating nominal wage patterns during the antebellum period, further insights require additional research on prices, particularly at the retail level. Section 4.3 discusses a new data source on antebellum wages, based on military records, which is used in conjunction with previously collected data on wholesale prices to chart region- and occupation-specific movements in real wages from 1821 to 1856. Section 4.4 compares the new estimates of real wages to earlier estimates, concluding that previous work has overstated real wage growth in the 1830s and understated real wage declines in the early 1850s. Section 4.5 presents evidence on regional real wage gaps in the North, finding that real wages were higher in the Midwest and that population redistribution raised the northern growth rate above the regional rates. Section 4.6 examines fluctuations in real wages, concluding that "shocks" had persistent effects. A summary is presented in section 4.7.

4.1 Real Wages and the Standard of Living

Economists use real wage indices to measure short- and long-run movements in the standard of living. Such analyses, particularly for historical economies like the antebellum United States, pose well-known problems of measurement and interpretation.[2] With respect to measurement, the major issues concern the payment period and variations in wages and prices around the mean or mode.

Ideally the numerator of a real wage index should reflect annual earnings—the product of a wage *rate* (hourly or daily) times the amount of time worked per year. Annual wages are preferable to hourly or daily wages because the former implicitly adjust for fluctuations in unemployment or long-run trends in time worked per year. An ideal index is comprehensive: it recognizes that, historically (as well as today), wages, prices, and consumption patterns as reflected in budget shares (used in the construction of price deflators) differ across the population. A narrowly defined real wage index (for example, masons employed in urban areas in the northeastern United States) may accurately represent aggregate trends *if* wage differentials are unchanging in the short and long run, but there is no good reason to assume this was ever true for *any* historical economy. Provided enough detail is available on the distri-

---

2. For useful discussions of some of the problems, see David and Solar (1977) and the various papers in Scholliers (1989).

bution of wages, prices, budget shares, and the relevant population weights (the proportion of masons employed in the Northeast), the construction of an aggregate index of real wages is straightforward, if computationally burdensome.[3]

Assuming these measurement problems can be solved, there is a larger question: what does a real wage index mean? Economically speaking, a real wage index is supposed to represent an individual worker's "budget constraint"; if the constraint moves outward (real wages increase), the worker is "better-off." However, even if the index is comprehensive as previously defined, it may be a poor representation of the budget constraint. At best, a real wage index can measure only the budget constraints of wage workers: the self-employed and owners of capital are excluded. Just as it is not wise to assume that wage trends for a narrowly defined population group mimic the average, it is not wise to assume that trends in incomes of the nonwage labor force closely resembled real wage movements. In many historical economies wages were a small share of workers' total compensation: they were paid in kind, or were paid by the piece, not by a money wage per unit of time. Such payments should be included in a real wage index; in practice, it may be difficult to find reliable data. Individuals spend all or part of their working lives as part of households in which other members may contribute income. Thus an individual's consumption possibilities may differ drastically from his or her earnings as a wage worker.

Subtle issues of interpretation involve the relationship between real wage growth and economic development. According to some scholars, the introduction of the factory system led to deleterious changes in work organization and increasing intensity of work. To accept these changes, workers required higher real wages; unadjusted for them, real wage indices overstate the degree to which economic welfare was rising. Rapid urbanization in the nineteenth century, which was associated with industrialization, led to reductions in nutritional status and health, at the same time that real wages may have been increasing (Fogel 1986).

As will become apparent as the paper unfolds, research on the antebellum United States is far from meeting these ideals. With the exception of Lebergott (1964), Adams (1982), and Sokoloff (1986b), most studies have examined daily wages, not annual earnings, despite evidence that the length of the work year not only differed between agriculture and manufacturing but also increased over time in the nonfarm sector (Gallman 1975; Adams 1986). In addition, there is indirect evidence that annual fluctuations in the length of the work year were significant (Keyssar 1986; Goldin and Margo 1992). Little is

3. "Straightforward" is meant in a practical sense, not in the sense that all problems associated with the construction of real wage indices can be solved in a believable fashion. Even if the wage and price data were ideal, there still would be the classic index number problem of valuing new products.

known about the effects of personal characteristics (for example, literacy, age, work experience, ethnicity) on wages.[4] Although evidence is mounting that health and nutritional status deteriorated in the late antebellum period at the same time that real wages were rising (Margo and Steckel 1983; Fogel 1986), there has been little work at reconciling these different measures of living standards, or at measuring the impact of changing working conditions and work intensity on wages.

Lest this discussion seem too pessimistic, my opinion is that the situation is not hopeless. There is a (very) long historiographic tradition of using real wages as a proxy for living standards, and tradition counts for something. Data on wages and prices are useful for many purposes, not just to construct proxies for economic welfare. As recent work on the British industrial revolution has demonstrated (Lindert and Williamson 1983), none of the problems are intractable; what *is* really needed in the American case is a great deal more evidence. With that goal in mind, I now turn to a survey of previous work on antebellum wages and prices.

4.2 Antebellum Wages and Prices: A Survey

4.2.1 Wages

Except in a few scattered years, no comprehensive national surveys of American wages were taken before the Civil War. In their place scholars have turned to late-nineteenth-century documents containing retrospective evidence and to archival records. Although this effort has yielded a significant amount of valuable information, there are still major gaps in the historical record.

The most famous compilations of wages for the nineteenth-century United States are two federal government documents: the Weeks report, published as part of the 1880 census (Weeks 1886); and the Aldrich report, published in conjunction with a Senate investigation in the early 1890s (Aldrich 1893). The two reports differ somewhat in detail, but their basic structures are the same: both were collected from payroll records of firms, and both are *retrospective* surveys—the data are time series of wages paid by firms that existed at the time of the survey.[5] Because many of the firms in the surveys had been in business for many years, one can use either report to estimate time series going back well into the nineteenth century (Abbott 1905; Hansen 1925). The

---

4. Gender is an exception; see Goldin and Sokoloff (1982) and Adams (1986).

5. Some firms had been in business longer than others, and one can study whether the length of time firms were in business affects the calculation of, for example, real wage changes. Suppose one is studying wage growth between (say) 1870 and 1880. By varying which firms are in the sample (i.e., only firms in existence for those ten years, versus those in existence prior to the 1870s), one can gauge the importance of the length of time firms were in business. But one cannot study how firms that came into existence prior to either survey *and* failed to survive until 1880 or 1983 affect the calculation.

best-known modern studies based wholly or in part on either report are David and Solar (1977) and Williamson and Lindert (1980). In both sources wages are disaggregated by firm (thus industry), occupation, and frequency of payment (daily or hourly), but the Weeks report does not give the number of observations underlying the firm averages.[6]

Although a fairly convincing case can be made that either report can be used to study late-nineteenth-century wage movements, their usefulness in studying antebellum patterns is another matter, particularly before 1850. The numbers of observations per year declines very sharply before 1840 (for example, for common labor between 1830 and 1832 the Weeks report contains *one* observation). Although it is unclear a priori whether the selection induced by retrospectiveness produces bias, selectivity is potentially a problem because the number of firms with antebellum data is small. The antebellum data pertain almost solely to the Northeast; little can be gleaned from either report about wages in the Midwest or the South, at least prior to the 1850s.

Partly in response to the inadequacies of both surveys and partly for other reasons, economic historians have turned to archival records. One such study is Walter B. Smith's (1963) well-known compilation of wages paid on the Erie Canal. Drawing on canal payroll records, Smith constructed annual estimates of the nominal and real daily wages of common laborers, carpenters, masons, and "teamwork" on the canal from 1828 to 1881.[7] In addition to Smith, important archival contributions have been made by Layer (1955), Lebergott (1964), Zabler (1972), Adams (1968, 1970, 1982, 1986), Sokoloff (1986b), and Rothenberg (1988). Layer used firm payrolls to construct estimates of wages for textile manufacturing workers beginning in the late 1830s. Lebergott pulled together wage estimates for various occupations from a wide array of government documents and even presented a long time series of seamen's wages but stopped short of constructing an annual index of real wages (Lebergott 1964, 150, provides educated guesses at real wage movements over medium-length periods, such as 1835 to 1850). Zabler used firm records to estimate occupation-specific wages in the iron industry in rural Pennsylvania from 1800 to 1830.

Without question the most prolific scholar in this area has been Donald Adams. In his 1968 and 1970 papers Adams used account books and firm records to estimate occupation-specific nominal wages in Philadelphia from 1780 to 1830. Adams also used wholesale prices for Philadelphia to construct indices of real wages over the same period. Adams (1982) used business records to estimate daily and annual earnings of manufacturing and farm labor

6. Early work favored the Aldrich report on these grounds (Abbott 1905) but Lebergott (1964) worked instead with the Weeks data, arguing that its coverage was better and it was less affected by sampling variability.

7. Smith's estimates are modes, not means, which complicates comparisons with other studies as well as any time-series analysis of the Erie Canal data (i.e., the mode is more stable than the mean).

in the Brandywine region around Philadelphia from 1800 to 1860. He concluded that, while there were substantial long-run increases in real daily wages and annual earnings, there were also significant short-run fluctuations. He also found rather large wage gaps between agriculture and manufacturing, suggesting that the sectoral shift of labor out of farming raised per capita income (later I discuss an analogous effect involving interregional migration). Adams (1986) presents estimates of wages of farm labor for Maryland from 1750 to 1850, finding an *absence* of real wage growth for farm labor from roughly 1820 to 1850.

Using the 1832 McLane report and the manuscript schedules of the federal manufacturing censuses of 1820, 1850, and 1860, Sokoloff (1986b) estimated average annual earnings of manufacturing workers at four benchmark dates. In addition to finding large increases in nominal and real earnings, Sokoloff also discovered a narrowing of urban-rural wage gaps in the Northeast, suggesting an improvement in the spatial efficiency of labor markets. Rothenberg (1988) mined account books to estimate nominal and real wages of farm labor in Massachusetts from 1750 to 1855. Like Sokoloff, Rothenberg also found evidence of an improvement in the spatial efficiency of farm labor markets.

These various studies illustrate the pluses and minuses of archival evidence. Use of archival records solves the problem of retrospectiveness. Archival records may contain great detail on the characteristics of workers and jobs, which is necessary for constructing wage estimates free of compositional changes over time or for regression studies of the cross-sectional determinants of wages (for example, Margo and Villaflor 1987). Unfortunately, the archival records that have been examined to date typically have pertained to a single employer or a small number of employers located in the Northeast. While further work on the Northeast would be valuable, archival research would make the greatest contribution by shifting attention to the Midwest or the South.

4.2.2 Prices

Antebellum data on prices have received less attention recently by economic historians. The major exceptions are Rothenberg (1979), who presents a price index for rural Massachusetts, and Adams (1986), who provides evidence on meat and grain prices in Maryland. Although much is known about wholesale prices in a few key markets, very little is known about retail prices. Available evidence on both is discussed in turn (see also Hoover 1958).

Wholesale prices. Relatively early in American history wholesale markets developed in several ports and inland cities located on navigable waterways. The activities of these markets generated an abundance of price quotations in newspapers, in documents known as "Prices Current," and in government and firm records (Hoover 1958). A vast number of quotations were compiled by Benzanson, Cole, Warren, and Pearson, and their various associates (Cole

1938). From these data wholesale price indices for New York, Philadelphia, Charleston, and Cincinnati were constructed (U.S. Bureau of the Census 1975). Because the wholesale price data are of high quality (compared with quantity data from the period), inferences about antebellum business cycles have frequently been gleaned from their annual movements (Smith and Cole 1935).

The general trend in wholesale prices before 1860 is well-known. Although long-term drift was downward (at least from the early 1820s), short-term movements were highly variable. Prices rose in the mid-1830s, peaked in the late 1830s, and then declined sharply during the early 1840s. The next big upward surge in prices occurred in the early 1850s, followed again by a decline. Perhaps the major exception to a long-term downward drift occurred in the Midwest. Improvements in internal transportation caused the Midwest to experience a long-term rise in its terms of trade—prices of agricultural goods produced in the Midwest rose relative to the price of nonagricultural goods (Berry 1943). Although the improvement in the terms of trade raised the incomes of midwestern farmers, it appears to have hurt nonfarm workers in the region, who produced substitutes for nonfarm goods imported from the Northeast and for whom food was a major item of household budgets. Real wages in the Midwest grew less rapidly before the Civil War than in the Northeast, in part because of the terms of trade effect (Ross 1985; Margo and Villaflor 1987).

Studies of real wages have frequently used wholesale price data to construct price deflators (Hansen 1925; Adams 1968; Williamson and Lindert 1980). The major problems in doing so are discussed later. For now, I would note that, although the cities covered by the wholesale data were the major wholesale markets, they were far from being the only wholesale markets. Thus, for example, using New York price data to deflate nominal wages in Syracuse or Albany (the Erie Canal) presumes that markets in the two locations were spatially integrated. Rothenberg's (1981) finding of a strong positive correlation between her price index for rural Massachusetts and wholesale prices in New York City and Philadelphia suggests this assumption is not totally unreasonable, at least for markets in close geographic proximity. However, it remains to be seen if the assumption is valid for other parts of the country, such as the Midwest or the South.

Retail prices. Compared with wholesale price data, antebellum data on retail prices are sparse. Virtually all attempts to construct an antebellum cost-of-living index based on retail prices have relied on T. M. Adams's (1939) pioneering study of prices paid by Vermont farmers. Although Adams's study is valuable, there are serious (and well-known) problems with the Vermont data. Foods consumed by working-class nonfarm households are not covered in the Vermont data. The Vermont data show a steep long-term downward trend from the early 1820s that some scholars (Lebergott 1964) believe to be exaggerated. Price deflators based on the Vermont data thus might be expected to produce relatively large increases in real wages, at least compared with deflators based on wholesale prices (see section 4.4).

Other significant contributions have been made by Brady (1966) and Hoover (1960). Using data compiled originally by the Massachusetts Department of Labor and by herself from Pennsylvania account books and store records, Brady calculated average retail prices for a large number of goods for six benchmark dates: 1809, 1834, 1836, 1839, 1844, and 1849. Based on data from the Weeks report, Hoover (1960) constructed a retail price index covering the period 1851 to 1880, later extending the index back to 1800 (U.S. Bureau of the Census 1975).

David and Solar (1977) used the Vermont data, Brady's benchmark figures, Hoover's index, and wholesale prices from Philadelphia to construct a cost-of-living index going back to 1774. Because neither the Vermont data nor Brady provided evidence on housing prices, David and Solar constructed a proxy for annual reproduction costs of housing, using data on common labor wages and building materials prices. David and Solar's index (1821 to 1986) is plotted in figure 4.1.

Although carefully constructed from the available evidence, the David-Solar index has serious limitations. To fill the gaps between Brady's benchmark dates, David and Solar interpolated using the Vermont data. The interpolation was trend-corrected (adjusted for the different long-run trends in the Vermont and Brady's data), but it is unclear whether the Vermont data should be used for this purpose (see section 4.4). The David-Solar index is a hybrid between a northeastern (pre-1850) and a national (post-1850) price index. Thus, while it may be used to deflate nominal wages for the Northeast (at least before 1850) using it to deflate wage estimates for other regions is dubious, especially in light of known regional differences in wholesale price trends (Berry 1943).

The most serious problem with the David-Solar index is its proxy for housing costs. David and Solar justify their proxy by arguing that most housing during the period depreciated very rapidly (for example, the balloon-frame house). Consequently, an index of annual reproduction costs would appear to be appropriate. Even if this assumption were tenable, the adequacy of a proxy based on common laborers' wages and building materials remains to be demonstrated (see David and Solar 1977, 45–46, for an attempt to do so). However, much of the wage data for the Northeast pertains to urban locations, or to locations where housing was of a more permanent nature. There is considerable qualitative evidence that rental prices of housing deviated from reproduction costs in the short run, particularly during periods of high immigration (Lebergott 1964; Fogel 1989; Blackmar 1989). There is also evidence that the rental component of Hoover's price index grossly understates increases in housing prices in the Northeast in the early 1850s (Fogel, Galantine, and

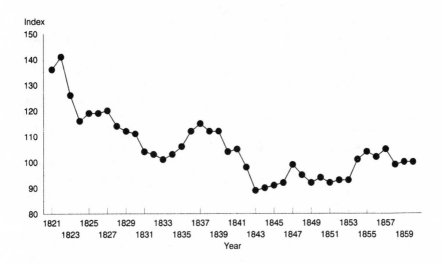

Fig. 4.1   David-Solar price index (1860 = 100)
Source: David and Solar (1977).

Manning 1992). Thus the usefulness of David and Solar's proxy for housing costs is questionable.

4.3   Civilian Wage Data in Military Records

Since its inception the U.S. Army has hired civilians to perform various tasks at military installations.[8] Quartermasters were responsible for the hiring, and they also were required to keep duplicate monthly records, one copy of which was eventually sent to Washington. Extent civilian payrolls covering the period 1818 to 1905 are called the *Reports of Persons and Articles Hired* and are currently lodged at the National Archives in Record Group 92. A large sample of payrolls covering the period 1818 to 1856 has been collected and put on computer tape (Margo and Villaflor 1987). The unit of observation is a "person-month"—for example, if a man was hired as a teamster for three months at $15 per month, he contributes three observations to the sample.

Because the army was charged with forging a path to the frontier, the composition of the *Reports* sample with respect to location, timing, and occupation differs from what a purely random sample of the antebellum population would yield (Margo and Villaflor 1987, 875–76). For example, frontier locations—the west North Central and west South Central regions—are overrep-

8. In addition to data on civilian wages at army installations, there are considerable wage data for arsenals and naval yards; see Heppner and John (1968).

resented. The number of observations per decade is generally large, except in the 1820s and in the Northeast and South Atlantic regions in the 1850s. Although most of the tasks civilian workers performed had their counterparts in the civilian economy, occupations in the building trades (and clerical occupations) are overrepresented relative to the civilian population.

Perhaps the most serious problem with the *Reports* is whether the army paid competitive wages. The forts were not competitive firms. Quartermasters had few incentives to hire the best workers at the lowest cost. This issue can be investigated by comparing wages at the forts with wages in the same location from purely civilian records. Based on comparisons made thus far, it appears that wages at the forts were similar in level to purely civilian wages (Margo and Villaflor 1987, 877). I stress this conclusion is a limited one. Systematic comparisons have been made only for a few locations (for example, upstate New York forts and the Erie Canal) or for isolated years (between the *Reports* and 1850 census data). More work needs to be done comparing the *Reports* with purely civilian sources, particularly for locations in the Midwest and the South.

By comparison with other archival sources for the antebellum period, the spatial, temporal, and occupational coverage of the *Reports* sample is quite good.[9] It is not good enough, however, to produce finely disaggregated wage series for the entire 1821 to 1856 period, for example, by simple averaging of the original data. Instead, hedonic wage regressions were estimated, and the regression coefficients form the basis for annual dollar estimates of nominal wages of common laborers/teamsters, and skilled artisans for the four census regions (Northeast, Midwest, South Atlantic, and South Central). Because the regressions reveal a good deal of information about the cross-sectional determinants of antebellum wages and because the methodology differs from that used in previous research on antebellum wages, the details are reported here in an appendix.

To convert one of the nominal wage series into an index of real wages, one must deflate by an index of prices. Since the wage series are region-specific, so should the price indices be. The only available region-specific price data pertain to wholesale prices (see section 4.2.2). Using these data, Goldin and Margo (1992) estimated region-specific price deflators.[10] For the purposes of deflating nominal wages, the new price indices are superior to those previously constructed from wholesale price data, because the new indices are based on a set of commodities consumed by households (for example, flour, pork, coffee) and exclude commodities like iron bars and so forth that were

9. The *Reports* are not, however, comprehensive with respect to the variety of occupations found in the antebellum United States, for example, in the 1850 census. Thus the *Reports* cannot be used to reconstruct the antebellum wage structure in fine detail.

10. The price indices are geometrically weighted aggregates of price indices of specific goods; see Goldin and Margo (1992).

not consumed by households (but that were included in other wholesale price indices).[11]

The limitations of the new price indices are serious and should be kept in mind. *No* adjustment has been made for housing prices. It is assumed in the construction of the indices that wholesale price data for, say, New Orleans provides a usable price deflator for the entire South Central region. The wholesale price data do not give prices of finished textile products for all regions. It is therefore necessary to assume, for example, that long-term trends in retail prices of shoes were the same as long-term trends in wholesale leather prices. This assumption is false, because it ignores productivity growth in finished textile production (Sokoloff 1986a). Fuel prices are proxied by the wholesale price of coal even though wood was widely used in rural areas and wood and coal prices diverged in the long run (David and Solar 1977). Budget shares are assumed to be the same in every region, even though relative prices differed geographically.

The real wage indices are graphed in figures 4.2–4.5 (the indices are reported in table 4A.1). In general, real wage growth was less in the South than in the North. Real wages also grew more slowly in the Midwest than in the Northeast, but the opposite pattern occurred in comparing the South Atlantic and South Central regions. Real wage growth was more rapid in the 1840s than in the 1830s or early 1850s.

Williamson and Lindert (1980; see also Kuznets 1955 and Lindert and Williamson 1982) investigated whether income inequality in the United States worsened between 1820 and 1860. Because there are no income statistics for the period, Williamson and Lindert used skill differentials—the ratio of skilled to unskilled wages—as a proxy for inequality, arguing that skill differentials increased in the late antebellum period (for a contrary view see Grosse 1982). Data from the *Reports,* however, suggest that real wages of common laborers/teamsters grew faster (or at about the same rate) as the real wages of artisans, and thus provide no evidence that a surge in skill differentials took place.[12]

Table 4.1 gives estimates of the long-run rate of growth of real wages. Three different methods are used to estimate the long-run growth rate: a regression of the (log) real wage on a linear trend, a straight-line interpolation between decadal averages (1851–56 compared with 1821–30), and the mean of the growth rates (the mean of the first difference of the log wage). Using the regression method, the estimated growth rates range from a low of 0.4 percent per annum (midwestern artisans) to a high of 1.6 percent (laborers in the Northeast). The regression method gives higher growth rates than either

---

11. In this respect they are similar to the price deflators employed by Hansen (1925), Adams (1968), and Williamson and Lindert (1980).

12. Goldin and Margo (1992) show that wages of clerks increased more than wages of common laborers/teamsters, providing some support for the surge hypothesis.

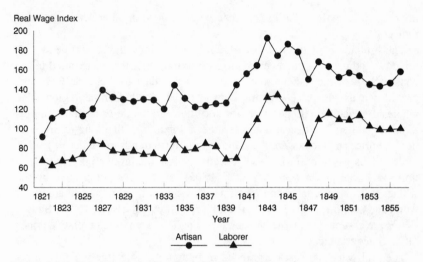

Fig. 4.2   Real wages in the Northeast (common laborer/teamster, 1856 = 100)
Source: See text.

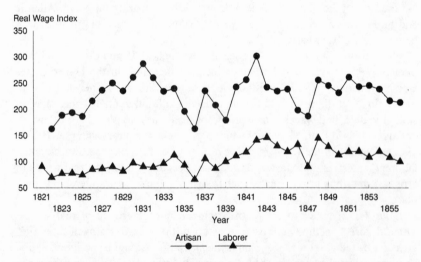

Fig. 4.3   Real wages in the Midwest (common laborer/teamster, 1856 = 100)
Source: See text.

the decadal averages or mean of the growth rates. This difference reflects the fact that real wages in every region fell in the early 1850s. Regional and occupational differences, however, are generally the same regardless of the method used to estimate the long-term trend.

The new evidence confirms that real wages in the United States were higher in the 1850s than in the 1820s. Growth, however, was uneven geographically

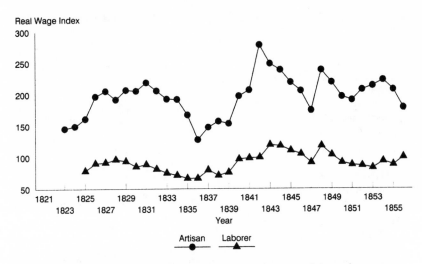

Fig. 4.4   Real wages in the South Atlantic states (common laborer/teamster, 1856 = 100)
Source: See text.

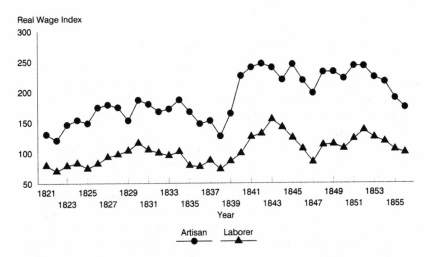

Fig. 4.5   Real wages in the South Central states (common laborer/teamster, 1856 = 100)
Source: See text.

and differed across occupations. Further, real wages did not increase in a steady fashion from year to year. Rather, growth was highly erratic, sometimes rising or falling very sharply in short periods of time (similar findings were reported by Adams 1982). I shall return to the erratic nature of real wage growth in section 4.6.

Table 4.1   Real Wage Growth during the Antebellum Period

	Artisans	Common Laborers/ Teamsters
Coefficient on trend (ln $w = \alpha + \beta t$)		
Northeast	0.0114	0.0155
Midwest	0.0038	0.0142
South Atlantic	0.0043	0.0059
South Central	0.0140	0.0120
Decadal averages (1821–30/1851–56)		
Northeast	0.0081	0.0121
Midwest	0.0036	0.0107
South Atlantic	0.0039	0.0001
South Central	0.0112	0.0106
Mean of growth rates		
Northeast	0.0156	0.0113
Midwest	0.0081	0.0027
South Atlantic	0.0062	0.0077
South Central	0.0082	0.0067

Source: See text.

Note: Figures are average annual changes in the log of real daily wage, 1821–56.

4.4   Comparing Different Estimates of Real Wage Growth

Because there are no alternative series for the antebellum South or Midwest, it is difficult to assess the novelty of the insights provided by the real wage indices presented in the previous section. It is possible, however, to compare the new index of unskilled wages for the Northeast to previously constructed indices.

The basic issues are as follows: the Margo-Villaflor (hereafter MV) index shows relatively little real wage growth in the 1830s, considerable growth in the 1840s, and a sharp decline in real wages in the early 1850s (see also Hansen 1925). By comparison, the index of unskilled wages constructed by David and Solar (1977; hereafter DS) shows a steady rise from decade to decade. The unskilled index constructed by Williamson and Lindert (1980; hereafter WL) shows considerable growth in the 1830s and a decline in the early 1850s.

These discrepancies lead to radically different pictures of the antebellum economy. The 1820s and 1830s (before the Panic of 1837) are frequently characterized as years of economic expansion, yet the MV index implies that unskilled nonfarm workers gained little from that expansion. The decline in real wages in the early 1850s shown by the MV and WL indices (but not the DS index) has recently been given considerable weight in explanations of the political realignment of the 1850s (Fogel 1990).

Table 4.2 shows the differences in decadal averages between the three series. The MV index shows a smaller increase in nominal wages in the 1830s

Table 4.2   **Explaining Different Estimates of Real Wage Growth; Unskilled Labor, 1821–56**

Nominal wages

	Margo-Villaflor	David-Solar	Williamson-Lindert
1821–30	100.0	100.0	100.0
1831–40	108.9	109.6	130.0
1841–50	119.8	104.5	129.0
1851–56	138.1	121.5	141.8

Margo-Villaflor real wage index with different price deflators

	David-Solar	Goldin-Margo
1821–30	100.0	100.0
1831–40	122.4	103.7
1841–50	153.9	152.8
1851–56	171.0	140.5

David-Solar real wage index with different price deflators

	David-Solar	Goldin-Margo
1821–30	100.0	100.0
1831–40	122.7	104.1
1841–50	133.3	132.8
1851–56	150.6	123.9

Williamson-Lindert real wage index with different price deflators

	David-Solar	Goldin-Margo
1821–30	100.0	100.0
1831–40	146.0	123.6
1841–50	164.8	163.0
1851–56	175.4	143.9

than either the DS index or especially the WL index. In the 1840s, the MV index shows another increase, while the DS and WL indices both show declines. Growth in nominal wages from 1841–50 to 1851–56 is about the same in the MV and DS indices but is smaller in the WL index.

The remainder of the table shows the decadal average of real wages using either the DS or Goldin and Margo (1992; hereafter GM) price deflator. Clearly the major difference between the MV and DS indices in the 1830s is a consequence of the price deflator. If the DS price deflator is used with the MV nominal wage index, real wages growth is just slightly less than that shown by the DS real wage index. However, the WL nominal wage index shows much greater real wage growth in the 1830s than either the DS or MV indices.

Comparing the 1840s to the 1830s all of the indices show much less real wage growth using the DS price deflator than using the GM price deflator. The GM price deflator is also primarily responsible for the decline in real wages in the early 1850s; if the DS price deflator is used instead, all of the indices show growth. It is also clear that the GM price deflator gives a somewhat lower long-run rate of growth (comparing the 1850s to the 1820s) than the DS price deflator.

As a first step toward reconciling the differences across the real wage indices, I consider how the WL and DS indices of nominal wages were derived. For 1821 to 1830 DS used data originally collected by the Massachusetts Bureau of Labor Statistics. For 1831 to 1839 DS used geometrically weighted averages for Erie Canal and Abbott's (1905) calculations of average wages from the Weeks report. From 1840 to 1880 DS spliced into the Weeks data. For 1821 to 1834 the WL index consists of quotations from Adams's (1939) Vermont data. For 1835 to 1839 WL spliced into Layer's (1955) wage series for *manufacturing* workers. From 1840 to 1860 the WL index consists of observations on common labor drawn from the Aldrich report.

It is likely that splicing accounts for the differences between the MV and the DS and WL nominal wage estimates. Although DS purport to rely on wage observations from the Northeast for the pre-1840s part of their index, the Weeks quotations for 1836 to 1838 actually pertain to St. Louis, which had much higher than average nominal wages (see the Midwest regressions in the Appendix). The WL index shows an abrupt increase in nominal wages in 1835 (the point of the splice to Layer), an increase not present in the other indices. The DS and WL indices overstate nominal wage growth in the 1830s. This overstatement, in turn, causes both indices to show less real wage growth from the 1830s to the 1840s than does the MV index.[13]

Differences in nominal wages, however, do not fully account for differences in real wage growth. The choice of a price deflator is crucial. As pointed out earlier, to construct the pre-1850 portion of their price index, DS relied on Vermont data and Brady's (1966) retail price quotations at benchmark dates. After 1850 DS spliced into Hoover's (1960) index, which was based on retail price quotations from the Weeks report.

Part of the difference between the DS and GM price deflators could be explained if wholesale prices were more variable in the short- and medium-run than retail prices. DS purport to show such a difference by graphing their index against the Warren and Pearson wholesale price index, and by estimating a regression of their index on an index of Philadelphia wholesale prices. These comparisons are questionable because the DS price index and the wholesale price indices are not based on a common set of goods (this is particularly true for the nonbenchmark years, since the Vermont data do not include price quotations for many of the goods regularly traded in wholesale markets). The correlation between short-run movements in wholesale and retail prices is discussed further in section 4.6. Here I simply wish to note again the neces-

---

13. The level of the WL real wage index in the 1840s (using the GM deflator) is higher than the MV real wage index level. This difference is primarily due to WL's use of Vermont nominal wages, which are lower in the 1820s than indicated by other sources.

sity of more and better retail price data in order to properly measure the relationship between retail and wholesale fluctuations.

This point aside, the basic reason the DS price deflator shows much larger real wage increases in the 1830s can be traced to two aspects of the index. First, the DS price index shows a much greater decline in prices from 1821–23 to 1831–33 than does the GM index. This is a consequence of the use of the Adams series as an interpolator, which shows an extremely steep rate of decline, much steeper than the decline in wholesale prices over the same period. Although DS corrected the Adams interpolator for its excessive downward trend relative to Brady's benchmark dates, they had no benchmark date for the early 1820s. That the Adams interpolator gives too steep a rate of price decline is confirmed by DS's regression of their index on Philadelphia wholesale prices. The *predicted* DS index from the regression shows a smaller decline in prices between 1821–23 and 1831–33 than the actual DS index. Until more evidence on retail prices from the early 1820s is found, it seems prudent not to rely on the DS price index for those years.

Second, the DS price index shows a smaller increase in prices from 1834 to 1839 (especially 1834 to 1836) than does the GM price index. Comparing 1834 to 1836, the GM index increases from 84.6 to 110.2, but the increase in the DS index is much less, 103 to 112. Some of this difference can be traced to Brady's data and to DS's expenditure weights. Brady's data show sharp declines in prices of coffee and tea (two consumption staples) between 1834 and 1836, declines not present in wholesale price data. Brady's data also show extraordinary short-run declines in the prices of several clothing items, such as hosiery, buttons, and cotton thread. In constructing their price index, DS gave a lower weight to food (39.5 percent) than is customary in nineteenth-century price indices. This tends to dampen price increases in the mid-1830s because Brady's data show larger increases in food prices between 1834 and 1839 than do her nonfood prices.[14] If one uses Brady's data, substitutes wholesale prices for coffee and tea, and excludes clothing items with extremely steep price declines, the revised DS index shows an increase in prices between 1834 and 1836 of about 18 percent. This is still a smaller increase than shown by the GM index; the remaining difference may be due to short-run differences in wholesale and retail price changes.

The next issue concerns the decline in real wages in the early 1850s. As is clear from table 4.2, this difference, too, is a consequence of the choice of a price deflator. The basic reason the DS price index results in an increase in real wages while the GM deflator results in a decrease turns on the behavior of the subindices making up the Hoover (1960) price index. First, the Hoover food price subindex shows a much smaller increase in food prices from 1851 to 1856 than does the GM price index and virtually no change in clothing

14. For example, Hoover's (1960) budget share for food was 59 percent.

prices over the same period, despite a 39 percent rise in the wholesale price of cotton and a 70 percent rise in the wholesale price of leather in the Northeast. Second, the Hoover index includes a rent component, which displays very little increase in housing prices between 1851 and 1856. Yet there is considerable anecdotal evidence of rising housing prices, particularly in northeastern cities in the early 1850s, due to massive immigration. The problem, as Lebergott (1964) observed some time ago (see also Fogel, Galantine, and Manning 1992), is that much of the Weeks data pertained to company stores and company-owned housing in small towns. Price movements in the Weeks data may be artificially dampened because of the nature of the sample; thus use of the Weeks price data leads to too rosy a picture for real wages in the early 1850s.

Thus far I have argued that the discrepancies between the various indices arise primarily because of biases in the DS an WL nominal wage indices and in the DS price index. Yet not all of the problems rest with the DS and WL indices. Because the MV index was derived from an hedonic regression that did not fit the data perfectly, some of the year-to-year variability in real wages is noise. The number of observations underlying certain estimates is small—sometimes smaller than the number available in the Aldrich or Weeks reports for particular years (this is especially true in the late 1840s and early 1850s). Even with these problems, the advantages of the new indices are considerable. They are not spliced from disparate data sources, and they control for changing sample composition from year to year.

The MV indices suggest that real wage growth may have been less than previously thought in the 1830s and that real wages fell in the early 1850s. It is important to stress that these conclusions rest on the choice of a price deflator. Although a case has been made here against the DS price deflator, the GM price deflator is far from perfect. It lacks a housing price component, and one is forced to assume that yearly changes in wholesale prices mimicked yearly changes in retail prices. Further work is necessary to determine if the conclusions implied by the new indices are sustained with better price deflators.

4.5   Regional Differences: The Northeast and the Midwest

The indices presented in section 4.3 do not show how real wage levels differed between regions. Here I estimate the ratio of real wages in the Midwest relative to the Northeast. Real wages were generally higher in the Midwest, and there was a slight but erratic downward trend in the Midwest/Northeast ratio of real wages. This downward trend is consistent with the direction of internal migration in the North and also suggests the (modest) beginnings of regional labor market integration. That real wages were higher in the Midwest implies that population redistribution raised the northern growth rate above the rate experienced in the Northeast or the Midwest.

To estimate the ratio of real wages in the Midwest relative to the Northeast, it is necessary to construct an index of relative regional prices. This index, like the ones constructed by Goldin and Margo (1992), is based on wholesale price data.

Basic findings are shown in figures 4.6 (artisans) and 4.7 (common laborers/teamsters). Among artisans, real wages were almost always higher in the Midwest than in the Northeast. The wage gap increased in the late 1820s but then declined in the early 1830s, consistent with the sharp increase in immigration into the Midwest during that period. The gap also declined in the early 1840s. The Midwest was hit harder by the depression of the early 1840s than the Northeast was (North 1966). The gap then increased in the late 1840s as recovery occurred. The decline in the gap in the early 1850s was a consequence of rising in-migration plus the temporary glutting of midwestern labor markets due to the ending of the railroad-building boom (Fogel 1989).

The results for common laborers/teamsters indicate greater regional similarity, but this conclusion is heavily influenced by the inclusion of Pittsburgh in the Midwest. Unskilled wages were much lower in Pittsburgh than at other forts in the Midwest (see the Appendix). If Pittsburgh were included in the Northeast, the real wage gap would have been substantial.

The notes to the figures show regressions of the regional real wage ratio on a time trend. The negative coefficient on the time trend for artisans suggest the beginnings of regional labor market integration. Rosenbloom (1990) recently investigated labor market integration in the North in the late nineteenth century. If one uses the regression in figure 4.5 to predict the regional wage gap in the mid-1870s, the gap is predicted to be about 7 percent, which is quite close to Rosenbloom's estimate of the regional gap (8.5 percent for building tradesmen). Thus, while integration of regional labor markets for skilled artisans began in the antebellum period, the pace at which integration took place was rather slow. For common laborers/teamsters, there is little evidence of regional integration at all.

The principal implication of these results concerns the difference between aggregate (northern) rates of growth of real wages and regional rates of growth. Because real wages were higher in the Midwest than in the Northeast, the shift of population from the Midwest to the Northeast raised the overall growth rate of real wages in the North.[15] The result confirms other research showing that per capita income growth in the North was accomplished with the aid of interregional migration (Fogel 1989) and that the existence of sectoral shifts in the context of wage gaps contributed to antebellum growth (David 1967; Adams 1982).

---

15. Because regional differences were much smaller by the early twentieth century (Rosenbloom 1990), improved labor market integration contributed to economic growth in the North over the nineteenth century. Calculating the size of this contribution would be difficult, however, because it would be necessary to determine how much of the regional wage gap was a *disequilibrium* rather than a compensating differential for mobility costs.

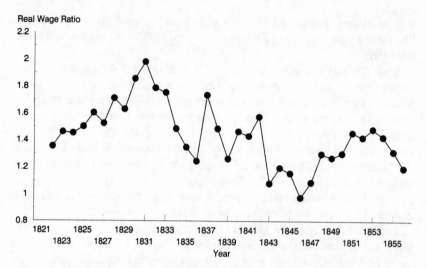

Fig. 4.6   Real wage ratio, artisans, Midwest/Northeast
ln (ratio) = 0.501 − 0.0079*Time R^2 = .23
Source: See text.

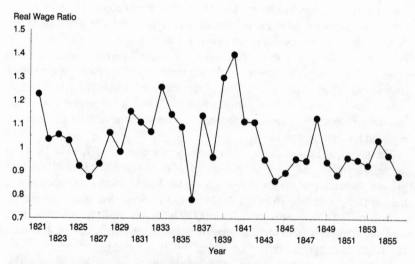

Fig. 4.7   Real wage ratio, laborers, Midwest/Northeast
ln (ratio) = 0.083 − 0.0034*Time R^2 = .053
Source: See text.

4.6   The Short-Run Behavior of Wages and Prices

It is clear from the evidence presented earlier that the growth rate of real wages fluctuated a great deal in the short and medium run. Antebellum growth in real wages was not a continuous affair. Rather, growth was uneven from year to year, punctuated by periods of sharp increases and equally sharp declines.

These fluctuations were not randomly timed over the antebellum period. The fluctuations were correlated with short-run movements in prices and with real shocks. Nominal wages did not adjust instantaneously—when prices rose, as in the mid-1830s, real wages fell; when prices fell in the early 1840s, real wages rose.[16] Declining real wages in the early 1850s appear to have been a combination of nominal wages lagging behind rising prices and downward pressure on nominal wages caused by a sudden wave of immigration and other real shocks (Fogel 1989).

The short-run behavior of wages and prices may have important implications for understanding the antebellum macroeconomy. Even if, in the long run, real wages followed an equilibrium growth path determined by real factors (productivity growth and the growth of factor supplies), real wages in the short run could have been persistently below or above their long-run level. If they were, it is possible that fluctuations in employment could have been large. Although some economic historians have argued against such a view of antebellum business cycles (Temin 1969), others have attached great importance to short-run fluctuations (Fogel 1989, 1990).

In a recent paper, Goldin and Margo (1992) examined the time-series properties of the MV real wage series. The basic issue was whether real wages followed a long-run growth path dictated by long-run movements in real factors, which were captured by a linear time trend or by a proxy for per capita GNP.[17] No evidence was found against the view that real wages did follow such a path. But Goldin and Margo also found that short-run deviations from the long-run path were quite persistent—for example, up to five years were needed to restore equilibrium after a price (or other) shock.[18] Deviations were

16. The stability of nominal wages in the face of wide fluctuations in commodity prices is a very old (and apparently universal) problem in economic history; see, for example, the various papers in Scholliers (1989).

17. Posed somewhat differently, this question was also investigated by David and Solar (1977, 37–39), Sokoloff (1986b), and Rothenberg (1988). Using very different methods, similar results were obtained for a number of nineteenth-century European economies by Bairoch (1989).

18. Williamson (in his comment to this paper) speculates that the result may be an artifact of the use of hedonic regressions to construct the nominal wage indices. But a regression is merely a particular way of obtaining an average. Hence, if nominal wages are stable from year to year while prices fluctuate *and* the fit of the regression is less than perfect (which was the case), it follows that some wage changes at the individual level were *opposite* in sign to contemporaneous price changes. Disaggregating to the individual level will not answer the question why shocks were persistent *on average,* which is the question posed by Goldin and Margo (1992). The persistence of shocks is largely the consequence of a few episodes in which large nominal or real shocks occurred.

more persistent in the Northeast than in the North Central region, and for skilled labor than for unskilled labor. Goldin and Margo also found that deviations were largely transitory for agricultural labor, which suggests that the large farm sector may have served as an important buffer against urban unemployment during economic downturns (Temin 1969; Keyssar 1986).

Persistence of shocks to real wages may not seem very surprising, given similar findings for the post-1860 period (DeCanio and Mokyr 1977; James 1989; Hanes 1990). But it leaves open the question as to why, in an economy previously characterized as satisfying textbook properties of flexibility (Temin 1969), persistent effects of shocks should be present at all.

One possibility is imperfect information (Lucas 1981). Antebellum firms may have confused absolute price changes—inflation or deflation—with relative price changes. Thinking that absolute change was specific to their industry, firms may have been led to adjust real quantities (labor) rather than nominal quantities (wages). Although the Northeast had the most developed markets of the period, the difficulty of distinguishing relative and absolute price changes may have been greater in regions, such as the Northeast, with more heterogeneous goods than in simpler economies such as the Midwest.

With modern data, a standard way of testing for such an effect is to examine the relationship between average price changes (inflation or deflation) and changes in relative price dispersion (the variance of relative prices). If average price changes were neutral, they should bear no systematic relationship with the variance of relative prices. Recent research tends to reject this conclusion, generally finding a significant positive relationship between the variance of price changes and the mean price change (see the references cited in Quddus, Liu, and Butler 1988).

Using wholesale price data for New York City, relative price dispersion is defined to be the variance of the first difference of the logarithm of annual price changes for ten commodities. The overall rate of price change is the square of the unweighted average of the individual price changes, or the rate of change of the Warren-Pearson price index.

A positive correlation between average price change and relative price dispersion is revealed by simple regressions of the variance of price changes (VR) on the squared mean price change (unweighted average, UA, or Warren-Pearson, WP):

$$VR = 0.004 + 0.679UA$$
$$(4.459) \quad (7.336) \quad R^2 = .47$$

$$VR = 0.005 + 0.287WP$$
$$(4.851) \quad (3.507) \quad R^2 = .16$$

A positive correlation, however, is not the same as causation. Causation can be investigated using a Granger causality test. If the theory were correct, one would expect the causality to run from average price changes to increased relative price dispersion. However, the results are exactly the opposite—causality runs from relative price dispersion to average price changes.[19]

Although the causality result may appear puzzling, it is consistent with accounts of antebellum business cycles, particularly the Panic of 1837. During the 1830s the United States was on a specie standard together with free banking. In the early 1830s favorable harvests in Great Britain and rising British prices led to capital exports to the United States and a trade deficit. To restore equilibrium, American prices—particularly cotton prices—had to rise. For prices to rise the money supply had to increase, and most of the increase (in the mid-1830s) resulted from an inflow of specie. The increase in the money supply, in turn, caused wholesale prices to rise, with a slight lag. Thus the causality ran from a real shock in Great Britain—good harvests—to relative price dispersion in the United States, an increase in the money supply, and ultimately to a higher American price level (Temin 1969).

The causality test does not rule out an imperfect information explanation of persistence, but it does suggest that other factors were involved. One possibility involves the time-series properties of the antebellum price level. Recent work suggests the antebellum price level can be approximated by an integrated time series (Goldin and Margo 1992). An integrated time series is nonstationary—it does not return to a fixed mean, unlike a stationary series. An example of an integrated time series is a random walk. Were the price level a true random walk, price changes—inflation or deflation—would be white noise—a mean-zero, serially uncorrelated time series. In thinking about this possibility, keep in mind that it is extremely difficult to distinguish an integrated series from a near-integrated series (which is still stationary), yet this distinction may have been crucial to behavior. Also, standard tests can reject stationarity even if the series is stationary over subperiods but the mean shifts from one subperiod to the next (see below).

It is easy to see how random walk–like movements in prices could lead to wild ex post fluctuations in real wages in the short run. Consider a worker hired for, say, a six-month period. During the period of the contract the worker may consume all sorts of goods whose prices fluctuate unpredictably in the short run. Even if it were costless to continuously renegotiate labor contracts, price fluctuations might be tolerated by the worker because (if average price changes were truly white noise) the real wage will be constant, on average, over the period of the contract. Ex post, the real wage fluctuates a great deal within the period. If it is difficult to determine if a particular sequence of price changes is serially correlated (is persistent) and if it is costly to renegotiate labor contracts, one might observe persistent deviations in real wages from

19. Tests of Granger causality from mean price changes to relative price dispersion yielded F-statistics of 0.24 (UA) and 0.56 (WP). Tests of Grander causality from relative price dispersion to mean price changes yielded F-statistics of 5.01 (UA) and 2.82 (WP). The latter two statistics are significant at the 5 percent level. The lag length for the tests was set at 3 (three years).

long-run equilibrium values. Only when inflation or deflation became abundantly clear would nominal wages adjust, possibly abruptly.

This analysis may be relevant for the antebellum period. Although labor contracts were generally quite brief during the period, in the sense that workers might be hired by the day or the month, it does not follow that all parameters of such contracts, such as the nominal wage, would be renegotiated continuously. This is especially true if, as was the case during the antebellum period, the price level might be close to stationary (or stationary around a downward trend) for several years, only to suddenly shift upward or downward. During the inflation of the mid-1830s, strikes by journeyman cabinetmakers in New York are said to have been motivated by the fact that "the price book [giving journeymen's wages] used by their masters was more than a quarter of a century old. . . . the old book failed to keep up with the cost of living" (Wilentz 1984, 231). It was these sudden shifts, due to international events (the 1830s) or gold discoveries (1850s), that led first to confusion, then to a revision of price expectations, and ultimately to nominal wage adjustments.

Nor is the point relevant for just the antebellum period. After the Civil War (1870 to 1897) deflation became a fact of economic life. Then in 1898, gold discoveries led to rapid price increases. Expectations did not adjust immediately, and real wages fell. The adjustment lag was not necessarily irrational. Barsky and De Long (1988) have recently shown that sophisticated economic agents, given the information available at the time, might have concluded there was no necessary positive relationship between changes in specie production and changes in the price level.[20] Ex post they were wrong, but not necessarily ex ante.

4.7 Summary

This paper has surveyed recent work on prices and wages before the Civil War. Although there are serious shortcomings in the available data, the evidence suggests that, with notable exceptions, long-run growth in real wages was substantial before the Civil War. Because real wages were higher in the Midwest than in the Northeast, population redistribution raised the average rate of growth of real wages in the North.

But the research also suggests that real wage growth was erratic in the short run, and that shocks to real wages had persistent effects. Historians have emphasized the importance of these fluctuations to the social, labor, and political history of the period, and rightly so. But a comprehensive explanation of the persistence of shocks to real wages during the antebellum period remains to be developed.

20. As Barsky and De Long (1988) demonstrate, it is this adjustment lag that causes late-nineteenth-century interest rates to violate the "Fisher" equation, namely, that the real interest rate equals the nominal rate plus the expected rate of change in the price level.

Appendix
Nominal Wage Estimates

This appendix describes the nominal wage estimates used in the construction of the real wage indices (see table 4A.1).[21] The hedonic wage regressions are reported in tables 4A.2–4A.5.

Weighting Procedure

The idea is to attach to each fort location a decade-specific share of the region's population and to each occupation (within the skilled and unskilled groups) an occupational share. The weight for the variables MONTHLY, HIGH, LOW, and SLAVE (South Atlantic and South Central) is zero; for SPRING, SUMMER, and FALL the weight is 0.25.[22] The wage estimates refer to ordinary skilled or unskilled workers, hired on a daily basis, averaged over the year to account for seasonal variations. The fort location and occupation weights are shown in table 4A.6.

The fort weights were derived from population figures in U.S. Bureau of the Census (1975, ser. A 195–209) and are decade-by-decade averages. For example, the fort weight for southern New England for the 1820s (0.244) is the average of the share of the northeastern population living in Massachusetts, New Hampshire, Connecticut, and Rhode Island in 1820 and 1830. Similarly, the 1830s weight is an average of the 1830 and 1840 population shares; the 1850 weight, the 1850 and 1860 population shares.[23]

The occupational weights are derived from the 1850 census. For example, the weight for teamsters (0.04) reflects the fact that, of all persons in the Northeast reporting an occupation of teamster or common laborer in 1850, 4 percent were teamsters.

The principal advantage of the weighting procedure is that it adjusts for the geographic and regional differences between the sample and the antebellum population. The procedure is crude: it assumes that the labor market to which the fort belonged was proportional in size to the population of the area in which the fort was situated, and no adjustments are made for changes in the occupational distribution over time. A key advantage of the hedonic approach, however, is that other economic historians are free to use whatever weights they wish to generate a different set of estimates from the regressions

21. The estimates themselves are reported in Margo and Villaflor (1987, 893–94).

22. Rations were valued at 12 cents each; see Margo and Villaflor (1987, 878). The only exception was the South Central common laborer/teamster regression, in which the number of rations was included as an independent variable. In constructing the South Central wage estimates, the rations weight was set equal to its sample mean, 0.055.

23. The notes to the fort location tables give the geographic areas identified with each coefficient in the construction of the fort location weights. For example, in the Northeast table, the coefficient for Carlisle, Pennsylvania, is identified with "rural Pennsylvania"; this means the Carlisle coefficient was weighted by the share of the northeastern population living in rural Pennsylvania.

Table 4A.1   Real Wage Indices

	Artisans				Common Laborers/Teamsters			
	New England	Midwest	South Atlantic	South Central	New England	Midwest	South Atlantic	South Central
1821	91.4			130.5	67.4	90.9		79.1
1822	110.6	162.4		120.7	62.1	69.7		69.9
1823	117.5	188.4	145.7	146.2	66.9	77.5		78.7
1824	120.7	193.4	149.4	153.9	68.7	78.2		82.9
1825	112.9	186.3	161.5	148.5	73.6	74.5	78.7	74.3
1826	120.3	216.1	197.0	174.4	87.2	85.5	90.4	82.2
1827	139.9	236.5	205.6	178.9	83.6	86.7	91.8	92.9
1828	132.1	250.3	192.1	174.6	77.0	90.6	96.6	97.4
1829	129.8	235.1	207.2	153.0	75.1	81.9	93.7	103.5
1830	127.7	261.1	205.8	186.6	76.9	97.7	85.4	116.2
1831	129.8	286.9	219.0	179.8	73.5	90.8	88.6	105.0
1832	129.1	260.2	206.0	167.6	74.3	89.4	81.4	99.9
1833	120.0	234.2	192.8	172.0	69.1	96.7	75.1	95.4
1834	144.3	239.6	192.3	186.9	88.2	112.5	71.4	102.1
1835	130.9	195.9	167.5	167.3	77.4	93.5	66.6	78.8
1836	121.9	162.7	127.8	147.6	78.8	66.0	66.7	77.2
1837	123.2	235.2	147.7	152.5	84.6	105.7	79.7	87.3
1838	125.3	207.7	157.3	127.1	81.4	87.2	71.1	72.9
1839	126.2	179.0	153.6	164.3	68.6	100.2	75.8	85.9
1840	144.6	242.9	197.4	226.4	69.4	111.0	96.9	99.1
1841	155.9	256.3	206.7	240.2	92.6	118.3	98.4	126.0
1842	164.3	301.1	279.0	246.3	109.2	140.9	99.5	131.2
1843	192.3	242.0	248.8	240.0	131.8	145.9	119.4	154.6
1844	174.3	234.5	238.9	220.0	134.1	130.0	117.8	141.4
1845	186.2	238.3	219.2	245.0	120.2	119.1	110.3	124.1
1846	178.2	198.0	205.7	218.7	122.1	132.5	105.0	106.4
1847	150.2	186.8	174.5	197.5	84.0	90.8	91.4	84.3
1848	168.1	255.9	238.8	232.6	109.4	144.5	117.8	112.5
1849	163.1	245.3	219.3	233.0	115.6	128.7	103.4	113.8
1850	152.3	231.6	196.5	222.4	109.4	113.0	91.5	107.0
1851	156.8	261.5	190.9	242.7	108.6	119.2	87.6	122.7
1852	153.9	243.4	207.7	242.4	113.4	119.8	86.5	136.9
1853	145.1	246.5	213.8	224.1	102.5	108.4	82.8	124.8
1854	143.2	239.1	223.0	216.8	98.7	119.5	93.5	118.0
1855	146.4	217.0	207.7	189.5	99.1	108.0	88.0	105.1
1856	158.1	213.9	179.0	174.2	100.0	100.0	100.0	100.0

Source: See text.

Notes: The artisan indices are relative to a region-specific base of 100 for common laborers/teamsters in 1856. For example, the 1854 index number for northeastern artisans (143.2) means that real wages of artisans in 1854 were 43.2 percent higher than the real wage of common laborers/teamsters in 1856.

Table 4A.2   **Regressions of Nominal Daily Wage Rate, Northeast**

Variable	Artisan		Common Laborer/Teamster	
	β	t-statistic	β	t-statistic
Constant	0.558	13.558	0.219	3.385
Fort location				
Upstate New York	−0.0001	−0.008	−0.068	−2.040
Philadelphia	−0.025	−1.065	0.079	2.650
Carlisle, Pennsylvania	−0.176	−8.358	0.008	0.214
Southern New England	0.148	5.862	−0.017	−0.360
Northern New England	0.340	17.277	0.353	6.483
Worker or job characteristics				
High	0.391	22.597	0.664	4.454
Low	−0.569	−15.275		
Paid monthly	−0.159	−7.137	−0.096	3.885
Season				
Spring	0.088	3.978	−0.125	−1.865
Summer	0.016	0.815	−0.015	−0.291
Fall	0.071	3.599	−0.046	−0.868
Occupation				
Mason	0.118	11.474		
Painter-plasterer	0.086	5.188		
Blacksmith	0.017	0.809		
Teamster			0.104	4.324
Year				
1820	−0.231	−3.627		
1821	−0.574	−4.665	−0.410	−3.527
1822	−0.339	−4.084	−0.445	−3.587
1823			−0.445	−3.587
1823–24	−0.351	−4.063		
1824			−0.449	−3.730
1825–26	−0.432	−5.216	−0.281	−4.242
1827	−0.297	−3.714	−0.335	−4.545
1828	−0.373	−6.697	−0.442	−6.230
1829	−0.420	−9.376	−0.499	−5.428
1830	−0.463	−9.992	−0.493	−5.340
1831	−0.409	−4.719	−0.507	−6.920
1832	−0.372	−5.924	−0.458	−6.274
1833	−0.388	−6.667	−0.471	−5.844
1834	−0.266	−4.854	−0.292	−3.078
1835	−0.349	−5.396	−0.292	−3.078
1836	−0.473	−9.442	−0.298	−3.093
1837	−0.395	−7.456	−0.126	−1.499
1838	−0.253	−6.847	−0.221	−3.716
1839	−0.192	−5.089	−0.335	−6.040
1840	−0.254	−6.632	−0.527	−9.280
1841	−0.254	−6.652	−0.313	−5.397
1842	−0.346	−9.044	−0.296	−5.057
1843	−0.282	−6.958	−0.204	−3.401
1844	−0.400	−9.748		
1844–45			−0.204	−3.072

Table 4A.2   (continued)

Variable	Artisan		Common Laborer/Teamster	
	β	t-statistic	β	t-statistic
1845	−0.223	−4.202		
1846	−0.263	−5.985	−0.181	−3.636
1847	−0.243	−4.102	−0.365	−5.603
1848	−0.301	−6.605		
1848–50			−0.132	−2.426
1849–50	−0.287	−5.947		
1851	−0.299	−6.162	−0.214	−2.016
1852			−0.116	−1.539
1852–53	−0.229	−3.182		
1853			−0.127	−1.276
1854			−0.079	−1.111
1854–55	−0.106	−2.440		
1855			−0.046	−0.782
N	3,555		2,364	
R²	0.61		0.44	

Notes: Artisan: constant term represents an ordinary carpenter, hired on a daily basis without rations in the winter at a fort in or nearby New York City in 1856. *Common laborer/teamster:* constant term represents a common laborer hired on a daily basis without rations at a fort in or near New York City in 1856.

Table 4A.3   **Regressions of Nominal Daily Wage Rate, Midwest**

Variable	Artisan		Common Laborer/Teamster	
	β	t-statistic	β	t-statistic
Constant	0.867	25.427	0.022	0.895
Fort location				
Pittsburgh	−0.223	−2.967	−0.382	−8.872
Cincinnati	−0.081	−1.432	0.031	0.432
Detroit	−0.319	−9.359	0.118	3.933
Michigan (other than Detroit)	−0.122	−4.234	0.280	4.127
Iowa, Wisconsin, Minnesota	−0.088	−4.088	0.143	3.998
Ft. Leavenworth	−0.135	−6.491	0.365	16.829
Kansas (other than Ft. Leavenworth)	−0.050	−2.020	0.346	9.504
Worker or job characteristics				
High	0.470	20.106		
Low	−0.485	19.122		
Paid monthly	−0.113	−6.598	−0.389	−19.341
Season				
Spring	−0.025	−0.839	0.049	1.799
Summer	−0.016	−0.646	0.047	2.213
Fall	−0.007	−0.247	0.150	6.122
Occupation				
Mason	0.043	3.012		
Painter-plasterer	0.091	3.908		
Blacksmith	0.106	6.757		
Teamster			−0.025	−2.126

Table 4A.3   (continued)

Variable	Artisan		Common Laborer/Teamster	
	β	t-statistic	β	t-statistic
Year				
1820			−0.168	−1.812
1821			−0.147	−1.382
1822	−0.361	−5.000	−0.350	−3.999
1823			−0.399	−4.974
1823–26	−0.388	−5.688		
1824			−0.423	−6.885
1825			−0.427	−6.879
1826–27			−0.450	−7.245
1827–29	−0.163	−4.369		
1828			−0.382	−5.133
1829			−0.341	−4.783
1830	−0.152	−2.606	−0.304	−2.886
1831	−0.044	−0.746	−0.360	−4.903
1832	−0.064	−0.821	−0.304	−4.911
1833	−0.125	−3.476		
1833–34			−0.069	−1.822
1834	−0.141	−2.834		
1835			−0.071	−1.276
1835–36	−0.172	−2.312		
1836			−0.248	−3.851
1837	0.134	2.917	0.160	6.442
1838	−0.075	−1.534	−0.121	−1.889
1839	−0.175	−7.078	0.071	3.467
1840	−0.166	−5.843	−0.161	−4.493
1841	−0.229	−9.279		
1841–42			−0.268	−10.450
1842	−0.306	−9.581		
1843	−0.481	−15.105	−0.190	−5.990
1844	−0.420	−14.113		
1844–45			−0.257	−9.253
1845	−0.359	−9.275		
1846	−0.509	−15.708	−0.118	−3.200
1847	−0.372	−9.561	−0.303	−6.539
1848	−0.316	−8.809	−0.097	−2.155
1849–50	−0.236	−8.768	−0.194	−7.489
1851	−0.110	−2.818		
1851–52			−0.089	−3.400
1852	−0.134	−2.694		
1853	−0.066	−2.524	−0.130	−5.956
1854	−0.053	−1.850	0.005	−0.222
1855	−0.019	−0.664	0.037	1.546
N	3,494		4,900	
R²	0.574		0.620	

Notes: Artisan: constant term represents an ordinary carpenter, hired on a daily basis without rations during the winter at a fort at or near St. Louis in 1856. *Common laborer/teamster:* constant term represents a common laborer hired on a daily basis without rations at a fort at or near St. Louis in 1856.

Table 4A.4   **Regressions of Nominal Daily Wage Rate, South Atlantic States**

Variable	Artisan		Common Laborer/Teamster	
	β	t-statistic	β	t-statistic
Constant	0.519	4.689	0.140	1.410
Fort location				
Baltimore	−0.108	−3.091	0.279	6.484
Savannah, Georgia	0.089	2.364	0.142	2.196
North Carolina	0.022	0.456	−0.226	−3.514
South Carolina	0.141	3.790	−0.254	−5.210
Worker and job characteristics				
High	0.406	15.083	0.750	3.608
Low	−0.775	−22.669	−0.019	−0.328
Paid monthly	0.141	2.578	−0.053	−1.492
Slave	−0.246	−9.952	−0.108	−4.517
Season				
Spring	−0.0005	−0.013	0.050	0.928
Summer	−0.023	−0.683	−0.028	−0.590
Fall	0.056	1.463	−0.089	−1.908
Occupation				
Mason	0.014	0.629		
Painter-plasterer	0.071	2.521		
Blacksmith	0.137	2.798		
Teamster			−0.170	5.747
Year				
1823	−0.191	−1.645		
1823–24	−0.236	−2.118		
1824–26			−0.275	−2.629
1825–26	−0.043	−0.377		
1827	−0.010	−0.090	−0.251	−2.420
1828	−0.122	−1.051	−0.231	−2.228
1829	−0.066	−0.599		
1829–30	−0.037	−0.323		
1830–31			−0.351	−3.398
1831–32			−0.406	−3.928
1832–34	−0.044	−0.399		
1833–34			−0.449	−4.600
1835	−0.015	−0.124	−0.392	−3.871
1836	−0.095	−0.714	−0.171	−1.728
1837			−0.132	−1.341
1837–39	−0.069	−0.539		
1838			−0.297	−3.015
1839			−0.209	−1.894
1840–41	−0.077	−0.617	−0.243	−2.378
1842	−0.046	−0.417	−0.501	−4.394
1843	−0.174	−1.604	−0.324	−2.889
1844–46	−0.163	−1.369	−0.267	−2.108
1847	−0.186	−1.114	−0.254	−2.345
1848	−0.151	−1.204	−0.276	−2.628
1849–50			−0.327	−3.160
1849–51	−0.115	−1.021		

Table 4A.4   (continued)

Variable	Artisan		Common Laborer/Teamster	
	β	t-statistic	β	t-statistic
1851–53			−0.352	−2.507
1852–55	0.161	1.411		
1854–55			−0.112	−0.490
N	1,906		2,071	
R²	0.60		0.54	

Notes: Artisan: constant term represents an ordinary carpenter, hired on a daily basis without rations during the winter at Fort Monroe, Virginia in 1856. *Common laborer/teamster:* constant term represents a common laborer hired on a daily basis without rations during the winter at Fort Monroe, Virginia, in 1856. *Slave* = 1 if the person was a slave, 0 otherwise.

Table 4A.5   **Regressions of Nominal Daily Wage Rate, South Central States**

	Artisan		Common Laborer/Teamster	
Variable	β	t-statistic	β	t-statistic
Constant	0.734	10.982	0.424	22.678
Fort location				
Baton Rouge, Louisiana	0.069	2.804	−0.445	−31.543
Arkansas	−0.132	−5.806	−0.343	−26.715
Kentucky	−0.348	−9.992	−0.272	−10.846
Tennessee	−0.577	−8.826	−0.015	−0.564
Alabama, Mississippi	0.075	1.268	−0.328	−10.639
Worker or job characteristics				
High	0.495	21.056	0.425	10.890
Low	−0.674	−20.674	−0.720	−17.129
Paid monthly	−0.108	−4.784	−0.191	−17.642
Number of rations			−0.066	−3.537
Slave	−0.220	−5.119	−0.073	−3.930
Season				
Spring	−0.032	−1.050	−0.004	−0.194
Summer	0.014	0.553	0.048	2.667
Fall	−0.019	−0.718	−0.017	−0.982
Occupation				
Mason	0.013	0.740		
Painter-plasterer	0.031	1.110		
Blacksmith	0.080	3.374		
Teamster			0.025	2.502
Year				
1820	−0.221	−1.914	−0.302	−7.716
1821			−0.225	−6.334
1821–22	−0.131	−1.435		
1822–24			−0.208	−7.236
1823	−0.042	−0.389		
1824	−0.059	−0.716		
1825–26			−0.262	−4.092
1826–28	0.110	1.612		

Table 4A.5   (continued)

Variable	Artisan		Common Laborer/Teamster	
	β	t-statistic	β	t-statistic
1827–29			−0.049	−1.202
1829	−0.106	−1.096		
1830	−0.051	−0.641	−0.023	−0.304
1831			−0.096	−1.288
1831–32	−0.086	−1.150		
1832			−0.102	−1.360
1833			−0.121	−1.748
1833–34	0.028	0.428		
1834			−0.079	−1.639
1835	0.077	1.215	−0.176	−6.278
1836	0.147	1.965	−0.002	−0.120
1837	0.084	0.928	0.022	0.544
1838	−0.103	−1.634	−0.163	−10.847
1839	0.101	1.623	−0.044	−2.202
1840			−0.096	−1.288
1840–41	0.219	3.614		
1841			0.011	0.488
1842	0.106	1.707	−0.008	−0.461
1843	−0.129	−2.177	−0.023	−1.257
1844	−0.167	−2.512	−0.074	−0.875
1845	−0.036	−0.564		
1845–46			−0.310	−14.615
1846	−0.128	−1.993		
1847	−0.008	−0.111	−0.322	−9.831
1848	−0.069	−0.825	−0.241	−7.899
1849–50	0.090	1.335	−0.092	−4.393
1851			−0.032	−1.696
1851–53	0.099	1.520		
1852			0.077	2.561
1853			0.055	0.919
1854	0.063	0.849	0.009	0.511
1855	0.082	0.862	0.048	2.678
N	2,898		4,728	
R^2	0.65		0.65	

Notes: Artisan: constant term represents an ordinary carpenter, hired on a daily basis without rations in the winter in New Orleans in 1856. *Common laborer/teamster:* constant term represents a common laborer hired on a daily basis without rations during the winter in New Orleans in 1856. *Slave* = 1 if the person was a slave, 0 otherwise.

Table 4A.6   **Weights for Nominal Wage Estimates**

Panel A: Fort Location Weights

	1820s	1830s	1840s	1850s
Northeast				
Upstate New York	0.291	0.294	0.275	0.239
Philadelphia	0.043	0.050	0.066	0.090
Carlisle, Pennsylvania	0.260	0.255	0.251	0.241
Southern New England	0.244	0.221	0.212	0.210
Northern New England	0.118	0.120	0.111	0.097
Midwest				
Pittsburgh	0.629	0.517	0.410	0.304
Detroit	0.000	0.002	0.004	0.008
Michigan (other than Detroit)	0.015	0.042	0.069	0.076
Iowa, Wisconsin, Minnesota	0.000	0.011	0.057	0.130
Kansas (other than Ft. Leavenworth)	0.000	0.000	0.000	0.060
Ft. Leavenworth	0.000	0.000	0.000	0.000
South Atlantic				
Baltimore	0.036	0.041	0.053	0.068
Savannah, Georgia	0.003	0.004	0.007	0.011
North Carolina	0.234	0.219	0.203	0.197
South Carolina	0.253	0.272	0.277	0.269
South Central				
Baton Rouge	0.041	0.038	0.045	0.054
Arkansas	0.013	0.026	0.046	0.074
Kentucky	0.385	0.305	0.264	0.246
Tennessee	0.346	0.318	0.275	0.244
Alabama, Mississippi	0.203	0.297	0.352	0.362

Panel B: Occupational Weights

	Northeast	Midwest	South Atlantic	South Central
Mason	0.21	0.19	0.18	0.17
Blacksmith	0.16	0.04	0.08	0.03
Painter-plasterer	0.10	0.06	0.08	0.03
Teamster	0.04	0.03	0.02	0.02

Source: See text.

Notes: Identification of fort location coefficients with population shares: upstate New York = rural New York; Philadelphia = urban Pennsylvania (eastern) and New Jersey; Carlisle = rural Pennsylvania; southern New England = Massachusetts, New Hampshire, and Connecticut; northern New England = Maine and Vermont; Pittsburgh = western Pennsylvania and rural Ohio; Cincinnati = urban Ohio and Indiana; Detroit = urban Michigan; Baltimore = urban Maryland and District of Columbia; Savannah = urban Georgia; Baton Rouge = Louisiana except New Orleans; North Carolina, South Carolina, Arkansas, Kentucky, Tennessee, and Alabama and Mississippi = state population shares.

(for example, estimate wage series for each fort and then produce regional series by taking *unweighted* averages of the fort-specific estimates).[24]

Step-by-Step Calculation of Estimates

To derive the wage estimates, multiply the fort coefficients by the decade-specific fort weights, the occupational coefficients by the occupational weights, and the seasonal coefficients by the seasonal weight (0.25), and add together. Take the sum and add the constant term to it: call the result α. To α add the coefficient of the time-period dummy, and exponentiate the result.

As a specific example, the wage estimate for unskilled labor in the Northeast in 1822 is $0.78. Multiplying the coefficients of the fort dummies by the fort weights for the 1820s ($-0.068 \times 0.291 + 0.079 \times 0.043 + 0.008 \times 0.260 - 0.017 \times 0.244 + 0.353 \times 0.118$), the teamster coefficient by the teamster weight (0.104×0.04), and the seasonal coefficients by the seasonal weight ($-0.125 \times 0.25 - 0.015 \times 0.25 - 0.046 \times 0.25$) and adding together with the constant term gives $\alpha = 0.200$. Adding to α the coefficient of the 1822 time dummy (-0.445) and exponentiating gives the estimated wage of $0.78 ($= \exp[-0.245]$).[25]

This procedure must be modified when the time-period dummy refers to a group of years rather than a single year. If the group refers to two years (for example, 1824–25), the estimated wage is assumed to refer to the second year (1825), and the estimate for the first year is a linear interpolation of the preceding year's estimate (1823) and the second year's estimate (1825). If the group refers to three or more years (1824–26), the estimated wage is assumed to refer to the midpoint of the group of years (1825.5), and the estimates for surrounding years are again calculated by linear interpolation. All estimates for 1849 are interpolated because no reports have been found for that year.

Northeast: Adjustment of 1835–37 Estimates

Based on an extensive analysis of the original data and other evidence, the Northeast coefficients of the time dummies for 1835–37 for skilled labor and for 1836 for unskilled labor were deemed to be unreliable. To estimate wage changes from 1835 to 1837, data pertaining to workers at the Boston Naval Yard was used ("Naval Hospital Payrolls," Bureau of Yards and Docks, Record Group 71, National Archives). It is important to note that these workers were building hospitals and other buildings at the yard, *not* ships (ship carpenters earned a premium above ordinary carpenters). Average wage rates

---

24. Or no weights at all: because the dependent variable is the log of the daily wage, the coefficients of the time dummies can be used directly to construct nominal wage *indices* (relative to a value of 1.0 for the base year, 1856). For example, the index number for artisans in the South Atlantic states in 1823 is $0.826 ($= \exp[-0.191]$).

25. This procedure ignores the fact that, while the prediction error, e, of the regression has a mean value of zero ($E[\hat{e}] = 0$), $E(\exp[\hat{e}])$ is nonzero. The appropriate adjustment was too small to affect the results, however, and was ignored throughout.

for skilled artisans (carpenters, masons, painters, and plasterers) and common laborers were calculated for each year at the yard, and the resulting percentage changes in wages were used to generate new estimates of the coefficients of the time dummies. The coefficient estimates are for skilled laborers for 1835–37 -0.236, -0.167, and -0.218 and for unskilled laborers for 1836 -0.206.

South Central: Adjustment of Fort Location Coefficients, Unskilled Regression

Based on extensive comparisons with the original data, it appears that the unskilled regression significantly overpredicts wages at forts in Kentucky, Tennessee, Alabama, and Mississippi. New coefficients for these forts were derived directly from the data, by forming the ratio of wages at the forts to wages at New Orleans for specific years. The new coefficients are Kentucky, -0.484, Tennessee, -0.484, and Alabama-Mississippi, -0.471.

References

Abbott, Edith. 1905. The Wages of Unskilled Labor in the United States, 1850–1900. *Journal of Political Economy* 13 (June): 321–67.

Adams, Donald R., Jr. 1968. Wage Rates in the Early National Period: Philadelphia, 1785–1830. *Journal of Economic History* 28 (September): 404–26.

———. 1970. Some Evidence on English and American Wage Rates, 1790–1830. *Journal of Economic History* 30 (September): 499–520.

———. 1982. The Standard of Living during American Industrialization: Evidence from the Brandywine Region, 1800–1860. *Journal of Economic History* 42 (December): 903–17.

———. 1986. Prices and Wages in Maryland, 1750–1850. *Journal of Economic History* 46 (September): 625–45.

Adams, T. M. 1939. *Prices Paid by Farmers for Goods and Services and Received by Them for Farm Products, 1790–1871.* Burlington, VT: Vermont Agricultural Experiment Station.

Aldrich, Nelson W. 1893. *Wholesale Prices, Wages, and Transportation.* 52d Cong., 2d sess., S. Rept. 1394. Washington, DC: U.S. Government Printing Office.

Bairoch, Paul. 1989. Wages as an Indicator of Gross National Product. In *Real Wages in Nineteenth and Twentieth Century Europe: Historical and Comparative Perspectives,* ed. Peter Scholliers, 51–60. New York: Berg and St. Martin's Press.

Barsky, Robert, and J. Bradford De Long. 1988. Forecasting Pre–World War I Inflation: The Fisher Effect Revisited. NBER Working Paper no. 2784. Cambridge, MA: National Bureau of Economic Research.

Berry, Thomas S. 1943. *Western Prices before 1861.* Cambridge, MA: Harvard University Press.

Blackmar, Elizabeth. 1989. *Manhattan for Rent, 1785–1850.* New York: Cornell University Press.

Brady, Dorothy S. 1966. Price Deflators for Final Product Estimates. In *Output, Employment, and Productivity in the United States after 1800,* ed. Dorothy S. Brady,

91–115. NBER Studies in Wealth and Income, 30. New York: Columbia University Press.

Cole, Arthur H. 1938. *Wholesale Commodity Prices in the United States, 1700–1861.* Cambridge, MA: Harvard University Press.

David, Paul. 1967. The Growth of Real Product in the United States before 1840: New Evidence, New Conjectures. *Journal of Economic History* 27 (June): 151–97.

David, Paul, and Peter Solar. 1977. A Bicentenary Contribution to the History of the Cost of Living in America. *Research in Economic History* 2: 1–80.

DeCanio, Stephen, and Joel Mokyr. 1977. Inflation and the Wage Lag during the American Civil War. *Explorations in Economic History* 14 (October): 311–36.

Engerman, Stanley L., and Robert E. Gallman. 1983. U.S. Economic Growth, 1783–1960. *Research in Economic History* 8: 1–46.

Fogel, Robert W. 1986. Nutrition and the Decline in Mortality since 1700: Some Preliminary Findings. In *Long-Term Factors in American Economic Growth,* ed. Stanley L. Engerman and Robert E. Gallman, 439–527. NBER Studies in Income and Wealth, 51. Chicago: University of Chicago Press.

———. 1989. *Without Consent or Contract: The Rise and Fall of American Slavery.* New York: W. W. Norton.

———. 1990. Modelling Complex Dynamic Interactions: The Role of Intergenerational, Cohort, and Period Processes and of Conditional Events in the Political Realignment of the 1850s. NBER Historical Working Paper no. 12. Cambridge, MA: National Bureau of Economic Research.

Fogel, Robert W., Ralph A. Galantine, and Richard L. Manning, eds. 1992. *Without Consent or Contract: The Rise and Fall of American Slavery.* Vol. 2, *Evidence and Methods.* New York: W. W. Norton.

Gallman, Robert E. 1975. The Agricultural Sector and the Pace of Economic Growth: U.S. Experience in the Nineteenth Century. In *Essays in Nineteenth Century Economic History,* ed. David C. Klingaman and Richard K. Vedder, 35–76. Athens: Ohio University Press.

Goldin, Claudia, and Robert A. Margo. 1992. Wages, Prices, and Labor Markets before the Civil War. In *Strategic Factors in Nineteenth Century American Economic History,* ed. Claudia Goldin and Hugh Rockoff, 67–104. Chicago: University of Chicago Press.

Goldin, Claudia, and Kenneth Sokoloff. 1982. Women, Children, and Industrialization in the Early Republic: Evidence from the Manufacturing Censuses. *Journal of Economic History* 42 (December): 741–74.

Grosse, Scott. 1982. On the Alleged Antebellum Surge in Wage Differentials: A Critique of Williamson and Lindert. *Journal of Economic History* 42 (June): 413–18.

Habakkuk, H. J. 1962. *American and British Technology in the Nineteenth Century.* New York: Cambridge University Press.

Hanes, Christopher. 1990. Explaining a Decrease in Cyclical Wage Flexibility in the Late Nineteenth Century. Department of Economics, University of Pennsylvania. Manuscript.

Hansen, Alvin. 1925. Factors Affecting the Trend in Real Wages. *American Economic Review* 15 (March): 27–42.

Heppner, Francis, and Harry John. 1968. Wage Data among Nineteenth Century Military and Naval Records. National Archives, Washington, DC. Manuscript.

Hirsch, Susan E. 1978. *Roots of the American Working Class: The Industrialization of Crafts in Newark, 1800–1860.* Philadelphia: University of Pennsylvania Press.

Hoover, Ethel D. 1958. Wholesale and Retail Prices in the Nineteenth Century. *Journal of Economic History* 17 (September): 298–316.

————. 1960. Retail Prices after 1850. In *Trends in the American Economy in the Nineteenth Century,* ed. William N. Parker, 141–86. NBER Studies in Income and Wealth, 24. Princeton: Princeton University Press.

James, John A. 1989. The Stability of the Nineteenth Century Phillips Curve Relationship. *Explorations in Economic History* 26 (April): 117–34.

Keyssar, Alexander. 1986. *Out of Work: The First Century of Unemployment in Massachusetts.* New York: Cambridge University Press.

Kuznets, Simon. 1955. Economic Growth and Income Inequality. *American Economic Review* 45 (March): 1–28.

Layer, Robert. 1955. *Earnings of Cotton Mill Operatives, 1825–1914.* Cambridge, MA: Harvard University Press.

Lebergott, Stanley L. 1964. *Manpower in Economic Growth.* New York: McGraw-Hill.

Lindert, Peter, and Jeffrey G. Williamson. 1982. Antebellum Wage Widening Once Again. *Journal of Economic History* 42 (June): 419–22.

————. 1983. English Workers' Living Standards during the Industrial Revolution: A New Look. *Economic History Review* 36 (February): 1–25.

Lucas, Robert. 1981. *Studies in Business Cycle Theory.* Cambridge, MA: MIT Press.

Margo, Robert A., and Richard Steckel. 1983. Heights of Native-Born Whites during the Antebellum Period. *Journal of Economic History* 43 (March): 167–74.

Margo, Robert A., and Georgia C. Villaflor. 1987. The Growth of Wages in Antebellum America: New Evidence. *Journal of Economic History* 47 (December): 873–95.

North, Douglass C. 1966. *The Economic Growth of the United States, 1790–1860.* New York: W. W. Norton.

Quddus, Munir, Jin-Tan Liu, and J. S. Butler. 1988. Variability of Inflation and the Dispersion of Relative Prices: Evidence from the Chinese Hyperinflation of 1946–1949. *Economics Letters* 27: 239–44.

Rosenbloom, Joshua L. 1990. One Market or Many? Labor Market Integration in the Late Nineteenth-Century United States. *Journal of Economic History* 50 (March): 85–107.

Ross, Stephen J. 1985. *Workers on the Edge: Work, Leisure, and Politics in Industrializing Cincinnati, 1788–1890.* New York: Columbia University Press.

Rothenberg, Winifred B. 1979. A Price Index for Rural Massachusetts, 1750–1855. *Journal of Economic History* 39 (December): 975–1001.

————. 1981. The Market and Massachusetts Farmers, 1750–1855. *Journal of Economic History* 41 (June): 283–314.

————. 1988. The Emergence of Farm Labor Markets and the Transformation of the Rural Economy: Massachusetts, 1750–1855. *Journal of Economic History* 48 (September): 537–66.

Scholliers, Peter, ed. 1989. *Real Wages in Nineteenth and Twentieth Century Europe: Historical and Comparative Perspectives.* New York: Berg and St. Martin's Press.

Smith, Walter B. 1963. Wage Rates on the Erie Canal. *Journal of Economic History* 23 (September): 298–311.

Smith, Walter B., and Arthur H. Cole. 1935. *Fluctuations in American Business, 1790–1860.* Cambridge, MA: Harvard University Press.

Sokoloff, Kenneth. 1986a. Productivity Growth in Manufacturing during Early Industrialization: Evidence from the American Northeast, 1820–1860. In *Long-Term Factors in American Economic Growth,* ed. Stanley L. Engerman and Robert E. Gallman, 679–729. NBER Studies in Income and Wealth, 51. Chicago: University of Chicago Press.

————. 1986b. The Puzzling Record of Real Wage Growth in Early Industrial America: 1820–1860. Department of Economics, University of California, Los Angeles. Manuscript.
Temin, Peter. 1969. *The Jacksonian Economy.* New York: W. W. Norton.
U.S. Bureau of the Census. 1975. *Historical Statistics of the United States.* Washington, DC: U.S. Government Printing Office.
Weeks, Joseph D. 1886. *Report on the Statistics of Wages in Manufacturing Industries with Supplementary Reports.* Washington, DC: U.S. Government Printing Office.
Wilentz, Sean. 1984. *Chants Democratic: New York City and the Rise of the American Working Class, 1788–1850.* New York: Oxford University Press.
Williamson, Jeffrey G., and Peter H. Lindert. 1980. *American Inequality: A Macroeconomic History.* New York: Academic Press.
Zabler, Jeffrey. 1972. Further Evidence on American Wage Differentials, 1800–1830. *Explorations in Economic History* 10 (Fall): 109–17.

Comment   Jeffrey G. Williamson

Some Preliminaries

We all seem to agree that real wages of common labor were higher in America than in Britain in the 1820s. Indeed, that's why English emigrants came to North America, and that's why visitors to colonial Philadelphia called America the "best poor man's country in the world" (Nash 1976, 545). Although the data are nowhere near as good for 1825 or 1855 as they are for 1895, especially for adjustments to purchasing-power parity and real wage comparisons, we do have some strong priors. H. J. Habakkuk (1962, 11) thought that real wages of American common labor might have been 50 percent higher than those of the British early in the nineteenth century. John James and Jonathan Skinner (1985, table 5, 529) imply that real wages of common labor were at least 58 percent higher late in the antebellum period. My own estimates, summarized in table 4C.1, constructed using Margo's antebellum estimates for the United States, suggest that those Anglo-American wage gaps were even higher than Habakkuk thought. If Margo's estimates are correct, they suggest that America's superior position was strongly reinforced during the antebellum surge, American real wages rising to about 97 percent above the British in the mid-1850s.

Some part of that American real wage superiority was lost in the half century that followed, falling to 44 percent above the British in 1895 and 54 percent above the British in 1900. When and why did real wages of American common labor lose some of their striking superiority over Britain across the late nineteenth century? Part of the erosion took place during the Civil War decade, when real wages slumped in America (Williamson 1974, table 7,

Jeffrey G. Williamson is the Laird Bell Professor of Economics at Harvard University.

Table 4C.1   **Anglo-American Real Wage Gaps for Unskilled Labor, 1830–1913 (England = 100)**

1830	140	1858	156	1886	148
1831	139	1859	157	1887	147
1832	133	1860	184	1888	143
1833	118	1861	184	1889	146
1834	130	1862	156	1890	149
1835	120	1863	132	1891	149
1836	157	1864	120	1892	149
1837	178	1865	130	1893	147
1838	190	1866	144	1894	137
1839	165	1867	165	1895	144
1840	153	1868	166	1896	138
1841	160	1869	155	1897	142
1842	168	1870	167	1898	146
1843	170	1871	172	1899	145
1844	193	1872	167	1900	154
1845	177	1873	161	1901	157
1846	183	1874	159	1902	160
1847	167	1875	158	1903	164
1848	160	1876	158	1904	163
1849	158	1877	138	1905	167
1850	154	1878	135	1906	156
1851	151	1879	130	1907	158
1852	157	1880	132	1908	155
1853	183	1881	136	1909	161
1854	196	1882	151	1910	162
1855	198	1883	152	1911	160
1856	196	1884	150	1912	163
1857	175	1885	147	1913	154

Source: Williamson (1992, tables A2.1, A2.2). The data base uses purchasing-power-parity deflators and daily wage rates for unskilled in the building trades to establish a truly comparable real wage benchmark around the turn of the century. The real wages are then projected backward to 1830, using nominal wage series and cost-of-living deflators. Margo's data in chapter 4 of this volume underlies the antebellum estimates for America.

660), falling by 25–30 percent up to 1864, and recovering their 1860 levels only by about 1869. America lost a decade of real wage growth during the 1860s, while British real wages rose by 22 percent (Williamson 1985, table 2.13, 30). America regained much of what it had lost by the early 1870s, only to lose a good share of it again in the following quarter century. By the 1890s, American wages were 40 or 50 percent higher than those in Britain.

These calculations imply that American real wage growth surged ahead of Britain in the antebellum period, confirming Robert Margo's assertion that American real wage growth was "substantial." If we have the facts right, why the rise in the Anglo-American wage gap during the antebellum decades and the fall thereafter? Tim Hatton and I have been exploring this question for the Anglo-American gap, as well as for other pairs of countries representing the

Old and New World, as an integrated global labor market gradually emerged during the nineteenth century. The forces that contributed to the integration of trans-Atlantic labor markets certainly included the rising international migrations, which served to strengthen the links between national labor markets. They also must have included the evolution of better-integrated commodity markets (a substitute for migration via factor-price equalization effects: O'Rourke and Williamson 1992). Some might argue that it also would include technological diffusion along the lines of Gerschenkron and Baumol, Blackman, and Wolff (1989), as well as better-integrated capital markets (another substitute for migration). However, these two arguments are unlikely to account for the eroding Anglo-American gap after the mid 1850s, since American GNP per capita, driven by accumulation and technical progress, was catching up with and surging ahead of Britain, not falling behind. These two arguments may be stronger, of course, in accounting for other international wage gaps: for example, between western Europe, on the one hand, and Scandinavia, the Mediterranean, and eastern Europe, on the other.

The Missing Ingredient: Comparative History

This has been a long-winded introduction to my comments on Robert Margo's paper, but I think the trip was necessary. American economic historians don't think comparatively as often as European economic historians do. They ought to do it more frequently. Such thinking would certainly help assess the implications of Margo's paper. What's "big" real wage growth? What's "significant" regional wage integration? Were wages really sticky? How important is the omission of rents from the cost-of-living index? These questions are hard to answer without applying a comparative standard, like the one invoked in the previous section. Furthermore, the thriving standard of living literature on industrializing nineteenth-century Europe might help place the antebellum American experience in perspective. Let me illustrate with some examples from the first industrial revolution.

First, how important is the omission of rents from Margo's cost-of-living deflator? Margo is quite aware of the flaws in his cost-of-living index, and he takes pains to emphasize similar flaws in other antebellum consumer price proxies. These include the unfortunate use of producers' rather than consumers' goods, wholesale rather than retail prices, and tradable goods to the exclusion of nontradable services. If the relative price of each was fairly stable over time, the flaws can be ignored. But it seems unlikely. One relative price that increases sharply during the industrial revolution is rents. There are three reasons for this. First, housing construction is labor-intensive, and the relative price of labor rises during industrialization—after all, real wages do rise "substantially" during the antebellum years. Second, urban housing is space-intensive, and rising urban land scarcity is a fact of life during all industrial revolutions, past and present. Third, the rate of total factor productivity growth in the building trades is slower than that of commodity production even today (Baumol, Blackman, and Wolff 1989, chap. 4). All of these factors should serve to raise the relative cost of housing as industrialization unfolds. It is manifested by a rise in rents, and it is manifested by families saving on rental expenditures by moving into smaller dwellings and by the dwellings themselves packing in closer together, events that served to raise nineteenth-century mortality and morbidity while lowering the quality of life. To the extent that quality-adjusted rents are excluded from the cost-of-living index, estimated real wage growth during the antebellum years is overstated in Margo's figures. In contrast, the British estimates in table 4C.1 include the impact of rising rents.

So much for theory. What about fact? Did the likely rise in city rents serve to suppress real wage growth in antebellum America? While such evidence may be missing for almost every year covering Margo's time series 1821–56, it is available starting with the late 1850s (Williamson and Lindert 1980, chap. 5), so that Margo could assess its contribution to trends in the cost-of-living index shortly after the mid-1850s, using such insights to help assess its potential impact on antebellum trends. Furthermore, such evidence is also available for Britain during its industrial revolution (Williamson 1990, 188, 235–38). From the 1790s to the 1840s, real rents (nominal rents relative to the cost of living) in Leeds, Black Country towns, and a village in Staffordshire rose by 2.5 percent per annum, for a whopping 30 percent per decade. Since rents accounted for about 20 percent of the common laborer's budget, this explosion in urban dwelling expense served to raise the cost-of-living growth rate by perhaps as much as 0.5 percent per year. If the British experience was shared by American cities and towns, Margo's estimates of real wage growth are exaggerated by no small measure.

Second, while this is a conference on antebellum living standards, Margo's paper only discusses wages. The European economic historian would be surprised by this limited focus, since the age-old literature there has included debate over urban disamenities, work hours and leisure, safety nets, and unemployment incidence, to name only a few. Some of these turn out to matter in making assessments about the rate of improvement in living standards (Lindert and Williamson 1983). Why is American antebellum debate so quiet on these issues?

Third, America isn't the only country that has a fixation on regions and "sections." While England never had a Frederick Jackson Turner, it has always been acutely aware that wages differed across regions during the industrial revolution. London always had higher wages than other cities, even after taking account of the fact that it was an expensive place to live. And the rural south of England had lower real wages than did the rural north. Given these regional wage differentials, debates have raged surrounding two issues (just as in America): When do truly national labor markets begin to emerge? What role did interregional migration play (workers seeking out high-wage labor markets) in contributing to real wage growth economy-wide? The answer to the first question is that it depends. If we are talking about cities and large towns, then it appears that there was a well-integrated labor market very early in the industrial revolution (Williamson 1990, chap. 5). If we are talking about farms and rural villages, then the labor market was very poorly integrated, and it was manifested by rising farm-city wage gaps (Williamson 1990, chap. 7). Was antebellum experience in America any different than experience in England from the 1790s to the 1850s? Comparative questions like this would enrich our understanding of American experience with real wage performance.

Fourth, how comprehensive is the occupational coverage offered by Margo's fort wage records? The evidence he (and Georgia Villaflor) extracts so skillfully from those wage records deals with the building trades and clerks only. There is no evidence from other nonfarm service activities, from farms, or from any factories. Thus, Margo's evidence is relevant to real wage growth only if the structure of wages was stable during these antebellum decades of dramatic industrialization. While the debate over alleged "wage-stretching" between skilled and unskilled labor during early nineteenth-century industrial revolutions still rages for both America and Britain, no one in either camp has argued that the wage structure was stable. The wage gap between farm and city rose sharply in Britain. If the same was true for antebellum America, then Margo's real wage growth estimates are overstated. If skilled factory wages rose relative to the building trades, then Margo's real wage growth estimates are understated. While I applaud Margo's effort to develop an alternative wage data source, caution is warranted in making the leap from statements about building wage trends to average real wage trends. And to the extent that the wage structure did change over the antebellum decades, we want to know why.

Sticky Wages?

Margo spends a number of pages at the end of his admirable survey on wage stickiness in the short run. It draws on a collaboration with Claudia Goldin (Goldin and Margo 1992), which has been stimulated by similar questions raised by macroeconomists on twentieth-century experience. Other American economic historians have been doing the same (e.g., see Hanes 1990; James 1989). The basic finding is this: "Nominal wages did not adjust instantaneously—when prices rose, as in the mid-1830s, real wages fell." Based on conventional thinking, macroeconomists will be surprised by this antebellum finding. Led by Jeffrey Sachs and Robert Gordon, macroeconomists have persuaded themselves that sticky wages are a twentieth-century phenomenon, and that they evolved that way due to the rise of unions and formal unemployment insurance schemes. Chris Hanes (1990) has shown this view to be wrong, since sticky wages were on the rise in the late nineteenth century long before the appearance of unemployment insurance schemes and when little of the labor force was unionized. Hanes finds, however, a sharp discontinuity in the late 1880s: prior to those years, wages in manufacturing were flexible; after those years they became increasingly sticky. Hanes has developed an explanation for the institutional evolution that hinges on the increase in firm size and concentration along Chandlerian lines. Given these findings, how is it that Margo (and Goldin) find wage stickiness in the antebellum decades?

My role is to pose this question, while I will let those more expert debate the answers. However, I cannot resist making two points.

First, are the cost-of-living figures likely to yield that result by construction? Margo has already listed the flaws in the price index, and they are likely to imply far greater instability over booms and busts than would a true cost-of-living index. Why? Well, it excludes services like rents, and they are notoriously stable over booms and busts. And it also uses wholesale prices, rather than retail prices. The former is more unstable over booms and busts than the latter, and it's the latter that's relevant to wage stickiness tales. And it also uses raw material prices (e.g., leather) to proxy consumer goods prices (e.g., shoes). Once again, the former is more unstable than the latter over booms and busts, and it's the latter that's relevant to wage stickiness tales. To repeat, Margo may have fabricated sticky wages by construction.

Second, let's remember whose wages Goldin and Margo are talking about. Farm wages, based on Winifred Rothenberg's (1988) Massachusetts evidence, are not sticky at all, a result that we all thought was true anyway (see Hatton and Williamson 1992 for confirmation on U.S. experience 1890–1941). Clerks, on the other hand, had sticky wages, a finding that makes sense since they were in one of the few occupations that had long-term contracts. They also report sticky wages for the building trades drawn from those fort wage records. I think Margo should be more cautious at this point. He has to persuade me that the result was not constructed. After all, the fort wage data are constructed by regression analysis, which minimizes variance. Does that fact create an illusion of stickiness that was never present? Furthermore, there were missing years and missing forts in the data base that, as I understand it, were filled by interpolation. Does that fact also create an illusion of stickiness that never was present? Finally, we should remember that the building trades were the first to unionize. That statement applies to cities and not necessarily to the forts, but since Margo has already invoked the assumption of competitive labor markets between the forts and civilian labor markets elsewhere in the region, he should find no objection to the statement. Building trade craft unions appeared long before the rise of industrial unions late in the century; these craft unions were the first to experiment with strikes (and strike threats); and these unions were the first to demand no wage cuts during periods of industrial crisis.

So, we must be cautious. Much of the wage stickiness that Margo sees in the antebellum period may be wage stickiness in one sector, the building trades, and much of the stickiness even there may be by construction.

References

Baumol, W. J., S. A. B. Blackman, and E. N. Wolff. 1989. *Productivity and American Leadership*. Cambridge, Mass.: MIT Press.

Goldin, C., and R. A. Margo. 1992. Wages, Prices, and Labor Markets before the Civil War. In *Strategic Factors in Nineteenth Century American Economic History*, ed. C. Goldin and H. Rockoff. Chicago: National Bureau of Economic Research.

Habakkuk, H. J. 1962. *American and British Technology in the Nineteenth Century*. Cambridge: Cambridge University Press.

Hanes, C. 1990. Explaining a Decrease in Cyclical Wage Flexibility in the Late Nineteenth Century. Paper presented to the Thirtieth Annual Cliometrics Conference, University of Illinois, May 18–20.

Hatton, T. J., and J. G. Williamson. 1992. "What Explains Wage Gaps between Farm and City? Exploring the Todaro Model with American Evidence, 1890–1941. *Economic Development and Cultural Change* 40 (January): 267–94.

James, J. A. 1989. The Stability of the Nineteenth Century Phillips Curve Relationship. *Explorations in Economic History* 26: 117–34.

James, J. A., and J. S. Skinner. 1985. The Resolution of the Labor-Scarcity Paradox. *Journal of Economic History* 45: 513–40.

Lindert, P. H., and J. G. Williamson. 1983. English Workers' Living Standards during the Industrial Revolution: A New Look. *Economic History Review*, 2d ser., 36: 1–25.

Nash, G. B. 1976. Urban Wealth and Poverty in Pre-revolutionary Philadelphia. *Journal of Interdisciplinary History* 6: 545–84.

O'Rourke, K., and J. G. Williamson. 1992. Were Heckscher and Ohlin Right? Putting History Back into the Factor Price Equalization Theorem. Paper presented to the Cliometrics Conference, Miami University, Oxford, Ohio: May 15–17.

Rothenberg, W. B. 1988. The Emergence of Farm Labor Markets and the Transformation of the Rural Economy: Massachusetts, 1750–1855. *Journal of Economic History* 48 (September): 537–66.

Williamson, J. G. 1974. Watersheds and Turning Points: Conjectures on the Long-Term Impact of Civil War Financing. *Journal of Economic History* 34: 636–61.

———. 1985. *Did British Capitalism Breed Inequality?* London: Allen and Unwin.

———. 1990. *Coping with City Growth during the British Industrial Revolution*. Cambridge: Cambridge University Press.

———. 1992. The Evolution of Global Labor Markets in the First and Second World since 1830: Background Evidence and Hypotheses. NBER/DAE Working Paper no. 36. Cambridge, Mass.: National Bureau of Economic Research, February.

Williamson, J. G., and P. H. Lindert. 1980. *American Inequality: A Macroeconomic History*. New York: Academic Press.

5   Consumer Behavior, Diet, and the Standard of Living in Late Colonial and Early Antebellum America, 1770–1840

Lorena S. Walsh

Did living standards as measured by trends in consumption patterns improve, remain static, or decline in the decades following the American Revolution? My aim in this paper is to survey what we know and what we don't know about patterns of consumer behavior as these may have influenced the diet of inhabitants of the early republic. The sources included in the survey are probate inventories, widows' allowances, culinary history, archaeology, and account books. While these sources—especially in combination, since each by itself supplies an incomplete picture—hold great promise for future research, none offer quick or easy answers about continuity and change in diet.

Conclusions that can be drawn from recent research in several disciplines are more tentative than one would wish, but nonetheless suggest that in the early nineteenth century many Americans maintained the levels of consumption of household goods and of foods that they had achieved at the end of the colonial era. Moreover, for wealthy and middle classes in both rural and urban areas, household amenities, variety in diet, and the means to prepare foods increased, while seasonal variations in the foods available diminished. Among the groups that we know the least about—those at the bottom of the income distribution, and especially the urban poor—living standards most likely did

Lorena S. Walsh is a historian in the Research Department at the Colonial Williamsburg Foundation and adjunct lecturer in American Studies at the College of William and Mary.

The debts incurred in writing this paper are many. Barbara Carson, James Henretta, Jack Larkin, Jean Lee, and Michael Zuckerman kindly shared references to the historical literature. Joanne Bowen, Julia King, Henry Miller, and Dennis Pogue were helpful in explaining the archaeological materials and in providing references to relevant site reports. Patricia Gibbs supplied a quick but thorough review of culinary history literature, as well as lending me a good part of her personal library. Winifred Rothenberg provided data on livestock slaughter weights. Many scholars generously shared preliminary reports and drafts of works in progress. Doubtless some of the preliminary findings and early drafts will be revised before publication. This is of course the prerogative of the various authors, and I am solely responsible for inaccuracies of summary or interpretation.

not improve, and may have declined. Unfortunately, evidence about levels of consumption among households of varying wealth are firmest for the late colonial period. Thereafter, results become increasingly more tentative, and the years after 1830 are truly a "dark age." This results not from lack of relevant materials but from failure to study them. Here is a major area for future research.

I'll begin with a series of gross generalizations that seem warranted from the available materials. These will be treated in greater detail in later discussions of the different sources. (1) Living standards, as measured by quantity and variety of household equipment, appear to have improved for the urban middle classes and for farmers who had access to hired or bound labor between 1790 and 1830. The situation of urban poor, of farmers without extra labor, and of landless rural residents is uncertain; there were clearly no major improvements. (2) The life styles of the urban and rural upper and middle classes followed increasingly diverging paths. (3) Cooking and food preservation technology remained basically unchanged everywhere for all groups until the 1830s and, for many places and groups, did not change significantly until after the Civil War. (4) Systems of food distribution may have changed (or failed to do so) in ways that affected both urban and rural diets. Too little research has been done on this topic to permit generalization. This is an area that deserves particular attention in future. (5) Consumption of vegetables increased throughout the population. (6) Consumption of alcohol rose dramatically between 1790 and 1820, then declined markedly after 1830, especially in New England among all consumers, and probably among women and children elsewhere. (7) Coffee drinking increased, while tea drinking remained relatively constant. The social connotations of use of these beverages (especially tea) continued to be a prime consideration for their adoption, separate from their nutritional role. (8) Despite many assertions to the contrary, people of all classes ate at least as much beef as they did pork. Because beef was generally eaten as fresh rather than preserved meat, it is seldom mentioned in some kinds of sources, and its importance in the diet has been greatly underestimated. (9) Food supplies became somewhat less dependent on season as improved systems of harvesting and distribution and marginally improved preservation techniques afforded a greater range of foods across the calendar year. (10) Consumption of fish and to a lesser extent shellfish increased above levels prevailing between circa 1725 and 1775 throughout older parts of the country. (11) Wheat flour was increasingly substituted for other cereal grains, especially in New England. (12) Production of dairy products, especially butter, rose substantially in New England, the Middle Atlantic, the Midwest, and the Upper South.

I wish also to raise at the outset two other considerations. First, evaluation of the production, procurement, preparation, preservation, and consumption of food must take into account changing roles and responsibilities by gender. Expectations for women's role in the family, in the general society, and in opportunities or necessities for various kinds of work in or outside the home were changing at least as quickly as were those of men, and perhaps more quickly. Women were almost exclusively responsible for preparing and serving meals, along with numerous other productive and reproductive responsibilities. Changes in the time women had available for raising, processing, and cooking food as opposed to other pursuits had significant impact on what families ate. From the mid-eighteenth century, women who wished their families to adopt genteel manners and genteel styles of taking meals effected changes in their home environments and in mealtime content and rituals. By the early nineteenth century, the ideology of domesticity enjoined a limited and sex-specific role for women, primarily in the sphere of the home (as opposed to the outside world of waged work and commerce), with particular emphasis on wives' and mothers' roles in nurturing children, and in uplifting society through private moral influence and religious example exercised largely within the family. Homemaking and housekeeping acquired an enhanced and sentimentalized role. Urban middle-class women, most influenced by domestic ideology, certainly devoted more time to the preparation of increasingly complex and elaborate meals, and some to fashionable entertainments. Rural women used their time differently, but the major shift seems to have been to other commercial pursuits, rather than to significantly increased time in the kitchen and about the table. In New England and the middle states, many rural women shifted out of textile production shortly after the close of the Revolution, devoting more of their time instead to dairying or various sorts of craft outwork. In the South, textile production gained in importance in all but the wealthiest households through the War of 1812. (I'm uncertain as to the dating of a downturn in household production.) Women from poor urban and rural families devoted increasing time to a variety of wage labor or outwork in order to supplement family incomes. These competing demands cut into the time available to produce or procure and to prepare and preserve foodstuffs. Women's income from such activities as factory work; spinning; weaving; knitting; sewing; washing; taking in boarders; making buttons, shoe parts, or palm hats; dairying; and the like were often critical to maintaining family income. Opportunities for such work were surely increasing during this period, just as those for gardening, animal raising, gathering wild foods, and scavenging firewood were diminishing (Blackmar 1989, chap. 4; Clark 1990, chaps. 4, 8; Geib 1981, chaps. 3, 6; Hood 1988, chaps. 1, 4; Jensen 1986, chap. 3; Larkin 1988, chap. 1; McMahon 1981, introduction, chaps. 5, 6, 1989b; Matthews 1987, chap. 1; Shammas 1990, 186–88; Williams 1985). To date, European historians have paid more attention to the implications of such changes, especially among marginal groups. American historians might profit from their example (Boserup 1985; Goody 1982; Humphries 1990; Mintz 1985, chap. 3; Tilly 1985).

Second, the myth of self-sufficiency, while attenuated by recent research, still exerts a powerful and often deadening influence on inquiries into diet.

Many studies of rural foodways based either on probate inventories or archaeology tend to assume that observed foodstuffs were produced by the individual household for private consumption. This assumption is demonstrably false for households both at the top of the wealth structure and at the lower end. Only the more substantial farmers achieved self-sufficiency in food and, in the process of achieving this goal, produced a superfluity of at least some foodstuffs that were either sold or expended in entertaining. Nonlandowners, along with some tenant farmers and freeholders with minimal acreage, had to purchase some foods. Freeholding farmers of middling economic and social status may have been more self-sufficient, but this is much more bold assumption than certain knowledge. Given the amount of work required to raise, prepare, and cook food and otherwise to maintain a home, for an individual to live in accord with prevailing standards of decency in the early nineteenth century, he or she needed to be a member of a larger, cooperating household. The strategies households at varying levels of wealth adopted for making a living were increasingly varied; most involved either greater dependence on wage labor or on market exchange than had been the norm in the colonial period. Changes in the labor system, especially in New England and the middle colonies, brought about changes in household subsistence strategies. In the South, labor systems changed somewhat less dramatically, but alterations in crop mix and commodity markets also encouraged change in household production and consumption strategies (Bowen 1990, chaps. 2, 3; Clark 1990, chap. 1; Clemens and Simler 1988; Gross 1982; Pruitt 1984; Shammas 1990, chap. 3).

5.1   General Trends in Material Culture Gleaned from Probate Inventories

5.1.1   Inventory Studies, circa 1770 to 1789

Studies of probate inventories are most plentiful for the colonial era. Many of them have benefited from long-term, cooperative research strategies including the sharing of promising analytical categories and information on varying colonial monetary systems. These suggest a slowly rising standard of living from the middle of the eighteenth century. By circa 1770 colonial elites owned a number of household amenities and had the equipment to prepare a varied and rich dietary fare. Those of middling wealth had also acquired more household comforts, along with a few amenities that had formerly been luxury items available only to the elite. The rural poor functioned with much less in the way of household goods, continuing styles of life that had changed only incrementally since the seventeenth century. Still, they made some progress over time in acquiring a somewhat broader range of cooking and dining equipment, preserved foods, bedding, chairs, and tables. Status-laden foods, especially tea and sugar, exerted an ever-increasing appeal among all wealth groups. In general, most households achieved a slowly rising level of comfort without spending a greater proportion of family wealth on home furnishings (Carr and Walsh 1978, 1980, 1988b, n.d.; Carson and Walsh n.d.; Jones, 1980; Main 1988; Main and Main 1988; Shammas 1980, 1982, 1990; Walsh 1983, 1988).

5.1.2   Inventory Studies, 1790–1830

An initial caution on the quality of the data is in order. Inventory studies for this period are few and far between and are sometimes difficult to compare. Most are based on relatively small numbers of decedents. Biases in coverage are seldom tested rigorously, if tested at all. Both the categories chosen for scrutiny and the methods of analysis vary widely. As the national economy grew in size and complexity, it becomes increasingly difficult to place the relative standing and economic roles of particular localities within the context of the wider regions of which they were a part, at least until national agricultural censuses are available. Few studies assess the proportion of personal wealth devoted to household equipment and furnishings, so possible shifts in allocations between producer and consumer goods cannot be evaluated. In addition, a bewildering variety of currencies of account—pounds, shillings, and pence in pre- or postwar state currencies of differing and shifting values against sterling and/or the Spanish dollar, coexisting with, but not supplanted by, U.S. dollars and cents before 1820—present individual scholars with exceedingly difficult problems in making inventory values comparable over time within a locality, much less within a region.[1]

Probate record series are scanty and sometimes nonexistent for many states during the later years of the American Revolution. Rapid inflation of the multiple currencies of account between 1777 and 1781 render stated values in existing inventories exceedingly difficult to interpret. Other sources such as account books and private correspondence make clear, however, that general living standards declined during the war, and that postwar economic recovery was slow and halting (McCusker and Menard 1985, chap. 17; Clemens 1990; Walsh n.d.). Fuller runs of inventories are available in most places from the mid- to late 1780s, coinciding with the onset of better times and with various localities stabilizing their postindependence court and probate systems.

Among studies of inventoried decedents in the colonial period, the proportion of households judged to be among the elite usually range between 5 and 10 percent of those inventoried and, in some places where reporting rates are low, as many as 20 percent. Middling farmer, planter, and artisan households are usually between 30 and 45 percent, and the poor (those at or below the median inventory value) 30 to 40 percent (Carr and Walsh 1988b; Main 1988).

---

1. John J. McCusker (1978) has provided students of colonial history with an invaluable resource that permits comprehensive standardization of monetary values over place and time. Students of the early national period are not so fortunate. Some specialists in price history are attempting to standardize currencies of the colonial and early national periods, at least for some states, but not all the results are yet published.

Roughly similar proportions appear in some postrevolutionary inventory studies. However, reporting rates appear to have declined in many places after independence, with the poor increasingly less well represented. Given the biases of inventories toward richer and older households, these proportions do not reflect the distribution of wealth among all free households in the living population. There the poor made up a much higher proportion. The paucity of information on wealth distributions among the living population in the colonial period requires that scholars make heroic assumptions in order to generalize from the decedent to the living population. Sources for the living population are more plentiful for the early national period. Unfortunately, to date, comparisons of probated to general populations after the Revolution are too few to permit meaningful comparisons.

The available studies from circa 1790 to 1830 show a modest increase in the standard of living in older areas, especially among landowning farmers and more-propertied tenants. Such improvements, however, must be interpreted in the context of substantial outmigration that removed many families with lesser prospects from older areas. The migrants had greater chances for improving their fortunes through farm building or wage labor in newer areas, but at the price of lower levels of material comfort for some years after they moved. Some eastern tenant farmers also improved their fortunes, but it is likely that the social and economic characteristics of tenants changed. Many post–Revolutionary War tenants had access to greater resources than did the typical prewar tenant farmer, but most of them were children of landowners or immigrants who arrived with some capital (Clemens 1990; Marks 1979; Walsh 1985).

While subject to the limitations noted above, the findings for older areas are surprisingly consistent. Farm families appear to have achieved some improvements in levels of domestic comfort. Most postwar households, in contrast to the earlier years, were equipped with at least one table, one wooden bedstead, several chairs, and some ceramic or pewter plates. Most houses, however, were still often dark (given the expense of candles) and cold (given the rising price of firewood). Middling rural households were also more likely to boast a piece or two of case furniture, a timepiece, a looking glass, some ceramic table- and teawares, and a few more kitchen conveniences, especially Dutch kettles and roasting ovens that facilitated preparation of quick hot breads, whole fowls, and larger cuts of meat. At lower levels of wealth, householders concentrated on building up basic furnishings—chairs, tables, and bedsteads (Bushman 1987; Clemens 1990; Cook 1989, chap. 4; Jensen 1986, 219–20; Kessel 1981, 14–59; Larkin 1988, 132–38; Martin 1989; Sweeney 1984; Walsh 1982).

Differences in household arrangements between urban and rural areas, already noted for the colonial period, became ever more pronounced in the early republic. Most elite and a goodly proportion of upper-middle-class town dwellers accumulated a burgeoning array of mahogany furnishings, sideboards, silver plate, decorative items, musical instruments, and elaborate dining and cooking equipment designed for entertainment and display. Lower-middle-class urbanites, along with a lesser proportion of poor urban property-holders, followed suit, to the extent that resources permitted or aspirations supported. For example, in York County, Virginia, in 1815 the poorest ratepayers in the town of Williamsburg—those with assessed property below the median value—paid thirteen times the taxes on luxury goods as did rural taxpayers of equivalent assessed wealth. Two-thirds of all Williamsburg taxpayers had at least one luxurious household furnishing (as defined by current law), but only a quarter of rural families were so assessed. Rural households, with the exception of a few extraordinarily rich planters or merchants, almost never adopted the extravagant display characteristic of urban elites (Smart 1986).[2] Even in a frontier state such as Tennessee in the 1790s, the state capital of Knoxville was the scene of genteel entertainments, while most rural residents were subsisting with little more than the bare essentials of decent but unpretentious living (Gump 1989, chap. 1).

However, scholars, who have relied more on prescriptive literature than on inventory analysis, have often overstated the levels of display that urban families adopted. A new study of dining in Washington, D.C., between 1818 and 1826 shows that few urban households had full sets of equipment for serving high-style dinners for as many as ten guests. Only 13 percent of inventoried households possessed all the furniture, serving equipment, cutlery, and sets of plates and glasses that the prescriptive literature suggested was necessary for such a meal, and only 4 percent of these decedents could entertain twenty or more in style. Such entertainments also required more space in the house and increasingly took place in separate dining rooms. Many urban homes were simply too small. Below these privileged few, 48 percent of the inventoried households could dine decently but unpretentiously with individual knives, forks, and plates, put a cloth on the table, and present several dishes in appropriate serving wares. Most couples may have decided not to acquire all the props needed for stylish dining because, rather than serving as a focus for family interaction, high-style urban dinners were often virtually all-male affairs, with the hostess the only woman present. Many upper-class women questioned the rewards for themselves of such entertainments and got more enjoyment from less formal teas and evening suppers that required less elaborate preparations (Carson 1990; cf. Smart 1986; Martin 1987b; Wenger 1991; the male-dominated high-style dinner became a fashionable form of entertainment in most larger cities, not just in the nation's capital).

Families who moved west to build farms on the frontier suffered a decline in comfort as well as in quality of diet, at least in the initial years. Houses were small and crude, with little in the way of furnishings. In places where

---

2. Smart's data base is a tax list rather than probate inventories, but her findings are similar to those from inventory studies.

there were few established farms, few foods were available year-round aside from corn, salt pork, coffee, tea, and alcohol. The length of time an area remained a frontier (in terms of limited availability and high costs of consumer goods) varied, depending on such factors as pace of in-migration, development of cheap transport, and discovery and development of cash crops or other marketable natural resources (Arnow 1960, chap. 14; Miller and Hurry 1983). Frontier housewives, lacking both equipment and ingredients, prepared simple meals—mostly boiled or fried dishes accompanied by quick breads baked on the hearth. Few frontier cabins had built-in ovens or roasting spits and at least half also lacked ceramic or pewter plates, cutlery, serving dishes, or for that matter, chairs and tables. Migrant women could not take with them the cooking and dining equipment necessary to create a separate sphere of feminine influence. On the whole, frontier women seem to have attached more importance than men did to such amenities as plates, teaware, and ingredients that added variety to diet, as well as to civilized table manners. According to McMahon's recent analysis of settlers' later recollections of their daily fare, most men who moved West did not care much about what they ate or the circumstances in which they consumed their meals, so long as their stomachs were full (McMahon 1989b; cf. Arnow 1960, chaps. 13, 14; Gump 1989, chap. 5). As frontier areas matured, better-off residents achieved a life style (and presumably diet) similar to that common in older areas. Perkins's study (1991) contrasting Kentucky inventories of 1801–4 with those of 1781–83 shows that by the turn of the century the majority of decedents in the upper two-thirds of the wealth distribution had acquired the sorts of furniture, ceramics, cutlery, teawares, and other amenities popular in the East. However, while decedents in the bottom third were better equipped than most of the poorest early settlers, at the turn of the century fewer than half of such households had tables, chairs, bedsteads, crude ceramics, or knives and forks. Their style of life was similar to that of poorer eastern households fifty years earlier.

Findings that relate specifically to diet in the early republic include the following. In New England and the Upper South, corn was the primary breadstuff, while wheat predominated in the middle colonies. Rye was the second most important grain in New England and in parts of the middle colonies where German immigrants were influential. In most households of median wealth, boiling and frying (rather than baking and roasting) were the predominant methods of food preparation. The lower the household's wealth, the more limited were stocks of preserved food and food storage equipment, indicating a need for frequent purchase of some foodstuffs, especially meat. Stocks of preserved meat increased in late-eighteenth-century Massachusetts inventories. Period account books, however, suggest that poor householders still turned to the market for some or perhaps the bulk of their meats. While most poor rural households kept a cow for milk, few engaged in butter or cheese making. Most family farms produced sufficient grains to meet the family's minimum yearly caloric requirements. If the family wished to eat a reasonable quantity of meat, however, they had to obtain it from more prosperous farmers. Qualitative sources imply that poor and lower middling households opted for more meat instead of a more varied fare. True consumption patterns remain undocumented.

Households above median wealth were more self-sufficient in foodstuffs. The greater the household's wealth, the greater the quantity and variety of preserved meat, grain, cider, fruit, and vegetables. Equipment for preserving, pickling, and dairying was also more often available, as were utensils for roasting and oven baking. Elite and some middling householders also purchased imported items, such as spices, dried fruits, sugar, rum, and wines, and sold much of the grain and meat they produced either to neighbors, in towns, or for the coastwise and export trades. A proliferation of country stores that accepted payment in locally raised produce such as butter, eggs, poultry, and vegetables made these items, as well as imported groceries, more widely available to rural consumers of lesser status (Geib 1981, chap. 3; McMahon 1981).

Overall, the composition of most Americans' diets changed in two major ways between the late 1780s and the 1830s. First, vegetable consumption appears to have risen for all groups, with increasing evidence after about 1790 of more widespread use of white potatoes and more careful preservation of root crops and greens. Greater frequency of appearance of vegetable stocks in inventories overall, accompanied by more careful enumeration by variety (rather than lumping all as "sauce"), suggests vegetables were more often prepared as individual dishes, rather than just boiled together as a secondary ingredient in a one-pot meal. This development was probably confined largely to upper and middling wealth groups, where inventoried vegetable listings (aside from potatoes) were concentrated. A limited number of cooking vessels and limited preparation time probably precluded serving vegetables as a separate dish among the poor. Period garden and farm diaries suggest that both elite and middle-class families began to value greater variety in their diet more highly, and were willing to invest considerable effort in truck gardening for household use, as well as purchasing more fruits and vegetables either in town markets or from rural peddlers. Poorer folk may have eaten more vegetables out of necessity. Rising grain prices at the turn of the century made cereals less affordable for independent households, farm size decreased among landowners, fewer tenants had access to rented farms of a viable size, and managers of city hospitals, rural almshouses, and local jails needed to cut the costs of inmate's meals (Marks 1979, chap. 3; McMahon 1981, chap. 3, 1985, 1989a, 1989b; Sarudy 1989, 1990; Ulrich 1990, 323–29; Walsh n.d.).

Second, meal ingredients varied less by season than in the mid-eighteenth century. Stocks of preserved meat, vegetables, and cider, where present at all, lasted through most of the year, and springtime shortages became less evident than in the seventeenth and early eighteenth centuries. The scheduling of the harvesting of meat and dairy resources was so arranged that fresh meat was available nearly year-round. (See section 5.5.) Dairy products, vegetables, and fruits were preserved more often and more carefully. The number of inventories with vinegar and pickles increased dramatically by the 1830s, as did the amount of space cookbooks devoted to preservation instructions for meats, vegetables, and fruits (McMahon 1981, 1989a, 1989c). McMahon concluded that "households with the most ample resources broke through the previous plateaus in dietary standards as they produced both an abundant and increasingly varied yearly diet" (1981, 305).

Evidence for increasing interest in obtaining a more varied, attractively presented fare among middling and elite households (and, by implication, in acquisition of genteel manners appropriate to the equipment) appears in the majority of period eastern United States inventories. Families who could live in some degree of comfort acquired more dining ware, including individual plates, knives and forks, and specialized serving pieces. Change was most pronounced in urban areas, but appeared also in lesser degree throughout the countryside. The ability to entertain with some style, long critical to gentry culture, became an increasingly important goal of middle-class respectability as well, and the knowledge of how to eat properly became essential. Rituals of dining and taking tea among the upper classes became more complicated and formalized in the early republic. For people hoping to enhance social status, appropriate manners and knowledge of how to properly use increasingly specialized dining and drinking wares and cutlery were critical to success. As politics became more democratic, education more widespread, and more middling folk aspired to gentility, the old social and economic elite closed ranks. They developed more intricate rituals and rules of etiquette centered on dinners and other entertainments involving the serving of foods that were designed to exclude aspiring social climbers with new wealth or new political position but less than gentle upbringing. The act of dining carried increasingly high ritual stakes, and advice manuals proliferated beginning in the 1830s to instruct the aspiring in the rudiments and a few of the intricacies of civilized behavior. Carson's (1990) relation of the hazards and triumphs of "power dining" in the nation's capital reveals that such apparently insignificant details as whether one used two-tined or multitined forks had real social significance that could even, on occasion, affect political standing. Changes in some aspects of diet among the better-off were intricately linked to social and political changes (Bushman 1987; Carson 1990; Kasson 1987; Williams 1985, chap. 1).

Contrasts in living standards between the urban rich and reasonably well-off and the urban poor were greater than between poor and most middling folk in the countryside. Even though many rural poor failed to leave probate records, sufficient numbers of inventories survive to provide an approximation of their living conditions, if not of their true proportion among all decedents. This seems not to have been the case in larger towns. In his study of Philadelphia's laboring classes between 1750 and 1800, Billy Smith found almost no probate records for lesser artisans, manual laborers, and mariners. In order to assess their living standards, he had to construct likely household budgets using records of daily purchases by the Pennsylvania Hospital to provide retail prices, proportions of foods eaten by hospital inmates for weighting those prices, and assumptions about necessary caloric intakes to establish average family needs and their relative costs. Expenditures for rum, taxes, medical services, burial fees, and household furnishings were not considered. Extant wage series for the various groups supplied information on income. This exercise demonstrated that for families of unskilled and lesser-skilled Philadelphia workers the expense of living independently in rented quarters with a diet similar to that of prisoners and clothing equivalent to that of almshouse inmates usually exceeded the likely annual income of the primary wage-earner. The costs of food, fuel, and rent escalated in the 1790s, and while wages rose, they did not rise as much (Smith 1990, chap. 4, appendix F).

In Carson's study of inventoried Washington, D.C., residents between 1818 and 1826, free blacks (who were between 10 and 17 percent of the free population between 1810 and 1830) were virtually unrepresented, as were an unknown percentage of poor white decedents. Consequently, many of the poorest town dwellers are missing from the analysis. Still, Carson found that 20 percent of the householders (most of them at the lowest level of portable inventoried wealth) ate without benefit of knives, forks, or even spoons, had no table linen, and owned few ceramics of any kind; possibly they may have been sitting on the floor eating out of the cooking pot with their hands.[3] (Surveys of available housing indicate that many families were crowded into one- or two-room temporary shanties, or in slightly more permanent dwellings that offered little more space.) Another 19 percent of District householders (many also poor, but others with sufficient assets to make a choice) ate their meals seated at a table with individual spoons, but eschewed knives and forks and had only a minimal assemblage of tablewares. These findings too suggest that in larger towns the very poor, as well as some of those a rung or two up from the bottom, continued to live in impoverished conditions where simply finding sufficient food was a constant struggle. Lack of fuel, as well as of time and cooking equipment, may have forced poor townfolk to rely primarily on cold meals—bread, cheese, and when they could afford them, carryout pies supplied by early purveyors of fast food (Carson 1990). Blackmar (1979, 1989) presents a similarly dismal survey of lower-class housing in New York City between 1780 and 1850.

---

3. The criterion employed for differentiating a householder from a boarder or lodger is the presence in the inventory of both one or more beds and one or more cooking vessels, indicating that the owner could fulfill both of the functions basic to any household of sleeping and cooking.

5.1.3   1830 and After

Inventory studies for the period after 1830 are even fewer in number and more limited in the time covered, and almost none have been published.[4] No general conclusions about living standards for various groups are yet possible. Consequently, some of the more likely trends in consumer behavior and diet will be discussed instead in section 5.3 as part of culinary history. A major unresolved question concerns the influence of the cult of domesticity on family life styles. To what extent did new perceptions of women's roles bring about a reallocation of their labor time within the household? Did new attitudes about the cultural importance of the home cause families to allocate their resources differently? Larkin (1988, 138–48) reports that in rural New England further improvements in domestic comforts appeared in the 1830s and 1840s.[5] These include improved lighting, more on-the-road vehicles, greater segregation of sleeping from daytime living facilities, and elements of the parlor culture associated with the cult of domesticity—window curtains, wallpaper, carpets, clocks, musical instruments, sofas, heating stoves, and the like. Cook (1989, chap. 6) provides corroborating, albeit less detailed, evidence for New Hampshire. Acquisition of these goods was presumably accompanied by changes in the diet and in women's roles in the household, and by a drop in the size of completed families.

Blumin (1989, 183), among others, finds a similar "more refined middle-class culture revolving around the well-furnished, female-directed middle-class home" in northeastern cities by midcentury. This development was, however, limited to nonmanual middle-class families. Urban middle-class housing seems to have improved by the 1830s, facilitating many of the changes associated with the cult of domesticity, for example, more space for entertaining and display and more elegant entrances. But housing standards changed little if at all for less privileged workers, and many of the very poor still subsisted with little or no furniture, no artificial light, no indoor toilets or running water, and presumably little change in women's work in the home and no better diets (cf. Blackmar 1989; C. E. Clark 1987; Larkin 1988; Williams 1985; Wright 1981, 34–40). Middle-class families in the rural Middle Atlantic and southern states and in newer areas of the West were much slower to adopt these trends, if at all, if household possessions provide evidence (Fox-Genovese 1988, 61–82, chap. 2; Jensen 1986, chap. 7). Links between

---

4. Part of this lacuna doubtless flows from my lack of familiarity with both the published literature and works in progress for this period. The material culture specialists whom I consulted reported few studies in progress, however, and bibliographies from period studies provided few additional references. Several of the analyses cited by scholars come from ongoing working files assembled by historical museums, not yet complete enough for publication. In addition, recent programs of the Economic History Association and Social Science History Association, among others, showed little current work in the field.

5. A study of prescriptive literature (Matthews 1987) suggests the same timing for rural New England as Larkin found in inventories. Jaffee (1991) and Garrison (1991) are also suggestive.

changes in domestic equipment, family size, perceptions of women's roles, and social emulation require further study.

Mass production of some household goods lowered costs of such items as chairs, window glass, textiles, clocks, ceramics, pressed glassware, and electroplated silver utensils between 1790 and 1850, and especially between 1830 and 1850 (Larkin 1988, chap. 5; Martin 1942, chap. 4; Jaffee 1991; G. L. Miller 1980, 1984a, 1984b, 1990; Shammas 1990; Williams 1985, chap. 3). Price and purchasing trends in ceramics are the most thoroughly studied. As prices declined, consumers substituted ceramics for more expensive metalwares, upgraded the type of ceramics they purchased, and bought more kinds of vessels in a greater variety of sizes. While families devoted only a minuscule fraction of their household expenditures to ceramics, tablewares are important indicators of more significant changes in consumption patterns of foods and beverages (G. L. Miller 1984a, 1984b, 1990; Miller, Martin, and Dickinson n.d.; Shammas 1990).

Some families may have been able to raise standards of comfort without spending more on household goods, a pattern that began in the mid-eighteenth century[6] (Carr and Walsh 1988b, n.d.; Main 1988; Shammas 1990, chap. 4). Spending more, less, or the same of course depended not just on changing costs of goods but also on competing uses of income, including the costs of rent, fuel, and food. Studies of postrevolutionary inventories do not consider the question of allocations of portable wealth among various capital and noncapital uses; hence it is impossible to determine whether these shifted over time.[7]

For the urban poor, the ability to keep poultry, a pig, or a cow or to raise garden vegetables doubtless often made the difference between sufficient food or scanty fare. These opportunities were diminishing in larger cities after 1830, but there is little firm evidence on the extent of the practice (Bushman 1981; Levenstein 1988, chap. 2; Marks 1979, 130; McMahon 1981, chap. 3; Strasser 1982, chap. 1).

Some rudiments of cleanliness, like polite table manners, were also becoming part of gentry and to some extent of middle-class respectability between 1800 and 1850. Some families, mostly gentry and middle-class professionals, took up routine washing of at least faces and hands. A few rural householders began to dump refuse in pits rather than scattering it broadcast, and the market

6. Shammas (1990, chap. 4) found few changes in spending on consumer durables from the eighteenth century to the present. These accounted for about 25 percent of inventoried movable wealth in eighteenth-century inventories, as they did in a 1979 survey of household wealth in America.

7. Marks (1979, chap. 6) is an exception. She found that inventoried decedents in rural southern Maryland spent a slightly lower percentage of portable wealth on household furnishings between 1821 and 1840 than they had between 1790 and 1820. Intended allocations may have changed little, however, as rising slave values alone accounted for the alteration. Colonial spending patterns demonstrated very little change over time (Carr and Walsh 1988b, n.d.; Main 1988).

for mass-produced Connecticut Valley brooms grew phenomenally. Store-keepers carried more ceramic toilet wares by the 1850s. Household advice books began to include more information on cleaning houses and kitchen utensils. On the other hand, widespread tolerance for dirt, both in homes and on bodies, remained the norm rather than the exception. Improvements in personal hygiene and household sanitation were probably insufficient to improve prospects for better health for most families. (Bushman and Bushman 1988; Larkin 1988, 127–32; G. L. Miller 1990, 6). (But see section 5.4.)

5.1.4   Opportunities and Limitations

As McMahon's pioneering work demonstrates, probate inventories are indeed valuable for establishing general trends in diet over time, especially what types of foods were produced or could be purchased by families of varying wealth, and changing seasonal patterns of scarcity or plenty. On the other hand, I conclude that inventories are of limited use for estimating per capita consumption of foodstuffs. For a number of reasons, listings of stocks of food are sporadic, and information on potential consumers of the enumerated stock inadequate.

First, there is the problem of what was recorded and what was omitted. Stocks of preserved foods vary greatly by the season in which the inventory was made, and these variations must be taken into account. Second, there were often unwritten local practices for excluding from an inventory a portion of the stocks required for family consumption. One cannot be certain to what extent recording practices varied from one locality to another, nor for that matter, from one appraisal to another. Some estate creditors may have insisted that the appraisers include all assets in the inventory, while others may have agreed to leave some food stocks aside for the subsistence of distressed widows and orphans. Thus, listings for small estates are more likely to be incomplete than those for large ones. Third, the crops produced in the year the decedent died may not be included in the inventory, or may be reported only in subsequent estate accounts, a record type that is preserved less systematically than inventories. And the more the family depended on the efforts of the primary breadwinner alone, the more year-of-death output may have been diminished by the increasing incapacitation of the farmer. Crop production as reported in inventories, especially on farms with little additional labor, may represent minimal yields. Fourth, perishables were usually omitted from inventories in all seasons. Consequently, generalizations about the monotony of daily fare based on analysis of stocks of preserved foods may be exaggerated. For fruits and vegetables that were available only for a limited season this is not a major distortion, but not so for meat. Beef (and, to a much lesser degree, mutton) was almost always eaten fresh and hence does not appear in inventories except as livestock. Archaeological studies and studies based on account books introduce a major modification to findings from inventories. Sites from a variety of regions and classes all show consumption of beef and pork to have been roughly equal. (See, for example, H. M. Miller 1988; Bowen 1990.)

The second problem in using inventories to estimate consumption involves the composition of the consuming household. One seldom knows the numbers and ages of family members, whether or not all were present in the household throughout the year, or alternatively whether nonfamily boarders or found workers were present for all or part of the year. Neither does one know whether the foodstuffs were intended for family consumption, for entertainment of others, or for sale. Where slaves were present, it is sheer guesswork to allocate food stocks among them in the absence of knowledge of the particular rationing practices of the owners.

On the other hand, inventories have some underexploited strengths. While enumerations of stored foods vary by season, listings of equipment for food storage, preservation, preparation, and service appear consistently. Analysis of available kitchen equipment by time, place, and wealth group can provide much information about the most common methods of cooking and likely components of the diets of various groups. The presence of more specialized cooking and serving ware can supplement information from cookbooks to better define which groups were adding variety to their meals and adopting new foods (especially non-European grocery items) and new methods of preparation and preservation, and were placing more emphasis on presentation and display (cf. Martin 1987a, 1988; Shammas 1990, chap. 4). The increasing presence of tea and coffee pots, kettles, and wares, for example, helps to trace differing households' adoption of imported beverages with status connotations. High desirability of these caffeinated beverages is underscored in that wares for serving them made up over half of all ceramic vessels imported from England by American merchants between 1783 and 1855, and in that consumers tended to purchase more costly teawares than tablewares (Miller, Martin, and Dickinson n.d.). Finally, presence or absence of food storage and dairying equipment helps to determine levels of self-sufficiency or necessary recourse to frequent small purchases of foodstuffs. While inventories are not likely to yield reliable estimates of per capita consumption, they do provide the greatest amount of information for a broad range of families consistent over time and place.

5.2 Consumption Estimates from Widows' Allowances and Institutional Records

Widows' allowances, occasionally stated in wills, are a more promising source for measuring actual levels of consumption of various foodstuffs. Amounts of major foods intended for one person are clearly stated, as well as rights of access to less readily quantified produce from gardens and orchards. Lemon, McMahon, and Kessel report an average yearly consumption between circa 1750 and circa 1830 of 150 to 200 pounds of meat, 13 to 23 bushels of the most commonly consumed grains, and some vegetables and dairy products or pasturage for a cow and ground for a garden (Kessel 1981, 242–47; Klingaman 1971; Lemon 1967, 1972, chap. 6; McMahon 1981, chap. 1).

Unfortunately, this source has its limitations. The custom was a restricted one, pertaining mainly to older wives of farmers of middling status in parts of New England and the Middle Atlantic states. The practice was not very common until the last half of the eighteenth century, and it is not clear how long it continued into the nineteenth century; so far analyses end in 1830. The numbers cited in studies to date are so small that one is uncertain how far to stretch generalizations, especially if the observations are broken down over time, as they must be to isolate potential change (Klingaman 1971; Pruitt 1984). In addition, widows' allowances, especially of grain, may have included some surplus that could be traded for other goods or to fatten livestock. (The higher grain allowances include more than anyone was likely to have consumed.)[8] Preserved meat allowances may reflect minimal rather than normal consumption patterns, which almost certainly included some fresh as well as salted meats.

In a related study, estimates of per capita food consumption derived from estate administration accounts and from the 1840 agricultural census were compared for a rural southern Maryland county. While calculations from the agricultural production and population schedules indicated 300 pounds of meat were available per capita in 1840, administration accounts dating from 1798 to 1839 (which record the foods actually consumed by widows, dependent children, and slaves of deceased farmers) showed a much lower consumption of only 70 pounds of meat per capita plus some salt fish. The accounts also showed per capita consumption of 15 bushels of corn, the traditional standard allowance, supplemented with 2.7 bushels of wheat and 1 of potatoes. Farmers' inventories for the same county presented a different picture, with listings of food stocks increasing after the 1780s, and especially between 1820 and 1840. Increases in vegetables, poultry, and dairy products were most pronounced. This may reflect both increased on-farm consumption and the greater likelihood of such produce being included in an inventory, as possibilities for selling to country stores raised the value of perishables. As in New England, however, wealthy farmers were the ones improving their diets. Food items other than poultry, corn, bacon, and pork were largely absent in inventories worth less than $500 and increased greatly in those worth over $2,000. The allowances in the administration accounts suggest the diet of poor farmers was similar to that of area slaves who generally consumed rations of two pounds of meat (or occasional salt fish) and one peck of cornmeal per week, supplemented with poultry and garden produce they raised themselves (Marks 1979, 113–33).

8. Not all of the studies clearly report average total allowances of all grains.

Institutional records, in addition to estate administration accounts, are another promising but so far little used source for estimating per capita consumption of various foods. Detailed records of the amounts and types of foods purchased by almshouses, hospitals, and colleges are available, along with information on individual rations allotted to prisoners, seamen, and men in military service. These merit systematic study (cf. Shammas 1990, 134–45).

Most British American colonists clearly had an advantage over their English contemporaries both in access to staple foods and in the proportion of family income needed to secure a calorically adequate diet. Many more colonial families owned cattle and hogs than did contemporary English families, insuring some supply of meat and dairy products. And the proportion of household income colonists spent on food was probably about 10 percent less than that spent by English families (Shammas 1990, chaps. 2, 3, 5, 10). It now seems likely that relatively high standards of consumption for grains and meat were established in the Chesapeake colonies in the seventeenth century and in New England and the Middle Atlantic by the early eighteenth century (Carr, Menard, and Walsh 1991; McMahon 1981). From then until 1840, as the following sections elaborate, wealthy households made some further gains in dietary quantity and especially in dietary variety. Dependent laborers and slaves in particular were allotted much less generous fare, a shortfall they worked diligently, if not always successfully, to rectify. As the American population expanded and urbanization increased, it is doubtful that earlier standards were surpassed for the average American, and many individuals were hard-pressed to maintain them.

5.3 Culinary History

In the category of culinary history, I have included literature on cookbooks, culinary history, vernacular cookery, kitchen and dining equipment, contemporary travellers' accounts and diaries, and miscellaneous general sources on foodways and diet.

Bibliographies and analysis of published cookbooks reveal a shift during the mid-eighteenth century, especially in Britain, from cookbooks describing court cookery to cookbooks increasingly written by and directed to upper-middle-class women. These works provide directions for gentry and upper-middle-class family meals and company entertainments rather than for courtly banquets. Their advertised emphasis on "economical fare" was intended to bring the menus within the means of groups somewhat below the elite and, in the case of English cookbooks, reflected a reaction to complicated, high-style French cookery that emphasized use of expensive ingredients. Stated aims of joining "oeconomy with neatness and elegance," or of providing "elegant, cheap, and easy methods of preparing most of the dishes now in vogue," indicates the intended audience (Maclean 1981, 122, 130). The more popular of these books were available (sometimes reprinted) in the American colonies, and they can be found fairly frequently in the inventories of the upper classes from about 1760. French cookbooks underwent a similar evolution but were little used in the United States. The influence of French styles of cookery, in vogue among some elite circles, arrived indirectly through British sources. Limited female literacy, as well as multiple demands upon women's time, restricted the groups to which cookbooks appealed (Carson 1985; Goody 1982, 148–52; Maclean 1981; Mennell 1985, chaps. 4, 8; Quayle 1978; Wheaton 1983).

The first cookbook written by an American appeared in print in 1796 and was followed in the 1820s, 1830s, and 1840s by a series of frequently reissued regional cookbooks. To the extent these books were directed to middle-class urban women who lacked training in traditional cookery, featured regional and ethnic specialties, and incorporated the contributions of unlettered African-American cooks, they increasingly describe the ideal cuisine of middling Americans and provide occasional examples of more ordinary fare. The first American cookbook addressed to women of humble means appeared in 1832. Rising female literacy in the first half of the nineteenth century doubtless enlarged the market for such books, as did an increase in social entertaining and in women's nurturing role within the family (Randolph 1824; Bryan 1839; Rutledge 1847; Wilson 1957; Hess and Hess 1972, chaps. 6, 7; Weaver 1981, 1982; Carson 1985; Fordyce 1987; Wheaton and Kelly 1988, 308–13, 336–39; Haskell 1990).

British cookbooks published during the Napoleonic Wars reflect the severe food crises that the English poor experienced, especially in 1794–96 and 1799–1801. A series of pamphlets appeared advocating the substitution of broths and vegetables for prohibitively expensive wheat bread that was the staple food of the laboring poor, especially in southern England. Cookbooks directed to middling housewives included instructions for making stews out of pot liquor, meat scraps, vegetables, and scrapings from the family's plates to be distributed to the poor (Wells 1988; Mennell 1985, 214–29; Maclean 1981; Burnett 1966, chap. 3). Americans experienced no acute wartime shortages (although high grain prices did elevate the cost of bread), and domestic cookbook authors of the 1790s included no such instructions. In the aftermath of the Panic of 1819, however, both urban and rural poor were unable to buy sufficient food. Soup kitchens opened in Washington, D.C., for example, and charitable organizations distributed cornmeal in rural southern Maryland (Carson 1990; Marks 1979). A Middle Atlantic cookbook of 1845 included advice on making cheap stews to be given to poor neighbors, suggesting hunger continued to be a problem among some groups (Weaver 1982, 281–82).

Like practitioners of other literary genres, authors of cookbooks tended to borrow heavily from earlier publications and to include certain expected, stereotyped elements. Many period cookbooks, for example, include elaborate seasonal bills of fare that represented highly ambitious company entertainments rather than everyday family fare; directions for marketing, applicable to larger English towns but not, at least until the second quarter of the century, to urban Americans; and advice on the management of household servants.[9] This material depicts the ideal rather than reality, and it seems to me that so far analyses of American materials have insufficiently addressed the question of what was simply borrowed from European sources and what addressed the actual circumstances of American housewives.

Students of cookbooks have been more comfortable in isolating what was new in the evolving literature of cookery, fearing recipes retained through numerous editions might have become outmoded (Hörandner 1981). Unfortunately for those interested in general trends in diet, what was new was generally the preserve of the elite. The trends identified in early-nineteenth-century cookbooks toward more, and more elaborate, desserts, ice cream, and so forth, required ingredients and equipment that ordinary people could not readily afford, or lacked the time to make. Many of the meals suggested for the entertainment of company could be prepared only with the help of one or more servants, and required a stock of dining and serving equipment that few families, including members of the economic elite, possessed. Consequently, much of what appears in the cookbooks represents the fare of the already well-fed, if not the overly well-fed. Much of the available literature, after a nod or two to the "common sorts," quickly retreats to a fulsome treatment of elite company cuisine (Wheaton 1983, introduction; Williams 1985; Belden 1983; McMahon 1981, chaps. 5, 6; Strasser 1982, chap. 9; Wright 1981, 111–12).

Manuscript recipe books do show choices made among available published recipes and some unpublished ones, identify the things mothers wanted to pass on to daughters, and occasionally identify sources of information—friends, slaves, newspaper clippings, and so forth. They also reflect changes in taste and the introduction of new techniques and products more swiftly than printed works (Schmit 1982, introduction; Hörandner 1981; Hess 1981; Hooker 1984; Oliver 1990b). So far, not many have been analyzed.

More popular surveys of American eating and drinking habits contain some useful information on food preparation and availability. However, they tend either to collapse time or to be vague about the economic status of consumers or both (for example, Hooker 1981; Taylor 1982). Such surveys usually cite occasional references from diaries but rely most heavily on contemporary travellers' accounts, which in turn dwell on the meals served in country inns and taverns. Rural innkeepers could not readily predict the arrival time or the numbers of their customers, so they must have served primarily preserved foods, especially salted meat. Studies of contemporary accounts of American eating habits would be more useful if reported meals were carefully categorized. Which were eaten in private homes, and what was the social and economic status of the family serving them? Were they holiday meals or ordinary

---

9. The first manual for house servants written in the United States was Robert Robert's 1827 publication directed especially to residents of Washington, D.C. (Belden 1983, 24–27).

daily fare? What were the similarities and differences between meals served in private households and those served in public inns and taverns? Were there contrasts between what was available in large cities and in the countryside? Brown et al. (1990, 179–83) provides one such analysis of differences between public and private meals in the eighteenth-century Chesapeake.[10] Among the better regional studies, Conlin (1986) supplies a useful summary of Americans' diets in the mid-nineteenth century (as well as a fascinating account of eating on the western mining frontier), while Arnow (1960, chap. 14) has a good discussion of food procurement and preparation in middle Tennessee in the early national period (cf. Crump 1991).

The question of possible differences in the social meaning of various foods among poor as opposed to upper and middling groups might also be profitably explored. British sources suggest several avenues for study. Did urban workers increasingly rely on wheat bread and begin to consider it an entitlement (Wells 1988, chap. 2)? Did they use tea, coffee, and sugar in different ways than more privileged families (Burnett 1966, chaps. 1, 3; Mintz 1985)? Did women and children eat less than their proportional share of food in order to provide the principal male breadwinner with sufficient calories to better enable him to work (Burnett 1966, chap. 3; Wells 1988, chap. 18)?

How to translate cookbook cookery into vernacular cookery is a problem only hesitatingly addressed. The most commonly replicated recipes were for dishes that were new and novel, that were made infrequently (such as pickled meats, pickles, and preserves), or that required precision in execution (such as cakes and other farinaceous dishes), the mastery of which was thought to raise a housewife's reputation. There was little need or incentive to include instructions on how to prepare the simple dishes that probably provided the bulk of the average American's daily fare. An assessment of the early-nineteenth-century diet based on Amelia Simmons and Mary Randolph may be somewhat closer to reality than an assessment of present-day diet based on *Gourmet* magazine and the several *Silver Palate* cookbooks, but perhaps only marginally so.

Foodways programs in various outdoor historical museums provide some guidance, although results are just beginning to appear. Practical experience

---

10. In addition to the works cited in the text, four foodways journals are worth following. *Food and Foodways* addresses important issues including the historic and cultural roles of food and nutritional values. But so far only one article has dealt with the United States. *Petits Propos Culinaires* is more strictly a journal of culinary history. Articles occasionally provide useful information on kitchen equipment and the history of the preparation of particular dishes, but in general are too specialized to be of much use to economic historians (Middle Eastern recipes for preparing cattle udders and penises being the most exotic example). *Foodtalk* concentrates on more recent time periods, but occasional articles dealing with specific types of foods may prove helpful. *Food History News* explores vernacular American cooking. There is again much on the specifics of particular dishes, but reports on museum foodways programs supply useful information on the composition and preparation of the fare of ordinary folk. For a recent bibliography see Benes (1984).

in regularly cooking full meals in a period house, equipped with a set of kitchen equipment and stock of food typical of families at varying levels of wealth, can provide crucial insights into opportunities and constraints of materials, technology, and time. The reluctance of these programs to depart from known recipes precludes inappropriate use of later cooking methods, but also limits possible insights from learning by doing. How best to recover the "orally transmitted basic knowledge, which must always be taken into account in the assessment of a recipe book as a source" (Hörandner 1981, 124), is an unsettled issue (Oliver 1990a).

Some museums have tried time/motion/environment studies that supply invaluable insight into the conditions in which housewives had to function. On a midsummer's day in a reconstructed eighteenth-century kitchen in Williamsburg, for example, the temperature at the open hearth while the major midday meal was being prepared reached 170 degrees, making a brief respite to the far side of the room where the temperature dropped to a mere 90 a delightful refreshment. Conversely, cooking experiments conducted in early December in a reconstructed one-room tenant farmer's house at St. Mary's City revealed that the immediate hearth area where the temperature was 120 degrees was the only part of the room warmer than the outside temperature of 46 degrees, practically demonstrating acute levels of discomfort to present-day recreators, and documenting the reason for the location of root cellars for storage of winter vegetables just in front of the hearth (Gibbs 1982, 1989). Practical considerations limit such insights largely to the actual cooking process. Resource constraints prevent a full replication of the time and effort involved in seeding, nurturing, weeding, and harvesting of vegetables; milking cows and churning butter; milling grain; or catching and slaughtering, skinning, butchering, plucking, and/or scaling of livestock and game (cf. Goody 1982, chap. 3).

Culinary literature and studies based on inventories are in general agreement that most early-nineteenth-century innovations in food cooking and preservation remained sufficiently expensive to limit their use to the elite before circa 1850 and, to a large extent, until after the Civil War. These include stoves, refrigeration, and canning (Roberts 1981; Strasser 1982, chaps. 1, 2; Martin 1942, chap. 3; McMahon 1981, chap. 6; Keuchel 1972; Belluscio 1984; Goody 1982, chap. 5; Larkin 1988, 51–52; Garrison 1991, chap. 7). Open-hearth cooking remained the norm throughout most of the country until 1850 or later. Families were slow to change the utensils with which they prepared food, and in turn limitations of equipment precluded widespread adoption of many new types of foods. Stoves did appear around 1820 in prosperous urban homes and by the late 1830s among some middling city families and northern commercial villages. Stoves saved stooping, firewood, and time in tending fires, but an 1899 study showed that it still took almost one hour per day to care for an up-to-date stove (Strasser 1982, chap. 2). However, stoves remained uncommon in many areas until the 1850s or 1860s (Larkin 1988, chap. 4; Martin 1942, chap. 2).[11] Consequently, the food types to which stoves were especially suited—cakes and white sauces, for example—were also uncommon except on the tables of the rich (Hess and Hess 1972, chap. 7; Weaver 1986). Similarly, while various sorts of iceboxes were available from the 1820s, few households acquired them, aside from the urban elite. Consequently, in hot weather most families had to purchase meat and milk often and in small quantities. Iced beverages and desserts were likewise confined to elite homes.

Ordinary families also apparently failed to buy much in the way of purported labor-saving kitchen gadgetry, the mechanical eggbeater being the main exception. Many of the early-nineteenth-century gadgets did not perform very well, remained decidedly expensive relative to wages, and were intended for the preparation of somewhat costly ingredients. In addition, domestic mass-produced lightweight metal cookwares were often inferior in performance to older, heavier cooking implements, and were not widely available until the middle of the century (Levenstein 1988, chap. 2; Strasser 1982, chap. 2; W. W. Miller 1987).

Changes in consumption patterns of particular foods include the following.

Alcohol. At the time of the Revolution annual per capita consumption has been estimated at 3½ gallons pure alcohol. After 1790 men began to drink more, especially cheap western whiskey that supplanted imported or domestically produced rum as the common people's drink during the war for independence. Per capita consumption reached 4 gallons by the late 1820s. After 1840, with the influence of the temperance movement, consumption declined by two-thirds for the nation as a whole to 1½ gallons. It was rural New Englanders who were most likely to give up drink (including cider to some degree). By the 1840s liquor was seldom sold in New England country stores. Throughout the country, women and children probably curtailed their consumption of alcoholic beverages by the second quarter of the century. On the other hand southern, western, and some urban men continued to imbibe more freely. Neither beer nor wine appears to have became widely popular beverages before 1850 (Rorabaugh 1979, 1987; Larkin 1988, chap. 5; McMahon 1981, chap. 1; Geib 1981, chap. 3; Clark 1990, chap. 6; Arnow 1960, chap. 14).

Sugar. Sugar remained relatively expensive until after the Civil War, and consumption rose slowly, from an estimated 16.8 pounds in 1772 (plus 4.9 gallons of molasses) to 30 to 35 pounds per capita in 1860. Nonetheless, its use was widespread. Poorer folk generally used sugar in connection with cof-

---

11. Jensen (1986, 219–20) shows almost half of Chester County, Pennsylvania, and New Castle, Delaware, inventoried decedents as owning stoves and/or ovens in 1790, a much higher percentage of stove ownership than reported in any other source. Since the percentage of households owning other fireplace cooking equipment was the same as in 1750, I conclude she lumped cast-iron stoves (which were likely found in a much smaller percentage of inventories) with new open-hearth equipment—dutch ovens and roasting ovens.

fee and tea, beverages that were cheaper than milk and that even urban laborers were coming to consider necessities. The sweetener remained a luxury for slaves. Owners usually provided it only for the sick, but slaves increasingly bought some sugar along with tea and coffee on their own account. Use in desserts was largely confined to the middle and upper classes (Larkin 1988, 174–75; Williams 1985, chap. 4; Martin 1942, chap. 2; Shammas 1990, chap. 4; Smith 1990, 98–99; Adams 1982; Mintz 1985; Austen and Smith 1990).

Coffee/tea. By 1773 sufficient tea was imported or smuggled into the colonies to permit at least two-thirds of white adults to drink it daily. Inventories suggest that by 1800 half or more households had ritual tea equipment, and even more families could brew and drink tea more informally. In the early nineteenth century, more families purchased teawares than new dining wares. By 1840 tea consumption roughly doubled in per capita terms. In the same four decades, coffee consumption rose fivefold, overtaking tea in popularity by 1830. (This change doubtless reflected steadily falling coffee prices from the 1830s.) These beverages and their associated equipment were minor luxuries that the poor could afford, and their appeal was intense. Once firmly entrenched in their diets, consumers were unwilling to forgo caffeinated beverages. Tea remained a metaphor for refined behavior and was the primary way in which the poor could participate in the rising culture of respectability. How tea was presented (as well as the grades of tea and sugar used), however, continued to separate the rich from the poor. In addition to their status connotations, tea and coffee, especially when taken with sugar, provided a quick energy boost and suppressed hunger (Austen and Smith 1990; Mintz 1985, chaps. 2, 3; Williams 1985, chap. 4; Martin 1942, chap. 2; Adams 1982; Martin 1988; Larkin 1988, 174–75; Shammas 1990, chap. 4).

Flour. Wheat flour became increasingly available in New England beginning in 1825 with the opening of the Erie Canal. At first its use was most common in commercial and industrial towns; it remained a luxury in rural areas. By 1840 New York and Ohio flour had largely replaced the traditional New England breadstuffs of corn and rye (McMahon 1981, chap. 1; Larkin 1988, chaps. 1, 4; Clark 1990, 150–52). In the South, wheat did not displace corn as the primary bread. Although wheat was a major crop in the Upper South, much of it was sold for export elsewhere. Slaves and poor farmers ate little besides corn (and some rice in the Lower South). Better-off southern families enjoyed some wheat breads and pastries, but did not opt for wheat over corn as the primary starch. Even as wheat flour increased in popularity, affordability, and availability throughout much of the country, it probably declined in nutritional value. By the 1840s flour-milling technology changed, with the wheat germ being extracted in advance, removing nutrients that were often replaced with adulterants (Hess and Hess 1972, chap. 5).

Dairy products. As the urban population rose, dairying became an important occupation for most farm women in New England, the Middle Atlantic, and the Midwest, and among the more prosperous in the Upper South and parts of the West such as Tennessee. Cheese making was more specialized, concentrated mostly in New England, where it was a significant item of exchange. This major shift was possible because more and more women left off home textile production and turned instead to making butter. Butter production rose on most farms from the 1790s, and by 1850 many New England farms were specializing in dairying (Larkin 1988, chap. 5; Arnow 1960, chap. 14; Gump 1989, chap. 5; Marks 1979, 122; Geib 1981, chaps. 3, 7; McMahon 1981, chaps. 1, 3; Clark 1990, chaps. 3, 4, 8; Jensen 1986, chaps. 5, 6; Gross 1982; Atack and Bateman 1987, chaps. 9, 12).

5.4 Findings from Archaeology

Studies of diet from recovered artifacts are largely based on analysis of faunal remains, a branch of archaeology that has only recently developed. Faunal remains provide systematic information on the relative dietary importance of different animals and differing cuts of meat, butchery practices, and animal husbandry. Meat was a central element of the traditional British diet, and meat consumption carried a high cultural value that was shared by those who immigrated to America (H. M. Miller 1988; Bowen 1990; Reitz 1987).[12] Analysis of ceramic assemblages provides some additional insights. A high proportion of bowls among recovered dining and serving wares, for example, suggests primary reliance on stews and porridges, while greater numbers of flatware—plates, platters, and so forth—indicates a greater variety of cooking methods, including roasting. Similarly, a higher proportion of serving, storage, and preparation vessels reflect value placed on the appearance of the table, and means to accumulate surplus food for storage (Kelso 1984; Smith 1987).[13]

To date, most investigations have concentrated on the seventeenth and later nineteenth centuries, with a marked gap for sites dating between 1750 and 1880. There is little information available for the period under investigation. Most of the sites that have been analyzed concentrate on the diet of slaves and

12. Two unresolved interpretative problems include historical definitions of high- and low-status meats (Lyman 1987) and comparisons of faunal remains between poor households where grains and dairy products were the predominant food source as opposed to better-off households where meat was a more significant part of the diet (Bowen 1990). Other problems encountered in making comparisons include small sample sizes, inappropriate recovery methods, incomplete or incomparable analyses, uncertain identification of the socioeconomic status and ethnic origins of site inhabitants, and difficulties in identifying faunal remains to a particular species. (Many remains can be identified only as coming from some sort of fish, or from mammals of small, medium, or large size; Reitz, Gibbs, and Rathbun 1985).

13. Reliance on ceramics may present some problems. Pewter vessels, which could be melted down and recycled, are seldom found in trash pits, although probate inventories show widespread use of pewter dining wares and kitchenwares through the 1790s. Distributions of various types of pewterwares by wealth do not show the same economic and status correlations as do ceramics (Martin 1989).

the planter elite in the Lower South. New England, the Middle Atlantic, the Upper South, and urban sites are poorly represented. Two other promising areas of study, analysis of plant remains and of human skeletons, have so far been neglected, the first for reasons of technology and cost, the second for reasons of widespread public distaste (Reitz, Gibbs, and Rathbun 1985). In future, studies of plant remains promise better evidence of the vegetable part of the diet. Skeletal analysis can reveal much, not only about diseases and nutritional stress, but also about the ratios of various plants and animals eaten during the lifetime of the individual (Brown 1990).

Other promising new archaeological undertakings include studies of the distribution of the remains of other, more minute kinds of fauna that played important roles in the overall health environment, particularly in urban areas. Elite households may prove to have been more successful in maintaining higher standards of hygiene than poorer ones. Rat carcasses (commensals, in archaeological parlance), for example, are fewer on wealthy Charleston, South Carolina, sites than on lots inhabited by poorer people. Analysis of helminth remains (the preserved egg sacs of intestinal parasites) and other evidence from urban privies in Newport, Rhode Island, and Williamsburg, Virginia, show more careful disposal of human wastes on elite sites, less overall (although still endemic) parasite infestation, and differences in the most prevalent parasite species. The microecologies of some urban house lots, for example, rendered their human inhabitants more susceptible to the giant human whipworm, while other households living nearby suffered greater infestations of roundworms (Brown 1990; Reinhard, Mrozowski, and Orloski 1986).

Generalization has not been the strong suit of historical archaeologists. The number of excavations for the later eighteenth and early nineteenth century are limited, and so far most reports are preliminary and have of necessity been largely devoted to description of the sites and artifacts. Few clear patterns have been detected among findings from reported sites. Otherwise, much effort has been placed on elucidating differences in status among artifacts left by households of varying ethnic origins and wealth, a major concern of the profession but a topic of less interest to economic historians. Finally, many earlier studies tended to assume that rural households were self-sufficient in foodstuffs, and so have paid inadequate attention to the possibility of exchange.

A notable exception to the lack of generalization is the work of Henry Miller. Miller has so far concentrated on the tidewater Chesapeake in the seventeenth and early eighteenth century, but his findings have provided an interpretive framework for most subsequent faunal studies. From a comparison of faunal remains on seventeenth- and early-eighteenth-century sites in Maryland and Virginia, Miller concluded that early settlers relied heavily on fish and game for protein. Wild animals accounted for as much as 40 percent of the meat diet at early sites. Colonists utilized wild resources especially in

summer and fall, and turned to domestic meats—primarily hogs and cattle—
in the colder months. Cooking methods were simplified over traditional British methods, with more boiling and frying and considerably less roasting.

Beginning about 1660 when stocks of farm animals became adequate, colonists relied more on domestic livestock, now including some sheep and poultry. The contribution of wild foods dropped to about only 10 percent of the
meat diet. After 1700 colonists harvested little game, and strikingly reduced
fish consumption. Seasonal variations in diet largely disappeared. Beef accounted for two-thirds of the meat diet and pork one-quarter. More uniform
patterns of animal husbandry emerged, with cattle being kept to greater ages
and hogs uniformly slaughtered at ages that yielded the most weight for the
least supplemental feed. Meat was relatively abundant. Independent landowners of varying levels of wealth all consumed meats of similar quality. There
were differences in food preparation and dining style, but the basic ingredients
were the same. Cattle and hogs were dependable resources that could be inten-
sively exploited, and all landowners had sufficient space to raise enough livestock to supply their households. Information on poor freeholders and bound
laborers is less abundant, but slaves and servants probably ate beef from low-
quality cuts, and supplemented meat rations with a few small wild mammals
(H. M. Miller 1984, 1986, 1988, n.d. cf. Garrow and Wheaton 1986, 570–
71, 640–42).

A consistent finding from all later seventeenth-, eighteenth-, and early-
nineteenth-century archaeological sites is the importance of beef in the diets
of all groups. This is a major revision of evidence from culinary histories and
studies based on probate inventories and even widows' allowances. Meat,
when available, was not always a monotonous round of salt pork upon salt
pork. From estimates of the weights of meat represented by recovered bones,
everywhere beef and pork were eaten in roughly equal proportions. Most beef
was eaten fresh and hence does not appear as stored food in inventories. Fresh
beef distributed to slaves is very likely underrepresented in accounts of standard rations; most slave sites show the same relatively equal proportions of
beef and pork that appear in free households.[14]

The archaeological record also demonstrates that in general meat diets were
more diverse than documentary sources suggest. On the southern Atlantic
coastal plain, diets of the rich and of the poor were perhaps more varied than
those of middling folk. Town dwellers apparently ate more domestic meat
than rural residents but used a greater variety of species, especially birds.
Residents of towns like Charleston and Savannah could purchase fresh meat
year-round, since town populations were sufficiently large to permit quick sale
of whole carcasses. Imported meats were also available. Farmers, on the other

14. The technology of pork preservation introduces possible problems. Some pork may have
been deboned before pickling, and pickled bones may have decomposed more rapidly than fresh
ones. Hence pork consumption may be underrepresented in faunal remains. Preserved fish also
leaves few remains (Reitz 1987).

hand, had to schedule slaughtering times carefully in order to use an entire animal carcass before it spoiled (Brown 1990; Brown et al. 1990; Reitz 1986, 1987; Reitz and Honerkamp 1983; Rothschild 1989).

In nineteenth-century New England towns, urban dwellers probably had access to a more limited range of meats than did countryfolk. Wild resources were seldom available. In eighteenth-century Portsmouth, New Hampshire, most households butchered calves and pigs on their house lots, while purchasing smaller portions of mature cattle and hogs. Evidence of urban butchering begins to disappear around the turn of the century, forcing most urban residents to buy only what cuts were available in town markets (Pendery 1984). Some African-Americans in early-nineteenth-century Boston consumed the same fleshier cuts of meat as did richer folk, but probably in limited quantity and in part because market restrictions curtailed their ability to purchase cheaper pieces.[15] Richer town dwellers in fact apparently had greater access to variety meats; for example, a comparison of household refuse showed that a contemporary Salem merchant's family ate many more calf and pig heads than did the free blacks (Bowen 1989). A documentary study of Boston slaughterhouses indicates that city butchers at first sold beef offal to almshouses and donated them the offal of other animals, but increasingly bones, heads, hooves, tallow, and the like were sold to local industries (Smith and Bridges 1982). Differing market regulations and offal disposal patterns clearly had some effect on the cost and availability of meats for city dwellers.

So far there is not enough archaeological evidence available to prove that consumption of fish and shellfish increased after the Revolution. However, I think that the documentary evidence is so strong that this will prove to be the case. My research in Maryland and Virginia agricultural account books and planter correspondence shows an increase in seine fishing both in Chesapeake Bay and freshwater streams. Salt fish did not appear in slave rations until the 1760s but was increasingly common after the Revolution. Much of the fish was caught and processed locally, but planters also bought salt fish from New England ship captains and later from Baltimore merchants. Account books also show a growing number of local men selling oysters and fish to large planter households. In prerevolutionary probate inventories, seines and oystering and crabbing equipment appear very infrequently. But in inventories for the years 1790 to 1820 for St. Mary's County, Maryland, and York County, Virginia, fishing and/or shellfish paraphernalia is present in about a quarter of

15. In helping to explain changes and differing patterns among various economic and ethnic groups in the composition of faunal remains, archaeologists have first investigated urban marketing regulations. For a further discussion of the implications of changing regulations, see section 5.5. Examination of urban household account books would also prove useful, as would investigation of varying sources of supply. Brown et al. (1990), for example, report differences in the ages of domestic animals purchased by tavernkeepers in Williamsburg (younger animals raised specifically for meat), and by a private householder who later lived on the same property (older animals butchered when they were no longer useful for other purposes and presumably purchased in small cuts from town butchers).

the inventories, perhaps on nearly every farm located along waterways (Walsh 1991). Connecticut account books for the same period also show intense harvesting of spring fish runs (Bowen 1990). Once railroads spread into rural Pennsylvania in the 1840s, fresh fish and shellfish were readily available (Weaver 1981). This likely increase in use of marine resources probably reflected both a response to growing urban markets and a shift among farmers to lower-cost sources of protein in a period of rising grain prices (cf. Adams 1982). High grain prices also raised the cost of meats, and farmers may either have fattened fewer animals or have sold a greater proportion of surplus stock.

For the period 1790–1860 most archaeological evidence comes from Lower South plantations.[16] In coastal South Carolina, Georgia, and Florida, both planters and slaves relied heavily on wild resources. Planters harvested their stocks of cattle, hogs, and sheep but also regularly assigned slaves to hunting and fishing over considerable distances, supplying them with guns, boats, and fishing equipment. Consequently, planters could stock their tables with venison and deep-water fish, along with shellfish and a variety of wild birds and smaller mammals. Everywhere, planters also commonly roasted their meat or ate large cuts of boiled meat (Kelso 1984, 176–97; Otto 1984; Reitz 1986).

Standard meat rations for slaves varied widely depending on place, the custom of individual plantations, and whether a task or a gang system prevailed. Other factors affecting slave diet included the amount of free time, the age and sex composition of the work force, the intensity of work, the ability of slaves to produce food for themselves, the amount of food the slaves could barter, purchase, or steal, and the livestock mix on the plantation.[17] Maryland and Virginia planters issued regular rations of salt pork or fish, supplemented with any butchery offal they did not choose to consume, and occasionally slaughtered cattle and sheep to provide slaves fresh meat. Lower South long-staple cotton and rice planters were more stingy with meat rations, and there many slaves had to catch small wild mammals, turtles, and fish in order to enjoy any regular source of protein. (Wild foods, for example, made up half of the meat diet at one sea-island slave site.) Slaves' procurement strategies differed from those of the planters. Given limited time and limited mobility, slaves had to rely on the wild species that they could catch or trap near their quarters. On plantations as widely scattered as Washington's Mount Vernon and the Georgia sea islands, planter household refuse contains more deep-water fish caught with seines and boats, while slave deposits have more smaller fish caught in shallower waters with hook and line. Upland slaves had access to a narrower range of wild resources, for which planters may or may not have compensated

16. My survey of the relevant archaeological literature is far from comprehensive, especially for unpublished reports. Singleton (n.d.) promises a more comprehensive bibliography of sources pertaining to African-American archaeology.

17. Planters who raised many sheep, for example, distributed inferior animals among their slaves, while those who raised few sheep apparently kept all the lamb and mutton for their own tables.

with larger rations of domestic meats (Reitz, Gibbs, and Rathbun 1985; Moore 1989; Pogue 1990; Gaynor 1989; Hughes 1991; Zierden, Drucker, and Calhoun 1986).

Other findings from slave sites confirm that they had few storage or cooking vessels. Meals had to be simply prepared, primarily by boiling, and most of the food they secured was eaten promptly (Kelso 1984, 176–97; Reitz, Gibbs, and Rathbun 1985). Available meat was hacked into small pieces for cooking, and the bones thoroughly scraped or pulverized to extract marrow. The cuts of domestic livestock that slaveowners provided were also usually of low quality, especially heads and feet. Documentary sources indicate these were occasionally supplemented with butchery offal, which leaves few detectable traces. Crude butchery techniques on occasional larger bones suggest that slaves had limited familiarity with more desirable parts of animal carcasses (Kelso 1986a, 1986b; McKee 1987; Davis 1987).

Archaeological evidence demonstrates that slaves tried mightily to supplement allotted rations by hunting, fishing, raising poultry, and gardening. What is unclear is how satisfactory these supplements were, either to provide a sufficiency of food or to supply nutrients absent in corn and salt-meat rations. Long cooking and frequent reheating of foods lost much of the vitamin content (Reitz, Gibbs, and Rathbun 1985).

Diets of free blacks probably varied widely, depending both on urban or rural residence and on family income. The household goods free blacks chose to acquire and some of the foods they chose to eat differed from the remains found at slave sites. Evidence for a well-off family comes from the Banneker farm in Baltimore County, Maryland. The family was unusually privileged in that they owned their own farm, and the celebrated almanac writer earned an unusually high income. The Banneker family at first relied on both domestic livestock and wild game, but as Benjamin Banneker's career developed, the family gave over hunting and eventually began to purchase some meat from a local store. They also started out using mostly wood, pewter, and coarse earthenwares for food preparation, storage, and dining but, with increased purchasing power after about 1775, acquired more ceramics (Hurry 1989). Excavation of three rental properties in a free black neighborhood in Alexandria, Virginia, revealed that antebellum tenants placed a high priority on acquiring inexpensive ceramic tea- and coffeewares and on miscellaneous plates for dining, presumably also consuming more of the popular stimulating beverages than did slaves and perhaps serving meals in different ways. Their meat diets were less varied than those of contemporary middle-class white Alexandrians, and included a much higher proportion of pork. (Upper-middle-class whites consumed both more wild meats and more beef, sheep, and poultry.) In the early nineteenth century the black tenants ate some fish, oysters, and small wild mammals, and some poultry, which they probably kept at home, along with a cow. But the primary source of meat was pork purchased from butcher shops, especially heads, feet, stew meat, and, more rarely, ribs (Cressey 1985).

5.5   Account Books and Studies of Food Distribution Systems

5.5.1   Account Books

Studies of account books offer yet another perspective on diet. The potential is most promising, yet this source has been underutilized. So far most studies of account books have concentrated on the character (capitalistic or communal) of the transactions, rather than on their content. Joanne Bowen's work on Suffield, Connecticut, account books between 1770 and 1810 represents a major advance in the study of diet, and provides an important critique of findings derived from probate inventories (Bowen 1990). Concentrating on meat-related exchanges appearing in selected account books, Bowen found that farmers had developed an intricate system of harvesting resources in order to insure a year-round supply of fresh meat to supplement salt pork, the ordinary staple. For the wealthy, fresh meat was available year-round. The process of meat supply began in early winter with the slaughter and preserving of hogs. As temperatures dropped, cattle were killed for fresh winter meat. Large pieces of beef were distributed through a complex network of exchange. In warm weather these rural exchange networks were not wide enough to absorb an entire beef carcass without spoilage, so cattle were not killed in summer. In early spring, salmon and shad fishing provided protein for immediate consumption and some preservation for later use. As it grew warmer, families turned to their stocks of salted pork, and added fresh meat by killing lambs, calves, and old sheep that were small enough to be consumed quickly within a few households. Dairy products provided additional protein, especially in summer, and in more limited quantities throughout the year. Local rural exchange networks served as a "social refrigerator."

Bowen also investigated the social and economic relationships of the people buying and selling meat, using local histories to identify relationships and tax lists and probate records to determine economic standing. Large farmers generated the surplus livestock and dairy products and sold meat in both local and distant markets. Many local sales were to wage laborers who did occasional work for the sellers. The laborers made frequent small purchases, mostly of preserved meats and cheese. Lower middling households, in contrast, engaged in by-employments rather than wage labor to supplement income and food stocks produced on small farms. They may have satisfied themselves with whatever fresh meats they could raise, and relied on the ubiquitous salt pork to augment a diet heavy on potatoes, cornmeal, and beans. Bowen found that better-off middling landowning farmers (with the exception of those related to wealthy producers) were notably absent from the account books. They may have raised sufficient meat for their households or else made exchanges with other families of equal status. Bowen could find no surviving account books kept by middling Connecticut farmers, so the question remains unresolved.

Exchanges of fresh meat or dairy products were infrequent among large farmers, probably a matter of occasional mutual accommodation. Most local fresh meat sales were made to relatives, including a number of poorer ones. Most of the buyers were related to the sellers either by blood or by marriage, and most exchange partners lived within walking distance of each other. Access to fresh meat for those who could not raise enough livestock to supply their own tables apparently depended on kin connections. As wealthier farmers began to hire more wage laborers (usually unrelated workers) and to rely less on mutual exchanges of work with kinfolk, less prosperous but still semi-independent relatives may have had to lessen their consumption of fresh meats or else attempted to become more self-sufficient. Poor rural folk who moved away from their families of origin were at a disadvantage for procuring a varied protein diet, perhaps especially residents of factory villages who were viewed by older residents as complete outsiders (Clark 1990, chap. 7).

Chesapeake account books and farm diaries for the same period reveal parallel patterns. Large slave owners followed similar strategies of resource harvesting to insure a year-round supply of fresh meats. Patterns of social and economic exchange were also similar. Big planters supplied dependent laborers and parish pensioners with frequent small amounts of grain and preserved meat. Meat exchanges with other large planters were infrequent. Small and middling planters did not often buy meat from large slave owners, and they too did not keep account books that would clarify procurement strategies (Walsh n.d.).

Account books and farm diaries also provide data on livestock slaughter weights that indicate the amounts of meat obtained per animal and identify periods of change in livestock feeding and marketing practices. Table 5.1 shows net slaughter weights of hogs in the Chesapeake between 1678 and 1820 and in Massachusetts between 1760 and 1840. Hogs that were left to forage for themselves until a brief fattening with supplemental corn for a few weeks prior to slaughter produced low net carcass weights. In the seventeenth century, when the age at which hogs were harvested varied, net slaughter weights averaged 130 pounds. Weights dropped to 100 pounds in the early eighteenth century, when uniform earlier slaughter ages (eighteen to twenty months) became the norm. Beginning in the 1750s, when more planters were raising surplus corn, net slaughter weights returned to about 130 pounds, although the age of slaughter remained the same. There was no change in slaughter weights or, by inference, in feeding practices through 1820 (Walsh n.d.). Massachusetts farmers apparently followed similar minimal fattening practices until about 1790. Then they began to slaughter hogs at both younger and at older ages, and overall to raise much heavier hogs. There net slaughter weights doubled by 1840 (Rothenberg 1981, 305–10).

Much less data is available for net slaughter weights of beef cattle. These varied widely, depending on the age and sex of the animal, the season of killing, and whether the animal was range-fed or stall-fed. Until urban markets

Table 5.1   Net Hog Slaughter Weights, Chesapeake Region and Massachusetts, 1678–1840

Chesapeake Region			Massachusetts		
Years	N	Net Pounds	Years	N	Net Pounds
1678–99	48	131	1760–89	8	120
1700–1749	408	104	1790–1809	22	187
1750–74	2,032	128	1810–20	33	198
1775–89	3,514	124	1821–40	181	248
1790–1809	2,933	130			
1810–20	1,723	128			

Sources: For the Chesapeake, net slaughter weights from plantation account books cited in Walsh (n.d.); for Massachusetts, data supplied by Winifred Rothenberg. Rothenberg's live weights were converted to net weights by multiplying by 0.7. (See Rothenberg 1981, 305–10).

became important in the early nineteenth century, whole animals were seldom sold to a single buyer, scales were often inadequate for weighing an entire carcass, and sellers were often content to eyeball estimated slaughter weights. Weights for a single quarter may under- or overstate full carcass weights, and it is not always clear whether weights given for whole animals include only the four quarters of saleable meat or whether the fifth quarter (tallow and hide) is also included. (See Smith and Bridges 1982, 6.) Table 5.2 shows trends in net slaughter weights for Chesapeake cattle (four quarters only) between 1749 and 1820. Before 1790, beef cattle averaged only about 350 pounds net. Thereafter, cattle weights rose steadily, although, given the small number of observations, it is uncertain by how much. Many of the heavier animals were raised by farmers who were selling fattened cattle to urban markets. A trend to fatter animals for the town trade is clear, but it is unlikely that cattle weights overall nearly doubled between 1790 and 1820. Doubtless families who killed only barren cows and old oxen for their own use realized fewer gains in meat per animal. Even if the analysis is restricted to cattle consumed on the plantation, however, net slaughter weights still rose about 100 pounds at the turn of the century.

Analysis of food-purchasing patterns from country stores is another promising use of account books. A small-scale study of store accounts in Deerfield, Massachusetts, for 1710–1800 turned up seasonal purchasing patterns of butter, cheese, vinegar, salt, and fresh and preserved meats that both confirm Bowen's findings on seasonality and suggest additional food preservation and procurement strategies. Deerfield customers who relied on the stores for meat supplies bought much more pork than other meats, again suggesting that fresh meat moved through a specialized distribution network. The study also confirms growing availability toward the end of the eighteenth century of imported groceries, and more regular ties with Boston markets (Derven 1984).

Similarly, George Miller used invoices of ceramics purchased by country

Table 5.2   **Net Cattle Slaughter Weights, Chesapeake Region, 1749–1820**

Years	N	Net Pounds
1749–79	37	368
1780–89	119	344
1790–1809	84	450
1810–20	53	681

Source: Plantation account books cited in Walsh (n.d.).

Note: The data are limited to observations for an entire carcass consisting of four quarters.

storekeepers in the late eighteenth and early nineteenth centuries to determine community consumption patterns of food preparation and dining wares (G. L. Miller 1984a, 1990). Ann Martin found store accounts helpful in tracing changes in cuisine among middling and lesser planters as indicated by purchases of nonnative spices, citrus fruits, and new kinds of food preparation and serving equipment, as well as for signs of a shift from eating meals off individualized dining wares rather than out of shared communal vessels. (Dinner plates, for example, rose from a negligible 8 percent of food-related objects carried in country store inventories in the first quarter of the eighteenth century, to 15 to 20 percent in the third quarter, and by 1800 constituted 40 percent of the merchants' food-related wares; Martin 1987a, 1987b). A study of country store accounts in Kentucky in the 1790s suggests that frontier consumers were perhaps less likely than New Englanders to purchase basic foodstuffs (this issue is not closely addressed), but definitely eager to purchase whiskey, sugar, coffee, tea, and teawares (Perkins 1991). Similarly, a study of Ohio's Western Reserve between 1800 and 1825 found brides willing to travel three days on horseback in order to purchase a few pieces of crockery and teaware with which to begin housekeeping (Miller and Hurry 1983). While at first glance such bits and pieces of information do not seem of much importance, well-structured studies of consumer choices among country store buyers can provide valuable insights into the purchasing patterns and dietary preferences of ordinary folk.

The distribution effects of elite hospitality also merit consideration. A run of extremely detailed accounts from 1777 to 1790 for the family of a wealthy merchant in the small port town of Chestertown, Maryland, raises interesting questions. Complexities of settling the estate required that the administrator keep exact records of all the provisions the town-dwelling widow received from three nearby plantations. The plantation overseers kept running accounts of what they supplied, including beef, poultry, eggs, dairy products, and vegetables. The ages of the children are known, as are the numbers and ages of household slaves and indentured servants. The widow maintained the style of life to which she had been accustomed while her husband was alive, including keeping a carriage and much local visiting and entertaining at home. In a preliminary analysis, I assumed children under sixteen consumed half the food of an adult, and (probably unrealistically) that the slaves and servants ate the same food as the merchant's family. The results show average per capita meat consumption of six hundred pounds per year, plus fifty pounds of butter. Perhaps members of this household did indeed consume over a pound and a half of meat each day, but it is more likely that gentry hospitality was not reciprocal. That is, food expended for entertainments at home was not balanced by equivalent meals a gentry family ate in neighbors' houses. The need to care for several young children precluded extended travel for the widow, but a succession of visiting relatives and other guests, many of them not yet married, probably fared much better at her table than at home. The slaves likely shared leftovers among themselves and with friends and kin living nearby. I'm uncertain how important the redistributive effects of gentry entertaining may have been.[18] Like Bowen's finding of differential access to fresh meat based on kin relationships, this account suggests that a variety of connections to gentry households, either as guest or servant, may have improved the diets of those so connected.

5.5.2   Food Distribution Systems

How well or badly the food distribution system worked had the greatest effect on urban residents, and the larger the city, the greater was the effect. Depending on where they lived, changes in distribution networks changed the dietary prospects of some country folk as well. As Komlos (1987) has suggested, in the absence of other explanatory variables for significant changes in height such as disease, sanitation, or harvest failures, the distribution system merits close scrutiny. So far, with a few exceptions (Friedmann 1973; Smith and Bridges 1982; Usner 1986; G. J. Brown 1987), economic historians have ignored distribution networks.

It seems likely that at least until 1820 urban distribution systems were poorly developed. For example, foreign travellers to the Chesapeake complained repeatedly of the poor quality, scant quantity, and high prices of meat, hay, dairy products, and produce in town markets. Farmers, they asserted, were not responding to an obvious opportunity. In those same years, farmers who did produce fruits, vegetables, and butter or caught fish for sale in the towns complained that markets were so easily glutted that they could not count on selling enough to justify the time and effort required to haul the goods to town and hawk them about. Wealthy plantation owners who spent part of the year in town and might have been major buyers instead supplied their kitchens almost entirely from their home plantations, shipping or hauling, often from long distances, not only preserved meat, livestock, and grain,

18. Convention required that a dinner table be set with a sufficient number of dishes to occupy its entire space. In 1789 George Washington's secretary, Tobias Lear, sought to purchase an elaborate set of plateau mirrors to ornament the center of the dinner table "to occupy the place which must otherwise be filled with dishes of meat, which are seldom or never touched" (quoted in Carson 1990, 51; on quantities of food in elaborate meals see Belden 1983, chap. 1).

but also fruits, vegetables, nuts, and even herbs (Walsh n.d.). The urban poor, usually living in extremely crowded quarters, often with little cooking equipment and not enough money to buy firewood, apparently bought little besides bread and occasionally meat (Carson 1990).

By the 1830s larger cities were better supplied, but they began to impose marketing regulations that worked to the disadvantage of both the urban and rural poor. Restrictions on keeping livestock in town proliferated. Butchers were not allowed to vend quick-spoiling offal. Instead, heads, feet, and tallow were increasingly put to industrial uses. Such measures may have improved sanitation, but poor consumers were also deprived of a source of cheap protein. Similarly, regulations curtailing the activities of strolling hawkers and peddlers, and requirements that vendors rent market stalls both raised food prices and excluded the poorest producers, especially slaves and free blacks (Hooker 1981, 98–101; Usner 1986; Bowen 1989; Bushman 1981; Smith and Bridges 1982; Pendery 1984). Qualitative sources assert that before the Civil War urban residents (except perhaps in major cities) could purchase milk, fruit, and vegetables only within a limited season (Strasser 1982, chap. 1; Levenstein 1988, chap. 2; Martin 1942, chap. 2). In addition, as direct links between producers and consumers diminished, opportunities for food manufacturers and retailers to adulterate their wares multiplied. Adulterated foods, especially in urban areas and particularly among the urban poor, became a major problem in Britain in the first half of the nineteenth century (Burnett 1966, chap. 5). This was doubtless the case as well in urban distribution systems in the United States.

Too few studies have been undertaken to permit assessment of the impact of growing urban markets on the rural poor. My work on Chesapeake agriculture suggests some changes in slave diet did occur. By custom, whenever an animal was slaughtered on the plantation, either for on-site consumption or for local sale, the slaves were given all the offal the planter family did not choose to eat. As more animals were driven to town markets for slaughter, rural slaves lost out. On the other hand, on plantations where the owners were raising or harvesting produce for town markets, slaves may have had access to more fruits, vegetables, and fish. The slaves probably ate any produce too inferior to market, along with any surplus that failed to sell. Urban markets also provided slaves and free blacks with increased opportunities to sell poultry, vegetables, fish, and oysters. Again, the results for their own diet is uncertain. Earnings may have been used to make marginal improvements in their living conditions. But some may have sold foodstuffs they would otherwise have eaten, and spent the proceeds on clothing, tobacco, and alcohol, further impoverishing nutritional levels (Walsh n.d.).

In New England, growing industrialization and urbanization brought even greater economic change. As fewer farm households produced either textiles or bread grains or raised livestock, the need to earn income to buy these essentials may have left rural families hard-pressed, especially when prices of cash crops fell. In addition, country storekeepers extended less and less credit, and demanded cash rather than country pay. Poorer folk had to take goods in small amounts at high prices and could not realize economies from bulk purchases (C. Clark 1990). Clearly there is much to learn about what consumers in various places and at varying levels of wealth could buy, and out of that which was available, what they chose to buy.

Finally, such evidence as exists for improving living standards must be evaluated within the context of likely increases in the intensity or duration of work for many Americans. Some members of the middle classes may have gained leisure time, but ordinary farm men and women and slaves probably had less. Overall, by the 1840s some aspects of living standards, for example, housing, furnishings, and hygiene, may have improved incrementally over those of the 1770s. Work conditions for many, on the other hand, had almost certainly declined (Gross 1982; Larkin 1988, chap. 7; G. Clark 1987; C. Clark 1990; Carr and Walsh 1988a; Walsh 1989).

5.6 Conclusion

All the sources surveyed—probate inventories, widows' allowances, culinary history, archaeological studies, and account books—provide differing perspectives on American diets between 1770 and 1840, some complementary and some conflicting. In general, less work has been done for 1780–1860 than for either the colonial or postbellum period, so conclusions remain tentative.

The level of consumption of household goods and style of life of the wealthy and middle classes in both rural and urban areas clearly improved. Some independent farmers and middle-class city dwellers also achieved improvements in their year-round diet, adding variety and to some extent increasing availability of more foods over a greater part of the year. Beef consumption was higher than previously thought, and distribution networks existed to provide year-round fresh meat to a significant portion of the population.

On the other hand, our knowledge about living conditions of people of lesser wealth is inadequate. There is no evidence for major improvement in household equipment, and a possibility for declines in diet. There were few changes in cooking methods or in food preservation technology that would have facilitated major changes in daily fare. Changes in food distribution networks probably disadvantaged rather than enhanced the diets of the poor. Less wealthy families who lacked access to land, a growing proportion of the population, were hard-put to maintain consumption levels typical of the late colonial period, as were slaves and other laborers who were forced to work longer and harder with no offsetting improvements in quantity or quality of rations. In cities, poor families may have been worse off than in earlier years; high rent and fuel costs probably precluded improvements in diet. Bowen's finding that even in rural areas of New England ready access to fresh meat depended on kin connections shows that trends in prices, wages, and family incomes are but part of the story.

At present, needs and opportunities for further research outweigh established results for early-nineteenth-century America. The overall standard of living in the early republic is as yet imperfectly understood, trends in consumer behavior only tentatively identified, and the relationship between living standards and diet for all but the rich insufficiently explored.

References

Adams, D. R., Jr. 1982. One Hundred Years of Prices and Wages: Maryland 1750–1850. *Working Papers from the Regional Economic History Research Center* 5, no. 4: 90–129.

Arnow, H. S. [1960] 1983. *Seedtime on the Cumberland*. Rev. ed. Lexington: University Press of Kentucky.

Atack, J., and F. Bateman. 1987. *To Their Own Soil: Agriculture in the Antebellum North*. Ames: Iowa State University Press.

Austen, R. A., and W. D. Smith. 1990. Private Tooth Decay as Public Economic Virtue: The Slave-Sugar Triangle, Consumerism, and European Industrialization. *Social Science History* 14: 95–115.

Belden, L. C. 1983. *The Festive Tradition: Table Decoration and Desserts in America, 1650–1900*. New York: W. W. Norton.

Belluscio, L. J. 1984. Brick Ovens in the Genessee Country, 1789–1860. In *Foodways in the Northeast*, ed. P. Benes, 64–79. Boston: Boston University Press.

Benes, P. 1984. Foodways Bibliography. In *Foodways in the Northeast: The Dublin Seminar for New England Folklife Annual Proceedings 1982*, ed. P. Benes, 130–39. Boston: Boston University Press.

Blackmar, B. 1979. Re-walking the "Walking City": Housing and Property Relations in New York City, 1780–1840. *Radical History Review* 21: 131–48.

———. 1989. *Manhattan for Rent, 1785–1850*. Ithaca: Cornell University Press.

Blumin, S. M. 1989. *The Emergence of the Middle Class: Social Experience in the American City, 1760–1900*. Cambridge: Cambridge University Press.

Boserup, E. 1985. The Impact of Scarcity and Plenty on Development. In *Hunger and History: The Impact of Changing Food Production and Consumption Patterns on Society*, ed. R. I. Rotberg and T. K. Rabb, 185–209. Cambridge: Cambridge University Press.

Bowen, J. V. 1989. Urban Household Subsistence: A Comparative Analysis of a Black American and Upper-Class White Household. Colonial Williamsburg Foundation, Williamsburg, VA. Manuscript.

———. 1990. A Study of Seasonality and Subsistence: Eighteenth-Century Suffield, Connecticut. Ph.D. diss., Brown University.

Brown, G. J. 1987. Marketing Meat and Fish in the Eighteenth-Century Tidewater: The Documentary Evidence for the Existence of Markets in Early Peninsula towns. Occasional Papers from the Research Division, Colonial Williamsburg Foundation, Williamsburg, VA. Manuscript.

Brown, G. J., T. F. Higgins, D. F. Muraca, S. K. Pepper, and R. H. Polk. 1990.

Archaeological Investigations of the Shields Tavern Site, Williamsburg, Virginia. Williamsburg, VA: Colonial Williamsburg Foundation.

Brown, M., III. 1990. Digging the Urban Places of Colonial Virginia: The Perspective of Environmental Archaeology. Manuscript.

Bryan, L. 1839. *The Kentucky Housewife.* Cincinnati: Shepard and Stearns. Reprint. Paducah, KY: Collector Books, n.d.

Burnett, J. [1966] 1979. *Plenty and Want: A Social History of Diet in England from 1815 to the Present Day.* Rev. ed. London: Scolar Press.

Bushman, R. L. 1981. Family Security in the Transition from Farm to City, 1750–1850. *Journal of Family History* 6: 238–56.

———. 1987. The Gentrification of Kent County, Delaware, 1740–1776. Paper presented to the Washington Area Seminar in Early American History, University of Maryland, April.

Bushman, R. L., and C. L. Bushman. 1988. The Early History of Cleanliness in America. *Journal of American History* 74: 1213–38.

Carr, L. G., R. R. Menard, and L. S. Walsh. 1991. *Robert Cole's World: Agriculture and Society in Early Maryland.* Chapel Hill: University of North Carolina Press.

Carr, L. G., and L. S. Walsh. 1978. Changing Life Styles in Colonial St. Mary's County. *Working Papers from the Regional Economic History Research Center* 1, no. 3: 73–119.

———. 1980. Inventories and the Analysis of Wealth and Consumption Patterns in St. Mary's County Maryland, 1658–1777. *Historical Methods* 13: 81–104.

———. 1988a. Economic Diversification and Labor Organization in the Chesapeake, 1650–1820. In *Work and Labor in Early America,* ed. S. Innes, 144–88. Chapel Hill: University of North Carolina Press.

———. 1988b. The Standard of Living in the Colonial Chesapeake. *William and Mary Quarterly,* 3d ser., 45: 135–59.

———. N.d. Consumer Behavior in the Colonial Chesapeake. In *Of Consuming Interests: The Style of Life in the Eighteenth Century,* ed. C. Carson, R. Hoffman, and P. J. Albert. Charlottesville: University Press of Virginia, forthcoming.

Carson, B. G. 1990. *Ambitious Appetites: Dining, Behavior, and Patterns of Consumption in Federal Washington.* Washington, DC: American Institute of Architects Press.

Carson, C., and L. S. Walsh. N.d. The Material Life of the Early American Housewife. *Winterthur Portfolio,* forthcoming.

Carson, J. 1985. *Colonial Virginia Cookery: Procedures, Equipment and Ingredients in Colonial Cooking.* Williamsburg, VA: Colonial Williamsburg Foundation.

Clark, C. 1990. *The Roots of Rural Capitalism: Western Massachusetts, 1780–1860.* Ithaca: Cornell University Press.

Clark, C. E., Jr. 1987. The Vision of the Dining Room: Plan Book Dreams and Middle-Class Realities. *Dining in America, 1850–1900,* ed. K. Grover, 142–72. Amherst: University of Massachusetts Press.

Clark, G. 1987. Productivity Growth without Technical Change in European Agriculture before 1850. *Journal of Economic History* 47: 419–32.

Clemens, P. G. E. 1990. Material Culture and the Rural Economy in Burlington County, New Jersey: The Evidence from Probate Records, 1760–1820. History Department, Rutgers University, New Brunswick, NJ. Manuscript.

Clemens, P. G. E., and L. Simler. 1988. Rural Work and the Farm Household in Chester County, Pennsylvania, 1750–1820. In *Work and Labor in Early America,* ed. S. Innes, 106–43. Chapel Hill: University of North Carolina Press.

Conlin, J. R. 1986. *Bacon, Beans, and Galatines: Food and Foodways on the Western Mining Frontier.* Reno: University of Nevada Press.

Cook, E. M., Jr. 1989. *Ossipee, New Hampshire 1785–1985: A History.* Portsmouth, NH: Peter E. Randall.

Crader, D. C. 1984. The Zooarchaeology of the Storehouse and the Dry Well at Monticello. *American Antiquity* 49, no. 3: 542–58.

Cressey, P. J. 1985. The Alexandria, Virginia City-Site: Archaeology in an Afro-American Neighborhood, 1830–1910. Ph.D. diss., University of Iowa.

Crump, N. C. 1991. "Pragmatic Unpretentiousness": The Albemarle Diet. In *A Taste of the Past: Early Foodways of the Albemarle Region, 1585–1830,* ed. B. E. Taylor, 50–58. Elizabeth City, NC: Museum of the Albemarle.

Davis, B. 1987. Faunal Analysis. In Material Culture, Social Relations, and Spatial Organization on a Colonial Frontier: The Pope Site (44SN180), Southampton County, Virginia, ed. T. R. Reinhart, 85–96. Anthropology Department, College of William and Mary, Williamsburg, VA. Manuscript.

Derven, D. L. 1984. Wholesome, Toothsome, and Diverse: Eighteenth-Century Foodways in Deerfield Massachusetts. In *Foodways in the Northeast,* ed. P. Benes, 47–63. Boston: Boston University Press.

Food and Foodways: Explorations in the History and Culture of Human Nourishment. 1985–. Ed. M. Aymard, J.-L. Flandrin, and S. L. Kaplor.

Food History News. 1988–. Ed. S. L. Oliver.

Foodtalk: The Newsletter for People Who Enjoy Food for the Mind as Well as the Table. 1987–. Ed. E. D. Cohn.

Fordyce, E. T. 1987. Cookbooks of the 1800s. In *Dining in America, 1850–1900,* ed. K. Grover, 85–113. Amherst: University of Massachusetts Press.

Fox-Genovese, E. 1988. *Within the Plantation Household: Black and White Women of the Old South.* Chapel Hill: University of North Carolina Press.

Friedmann, K. J. 1973. Victualling Colonial Boston. *Agricultural History* 47: 189–205.

Garrison, J. R. 1991. *Landscape and Material Life in Franklin County, Massachusetts, 1770–1860.* Knoxville: University of Tennessee Press.

Garrow, P. H., and T. R. Wheaton, Jr., eds. 1986. Final Report Oxon Hill Manor Archaeological Site Mitigation Project I-95/MD 210/I-295. Vol. 2. Garrow and Associates, 4000 DeKalb Technology Parkway, Atlanta, GA. Manuscript.

Gaynor, J. B. 1989. Preliminary Notes on the House for Families Faunal Assemblage. Department of Archaeological Research, Colonial Williamsburg Foundation, Williamsburg, VA. Manuscript.

Geib, S. 1981. Changing Works: Agriculture and Society in Brookfield, Massachusetts, 1785–1820. Ph.D. diss., Boston University.

Gibbs, P. 1982. Notes on Cooking Experiments. Research Department, Colonial Williamsburg Foundation. Manuscript.

————. 1989. Re-Creating Hominy: The One-Pot Breakfast Food of the Gentry and Staple of Blacks and Poor Whites in the Early Chesapeake. In *Oxford Symposium on Food and Cookery 1988: The Cooking Pot: Proceedings,* 46–54. London: Prospect Books.

Goody, J. 1982. *Cooking, Cuisine, and Class: A Study in Comparative Sociology.* Cambridge: Cambridge University Press.

Gross, R. A. 1982. Culture and Cultivation: Agriculture and Society in Thoreau's Concord. *Journal of American History* 69: 42–61.

Gump, L. K. 1989. Possessions and Patterns of Living in Washington County: The Twenty Years before Tennessee Statehood, 1777–1796. M.A. thesis, East Tennessee State University.

Haskell, M. B. 1990. Cooks, Collectors, and Culinary Bibliography. *AB Bookman's Weekly* 86: 1765–71.

Hess, J. L., and K. Hess. 1972. *The Taste of America.* Harmondsworth, England: Penguin Books.

Hess, K., transcriber. 1981. *Martha Washington's Booke of Cookery.* New York: Columbia University Press.

Hilliard, S. 1972. *Hog Meat and Hoecake: Food Supply in the Old South, 1840–1860.* Carbondale: Southern Illinois University Press.

Hood, A. 1988. Organization and Extent of Textile Manufacture in Eighteenth-Century Rural Pennsylvania: A Case Study of Chester County. Ph.D. diss., University of California, San Diego.

Hooker, R. J. 1981. *Food and Drink in America: A History.* Indianapolis: Bobbs-Merrill.

———, ed. 1984. *A Colonial Plantation Cookbook: The Receipt Book of Harriott Pinckney Horry, 1770.* Columbia: University of South Carolina Press.

Hörandner, E. 1981. The Recipe Book as a Cultural and Socio-historical Document. In *Food in Perspective: Proceedings of the Third International Conference on Ethnological Food Research, Cardiff, Wales, 1977,* ed. A. Fenton and T. M. Owen, 119–44. Edinburgh: John Donald Publishers.

Hughes, C. T. 1991. African American Foodways at Lake Phelps. In *A Taste of the Past: Early Foodways of the Albemarle Region, 1585–1830,* ed. B. E. Taylor, 20–23. Elizabeth City, NC: Museum of the Albemarle.

Humphries, J. 1990. Enclosures, Common Rights, and Women: The Proletarianization of Families in the Late Eighteenth and Early Nineteenth Centuries. *Journal of Economic History* 50:17–42.

Hurry, R. J. 1989. An Archeological and Historical Perspective on Benjamin Banneker. *Maryland Historical Magazine* 84: 361–69.

Jaffee, D. 1991. Peddlers of Progress and the Transformation of the Rural North, 1760–1860. *Journal of American History* 78: 511–35.

Jensen, J. M. 1986. *Loosening the Bonds: Mid-Atlantic Farm Women, 1750–1850.* New Haven: Yale University Press.

Jones, A. H. 1980. *Wealth of a Nation to Be: The American Colonies on the Eve of the Revolution.* New York: Columbia University Press.

Kasson, J. F. 1987. Rituals of Dining: Table Manners in Victorian America. In *Dining in America, 1850–1900,* ed. K. Grover, 114–41. Amherst: University of Massachusetts Press.

Kelso, W. M. 1984. *Kingsmill Plantations, 1619–1800: Archaeology of Country Life in Colonial Virginia.* Orlando, FL: Academic Press.

———. 1986a. The Archaeology of Slave Life at Thomas Jefferson's Monticello: "A Wolf by the Ears." *Journal of New World Archaeology* 6, no. 4: 5–20.

———. 1986b. Mulberry Row: Slave Life at Thomas Jefferson's Monticello. *Archaeology* (Sept./Oct.): 28–35.

Kessel, E. A. 1981. Germans on the Maryland Frontier: A Social History of Frederick County, Maryland, 1730–1800. Ph.D. diss., Rice University.

Keuchel, E. F. 1972. Master of the Art of Canning: Baltimore, 1860–1900. *Maryland Historical Magazine* 67: 351–62.

Klingaman, D. 1971. Food Surpluses and Deficits in the American Colonies, 1768–1772. *Journal of Economic History* 31: 553–69.

Komlos, J. 1987. The Height and Weight of West Point Cadets: Dietary Change in Antebellum America. *Journal of Economic History* 47: 897–927.

Larkin, J. 1988. *The Reshaping of Everyday Life, 1790–1840.* New York: Harper and Row.

Lemon, J. T. 1967. Household Consumption in Eighteenth-Century America and Its Relationship to Production and Trade: The Situation among Farmers in Southeastern Pennsylvania. *Agricultural History* 41: 59–70.

————. 1972. *The Best Poor Man's Country: A Geographical Study of Early Southeastern Pennsylvania.* New York: W. W. Norton.

Levenstein, H. A. 1988. *Revolution at the Table: The Transformation of the American Diet.* New York: Oxford University Press.

Lyman, R. L. 1987. On Zooarchaeological Measures of Socioeconomic Position and Cost-Efficient Meat Purchases. *Historical Archaeology* 21, no. 1: 58–66.

McCusker, J. J. 1978. *Money and Exchange in Europe and America, 1660–1775: A Handbook.* Chapel Hill: University of North Carolina Press.

McCusker, J. J., and R. R. Menard. 1985. *The Economy of British America, 1607–1789.* Chapel Hill: University of North Carolina Press.

McKee, L. W. 1987. Delineating Ethnicity from the Garbage of Early Virginians: Faunal Remains from the Kingsmill Plantation Slave Quarter. *American Archaeology* 6: 31–39.

Maclean, V. 1981. *A Short-Title Catalogue of Household and Cookery Books Published in the English Tongue, 1701–1800.* London: Prospect Books.

McMahon, S. F. 1981. "A Comfortable Subsistence": A History of Diet in New England, 1630–1850. Ph.D. diss., Brandeis University.

————. 1985. "A Comfortable Subsistence": The Changing Composition of Diet in Rural New England, 1620–1840. *William and Mary Quarterly,* 3d ser., 42: 26–65.

————. 1989a. "All Things in Their Proper Season": Seasonal Rhythms of Diet in Nineteenth Century New England. *Agricultural History* 63: 130–51.

————. 1989b. The "Indescribable Care Devolving upon a Housewife": Gender Perceptions of the Preparation and Consumption of Food on the Midwestern Frontier, 1790–1860. Paper presented at a conference on Women and the Transition to Capitalism in Rural America, 1760–1940, Northern Illinois University, March.

————. 1989c. Laying Foods by: Gender, Dietary Decisions, and the Technology of Food Preservation in New England Households, 1750–1850. Paper presented at the annual meeting of the Social Science History Association, Washington, DC., November.

Main, G. L. 1988. The Standard of Living in Southern New England, 1640–1773. *William and Mary Quarterly,* 3d ser., 45: 124–34.

Main, G. L., and J. T. Main. 1988. Economic Growth and the Standard of Living in Southern New England, 1640–1774. *Journal of Economic History* 48: 27–46.

Marks, B. E. 1979. Economics and Society in a Staple Plantation System: St. Mary's County, Maryland, 1790–1840. Ph.D. diss., University of Maryland.

Martin, A. S. 1987a. "Dish It Up and Send It to the Table": Foodways at the Local Store. Paper presented at the Jamestown Conference on Foodways, Charlottesville, VA, May.

————. 1987b. "The Limits of the Possible": Availability and Costs of Tablewares in an Eighteenth-Century Virginia Store. Occasional Papers from the Research Division, Colonial Williamsburg Foundation, Williamsburg, VA. Manuscript.

————. 1988. "To Supply the Real and Imaginary Necessities": The Retail Trade in Table and Teawares, Virginia and Maryland c. 1750–1810. Final Report to the National Endowment for the Humanities, Grant #R0-21158-86. Department of Archaeological Research, Colonial Williamsburg Foundation, Williamsburg, VA.

————. 1989. The Role of Pewter as Missing Artifact: Consumer Attitudes toward Tablewares in Late Eighteenth Century Virginia. *Historical Archaeology* 23: 1–27.

Martin, E. W. 1942. *The Standard of Living in 1860: American Consumption Levels on the Eve of the Civil War.* Chicago: University of Chicago Press.

Matthews, G. 1987. *"Just a Housewife": The Rise and Fall of Domesticity in America.* New York: Oxford University Press.

Mennell, S. 1985. *All Manners of Food: Eating and Taste in England and France from the Middle Ages to the Present.* Oxford: Basil Blackwell.

Miller, G. L. 1980. Classification and Economic Scaling of Nineteenth Century Ceramics. *Historical Archaeology* 14, no. 1: 1–40.

———. 1984a. George M. Coates, Pottery Merchant of Philadelphia, 1817–1831. *Winterthur Portfolio* 19: 37–49.

———. 1984b. Marketing Ceramics in North America: An Introduction. *Winterthur Portfolio* 19: 1–5.

———. 1990. The "Market Basket" of Ceramics Available in Country Stores from 1780 to 1880. Paper presented at the Society for Historical Archaeology, Tucson, AZ, January.

Miller, G. L., and S. D. Hurry. 1983. Ceramic Supply in an Economically Isolated Frontier Community: Portage County of the Ohio Western Reserve, 1800–1825. *Historical Archaeology* 17, no. 2: 80–92.

Miller, G. L., A. S. Martin, and N. S. Dickinson. N.d. Changing Consumption Patterns, English Ceramics, and the American Market from 1770 to 1840. In *Everyday Life in Early America*, ed. Catherine Hutchins. New York: W. W. Norton, forthcoming.

Miller, H. M. 1984. Colonization and Subsistence Change on the Seventeenth Century Chesapeake Frontier. Ph.D. diss., Michigan State University.

———. 1986. Transforming a "Splendid and Delightsome Land": Colonists and Ecological Change in the Chesapeake, 1607–1820. *Journal of the Washington Academy of Sciences* 76: 173–87.

———. 1988. An Archaeological Perspective on the Evolution of Diet in the Colonial Chesapeake, 1620–1745. In *Colonial Chesapeake Society*, ed. L. G. Carr, P. D. Morgan, and J. B. Russo, 176–99. Chapel Hill: University of North Carolina Press.

———. N.d. Kingsmill Plantation Faunal Analysis Preliminary Statement. Historic St. Mary's City, St. Mary's City, MD. Manuscript.

Miller, W. W. 1987. Technology and the Ideal: Production, Quality and Kitchen Reform in Nineteenth-Century America. In *Dining in America, 1850–1900*, ed. K. Grover, 47–84. Amherst: University of Massachusetts Press.

Mintz, S. W. 1985. *Sweetness and Power: The Place of Sugar in Modern History*. New York: Penguin Books.

Moore, S. G. 1989. "Established and Well Cultivated": Afro-American Foodways in Early Virginia. *Virginia Cavalcade* 39, no. 2: 70–83.

Oliver, S. L. 1990a. State of the Art: Souply at Bixby. *Food History News* 1: 5–7.

———. 1990b. Vernacular Cooking. Lecture, Octagon House, Washington, DC.

Otto, J. S. 1984. *Cannon's Point Plantation 1794–1860: Living Conditions and Status Patterns in the Old South*. Orlando, FL: Academic Press.

Pendery, S. R. 1984. The Archeology of Urban Foodways in Portsmouth, New Hampshire. In *Foodways in the Northeast*, ed. P. Benes, 9–27. Boston: Boston University Press.

Perkins, E. A. 1991. The Consumer Frontier: Household Consumption in Early Kentucky. *Journal of American History* 78: 486–510.

Petits Propos Culinaires. 1979–.

Pogue, D. J. 1990. Washington's View of Mount Vernon: Transformation of an Eighteenth-Century Plantation System. Paper presented at a conference on Re-Creating the World of the Virginia Plantation, 2 June, Charlottesville, VA.

Pruitt, B. H. 1984. Self-Sufficiency and the Agricultural Economy of Eighteenth-Century Massachusetts. *William and Mary Quarterly*, 3d ser., 41: 333–64.

Quayle, E. 1978. *Old Cook Books: An Illustrated History*. New York: E. P. Dutton.

Randolph, M. [1824] 1984. *The Virginia House-wife*. Ed. K. Hess. Columbia: University of South Carolina Press.

Reinhard, K. J., S. Mrozowski, and K. Orloski. 1986. Privies, Pollen, Parasites, and

Seeds: A Biological Nexus in Historic Archaeology. *MASCA Journal* 4, no. 1: 31–36.

Reitz, E. J. 1986. Urban/Rural Contrasts in Vertebrate Fauna from the Southern Atlantic Coastal Plain. *Historical Archaeology* 20, no. 2: 47–58.

————. 1987. Vertebrate Fauna and Socioeconomic Status. In *Consumer Choice in Historical Archaeology*, ed. S. M. Spencer-Wood, 101–19. New York: Plenum Press.

Reitz, E. J., T. Gibbs, and T. A. Rathbun. 1985. Archaeological Evidence for Subsistence on Coastal Plantations. In *The Archaeology of Slavery and Plantation Life*, ed. T. A. Singleton, 163–91. Orlando, FL: Academic Press.

Reitz, E. J., and N. Honerkamp. 1983. British Colonial Subsistence Strategy on the South East Coastal Plain. *Historical Archaeology* 17, no. 2: 4–26.

Roberts, H. D. 1981. *Downhearth to Bar Grate: An Illustrated Account of the Evolution in Cooking due to the Use of Coal instead of Wood*. Marlboro, Wiltshire: Wiltshire Folklife Society.

Rorabaugh, W. J. 1979. *The Alcoholic Republic: An American Tradition*. Oxford: Oxford University Press.

————. 1987. Beer, Lemonade, and Propriety in the Gilded Age. In *Dining in America, 1850–1900*, ed. K. Grover, 24–46. Amherst: University of Massachusetts Press.

Rothenberg, W. 1981. The Market and Massachusetts Farmers, 1750–1855. *Journal of Economic History* 41: 283–314.

Rothschild, N. A. 1989. The Effect of Urbanization on Faunal Diversity: A Comparison between New York City and St. Augustine, Florida, in the Sixteenth to Eighteenth Centuries. In *Quantifying Diversity in Archaeology*, ed. R. D. Leonard and G. T. Jones, 92–99. Cambridge: Cambridge University Press.

[Rutledge, S.] 1847. *The Carolina Housewife or House and Home*. Ed. A. W. Rutledge. Charleston, SC: W. R. Babcock. Reprint. Columbia: University of South Carolina Press, 1979.

Sarudy, B. W. 1989. Eighteenth-Century Gardens of the Chesapeake. *Journal of Garden History: An International Quarterly* 9, no. 3: 103–59.

————. 1990. Table Produce Grown and Sold in the Chesapeake Bay Region of Maryland during the Last Third of the Eighteenth Century. Box 247, Monkton, MD 21111. Manuscript.

Schmit, P. B., ed. 1982. *Nelly Custis Lewis's Housekeeping Book*. New Orleans: Historic New Orleans Collection.

Shammas, C. 1980. The Domestic Environment in Early Modern England and America. *Journal of Social History* 14: 3–24.

————. 1982. How Self-sufficient Was Early America? *Journal of Interdisciplinary History* 13: 247–72.

————. 1990. *The Pre-industrial Consumer in England and America*. Oxford: Oxford University Press.

Singleton, T. A. N.d. The Archaeology of African American Life: A Critical Review and Bibliography. In *Guides to the Archaeological Literature of the Immigrant Experience in America*, no. 2, comp. T. A. Singleton and M. Bogard. Society of Historical Archaeology, forthcoming.

Smart, A. M. 1986. The Urban/Rural Dichotomy of Status Consumption: Tidewater Virginia, 1815. M.A. thesis, College of William and Mary.

Smith, B. G. 1990. *The "Lower Sort": Philadelphia's Laboring People, 1750–1800*. Ithaca: Cornell University Press.

Smith, D. C., and A. E. Bridges. 1982. The Brighton Market: Feeding Nineteenth-Century Boston. *Agricultural History* 56: 3–21.

Smith, M. E. 1987. Household Possessions and Wealth in Agrarian States: Implications for Archaeology. *Journal of Anthropological Archaeology* 6: 297–335.

Strasser, S. 1982. *Never Done: A History of American Housework*. New York: Pantheon Books.

Sweeney, K. M. 1984. Furniture and the Domestic Environment in Wethersfield, Connecticut, 1639–1800. *Connecticut Antiquarian* 36: 10–39.

Taylor, J. G. 1982. *Eating, Drinking, and Visiting in the South*. Baton Rouge: Louisiana State University Press.

Tilly, L. A. 1985. Food Entitlement, Famine, and Conflict. In *Hunger and History: The Impact of Changing Food Production and Consumption Patterns on Society*, ed. R. I. Rotberg and T. K. Rabb, 135–51. Cambridge: Cambridge University Press.

Ulrich, L. T. 1990. *A Midwife's Tale: The Life of Martha Ballard, Based on Her Diary, 1785–1812*. New York: Alfred A. Knopf.

Usner, D. J., Jr. 1986. Food Marketing and Interethnic Exchange in the Eighteenth-Century Lower Mississippi Valley. *Food and Foodways* 1: 279–310.

Walsh, L. S. 1982. Initial Report on Talbot County Inventories for the 1790's. Manuscript.

———. 1983. Urban Amenities and Rural Sufficiency: Living Standards and Consumer Behavior in the Colonial Chesapeake, 1643–1777. *Journal of Economic History* 43: 109–17.

———. 1985. Land, Landlord, and Leaseholder: Estate Management and Tenant Fortunes in Southern Maryland, 1642–1820. *Agricultural History* 59: 373–96.

———. 1988. Questions and Sources for Exploring the Standard of Living. *William and Mary Quarterly* 3d ser., 45: 116–23.

———. 1989. Rural African Americans in the constitutional era in Maryland, 1776–1810. *Maryland Historical Magazine* 84: 327–41.

———. 1991. Report on Selected Agricultural and Food-related Items in York County, Virginia, and St. Mary's County, Maryland Inventories, 1783–1820. Research Department, Colonial Williamsburg Foundation. Manuscript.

———. N.d. *"To Labour for Profit,"* A book-length study of plantation management in the Chesapeake, 1620–1820. Forthcoming.

Weaver, W. W. 1981. Die Geschickte Hausfrau: The First Ethnic Cookbook in the United States. In *Food in Perspective: Proceedings of the Third International Conference on Ethnological Food Research, Cardiff, Wales, 1977*, ed. A. Fenton and T. M. Owen, 343–63. Edinburgh: John Donald Publishers.

———. 1982. *A Quaker Woman's Cookbook: The Domestic Cookery of Elizabeth Ellicott Lea (1793–1858)*. Philadelphia: University of Pennsylvania Press.

———. 1986. White Gravies in American Popular Diet. In *Food in Change: Eating Habits from the Middle Ages to the Present Day*, ed. A. Fenton and E. Kisban, 41–52. Edinburgh: John Donald Publishers.

Wells, R. 1988. *Wretched Faces: Famine in Wartime England, 1763–1803*. New York: St. Martin's Press.

Wenger, M. R. 1991. Gender and the Eighteenth-Century Meal. In *A Taste of the Past: Early Foodways of the Albemarle Region, 1585–1830*, ed. B. E. Taylor, 26–33. Elizabeth City, NC: Museum of the Albemarle.

Wheaton, B. K. 1983. *Savoring the Past: The French Kitchen and Table from 1300 to 1789*. Philadelphia: University of Pennsylvania Press.

Wheaton, B. K., and P. Kelly. 1988. *Bibliography of Culinary History: Food Resources in Eastern Massachusetts*. Boston: G. K. Hall.

Williams, S. 1985. *Savory Suppers and Fashionable Feasts: Dining in Victorian America*. New York: Pantheon Books.

Wilson, M. T. 1957. Amelia Simmons Fills a Need: *American Cookery*, 1796. *William and Mary Quarterly*, 3d ser., 14: 16–30.

Wright, G. 1981. *Building the Dream: A Social History of Housing in America*. New York: Pantheon Books.

Zierden, M. A., L. M. Drucker, and J. Calhoun. 1986. Home Upriver: Rural Life on Daniel's Island, Berkeley County, South Carolina. Contract study produced for the South Carolina Department of Highways and Public Transportation by Carolina Archaeological Services and the Charleston Museum.

Comment   Gloria L. Main

Most of the papers presented at this conference argue for substantial real growth of the American economy in the early nineteenth century. Economists are accustomed to thinking that such gains imply corresponding improvements in the "standard" of living, at least in the long run. Such optimism appears warranted by the work of Soltow and Margo, who find no evidence of increasing inequality in the distribution of some of the benefits of that growth. As we know, however, all was not sweetness and light in the years between independence and civil war. Slavery expanded, entire nations of Indians lost their homelands, and degradation of the natural environment proceeded apace. Even the white population paid a price for progress as their mortality rates rose and the disamenities of urban life grew worse through overcrowding.

Any reasonable assessment of trends in our standard of living must, therefore, include the underside of economic growth as well as its benefits, and efforts should encompass a wide range of measures. Modern international agencies, for instance, not only collect data on conventional measures of economic resources but also report rates of infant mortality and life expectancy, the proportion of the population with access to clean water and health services, levels of literacy, and years of schooling. Steckel's paper at this conference discusses one such index: the study of human stature. In the process, he reminds us of the now-familiar downward slide in adult heights among men born between 1830 and 1880. That decline was closely associated with rising crude death rates, as reported at an NBER conference a few years ago.[1] Although the evidence derives from adults, the causes of diminished stature did their work in childhood and adolescence and presumably consisted of increasing incidence of infectious epidemical diseases, which interfere with the body's ability to convert nutrients into bone and muscle. Hence, the height data suggest that one major source of rising mortality among both whites and blacks lay in the spread of hostile microbes associated with urbanization and

Gloria L. Main is associate professor of history at the University of Colorado, Boulder.

1. Robert W. Fogel, "Nutrition and the Decline in Mortality since 1700: Some Preliminary Findings," in *Long-Term Factors in American Economic Growth*, ed. Stanley L. Engerman and Robert E. Gallman, NBER Studies in Income and Wealth, 51 (Chicago: University of Chicago Press, 1986).

foreign immigration. These first accelerated in the 1830s, the period of birth for the first cohorts showing declines in average height. If we look at the most recent work available on adult mortality rates, however, the actual rise may have taken place before the 1830s, particularly for women.[2] If true, the sources of that increased mortality were not associated with urban crowding and hordes of microbe-bearing immigrants, and we must look elsewhere for the culprit.

Whether due to new and more infectious epidemical diseases or to inadequate systems for distributing wholesome food or to heavier work loads among agricultural workers, the shorter adults of the nineteenth century were survivors of a milieu less hospitable than that in which their colonial predecessors had thrived. Hence, Walsh's pioneering exploration of diet, cooking styles, means of food preservation, and distribution systems in the early republic is doubly welcome. Not only has she pursued a broad range of subjects through the thickets of dissertations, conference papers, journal articles, and museum shows, thus greatly extending our own conception of this aspect of the standard of living, but her paper allows us to explore, if not dismiss, the notion that the quantity or quality of food had altered sufficiently to affect adversely the well-being and life chances of significant portions of the population.

Walsh's survey suggests two things. First, the American diet did not change substantially between 1750 and 1840, but this statement must be modified in terms of class and locale. Modes of cooking and preserving had changed little since colonial times, as stoves, iceboxes, and canning equipment remained unavailable to all but the rich before circa 1850 or even into the post–Civil War era. Propertied classes ate better and more varied diets, and people living in frontier areas probably ate much the same as had the early settlers of the East Coast. City dwellers, on the other hand, may have been worse off than before, especially the poorer sort. Moreover, consumption of cheap whiskey among the general population reached peak levels soon after 1800 and may have seriously impaired the health of adults and children alike.

Second, compared to the colonial era, rural and urban poor whites and most blacks in the early nineteenth century worked harder and thus may have suffered from nutritional inadequacy in the face of higher bodily needs. Thus, it is possible that laborers generally were living closer to the nutritional edge, less because their diet had deteriorated than because of greater calorie needs.

Much of Walsh's paper reviews the varieties and availability of primary sources for this little-known period and suggests how they might be most efficiently mined. She herself has explored cookbooks, diaries, and probate records, among others, but finds them, and secondary works based on them, generally wanting. Diaries are scarce in any case, and few of them deal with

___

2. Clayne L. Pope, "Adult Mortality before the Twentieth Century: Current Evidence and New Sources," Department of Economics, Brigham Young University, Provo, Utah, 1989.

the mundane matters of the kitchen. Cookbooks do not seem to reflect actual practices. The scarcity of probate records is particularly bad news, but she reports more hopefully on two less familiar sources: archaeological digs and account books. The latter have generally been quarried for wages and prices as well as for information on the kinds of commodities entering local trade. However, their contents take on fresh meaning when people named in the books are identified in terms of family connections and economic rank in the local community. Thus, laconic notations concerning transactions in fresh meat revealed to one Connecticut student that kinship networks played vital distributory roles in providing access to perishable foods. Archaeologists can provide a good deal of evidence on diet, morbidity, and mortality by studying faunal remains, ceramic ware, and human skeletons, all of which become especially valuable when, as with account books, the human participants can be identified in terms of class or social rank. Most such studies currently available, however, come from seventeenth-century or late-nineteenth-century sites, too early or too late for our purposes. However, it would be very informative to compare heights and other kinds of evidence from skeletons of late Woodlands Indians, both coastal and interior, with those of whites and blacks of the colonial and early national period, young children as well as adults, and women as well as men.

Where does Walsh's heroic survey leave us, then? Pointing the way to the salt mines is a common ploy for scholars whose work generates questions rather than answers. Still, one of Walsh's major conclusions takes on great interest in the light of declining life expectancy of adults in America's rural population. Rising agricultural productivity in the older settled regions became possible as employers found ways to use labor profitably year-round, according to Rothenberg's research reported at this conference. Walsh found farm workers of both races and both sexes working harder than they had during the colonial period: putting in longer days and more days per year. One horrific measure of this effect is the high death rate of slave infants, whose mothers were severely overworked during pregnancy and given little time to nurse their infants after birth. Hence, not declining food intake but overwork, especially of women, may well have combined with changing disease patterns to raise adult mortality among poorer rural whites and slaves.

Hard evidence for the connection between overwork and mortality rates will not be easy to come by, but life expectancy at age thirty turned downward for both sexes born *before* 1790 in Pope's sample of family genealogies.[3] This is long before population densities could have played much of a role through overcrowding. Although the downturn reversed itself temporarily in the first decade of the nineteenth century, those born in succeeding decades again faced significantly shorter lives than had their colonial forbears, as urbanization and immigration aided the spread of disease.

3. Ibid., table 7.

Whether shorter lives and higher morbidity outweighed the gain in real annual incomes for the white population at the time remains unknown. Presumably no gains accrued to slaves or Indians. In the long run, of course, cumulative economic growth brought enormous benefits. From the advantage of many generations' distance and of a level of comfort and health little short of miraculous, the modern observer can only be grateful that the transition to industrialism did not exact an even greater cost.

6 Stature and Living Standards in the United States

Richard H. Steckel

The conceptual foundations and measurement of living standards have been enduring concerns for economists, human biologists, anthropologists, and other social scientists. Attempts to define and measure national income, for example, originated in the seventeenth century, while stature was used in the early nineteenth century to monitor health conditions. These and subsequent efforts to assess living conditions were sustained by several motives, including intellectual curiosity, nationalism, and desires to implement social and economic policies. The twentieth century has witnessed considerable progress in designing and implementing various measures of living standards, but scholars continue to research and debate the alternatives.

This paper briefly reviews the literature on the evolution of approaches to living standards and then applies the methodology discussed for stature to the United States from the late eighteenth through the early twentieth century. Section 6.1 of the paper emphasizes two major strands of the subject: national-income accounting and related measures, developed by economists and government policymakers, and anthropometric measures (particularly stature), developed by human biologists, anthropologists, and the medical profession. Until recently the practitioners of these seemingly diverse approaches apparently had little in common and certainly had little interaction. I compare and contrast these alternative approaches to measuring living standards and place anthropometric measures within the context of the ongoing debate over the system of national accounts.

Section 6.2 examines the relationship of stature to living standards, begin-

Richard H. Steckel is professor of economics at Ohio State University and a research associate of the National Bureau of Economic Research.

The author is grateful to Stanley Engerman, Robert Gallman, Howard Marvel, Carole Shammas, John Wallis, Thomas Weiss, the NBER conference participants, and seminar participants at the University of Pennsylvania and Ohio State University for discussion and comments.

ning with a discussion of sources of evidence and the growth process. A statistical analysis explores the relationship of stature to per capita income and the distribution of income using twentieth-century data.

Section 6.3 presents evidence on time trends, regional patterns, and class differences in height. The major phenomena discovered to date are the early achievement of near-modern stature, the downward cycle in stature for cohorts born around 1830 to near the end of the century, the height advantages of the West and the South, and the remarkably small stature of slave children. The secular decline in height is puzzling for economic historians because it clashes with firm beliefs that the mid-nineteenth century was an era of economic prosperity. I establish a framework for reconciling these conflicting views on the course of living standards and discuss possible explanations for the height patterns noted in the paper. The concluding section suggests directions for future research.

6.1   Intellectual History

6.1.1   National Income Accounting

The history of attempts to measure national income before the early twentieth century consists of sporadic efforts by individuals who used several different conceptual foundations and data that were often fragmentary.[1] The earliest attempts can be traced to England and France in the late seventeenth century. In 1665 Sir William Petty sought to measure a country's annual income as the sum of the annual value of labor and the annual proceeds of property. This approach anticipated the current distinction between labor income and capital income, the latter consisting of rent, interest, and profits. Shortly thereafter in France, Pierre Boisguillebert formulated a similar approach, defining national income in terms of a flow of goods and services and in terms of a flow of money incomes. In his view national income consisted of two nearly equal parts, income from labor, which was derived from peasants, artisans, factory workers, petty tradesmen, and professionals, and income from property, which consisted of land, houses, mills, toll houses, revenue-producing public offices, and money capital. Eighteenth-century scholars in England and France, who followed these pioneering efforts, tended to employ narrower concepts of national income. The French physiocrats, led by François Quesnay, defined national income in terms of consumable commodities alone and treated agriculture as the only productive occupation, while Adam Smith took a broader view, including agriculture, manufacturing, and trade but excluding services as productive. Comprehensive production and income

1. This section draws heavily on Studenski (1958), Kendrick (1970), Kendrick and Carson (1972), and United Nations Statistical Office (1980).

concepts were not firmly reestablished in this literature until Alfred Marshall set forth his ideas in the late nineteenth century.

By the beginning of the twentieth century attempts to estimate national income had filtered through much of the industrial or industrializing world. The time pattern of first attempts, presented in table 6.1, shows that the pace of diffusion was slow until the mid-nineteenth century. Although estimates were made for Russia in the late eighteenth century, these endeavors were uninfluential and largely unknown until they were rediscovered in the mid-twentieth century. In the United States the process began with George Tucker (1843), who based his estimate on the new categories of economic data first collected by the census of 1840, and continued with improvements by Ezra Seaman (1852, 1870), who made estimates for 1839, 1849, and 1859, and Edmund Burke (1848, 1849), who made estimates for 1847 and 1848.[2] In 1855 Tucker extended this work to data assembled by the 1850 census, but after the mid-nineteenth century attempts in the United States languished until the 1890s, despite the growing richness of census data collected under the direction of Francis A. Walker. By the end of the century first attempts to estimate national income extended to Austria, Germany, Australia, and Norway and by the end of World War I had reached Japan, Switzerland, the Netherlands, Italy, Bulgaria, and Spain. The Australian case in 1886 is notable as the first example of an estimate that was officially prepared and published by a government agency.

During the course of the twentieth century, national income accounting changed from the casual and sporadic activities of individual researchers to become a nearly universal, systematic endeavor sponsored by governments. The economic restructuring that followed World War I prompted interest in the subject during the 1920s. In the United States the National Bureau of Economic Research, founded in 1920, contributed substantially to the development of methodology. Desires to understand and to cope with the Great Depression stimulated progress in the 1930s. In 1932 the Senate instructed the Department of Commerce to prepare national income estimates, which were delivered in 1934 under the guidance of Simon Kuznets, who was leading the National Bureau's work in the area. Thereafter estimates were produced on an annual basis, and by the end of the decade these were supplemented by monthly and by state-level figures. By 1939 nine countries were preparing official estimates on a continuing basis. Government involvement accelerated during the 1940s with needs for fiscal and economic planning brought on by World War II. Soon after the conclusion of the war, international organizations such as the United Nations played an important role in standardizing concepts, in promoting the diffusion of government involvement in national income accounting, and in facilitating international compar-

2. For a discussion of these early estimates see Gallman (1961).

Table 6.1   First Attempts to Estimate National Income

Country	Estimator	Date or Preparation or Publication	Approach
England	Petty	1665	Value of labor and proceeds of wealth; expense of the people
France	Boisguillebert	1697	Details unavailable
Russia	Hermann (Austrian)	1790	Based on per capita consumption
United States	Tucker	1843	Net value of material production
Austria	Czoernig	1861	Net value of the principal branches of production
Germany	Rumelin	1863	Income tax statistics
Australia	Coghlan	1886	Net output
Norway	Unknown	1893	Unknown
Japan	Nakamura	1902	Net output
Switzerland	Geering and Holtz	1902	Income distributed
Netherlands	Bonger	1910	Income distributed
Italy	Santoro	1911	Net output
Bulgaria	Popoff	1915	Net output
Spain	Barthe	1917	Net output

Source: Compiled from Studenski (1958, pt. 1, "History").

isons.[3] The number of countries that systematically prepared estimates grew from 39 in 1945 to more than 130 in 1969.

During the 1920s and 1930s accounting methodology emerged as an important subject in university economics departments, and scholars debated alternative ways of conceptualizing the accounts. Controversies centered on the types of economic activity that should be included, the extent to which imputation should be used, distinctions between consumption and investment expenditures, the definitions of intermediate versus final products, the organization of subaccounts, and the classification and evaluation of government activities. One school of thought, represented by Simon Kuznets (1941, 1946, 1953), Joseph Davis (1945), and M. K. Bennett (1937), urged the development of welfare-oriented measures that would reflect the satisfaction of consumers. Kuznets argued that a welfare measure might begin with national income but that numerous refinements were necessary to incorporate items such as nonmarket activities, occupational costs, leisure, costs of urban civilization, and the distribution of the product among various groups in society. Ultimately many practical considerations were involved, and given pressures to implement a system useful for coping with the depression and wartime emergencies, the Commerce Department followed a narrower approach, defining national product as "the market value of the output of final goods and

3. On the last point see the methodology and results in Kravis, Heston, and Summers (1978), who develop an alternative to using exchange rates for converting GDPs of different countries into a common currency.

services produced by the nation's economy." This definition is useful for investigating macroeconomic matters such as savings, investment, productivity, and growth, but nonetheless is tangential to a welfare measure. Though it had recognized shortcomings, per capita gross national product soon emerged as a widely used measure of living standards.

With the major conventions of national income accounting more or less established by the 1940s, economic historians began to extend these concepts to the past.[4] By combining census data, market prices, and other sources with methods of imputation and interpolation, data series on national product and related components were constructed from the mid-nineteenth century onward for many countries. While important for understanding the extent and possible ingredients of long-run economic growth, these series typically began too late for analysis of the crucial early phase of the industrialization process. By the 1950s many economists believed that the major accounting questions had been resolved to the extent practical, and the emphasis in the emerging field of macroeconomics shifted to using the new results on national product and its components to study determinants of income, employment, and the price level. Organizations such as the Conference on Research in Income and Wealth and the United Nations continued to refine methods and to work on developing a comprehensive system of national accounts, but national income accounting lost its place as the preeminent field of research, and new cohorts of graduate students in the discipline were exposed less and less to the methodological debates and issues of earlier decades.

The 1970s witnessed a revival of interest in the methodology of social accounting. Moderation of business cycles and high rates of economic growth and accompanying disamenities in the form of urban sprawl, pollution, congestion, and crime stimulated interest in broad welfare measures. In an influential article of the early 1970s William D. Nordhaus and James Tobin (1973) asked whether growth was obsolete.[5] Taking issue with gross national product as a measure of production as opposed to welfare or consumption, they proposed a measure of economic welfare constructed by incorporating adjustments to GNP for capital services, leisure, nonmarket work, and disamenities. In a similar vein Edward Denison (1971) discussed possible components of a welfare measure and its relationship to GNP, while Richard Easterlin (1974) used surveys of human happiness to investigate whether economic growth improves the human lot.

International organizations and economists concerned with the lagging progress of the poor in Third World countries also expressed dissatisfaction in the 1970s with the focus on economic growth, urging a greater role for welfare considerations in the form of distribution and equity. The United Nations, the

---

4. See, for example, Conference on Research in Income and Wealth (1960).
5. This paper and others were presented in 1971 at the Conference on the Measurement of Economic and Social Performance. Moss (1973).

World Bank, and economists such as Irma Adelman and Cynthia Taft Morris (1973) have proposed what are called growth-with-equity or basic human needs approaches to living standards.[6] While there is some disagreement over the essential elements of basic needs, they may be interpreted in terms of minimum amounts of food, clothing, shelter, water, and sanitation that are necessary to prevent ill health and undernourishment (Streeten 1981). Morris (1979) took up the task of quantifying these concerns in the form of a Physical Quality of Life Index based on the infant mortality rate, the literacy rate, and life expectation at age one. In 1990 the World Bank hosted an International Society for Ecological Economics conference, "The Ecological Economics of Sustainability," which included discussion of accounting frameworks that would incorporate environmental losses.[7]

The concept of measuring results in terms of health rather than using only inputs to health has the advantage of incorporating the supply of inputs to health as well as demands on those inputs, a consideration high on the agenda of Amartya Sen's (1987) approach to the standard of living. Sen rejects the notion that the standard of living can be portrayed in terms of opulence or commodities alone, though it is influenced by them, in favor of the idea that one must consider the balance between functionings (the various living conditions that one can or cannot achieve) and capabilities (the ability to achieve various living conditions). Using the example of nutrition he observes that "to reach the same level of nutrition as another, one needs a larger command over food if one has a higher metabolic rate (or a larger body frame), or if one is pregnant (or breast-feeding), or if one has a disease that makes absorption more difficult, or if one lives in a colder climate, or if one has to toil a lot, or if food has other uses (such as for entertainment, ceremonies, or festivals)" (1987, 16). Sen (17) extends the concept of the standard of living in terms of functionings and capabilities by noting the views of Adam Smith, who discussed functionings such as not being "ashamed to appear in public." The commodities needed for this achievement vary with social customs.

While research on living standards by economists in the past two decades has moved toward welfare matters, historians have traditionally dealt with the complexity and diversity of the subject. Those who study the past, particularly the period before governments became heavily involved in data gathering, have been forced by the lack of systematic evidence into foraging among the remains of diverse sources. European historians and scholars of the colonial period in America, for example, have used sources such as probate inventories, yield-to-seed ratios, tax lists, grain reserves per family, and measures of real wages as proxies for a component of the standard of living (see, for example, Deane and Cole 1967; Jones 1980; Cipolla 1980; Lindert and Williamson 1983; and McCusker and Menard 1985).

6. See Johnston (1977) for a discussion of issues.
7. See Constanza et al. (1990) for a discussion of issues, a list of papers, and abstracts of work in the area.

6.1.2   The Evolution of Thought and Use of Stature

The history of national income accounting and that of auxology (the study of human growth) have two things in common: the first substantial efforts occurred in the seventeenth and eighteenth centuries and the early studies were sporadic, imprecise attempts made by individuals. Unlike national income, however, useful measurements of height and related attributes could be made on a small scale. Systematic national income data awaited government involvement and support in the twentieth century, while important progress in auxology had been made before the end of the nineteenth century.

Although desires to monitor social conditions or to engage in the therapeutic treatment of children have sponsored many growth studies in the past, interest in anthropometry, or measurement of the human body, did not originate with science or medicine but with the arts; painters and sculptors needed human measurements to create lifelike images.[8] Artists in this tradition were interested primarily in relative proportions rather than in absolute size, however, and the data they gathered during the Renaissance had little value for understanding processes of human growth.

Table 6.2 charts milestones in anthropometry from the perspective of human biology. The table shows that initial steps were taken in the seventeenth and eighteenth centuries, but progress was slow until the second quarter of the nineteenth century. The first person to use measurements for medical purposes may have been Sigismund Elsholtz, who tried to relate body proportions to health in the mid-seventeenth century. In the next century early attempts at systematic anthropometry appeared in the form of Jampert's measurements of orphans of various ages, Roederer's study of newborns, and the growth table of Montbeillard's son from birth to maturity.

Substantial impetus to growth studies appeared in the 1820s and 1830s when scholars realized that environmental conditions systematically influenced growth. The rise of auxological epidemiology can be traced to France, where Villerme studied the stature of soldiers; to Belgium, where Quetelet measured children and formulated mathematical representations of the human growth curve; and especially to England, where Edwin Chadwick inquired into the health of factory children. After examining the heights of soldiers in France and Holland and studying the economic conditions in their places of origin, Villerme concluded in 1829 that poverty was much more important than climate in influencing growth. The idea that human growth reflected health was put into action in reports on the stature of factory children that were submitted to Parliament in 1833. Legislation in that year incorporated stature as a criterion in evaluating minimum standards of health for child employment.

The greatest strides in the modern study of human growth occurred in the late 1800s and early 1900s with the work of Charles Roberts, Henry Bow-

---

8. This section draws heavily on material in Tanner (1981).

Table 6.2   **Milestones in Auxology**

Country	Investigator	Year	Events or Developments
Germany	Elsholtz	1654	Graduation thesis on anthropometria
Germany	Jampert	1754	Cross-section measurements of stature by age
Germany	Roederer	1754	Measured and weighed newborns
France	Montbeillard	1777	First longitudinal study from birth to adult
France	Villerme	1829	Studied environmental influences on growth
England	Chadwick	1833	First survey of factory children
Belgium	Quetelet	1842	First mathematical formulation of growth
England	Roberts	1876	Used frequency distributions to assess fitness; studied growth by social class
United States	Bowditch	1877	School surveys; analyzed velocity of growth
Italy	Pagliani	1879	Longitudinal studies; school surveys
England	Galton	1889	Studied inheritance of height; introduced regression coefficient
France	Budin	1892	First infant welfare clinic established
United States	Boas	1892–1932	Tempo of growth; concept of developmental age; growth studies in anthropology; standards for height and weight
France	Godin	1903	Detailed growth surveillance
United States	Baldwin	1921	Supervised the first large longitudinal study
England	Douglas	1946	First national survey of health and development
England	Tanner	1952	Models underlying clinical standards

Source: Compiled from Tanner (1981).

ditch, and especially, Franz Boas. Roberts's work in the 1870s increased the sophistication of judging fitness for factory employment with the use of frequency distributions of stature and other measurements, such as weight-for-height and chest circumference. Bowditch assembled longitudinal data on stature to establish the prominent gender differences in growth. In 1875 he supervised the collection and analysis of heights from Boston school children, a data set on which he later used Galton's method of percentiles to create growth standards. In a career that spanned several decades, Boas identified salient relationships between the tempo of growth and height distributions and in 1891 coordinated a national growth study, which he used to develop national standards for height and weight. His later work pioneered the use of statistical methods in analyzing anthropometric measurements and investigated the effects of environment and heredity on growth.

From the late nineteenth century onward there has been a substantial increase in the volume and quality of evidence on human growth. The school surveys of the 1870s and 1880s, noted earlier, were merely the first in a series of large-scale collection efforts. In the United States these endeavors continued with Bird T. Baldwin at the Iowa Child Welfare Research Station beginning in 1917, W. F. Dearborn and the Harvard Growth Study that began in 1922, and the studies initiated in the 1930s in response to the Great Depression, such as the Longitudinal Studies of Child Health and Development of the Harvard School of Public Health, the Child Research Council studies at the University of Colorado, and the Brush Foundation longitudinal study at Western Reserve University. The largest and longest North American longitudinal study was sponsored by the Fels Foundation and investigated Ohio families beginning in 1929. The first in a series of national studies of growth and development was begun in 1946 by England's Royal Commission of Population. The results of an explosion of growth studies throughout the world beginning in the 1950s are contained in the volume by Phyllis Eveleth and J. M. Tanner, *Worldwide Variation in Human Growth* (1976).

6.2 Stature and Living Standards

These movements devoted to assessing human welfare—national income accounting and anthropometric measures—have long, distinguished intellectual traditions that emanated to an important extent from humanitarian considerations, yet until recently there has been virtually no overlap of personnel or cross-fertilization of ideas.[9] Casual inspection of tables 6.1 and 6.2 shows that none of the major players in either field was involved in an important way in the other field.[10] Why these movements unfolded in isolation remains to be explained. Perhaps the demands of understanding and making important contributions to economics and national income accounting (or to auxology) precluded forays into other, seemingly distant areas. Perhaps the greatest flurries of activity occurred at times when these fields were particularly remote; national income accounting advanced rapidly in the 1930s and 1940s, a time when the data gathering and analysis in auxology were centered in medical enterprises and in institutions devoted to the study of child welfare, which were removed from the economics profession. Perhaps the national income accountants of the 1930s and 1940s were repelled by the perversion of human measurements and study of human form that occurred in Hitler's Germany. Whatever the explanation, I will argue the case for collaboration.

Figure 6.1 is a useful organizing device for exploring the relationship of average height to living standards. The top portion of the figure shows a circular chain of causation or influence. One portion of the chain goes from left to right: stature is a function of proximate determinants such as diet, which in turn are functions of socioeconomic variables such as income. In addition, human growth may have functional consequences for health, mental development, and personality, which in turn may influence socioeconomic conditions.

9. It may be interesting to speculate on developments that might have occurred if Franz Boas and Simon Kuznets had been collaborators.

10. It is possible, but unlikely, that an extensive study of lesser contributors in these fields would alter this conclusion that collaboration or interchange was rare, if not entirely lacking, in the past.

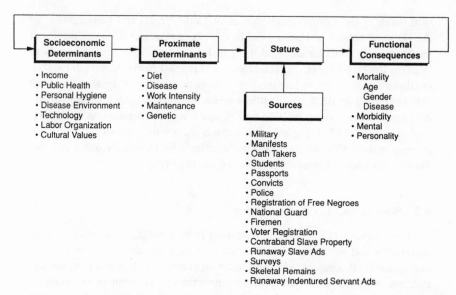

Fig. 6.1   Relationships involving stature

6.2.1   Sources of Evidence on Stature

Height can be used as a measure of living standards because measurements were widely collected from the mid 1700s onward, often as part of an identification or registration scheme for soldiers, students, slave cargoes, oath takers, or travellers. In the absence or high cost of photography, identification procedures before the present century usually relied on personal characteristics such as age, height, hair color, and complexion. Military organizations recorded stature as part of the physical exam of the mustering process, and the results were used to track deserters, to assure that compensation went to the proper individuals, and to assess the fighting capability of regiments. Heights were also useful for the manufacture of uniforms and the estimation of standard food rations. Authorities extended the physical exam and related procedures to students enrolled in military preparatory schools such as West Point. In an effort to prevent smuggling from Africa after 1807, Congress required ship captains to record slave heights on cargo manifests of the coastwise trade in the United States. Comparison of slaves in the cargo at the port of destination with the characteristics enumerated on the manifest confirmed that the slaves originated within the country. Since most black people were slaves in the antebellum American South, many localities required free blacks to register or to carry identification papers that proved their status as free persons of color. During the Civil War the Union Army collected identifying information, such as age, height, and value, on contraband slaves. Beginning in 1863 the president and Congress established an amnesty program for residents of states that were in rebellion; by confirming allegiance to the government of the United States the oath-takers regained rights as citizens. In addition, skeletal remains have proven useful for documenting stature and the nature of work, nutrition, and disease in the past.

Minimum height standards, age and height heaping, ethnic differences in growth potential, and selectivity of those measured complicates the interpretation of stature, but techniques have been devised to address these problems. Military organizations often applied minimum height standards that led to an undersampling of short individuals. The standards varied with manpower needs, and because they were flexibly enforced, the lower tail of the height distribution was eroded rather than truncated. Based on the assumption that the underlying distribution was normal or Gaussian, techniques such as the quantile bend estimator and the reduced-sample maximum likelihood estimator have been devised to identify the height below which standards were applied and to compensate for those who were omitted (Wachter and Trussell 1982).

Heaping, or concentrations of measurements at whole feet or meters, at even-numbered ages or units, and at ages or units ending in zero, plagues many data sources, including some modern studies (Fogel et al. 1983). But simulations of several cases suggest that these adverse aspects were relatively minor for estimates of sample means, primarily because their effects are largely self-cancelling. Rounding error may have affected calculated means depending on tendencies to round upward or downward to whole units of height. Rounding by the military during World War II probably biased average heights by approximately 0.5 centimeters below the actual mean. In any event, rounding practices that were uniform over time and across space would not distort comparisons of relative height averages. In addition, smoothing techniques such as the Preece-Baines models help to overcome heaping irregularities that contaminate the picture of the growth profile (Preece and Baines 1978).

It was seldom the case that the individuals measured represented the entire population about which investigators would like to draw inferences. Army volunteers, for example, typically included more unskilled and more foreign-born relative to the adult male population, and it has been alleged that slaves who were transported in the coastwise trade were rejects in poor health. Questions of sample selectivity can be addressed in three ways. One is to compare different samples from the same population. For example, the average heights of U.S. Colored Troops and slaves shipped in the coastwise trade were nearly identical, a finding that reinforces the credibility of both samples (Margo and Steckel 1982). Second, it may be possible to assign population weights to components of the sample. If laborers made up a disproportionate share of army volunteers, for example, the population mean could be calculated by appropriately reducing the weight given to their average stature. Third, in a few cases, such as Sweden beginning in 1840 and the United States during the

Civil War, all (or nearly all) men of a particular age were measured, which makes possible study of the labor market for volunteers and the characteristics of rejects. Results of this type of study may provide insights into the recruiting process elsewhere.

6.2.2   The Growth Process

The growth process following birth is organized into two periods of intense activity (Tanner 1978). The change in height, or velocity, is greatest during infancy, falls sharply, and then declines irregularly into the preadolescent years. During adolescence velocity rises sharply to a peak that equals approximately one-half of the velocity during infancy, then declines rapidly and reaches zero at maturity. In girls the adolescent growth spurt begins about two years earlier than for boys, but the magnitude of the spurt is smaller. Girls and boys are about the same height at a given age prior to adolescence in girls, but during their spurt girls temporarily overtake boys in average height. Males eventually emerge taller than females primarily because they have approximately two additional years of growth prior to their adolescent growth spurt.

The height of an individual reflects the interaction of genetic and environmental influences during the period of growth. According to Eveleth and Tanner (1976, 222),

> Such interaction may be complex. Two genotypes which produce the same adult height under optimal environmental circumstances may produce different heights under circumstances of privation. Thus two children who would be the same height in a well-off community may not only be smaller under poor economic conditions, but one may be significantly smaller than the other. . . . If a particular environmental stimulus is lacking at a time when it is essential for the child (times known as "sensitive periods") then the child's development may be shunted as it were, from one line to another.

Although genes are important determinants of individual height, studies of genetically similar and dissimilar populations under various environmental conditions suggest that differences in average height across most populations are largely attributable to environmental factors. In a review of studies covering populations in Europe, New Guinea, and Mexico, Malcolm (1974) concludes that differences in average height between populations are almost entirely the product of the environment. Using data from well-nourished populations in several developed and developing countries, Martorell and Habicht (1986) report that children from Europe or European descent, Africa or African descent, and India or the Middle East have similar growth profiles. Comparisons involving European and Far Eastern children or adults are an exception that may have a substantial genetic basis; well-off Japanese, for example, reach on average the fifteenth height percentile of the well-off in Britain (Tanner et al. 1982). Important for interpreting stature in the United States during the eighteenth and nineteenth centuries is that Europeans and people of European descent and Africans and people of African descent who grew under good nutritional circumstances have nearly identical stature (Eveleth and Tanner 1976, appendix).

It is important to realize that height at a particular age reflects an individual's history of *net* nutrition. A substantial share of food received by the body is devoted to maintenance, and other claims on the diet are made by work or physical activity and by disease. The nutrition left over for growth may be further reduced by a synergistic effect of malnutrition and illness (Scrimshaw, Taylor, and Gordon 1968). Poorly nourished children are more susceptible to infection, and infection reduces the body's absorption of nutrients. The character of stature as a net measure implies that explanations for temporal or geographic patterns must recognize not only inputs to health such as diet and medical care but also the implications of work effort and related phenomena such as methods of labor organization for growth. Similarly, researchers must attempt to understand ways that exposure to infectious disease may have placed claims on the diet.

The sensitivity of growth to deprivation depends on the age at which it occurs. For a given degree of deprivation, the adverse effects may be proportional to the velocity of growth under optimal conditions (Tanner 1966). Thus, young children and adolescents are particularly susceptible to environmental insults. At the end of a period of slow growth, normal height may be restored by catch-up growth if nutritional conditions are adequate.[11] If conditions are inadequate for catch-up, normal adult height may be approached by an extension of the growing period by as long as several years. Prolonged and severe deprivation results in stunting, or a reduction in adult size.

6.2.3 Relationship of Stature to Per Capita Income and Its Distribution

While it will be argued that income is a potent determinant of stature that operates via diet, disease, and work intensity, one must recognize that other factors may be involved. The disease load is a function of personal hygiene, public health measures, and the disease environment, while technology and methods of labor organization influence work intensity. In addition, cultural values such as the pattern of food distribution within the family, methods of preparation, and tastes and preferences for foods may also be relevant. Income is probably the most important determinant of diet (Caliendo 1979; Berg 1973). Extremely poor families may spend two-thirds or more of their income on food, but a high proportion of very low income purchases few calories. Malnutrition associated with extreme poverty is known to have a major impact on height. Once calorie requirements are satisfied, additional expenditures on food purchase largely variety, palatability, and convenience.

Impoverished families can afford little medical care, and additional income

---

11. Ingestion of toxic substances, such as alcohol or tobacco, in utero or in early childhood may create permanent stunting regardless of nutritional conditions.

may have an important effect on health through control of infectious diseases. While tropical climates have acquired a bad reputation for diseases, Maurice King (1966) argues that poor health in developing countries is largely a consequence of poverty rather than climate. There is a group of diseases that are spread by vectors that need a warm climate, but poverty is responsible for the lack of doctors, nurses, drugs, and equipment to combat these and other diseases. Poverty, via malnutrition, increases the susceptibility to disease.

Gains in stature associated with rising income are not limited to developing countries. Within industrialized countries height rises with socioeconomic class (Eveleth and Tanner 1976, 34). These changes in height may be related to improvements in the diet, reductions in physical work loads, and better health care. Expenditures on health services rise with income, and there is a positive relationship between health services and health (Fuchs 1972).

At the individual level, extreme poverty results in malnutrition, retarded growth, and stunting. Higher incomes enable individuals to purchase a better diet, and height increases correspondingly, but once income is high enough to satisfy caloric requirements, there is little further increase related to change in the diet. Height may continue to increase with income because more or better medical care services are purchased. As income increases, consumption patterns change so that more and more of a person's genetic potential is realized, but once the potential is reached, environmental variables have no more effect. The limits to this process are clear from the fact that people who grew up in very wealthy families are not physical giants.

If the relationship between height and income is nonlinear at the individual level, then the relationship at the aggregate level depends upon the distribution of income. Average height may differ for a given per capita income depending on the fraction of people with insufficient income to purchase an adequate diet. Since the gain in height at the individual level increases at a decreasing rate as a function of income, one would expect average height at the country level to rise, for a given per capita income, with the degree of equality of the income distribution (assuming there are people who have not reached their genetic potential). Therefore one should proceed with caution to estimate and interpret the relationship between per capita income and average height at the aggregate level.

The aggregate relationship between height and income can be explored by matching the results of the extensive height studies tabulated in Eveleth and Tanner (1976) with per capita income data compiled by Summers, Kravis, and Heston (1980) for market-oriented economies and by the World Bank (1980) for centrally planned economies.[12] The tables in the appendix of the Eveleth and Tanner volume give the same type of information for each study, includ-

---

12. The method of comparative evaluation is an issue in the use of per capita income data for various countries. It would be desirable to have data based on detailed price and output comparisons, as suggested in Summers, Kravis, and Heston (1980), but the number of countries for which data are available is insufficient for the type of analysis undertaken here.

ing country, the people or place, height by year of age up to age eighteen (heights are not available for some ages), and adult height. The volume includes several national studies of height as well as studies of numerous smaller groups within these populations, such as rural, urban, student, military, poor, and rich residents. Despite the large number of factors that may influence average height at a given level of per capita income, there is a high correlation between these variables. Table 6.3 shows that simple correlations between average height and the log of per capita income are in the range of 0.84 to 0.90.[13]

The analysis of average height can be expended to include studies of various subsets of a country's population by employing a regression framework. I examine adolescents and adults separately because the independent variables may have different effects on the heights of these groups. The independent variables available, in addition to the log of per capita income, include a Gini coefficient, which is a measure of income inequality that varies from zero (complete equality) to one (complete inequality), and dummy variables representing poor, rich, urban, rural, university student, and military residents.[14] The urban, rural, and student variables may operate as proxies for income; the poor tend to be located in rural areas, and university students tend to come from high-income families. The effects of military employment are unclear; some countries have minimum height standards while others have universal service, and the bulk of the personnel in many countries is drawn from lower socioeconomic classes. The height studies include populations of Europeans, Africans, Asians, Indo-Mediterraneans, and people with European ancestry or African ancestry.[15] The ethnic variables could measure genetic factors or environmental influences (other than income) such as food prices, health care availability, the disease environment, cultural factors affecting food use, and so forth. The equation for children includes those from ten to fourteen years, ages at which growth is particularly sensitive to environmental influences.

Table 6.4 sets forth the estimated equations.[16] The income variable, the

13. The functional form of the relationship was explored by regressing average height on various polynomials in per capita income and the log of per capita income. There is a substantial improvement in fit by going from the linear to the quadratic formulation and a slight additional improvement from the quadratic to the cubic. Because the semilog form fits approximately as well as the cubic but is simpler, results are reported for the semilog formulation.

14. Attained height is a function of income during the years of height growth, and a more elaborate model would include several lagged values of per capita income. In view of the large differences in per capita income across countries, lagged values would probably add little to the analysis, and one may question whether their inclusion would justify the additional complexity. It should be noted that some research on the lagged relationship between income and stature, which is discussed below, has gone forward for the Netherlands (Brinkman, Drukker, and Slot 1988).

15. There are no observations on adult Africans due to a lack of income distribution data.

16. While it is safe to argue that causation runs one way from per capita income to the heights of children, per capita income and adult height are jointly determined. Height is an index of health and nutrition, and the health and nutrition of workers are known to affect output (see, for example, Weisbrod 1961; Mishkin 1962; Perlman 1966; Meeker 1974). Healthy workers have greater physical vigor, fewer days lost from work, and longer working lives. By using two-stage least squares

Table 6.3   **Correlations between Average Height and the Log of Per Capita Income**

Group	Correlation	Number of Countries
Boys aged 12[a]	0.90	16
Girls aged 12[a]	0.89	15
Adult men[b]	0.84	16
Adult women[b]	0.90	17

Sources: Calculated from data in Eveleth and Tanner (1976), Summers, Kravis, and Heston (1980), and World Bank (1980). The results are reproduced from Steckel (1983).

[a]The countries represented for boys and girls are Czechoslovakia, Egypt, German Democratic Republic, Ghana, India, Japan, Lebanon, the Netherlands, New Zealand, Republic of Korea, Soviet Union, Taiwan, United States, and Uruguay; the boys also include Mozambique. The United States has two height studies.

[b]The countries represented for adults are Bulgaria, Czechoslovakia, India, Indonesia, the Netherlands, Paraguay, Soviet Union, Taiwan, and the United States. The adult men sample also includes Denmark and Zaire, and the adult women sample also includes France, New Zealand, Republic of Korea, and Ireland. India and Zaire have multiple height studies.

Gini coefficient, and the rural, poor, and rich variables have the expected signs.[17] The findings on per capita income and the Gini coefficient are noteworthy results that are discussed at various points in the remainder of the paper. The negative sign of the urban variable may reflect inflows of short people from rural to urban areas; many urban areas also have large numbers of poor people and congested living conditions that spread communicable diseases. Minimum height standards may dominate the effects of the military variable. The coefficient of the gender variable is positive among adolescents,

---

it is not necessary to specify the complete model involving adult height and per capita income; exogenous variables excluded from the height equation must be used, though, to identify the height equation. Any reasonable model of per capita income determination would probably include the value of the capital stock per worker, a measure of human capital per worker, and the percentage of the population of working age. Reliable estimates of the capital stock per worker are available for only a few countries, and therefore the other exogenous variables are used to identify the height equation. The adult literacy rate is used as a measure of human capital.

In the data of this study the correlation between expectation of life at birth and the log of per capita income is about .88. Consequently, estimates of the separate effects of these variables on height are unreliable. Although the regressions include only the log of per capita income, the estimated coefficients of this variable reflects the effects of both income and health.

17. One cannot rule out the possibility that the Gini coefficient is an indicator for other variables. It has been argued, for example, that income eventually becomes more evenly distributed during the course of economic growth (Kuznets 1955). The correlation between the log of per capita income and the Gini coefficient is only about −.17 in these data. The range of the Gini coefficient is .314 to .568 in the adult regression and .204 to .537 in the adolescent regression.

The results for adults are not sensitive to the method of estimation. Ordinary least squares estimates are similar to the two-stage least squares estimates reported for adults in table 6.4. The OLS coefficients of the Gini and the log of per capita income variables are −36.2 and 3.1, respectively.

Coefficients for "poor" and "rich" variables are absent in the adult regressions because height studies were lacking for these classes of residents in the data sources for adults.

Table 6.4   **Regressions of Average Height on Per Capita Income, Gini Coefficient, Place of Residence, Gender, Ethnic Group, and Age**

Variable	Adolescents		Adults	
	Coefficient	t-value	Coefficient	t-value
Intercept	116.0	33.38	160.5	13.99
Log per capita income	3.545	7.644	3.490	2.223
Gini coefficient	−8.260	1.283	−36.74	4.408
Urban	−0.3085	0.3591	−0.1478	0.0909
Rural	−3.392	3.539	−2.524	1.315
Poor	−7.968	4.938		
Rich	5.483	6.426		
Student			1.225	1.148
Military			2.599	1.765
Female	0.1171	0.2637	−11.24	16.05
European ancestor	−4.452	3.313	−1.170	0.5954
African	−0.6789	0.3187		
African ancestor	−3.328	2.010	−1.903	0.9970
Asian	−6.315	4.582	−1.673	0.6294
Indo-Mediterranean	−4.531	2.166	2.321	0.7658
Age 11	5.250	7.961		
Age 12	11.11	16.85		
Age 13	16.81	24.80		
Age 14	21.43	31.32		
R^2	0.92			
N	163		30	
Method	OLS		2SLS	

Sources: Calculated from data in Eveleth and Tanner (1976), Ginsberg (1961), Jain (1975), Summers, Kravis, and Heston (1980), UNESCO (1957), and World Bank (1980). The results are reproduced from Steckel (1983).

Notes: Dependent variable = average height in centimeters. Income is measured in 1970 U.S. dollars for the year that the height study was published. The omitted class refers to a national height study of Europeans. Age ten is an excluded variable in the regression on adolescent height. Observations on "poor" and "rich" groups do not exist for the adults.

The countries represented for adolescents are Argentina, Egypt, German Democratic Republic, Hong Kong, India, Japan, Republic of Korea, Lebanon, Malaysia, New Zealand, Spain, Sudan, Taiwan, United States, Uruguay, and Yugoslavia. The countries represented for adults are Egypt, France, Hong Kong, India, Republic of Korea, New Zealand, Taiwan, Thailand, Turkey, United Kingdom, and the United States. Several counties have more than one height study.

probably because girls begin the growth spurt earlier than boys. The ethnic variables may capture possible genetic differences, but in view of the important role attributed to environment by human biologists, environmental factors may underlie the results. Among adults the ethnic variables have no statistically significant effect, but among children all ethnic variables are negative, and four out of five are statistically significant. This finding may reflect the fact that children are relatively sensitive to the environment; some deprivation in childhood may be overcome by an extension of the growing period. Our understanding of environmental consequences would be improved by analysis of individual level data.

Table 6.5 depicts the estimated relationship between average height and per capita income derived from the regressions in table 6.4 under the assumptions that the Gini coefficient was evaluated at the sample mean and the group was people with European ancestors. Height is particularly sensitive to income at low income levels. Among boys aged 12, for example, height increases by 6.7 centimeters as per capita income increases from $150 to $1,000, whereas the gain is 5.7 centimeters as per capita income increase from $1,000 to $5,000.

The relationships given in table 6.5 suggest that it may be feasible to use data on average height to infer levels of per capita income. Because other factors also influence height, one should proceed with caution in this endeavor. A reduction in the Gini coefficient of 0.2, for example, increases average adult height by more than 7 centimeters. Moreover, changes or differences in public health measures, personal hygiene, the disease environment, or methods of labor organization could lead to different levels of average height for a given per capita income. Despite this possibility, Roderick Floud's (1984) study of per capita income and average heights in Europe from the mid-nineteenth through the mid-twentieth century, using an analysis similar to that in Steckel (1983), suggests that the relationship may have been relatively stable. The pattern of Floud's results, given in table 6.6, is remarkably similar to that reported in table 6.5. This stability gives credence to more recent attempts to "backcast" per capita income using a polynomial distributed lag model. Brinkman, Drukker, and Slot (1988) estimate such a model for the Netherlands, based on data for the years 1900 to 1940, to predict levels of per capita income beginning in 1845. Their results challenge claims that substantial economic development, as measured by per capita income, occurred in the Netherlands before the mid-1800s.

Table 6.5   **Estimated Relationship between Average Height (centimeters) and Per Capita Income**

Per Capita Income (1970 U.S. $)	Boys Aged 12	Girls Aged 12	Adult Men	Adult Women
150	137.1	137.2	160.9	149.7
250	138.9	139.0	162.7	151.4
500	141.4	141.5	165.1	153.9
1,000	143.8	143.9	167.5	156.3
2,000	146.3	146.4	169.9	158.7
3,000	147.7	147.8	171.4	160.1
4,000	148.7	148.8	172.4	161.1
5,000	149.5	149.6	173.1	161.9

Source: Calculated from table 6.4, assuming a national study for a population with European ancestors and a Gini coefficient evaluated at the sample mean.

Table 6.6   **Relationship between Height and Per Capita Income in Europe**

Per Capita Income (1970 U.S. $)	Average Height (centimeters)
500	163.8
1,000	166.9
2,000	169.9
3,000	171.7
4,000	173.0

Source: Floud (1984, table 3). The results are calculated assuming a national height study for Italy using a semilog model.

In contrast, the data for the United States (discussed below) show that native-born Americans were tall despite their low per capita income. If plausible levels of per capita income that existed in 1800 (Weiss, chap. 1 of this volume; converted to 1970 dollars using U.S. Bureau of the Census 1975) were substituted into table 6.5, for example, predicted stature would be roughly 9 centimeters below the level observed. While no firm answer to this question is currently available, there are several promising potential explanations. First, the degree of wealth or income inequality in early America may have been low compared with developing countries, a line of inquiry made attractive by the finding that average height is sensitive to the Gini coefficient. Many developing countries are characterized by considerable income inequality, and probate records suggest that inequality in wealth was modest in the late-eighteenth-century America (Jain 1975; Jones 1980). Second, the relationship between height and per capita income expressed in table 6.5 depends upon income comparisons calculated using exchange rates, but work by Summers and Heston (1991) using purchasing-power-parity concepts shows that exchange rates systematically underestimate the real income of poor countries compared with rich ones. A sense of the importance of this methodology for understanding height comparisons in the United States can be obtained by substituting relative per capita GNP in the United States in 1800 into the framework of results obtained by Summers and Heston. U.S. GNP per capita in 1800 (Weiss, table 6) adjusted for price changes (U.S. Bureau of the Census 1975, ser. E 135–166; U.S. Department of Labor 1991) was about 5.5 percent of that in 1980 (World Bank 1982). At this level of income relative to that in the United States in 1980, real income measured by purchasing power parity is, on average, roughly double that measured by exchange rates (Summers and Heston 1991, figure 1), which would explain about one-quarter of the 9-centimeter difference between predicted (according to the height-income relationship expressed in table 6.5) and observed heights given per capita income that prevailed in 1800. These calculations assume, among other things, that incomes in the early-nineteenth-century United States can be treated like the per capita incomes of poor countries today within the Summers-Heston framework, something that awaits verification. While these calculations should be refined and their underlying assumptions investigated, these preliminary results suggest that the method of comparing incomes is relevant, but not a dominant factor in understanding the early achievement of near-modern stature in the United States.

A third line of investigation (discussed in more detail below) would explore differential experience made by claims on the diet associated with disease. Given the relatively low density of population in the late eighteenth century, it is plausible that Americans were exposed less to communicable diseases than the typical resident of a developing country in the twentieth century. Moreover, the temperate climate of America may have fostered lower levels of exposure to disease than the tropical or semitropical climate characteristic of many developing countries.

6.2.4   Stature and the Intellectual Tradition of Living Standards

Given that average height is highly correlated with per capita income, it is appropriate to ask how average height fits in with the intellectual tradition of measuring living standards as devised by economists. The earlier discussion noted that the welfare basis of the national income accounts was widely debated in the 1930s, but for practical reasons and desires to establish methods that would help in the management of fluctuations in income and employment, the accounts have a narrower focus on production. However, a revival of interest in these issues occurred in the 1970s with economists proposing welfare measures. Average height is particularly adept at assessing degrees of deprivation, a feature that places the measure nicely within the basic-needs approach to living standards. While the basic-needs approach has been criticized for the conceptual problems associated with ascertaining what is basic, in many ways average height finesses this problem because it is a measure of net nutrition. Average height incorporates the extent to which individuals have greater needs created by factors such as a harsher disease environment or greater work loads. In this vein, average height is also conceptually consistent with Sen's framework of functionings and capabilities, though, of course, height registers primarily conditions of health during the growing years as opposed to one's status with respect to commodities more broadly.

Average height also meets satisfactorily the criteria set forth by Morris Morris (1979, chap. 4) for an international standard of the physical quality of life:

1. It should not assume that there is only one pattern of development. In other words the measure should be adaptable to diverse societies including those with modern economic structures, village economies, or tribal systems.
2. It should avoid standards that reflect the values of specific societies.
3. It should measure results, not inputs.
4. It should be able to reflect the distribution of social results.

5. It should be simple to construct and easy to comprehend.
6. It should lend itself to international comparison.

Stature obviously measures results, not inputs, and the regression analysis presented in table 6.4 made clear that the measure is sensitive to the distribution of income. Moreover, measurements of stature are simple to construct, easy to comprehend, and amenable to a variety of economic structures and to international comparison once differences in genetic potential, if relevant, are recognized. One can allow for genetic differences by comparing stature relative to percentiles attained on the appropriate local height standards. It may be possible to question average height on grounds of point 2 in the sense that the measure may imply that "bigger is better," which could be construed as a cultural value. It is claimed, however, not that stature is an end in itself but that it is merely an indicator of health.

6.3   Stature and the Standard of Living in America

It was stature's versatility in measuring living standards in diverse societies that led to its first application in historical debates of the mid-1970s. Progress on the controversy over the sexual mores of American slaves hinged on knowledge of the age at which slave women had children, relative to when they could have had children (Trussell and Steckel 1978). Heights collected as part of an identification scheme on shipping manifests were useful for this purpose because menarche typically occurs within a year or so following the peak of the adolescent growth spurt. From this application the use of stature spread to issues of slave health more generally (Steckel 1979) and to the health of other populations (see Fogel et al. 1983 for additional discussion). While the study of average heights in the past has confirmed some widely held beliefs, such as the poor living conditions of urban areas in the eighteenth and nineteenth centuries, the most interesting applications involve challenges to traditional beliefs. This sections discusses examples in American history.

6.3.1   Long-Term Trends

Table 6.7 presents evidence on the long-term trend of heights of the native-born in the United States. The most surprising feature of the table is the early achievement of nearly modern stature. Contrary to the popular assumption that there was a secular increase in stature, troops measured during the mid- to late 1700s were nearly as tall as those who were measured over a century and a half later. Soldiers in the French and Indian War attained a mean of about 172.1 centimeters, or the thirty-fifth percentile of modern standards (as tabulated in Tanner, Whitehouse, and Takaishi 1966), and those who participated in the American Revolution reached, on average, the thirty-ninth percentile.

The situation during the late colonial period was remarkable not only compared with twentieth-century America but also compared with contemporary European populations. During the third quarter of the eighteenth century,

Table 6.7   Heights of Native-Born White Males

Dates of Measurement	Age	Sample Size	Mean	Source
1755–63	24–35	767	172.0	Sokoloff and Villaflor (1982, 459)
1755–63	21–30	885	172.2	Steegmann and Haseley (1988, 415)
1775–83	24–35	968	172.9[a]	Sokoloff and Villaflor (1982, 457)
1861–65	25–30	123,472	173.2	Gould (1869, 104)
1916–18	21–30	868,445	171.4[b]	Davenport and Love (1921, 67)
1943–44	20–24	119,443	173.2[c]	Karpinos (1958, 300)

[a]Adjusted for minimum height standards.
[b]Includes foreign-born.
[c]Tallest age group.

Swedish troops attained about 166 to 168 centimeters (Sandberg and Steckel 1987), while those from Britain and from the Habsburg Empire were 162 to 168 centimeters (Floud, Wachter, and Gregory 1990; Komlos 1989). Although the Swedes and the British experienced substantial but temporary gains to approximately 170 centimeters following the Napoleonic Wars, they did not reach the American stature of the late colonial period until the late 1800s.

The data of table 6.7 alone suggest a temporal stability that did not exist in the American record. If the heights are arranged by birth cohort, as shown in figure 6.2, then cycles or fluctuations are a better characterization of the American experience than is the high plateau evident from the table. The first identifiable surge began in the two or three decades before the French and Indian War. Heights were approximately constant at about 171 to 172 centimeters for those born between 1720 and 1740, but those born in the mid-1750s had gained about 1.0 centimeter over their predecessors. The evidence has not been gathered for some cohorts, and interpolation is required, but the available data indicate that the spurt of the mid-1700s was followed by a plateau of about 172.5 to 173.5 centimeters from births of 1780 to 1830. Thereafter heights declined irregularly to a low of approximately 169 centimeters for births in the late 1800s, which was followed by the more familiar secular improvement of the twentieth century.

The heights of adult slaves recorded on the coastwise manifests also displayed cycles. Those born in the 1770s reached, on average, about 171.3 centimeters, which corresponds to the thirtieth percentile of modern standards. Then the mean declined to 169.6 for those born in the early 1790s, after which there was an irregular recovery to about 171.5 centimeters by those born in the late 1820s. The measurements of children point to increasing net nutritional hardship for those born after 1830; the stature of adolescents aged 12 to

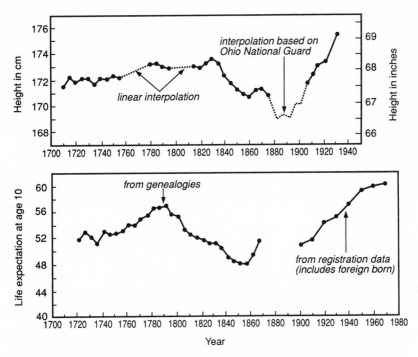

Fig. 6.2 **Average height of native-born white males by year of birth and the trend of their life expectancy at age ten**
Sources: Fogel (1986); Steckel and Haurin (1990).
Note: See table 6.8 for data.

17 who were born in the early 1840s was over 5 centimeters below that of children the same age born only 10 to 15 years earlier. Since those born in the early 1840s did not reach adulthood before the recording system was abolished, it is unknown whether these children were stunted as adults.

6.3.2 Geographic Differences

Several studies have noted differences in height by state or region. Small stature for those born or living in the Northeast was an enduring pattern, while residents of the South or the West were frequently tall. This pattern may have begun as early as the colonial period. Sokoloff and Villaflor (1982) report that among troops of the French and Indian War, southerners were 0.5 centimeters taller than those from the Middle Atlantic states. The North-South gradient also appeared during the American Revolution when southerners were 0.8 above those from the Middle Atlantic states, and 1.3 centimeters taller than New Englanders. Using a different sample and a more refined geographic grid, Steegmann and Haseley (1988) report, however, that heights of French and Indian War troops were tallest (173.5 centimeters) from noncoastal east-

Table 6.8   **Data for Figure 6.2**

Life Expectation at Age 10		Stature	
Years on Which Observation Is Centered	No. of Years	Year on Which Observation Is Centered	Height (centimeters)
1720–24	51.8	1710	171.5
1725–29	52.7	1715	172.2
1730–34	52.0	1720	171.8
1735–39	51.2	1725	172.1
1740–44	52.9	1730	172.1
1745–49	52.3	1735	171.7
1750–54	52.5	1740	172.1
1755–59	52.9	1745	172.0
1760–64	53.9	1750	172.2
1763–69	53.7	1755	172.1
1770–74	54.8	1760	
1775–79	55.2	1765	
1780–84	56.4	1770	
1785–89	56.5	1775	
1790–94	56.7	1780	173.2
1795–99	55.4	1785	173.2
1800–1804	55.2	1790	172.9
1805–9	53.0	1795	172.8
1810–14	52.3	1800	
1815–19	51.9	1805	
1820–24	51.4	1810	
1825–29	51.1	1815	173.0
1830–34	51.0	1820	172.9
1835–39	50.2	1825	173.1
1840–44	48.7	1830	173.5
1845–49	48.2	1835	173.1
1850–54	47.9	1840	172.2
1855–59	47.8	1845	171.6
1860–64	49.2	1850	171.1
1865–69	51.4	1855	170.8
1870–74		1860	170.6
1875–79		1865	171.1
1880–84		1870	171.2
1885–89		1875	170.7
1890–94		1882.5	168.9
1901	50.6	1887.5	169.2
1910	51.3	1892.5	169.0
1920	54.1	1897.5	170.0
1930	55.0	1902.5	170.0
1940	57.0	1906.5	171.6
1950	59.0	1911	172.2
1960	59.6	1916	172.9
1970	59.8	1921	173.2
		1931	175.5

Sources: Fogel (1986); Steckel and Haurin (1990).

ern Massachusetts, noncoastal Connecticut, and the mid–Hudson valley and declined as one moved south to 169.2 centimeters for these from Delaware, southeastern Pennsylvania, and eastern Maryland.

The disadvantage of the Northeast was clear during the Civil War, World War I, and World War II. At ages 27 to 30 Union troops from Kentucky and Tennessee were tallest (175.5), followed by other slave states and the Midwest at approximately 174.7, New England (173.4), and the Middle Atlantic states at 172.8 (Gould 1869, 123). The World War I recruits were shortest from the Northeast (about 169.5) and tallest from South at approximately 173.0 (Davenport and Love 1921, 75). During World War II inductees were largest from the West (174.6), followed by the South Central (174.2), the North Central (173.2), the Southeast (173.1), and the Northeast (171.6; Karpinos 1958). During the mid-1800s West Point cadets from the South were about 1 percent taller than those from the Middle Atlantic states and the West (Komlos 1987). It should be noted that the secular decline in stature of the nineteenth century, noted above, occurred despite the relative shift of population out of the low-stature states of the Northeast and into the high-stature states to the west.

Among southern whites who signed amnesty oaths during the 1860s, those from the interior states of Kentucky, Tennessee, Missouri, and Arkansas tended to be 0.8 to 1.8 centimeters taller than residents from the lower coastal states such as Alabama, Louisiana, South Carolina, and Texas (Margo and Steckel 1992). A similar but less pronounced regional pattern existed among ex-slave recruits. The former slaves from South Carolina were particularly small, falling 2.3 centimeters below those from Kentucky or Tennessee.

The slight growth advantage observed for people from urban areas in studies on modern data is probably a new phenomenon. As recently as World War II the stature of troops declined by 1.2 centimeters as their community size increased from a population of under 2,500 to 500,000 or more. Ohio National Guard recruits from rural areas were about 0.5 centimeters taller than urban recruits (Steckel and Haurin 1990).The advantage of rural residence was larger earlier in the century, as evident from Civil War troops from cities and towns of 10,000 or more people who were 1.3 centimeters shorter than their country counterparts. A similar advantage for rural residents prevailed among regular army troops who were measured between 1815 and 1820, but a half a century earlier that were no statistically significant urban-rural differences.

6.3.3   Socioeconomic Patterns

Systematic height differences existed by occupation, foreign birth, and condition of the population (whether free white, free black, or slave). As a general pattern the occupational differences were larger during the nineteenth century than during the present century or the late colonial period. Among World War II recruits, all but the shortest occupation were tightly packed within 0.5 centimeters, and the tallest, farmers and farm laborers, was only 1.2 centimeters larger than the shortest, clerks and kindred workers (Karpinos 1958). Half a century earlier in Ohio the range exceeded 2 centimeters; professionals were tallest at 175.5 followed by farmers (174.7), clerical and skilled workers (174.0), and laborers (173.3). Union troops who were farmers were 0.4 centimeters taller than white collar workers, who were 0.8 centimeters taller than skilled artisans, who were 0.9 centimeters taller than laborers. West Point cadets whose fathers were farmers were 1.1 percent taller than the shortest group, whose family background was in blue collar work (apparently children of laborers did not enter the academy). The results during the late colonial period are mixed with respect to occupation. In the French and Indian War sample farmers were about 1.5 centimeters taller than artisans or laborers, but the occupational differences vanished among troops of the American Revolution.

Since European residents were several centimeters shorter than Americans, the result that the foreign-born were smaller than the native-born throughout the period is not surprising. Yet the advantage of the native-born was substantially less than the difference in average heights between Europe and America, which indicates that trans-Atlantic migrants may have been taller and in better health than those who remained behind. It is also possible that newcomers from Europe who had not yet reached adult height benefited from improved nutrition after arriving in America. The native-born Ohio National Guard recruits, for example, were 2.1 centimeters taller than those who were foreign-born. The difference in favor of the native-born was about 3.2 centimeters for Union Army recruits, and 2 to 4.8 centimeters for troops of the French and Indian War or the American Revolution.

Although the differences in adult stature between native-born whites, free blacks, and slaves existed during the early and mid-1800s, the contrasts were less than observed between native and foreign-born and across occupations. Adult male free blacks in Virginia were only 0.7 centimeters smaller than northern whites, and at 170.6 centimeters slaves were 1.9 centimeters shorter than the free blacks. Yet comparisons of growth profiles from early childhood to maturity make clear that slaves were remarkably different (Steckel 1986c, 1987a). The slave children were extraordinarily small, approaching the early childhood heights of the Bundi of New Guinea. Slaves fell below the first percentile of modern height standards before age 6 and reached less than the second percentile before age 10. Average heights in this neighborhood are sometimes observed in poor developing countries or in poor countries of the past, but if the children were small, the adults in these populations were also small. Similarly, if the children were large, the adults tended to be large. The American slaves were remarkable because the children were small and the extent of catch-up growth was large if not unprecedented. The catch-up accelerated during adolescence and the age at maximum increment was 13.3 in females and 14.8 in males, only 1 to 1.5 years after that for well-nourished modern populations. Prolongation of growth helped bring slave adults to the twenty-seventh (male) or twenty-eighth (female) percentile of modern standards.

6.3.4   Discussion

Because study of socioeconomic, geographic, and temporal patterns is still at an early stage, the findings reported here should be regarded as preliminary. Nevertheless, enough is understood to report more than an agenda for research. The discussion emphasizes the unusual pattern of slave growth, the early achievement of near-modern stature, and cycles in height.

Examination of materials relevant to the unusual pattern of slave growth suggests that newborns got a poor start in life. The infant mortality rate was probably in the neighborhood of 350 per thousand or more, and losses for those aged 1 to 4 were about 201 per thousand on large plantations (Steckel 1986a, 1986b). Poor medical knowledge and practices of the era claimed many children, but slave losses before age 5 were roughly double those of whites who lived in the United States from 1830 to 1860. Regional differences in the survival rates of whites suggest that only a portion of the excess losses (perhaps 15 to 30 percent) could be attributed to a harsh disease environment and other factors affiliated with residence in the South (Steckel 1988). Although the vigorous adolescent growth spurt indicates that workers were well-fed, seasonal patterns of neonatal mortality and plantation work records indicate that pregnant women had an arduous work routine during peaks in the demand for labor, such as the plowing, planting, and harvesting seasons. The labor demands of the institution are clear from estimates that slaves produced about 30 percent more output per year than free farmers (Fogel and Engerman 1974). A number of features of slave skeletons from the colonial and antebellum periods document the strenuous physical labor demands, particularly in areas of the shoulders, hips, and lower vertebrae (Kelley and Angel 1987; Rathbun 1987). Claims on the diet placed by work were made worse by malaria and other fevers common during the "sickly season" of late summer and early autumn. It is also likely that certain vitamin and mineral deficiencies, such as for iron, calcium, vitamin C, and niacin, aggravated overall maternal ill health. Since stillbirths and neonatal deaths are sensitive to deprivation at or near conception, and neonatal deaths are elevated by deprivation during the third trimester, this evidence points to seasonal nutritional deprivation of the fetus as an important ingredient in poor infant health.

Although poor prenatal care and low birth weights underlay many neonatal deaths and contributed to high losses in the postneonatal period and beyond, a poor diet and infections also entered the picture. Slave women usually resumed regular work within three to five weeks after delivery, and while mothers were in the field, the young children typically remained in the nursery. Initially the mothers returned to the nursery two or three times per day for breast-feeding, but within three months after delivery their productivity in the fields reached normal levels, which suggests that one or more of the daytime breast-feedings were eliminated. As a substitute the infants received starchy paps and gruels, often contaminated or fed using contaminated utensils. Thus, young children who survived the hazardous neonatal period faced a poor diet and diseases that were often related to poor nutrition. The child's diet emphasized hominy and fat, and owners and medical practitioners frequently cited whooping cough, diarrhea, measles, worms, and pneumonia as causes of death. Concentrations of children on medium and large plantations probably promoted the spread of these diseases.

By ages 8 to 12 work entered the picture of slave health. Other things being equal, increased physical activity would have placed a claim on the diet that retarded growth. Yet it was at ages that work usually began, initially as a light activity, that some catch-up growth occurred. Other things must not have been equal. Specifically, slave workers received regular rations of meat (about one-half pound of pork per day) and other foods that may have been supplemented by garden produce, chickens, pigs, and game. In addition, as slaves matured they may have become more experienced and efficient at their work (using less wasted motion), thereby leaving more nutrition from a given diet for growth. A substantial incidence of Harris lines on leg bones uncovered from a South Carolina plantation points to late childhood and adolescence as the major period of recovery from deprivation (Rathbun 1987). The strong catch-up growth as teenagers and workers reinforces the view that nutrition was at least adequate, if not exceptional, for the tasks performed by slaves.

Caribbean slave children were approximately as small as slave children in the United States, but the Caribbean population displayed much less recovery, attaining only the third to the fourteenth percentile of modern standards as adults (Higman 1984). In the Caribbean the age at maximum increment was about 14.7 years for males and 13 years for females. The pattern of stunting with relatively little delay may have been caused by liberal rations of rum given to all working slaves, including pregnant women. It is also possible that the strenuous work of Caribbean sugar plantations that began in adolescence contributed to the meager catch-up growth.

Why did Americans achieve nearly modern heights as early as the mid-1700s while Europeans lagged behind a century or more? A substantial answer to this question is not yet available, but the evidence points to several ingredients of an interpretation that emphasize sources of good nutrition, a relatively low incidence of epidemic disease, and widespread access to land and other resources. First, the abundance of good land in America enabled farmers to choose only the most productive plots for cultivation, possibly allowing them to exert less physical effort, after clearing the land, for a given amount of output compared with European farmers. Second, most of the population was nestled along the coast between two abundant sources of protein—fish from the Atlantic and game from the forests. Third, the land was lightly populated in America, which tended to reduce the spread of communicable diseases that lessened the ability to work and that claimed nutrition from the diet. The benefits of isolation, low population density, and little commercial development for stature have been noted for outlying areas of Sweden, Austria-Hungary, Japan, and the American South (Sandberg and Steckel 1987; Komlos 1989; Shay 1986; Margo and Steckel 1982, 1992). Finally, the available evidence suggests that income and wealth were more equally distributed in the United States during the late colonial period than at any time except the mid-twentieth century and that inequality in the 1700s was probably much less in the United States compared with Europe (Gallman 1978; Jones 1980; Williamson and Lindert 1980). As noted earlier, a move toward equality in access to resources at a given level of income tends to increase the average height of a population, because a given income distributed from the rich to the poor will decrease the heights of the rich by less than the increase in the heights of the poor, assuming, of course, that the poor had not reached their growth potential. Given that average incomes were growing during the mid-nineteenth century, the redistribution argument is effective in explaining the height decline only if inequality increased fast enough to more than offset the health gains attributable to rising average incomes.

Several countries, including Sweden, England, Austria-Hungary, and the United States, have experienced cycles in heights. Although cycles are not unusual, the episode of stature decline that began in the United States during the second quarter of the nineteenth century is particularly interesting to economic historians because it challenges firm beliefs that the middle decades of the nineteenth century were prosperous by conventional income measures, estimates of real wages, productivity measures, and capital stock estimates. The United States began the process of industrialization in the Northeast during this era, and the economy achieved what is called "modern economic growth," or sustained increases in real per capita income at rates on the order of 1 to 1.5 percent or more per year (Gallman 1966). Estimates of real wages suggest that this measure of living standards increased by roughly 50 percent between 1820 and the late antebellum period (Margo and Villaflor 1987; Margo, chap. 4 in this volume). The antebellum period also witnessed productivity improvements in agriculture and manufacturing and increases in the capital stock per capita (Rothenberg, chap. 7 in this volume; Gallman, chap. 1 in this volume). Regional estimates of per capita income indicate that the Northeast was highly prosperous in the mid-1800s, yet the military data show that this region had the lowest average stature (Easterlin, 1961).

How can the height decline and the regional patterns be reconciled with the evidence of economic prosperity? One answer dismisses the height data as inaccurate, unrepresentative, or responding to genetic changes. While possible, I find this answer unappealing because the cycle registers in several data sources, including Civil War muster rolls, regular army recruits, West Point cadets, adolescent slaves, skeletal evidence, and mortality records. While one may quibble with estimates of short-term fluctuations from these sources, the existence of a substantial secular decline in the mid-to-late nineteenth century is well established. Large samples from the Civil War muster rolls and evidence from West Point cadets show that the decline began for those born after approximately 1830, and data from regular army enlistments following the Civil War indicate that the decline continued for those born in the years immediately following the Civil War (see figure 6.2 and Komlos 1987). Although the evidence collected to date is thin for the next three decades, Ohio National Guard muster rolls show that the trough was reached for those born in the 1880s or early 1890s, and data for World War II troops arranged by year of birth show the modern secular increase in stature began around the turn of the century (see Steckel and Haurin 1990; Karpinos 1958). Skeletal evidence also identifies the recovery underway at the turn of the twentieth century and suggests that a low point in stature was probably reached among those born in the 1880s (Trotter and Gleser 1951). Moreover, mortality evidence from genealogies, given in figure 6.2, and from plantation records indicate that life expectation tended to deteriorate while heights declined during the antebellum period. The height disadvantage of the Northeast is well-established from abundant military records. Although genetic drift cannot be ruled out as a factor in the height patterns, it should be noted that modern populations show little evidence of drift in stature when living conditions are approximately constant.[18] Moreover, it is known that stature does respond to the environment, and progress has been made in linking the stature patterns of the eighteenth and nineteenth centuries to changes or differences in environmental conditions.

If the height data are credible, the search for explanations should recognize that traditional national income accounting measures, real wage series, and average heights focus on different aspects of living standards. None of these measures gives a comprehensive picture of the standard of living broadly construed; the first two emphasize market behavior and various imputations for productive activity, while average height reflects net nutrition and the distribution of income or wealth. Thus, a particular type of prosperity may have accompanied industrialization while other aspects of the standard of living deteriorated. Other things being equal, one would expect that the measured economic prosperity of the mid-1800s would have increased average stature. The secular height decline and the regional patterns suggest that other things must not have been equal. Specifically, nutritional liabilities (either claims on nutrition or lower nutritional intake) that more than offset the advantages bestowed by higher incomes must have accompanied the economic prosperity.

The search for understanding should recognize that most of the antebellum height decline occurred within the rural population. Thus, one cannot base an explanation primarily on urbanization and the adverse health conditions in the cities. Although the available evidence indicates that health conditions were poor in the cities, only a small share of the population lived in these areas

18. Genetic issues are discussed in Tanner (1978) and Eveleth and Tanner (1976).

before the Civil War, and the height differences were modest between farmers and residents of large urban areas. The share of the U.S. population living in places of 10,000 or more people was 6 percent in 1830, and as late as 1860 it was only 14.8 percent (U.S. Bureau of the Census 1975, ser. A 57–72). Soldiers who were born in urban areas of 10,000 or more population were approximately 1.3 inches, or 3.3 centimeters, shorter than farmers (Margo and Steckel 1983). Therefore, the increase in the share living in these urban areas of $14.8 - 6.0 = 8.8$ percent would explain only $0.088 \times 3.3 = 0.29$ centimeters of the height decline that was approximately 2.5 centimeters between 1830 and 1860.

In contrast with the evidence for the antebellum period, the data for the Ohio National Guard following the Civil War indicate that height declines were substantial in large urban areas. Compared with the heights of those born before 1880, the heights of cohorts born in 1880–96 declined 0.25 centimeters among farmers, 2.0 centimeters among the nonfarm rural population, 0.25 centimeters among residents in small cities, and 2.3 centimeters among residents in cities with 50,000 or more population (Steckel and Haurin 1990). The share of the population living in urban places of 50,000 or more population increased from 12.7 percent in 1870 to 22.3 percent in 1900 (U.S. Bureau of the Census, 1975, ser. A 57–72). This evidence suggests that urbanization played a supporting role in the height decline of the late nineteenth century.

Several additional explanations are worth investigation. One emphasizes the sensitivity of average heights to the distribution of income or wealth. Based on the regression reported in table 6.5, a rise of .17 in the Gini coefficient from 1830 to 1890 would have offset the rise in per capita income and account for a decline of 4 centimeters in average stature. This line of thought is appealing because there is evidence from many countries that inequality tends to rise and then decline during development (Kuznets 1955; Lindert and Williamson 1985). The modest evidence on inequality trends in the United States during the nineteenth century has evoked controversy, but it seems plausible that growth in inequality could have contributed significantly to the secular decline in stature (Margo and Villaflor 1987; Margo, chap. 4 in this volume; Soltow, chap. 8 in this volume; Williamson and Lindert 1980).[19]

John Komlos (1987) argues that the height decline may have been caused by a deterioration in the diet created by the sectoral shift in production that occurred during industrialization. According to this view, urbanization and the expansion of the industrial labor force increased the demand for food while productivity per worker and the agricultural labor force grew slowly, causing a decline in food production (especially meat) per capita. It would be possible to test the argument that declines in inputs to net nutrition were re-

19. Unfortunately, little information on the course of wealth or income inequality is currently available for the nineteenth century. However, within a couple of years I expect to have some results based on a methodology of matching census manuscript schedules with tax records for the period 1820 to 1910.

sponsible by examining information on diets, cooking and food preparation technology, and systems of food distribution. However, the most recent survey of research in this area does not suggest that dietary deterioration occurred after 1825, though more research is clearly needed (Walsh, chap. 5 in this volume). An indirect test of the hypothesis can be conducted using data on relative prices. If per capita food production declined, the relative price of food should have risen, which may have caused a decline in stature. Table 6.9 presents the ratio of the wholesale price index of foods to the wholesale price index of all commodities from the 1820s through the 1880s. Consistent with the height decline, the relative price of food rose from the 1820s through the 1830s. However, the relative price reached a peak in the late 1830s, declined in the early 1840s, and fluctuated moderately thereafter. This evidence suggests that the temporary rise in food prices may have prompted modest and short-lived reductions in nutritional intake during the early phase of the secular decline, but other factors were probably involved in the early phase, and certainly thereafter.

Other hypotheses that are under study include greater exposure to infectious disease brought on by higher rates of interregional trade, migration, and immigration, and the push of midwestern farming into marshy and river-bottom lands that hosted malaria. Migration and trade may increase morbidity and mortality by spreading communicable diseases and by exposing newcomers to different disease environments (Smillie 1955; May 1958; Curtin 1989). These adverse consequences could have been substantial before public health measures became effective. Indeed, prior to the late nineteenth century isolated, preindustrial populations in sparsely settled regions were often relatively tall, as discovered in Ireland, the interior of the American South, Austria-Hungary, Sweden, and Japan (Sandberg and Steckel 1987; Shay 1986; Komlos 1989; Nicholas and Steckel 1991; Margo and Steckel 1982, 1992). Consistent with the idea that increased concentration of population and growth of trade have adverse net nutritional consequences before the era of modern public health, evidence from human remains suggests that popula-

Table 6.9   **Ratio of the Wholesale Price Index of Foods to the Wholesale Price Index of All Commodities, 1821–1825 to 1886–1890**

Years	Ratio	Years	Ratio
1821–25	1.012	1856–60	1.068
1826–30	1.021	1861–65	0.977
1831–35	1.049	1866–70	1.031
1836–40	1.128	1871–75	0.963
1841–45	0.985	1876–80	1.020
1846–50	1.042	1881–85	1.020
1851–55	1.070	1886–90	0.998

Source: Calculated from the Warren and Pearson price indexes (U.S. Bureau of the Census 1975, Ser. E 52–63).

tions that entered settled agriculture had greater nutritional stress than their hunter-gatherer predecessors (Cohen and Armelagos 1984). These sources of greater exposure to infectious disease merit attention because interregional trade, migration, and immigration expanded substantially during the mid-nineteenth century. The cholera epidemics from the 1830s through the 1860s are well-known examples of disease transmission that illustrate this point (Rosenberg 1962). The epidemic of 1832, for example, entered the continent at New York, Quebec, and New Orleans, and spread by travellers along the major routes. The importance of immigration in nineteenth-century disease transmission is confirmed by positive correlations between immigration rates and urban mortality rates and by information that epidemics often spread from immigrant districts to other areas (Higgs 1979; Meckel 1985). The early and mid-nineteenth century also witnessed numerous epidemics of yellow fever, typhoid, typhus, and smallpox that were spread by population movements. The high degree of churning in population movements from rural to urban areas may help to explain the rural character of the height decline. Low persistence rates in moves from farms to cities and towns indicate that rural-to-urban migrants often returned after short periods of time, bringing communicable diseases with them (Steckel 1987b). Westward migration also led to encounters with malaria, particularly in the numerous marshy and river-bottom areas of the Midwest. Travel accounts, memoirs, army statistics, and medical journals establish that malaria was a substantial seasonal health problem in the Midwest until the late nineteenth century (Ackerknecht 1945). Since this region of the United States was settled largely after 1815, the explanation is consistent with the timing of the height decline, its recovery near the end of the century, and its rural character. Although this explanation of the secular trend fails to account for the height disadvantage of the Northeast, it should be noted that other factors, such as population churning and changes in labor organization noted elsewhere, might explain that situation.

Changes in labor organization that led to greater exposure to disease in the workplace and may have required more physical exertion by workers deserves some attention in a list of potential explanations for the mid-nineteenth-century decline in health reported in figure 6.2. The home manufacturing typical of the eighteenth century diffused geographic patterns of work and insulated the population from contagious disease. Those employed at home also progressed at their own pace. In contrast, factories and artisan establishments that emerged in the 1820s and 1830s concentrated employees in the workplace under conditions that increased the risk of exposure to infectious diseases. Claims on nutrition were made by long hours in work arrangements paced by machines, and numerous people crowded in dusty or humid environments, typical of textile mills, led to the spread of tuberculosis and pulmonary illnesses. These conditions are important for understanding the secular decline in stature of the mid-nineteenth century, because children made up a substantial share of the labor force during America's industrial revolution (Goldin and

Sokoloff 1982). By the 1830s and 1840s poor working conditions in New England mills and factories received the attention of groups such as the New England Association of Farmers, Mechanics, and Other Workingmen; the National Trades' Union; and the Massachusetts Medical Society (Rosen 1944). The geographic spread of industrialization to the midwest widened the scope of this claim on nutrition.

It is conceivable that new opportunities for trade reduced nutritional intake in rural areas. This could happen if the transportation revolution made manufacturing goods available at low cost, tempting farmers to trade so much of their products that nutritional intake diminished. If rural residents placed extraordinarily high value on manufactured goods, their utility could have increased while their diet deteriorated. The abundance of land and growth in agricultural productivity in the mid-nineteenth century suggest that this effect, if it existed, was weak. However, it is a line of argument that is probably worth exploring.

The puzzle of height decline in the face of economic growth that the middle decades of the nineteenth century poses for economic historians also applies to the height disadvantage of northeastern residents. Although per capita incomes were relatively high in states of the region, the population was less well-off as measured by stature. One possible explanation of the pattern notes the dense settlement, high rate of commerce, industrialization, and substantial immigration into the area. The growing concentration of population in cities and towns after 1820 reinforced the harmful aspects of this disease environment. The region also had a smaller supply of good farmland per person than did the Midwest or the South, which may have been an important consideration before the substantial interregional trade of the mid-1800s.

The decline in adult heights of slaves born after 1775 and the subsequent recovery for those born after the mid-1790s may have been affiliated with changes in the concentration of the African-born in the American slave population. The African-born were 5 to 10 centimeters shorter than native-born or creole slaves (Eltis 1982; Higman 1984), and the annual rate of importation was at its highest level from 1780 to 1807. Unfortunately the share of African-born is unknown from the slave manifests, but an increase of 15 percentage points in this share could have accounted for about three-quarters of the decline. Since the African slave trade was outlawed after 1807 and smuggling was probably a minor or negligible part of population growth thereafter, the downturn in adolescent heights after 1830 had causes largely unrelated to the African-born. Possible explanations include rapid westward migration of the 1830s, which helped to spread communicable diseases, the rise of larger plantations, which had more demanding work routines and greater concentrations of children, and the appearance of epidemic diseases such as cholera. It is also possible that owners reduced rations and increased work requirements in response to the agricultural depression of the late 1830s and early 1840s.

6.4 Concluding Remarks

This paper reviews the intellectual history of living standards from the approaches of national income accounting and of auxology. Although the earliest efforts in these methods of assessing human welfare extend back to the seventeenth century, collaboration in these fields has occurred only recently. Since the mid-1970s economic historians have compared and contrasted these measures, collected data on stature, developed analytical techniques, and sifted output for novel comparative results. The typical American of the eighteenth and nineteenth centuries was nutritionally well-off compared with the average European, but diversity in the United States existed by social class, region, and time period. Young slaves, who were among the smallest children ever measured, had extraordinarily poor health. In the nutritional sense slave children had the worst living conditions of any ethnic group in America and were at least as badly off as any population in Europe. The free population was relatively tall in the South but short in the Northeast, and the stature of the native-born declined for over half a century for cohorts born after 1830. The geographic patterns and the secular decline appear to conflict with substantial evidence of economic prosperity. Although researchers should continue to probe the factual basis of these measures of living standards as an explanation for their apparent conflict, it should also be noted that they measure different aspects of living conditions. Economic conditions could improve while nutritional circumstances decline if greater claims were made on the diet by factors associated with the economic conditions, such as greater inequality in the distribution of income or wealth, more work effort, and increased exposure to infectious disease. If economic prosperity, measured by traditional means such as per capita income, increased claims on the diet, then it is important to adjust those measures for the loss in human welfare. Research is just beginning on the methodology appropriate for this purpose. Jeffrey Williamson's (1981b) use of the bribery principle to estimate the disutility of industrialization represents an important step in this direction. The resulting debate (Pollard 1981; Williamson 1981a) over assessment of risks, the accuracy and suitability of mortality estimates, and the equilibrating processes in labor markets serve as a guide for future research on this important issue of assessing human welfare.

The gathering and analysis of height data and related anthropometric measures, such as weight, will undoubtedly be an important academic enterprise in coming years, particularly since substantially more data are available, but I expect that future research will place greater emphasis on the functional consequences of height and related anthropometric measures. This aspect of research is important because many social scientists have little or no clinical experience with stature, and those not participating in height research or something related, such as physical anthropology, have read little or none of the underlying literature on human biology. As a consequence most social scientists find this measure difficult to interpret in isolation; average height has meaning only in relation to more familiar measures such as per capita income, Gini coefficients, real wages, labor productivity, human capital, social class, mortality, and fertility. Moreover, it is in terms of these measures that they have defined problems, framed hypotheses, and taken positions in debates. Social scientists will have an incentive to learn about the underpinnings of this line of work if height is accepted as a proxy or at least a measure similar to variables and concepts in which there is an established interest.

Some progress has been made in documenting the relationship of height to mortality and to labor productivity. Work on the slave registration data of Trinidad has measured the effect of height on the chances of survival (Friedman 1982; John 1988). Analysis of data from contraband slaves in the Civil War demonstrates that value increased with height, probably because taller slaves were stronger and lived longer (Margo and Steckel 1982). These examples portend the direction of this type of research, but scholars have merely scratched the surface of the available data. Pension records of former soldiers, for example, hold great promise for understanding the consequences of height for occupational choice, labor productivity, disability, and disease-specific causes of death. Stature could be used as the basis for extending per capita income estimates in several countries to the early industrial and, in some cases, the preindustrial eras, but one must be wary in this research. The conflicting patterns of stature and per capita income discussed for the United States in the nineteenth century suggest that other factors, such as the distribution of income or wealth and claims on the diet made by work or disease, must be taken into account. Projects are underway to document the course of birth weights from hospital records, such as the Lying-in Hospital in Montreal (Ward and Ward 1984) and the Philadelphia Alms House (Goldin and Margo 1989). Work has yet to begin on historical relationships among stature, nuptiality, and fertility. As an aid to this entire research agenda, economic historians have only begun to exploit information that may be available about stature and its consequences from skeletal evidence and from populations in developing countries.[20]

Efforts should also be made to extend the portion of the life span over which information is collected on the biological quality of life. Heights inform us about the history of health during the growing years, particularly every childhood and adolescence, but are silent on conditions after adult height is attained. Weight-for-height measures, such as the body mass index (weight in kilograms divided by the square of height in meters), is a useful measure of health risks among adults (Fogel 1991). Waaler (1984) reports that death rates

20. Efforts to use skeletal remains were made at a conference, "Diet, Disease, Work, and History: Techniques of Physical Anthropology and Historical Methods in the Reinterpretation of the Past," which was held in November 1990 at the Economics Department of Ohio State University.

among Norwegian men rose substantially among those whose body mass indexes exceeded 28 or fell below 22. Unfortunately, use of the body mass index on historical problems is limited because information on both height and weight was rarely reported before the late nineteenth century.

I propose that research efforts be devoted to defining and estimating a measure of the biological standard of living throughout the life span. The foundations of such a measure should be (1) the length of life and (2) the biological quality of life at each age while living. In designing this measure one could take a cue from the work of medical examiners and physicians who assigned pensions to Civil War veterans based on an individual's degree of disability. Courts that estimate the loss of a person's biological capacity following accidents operate on similar principles. For example, the biological standard-of-living index for individual j (I^j_{bsl}) could be defined as follows:

$$I^j_{bsl} = \sum_{i=1}^{100} Q^j_i \quad \text{where } Q^j_i = Q_i(x^j_1, x_2, \ldots, x^j_k),$$

i denotes the year of life, and Q_i is a function whose arguments are measures of the biological quality of life. The function Q_i, which takes on values from 0 to 1, measures the biological quality of life in year of life i. Excellent health is indicated by a function value of 1 and very poor health by a function value near 0. At death the function Q_i takes on a value of 0.0. A person who had excellent health throughout life and died at exactly age one hundred would have an index value of 100, but an individual who lived forty years in moderately poor health ($Q_i = 0.5$ for all ages from birth to death) would have an index value of 20. Age 100 is an approximate upper limit to the life span in most populations, and it provides a convenient maximum numerical value for the index.[21] Average values for the index could be used in comparative analyses, and since the index is based on individual data, one could use the measure to study inequality in the biological standard of living in much the same way that economists study inequality of wealth or income. Major research questions for this framework are the specification of the Q_i functions (perhaps some form of a logistic function would be suitable) and sources of data on indicators of the biological quality of life. One would like to have longitudinal data on a person's state of health from birth to death. A sequence of annual physical examinations would achieve this purpose, but more refined measurements, such as monthly, weekly, or even daily observations on health, would be desirable.[22] Unfortunately, such data are rare, even in modern populations. Alternatively, an individual's record of health could be approximated using information from skeletal remains. Although the skeletal record provides an incomplete picture of health, emphasizing chronic as opposed to acute condi-

---

21. Obviously the index could be scaled on the basis of a longer life span.
22. A device, implanted in the body, that continuously monitored an individual's state of health would be ideal for this purpose.

tions, it nonetheless provides a consistent way of measuring important aspects of health across diverse populations (Steckel and Rose 1991).

Although poverty and inequality have been enduring concerns for social scientists and there is a huge literature on methods of assessment and on the extent to which these phenomena exist (see, for example, Jencks 1979; Lebergott 1976; Taubman 1978; Tullock 1986), attempts to use height in monitoring living standards and to evaluate the efficacy of social policy have been rare. However, a growth surveillance program (National Study of Health and Growth) for this purpose has existed in England since 1972 (Rona 1989, 1991). There is a clear need for health surveillance in poor countries, and the World Bank recommends that stature be included as a component of living standards surveys in developing countries, but few systematic efforts are in place in industrialized countries.[23] Even in wealthy societies there are disadvantaged groups that are exposed to fluctuations in socioeconomic circumstances, which creates a need for a program for assessing nutritional status. Such a program has a sound methodological base and, I expect, would be sensible, given the ease of collecting anthropometric data. I therefore conclude with a call for study of the costs and benefits of incorporating measures of the biological standard of living into our social accounting apparatus.

References

Ackerknecht, Erwin H. 1945. Malaria in the Upper Mississippi Valley, 1760–1900. *Supplements to the Bulletin of the History of Medicine,* no. 4: 1–142.

Adelman, Irma, and Cynthia Taft Morris. 1973. *Economic Growth and Social Equity in Developing Countries.* Stanford: Stanford University Press.

Bennett, M. K. 1937. On Measurement of Relative National Standards of Living. *Quarterly Journal of Economics* 51: 317–35.

Berg, Alan D. 1973. *The Nutrition Factor.* Washington, DC: Brookings Institution.

Brinkman, Henk Jan, J. W. Drukker, and Bridgett Slot. 1988. "Height and Income: A New Method for the Estimation of Historical National Income Series." *Explorations in Economic History* 25: 227–64.

Burke, Edmund. 1848. *Annual Report of the Commissioner of Patents.* 30th Cong., 1st sess. H. Doc. 54, 558–61.

———. 1849. *Annual Report of the Commissioner of Patents.* 30th Cong., 2d sess. H. Doc. 59, 719–27.

Caliendo, Mary Alice. 1979. *Nutrition and the World Food Crisis.* New York: Macmillan.

Cipolla, Carlo M. 1980. *Before the Industrial Revolution: European Society and Economy, 1000–1700.* New York: W. W. Norton.

Cohen, Mark Nathan, and George J. Armelagos. 1984. *Paleopathology at the Origins of Agriculture.* New York: Academic Press.

Conference on Research in Income and Wealth. 1960. *Trends in the American Econ-*

---

23. For discussion of living standards surveys that include height see Ho (1982).

omy in the Nineteenth Century, ed. William N. Parker. NBER Studies in Income and Wealth, 24. Princeton: Princeton University Press.

Constanza, Robert, Ben Haskell, Laura Cornwell, Herman Daly, and Twig Johnson. 1990. The Ecological Economics of Sustainability: Making Local and Short-Term Goals Consistent with Global and Long-Term Goals. World Bank Environment Working Paper no. 32. Washington, DC.

Curtin, Philip D. 1989. *Death by Migration.* Cambridge: Cambridge University Press.

Davenport, M. W., and A. G. Love. 1921. *The Medical Department of the United States Army in the World War.* Vol. 15, *Statistics.* Part I, *Army Anthropology.* Washington, DC: GPO.

Davis, Joseph S. 1945. Standards and Content of Living. *American Economic Review* 35: 1–15.

Deane, Phyllis, and W. A. Cole. 1967. *British Economic Growth, 1688–1959: Trends and Structure.* Cambridge: Cambridge University Press.

Denison, Edward F. 1971. Welfare Measurement and the GNP. *Survey of Current Business* 51: 13–16, 39.

Easterlin, Richard A. 1961. Regional Income Trends, 1840–1950. In *American Economic History,* ed. Seymour Harris, 525–47. New York: McGraw-Hill.

———. 1974. Does Economic Growth Improve the Human Lot? Some Empirical Evidence. In *Nations and Households in Economic Growth,* ed. Paul A. David and Melvin W. Reder, 89–125. New York: Academic Press.

Eltis, David. 1982. Nutritional Trends in Africa and the Americas: Heights of Africans, 1819–1839. *Journal of Interdisciplinary History* 12: 453–75.

Eveleth, Phyllis B., and J. M. Tanner. 1976. *Worldwide Variation in Human Growth.* Cambridge: Cambridge University Press.

Floud, Roderick. 1984. The Heights of Europeans since 1750: A New Source for European Economic History. NBER Working Paper no. 1318. Cambridge, MA: National Bureau of Economic Research.

Floud, Roderick, Kenneth W. Wachter, and Annabel S. Gregory. 1990. *Height, Health, and History: Nutritional Status in the United Kingdom, 1750–1980.* Cambridge: Cambridge University Press.

Fogel, Robert W. 1991. New Sources and New Techniques for the Study of Secular Trends in Nutritional Status, Health, Mortality, and the Process of Aging. NBER Historical Factors in Long-Run Growth Working Paper no. 26. Cambridge, MA: National Bureau of Economic Research.

———. 1986. Nutrition and the Decline in Mortality since 1700: Some Preliminary Findings. In *Long-Term Factors in American Economic Growth,* ed. Stanley L. Engerman and Robert E. Gallman, 439–527. NBER Studies in Income and Wealth, 51. Chicago: University of Chicago Press.

Fogel, Robert W., and Stanley L. Engerman. 1974. *Time on the Cross: The Economics of American Negro Slavery.* Boston: Little, Brown.

Fogel, Robert W., Stanley L. Engerman, Roderick Floud, Gerald Friedman, Robert A. Margo, Kenneth Sokoloff, Richard H. Steckel, James Trussell, Georgia C. Villaflor, and Kenneth W. Wachter. 1983. Secular Changes in American and British Stature and Nutrition. *Journal of Interdisciplinary History* 14: 445–81.

Friedman, Gerald C. 1982. The Heights of Slaves in Trinidad. *Social Science History* 6:482–515.

Fuchs, Victor R. 1972. The Contribution of Health Services to the American Economy. In *Essays in the Economics of Health and Medical Care,* ed. Victor R. Fuchs, 3–38. New York: National Bureau of Economic Research.

Gallman, Robert E. 1961. Estimates of American National Product Made before the Civil War. *Economic Development and Cultural Change* 9: 397–412.

————. 1966. Gross National Product in the United States, 1834–1909. *Output, Employment, and Productivity in the United States after 1800,* ed. Dorothy S. Brady, 3–90. NBER Studies in Income and Wealth, 30. New York: Columbia University Press.

————. 1978. Professor Pessen on the Egalitarian Myth. *Social Science History* 2: 194–207.

Ginsberg, Norton Sydney. 1961. *Atlas of Economic Development.* Chicago: University of Chicago Press.

Goldin, Claudia, and Robert A. Margo. 1989. The Poor at Birth: Birth Weights and Infant Mortality at Philadelphia's Almshouse Hospital, 1848–1873. *Explorations in Economic History* 26: 360–79.

Goldin, Claudia, and Kenneth Sokoloff. 1982. Women, Children, and Industrialization in the Early Republic: Evidence from the Manufacturing Censuses. *Journal of Economic History* 42: 741–74.

Gould, Benjamin A. 1869. *Investigations in the Military and Anthropological Statistics of American Soldiers.* Cambridge: Riverside Press.

Higgs, Robert. 1979. Cycles and Trends of Mortality in Eighteen Large American Cities, 1871–1900. *Explorations in Economic History* 16: 381–408.

Higman, Barry W. 1984. *Slave Populations of the British Caribbean, 1807–1834.* Baltimore: Johns Hopkins University Press.

Ho, Teresa J. 1982. Measuring Health as a Component of Living Standards. LSMS Working Papers no. 15. Washington, DC: World Bank.

Jain, Shail. 1975. *The Size Distribution of Income: A Compilation of Data.* Washington, DC: World Bank.

Jencks, Christopher. 1979. *Who Gets Ahead? The Determinants of Economic Success in America.* New York: Basic Books.

John, A. Meredith. 1988. *The Plantation Slaves of Trinidad, 1783–1816: A Mathematical and Demographic Enquiry.* Cambridge: Cambridge University Press.

Johnston, Bruce F. 1977. Food, Health, and Population in Development. *Journal of Economic Literature* 15: 879–907.

Jones, Alice Hanson. 1980. *Wealth of a Nation to Be.* New York: Columbia University Press.

Karpinos, Bernard D. 1958. Height and Weight of Selective Service Registrants Processed for Military Service during World War II. *Human Biology* 30: 292–321.

Kelley, Jennifer Olsen, and Angel, Lawrence J. 1987. Life Stresses of Slavery. *American Journal of Physical Anthropology* 74: 199–211.

Kendrick, John W. 1970. The Historical Development of National-Income Accounts. *History of Political Economy* 2: 284–315.

Kendrick, John W., and Carol S. Carson. 1972. *Economic Accounts and Their Uses.* New York: McGraw-Hill.

King, Maurice Henry. 1966. *Medical Care in Developing Countries.* Nairobi: Oxford University Press.

Komlos, John. 1987. The Height and Weight of West Point Cadets: Dietary Change in Antebellum America. *Journal of Economic History* 47: 897–927.

————. 1989. *Nutrition and Economic Development in the Eighteenth-Century Habsburg Monarchy.* Princeton: Princeton University Press.

Kravis, Irving B., Alan Heston, and Robert Summers. 1978. *International Comparisons of Real Product and Purchasing Power.* Baltimore: Johns Hopkins University Press.

Kuznets, Simon. 1941. *National Income and Its Composition, 1919–1938.* New York: National Bureau of Economic Research.

————. 1955. Economic Growth and Income Inequality. *American Economic Review* 45: 1–28.

————. 1946. *National Income: A Summary of Findings.* New York: National Bureau of Economic Research.

————. 1953. National Income and Economic Welfare. *Economic Change: Selected Essays in Business Cycles, National Income, and Economic Growth,* 192–215. New York: W. W. Norton.

Lebergott, Stanley L. 1976. *The American Economy: Income, Wealth, and Want.* Princeton: Princeton University Press.

Lindert, Peter H., and Jeffrey G. Williamson. 1983. Reinterpreting Britain's Social Tables, 1688–1913. *Explorations in Economic History* 20: 94–109.

————. 1985. Growth, Equality, and History. *Explorations in Economic History* 22: 341–77.

McCusker, John J., and Russell R. Menard. 1985. *The Economy of British America, 1607–1789.* Chapel Hill: University of North Carolina Press.

Malcolm, L. A. 1974. Ecological Factors Relating to Child Growth and Nutritional Status. In *Nutrition and Malnutrition: Identification and Measurement,* ed. Alexander F. Roche and Frank Falkner, 329–52. New York: Plenum Press.

Margo, Robert A., and Richard H. Steckel. 1982. The Heights of American Slaves: New Evidence on Slave Nutrition and Health. *Social Science History* 6: 516–38.

————. 1983. Heights of Native-Born Whites during the Antebellum Period. *Journal of Economic History* 43: 167–74.

————. 1992. The Nutrition and Health of Slaves and Antebellum Southern Whites. In *Without Consent or Contract: Technical Papers on Slavery,* ed. Robert W. Fogel and Stanley L. Engerman. New York: W. W. Norton.

Margo, Robert A., and Georgia C. Villaflor. 1987. The Growth of Wages in Antebellum America: New Evidence. *Journal of Economic History* 47: 873–95.

Martorell, Reynaldo, and Jean-Pierre Habicht. 1986. Growth in Early Childhood in Developing Countries. In *Human Growth: A Comprehensive Treatise,* ed. Frank Falkner and J. M. Tanner, 3: 241–62. New York: Plenum Press.

May, Jacques M. 1958. *The Ecology of Human Disease.* New York: MD Publications.

Meckel, Richard A. 1985. Immigration, Mortality, and Population Growth in Boston, 1840–1880. *Journal of Interdisciplinary History* 15: 393–417.

Meeker, Edward. 1974. The Social Rate of Return on Investment in Public Health, 1880–1910. *Journal of Economic History* 34: 392–419.

Mishkin, S. 1962. Health as an Investment. *Journal of Political Economy* 70 (supp.): 129–57.

Morris, Morris David. 1979. *Measuring the Condition of the World's Poor: The Physical Quality of Life Index.* New York: Pergamon Press.

Moss, Milton, ed. 1973. *The Measurement of Economic and Social Performance.* NBER Studies in Income and Wealth, 38. New York: National Bureau of Economic Research.

Nicholas, Stephen, and Richard H. Steckel. 1991. Heights and Living Standards of English Workers during the Early Years of Industrialization, 1770–1815. *Journal of Economic History* 51: 937–57.

Nordhaus, William D., and James Tobin. 1973. Is Growth Obsolete? In *The Measurement of Economic and Social Performance,* ed. Milton Moss, 509–32. NBER Studies in Income and Wealth, 38. New York: National Bureau of Economic Research.

Perlman, Mark. 1966. On Health and Economic Development: Some Problems, Methods, and Conclusions Reviewed in a Perusal of the Literature. *Comparative Studies in Society and History* 8: 433–48.

Pollard, Sydney. 1981. Sheffield and Sweet Auburn: Amenities and Living Standards in the British Industrial Revolution: A Comment. *Journal of Economic History* 41: 902–4.

Preece, M. A., and M. J. Baines. 1978. A New Family of Mathematical Models Describing the Human Growth Curve. *Annals of Human Biology* 5: 1–24.

Rathbun, Ted A. 1987. Health and Disease at a South Carolina Plantation, 1840–1870. *American Journal of Physical Anthropology* 74: 239–53.

Rona, R. J. 1989. A Surveillance System of Growth in Britain. In *Auxology 88: Perspectives in the Science of Growth and Development*, ed. J. M. Tanner, 111–19. London: Smith-Gordon.

———. 1991. Nutritional Surveillance in Developed Countries using Anthropometry. In *Anthropometric Assessment of Nutritional Status*, ed. J. H. Himes. New York: Wiley-Liss.

Rosen, George. 1944. The Medical Aspects of the Controversy over Factory Conditions in New England, 1840–1850. *Bulleton of the History of Medicine* 15: 483–97.

Rosenberg, Charles E. 1962. *The Cholera Years*. Chicago: University of Chicago Press.

Sandberg, Lars G., and Richard H. Steckel. 1987. Heights and Economic History: The Swedish Case. *Annals of Human Biology* 14: 101–10.

Scrimshaw, N. S., C. E. Taylor, and J. E. Gordon. 1968. *Interactions of Nutrition and Disease*. WHO Monograph Series, no. 52. New York: United Nations.

Seaman, Ezra C. 1852. *Essays on the Progress of Nations: In Civilization, Productive Industry, Wealth, and Population*. New York: Charles Scribner.

———. 1870. *The American System of Government*. New York: Charles Scribner and Co.

Sen, Amartya. 1987. *The Standard of Living*. Cambridge: Cambridge University Press.

Shay, Ted. 1986. The Stature of Military Conscripts: New Evidence on the Standard of Living in Japan. Paper given at the 1986 Social Science History Association meetings, St. Louis, MO.

Smillie, Wilson G. 1955. *Public Health: Its Promise for the Future*. New York: Macmillan.

Sokoloff, Kenneth L., and Georgia C. Villaflor. 1982. The Early Achievement of Modern Stature in America. *Social Science History* 6: 453–81.

Steckel, Richard H. 1979. Slave Height Profiles from Coastwise Manifests. *Explorations in Economic History* 16: 363–80.

———. 1983. Height and Per Capita Income. *Historical Methods* 16: 1–7.

———. 1986a. Birth Weights and Infant Mortality among American Slaves. *Explorations in Economic History* 23: 173–98.

———. 1986b. A Dreadful Childhood: The Excess Mortality of American Slaves. *Social Science History* 10: 427–65.

———. 1986c. A Peculiar Population: The Nutrition, Health, and Mortality of American Slaves from Childhood to Maturity. *Journal of Economic History* 46: 721–41.

———. 1987a. Growth Depression and Recovery: The Remarkable Case of American Slaves. *Annals of Human Biology* 14: 111–32.

———. 1987b. Household Migration, Urban Growth, and Industrialization: The United States, 1850–1860. NBER Working Paper no. 2281. Cambridge, MA: National Bureau of Economic Research.

———. 1988. The Health and Mortality of Women and Children, 1850–1860. *Journal of Economic History* 48: 333–45.

Steckel, Richard H., and Donald R. Haurin. 1990. Health and Nutrition in the American Midwest: Evidence from the Height of Ohio National Guardsmen, 1850–1910. Ohio State University, Columbus. Manuscript.

Steckel, Richard H., and Jerome C. Rose. 1991. Bioarcheology and the Reinterpretation of the Past: A Research Project on the History of Health and Nutrition in the Western Hemisphere. Ohio State University, Columbus. Manuscript.

Steegmann, A. Theodore, Jr., and P. A. Haseley. 1988. Stature Variation in the British American Colonies: French and Indian War Records, 1755–1763. *American Journal of Physical Anthropology* 75: 413–21.

Streeten, Paul. 1981. *First Things First: Meeting Basic Human Needs in the Developing Countries.* New York: Oxford University Press.

Studenski, Paul. 1958. *The Income of Nations: Theory, Measurement, and Analysis: Past and Present.* New York: New York University Press.

Summers, Robert, and Alan Heston. 1991. "The Penn World Table (Mark 5): An Expanded Set of International Comparisons, 1950–1988." *Quarterly Journal of Economics* 106: 327–68.

Summers, Robert, Irving B. Kravis, and Alan Heston. 1980. International Comparisons of Real Product and Its Composition. *Review of Income and Wealth* 26: 19–66.

Tanner, J. M. 1966. Growth and Physique in Different Populations of Mankind. In *The Biology of Human Adaptability,* ed. Paul T. Baker and J. S. Weiner, 45–66. Oxford: Oxford University Press.

———. 1978. *Fetus into Man: Physical Growth from Conception to Maturity.* Cambridge: Harvard University Press.

———. 1981. *A History of the Study of Human Growth.* Cambridge: Cambridge University Press.

Tanner, J. M., T. Hayashi, M. A. Preece, and N. Cameron. 1982. Increase in Length of Leg Relative to Trunk in Japanese Children and Adults from 1957 to 1977: Comparisons with British and with Japanese Americans. *Annals of Human Biology* 9: 411–23.

Tanner, J. M., R. H. Whitehouse, and M. Takaishi. 1966. Standards from Birth to Maturity for Height, Weight, Height Velocity, and Weight Velocity, British Children, 1965, Part II. *Archives of Disease in Childhood* 41: 613–35.

Taubman, Paul. 1978. *Income Distribution and Redistribution.* Reading, MA: Addison-Wesley.

Trotter, M., and G. C. Gleser. 1951. Trends in Stature of American Whites and Negroes Born between 1840 and 1924. *American Journal of Physical Anthropology* 9: 427–40.

Trussell, James, and Richard H. Steckel. 1978. The Age of Slaves at Menarche and Their First Birth. *Journal of Interdisciplinary History* 8: 477–505.

Tucker, George. 1843. Progress of Population and Wealth in the United States, in Fifty Years, as Exhibited by the Decennial Census Taken in That Period. *Merchants' Magazine and Commercial Review* 9: 136–44, 220–43.

Tullock, Gordon. 1986. *The Economics of Wealth and Poverty.* New York: New York University Press.

UNESCO. 1957. *World Illiteracy at Mid-century.* New York: United Nations.

United Nations Statistical Office. 1980. Towards More Effective Measurement of Levels of Living, and Review of Work of the United Nations Statistical Office (UNSO) Related to Statistics of Levels of Living. LSMS Working Papers no. 4. Washington, DC: World Bank.

U.S. Bureau of the Census. 1975. *Historical Statistics of the United States, Colonial Times to 1970.* Washington, D.C.: U.S. Government Printing Office.

U.S. Department of Labor. 1991. *CPI Detailed Report.* Washington, D.C.: U.S. Government Printing Office.

Waaler, Hans Th. 1984. Height, Weight, and Mortality: The Norweigan Experience. *Acta Medica Scandinavica,* supp. 679.

Wachter, Kenneth W., and James Trussell. 1982. Estimating Historical Heights. *Journal of the American Statistical Association* 77: 279–93.

Ward, W. Peter, and Patricia C. Ward. 1984. Infant Birth Weight and Nutrition in Industrializing Montreal. *American Historical Review* 89: 324–45.

Weisbrod, Burton A. 1961. *Economics of Public Health: Measuring the Economic Impact of Disease*. Philadelphia: University of Pennsylvania Press.

Williamson, Jeffrey G. 1981a. Some Myths Die Hard: Urban Disamenities One More Time: A Reply. *Journal of Economic History* 41: 905–7.

———. 1981b. Urban Disamenities, Dark Satanic Mills, and the British Standard of Living Debate. *Journal of Economic History* 41: 75–83.

Williamson, Jeffrey G., and Peter H. Lindert. 1980. *American Inequality: A Macro-economic History*. New York: Academic Press.

World Bank. 1980. *World Development Report, 1980*. Washington, DC: World Bank.

———. 1982. *World Development Report, 1982*. Washington, D.C.: World Bank.

Comment   Carole Shammas

Over the past decade, economic historians have greatly expanded our knowledge of past living standards by using height as an indicator of nutritional status. Richard Steckel, a prominent researcher in this area, has presented a comprehensive overview of this work and makes a strong argument for including stature as a measure of material well-being worldwide.

Steckel traces the parallel but never intertwining development of national income accounting and measures of human growth, pointing out that in the national income accounts concerns about living standards have tended to take a backseat to issues relating to industrial production. Considering that preoccupation, it is perhaps not surprising that no links between per capita income measures and human growth emerged. What I find more puzzling is that those income analysts who used household budgets to study consumption had no contact with auxology research, given their prime interest in the percentage of income spent on diet.

Steckel is right to stress the great advantages of height records as a measure of living standards during the past three hundred years. These data go back further in time and are more continuous than income statistics. They are easily compared over time and space without the messy cost-of-living problems involved in evaluating income. There are disadvantages, though. Without information on weight, stature can only provide evidence about childhood deprivation, not current health status. The preponderance of military records as sources for height information, moreover, mean that women are usually excluded from the calculations. Given the patriarchal nature of most societies, past and present, and the strong preference for sons rather than daughters, one cannot assume that trends in male stature are the same as trends in female stature.

Carole Shammas is professor of history at the University of California, Riverside.

Perhaps the most controversial finding that has come out of the research on stature is the great impact of environment and the much lesser role of genes in explaining variation. Steckel estimates correlations of .9 between per capita income and mean heights, meaning that, generally, the richer the nation the taller the people. There is, of course, currently much intercorrelation between per capita income and race. The fact that the Japanese, one of the few Asian groups with living standards on a par with the United States and western Europe, do seem to have a genetic predisposition to being shorter will only feed the skepticism of the nature-over-nurture proponents.

In his cross-national analysis, Steckel discovers inequality had a strong effect on height attainment. He shows that a .10 increase in the Gini coefficient, his measure of inequality, results in a drop of 3 ⅔ centimeters or almost 1 ½ inches in a nation's average height. At the conference, there was much discussion about this result because of what it suggests about the costs of an unequal income distribution within a country.

This paper also provides a succinct summary of the major findings to date in research on height trends in the United States from the colonial period to the present. These findings have implications not only for standard-of-living questions but also for more traditional problems in political and economic history. Recent work has shown the "modern" height attainment of white eighteenth-century American soldiers and their clear physical advantage over their counterparts in the British forces. Did that translate into a military advantage? The disturbingly low heights recorded for slave children in the nineteenth century indicate very poor nutrition for African-Americans not yet in the field work force and abuse of pregnant and lactating mothers. If the children survived, American slave youth made up much of their loss in stature once they joined the field workers. The high infant and child mortality rates produced by these practices, however, suggest that earlier estimates of slavery's profitability have to be adjusted downward.

The height data relating to America have also strengthened the pessimist case against nineteenth-century economic development. The data show a drop in the average height of U.S. white males during the nineteenth century. Beginning with the cohort born after 1830 and continuing until the cohort born in the 1890s, mean height fell by about 4 centimeters. The drop seems to coincide with other standard-of-living indicators, including a rise in mortality. Attributing cause here, however, is trickier than it might seem. As was mentioned in conference discussion, scholars disagree as to whether increased inequality, produced by industrialization or by anything else, occurred in the middle third of the nineteenth century. Jeffrey Williamson and Peter Lindert have argued for such a rise, but Lee Soltow finds inequality as high a generation earlier, long before any deterioration in mean height levels. It also seems that urbanization and the movements of populations may have had more to do with the drop than did industrial activity per se, but what exactly was going on is unclear. Surprisingly, not until almost the mid-twentieth century did the urban disadvantage in heights disappear.

The problem of explaining the mid-nineteenth-century drop in heights leads to questions of just how robust this finding of discontinuity is. For example, in Lee Soltow's table on the heights of army recruits age 18–35 elsewhere in this volume, there seems little change in stature between recruits measured in 1799–1819 and during the Civil War. The Soltow data are not arranged by birth cohort, yet clearly the first group would have had to have been born by 1801 and nearly all of the Civil War recruits after 1830. Why no difference?

Whatever the answer may be, the imaginative work done in the 1980s on long-term trends in stature seems truly exceptional and of undeniable importance in the measurement of material well-being in the past.

7 The Productivity Consequences of Market Integration: Agriculture in Massachusetts, 1771–1801

Winifred B. Rothenberg

Two decades ago, Peter Temin proposed with a simple two-sector model to expose the logical fallacy in the labor-scarcity thesis.[1] If land is "free," he wrote, then "farmers will find themselves with more land than before, which they will use to produce agricultural products. As their workers will have more land to work, their productivity will rise. If their wages do not rise, it will pay the farmers to hire more workers. If their wages do rise, more workers will be attracted to agriculture. These new agricultural workers will come from the only other sector of the economy: manufacturing" (Temin 1971, 255 n. 5). But if land is "free," then capital—no less than labor—will also be attracted to agriculture where its productivity is enhanced by the abundance of complementary resources. Thus, free land in American agriculture "explains" capital scarcity as well as it "explains" labor scarcity, and therefore cannot motivate the capital-using bias in American manufacturing.

Implicit in Temin's argument was the assumption that the agricultural and manufacturing sectors are sufficiently alike to be treated alike, that labor and capital will shift between sectors in either direction. Useful as this model was for Temin's purpose, it ignored the central paradox of agriculture, and by ignoring it, alerts us: in the development process resources do not flow symmetrically between sectors; they do not flow into agriculture in response to the rising labor productivity achieved there. The response of a developing econ-

Winifred B. Rothenberg is assistant professor of economics at Tufts University.

The author acknowledges with gratitude the unfailing encouragement of Kenneth Sokoloff; the helpful comments of Jeremy Atack, Stanley Engerman, and Robert Gallman; and the generosity of Bettye Hobbs Pruitt, Jack Larkin, and Richard B. Lyman, Jr., whose willingness to share their data with her is deeply appreciated. The author thanks the American Council of Learned Societies for a fellowship supporting this research.

1. The labor-scarcity thesis holds that the preference for labor-saving machinery in American manufacturing "was fundamentally because the remuneration of American industrial labour was measured by the rewards and advantages of independent agriculture" (Habakkuk 1962, 11).

omy to rising productivity in agriculture—and uniquely in agriculture—is an *exodus* of resources from it. It is the paradox of the development process—but no less true for being a paradox—that while rising productivity in agriculture has been (and with the exception of oil- and mineral-rich countries still remains) the key to successful economic development, its function is to make possible the sector's declining output share.[2] Only growing productivity in agriculture can release the resources invested in it to still more productive sectors whose growth relative to agriculture is what we mean by economic development. And only growing productivity within agriculture can prevent the deleterious health and standard-of-living consequences of its sectoral decline.[3]

The sectoral decline of agriculture in the development process is necessary because, alone among the producing sectors in a market economy, the products of agriculture face implacable price and income inelasticities of demand. Expanded agricultural output, whatever its source, causes farm prices to fall disproportionately, and the earnings of farmers to lag further and further behind the growth of output and earnings in the rest of the economy. But should agricultural prices remain high because of a failure to achieve the very productivity growth that dooms it to falling prices, the short-run advantage the sector would experience in its terms of trade would lower real incomes and impede real growth in the rest of the economy. It is the combination of productivity growth, remorselessly low price and income elasticities of demand, falling prices, worsening terms of trade, and no-better-than-constant returns to scale that drives resources out of agriculture—a sector that grows, in effect, by feeding on its own tail![4]

That process in less developed countries today is driven, for better or worse, by deliberate government policy in the areas of commodity pricing, manpower training, relocation, housing, tariffs and trade, taxation, and subsidization; but in Massachusetts in the late eighteenth century the arbiter of that complex process was the market (Rothenberg 1981). It was the market economy that energized the farm sector to achieve labor's first productivity gains (Rothenberg 1988). It was the market economy that presided over the shift of resources into the nation's first industrial sector (Rothenberg 1985).

The process of initiating the transformation, of "getting agriculture mov-

2. Three-quarters of the twenty-three countries that in the 1970s experienced GDP growth of over 5 percent per annum had achieved growth rates in their agricultural sectors of over 3 percent per annum. With the exception of the oil-rich and mineral-based economies, no more than 2 percentage points separated the rates of agricultural and GDP growth in the successfully developing countries in the 1970s (World Bank 1982, 44–45, cited in Timmer 1988, 1: 277).

3. The quantity and quality of nutrients (especially proteins) in the diet is being discovered to be a good predictor of height, of life expectancy at age ten, of the capacity to work hard and protractedly, of resistance to epidemic diseases. Maternal nutrition also plays a major role in the birth weight and health of their infants (Fogel 1990; and Goldin and Margo 1989, especially 370–77).

4. I owe these very useful insights to C. Peter Timmer (1988, 276–331).

ing,"[5] of kicking the system off its suboptimal equilibrium, is not easy to observe, but once it does begin, the "Smithian" process that relates the extent of the market to the division of labor generates a feedback process that intensifies the use of inputs, increases output, expands markets, and—most relevant of all in premechanized agriculture—enhances what Moses Abramovitz has called "the effectiveness of labor hours" (Abramovitz 1989, 15). The total factor productivity growth[6] this feedback process made possible may well have "got agriculture moving" in Massachusetts. But how did it *begin?*

The trigger may well have been a shift in relative prices: in the late 1770s, crop prices, buoyed by wartime demand and inflation, rose more rapidly than farm wages for the first time in nearly three decades (figure 7.1).[7] Perhaps in this environment of rising prices for their products and falling "real" wages, farmers could afford to increase their use of underemployed labor services, "calling forth and enlisting for development purposes resources and abilities that [had lain] hidden, scattered or badly utilized" (Hirschman 1986, 56). They could afford to; the question is, did they? Did Massachusetts farmers respond to these market signals, and if so, how and when?

The motive and the cue for growth are first to be discovered in evidence that market outcomes informed the decisions respecting land use, output pricing, employment, the investment of rural savings, livestock holdings, and crop mix made individually by the approximately 50,000 farm households in Massachusetts in the late eighteenth century.[8] Thereafter one looks to find a way to measure the productivity consequences of that market penetration. I have been attempting for many years to do that, finding in microlevel sources—farm account books, daybooks, and probates—evidence that the end of the

5. "Getting agriculture moving" is a phrase that Timmer adopts from a book of that title by A. T. Mosher, with the subtitle "Essentials of Development and Modernization" (New York: Praeger, 1966).

6. The growth rate of output can be "decomposed into a portion contributed by 'total factor input,' which was the joint contribution of labor and capital (including land), and a portion contributed by 'total factor productivity.' The first was the sum of the growth rates of the factor inputs, each weighted by the share of its earnings in national income. The second was the difference between the growth rate of output and that of total factor input" (Abramovitz 1989, 14).

Depending on how this second "residual" portion is measured, it can be made to account for 99 percent, 70 percent, or 51 percent of the growth of output per worker; or for 36 percent (Edward Denison's estimates for the United States, 1948–79); or 24 percent of the growth of total output (Dale Jorgenson's estimates) (Abramovitz 1989, 15–19).

7. I say "inflation," not "hyperinflation." The hyperinflation during the Revolutionary War was a currency phenomenon in which prices skyrocketed in terms of the overissued and wildly depreciating paper Continental. But farm accounts, being repositories of long-term debt, were kept not in Continentals, but in Lawful Money or Old Tenor—the latter a paper currency recalled as a medium of exchange in 1750 but used by many farmers long thereafter as a unit of account. Account-book prices and wages were never hyperinflated.

8. I arrive at this estimate of 50,000 as follows: the surviving records of 38,000 rateable polls (nonexempt males age 16 and over) in 1771 are estimated by Bettye Hobbs Pruitt, editor of the 1771 tax valuation list, to constitute two-thirds of the taxable adult males, of which approximately 90 percent were "engaged in agriculture." I am deeply indebted to Dr. Pruitt for sharing with me the data for her pioneering analysis of the 1771 valuation list.

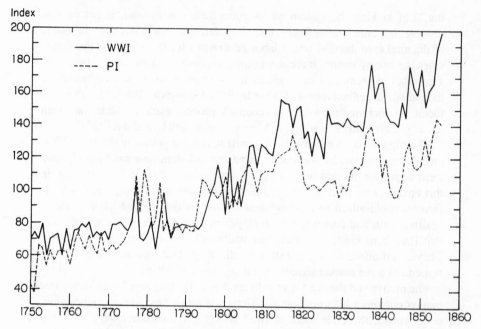

Fig. 7.1   Weighted wage index and price index, 1750–1855 (1795–1805 = 100)
Notes: WWI = Rothenberg weighted wage index of crop-related tasks; *PI* = Rothenberg farm commodity price index.
Source: Farmers' account books. The price index appears in Rothenberg (1979, 983–85). The wage index appears in Rothenberg (1988, figure 2, appendix 3).

Revolutionary War ushered in a period of profound economic transformation in the rural economy of Massachusetts. Expanding market orientation has not only been documented from the behavior of the relevant prices, but was found to have been linked to an upturn in the time trend of labor productivity as measured—not directly (by, say, output per man-day) because data of that kind for our period are lacking, but indirectly, by means of the dual, the ratio of a Massachusetts farm wage index to a Massachusetts farm commodity price index, which measures the real cost of labor to employing farmers (see figure 7.2).[9]

But the inquiry should not be left there. For one thing, it matters to the

9. "Movements of real wages—defining real wages as money wage rates divided by a cost-of-living index—are not, of course an appropriate indicator of the trend in the marginal physical productivity of labor employed in a particular sector or industry. What is relevant, assuming competitive or consistently imperfect product and labor market conditions, is the real cost of labor to employers in the industry under consideration; real wages received by farm workers could change merely as a result of changes in the farmer-employers' terms of trade with the rest of the economy, without any alteration in marginal labor productivity having taken place. Thus, for the present purpose, the relevant wage-deflator is an index of the prices received by farmers for those commodities in whose production hired labor was used" (David 1967, 179–80).

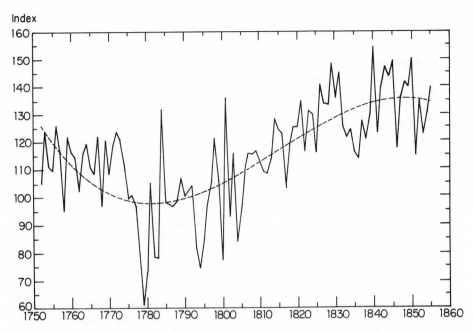

Fig. 7.2   Tracing the growth of agricultural labor productivity: the real cost-of-labor index, 1752–1855

Notes: The years 1750 and 1751 were omitted as outliers. The dotted line is the plot of the equation regressing the ratio of my weighted wage index to my price index on time.
Source: Farmers' account books. The indexes, regression equation, and plot appear in Rothenberg (1988, appendix 3, table 3, figure 4).

interpretation of the "real cost of labor index" whether its rise after 1785 is due to the rise of the productivity wage in the numerator, or to a decline of the commodity price index in the denominator. Even in highly evolved markets, structural changes—for example, lower transport costs—may have asymmetrical effects (at least in the short run): a significant impact upon farm prices but little if any on farm wages. This would compromise our interpretation of movements in the ratio between them. But even more to the point, the question—the timing of the productivity upturn in preindustrial Massachusetts—is of such critical importance to estimates of the pace of early American economic growth that it should not be left to hang on the dual. If it really happened, if Massachusetts farmers—presumably for the first time—experienced increasing output per worker, that fact should show up in other behavioral correlates.

In this paper I experiment with the use of data aggregated to the town level to confirm the turning point observed in figure 7.2, and to make more robust the case for the onset of productivity growth in Massachusetts agriculture before 1800. On the basis of town tax valuations for the years 1771, 1786, 1792, and 1801,[10] I advance the following propositions. (1) A significant improvement in Massachusetts agriculture can be confirmed from expanded output, diversification of crop mix, shift in land use, improved per acre yields, and increased emphasis on animal husbandry, all by 1800. (2) Growth in this agriculture was accompanied by the intersectoral shift of capital into commerce, banking, and infrastructure investments as required by the development process. (3) Widening differentials in rates of productivity growth exacerbate income inequalities within the rural economy, with serious political consequences. The 1786 tax valuations allow us to understand Shays's Rebellion in these terms.

The case for increased output and improved yields is made in table 7.1, where aggregate magnitudes are compared across tax valuations from 1771 to 1801. It should be acknowledged at the outset that intertemporal comparisons of tax lists are as problematic as intercensal comparisons. Much of the 1771 list has not survived, and part of what has survived is illegible. Many of the categories of taxable wealth are incommensurable across time: in 1786, no outputs (except cider) were taxed and consequently none (except cider) were enumerated; sheep and goats were counted in 1771, counted but not taxed in 1786, and not counted in 1792 and 1801, so that total livestock holdings cannot be compared across time; the age at which animals became taxable (and therefore enumerated), and the categories into which they were grouped, changed from valuation to valuation; and differences between valuations respecting the month in which property was assessed will much affect the number of animals found on the farms (Garrison 1987, 5). "Dooming"—that is, underreporting, tax evasion, and the systematic downgrading of land quality—although heavily penalized at the time, was extensive, particularly in the valuation for 1786, a depression year. The ubiquity of out-pasturing from valley farms to hill towns renders town pasture acreage an understatement and therefore overstates its "efficiency." The reconfigured map of Massachusetts— town boundaries redrawn, lands annexed, new counties carved out of old, new towns "hived off" from old—makes intertemporal comparisons of town outputs, town acreages, and therefore town yields, hazardous.[11] Nevertheless, the finding in table 7.1 that there was considerable improvement in all the magnitudes by 1801 appears robust enough to withstand problems in the data.

The output of grains by 1801 was nearly two and a half times what it had been only thirty years before. Corn was by far the principal grain, accounting for more than 50 percent of grain output.[12] "Rye-n-injun"—corn mixed with

10. The data are available on request from the author.
11. Indeed, it is just because working with these valuations is so perilous that data sets built from farm account books and probate inventories are so valuable.
12. Wheat, by contrast, accounted for only 4 percent. Black stem rust, a fungus, parasitic in one of its stages on the barberry bush, had appeared in 1660 and had virtually eliminated wheat cultivation in Massachusetts except in the western county of Berkshire, where it made up 20 percent of grain output.

Table 7.1   **Improvements in Agriculture, 1771–1801**

	Date of Tax Valuation			1771–1801,
	1771	1792	1801	% Change
No. of towns[a]	122	239	263	
Polls, rateable + unrateable[b]	34,648	79,949	87,842	+154
Tillage (acres)	99,280	191,802	208,822	+110
Combined grains (bushels)[c]	1,044,588	2,432,802	2,505,338	+140
Bushels of grain per acre tillage	10.5	12.7	12.0	+14
English/upland mowing (acres)	94,121	195,429	257,214	+173
English/upland hay (tons)	65,148	139,707	190,412	+192
No. of grazing animals	98,216	219,167	251,165	+156
Tons English hay per grazing animal	0.66	0.64	0.76	+15
Tons English hay per acre mowing	0.69	0.71	0.74	+7
Fresh meadow plus salt marsh (acres)	99,445	169,899	220,657	+122
Fresh meadow (acres)	82,896	140,609	190,149	+129
Salt marsh (acres)	16,534	29,190	30,508	+85
Fresh plus salt hay (tons)	53,168	147,279	167,531	+215
Tons fresh/salt hay per grazing animal	0.54	0.67	0.67	+24
Tons fresh/salt hay per acre meadow	0.53	0.87	0.76	+43
Pasture (acres)	200,934	568,534	751,128	+274
No. of cows pasture will "keep"	76,174	275,862	236,700	+211
No. of cows one acre pasture can keep	0.38	0.49	0.32	−17
No. of neat cattle[d]	81,473	185,820	205,140	+152
No. of horses	16,743	33,447	46,025	+175
No. of swine	46,176	80,248	84,949	+84
No. of sheep and goats	115,079	N.A.	N.A.	—
No. of total livestock[e]	144,392	299,515	336,114	+133

Sources: Town Tax Valuation Lists, 1771, 1801, Massachusetts State Archives; Felt 1847 for 1792 data.

[a]In addition to the 1771 town valuations that did not survive or are illegible, the towns in Maine, Cape Cod, Nantucket, and Martha's Vineyard are omitted from this table, as they are from this study as a whole.

[b]Includes taxable males sixteen to twenty-one years of age, taxable males twenty-one years of age and upward, male polls exempt from tax but not supported by the town (governor and lieutenant governor of Massachusetts, settled ministers, grammar school masters, and officers, faculty, students at Harvard), male polls exempt because supported by the town (paupers). Population is conventionally estimated by multiplying the number of polls by four. "Computing the polls in the ratio of 4½ [is] larger than usual" (Felt 1847, 165).

[c]The grains are wheat, rye, oats, corn, and barley.

[d]*Neat,* from an Anglo-Saxon root meaning "to use," includes oxen, cows, steers, and bulls. However, several of the valuations distinguish between oxen, cows, and neat cattle. In this table it is used to mean all bovine animals.

[e]Because the valuations of 1792 and 1801 did not count sheep and goats, I have, for the sake of comparability, omitted them from this total in 1771. In 1786, sheep and goats were enumerated but were not taxed.

rye—was the staple bread of farm family consumption, but as much as 60 percent of the corn output in 1800, by my estimate, was used as feed to fatten swine and as a supplement for cows in milk.[13]

While grain yields rose over 20 percent between 1771 and 1792, it will be observed in table 7.1 that they then fell back about 5 percent between 1792 and 1801. That drop in grain yields in the 1790s may testify to the depletion and predatory "mining" of the soil that foreign observers and agricultural reformers were fond of deploring. But less grain per acre of tillage may testify also to a diversification of output away from grains. By the turn of the nineteenth century, Massachusetts farmers had found many noncereal crops to grow on their tilled lands: potatoes, hops, flax, green herbs, celery, rutabaga, beets, winter squashes, pumpkins, carrots, parsnips, turnips, cabbages, onions, tomatoes, asparagus, string beans, green peas; and peaches, pears, rhubarb, new kinds of apples, strawberries, cherries, damson plums, quinces, cranberries, and wine grapes (McMahon 1985). Broomcorn (for brooms) and tobacco (for cigar wrappers) became the major agricultural exports of the Connecticut River valley.[14] Because none of these outputs (with the exception of peas and beans) is enumerated in the tax valuations for the period, their quantitative importance remains in doubt, but in view of this diversification away from grains it would be an error to make the case for declining *crop* yields on the basis of declining *grain* yields.

The improvement between 1771 and 1801 in aggregate grain output in table 7.1 should not be allowed to obscure the high variance among towns in both outputs and yields. While aggregate grain *output* expanded 140 percent, the experiences of individual towns varied between a more than fivefold increase in Blandford and a more than 50 percent decrease in Springfield. And while grain *yields* statewide increased 14 percent between 1771 and 1801, there were fifty towns where they increased far more than that—in four of them yields more than doubled—but thirty-three towns where they actually fell, in one case to nearly half the 1771 level. Some of that heterogeneity is caught in the differences between county-level yields in table 7.2.

Differential proximity to urban places, to waterways, to turnpikes—in short, to western competition—may account for the differential pace of diversification away from grains. It is likely, by increasing the variance, to have

13. My estimate of the proportion of corn used up for seed, to fatten swine, and as feed for cows in milk is discussed in Rothenberg (1979, 989–90).

14. As early as September 1738, Rev. Ebenezer Parkman, of Westborough, Massachusetts, noted in his diary a shipment of five hundred hogsheads of tobacco being sent down the Connecticut River to the West Indies. By 1860, Massachusetts farmers were growing 3.2 million pounds a year, chiefly for the New York market (Clark 1990, 294–303). Tobacco, having become important to the region when the broomcorn bonanza petered out, soon replaced it as the major agricultural staple of the antebellum period.

"The growing of broom corn dated from about the year 1800. In 1825 it had become a staple in the river towns; in the town of Hadley alone 1,000 acres were annually planted . . . . 'The mode of culture, in the towns on Connecticut river, is very similar to that of Indian corn, but it is said to require two or three times as much labour' " (Bidwell and Falconer 1925, 245).

Table 7.2   **Yields**

County	Date	Bushels of Grains per Acre Tillage	Tons of English Hay per Acre Mowing	Tons of Fresh/Salt Hay per Acre Meadow/Marsh	Cows Supportable per Acre Pasture
All towns	1771	11.8(3.9)	0.7	0.9	0.38
	1801	13.4(4.0)	0.8(0.4)	0.8	0.30
Suffolk/Norfolk	1771	14.5(2.7)	0.5	0.8	0.33
	1801	14.4(3.2)	0.5(0.1)	0.7	0.28
Essex	1771	14.7(2.6)	0.7	1.0	0.28
	1801	16.6(3.5)	0.9(1.3)	0.8	0.23
Middlesex	1771	13.7(3.5)	0.6	0.8	0.38
	1801	13.6(3.6)	0.7(0.1)	0.7	0.28
Hampshire	1771	7.7(2.3)	0.9	1.0	0.59
	1801	11.1(3.9)	1.0(0.2)	0.8	0.43
Plymouth	1771	11.0(2.6)	N.A.	N.A.	0.34
	1801	11.6(2.0)	0.6(0.1)	0.8	0.21
Bristol	1771	10.0(1.6)	0.6	0.8	0.31
	1801	11.1(2.1)	0.5(0.1)	0.7	0.24
Worcester	1771	14.1(2.4)	0.8	1.1	0.18
	1801	16.7(2.8)	0.8(0.1)	0.8	0.30
Berkshire	1771	8.4(1.6)	0.6	0.3	0.45
	1801	10.7(3.0)	0.9(0.1)	0.8	0.42

Source: Town Tax Valuation Lists, 1771, 1801, Massachusetts State Archives.

Note: The 1771 valuations are disaggregated by name of poll. Town totals for 1771 come from summing page totals where given in the original list, and, where those are missing, the totals are taken from the calculations made by Bettye Hobbs Pruitt for her compilation of the original data. She did not, however, calculate yields for English hay, salt hay, and meadow hay separately, but rather summed all three. The hay yields shown in this table are based on the towns for which there were totals in the original document. Because only five Plymouth County town valuations survive from 1771, there were too few English and meadow hay totals to enter. Standard deviations are in parentheses.

moderated the overall improvement of grain agriculture.[15] But more important than new tillage crops in the transformation of Massachusetts agriculture was the shift from tillage crops to grasses. Massachusetts farmers were moving away from cereals to specialize in hay, and this restructuring was happening in advance of significant western competition: long before through-rail service between Boston and the Midwest (1853), long before competition from the Cincinnati hog markets (1840s), and even long before the Erie Canal (1825). In fact, the shift, visible in table 7.1, from grains to grasses, and between grasses from the natural to the cultivated, can be observed in the act of happening, as it were, by 1801. While tillage acreage increased 110 percent over the period and fresh-meadow and salt-marsh[16] acreage (both natural grasses)

15. The reader will notice from table 7.1, for example, that the increase in grain output did not quite keep up with the increase in population (estimated as four times the number of polls).

16. Salt marsh hay, with phenomenal yields cited of up to ten tons per acre (more probably, two tons per acre), is the salt-tolerant grass that grows in coastal wetlands wherever a tidal rise and fall

increased 122 percent, the acreage in cultivated grasses (English and upland mowing) expanded by 173 percent. And English hay, which accounted for 46 percent of total hay tonnage in 1771, accounted for 53 percent thirty years later.

Hay was always of great significance to the New England economy in three respects: as primary input in the production of dairy products, meat, hides, urban livery services, and manure; as primary input in the production of livestock; and as a locally traded output protected from distant competition by its bulk and low value relative to bulk. But the grasses native to New England offered such poor nutrition that they constrained the expansion of the animal stock, and—as the principal constituent of manure—failed to enrich the soil. The most outstanding agricultural reform between 1750 and 1800 in the northern colonies was the diffusion of English grasses, which were probably brought to this shore accidentally, "the seeds buried in the fodder and bedding shipped across the Atlantic with the colonists' cherished livestock" (Stilgoe 1982, 183). The English grass—called "herdsgrass" in New England after John Herds, and "timothy" in New York, Maryland, and the Piedmont after Timothy Hansen—was mixed with redtop and clover and broadcast on upland meadows (called "mowing"), which careful farmers kept plowed and dressed with manure. In farm account books English hay was always twice as valuable as native hay[17]—selling for $10 a ton when fresh meadow hay sold for $5— and it diffused so rapidly that acreage in English and upland mowing came close to tripling in Massachusetts in the thirty years between 1771 and 1801. "Long after the first frost turned the native grasses brown . . . the English grasses remained true to their old climate and stayed green, providing pasturage into December . . . . [E]verywhere man shaped[,] the land was green and everywhere he left it untouched it was brown. Herd's grass or timothy announced the coming of civilization, of shaped land" (Stilgoe 1982, 184).

If the specialization in cultivated grasses was in fact occurring among the generality of Massachusetts farmers, we should see it in a shifting pattern of land use: a retreat from tillage and fresh meadow in favor of an increasing proportion of farm acreage devoted to mowing.[18] From the valuations of 1786 and 1801, table 7.3 aggregates to the county level the town data on land use

---

occurs. The fact that acreage in salt marsh was always taxed at a higher rate than fresh meadow suggests that it produces more hay, or perhaps a more valuable hay, although I have been unable to discover its nutritional properties. Animals grazing in the marshes or drawing the hay out were fitted with large flat "bog shoes." The hay was thrown onto "staddles" to dry and brought in when the marsh iced over in the winter (Smith et al. 1989).

17. According to Stilgoe, so valuable was the English hay that farmers put their fresh meadow hay in the barn and kept the stacks of English hay out in the meadow where they would be protected from barn fires lit by lightning (Stilgoe 1982, 184).

18. Changes in land use are measured in terms of *proportion* of acreage, not acreage itself, because of the constant redrawing of town boundaries and establishing of new towns from parts of the old that characterized this period. Between the valuations of 1786 and 1801, 116 towns gained or lost land, and some did both.

Table 7.3   **Acreage by Land Use as a Proportion of Total Acres**

County	Date	Tillage	Mowing	Meadow & Marsh	Pasture	Woodlands
All towns	1786	.06	.06	.06	.18	.53
	1801	.06	.08	.06	.22	.46
Hampshire	1786	.05	.03	.03	.05	.70
	1801	.07	.06	.04	.12	.57
Worcester	1786	.04	.05	.06	.13	.61
	1801	.04	.06	.07	.22	.51
Berkshire	1786	.08	.07	.01	.11	.58
	1801	.07	.07	.02	.15	.47
Suffolk/Norfolk	1786	.05	.10	.11	.32	.34
	1801	.05	.11	.09	.29	.35
Essex	1786	.09	.11	.11	.45	.18
	1801	.08	.11	.11	.44	.20
Middlesex	1786	.07	.07	.10	.21	.47
	1801	.07	.09	.09	.28	.42
Plymouth	1786	.06	.04	.06	.19	.48
	1801	.05	.06	.06	.19	.51
Bristol	1786	.08	.08	.06	.20	.50
	1801	.05	.09	.05	.21	.48

Source: Calculated from Town Tax Valuation Lists, 1786, 1801, Massachusetts State Archives.
Note: The rows do not sum to one hundred because of the omission of "unimproveable" acreage from this table.

as a proportion of *total* acreage.[19] Tillage and fresh meadow decreased as a percent of *improved* acreage in all counties, and mowing increased as a percent of *total*.

That the shift in the crop mix and land use from grains to hay, from tillage to grasslands, and from fresh meadows to upland mowing was a shift in the direction of higher-valued uses of land is confirmed in a comparison of differential tax rates on the several forms of taxable property (see table 7.4).[20]

19. Aggregating to the county level is not only a compact way to handle this large data set, but also makes good economic sense. In many respects the counties are more different from one another than are the towns within them, suggesting that they are good proxies for regions. Counties differed markedly in the proportions of wheat, rye, corn, oats, and barley in their grain output; in indexes of commercialization; and, of course, in the presence salt marsh.

The valuation of 1771 had to be omitted from table 7.3 because it did not count "woodland and unimproved" or "unimproveable" acres. "Unimproved" and "unimproveable" acres were counted in both 1786 and 1801. In table 7.3 I have not included "unimproveable" lands—much of which is land under water—in the total acres, and hence the rows do not sum to 100 percent. Thus, in table 7.3 "total" = tillage + English and upland mowing + fresh meadow + salt marsh + pasture + woodland and unimproved.

20. The valuation of 1771 had to be omitted from table 7.4 because it contains no tax rates.

The absolute level of tax rates bears no obvious relation to land values, but their levels relative to one another are suggestive. According to Harold Hitchings Burbank, the procedure for determining how the state direct tax should be apportioned among the towns was first to calculate the poll tax at one penny or ha'penny (1*d* or ½*d*.) per rateable poll, and then each town was compared to other towns with regard to real and personal property to determine how much should be added to each town's poll tax to fill its equitable share of the revenue sought from the tax. A town judged

Table 7.4   Tax Rates on Land Usage (in dollars per acre)

County	Date	Tillage	Mowing	Meadows	Pasture
All towns	1786	1.41	1.67	0.99	0.50
	1801	1.18	1.85	1.12	0.58
Suffolk/Norfolk	1786	1.86	2.11	1.05	0.72
	1801	1.54	2.25	1.17	0.73
Essex	1786	1.61	1.90	0.99	0.55
	1801	1.57	2.33	1.11	0.63
Middlesex	1786	1.48	1.70	1.03	0.51
	1801	1.27	2.11	1.36	0.68
Hampshire	1786	1.21	1.55	0.94	0.45
	1801	1.04	1.75	1.07	0.50
Plymouth	1786	1.26	1.52	0.96	0.38
	1801	1.06	1.67	1.01	0.49
Bristol	1786	1.39	1.60	0.99	0.45
	1801	1.05	1.73	1.00	0.52
Worcester	1786	1.39	1.64	0.83	0.49
	1801	1.12	1.69	1.01	0.56
Berkshire	1786	1.30	1.53	0.88	0.47
	1801	0.94	1.39	1.00	0.50

Source: Calculated from Town Tax Valuation Lists, 1786, 1801, Massachusetts State Archives.

While the tax rate on tillage in all towns declined between 1786 and 1801, the rates on all grasslands—on mowing, meadow, marsh, and pasture—rose; and mowing was taxed in each town as the most highly valued use of land.[21]

If agricultural improvement dictated a shift from native to cultivated grasses, we should also see a retreat from pasture—of all cleared acreage on Massachusetts farms, the most hilly, rocky, swampy, overgrown, "impoverished and skinned" (Bidwell and Falconer 1925, 102). Yet, for the state as a whole, acreage in pasture between 1771 and 1801 increased more than any of the other barometers we have been tracking, and increased as a proportion of

to be poor would derive more of its quota from the tax on polls than from the tax on property. Assessors in each town were instructed to come up with the full quota, but there was considerable room for discretion, for not all property was taxed and rates were seldom if ever assessed on full value. Even during the period when the law required full valuation—1777–81—the practice of 30–40 percent underassessing continued. The authority on this is still Burbank (1915). Pages 90–235 of this dissertation are available in typescript in the Massachusetts State Library, State House, Boston.

21. "Woodland and unimproved lands" paid increased taxes as well. It was the only land use taxed on an ad valorem basis—at 2 percent of market value. The increased burden of taxes on woodland came from a dramatic 37 percent rise in the market value of woodlands between 1786 and 1801.

Of course, to measure the real burden of rising per acre tax rates over time, comparisons should be made in constant dollars. According to my farm price index, there was a 21 percent increase in the level of farm-gate prices between 1786 and 1801. Thus, many of these tax rates increased less than the rate of inflation.

both improved and total farm acreage in most counties. There are several possible explanations for the expansion of pasture. First, keeping land in pasture for anywhere from three to seven years was a way to fallow tillage in rotation after two or three crops had been taken off, and to the extent that this was true, the increase in pasture would signal *more* careful husbandry—that is, more land in rotation—not less. Second, by 1801 the number of grazing animals (cattle, oxen, and horses) was more than two and a half times what it had been in 1771, and larger herds required more summer pasture even if considerable efforts were being made to stable and stall-feed animals for the rest of the year.

But these benign explanations for increased pasture acres fall before the farmers' own judgments concerning the quality of their pasture lands. Between 1771 and 1801 there was a 17 percent decline in the number of cows *per acre* that farmers reckoned their pasture "will keep"—a subjective but important measure. Whatever improvement in the carrying capacity of an acre of pasture had been realized between 1771 and 1792 was more than offset by the decline in its carrying capacity between 1792 and 1801 (see table 7.1). Pasture acreage had increased because pasture quality had unquestionably deteriorated, so that by 1800 more land was required to support each grazing animal.[22]

For the average farmer to have attempted to reclaim this, the uncultivated, overgrazed, exhausted 20 to 40 percent of his land,[23] would have required, at the very least, intensive manuring. Cattle can be viewed as curious machines: "they are the best machine for turning herbage into money" (Massachusetts Society for Promoting Agriculture [MSPA] Papers, 1807, 48), yes, but even more importantly, they turn herbage into manure. Each cow or ox that is stabled all winter consumes in that time two tons of hay from which it produces two loads of manure (at thirty bushels a load), and an additional load if yarded at night during the summer.[24] At thirty loads to the acre (the rate often cited for manuring tillage and mowing), it would have taken ten cows eating three tons of hay apiece for a year to manure one acre![25] There were horses, swine, chickens, and sheep to help, of course, and there were nonanimal sources of fertilizers, but with over 2,800 acres of pasture in the average Massachusetts town in 1801, the effort was formidable. Small wonder that one farmer from the hill country protested to the MSPA: "If you have rocky pas-

22. Perhaps "required" is an exaggeration. In a multiple regression analysis in which the dependent variable was "number of cattle owned" in 131 towns in the 1771 valuations, Bettye Hobbs Pruitt found that while "tons of hay" explained 89 percent of the variation of the dependent variable, the introduction of the variable "acres of pasture" increased the explanatory power of the regression by a mere 0.3 percent (Pruitt 1981, 183).

23. Bidwell goes so far as to say that the distinction the valuations made between pasture and woodlands—that is, between pasture and unimproved—"was probably not of great importance" (Bidwell and Falconer 1925, 120).

24. MSPA Papers, 1800–1807, responses to their "Inquiry" of 1800, questions 38–44.

25. In the 1790s, Dr. Nathaniel Ames of Dedham, brother of Fisher Ames, spread *400 loads of manure per acre* (at thirty bushels, or one yard cubed, to the load) to cover the soil three inches deep! His memorandum book is at the Dedham Historical Society.

ture, to subdue it would cost the whole value of the farm . . . . It makes no sense to cultivate [it] till our country shall count as China does its 270 million souls."[26]

Fortunately, improved animal husbandry in Massachusetts did not need to wait upon the reclamation of depleted pasturelands. The combination of summer out-pasturing in the hill country and stall feeding the rest of the year on corn and English hays, whose yields *per grazing animal* were rising, proved sufficient, even with inferior pastures, to support a very large increase in grazing stock. (Table 7.1 confirms both assertions.)

And it did more: livestock were increasing both in number and in *weight,* and the "edible weight" of hogs and beef cattle had a direct bearing upon the nutrition, health, and standard of living of the human population.[27] From farm account books and probate inventories I have collected 385 hog weights from 1750–1850. Standardizing slaughter and dressed weights to a live-weight basis,[28] the twenty-six observations that I found before 1800 averaged 164.5 pounds; the next twenty-six observations, from 1800 to 1816, averaged 287.3 pounds. The first 400-pound hogs appeared in 1801.

If it is indeed the case that "grain supplies offer clearer evidence of meat production capacity than do . . . animal inventories" (Gallman 1970, 18),[29] and if the weight gains in my small sample are representative, it suggests that we err in modeling grains and livestock, corn and hay, tillage and mowing as if they were *substitute* uses of resources. Animal husbandry is a thickly tex-

---

26. *New England Farmer,* August 3, 1822.

27. "[A]mericans achieved an average level of meat consumption by the middle of the eighteenth century that was not achieved in Europe until well into the twentieth century . . . . Americans achieved modern heights by the middle of the eighteenth century [and] reached levels of life expectancy that were not attained by the general population of England or even by the British peerage until the first quarter of the twentieth century" (Fogel 1990, 36). Fogel cites as his evidence of Americans' meat consumption Sarah F. McMahon's study of widows' portions in Massachusetts wills (McMahon 1981, 4–21). It is *Massachusetts farmers* who achieved this level of meat consumption.

28. I describe in Rothenberg (1981, 306) how I converted the sample of adult hog weights to live weights. For the convenience of the reader, I will repeat it here. In each case a determination had to be made as to whether the weight given in the farm account books was a live or dressed weight, and there are few clues in the sources themselves. I compared the per pound price of the hog (usually given) with the per pound price of fresh pork for that region in that year. If the per pound price of the hog was less than the price of fresh pork, the weight was called a live weight. If the per pound price of the hog equaled or exceeded the price of fresh pork, the weight was called dressed weight and divided by 0.70 to standardize all weights to live weights. The dressed weight/live weight ratio of 0.70 was chosen because it lies midway between the figure of 0.75 (or 0.76 used by some authorities) and 0.65 used by others.

At the time these calculations were being done, I assumed that dressed weight was the proper measure of the accessible nutriments in meat. Apparently there is still another correction to be made: to multiply dressed weight by 0.64 to reduce it to "edible weight" (Fogel 1990, 53 n. 14).

29. In Massachusetts it was not only grain supplies but skimmed milk, root crops, and legumes in animal feeds that determined meat production. As a consequence (presumably), Massachusetts hogs, fattened for one month, weighed more in 1800 than southern hogs, fattened for four months, weighed in 1860. The average live weight of Massachusetts hogs, calculated from probate inventory appraisals, was 224 pounds in 1780–1805; the average live weight of southern hogs, as estimated by Gallman, was 192 pounds in 1860 (Gallman 1970, 15).

tured web of complementarities made possible only by the increased yields achieved in tillage agriculture, which in turn is made possible only by the continuous improvement of manure achieved in animal husbandry. Corn, small grains, root crops, and legumes grown on richly manured soils were both consumption goods and intermediate products that along with nutritious grasses produced rich manures, fat cattle, dairy products, meats, hides, wool, energy, and the natural increase of animals after their kind. In addition to grasses, animals used every part of the cereal plants: the grains for feed, the straw and stover for fodder and for bedding; the stubble for forage, and what was not consumed by grazing livestock as "after-feed" was composted into "green manure" to augment animal manure. The process was profoundly circular.

A circular process was transformed into a growth process. It took the form of better management of livestock, manures, woodlots, fruit orchards, cultivated meadows, seed selection, stall feeding, and dairying. Legumes and root crops were both nutritious in feeds and nitrogen-fixing in rotation. Land clearing, fencing, and connecting farm buildings were part of the restructuring of farm space. None of these improvements required more capital, but all called for more labor inputs, more effective labor hours, the application of know-how learned by doing, and the reorganization of farm work. If, in the course of the development process, agriculture's share of the labor force goes down, then an increase in agricultural output per *capita* can be achieved only by a very great increase in agricultural output per agricultural *worker*.[30] Where is that increase to come from if, as late as the 1840s, there was virtually no capital deepening—that is, no technological change—in New England agriculture? From endogenously generated intensification in the use of labor. "Labor is the great thing in farming" (Larkin, 1989).

Lacking the kind of task- and crop-specific evidence of man-hour inputs that Parker and Klein (1966) and Atack and Bateman (1984, 1987) have collected for a later period, it is difficult to determine how the agricultural improvement visible in tables 7.1 and 7.2 was being achieved. But conspicuous among the techniques available to Massachusetts farmers to manage productivity growth was the employment of farm laborers (who usually lodged with the family) to do general farm work on monthly contract.[31] Workers paid a flat monthly wage for the duration of a long-term contract were accepting an implicit wage below the marginal productivity wage they might have negotiated

30. Paul David's "conjectural estimating equation" to measure growth in a two-sector economy is $O/P = LF/P \times [S_a(O/LF)_a + S_n \times k(O/LF)_a]$, where O/P is output per capita, LF/P is the labor force participation rate, S_a is the share of the labor force in agriculture, S_n is the share of the labor force in nonagriculture, both of which are weights on sectoral output per worker, and k is the ratio of the sectoral outputs per worker in the base year.

31. For a fuller discussion of the employment of contract labor in Massachusetts agriculture, 1750–1865, see Rothenberg (1992).

on a day-labor basis in season, in return for room, board, and an implicit wage above the value of their marginal product in the off-season (Lebergott 1964, 245; Goldin and Engerman 1991, 7, and table 2). Employing farmers, faced after the Revolution with wage competition from an increasingly integrated labor market, would have seen in the reorganization of farm labor an opportunity to hoard scarce labor, to minimize search costs, to hedge against the rising and increasingly differentiated wage structure that was emerging at the end of the eighteenth century (Rothenberg 1988, figure 1), and to increase the effectiveness with which labor was used.

Slavery and serfdom aside, the options available to farmers wherever wage labor is scarce are the same: cash tenancy, sharecropping, a cottager system, or labor contracts. Of these, Massachusetts farmers came increasingly to rely on labor contracts. I report briefly here on a larger study (Rothenberg 1992). The principal data come from a sample of 693 monthly contracts I have drawn from forty farm account books for the period 1750 to 1865. They are supplemented by a data base of 210 contract workers hired, beginning in 1787, to work on the Ward Farm in Shrewsbury, Massachusetts.[32]

Monthly contracts appeared in farm account books early in the eighteenth century,[33] but there was a threefold increase over time in their incidence, from an average of thirteen contracts per quinquennium before 1800 to an average of over fifty per quinquennium after 1800. The most rapid increase began at our "turning point," 1785: by 1814 the number of contracts per five-year period had soared from seven to seventy-three. That the acceleration in the use of monthly labor occurred at about the same time as the acceleration in the growth of labor productivity compels us to examine what relation may have existed between them. What role, if any, might this reorganization of the farm labor force have played in increasing total factor productivity?

The most obvious advantage of labor under contract is that it lessens search time (transactions costs) for both parties. Less obvious and more complicated is the impact of monthly labor contracts on seasonality in agriculture. To the extent that a live-in "hired hand" is (for the term of his contract) a piece of fixed capital—like a slave—the farmer's challenge is to keep him fully occupied. New England agriculture, which is so profoundly seasonal, would seem for that reason to be as unlikely a setting for a long-term contract as it was for slavery, and for some of the same reasons: an idle live-in worker was "an under-utilized asset which nonetheless required maintenance" (Anderson and Gallman 1977, 25). A surly young man of unknown family sleeping under

32. The Ward data base was compiled at Old Sturbridge Village under the direction of Jack Larkin, chief historian, in the Research Department, and generously made available to me by him.

33. The first agreement for monthly labor that I have found was in Boxford, Massachusetts, in 1713. Rev. Ebenezer Parkman of Westborough hired live-in labor on six-month contracts beginning in 1726 (Beales 1989). Joseph Barnard of Deerfield began regularly to hire monthly workers in 1753. In addition to Beales's study of Parkman's hired hands and Larkin's study of the Wards' farm laborers, volume 99 of the *Proceedings* of the American Antiquarian Society also contains Richard Lyman's study of workers on the Levi Lincoln farm in Oakham, Massachusetts.

your roof, eating (ravenously) at your table, wheedling to use your horse and to borrow cash against his wages, requiring of your wife that his clothes be washed and mended, posing a constant threat to your daughter, and expecting at the end of his term to be paid in full is a powerful incentive to organize your farm so that he is worked hard and continuously.[34]

If, despite the inexorable seasonalities of northern agriculture, Massachusetts farms were sufficiently diversified to employ a "fixed" labor force for much of the year, it would follow from the Anderson and Gallman argument that contract labor on Massachusetts farms, like slave labor on southern plantations, may have worked to enhance the productivity of the enterprise by compelling the reorganization of farm work to secure its year-round employment. Two kinds of evidence might be helpful here: Was there an increase in the length of labor contracts over time? Was there an increase in the frequency of off-season (winter) contracts, regardless of their length?

There is little evidence in my sample of any time trend in the average length of contracts. Although more than 10 percent of the contracts were for periods of nine to twelve months, there were only nine years when the average man-months per contract exceeded seven. This may speak to seasonalities in New England farming that resist efforts at distributing work more evenly across the year. Or it may have quite different implications.

Despite the obvious advantages of fixing a labor force in place, employing farmers may have been reluctant to lock themselves into lengthy and intimate commitments to unreliable men, strangers to the community, frequently absent, frequently drunk, and frequently quitters. Genealogical linking, by researchers at Old Sturbridge Village, of the sample of 210 farm laborers who worked on the Ward Farm in Shrewsbury reveals the following: half the day workers but only one-quarter of the contract workers were born in Shrewsbury; the average age of day laborers was 41.6 years, while the average age of contract workers was only 26.5 years; over 80 percent of the day workers were married, while over 86 percent of the contract workers were unmarried; the proportion of contract workers born abroad (England and Scotland at first, Ireland and French Canada after 1830) was more than double that of day workers.

I am suggesting that the *quality* of the agricultural labor supply—or the

---

34. I am put in mind, as they say, of an entry in Ebenezer Parkman's diary. On June 2, 1739, he was told of the "Rude and Vile conduct of John Kidney [his indentured servant] towards my Dauter Molly." (Molly—real name Mary—was fourteen at the time). Kidney had "button'd the Door and assaulted and Striven with her, thrown her on the Ground and was very indecent towards her, Yet was not suffer'd to hurt her—except what was by the Fright and bruising her arms in struggling with her. When disengag'd She ran out to go to her uncles, but he ran after her and forc'd her back and made her wash the Blood from her arms." John made promises but two weeks later was discovered to have stolen Mrs. Parkman's comb; he put on his best stockings to cut bushes in, and continued to exhibit "his Stubborn Stomach." Parkman threatened to send him to the house of correction, but in the end "accepted Johns Humiliation on his Knees with flowing Tears," and sold his indenture (Walett 1974, 64–65).

perception of their quality—may have deteriorated as a consequence of labor market integration,[35] creating not only a dual labor market in agriculture (at least in the short run),[36] but, increasingly over time, one that operated *perversely*.[37] Casual (part-time) day work was being done by stable men with roots in the community—kin, neighbors, and the sons of neighbors—while steady work on contract was, to a greater and greater extent, being done by casual men: transients, migrants, passersby who "come here to work," hired—quite literally in the case of the Wards—off the road (Larkin 1989, 197). Agreements frequently began cautiously, conditionally—"if he live with me a year," "no stated time agreed upon to stay," "if I want so long," "if we like," "if he is faithful and learns to work well"—with the starting wage to be raised if things worked out. The employing farmers were justifiably wary of long contracts; the record is strewn with sudden quits.[38]

Even if the average length of labor contracts in my sample did not increase to span the seasons, short-term contracts would have worked to offset seasonality if an increasing proportion of them were for off-season work. The number of winter contracts increased markedly from 4 in 1750s to 143 between 1800 and 1809. Overall, 24 percent of the man-months under contract in my sample were for winter work. Granted that no task made the manpower demands that haying did, farm work in Massachusetts was sufficiently varied to be almost a year-round enterprise. And to the extent that there was double-

35. It will be recalled from the Davis-Gallman-Hutchins project on whaling that whaling, too, suffered after 1820 from the deterioration in the quality of crews when alternatives ashore became more attractive. They estimate that productivity in whaling fell 0.3 points between 1820 and 1860 as a consequence of a 52 point increase in wages ashore (Davis, Gallman, and Hutchins 1989, 136).

36. I do not intend, by the use of the term "dual labor market," to engage in a political controversy over whether the market for rural labor "worked," in the neoclassical sense. After all, unlike race, ethnicity, gender, and educational deficits, the contract workers who were too young, too single, too uprooted, and too Irish would in time become as old, as married, and (even if not as rooted) as "American" as more respected workers. Nevertheless, in the short run they were identifiable as having limited options.

37. Dual labor market theory distinguishes between primary and secondary labor markets. A primary labor market is "composed of jobs . . . which tend to be better jobs—higher paying, more promotion possibilities, better working conditions, and more stable work. The secondary labor market . . . contains the low-paid jobs that are held by workers who are discriminated against and who have unstable working patterns" (Cain 1976, 1222).

"There are distinctions between workers in the two sectors which *parallel* those between jobs" (Doeringer and Piore 1971, 65; emphasis mine). In calling the market for rural labor "perverse," I wish to make the point that with respect to the steadiness of the work, the distinctions between workers in the two sectors (that is, between daily and monthly laborers) did *not* parallel those between the jobs.

38. The word *contract* is being used loosely throughout this section. What I am calling a contract is an entry in the employing farmer's account book or diary. (I have found only one instance when both the farmer and the worker signed their agreement.) The fact that over 10 percent of my sample contracts were terminated by worker quits would suggest that these arrangements were not legally binding. On the other hand, those state courts that denied relief to workers who sued for wages withheld when they quit took these agreements to be express contracts that barred an action on *quantum meruit*. For a debate on the judicial treatment of farm contracts in the early nineteenth century, contrast Horwitz (1977) and Karsten (1990).

cropping of winter rye and winter wheat—sown after the harvest in August and reaped in the spring—even grain farms needed labor "off-season."

Increments to the quantity and quality of factors of production will produce *growth,* but only structural change effects the transformation we call *development,* and it is structural change, more than mere growth, that distinguished the antebellum New England economy from all other regions in the country. Among the most important structural changes that take place in an agricultural economy is the shift of resources to sectors with economies of, and increasing returns to, scale. If these can seldom if ever be realized within the physical plant of a New England farm, we should look for signs of a shift of resources out of farming.

To seek evidence of developmental structural change within the limited categories of taxable property, we will judge those towns to be developing most rapidly where the agricultural sector bears a diminishing proportion, and nonagricultural property an increasing proportion, of the total tax burden.[39]

As early as 1647, the General Court authorized taxation not only on polls and real estate, but on the income from "mils, ships and all smaller vessels, merchantable goods, cranes, wharfes, and all sorts of cattell and all other visible estate" (Felt 1847, 237). In 1771, the state taxed (and therefore the valuations enumerated) shops, tanneries, slaughterhouses, pot- and pearl-ash works, warehouses, vessel tonnage, wharf footage, ironworks, bake houses, distilleries, sugar houses, gristmills, sawmills, slitting mills, fulling mills, stock in trade (goods in process and merchandise inventories), and money at interest (net of debts on interest). In 1786, money on hand (including bank deposits) and debts were added and taxed at 6 percent; and in 1801, annual income from holdings of U.S. and state securities, bank stock, and shares in bridges, toll roads, and turnpikes were added and taxed at 6 percent.

The expansion of the nonagricultural sector can be inferred from table 7.5, which shows that in all counties agricultural property, averaged across towns, paid a decreasing share—and nonagricultural property an increasing share— of taxes.[40] Within counties, the variance *among towns* in the same years, and for the same towns *between years,* is striking. Even excluding Salem and Boston, the range in 1786 extended from towns where agriculture paid over 90 percent of total taxes, to towns where agriculture paid less than 4 percent. While the range did not appreciably narrow by 1801, individual towns experienced the retreat of agriculture. The agricultural sector in Freetown (Bristol

---

39. By agriculture's share of the tax burden, I mean the share of each town's total tax liability accounted for by the taxes on acres of tillage, mowing, meadow, marsh, pasture, woodlands, and head of livestock. Cider was not included because, although it had been enumerated in all three valuations, it was not taxed in 1801 and hence had no tax rate in 1801.

40. Because the 1771 valuation list does not include tax rates at all, we can only trace the changes in tax rates between 1786 and 1801.

Table 7.5   **Taxes on Agriculture as a Percentage of Total Taxes**

County	Date	Mean	Range	
			Highest	Lowest
All towns[a]	1786	.74 (.14)		
	1801	.66 (.13)		
Hampshire	1786	.78 (.09)	.90 (Heath)	.55 (Springfield)
	1801	.71 (.07)	.89 (Shelburne)	.50 (Springfield)
Worcester	1786	.75 (.09)	.85 (Hubbardston)	.57 (Worcester)
	1801	.69 (.05)	.78 (Hubbardston)	.49 (Worcester)
Berkshire	1786	.82 (.05)	.92 (New Ashford)	.71 (Windsor)
	1801	.75 (.05)	.86 (Southfield)	.67 (Pittsfield & Stockbridge)
Suffolk/Norfolk	1786	.71 (.10)	.91 (Chelsea)	.52 (Hingham)
	1801	.61 (.10)	.46 (Chelsea)	.44 (Hingham)
Essex	1786	.55 (.22)	.76 (Lynnfield)	.03 Newburyport
	1801	.47 (.24)	.69 (Lynnfield)	.01 Newburyport
Middlesex	1786	.71 (.17)	.80 (Hopkinton)	.39 (Medford)
	1801	.66 (.11)	.79 (Boxborough)	.19 (Charlestown)
Plymouth	1786	.70 (.12)	.91 (Kingston)	.39 (Plymouth)
	1801	.56 (.15)	.78 (Halifax)	.20 (Plymouth)
Bristol	1786	.78 (.08)	.93 (Freetown)	.61 (Taunton)
	1801	.61 (.12)	.52 (Freetown)	.29 (New Bedford)

Source: Calculated from Town Tax Valuation Lists, 1786, 1801, Massachusetts State Archives.
Notes: Standard deviations are in parentheses. Taxes on agriculture are the sum of taxes on tillage, mowing, meadow and marsh, pasture, woodlands, and livestock.
[a]Boston and Salem, as in all these tables, are excluded from "all towns."

County) moved from paying 93 percent of taxes in 1786 to paying just over 50 percent; and in Kingston (Plymouth County) agriculture moved from paying over 90 percent of taxes in 1786 to just over 30 percent fifteen years later.

Stock in trade is of course only one index of commercialization, but it deserves special attention. It is the measure of inventory investment in the era before GNP accounting, measuring as it does the value of tools and goods in process found in artisanal shops,[41] and the magnitude of merchandise stocks in retail and wholesale shops. Shops and stores occupy places in a dendritic

41. A considerable literature is emerging on the transitional role played by artisanal shops in the industrialization of southern New England. Deeply rooted as they were in traditional rural society, they occupied a place on a continuum between farm and factory—part farmers, part craftsmen, part industrial worker. Shadrach Steere, a woodworker who made bobbins for the Slater mills in Rhode Island, continued to farm all his life. His farm protected him from the vicissitudes facing the urban artisan, while his craft protected him from the risks confronting New England farmers in the early nineteenth century (Sokoloff 1984, 351–82; Cooper 1987). I draw the reader's attention to the following as yet unpublished papers written for conferences at Old Sturbridge Village: Carolyn Cooper and Patrick Malone, "The Mechanical Woodworker in Early nineteenth Century New England as a Spin-off from Textile Industrialization" (1990); Robert B. Gordon, "Edge Tools in Context" (1990); Martha Lance, "Upper Quinebaug Mill Survey: Testing the Waters of Industrial Development" (1987).

marketing network.[42] When, around 1800, the little inland town of Shrewsbury found a market in Boston—ninety miles away—for its cheese, butter, chickens, veal, pork, and hay and in Brighton for its cattle, it was in large measure because Artemas Ward's General Store was a node in a proliferating network of symbiotic enterprises stretching from Worcester County to Boston along the two that ran through Shrewsbury. Stores, and peddlers as well, not only expanded the marketing perimeters of farmers qua suppliers, but played an important role in fashioning among farm families a demand for store-bought goods the insatiability of which may very well have been one of the "kicks" that got agriculture moving.[43]

Market-led productivity growth is a harsh process, one that produces both winners and losers. Presumably the towns in table 7.5 that lay on the yonder edge of developmental change, the towns that by 1801 still derived 70, 80, or 90 percent of their taxable wealth from farming, were among the losers. Perhaps the most politically significant group of losers in Massachusetts history were the followers of Daniel Shays, whose rebellion affords an opportunity to explore the economic contours of what is for me one of its most resonant attributes: the fact that it happened in 1786, *annus mirabilis* in the time path of rural market integration and agricultural productivity growth. Can differential access to the emerging market economy, and to the differential agricultural productivity growth that was its consequence, explain why some Massachusetts towns supported the insurrection, others supported the state, and still others produced leaders for both sides?

Table 7.6 relates proxy measures of agricultural productivity in "Shays country" to town sympathies in the rebellion.[44] While we are fortunate to have a tax valuation exactly contemporaneous with the event, two serious obstacles inhere in this source. First, because the 1786 valuations are aggregated to the town level, we are compelled to aggregate our two variables—both of which

42. On the importance of distribution networks in the growth of consumer demand, and the role that proliferating retail shops played in those networks, see Shammas (1990, 225–90).

43. "Peddlers were central to this process of creating a market structure in ante-bellum America . . . . They inaugurated a commercial revolution which swept away the village culture which had nourished them leaving us with some of their products and a rich folklore. Rural residents were less concerned with resisting the intrusion of capitalism than with articulating their own mode of indigenous commercialization. Peddlers were a part of this articulation as much as were farmers—their roles were different but they were part of the same world—a world which they were both unintentionally destroying" (Jaffee 1990).

44. I owe my attribution of town sympathies in the rebellion to Brooke (1992). Brooke determines the allegiance of towns in the three western counties on the basis of warrants, arrests, indictments, imprisonments, the Hampshire County Black List, and lists of militia leaders.

See also Marini (1986), who uses church histories, minutes of Baptist and Presbyterian associations, and sermons to characterize the town by characterizing its minister and his relation to his congregation. Marini also extends his analysis to the pockets of Shaysite sympathy in the eastern counties of Bristol and Middlesex.

Brooke has a sophisticated social-history (as distinguished from economic-history) interpretation of the rebellion in his *Heart of the Commonwealth* (1989, chap. 7).

Table 7.6   **Comparing Towns Supporting and Opposing Shays's Rebellion with Respect to Selected Agricultural Productivity Proxies**

	Shaysite	Militia & Conflicted
No. of polls	206	257
No. of barns	75	103
Tillage (acres)	673	938
Tillage assessment = acres × tax rate ($)	855	1,243
Mowing tax rate ($)	1.51	1.63
Meadow (acres)	342	669
Meadow tax rate ($)	0.85	0.91
Meadow assessment = acres × tax rate ($)	297	611
Pasture (acres)	1,177	1,611
Cider (barrels)	336	700
No. of head of livestock	1,320	1,589
Livestock assessment = no. head × tax rate ($)	592	761
Money on hand ($)	77	135
Debts ($)	438	2,151
Stock in trade ($)	259	1,176
Total tax ($)	4,948	6,934
Aggregate taxes on agriculture ($)	3,380	4,685

Source: Town Tax Valuation Lists, 1786, Massachusetts State Archives.

Notes: The 128 towns in "Shays Country" (the three western counties of Massachusetts in 1786) were partitioned into two groups according to the measures of allegiance cited in n. 44. For each category enumerated in the 1786 valuations, group means were calculated. The categories shown in this table are those for which the difference between the means is significant at the $<.05$ level (with the exception of number of head of livestock, where the difference between means was significant at the .09 level).

are, after all, decisions made on the individual level—to the town level. We are forced to say that the *town* has or does not have Shaysite sympathies, that the *town* is or is not realizing increases in farm labor productivity. The second major problem is the failure of the 1786 valuations to enumerate any outputs (except cider). This, of course, seriously compromises our efforts to generate productivity estimates. Lacking any alternative, I am compelled to argue that the striking variance in *tax rates* on land in the same use in different towns, and on lands in different uses in the same town, can serve as a proxy for the differential income-earning capacity of these lands.

The experimental design consists of testing, with respect to each of the taxable magnitudes in the valuations, the differences between the means and the variances of two groups of towns: those with Shaysite sympathies, on one hand, and on the other, those opposed, either because they supported the state militia or because they produced leaders for both sides. The magnitudes in the 1786 valuation that are not included in table 7.6 are those for which the means between the two groups of towns were not significantly different from one another at the 5 percent level.

The two-way contingency tables in table 7.7 rank the same two groups of

Table 7.7   **Two-Way Contingency Tables Relating Shaysite Sympathy to Agricultural Productivity Proxies**

	Total Tax		Agricultural Taxes		Agriculture/ Total Tax	
	0	1	0	1	0	1
Anti-Shays towns	31	44	33	42	32	43
Pro-Shays towns	26	8	26	8	21	13
Chi square	11.6		9.9		3.4	
Significance level	.001		.002		.06	

Sources: Town Tax Valuation List, 1786, Massachusetts State Archives, for the 128 western towns in "Shays Country." For attribution of town sympathies see sources at n. 44.

Note: "Anti-Shays towns" are those that supported the state militia and conflicted towns that produced leaders for both sides. "Agricultural taxes" are the assessments on tillage, grasslands, and livestock. "Agriculture/total tax" is the share of total assessments paid by taxes on agriculture.

towns by the frequency with which each group of towns fell above (1) or below (0) the mean of all 128 western towns in "Shays country" with respect to selected items in the 1786 valuation. The chi-square test results allow us to assert that the two groups of towns were significantly different from one another with respect to three proxy measures of the performance of agriculture.

Shaysite towns lay significantly below the mean (0), and non-Shaysite (militia and conflicted) towns lay significantly above the mean (1) with respect to total taxes assessed, the assessment on agricultural property, and the proportion of the tax paid by agricultural property. In other words, the towns that did not throw their lot in with the insurrection had significantly more prosperous agricultural enterprises than did the towns supporting the insurrection.[45] Given the intractabilities in the data referred to earlier, I interpret these results as confirming my surmise that whatever its significance as an event in anti-Federalist politics or democratic populism, Shays's Rebellion seems now to loom as a deeply conservative impulse, a fist shaken at impending change. The danger to the Shaysites came not from the "competitive capitalism of merchants,"[46] but from *within* the farm economy, poised, as it was quite literally in 1786, on the cusp of structural transformation.

Shays's Rebellion serves to illustrate the serious political consequences of uneven rural development, but my purpose in introducing this material at this time is to use the association confirmed in tables 7.6 and 7.7, between the

45. This does not contradict the discussion on pp. 329–31 measuring economic development by a *decline* over time in the proportion of total taxes paid by the agricultural sector. Recall that the movement out of agriculture has to do with the shift between 1786 and 1801, whereas this analysis of what we may call the economic origins of Shaysite sympathies has to do with the towns' relative status at a point in time, in 1786.

46. This is the view of David P. Szatmary (1980) and others who see the rebellion as an agrarian defense of the moral economy against merchant capitalism. I am suggesting that the enemy they faced was agrarian capitalism.

political polarities in 1786 and agricultural productivity measures, to reverse the direction of the inquiry. Having run a causal chain from agricultural improvement to partisanship in the insurrection, I propose now to run the chain backward, from partisanship in the insurrection to agricultural improvement, in order to suggest which towns may be presumed to have had access to the market in 1786 and which did not. Since the argument sounds circular, let me schematize it. There are three propositions here: A is a proposition about productivity; B is a proposition about market access; and C is a proposition about sympathies in the insurrection. I consider the link between A and C to have been demonstrated by the results in tables 7.6 and 7.7. I consider the link between A and B to have been demonstrated many times over in my published work. If C and B are both linked to A, then they are linked to each other, and allegiance can be used as presumptive evidence of market access, or the lack of it.

I suggest, then, that of the 128 towns in the western counties, the 34 towns loyal to the rebels were probably "locked out" of access to markets in 1786; and that the 75 anti-Shays towns, in addition to those that remained hors de combat, were in varying degrees "locked in " to a market economy, had in varying degrees embraced, as it were, the new dispensation, and were, by 1786, enjoying its consequences for productivity growth.

I have focused deliberately in this paper on a very narrow period—one I had elsewhere identified as a turning point in farm labor productivity—a point in time too narrow, I had feared, to register in the behavior of lumpy aggregates. But I submit that in this analysis, based principally on town tax valuations of 1771, 1786, 1792, and 1801, the turning point stands confirmed.

We might still ask, why? Why did the productivity turnaround happen at the end of the eighteenth century? Why did farmers choose that time to respond to market signals in a new way? Questions of that kind, if they have any answer at all, tend to have a great many answers. One was suggested at the beginning of this paper: the process may have begun as a Smithian feedback loop in which falling real wages, increased output, extended markets, and division of labor worked together to generate more of the same. But if so, that process was apparently embedded in a far more profound one: a change in climate regimes. The market-led transformation of Massachusetts agriculture was set against a major regional climate shift between 1750 and 1850. And the two phenomena, I suggest, may not have been unrelated. Confronted by a long transitional regime of hazardously unpredictable weather, reorganizing the farm to achieve total factor productivity growth may have been perceived as the only way to succeed by farming.

Weather happens both on a scale so large that we can speak of a "global climate" and on a scale so small that places a mile apart can have different "weathers." But that it is important to agriculture, even if not decisively so, goes without saying. (Which may explain why so far in this paper it has gone without saying!) Extremely important work on New England's climate history and its relationship to agricultural change is being done now, and the results, however preliminary, may cast light on dating the transformation of Massachusetts agriculture.[47]

The years 1750–1850 are identified by climate historian William R. Baron as a "change-over" period, an interval caught in the shift from one major climatic regime to another. The earlier regime, called the neoglacial, was "a time of somewhat cooler temperatures, prominent polar anticyclones, southwardly displaced depression tracts, and considerable blocking of upper winds by high pressure cells over Iceland and the northeastern Atlantic." The later regime was a "very different" pattern of warmer and more stable weather. Seventeen fifty to eighteen fifty, like all such transitional periods, was marked by great instability, by heightened variability in all the relevant parameters: in "growing season length, storm frequencies, snowfall, droughts, and harsh and unusual weather" (Baron 1990, 1). From the point of view of the farmer, it is this *variability* in the weather, far more than the weather itself, that increases his risks and endangers his enterprise. And risk there was: in thirteen out of the twenty-four years—more than half—between 1750 and 1774, there appear to have been too few "growing degree days" in Cambridge, Massachusetts, for the corn to mature at all.[48] The most extreme instance of eccentric weather was 1815, which had the longest growing season by far—240 days between killing frosts!—of any year between 1750 and 1970, followed the very next year, 1816, by the so-called year without a summer, which had a growing season of only 80 days, by far the shortest.[49] For any one year during the eighteenth century, a Massachusetts farmer could anticipate that the last killing frost before spring planting could happen anytime between the eleventh of March and the fourteenth of June; and that the first killing frost in the fall (which would destroy at least half his crop) could come anytime between the twenty ninth of August and the seventeenth of November (Baron 1984, 318).

Risks on this scale—uninsurable, random, devastating—dwarf the risks of producing for market. Confronted by a Nature that must certainly have appeared to play dice with the Universe, production for market becomes a *risk-averse* strategy. And in 1801, it must really have looked as though the enhanced yields, changes in output mix, intensified use of labor, spatial reo-

---

47. In the discussion of climate and weather to follow, I shall be summarizing, to the best of my ability, the work of William R. Baron, supervisor of the Historical Climate Records Office, Northern Arizona University, Flagstaff, Arizona 86011, and colleagues (Baron 1982a, 1982b, 1984, 1985, 1989, and 1990). I am deeply indebted to Prof. Baron for generously sharing his extraordinary work with me.

48. This is how I interpret Baron (1989, fig 1, p. 21).

49. The length of the growing season is one of the variables that can be expected to affect yields. It may therefore be relevant to the agricultural magnitudes in the valuations used in this study. At 212 days, 1771 had the longest growing season, save for the extraordinary summer of 1815; 1786 had 152 days; 1801 had 190 days.

rientation of farm functions, shift of capital out of agriculture, and perceptible gains in total factor productivity—all achieved under the aegis of the market—would indeed save Massachusetts agriculture.

References

Abramovitz, Moses. 1989. *Thinking about Growth and Other Essays on Economic Growth and Welfare.* New York: Cambridge University Press.

Anderson, Ralph V., and Robert E. Gallman. 1977. Slaves as Fixed Capital: Slave Labor and Southern Economic Development. *Journal of American History* 64, no. 2: 24–46.

Atack, Jeremy, and Fred Bateman. 1984. Mid-nineteenth Century Crop Yields and Labor Productivity Growth in American Agriculture: A New Look at Parker and Klein. In *Technique, Spirit, and Form in the Making of Modern Economies: Essays in Honor of William Parker,* ed. Gavin Wright and Gary Saxonhouse, 215–42. *Research in Economic History,* supp. 3.

———. 1987. *To Their Own Soil: Agriculture in the Antebellum North.* Ames: Iowa State University Press.

Baron, William R. 1982a. Eighteenth-Century New England Climate Variation and Its Suggested Impact on Society. *Maine Historical Society Quarterly* 21, no. 4: 201–18.

———. 1982b. The Reconstruction of Eighteenth Century Temperature Records through the Use of Content Analysis. *Climatic Change* 4: 385–98.

———. 1984. Frost-Free Record Reconstruction for Eastern Massachusetts, 1733–1980. *Journal of Climate and Applied Meteorology* 23, no. 2: 317–19.

———. 1985. A Reconstruction of New England Climate Using Historical Materials, 1620–1980. *Climatic Change in Canada* 5: 229–45.

———. 1989. Retrieving American Climate History: A Bibliographic Essay. *Agricultural History* 63, no. 2: 7–35.

———. 1990. A Comparative Study of Climate Fluctuation and Agricultural Practices in Southern New England. 1790–1850. Northern Arizona University. Manuscript.

Beales, Ross W. 1989. The Reverend Ebenezer Parkman's Farm Workers, Westborough, Massachusetts, 1726–1782. *Proceedings of the American Antiquarian Society* 99, no. 1: 121–49.

Bidwell, Percy W., and John I. Falconer. 1925. *History of Agriculture in the Northern United States, 1620–1860.* Washington, D.C.: Carnegie Institution of Washington.

Brooke, John L. 1989. *The Heart of the Commonwealth: Society and Political Culture in Worcester County, Massachusetts, 1713–1861.* New York: Cambridge University Press.

———. 1992. A Deacon's Orthodoxy: Religion, Class, and the Moral Economy of Shays's Rebellion. In *In Debt to Shays: The Bicentennial of an Agrarian Insurrection,* ed. Robert A. Gross. Charlottesville: University of Virginia Press.

Burbank, Harold Hitchings. 1915. The General Property Tax in Massachusetts, 1771–1792. Ph.D. diss., Harvard University.

Cain, Glen G. 1976. The Challenge of Segmented Labor Market Theories to Orthodox Theory: A Survey. *Journal of Economic Literature* 14, no. 4: 1215–57.

Clark, Christopher. 1990. *The Roots of Rural Capitalism: Western Massachusetts, 1780–1860.* Ithaca, N.Y.: Cornell University Press.

Cooper, Carolyn C. 1987. Thomas Blanchard's Woodworking Machines: Tracking

Nineteenth Century Technological Diffusion. *Journal of the Society of Industrial Archaeology* 13: 52–54.

Cooper, Carolyn C., and Patrick Malone. 1990. The Mechanical Woodworker in Early Nineteenth Century New England as a Spin-off from Textile Industrialization. Yale University. Manuscript.

David, Paul A. 1967. The Growth of Real Product in the United States before 1840: New Evidence, Controlled Conjectures. *Journal of Economic History* 27, no. 2: 151–97.

Davis, Lance E., Robert E. Gallman, and Teresa D. Hutchins. 1989. Productivity in Whaling: The New Bedford Fleet in the Nineteenth Century. In *Markets in History: Economic Studies of the Past,* ed. David W. Galenson, 97–147. New York: Cambridge University Press.

Doeringer, Peter B., and Michael J. Piore. 1971. *Internal Labor Markets and Manpower Analysis.* Lexington, Mass.: D. C. Heath.

Felt, Joseph B. 1847. *Statistics of Taxation in Massachusetts Including Valuation and Population.* Boston: American Statistical Association.

Fogel, Robert W. 1990. The Conquest of High Mortality and Hunger in Europe and America: Timing and Mechanisms. NBER Historical Factors in Long-Run Growth Working Paper no. 16. Cambridge, Mass.: National Bureau of Economic Research.

Gallman, Robert E. 1970. Self-Sufficiency in the Cotton Economy of the Antebellum South. *Agricultural History* 44, no. 1: 5–23.

Garrison, J. Ritchie. 1987. Farm Dynamics and Regional Exchange: The Connecticut Valley Beef Trade, 1670–1850. *Agricultural History* 61, no. 3: 1–17.

Goldin, Claudia, and Stanley L. Engerman. 1991. Seasonality in Nineteenth Century Labor Markets. NBER Historical Factors in Long-Run Growth Working Paper no. 20. Cambridge, Mass.: National Bureau of Economic Research.

Goldin, Claudia, and Robert A. Margo. 1989. The Poor at Birth: Birth Weights and Infant Mortality at Philadelphia's Almshouse Hospital, 1848–1873. *Explorations in Economic History* 26, no. 3: 360–79.

Gordon, Robert B. 1990. Edge Tools in Context. Paper presented at Old Sturbridge Village, Sturbridge, Mass.

Habakkuk, H. J. 1962. *American and British Technology in the Nineteenth Century: The Search for Labour-Saving Inventions.* Cambridge: Cambridge University Press.

Hirschman, Albert O. 1986. *Rival Views of Market Society and Other Recent Essays.* New York: Viking Press.

Horwitz, Morton J. 1977. *The Transformation of American Law, 1780–1860.* Cambridge, Mass.: Harvard University Press.

Jaffee, David. 1990. Peddlers of Progress and the Transformation of the Rural North, 1760–1860. City College of New York. Manuscript.

Karsten, Peter. 1990. "Bottomed on Justice": A Reappraisal of Critical Legal Studies Scholarship concerning Breaches of Labor Contracts by Quitting or Firing in Britain and the U.S., 1630–1880. *Journal of American Legal History* 34: 213–61.

Lance, Martha. 1987. Upper Quinebaug Mill Survey: Testing the Waters of Industrial Development. Paper presented at Old Sturbridge Village, Sturbridge, Mass.

Larkin, Jack, 1989. "Labor Is the Great Thing in Farming": The Farm Laborers of the Ward Family of Shrewsbury, Massachusetts, 1787–1860. *Proceedings of the American Antiquarian Society* 99, no. 1: 189–226.

Lebergott, Stanley L. 1964. *Manpower in Economic Growth.* New York: McGraw-Hill.

McMahon, Sarah F. 1981. Provisions Laid By for the Family, *Historical Methods* 14: 4–21.

———. 1985. A Comfortable Subsistence: The Changing Composition of Diet in Rural New England, 1620–1840. *William and Mary Quarterly,* 3d ser., 42, no. 1: 26–65.

Marini, Stephen A. 1986. The Religious World of Daniel Shays. Wellesley College. Manuscript.

Massachusetts Society for Promoting Agriculture. 1799–1816. Papers. Houghton Library, Harvard University, Boston.

Parker, William N., and Judith L. V. Klein. 1966. Productivity Growth in Grain Production in the United States, 1840–1860 and 1900–1910. In *Output, Employment, and Productivity in the United States after 1800,* ed. Dorothy S. Brady, 523–82. NBER Studies in Income and Wealth, 30. Princeton: Princeton University Press.

Pruitt, Bettye Hobbs, 1981. Agriculture and Society in the Towns of Massachusetts, 1771: A Statistical Analysis. Ph.D. diss., Boston University.

Rothenberg, Winifred B. 1979. A Price Index for Rural Massachusetts, 1750–1855. *Journal of Economic History* 39, no. 4: 975–1001.

———. 1981. The Market and Massachusetts Farmers, 1750–1855. *Journal of Economic History* 41, no. 2: 283–314.

———. 1985. The Emergence of a Capital Market in Rural Massachusetts, 1730–1838. *Journal of Economic History* 45, no. 4: 781–808.

———. 1988. The Emergence of Farm Labor Markets and the Transformation of the Rural Economy: Massachusetts, 1750–1855. *Journal of Economic History* 48, no. 3: 537–66.

———. 1992. Structural Change in the Farm Labor Force: Contract Labor in Massachusetts Agriculture, 1765–1865. In *Strategic Factors in Nineteenth Century American Economic Growth: A Volume to Honor Robert W. Fogel,* ed. Claudia Goldin and Hugh Rockoff, 105–34. Chicago: University of Chicago Press.

Shammas, Carole. 1990. *The Pre-industrial Consumer in England and America.* Oxford: Oxford University Press.

Smith, David C., William R. Baron, Ann E. Bridges, Janet TeBrake, and Harold W. Borns, Jr. 1982. Climate Fluctuation and Agricultural Change in Southern and Central New England, 1765–1880. *Maine Historical Society Quarterly* 21, no. 4: 179–200.

Smith, David C., Victor Konrad, Helen Koulouris, Harold W. Borns, Jr., and Edward Hawes. 1989. Salt Marshes as a Factor in the Agriculture of Northeastern North America. *Agricultural History* 63, no. 2: 270–94.

Sokoloff, Kenneth. 1984. Was the Transition from the Artisanal Shop to the Non-mechanized Factory Associated with Gains in Efficiency? Evidence from the U.S. Manufacturing Censuses of 1820 and 1850. *Explorations in Economic History* 21, no. 4: 351–82.

Stilgoe, John R. 1982. *Common Landscape of America, 1580–1845.* New Haven: Yale University Press.

Szatmary, David P. 1980. *Shays's Rebellion: The Making of an Agrarian Insurrection.* Amherst: University of Massachusetts Press.

Temin, Peter. 1971. Labor Scarcity in America. *Journal of Interdisciplinary History* 1 (Winter): 251–64.

Timmer, C. Peter. 1988. The Agricultural Transformation. In *Handbook of Development Economics,* ed. Hollis Chenery and T. N. Srinivasan, 1: 276–331. Amsterdam: North Holland Press.

Walett, Francis G., ed 1974. *The Diary of Ebenezer Parkman, 1703–1782.* Worcester, Mass.: American Antiquarian Society.

World Bank. 1982. *World Development Report.* New York: Oxford University Press.

Comment   Jeremy Atack

Writing in 1916, Percy Bidwell advanced what was then, or, certainly, what was to become, the conventional wisdom regarding New England agriculture at the start of the nineteenth century:

> it was most inefficiently, and, to all appearances, carelessly conducted. Very little improvement had been made over the primitive methods employed by the earliest settlers. As soon as the pioneer stage had passed and the clearing of the land had been accomplished, the colonists settled down to a routine husbandry, based largely on the knowledge and practices of English farmers of the early seventeenth century, but in many ways much less advanced than the agriculture of the motherland even at that early date . . . improvements of far-reaching significance had been introduced in English agriculture . . . yet the bulk of the farmers had shown no disposition to adopt the new methods. On their poorly cultivated fields little fertilizer of any sort was used, their implements were rough and clumsy, live stock was neglected, and the same grains and vegetables were raised year after year with little attempt at a rotation of crops, until the land was exhausted. (1916, 319)

This view has become so entrenched in our consciousness that it permeates the currently popular texts in economic history and is central to most models of U.S. regional specialization and development.[1] Surprisingly, it has also managed to avoid critical scrutiny for decades. Just as well—for it now appears to rest upon very shaky ground. Indeed, such views are no longer tenable, thanks in large part to the work of one scholar—Winifred Rothenberg.

Over the past fifteen years or so, she has assembled a large body of evidence from primary sources, both qualitative and quantitative, bearing on the condition of agriculture in the quintessential New England state—Massachusetts—between the late colonial period and the mid-nineteenth century. This evidence from farm account books, county records, and the like, her weaving of a coherent, consistent narrative theme, and her careful analysis of the quantitative data lead inescapably to the conclusion that farmers in Massachusetts, at least, were engaged in market production throughout the period, were responsive to market signals, mobilized capital, and were willing to change habits when the incentives were right.[2]

Rothenberg's paper here draws heavily upon her published work, especially her study of the farm labor market (1988). The crucial finding there was that

Jeremy Atack is professor of economics at the University of Illinois at Urbana-Champaign and a research associate of the National Bureau of Economic Research. This comment is on the paper as delivered at the conference.

1. For examples of this conventional wisdom in current American economic history texts, see Hughes (1990, 32–33) or Walton and Rockoff (1990, 49–50, 89). The best-known model of regional specialization and development in the United States during the nineteenth century is that of Douglass North. See North (1961, 1966). See also Field (1978).

2. Market production and responsiveness to market signals: Rothenberg (1981). Capital markets: Rothenberg (1985). Adaptability: Rothenberg (1988).

labor productivity, as measured by the farm labor wage rate deflated by a wage-good price index—actually Rothenberg's own farm-gate price index (1979)—was declining until about 1780 and rising from sometime after 1790 until perhaps the 1830s or 1840s (Rothenberg 1988, 558, figure 4). It is this result that Rothenberg seeks to buttress here.

The evidence she presents is in three forms. First, she finds evidence of increasing specialization in crops with higher labor value-added such as dairy products and hay. Second, she presents evidence showing that Massachusetts farmers changed the organization of farm labor. Third, she concludes that yields per acre were rising. However, as I shall explain below, each of these pieces of evidence, whether in isolation or together, fails to make a cast-iron case that labor productivity was rising at an average annual rate as high as 0.5 percent (Rothenberg 1988, 559n.35). This rate of growth is almost certainly biased upwards.

Nevertheless, I am unwilling to reject her conclusion that labor productivity was rising, if only because it is consistent with a growing body of evidence from other parts of the country about this time. For example, Ball and Walton find that there was very modest growth in total factor productivity in Chester County, Pennsylvania, agriculture before the Revolution, a slight setback during, and a modest resumption of growth immediately following the Revolution (1976, especially 110). Similarly, Adams's work on wages and prices in Maryland with commodity-deflated wage rates indexed to the 1780s implies rising labor productivity after that date (1986, especially 638, table 5). For the country as a whole, Gallman concludes that labor productivity in corn, oats, and wheat grew at about 0.3 percent per year between 1800 and 1850 (Gallman 1975, especially 47).

The crux of my critique derives from her use of the labor productivity defined as output, Q, per unit of labor input, L:

$$q_L = Q/L$$

Data constraints and the existence of multiple outputs, however, generally lead—as they do here—to the measurement of output by the aggregate value of output, that is Q is proxied by

$$\sum_i Q_i P_i$$

where Q_i is the output of the ith crop that sells for price P_i.

The obvious problem here is that price changes, driven by demand, may be confused with changes in physical output in this measure. But, we may be doubly sure that this is not the case here, for not only is Rothenberg's price index for farm products in Massachusetts but it is also for farm-gate prices—that is, it removes the effect of impact in transportation and distribution cost changes. Prices and price expectations, however, do play a crucial role in the allocation decision of farmers—how much to plant of each crop. Here, Rothenberg's argument is that Massachusetts farmers adopted higher revenue-producing crops and that this led to increased productivity. It seems unlikely that this technological shift identified by Rothenberg was an illusion even though much of the evidence is drawn from tax valuations.

Leaving aside the philosophical question of the impact of this implicit deviation from profit maximization upon productivity, the question is, why didn't farmers adopt the higher revenue-producing crop mix earlier? The answer is *not* that this option did not exist before: farmers were quite familiar with dairy and hay production long before they practiced them to the extent that they came to. Indeed, it was probably *because* they were familiar with these crops that they did not adopt them earlier! Although these crops produced higher revenues, they required greater effort. They are examples of Boserupian-innovations (Boserup 1965). Reluctance to put forth this increased effort then delays adoption until economic or physical survival makes it a matter of necessity. This issue thus bears upon the first two pieces of evidence used by Rothenberg.

The problem with this kind of technological change is easiest to see in the case of dairy production. The dairy demands year-round attention, twice-a-day milking, not to mention the cleaning of the milking shed, cooling the milk, churning, and so forth, and it also goes hand-in-hand with intensive stall feeding of hays and root crops, themselves more labor-intensive crops (see, for example, Bateman 1969). This intensification of effort—measured by more work effort per hour, increased hours per day, and more workdays per year—should, of course, be captured in the measure of labor input, L. The question, though, is, Is it?

I am not convinced that it is. Rothenberg's evidence pertains to labor contract terms and daily wages, not work intensity and man-hours. Are six one-month contracts the same quantity of labor as one six-month contract? I don't know, but I suspect not. One reason why is that rational employers would seek to retain the better worker by offering more attractive—such as longer—contract terms. Longer, and more frequent long-term, contracts are consistent with increased labor requirements throughout the year, and higher daily wages are consistent with either greater productivity or longer hours and greater effort. What is not mentioned is what happens to the farmer's own labor and that of unpaid family members, particularly his wife. Ideally what I would like to see is an accounting of labor hours by task (such as those reported for grain crops by Parker and Klein, 1966 later in the nineteenth century) for all paid and unpaid labor, including that of the farmer and that bound to the farmer by affection, filial devotion, or whatever and how this changes over time. If the necessary contemporary data do not exist in farmers' daybooks, the periodical literature, travelogues, and the like, perhaps time and motion studies at historic farm museums such as Old Sturbridge Village will offer some insight.

Rothenberg's third piece of evidence in defense of her argument that labor productivity was rising is that yields per acre were rising. If all land was currently under cultivation and remained in crops, increased yields necessarily imply increased output and hence higher labor productivity *ceteris paribus:*

$$\sum_i (Q_i/A_i)A_i P_i/L,$$

where A_i is acreage planted in the ith crop so that Q_i/A_i is the yield per acre for this ith crop. The evidence here, though, is very tenuous, being just for two year, 1771 and 1801. Nothing is said about conditions in these two years, though presumably some newspaper accounts of general weather conditions, the state of the harvest, and so forth, might be found. Even so, though, yield estimates contain large stochastic elements reflecting local weather variations that swamp any short, or even medium, -term trend. Indeed, yields show tremendous variations from farm to farm, township to township, year to year that a much, much longer run of data is needed before any broad sweeping statement is warranted.

Finally, while I am very sympathetic to the argument that Massachusetts agriculture was much less backward than the conventional wisdom has argued and believe that Rothenberg's evidence clinches the case, this paper contributes relatively little to this broader question. Although it starts out addressing the question of whether or not the real farm wage-farm labor productivity nexus holds and farm labor productivity was rising from the 1790s, its focus is actually upon a much narrower time frame from the late 1770s to the early 1780s—a period when fluctuations about the long-term trend are largest and the trend itself is obscured—with data that are themselves widely separated discrete observations.

References

Adams, Donald R., Jr. 1986. Prices and Wages in Maryland, 1750–1850. *Journal of Economic History* 46: 625–46.

Ball, Duane E., and Gary M. Walton. 1976. Agricultural Productivity Change in Eighteenth Century Pennsylvania. *Journal of Economic History* 36: 102–17.

Bateman, Fred. 1969. Labor Inputs and Productivity in American Dairy Agriculture, 1850–1910. *Journal of Economic History* 29: 206–29.

Bidwell, Percy Wells. 1916. Rural Economy in New England at the Beginning of the Nineteenth Century. *Transactions of the Connecticut Academy of Arts and Sciences* 20: 241–399.

Boserup, Ester. 1965. *The Conditions of Agricultural Growth.* London: Allen and Unwin.

Field, Alexander J. 1978. Sectoral Shift in Antebellum Massachusetts: A Reconsideration. *Explorations in Economic History* 15: 146–71.

Gallman, Robert E. 1975. The Agricultural Sector and the Pace of Economic Growth: U.S. Experience in the Nineteenth Century. In *Essays in Nineteenth Century Economic History,* ed. David C. Klingaman and Richard K. Vedder 35–76. Athens: Ohio University Press.

Hughes, Jonathan R. T. 1990. *American Economic History.* Glenview, IL: Scott Foresman.

North, Douglass C. 1961. *The Economic Growth of the United States, 1790–1860.* Englewood Cliffs, NJ: Prentice Hall.

———. 1966. *Growth and Welfare in the American Past.* Englewood Cliffs, NJ: Prentice Hall.

Parker, William N., and Judith L. V. Klein. 1966. Productivity Growth in Grain Production in the United States, 1840–60 and 1900–10. In *Output, Employment, and Productivity in the United States after 1800,* ed. Dorothy S. Brady, 523–82. NBER Studies in Income and Wealth, Princeton: Princeton University Press.

Rothenberg, Winifred B., 1979. A Price Index for Rural Massachusetts, 1750–1855. *Journal of Economic History* 39: 975–1001.

———. 1981. The Market and Massachusetts Farmers, 1750–1855. *Journal of Economic History* 41: 283–314.

———. 1985. The Emergence of a Capital Market in Rural Massachusetts, 1730–1838. *Journal of Economic History* 45: 781–808.

———. 1988. The Emergence of Farm Labor Markets and the Transformation of the Rural Economy: Massachusetts, 1750–1855. *Journal of Economic History* 48: 37–66.

Walton, Gary, and Hugh Rockoff. 1990. *History of the American Economy.* 6th ed. New York: Harcourt Brace Jovanovich.

8   Invention, Innovation, and Manufacturing Productivity Growth in the Antebellum Northeast

Kenneth L. Sokoloff

8.1   Introduction

Economic growth and advances in the standard of living are ultimately rooted in the processes by which improvements in techniques, organization, and products are discovered and implemented to make more productive use of available resources. These processes of invention, innovation, and the diffusion of technical change involve many aspects of social and economic behavior, and are fundamental to long-run progress in a population's material welfare. They appear to have first accelerated and become self-sustaining in the United States early in the nineteenth century, gaining strength in the Northeast and later spreading to other areas of the country. This initial phase of growth has long been associated with marked productivity growth in manufacturing, and the relative expansion of that sector. How, why, and to what extent manufacturing enterprise realized such gains at this time are thus central questions to any understanding of the onset of American industrialization and of the course of living standards.

Work on antebellum economic growth has been much influenced by a general controversy about the sources and potential for productivity advance in

Kenneth L. Sokoloff is professor of economics at the University of California, Los Angeles, and a research associate of the National Bureau of Economic Research.

The author has benefited from excellent research assistance by James Lin, Zorina Khan, Sukkoo Kim, John Majewski, and Geng Xiao, as well as from discussions with Jeremy Atack, Lance Davis, Stanley Engerman, Robert Gallman, Jean-Laurent Rosenthal, Viken Tchakerian, Michael Waldman, John Wallis, and participants at the NBER conference and at a seminar at Stanford University. The research was supported by the Center for Advanced Study in the Behavioral Sciences, the California Institute of Technology, and the Institute of Industrial Relations and the Academic Senate at UCLA.

manufacturing by preindustrial societies (Rostow 1960; Landes 1969; Marglin 1974; Wrigley 1988). One group of scholars has always been skeptical about the achievement of a rapid rate of growth before 1840 (Martin 1939; Taylor 1964; Chandler 1977). Although their views derive partially from the available national data series, they typically hold that only very limited increases in productivity were feasible prior to either major capital deepening or the introduction of a new generation of technologies and capital equipment quite different from those preceding. Since neither the use of machinery driven by inanimate sources of power nor highly capital-intensive techniques became widespread in manufacturing until the 1840s and 1850s, adherents of this position regard the possibility of substantial progress before then as quite unlikely. Others have suggested that changes in production methods or organization that did not involve new types of capital equipment were often implemented to undercut labor costs or autonomy, and questioned their effectiveness at increasing actual efficiency (Ware [1924] 1959; Dawley 1976; Faler 1981; Wilentz 1984).

Another intellectual tradition can be traced back at least as far as Adam Smith and has been represented in the dispute over the record of U.S. economic growth during the antebellum period by Simon Kuznets, among others (Smith [1776] 1976; Kuznets 1952; David 1967; Gallman 1971). This perspective views preindustrial economies as generally characterized by high transportation costs, low incomes, limited commercial development, and accordingly extensive opportunities for productivity and income growth without visibly dramatic alterations in technology. In particular, the extension of markets and shifts in expenditure patterns that accompany the beginning of economic growth stimulate economy-wide improvements in productivity through a variety of means, including more effective or intensified use of resources, scale economies, the introduction of new or higher-quality products, learning-by-doing and other forms of human capital accumulation, as well as increased specialization by factors of production. For example, I have argued in a series of articles that manufacturing industries drew on quite different sources of productivity growth during the first phase of American industrial development—often involving changes in the organization of workers or modest alterations in products or tools rather than major increases in capital intensity or mechanization—than they did later (Sokoloff 1982, 1984a, 1984b, 1986; Goldin and Sokoloff 1982). With these and similar advances in agriculture and other sectors, the U.S. economy was able to realize rapid and sustained growth by the 1820s (Gallman 1975; Rothenberg's chapter in this volume). They were followed by a perhaps more dramatic and enduring era of gains associated with widespread use of machinery driven by inanimate power sources.

These two streams of thought differ about the actual record of growth in the antebellum period, as well as in their basic conception of the process of technological change during early industrialization. The former emphasizes the primacy of radical innovations and downplays the returns to improvements in organization. Its proponents see such major technological breakthroughs as arising independently of Smithian processes, being embodied in capital equipment, clustered in a few key industries, and producing an unbalanced and highly discontinuous pattern of productivity increase (Rostow 1960; Chandler 1977; Crafts 1985; Wrigley 1988; Mokyr 1977, 1990). In highlighting the sweeping effects of a few specific advances such as the diffusion of inanimately powered machinery, the railroad, and the telegraph, this interpretation diminishes the significance of general mechanisms at work and focuses attention on the idiosyncratic aspects behind all singular events.

In contrast, what might be called the Smithian view focuses on the stimuli to increases in productivity provided by the expansion of markets (Landes 1969; Habakkuk 1962; Lindstrom 1978; Sokoloff 1986, 1988). Gains were realized through a variety of means, including changes in the utilization and organization of resources, the production process, and the design of products or capital goods. Although perhaps individually modest, the cumulative impact of an economy-wide series of incremental improvements of this sort was substantial. This perspective presumes that there was a broad potential to increase productivity while operating within the bounds of existing technical knowledge, and argues that the responses of firms to the increasing opportunities and challenges associated with the extension of markets involved an accelerated tapping of this potential. Once the process got under way, the people were not simply passive observers to these developments, but actively sought through both private and government intervention to promote and quicken their pace—say, by building roads and canals. This conception is one of rather balanced productivity growth, in which commercial development spurred advances that were realized and diffused gradually across a broad range of industries. Moreover, it allows for a greater flexibility of traditionally organized establishments and can more easily explain the persistence of regional differentials in performance.

Our understanding of manufacturing productivity growth during early American industrialization has been enhanced over the last decade by a number of studies based on material not previously examined systematically. This paper reviews these contributions, with particular attention to what the patterns of advance in measured productivity suggest about the sources of technical change and the circumstances that encouraged this progress. Overall, the evidence indicates that Americans were quite responsive to economic opportunities, and that the expansion of markets during the antebellum era stimulated a wide spectrum of producers to raise their commitments of resources to inventive activity and to squeeze out whatever increases in productivity could be obtained.

8.2 Data and Measurement

Scholars of antebellum manufacturing have benefited considerably from sharply falling costs in the collection and analysis of machine-readable data. Most prominent among the windfalls have been the samples of manufacturing-firm data drawn from various censuses or from archives of business records. Jeremy Atack, Fred Bateman, and Thomas Weiss have been pioneers in assembling such data sets for the mid- to late 1800s, and I as well as William Lazonick and Thomas Brush have followed in working with materials from the first half of the century (Atack 1976, 1977, 1985, 1987; Bateman and Weiss 1981; Sokoloff 1982, 1984a, 1984b, 1986; Lazonick and Brush 1985). These new bodies of evidence have made it possible to compute indexes of productivity across firm-specific characteristics—both cross-sectionally and over time. Information on individual establishments provides a much richer and more accurate understanding of how and why productivity varied than alternatives like state totals. The study of technical change has also been aided by the construction of samples of patent records linked to patentees and the localities in which they lived (Sokoloff 1988).

Of course the task of establishing the record of antebellum productivity growth in manufacturing has not yet been reduced to a matter of mere arithmetic. On the contrary, the measurement and analysis of productivity are always difficult, and the problems are especially severe in early industrial economies. At a basic level, the first censuses were conducted by and of a society with limited experience in such national efforts to gather comprehensive information. Not surprisingly, the surveys suffer from underenumeration, with the deficiencies in coverage varying systematically across classes of establishments (Fishbein 1973; Atack 1987; Sokoloff 1982, 1986). Questions of how to assemble a representative sample of observations afflict those working with other sources as well.

At a more global level, the major changes in technologies, the extent of markets, relative prices, and tastes that are characteristic of the onset of economic growth raise a special set of problems. Perhaps chief among them is the difficulty of distinguishing between changes in allocative efficiency and changes in the productivity of resources, given their allocation to a particular use. The expansion of markets, encompassing decreases in transaction and transportation costs, led to significant gains through greater specialization of factors, declines in seasonal unemployment, and other such improvements in the utilization of resources (Taylor 1951; Lindstrom 1978; Sokoloff and Dollar 1992). One would, for example, ideally like to decompose the substantial advance in the productivity of rural manufacturing between the portion due to the demise of inefficient producers driven by enhanced market competition and that attributable to the diffusion of or improvement in best-practice technology. Such calculations are challenging in any context, but are made immensely more complicated by the general lack in the antebellum censuses of a detailed accounting of the amount of time per year in which the designated inputs were actively involved in the manufacture of the specified output. Productivity is thus understated for enterprises operating part-time—where labor divided its year between agriculture and manufacturing.[1] Given the decline over the period in the prevalence of such establishments, the raw data yield biased estimates of productivity growth over time. Although the finding of rapid progress may not be sensitive to the choice between reasonable adjustments for this issue, the results concerning the relative significance of different sources of that progress almost certainly are.

Another sort of measurement problem stems from the inadequacies of the price indexes available for the deflation of reported current values of output over time to constant dollars. The principal issue is that the conventional indexes underestimate the rate of productivity growth, because they do not fully capture the improvements in the quality of goods over time (Brady 1964, 1966, 1972; Gordon 1990). The resulting bias could well be of a significant magnitude, because of the great increase in the variety and quality of goods and services made available for consumption during this phase of economic growth (Depew 1895; Larkin 1988). A second problem, however, is that high overland transportation costs often produced significant geographic differences in commodity prices, particularly between rural and urban districts. Without location-specific price indexes, cross-sectional productivity comparisons will be biased in favor of, and estimates of progress over time biased against, firms in areas with relatively high prices (Sokoloff and Villaflor 1992).

A further obstacle is that it is difficult to discern from census data much detail about the techniques and inputs in use at the firm level. Instead, one must rely on indirect inferences from the quantitative information provided on inputs and outputs. Without a knowledge of how firms differed with respect to technique, organization of production, equipment, products, social infrastructure, or the intensity of labor, however, there appears to be little hope of unambiguously establishing the contributions of specific changes in methods of manufacture to variation or increases in measured total factor productivity. Part of the problem is conceptual, because there are unresolved questions about how to treat phenomena like the increased intensity of labor, but most is due to the limitations of the bodies of evidence we have to work with.

---

1. A number of the northeastern establishments enumerated in the 1820 census of manufactures appear to have been operating part-time, either seasonally or irregularly throughout the year. Nearly all of these were located in rural areas. By 1832, however, well over 90 percent of the firms covered by the McLane Report were reported to be in full-time year-round production. The exceptions are overwhelmingly composed of putting-out establishments in the boot and shoes, tobacco, and palmleaf hats industries, or iron and steel establishments located on streams that froze during the winter months. In the census manuscripts for 1850 and 1860, few of the northeastern firms seem to have been operating part-time, but a great many in the South and Midwest evidently were—especially in the liquors and grain-milling industries. See Tchakerian (1990) for an extensive discussion of the latter, as well as Sokoloff (1982, 1986).

A final issue related to measurement is how to identify and better understand the processes generating the increases in manufacturing productivity during early industrialization. Competition in product markets and improvements in transportation can presumably explain the onetime gains due to greater specialization as well as the diffusion of innovations, but what accounted for the sustained acceleration of technical change? If a valid measure of invention were available, one could distinguish empirically between the view that the evolution of technological knowledge was driven by its own internal dynamic and was relatively independent of economic conditions, and the hypothesis that the expansion of markets was a major promoter of technical progress. Recent attempts, including my own, to use patent counts for this purpose have been very useful, but are obviously imperfect and quite controversial (Schmookler 1966; Sokoloff 1988; MacLeod 1988; Sullivan 1990; Mokyr 1990; Sokoloff and Khan 1990). Patents not only miss a good deal of, and probably most, invention but also include many valueless contributions. The variation in patenting in this particular context, however, may be at least qualitatively representative of the resources consumed in inventive activity. Since patent counts seem to provide the best measure currently available, they should be carefully examined rather than broadly dismissed (Griliches 1990). Alternative interpretations of their patterns of systematic variation can be more easily assessed in specific cases.

8.3   The Growth of Patenting and Inventive Activity

Americans were concerned with improving the material welfare of their families from the first days of settlement. They cherished a culture and set of social institutions that protected individual expression and the returns to enterprise, and defended them during the Revolution (Doerflinger 1986; Greene 1988). The debates over the early patent system reflected these sentiments, as well as an appreciation of the long-term social benefits of stimulating inventive activity through granting inventors limited property rights to the income yielded by their inventions (Machlup 1958). It was taken for granted that would-be inventors were influenced by the prospects of material gain. On that basis the drafters of the Constitution authorized a patent system whose establishment and improvement followed quickly in the laws of 1790 and 1793. From various alternative methods of rewarding inventors, a patent system was specifically selected. Both the designers and the judicial enforcers of the system intended and judged the increase in patents over time to manifest an increase in inventive activity. The recent use of patent records to investigate the growth of invention might thus be said to draw intellectual support from those who lived through the period.

As evident in figure 8.1, a sustained acceleration of patenting began during the first years of the nineteenth century, with the per capita rate rising more

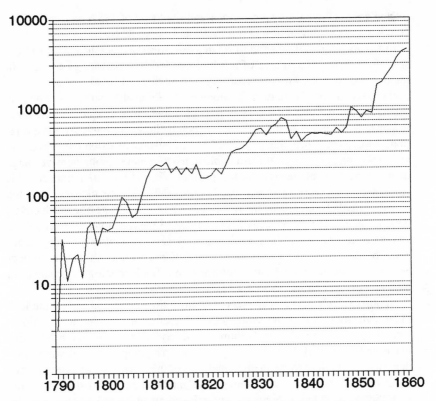

Fig. 8.1   Annual numbers of patents issued, logarithmic scale, 1790–1860
Source: U.S. Bureau of the Census (1975, ser. W99).

than fifteen times from 1790 to 1860. Conspicuous in virtually all industries and geographic districts, especially where markets were expanding, the increase was remarkable in scope as well as magnitude. The key issues about this development are whether the higher rates of patenting are representative of higher levels of inventive activity and, if so, what conditions accounted for the change. Although its sources are many and complex, I have argued that the extraordinary expansion of markets characteristic of the early stages of industrialization must have played a quantitatively important role (Sokoloff 1988). Several features of the evidence suggest this interpretation. First, the numbers of patents filed were quite sensitive to macroeconomic conditions, as seen in the sharp rise in activity before the War of 1812, when interruptions in the supply of foreign manufactures sparked a burgeoning of intraregional trade within the Northeast. This was an unusual source of boom times for domestic producers, but the remainder of the antebellum patent records was more conventionally procyclical, with downturns associated with the protracted contractions following the war and the Panic of 1837, and growth accompanying the long upturn of the 1820s and early 1830s.[2]

Even more compelling support of an association between patenting and the size of markets is the finding of much higher levels of patenting per capita in regions and counties with low-cost access to market centers as well as in urban centers (see table 8.1). In districts along the Erie Canal, where a more precise timing of the gaining of access is possible, there was a rapid and dramatic response in patenting to the opening of such facilities for low-cost transportation. Moreover, since the quantitative significance of extending navigable waterways on patenting was formidable in itself, a more comprehensive gauge of the expansion of markets would presumably yield a major impact. This combination of cross-sectional and longitudinal evidence indicates that the extent of markets influenced the rate of patenting, but the specific mechanisms remain unclear. These patterns could be due to the reactions of potential inventors or innovators to the greater commercial opportunities posed by larger pools of customers, the heightened competition arising from distant producers, improvements in the flow of information about technology, or changes in preferences and cultural attitudes.

Another salient aspect of the record of invention during the early American industrialization is that the same geographic areas maintained leadership in patenting throughout the antebellum period. By 1805–11, southern New England and New York had attained per capita patenting rates that were more than twice as high as those in any other part of the Northeast, and nearly three times the national average. Although the gaps had narrowed slightly by the mid-1840s, these two subregions still enjoyed an advantage of more than 50 percent over the next highest, Pennsylvania. By 1860, southern New England and New York were accounting for more than half of the nation's patents with only a fifth of its population. Southern New Englanders were especially inventive, with a rate that was 150 percent that of New Yorkers, 250 percent that of Pennsylvanians, and more than 300 percent that of northern New Englanders.[3] This persistent superiority of southern New England and New York cannot be attributed solely to more extensive transportation networks, larger

2. See Sokoloff (1988) for more discussion of the procyclicality and of how its variation in intensity across sectors and regions is very consistent with the view that the cycles were accounted for by market demand. The sharp rise in patenting during the late 1840s and 1850s may be more attributable to the nature of the technical change being realized at that time, however. In particular, these were years in which many new machines were developed and mechanization spread throughout the manufacturing sector for the first time. Patents for inventions embodied in capital equipment were easier to enforce.

3. The annual numbers of patents per million residents during the 1850s were 249.6 for southern New England, 166.0 for New York, 100.3 for the southern Middle Atlantic, 95.8 for Pennsylvania, and 75.0 for northern New England. Connecticut and Massachusetts had the highest rates—274.1 and 252.3, respectively. Overall, the leadership of southern New England, and Connecticut and Massachusetts in particular, increased from the 1840s to the 1850s in both absolute and percentage terms. See U.S. Patent Office (1891).

Table 8.1   **Annual Patent Rates per Million Residents, by Subregion, 1790–1846**

	1791–98	1799–1804	1805–11	1812–22	1823–29	1830–36	1836–42	1843–46
Northern New England								
Rural	0.7	4.5	13.0	15.4	33.8	69.1	28.1	16.3
Urban	—	—	9.8	11.4	9.9	50.2	42.1	27.6
Metropolitan	—	—	—	—	—	—	—	—
Total	1.9	7.5	15.2	15.1	33.0	65.5	32.9	20.0
Southern New England								
Rural	2.0	7.5	68.7	51.1	61.9	65.4	49.9	45.9
Urban	0.0	22.4	34.6	37.9	44.0	106.3	68.8	57.0
Metropolitan	11.9	78.5	291.5	244.9	160.0	226.9	213.9	265.5
Total	7.2	26.7	65.2	55.4	60.4	106.4	79.5	74.5
New York								
Rural	0.0	0.8	46.6	32.5	56.5	72.0	20.8	23.6
Urban	12.3	15.3	33.3	39.7	86.5	62.1	34.4	54.1
Metropolitan	24.8	68.0	121.4	116.0	159.7	196.7	131.9	148.4
Total	10.9	16.4	62.0	49.9	81.3	95.6	49.6	65.8
Pennsylvania								
Rural	0.0	0.0	11.9	11.3	20.3	38.1	18.8	22.8
Urban	0.0	8.6	17.3	8.7	8.4	31.4	20.7	22.1
Metropolitan	63.4	6.7	122.2	162.1	118.7	140.7	98.3	130.9
Total	17.2	14.5	29.7	33.6	32.2	53.3	32.9	42.5
Southern Middle Atlantic								
Rural	0.9	6.0	7.8	19.9	17.7	17.3	29.2	8.9
Urban	4.8	11.9	12.3	20.6	8.0	21.1	24.1	47.1
Metropolitan	17.6	35.2	131.7	108.7	105.6	134.4	82.1	111.8
Total	4.1	17.0	23.7	34.9	31.9	41.4	40.8	40.0
Other states	1.2	3.4	3.4	6.1	10.4	13.2	7.7	9.9
National average	5.2	11.3	23.9	22.9	30.0	41.8	24.5	27.3

Notes: Northern New England includes Maine, Vermont, and New Hampshire; southern New England includes Connecticut, Massachusetts, and Rhode Island; southern Middle Atlantic includes New Jersey, Delaware, Maryland, and District of Columbia. The counties were categorized for urbanization in each census year, and the reported figures for urban and rural districts are based on a rolling set of counties. Metropolitan counties, however, are composed in all years of those counties that contained a city of 50,000 or greater in 1840; urban counties are those that contained a city of at least 10,000 residents or were adjacent to a metropolitan county in the respective years. See Sokoloff (1988) for further information.

urban populations, or relative specialization on manufacturing. In regressions that control for these and other relevant variables, the higher patenting rates in southern New England and New York counties were estimated to be highly significant in a statistical sense (Sokoloff 1988).

To the extent that patenting is a meaningful gauge of inventive activity, these findings bear directly on the hypothesis that technical change depended on breakthroughs in mineral-based technologies and in the design of machinery. First is the matter of timing. Although major waves of diffusion of mechanization, steam power, and the railroad beginning in the late 1840s were accompanied by an upturn in patenting, the acceleration of the secular trend was by then forty years old. It was not therefore inspired by these heroic "macroinventions" (Mokyr 1990). Second, the responsiveness of patenting to market demand across a wide range of industries directly contradicts the claim that invention was exogenous with respect to economic conditions. Instead, the finding is consistent with the position that in early industrial America, where familiarity with the basic elements of technological knowledge was common among the population, valuable improvements in technique, organization, and design of product were induced by market pressures. Finally, the enduring leadership of southern New England and New York suggests that the more capital-intensive technologies of the late antebellum era evolved out of those in use during the preceding phase of Smithian growth.

The changes over time in the composition of patentees is consistent with this framework of two phases in technical change during the antebellum period. Merchants, professionals, and others from elite occupations had their share of patents fall substantially over the very beginning of the nineteenth century, with a growing contribution by artisans and other manual workers, those in the countryside, and individuals who had limited investments in technical skills or other invention-generating capital (Sokoloff and Khan 1990). This broadening of participation in patenting reveals a process in which an increasingly wide range of individuals was coming to redirect attention and resources toward commercial endeavors including invention and innovation (Gilmore 1989). Greater involvement by men with relatively ordinary endowments is suggestive of markets expanding opportunity for greater numbers rather than of technical breakthroughs facilitating further invention by the select few able to apply or refine them.

Although my work with Zorina Khan (1990) emphasized how the early rise in patenting was associated with a growing proportion of the population being involved in inventive activity, we also noted indications of the increasing importance over time of investment in what we termed "invention-generating capital." For example, trends toward greater specialization and increases in the number of lifetime patents by patentees were evident by the middle of the nineteenth century. We interpreted these findings as reflecting a rise in the return to, and investment in, invention-generating capital—and the beginning of the modern pattern in which the bulk of invention is carried out by factors specialized in that activity. Individuals with such investments would be expected to cluster in cities where there were greater incentives to specialize as well as a relative abundance of resources to support inventive activity or innovation. Indeed, we found that patentees in urban areas were more specialized and filed more patents over their lifetimes. Although the first phase of growth in patenting was marked by the democratization of invention, the later stages of development were characterized by the growing importance of technical expertise for effective invention.[4]

Despite the apparent relevance of patenting rates, some scholars have expressed skepticism about the usefulness of the information contained in the rates for the study of the origins of technical change. These reservations are generally based on either the variability in the value of inventions underlying patents or in the rates at which individuals choose to patent their inventions. Both of these conditions tend to erode the quality of patenting rates as a measure of inventive activity. To the extent that patents are representative of invention or other efforts to improve technique or products, however, there should be a relationship between these rates and productivity.

To explore this point, estimates of manufacturing productivity by geographic area are reported in table 8.2. Overall, they support the interpretation of patenting rates as reflective of inventive activity and of other efforts to improve efficiency, because manufacturing productivity was higher in areas with higher patenting rates. For example, southern New England had the highest number of patents per capita for virtually the entire antebellum period, and it stands out here as the subregion with the highest productivity, even after adjusting for urbanization. This superior performance by firms in southern New England is consistent across all four samples, and is generally statistically significant.[5] Another regularity in the data is that firms in urban counties were more productive than their rural counterparts, just as city residents outpatented their neighbors in the country. At the bottom of the scale, rural Pennsylvania and northern New England counties had both the lowest manufacturing productivity and patenting rates in the Northeast.[6]

Since cross-sectional variation in patenting across subregions was relatively stable over time, there is no effort here to explore whether comparisons be-

4. See Sokoloff and Khan (1990) for evidence on the greater specialization of patentees in urban areas and from more technical occupations. In research yet unpublished, we find a marked increase from the first to the second half of the nineteenth century in both specialization and the average number of career patents filed over a patentee's lifetime among a sample of 160 inventors whose inventions have been judged to be especially significant. Also see Thomson (1989) on this point. We also find that these "great inventors" disproportionately originated from areas with high patenting rates like southern New England and urban centers like New York, and that those born elsewhere were disproportionately inclined to migrate to these same districts.

5. The results from the 1820 sample diverge from the others in that the geographic differentials are uniformly lacking in statistical significance. The higher standard errors on the coefficients may reflect the effects of the severe economic contraction, which ended shortly before the census and had sharply reduced the demand for industrial products (Thorp 1926). Many of the enumerated establishments reported operating at far below capacity, and this could have increased the variance of the distribution of firms by productivity (Sokoloff 1982; Atack 1987). The results might also be partially due to the procedure by which likely "part-time" firms were identified and dropped from the analysis. See Sokoloff (1986) for details.

6. It is noteworthy that the rural counties in these two subregions had both their relative productivity and patenting rates decline significantly over the 1850s relative to those in southern New England and New York.

Table 8.2   **Indexes of Regional Manufacturing Productivity, 1820–1860**

	1820	1832	1850	1860
Northern New England				
Rural	88	87*	90*	83*
Urban	—	—	109	91*
Southern New England				
Rural	100	100	100	100
Urban	85	111*	114	106
New York				
Rural	91	—	89*	92
Urban	107	—	101	106
Pennsylvania				
Rural	88[a]	—	91*	74*
Urban	92[a]	—	98	98
Southern Middle Atlantic				
Rural	—[a]	—	104	91
Urban	—[a]	—	109	98

Sources: These indexes were computed from regressions estimated over the same subsamples of manufacturing firms examined in table 8.4. See the note to that table. The regressions employed only dummy variables for industries and for interactions between region and urbanization as independent variables. The logarithm of a value-added-based measure of total factor productivity served as the dependent variable. See Sokoloff (1986) for the selection of output elasticities.

Notes: Northern New England includes Maine, New Hampshire, and Vermont; southern New England includes Connecticut, Massachusetts, and Rhode Island; southern Middle Atlantic includes Delaware and New Jersey. Urban counties are those that contained cities with populations of 10,000 or greater and those adjacent to counties with cities of 25,000. Rural counties are the residual counties. Productivity in rural southern New England was set equal to 100 in each year, and productivity in other areas is reported relative to that standard. Asterisks indicate that the difference between the denoted districts and the standard of rural counties in southern New England is statistically significant.

[a]The Pennsylvania and southern Middle Atlantic observations were pooled in 1820, because of their small number.

tween productivity and current or lagged patenting activity would be more appropriate. Despite the lack of explicit attention to the issue of the rate of technological diffusion, the estimates do yield some insight on the subject. When product markets are in a stable competitive equilibrium, there should be no systematic regional differences in productivity. Then why are such differentials observed in the manufacturing data, and why are they correlated with patenting activity?

One possibility is that the differentials existed because transportation costs insulated certain areas from the market and allowed inefficient firms to survive in competition. That those same districts had lower patenting rates was strictly coincidental and did not contribute to the lower productivity. Another explanation is that the deviation from a competitive equilibrium was due to technical change being generated from investment in inventive activity at particular geographic sites and then slowly diffusing. At any point in time, the districts that were the technological leaders (i.e., southern New England) accordingly exhibited higher productivity. Firms in persistently backward areas were able to survive in competition, however, if they avoided or reduced the costs associated with acquiring new technologies by being a follower, or enjoyed lower factor costs. Although transportation costs undoubtedly protected pockets of inefficient establishments, the evidence seems to indicate that differences in inventive activity must have also played some role. It is hard, for example, to explain the roughly constant geographic differentials over time with transportation costs when the latter were declining. Moreover, the association between patenting rates and productivity held among urban counties, which were unlikely to be insulated from competition, as well as rural.[7]

8.4   Manufacturing

Increases in income from the reexport trade and gains in agricultural productivity stimulated expenditures on manufactures through the 1790s and into the first few years of the 1800s, but significant growth of domestic production appears not to have begun until just before the War of 1812. Domestic manufacturers had previously found it difficult to compete with British goods, but the interruptions of foreign trade greatly enhanced their effective opportunities (Cochran and Miller 1961; Spivak 1979). Due to the small scale of manufacturing enterprise, many firms could be quickly established in response, and production became concentrated in the Northeast. The lure of material benefit was reinforced by patriotic appeals and public sentiment in favor of national autonomy in manufactures. Also conducive were the extensive investments in transportation infrastructure undertaken privately but encouraged by government at all levels (Meyer, MacGill, et al. 1917; Goodrich 1960; Goodrich et al. 1961). As an increasing number of workers specialized in nonagricultural products, and as household incomes rose, the markets for farm produce in the Northeast expanded as well. The volume of intraregional trade grew rapidly, and areas that had previously been largely isolated economically were gradually drawn into a broad northeastern, if not national, market (Lindstrom 1978).

This growth in manufacturing production occurred from a very modest base. At the turn of the nineteenth century, even the cities relied on foreign sources for many high-value items. Rural residents produced many of their

---

7. In multivariate regressions, wage rates at the firm level were found to be positively and significantly related to local patenting rates and to firm productivity. Although relevant, this evidence does not help to discriminate between the two competing theories. On one hand, if the wage differentials pertained to identical workers, they could reflect the protection from competition provided by transportation costs to firms in outlying areas. If they were due to workers in counties with high patenting rates and high measured productivity having more human capital, however, then they might reflect a difference in the quality of labor required to operate with a new technology. In either of these cases, higher labor costs per worker might partially or even fully offset the advantage in measured productivity enjoyed by firms in the latter set of counties and slow the process by which the old-technology establishments were forced to upgrade or fail.

manufactured goods at home, or obtained them from travelling artisans who toured the countryside with their tools and materials. Because both the 1810 and 1820 censuses of manufactures are flawed by irregular enumeration, it is difficult to precisely identify how the number and organization of manufacturing establishments evolved over the first two decades of the nineteenth century in the dynamic Northeast (Sokoloff 1982). What is clear, however, is that manufacturing capacity expanded during the embargo and war years and was reflected in decreased household production as well as increased factory production (Tryon [1917] 1966). Though many of the new enterprises did not survive the severe economic contraction that followed the peace, the physical plants often endured and helped support the resumption of the industrial expansion during the 1820s (Ware 1931).

From the information on manufacturing firms contained in the manuscripts of the 1820 census, it is apparent that the great majority of establishments in that year continued to operate at small scales and rely on traditional production processes and capital. Textile mills were of course the prominent exception. Both cotton and wool manufacture were in the process of being transformed by major leaps in the design of machinery and other equipment, and large establishments using the new technologies were springing up throughout the Northeast (Cole 1926; Ware 1931). Virtually all other industries, however, were dependent on hand tools or simple water-powered devices, such as gristmills or trip-hammers, with which manufacturers had long been acquainted; land, structures, and inventories absorbed nearly all of the capital invested in these enterprises (Sokoloff 1984a). In rural areas, firms in such labor-intensive industries were quite small, with fewer than five adult males and perhaps an apprentice. It was typical in such "artisanal shops" for all workers to be skilled and involved in carrying out all steps in the production process (Sokoloff 1984b). Firms in or near urban counties were generally larger and organized differently. Although operating with essentially the same capital to labor ratios as those of the small shops, these manufactories or so-called non-mechanized factories were distinguished by work forces disproportionately composed of women and children, an extensive division of labor, a more intense pace of work, and greater standardization of output (Goldin and Sokoloff 1982).

Recent examinations of manufacturing-firm data have found substantial evidence that these manufactories were significantly more productive than artisanal shops (Sokoloff 1984b; Atack 1987). Cross-sectional analyses indicate significant differences in total factor productivity between the two modes of organization, with economies of scale being exhausted in labor-intensive industries at a size of about twenty employees. Other approaches to testing the hypothesis yield supportive results as well. For example, average firm size in such industries increased steadily over the antebellum period and was strongly related in cross-section to proximity to market. As their shares in output fell over time, the artisanal shops that survived the competition were increasingly located in small towns insulated by high transportation costs or were focused on satisfying narrow market niches like the demand for custom-made goods.

Detailed studies of the evolution of technology in industries such as boots and shoes, clocks, coaches and harnesses, furniture, glass, iron and steel, meat packing, paper, tanning, and cotton and wool textiles suggest a two-stage process in antebellum productivity growth (Hazard 1921; Cole 1926; Ware 1931; Davis 1949; Habakkuk 1962; Smith 1971; Hirsch 1978; Walsh 1982; Paskoff 1983; Hounshell 1984). The first stage was to occupy most of the sector for the first half of the nineteenth century, and was exemplified by the rise of manufactories. Their increases in technical efficiency stemmed from a series of improvements or refinements in the organization of production and from relatively subtle modifications of output and in traditional capital equipment. Just as the data from the manufacturing censuses reveal only a modest increase in the capital intensity of most industries until the 1850s, when mechanization diffused widely, industry studies highlight the gradual development of a more extensive division, with an accompanying intensification, of labor and the substitution of less-skilled workers for more-skilled as the most salient changes in technique prior to midcentury. Also noted are improvements in traditional tools and instruments like drills, lathes, and planes, as well as alterations in the product aimed at differentiation or at facilitating standardized production under the new organization of labor (Hounshell 1984; Smith 1977). As important as some of these changes proved to be, few outside of textiles seem to have either constituted or required a fundamental breakthrough in technical knowledge.

The second phase of technical change in manufacturing was distinguished by an increasing reliance on machinery driven by inanimate sources of power, although it also encompassed some modifications in organization to exploit the full potential of the more sophisticated capital stock (Lazonick and Brush 1985; Rosenberg 1963, 1972). Precisely where one draws the line in classifying a particular invention is not always clear, but those scholars who claim a revolutionary character to mechanization perceive a qualitative difference between the introduction of a new type of equipment and an alteration to a familiar tool. The textile industries are clearly the first to have entered into this stage of technical change, but many other industries had joined them by 1860. Judging both from industry studies and the degree of capital intensity revealed in firm data, the 1850s were the crucial decade of transition in the Northeast.

Estimates of the growth of labor and total factor productivity between 1820 and 1860 have been computed from the samples of manufacturing census manuscripts by class of industry for rural and urban counties in the Northeast. Perhaps the most important aspect of these figures, reported in table 8.3, is how rapid the rates of advance were. Despite the late diffusion of mechanization and inanimate power sources to most industries, total factor productivity in each of the categories grew over the entire period at almost the same rate as

Table 8.3   **Per Annum Growth Rates of Labor and Total Factor Productivity, by Classes of Manufacturing Firms, 1820–1860**

	1820–50	1850–60	1820–60
Mechanized Industries			
Labor productivity			
Rural	1.2%	3.5%	1.8%
Urban	2.8	2.0	2.6
All	2.1	2.4	2.2
Total factor productivity			
Rural	1.2	4.2	1.9
Urban	2.2	2.2	2.2
All	1.8	2.7	2.1
Less- or Non-mechanized Industries			
Labor productivity			
Rural	1.8%	4.3%	2.4%
Urban	0.5	3.7	1.3
All	1.5	3.9	2.1
Total factor productivity			
Rural	1.8	2.0	1.9
Urban	0.8	2.0	1.1
All	1.5	1.9	1.6
Capital-Intensive Industries			
Labor productivity			
Rural	1.4%	2.8%	1.8%
Urban	2.3	1.8	2.2
All	1.9	2.3	2.0
Total factor productivity			
Rural	1.2	3.3	1.8
Urban	1.8	1.9	1.8
All	1.6	2.5	1.8
Labor-Intensive Industries			
Labor productivity			
Rural	1.6%	5.6%	2.6%
Urban	0.7	4.4	1.7
All	1.7	4.5	2.4
Total factor productivity			
Rural	1.9	2.8	2.1
Urban	1.0	2.5	1.4
All	1.8	2.1	1.9

Notes and Sources: These estimates are for value-added-based measures of labor and total factor productivity. Similar qualitative results were obtained when using total value of output as the measure of product. The classification of firms as urban or rural was based on the population figures in the current censuses. A firm was treated as rural unless it was located in a county with a city of 10,000 people or greater, or in a county that was adjacent to a county with a city of more than 25,000. The mechanized industries consist of cotton textiles, wool textiles, paper, glass, flour milling, and iron and steel. The capital-intensive industries consist of cotton textiles, wool textiles, paper, flour milling, iron and steel, liquors, and tanning. The other industries included in the analysis are boots and shoes, coaches and harnesses, furniture and other wood-

Table 8.3   (notes, continued)

work, hats, and tobacco products. These estimates were computed with the same data and virtually identical procedures to those employed in Sokoloff (1986). See the notes in that paper to tables 13.7 and 13.12 in particular. The figures differ slightly; because of the small number of observations the glass industry was dropped from the calculations, and industry weights obtained from the subsample of firm data were used rather than those from the 1850 aggregates by state.

the long-term trend in manufacturing since 1860.[8] Skepticism about the centrality of capital equipment for technical change is further enhanced by the finding that total factor productivity rose in the labor-intensive and less-mechanized industries nearly as fast before the 1850s as in that decade of intense capital deepening and widening mechanization. Comparisons of the rates of labor and total factor productivity growth sow other doubts; in a growth accounting framework capital deepening explains little, and total factor productivity growth virtually all, of the substantial growth of labor productivity over the antebellum period—even in the most capital-intensive and mechanized industries. Only during the 1850s was capital deepening quantitatively important, accounting for more than half of the increase in the labor productivity of labor-intensive and less-mechanized industries.[9] Given that these same industries registered increases in total factor productivity that rivalled those of their counterparts, the clear implication is substantial technical change overall and a relatively limited role for physical capital accumulation within the manufacturing sector.

Disaggregating the record of productivity growth by class of district offers some insight into the spread of technical change. Of greatest interest is that between 1820 and 1860 the labor-intensive and less-mechanized industries realized more rapid total factor productivity growth in rural areas than in urban. The contrast is especially stark over the first thirty years, when progress was composed largely of changes in the organization of production and incremental improvement of tools and products. This pattern is consistent with the view that earlier access to broad markets had by 1820 already induced firms in cities to take advantage of scale economies as well as to explore these other means of increasing productivity. As falling transport costs expanded markets geographically over the next thirty years, rural firms were similarly stimulated to innovate, adopt, and make up ground on their urban competitors. Both sets of firms registered a sharp acceleration in technical change over the 1850s,

8. See Kendrick (1961) for his estimate that total factor productivity in manufacturing grew at 1.8 percent per annum between 1869 and 1953. See Sokoloff (1986) for further discussion.

9. In the framework adopted here in which value added serves as the measure of output and capital and labor are the only inputs, the contribution of capital deepening is equivalent to the rate of labor productivity growth minus the rate of total factor productivity advance. The striking increase in capital intensity and in the relative contribution of capital deepening during the 1850s is characteristic of virtually all of the relatively labor-intensive industries. See Sokoloff (1986), especially tables 18.8 and 13.13, for further discussion and evidence.

and their close-to-equivalent rates of progress may indicate a more rapid rate of diffusion for major advances embodied in capital equipment.[10]

The pattern was different among capital-intensive and mechanized industries. Here, the urban sector drew ahead between 1820 and 1850, but rural firms caught up with extraordinary 4.2 and 3.3 percent per annum rates of advance in total factor productivity over the next decade. Since the performances of the two sets of establishments were virtually identical over the period as a whole, one might be impressed by how quickly or evenly the early technological advances, such as power looms in textiles, had diffused between urban and rural areas. If one focuses on the unbalanced progress before and after 1850, however, the experience appears more consistent with invention or technological innovation originating in cities before spreading slowly to the countryside.

Some of the estimated rapid growth in manufacturing total factor productivity may be due to the realization of scale economies or to problems in measurement, but it is clear that taking account of such factors does not alter the qualitative results. Scale economies, for example, will not help explain the advances registered by firms in urban counties. Moreover, both Atack (1987) and I (1984b, 1986) have found that the extent of cross-sectional variation in total factor productivity with firm size pales relative to the estimated increase between 1820 and 1860.[11] As for part-time establishments, their declining prevalence is also unlikely to explain much of the pattern of widespread substantial advances. Not only were the growth rates computed from 1820 data that were carefully screened to exclude such firms, but information contained in the 1832 McLane Report indicates that they were no longer common in the Northeast.[12] Finally, because the price indexes underestimate the improvement over time in quality, as well as the fall in output prices for rural firms, the figures in table 8.3 likely understate, rather than overstate, productivity growth—especially for the rural establishments (Sokoloff and Villaflor 1992).

Given the robustness of the finding of rapid technical change to a consider-

10. See Hirsch (1978) for a detailed and well-documented discussion of the diffusion of technical change in many of these labor-intensive industries over the 1850s. Her evidence from the census manuscripts for Newark is quite consistent with the interpretation offered here.

11. Neither Atack nor I have presented a precise decomposition of the proportion of measured total factor productivity increase due to the realization of scale economies. Although one could be prepared, it would be unlikely to significantly advance the state of knowledge. The qualitative answer is already clear, and the deficiencies of the 1820 census complicate the task of obtaining a robust point estimate. Of particular concern are the unrepresentativeness of the firms enumerated in that census and the inclusion of establishments operating part-time.

12. See Sokoloff (1986) for a discussion of the procedures employed to identify and omit from the analysis those firms more likely to have been operating part-time. As mentioned in note 1, many of the firms enumerated in the McLane Report provided information about the number of weeks they operated each year. Long average workdays were also indicated (Atack and Bateman 1992). Based on both pieces of information, year-round full-time production appears to have been the norm by 1832, except for a few narrow categories of enterprises. Given the conventional understanding of what part-time operations pertain to, it appears unlikely that the decline in their prevalence could account for much of the increase in measured productivity.

ation of scale economies and measurement problems, the fundamental question to ask is from whence it came. The popular view that the onset of growth arose from a few key and exogenous inventions has been influential, but is it consistent with the available evidence? The record of manufacturing productivity suggests not. Instead of a strong association between mechanization or capital deepening and technical advance, the data indicate that more modest changes in organization and tools boosted productivity across a broad range of industries. Such gains seem unlikely to have been contingent upon a few exogenous breakthroughs. Rather, they were the sorts of improvements that would be expected if market conditions induced firms to experiment and develop better ways of carrying out production. Additional evidence of demand-induced or endogenous technological change comes from the demonstration that the growth in patenting rates was closely related to the expansion of markets and from the geographic correspondence across subregions between higher manufacturing productivity and higher patenting. If higher patenting rates do indeed reflect greater inventive activity or more of a commitment to searching for ways of improving productivity, what remains to be established is a linkage between firm productivity and local patenting rates that is robust to controlling for other variables.

Table 8.4 establishes such a linkage in presenting cross-sectional regressions estimated over samples of firm data for 1820, 1832, 1850, and 1860. The logarithm of total factor productivity is the dependent variable, and the independent variables include the logarithm of the current or most recent rate of patents per capita in the local county, as well as various dummies for industry, subregion, level of urbanization, and firm size. Although the size and significance of the coefficient varies somewhat across years, the central result of a positive relationship between firm productivity and local patenting rates is robust. With the 1820 and 1832 samples, for example, the qualitative finding is insensitive to reasonable changes in the time intervals used to identify current patenting rates, different definitions of urbanization, the inclusion of dummies for access to navigable waterways, and dropping establishments from mechanized industries out of the analysis.[13]

Since only a small fraction of inventions were ultimately patented, and

---

13. Many alternative specifications were estimated. The qualitative results are insensitive to the use of a measure of total factor productivity based on gross output as the measure of output, as well as to different methods of dealing with issues of firm size, urbanization, access to transportation, regional effects, and the time frame for current patenting rates. The only specifications that yield insignificant coefficients on the patenting rate are those that include a number of other collinear variables such as dummies for firm size, urbanization, subregion, and interactions. The results are slightly sensitive to introducing geographic restrictions on the subset of firms over which the regressions are estimated. Given the relatively small number of counties represented in the samples, however, this pattern is not disturbing. In general, the statistical relationship between productivity and local patenting rates is much stronger for labor-intensive industries than for highly mechanized industries like textiles. Hence, the qualitative results hold when the regression analysis is confined to the former, but not when it is confined to the latter.

Table 8.4 Cross-sectional Regressions with Total Factor Productivity as Dependent Variable, 1820–1860

	1820			1832			1850				1860			
	(1)	(2)	(3)	(4)	(5)	(6)	(7)	(8)	(9)	(10)	(11)	(12)	(13)	(14)
Constant	3.828 (39.85)	3.850 (37.44)	3.820 (33.66)	3.772 (19.44)	3.566 (17.46)	3.563 (17.19)	4.363 (44.09)	4.385 (42.85)	4.353 (42.20)	4.247 (41.05)	4.279 (39.18)	4.227 (37.44)	4.199 (37.44)	4.098 (35.48)
Log (patents per capita in local county)	0.024 (3.18)	0.027 (3.13)	0.028 (3.02)	0.105 (2.63)	0.106 (2.69)	0.078 (1.93)	0.013 (2.30)	0.011 (1.74)			0.022 (3.01)	0.012 (1.61)		
High patenting by 1820									0.175 (3.42)	0.098 (1.78)			0.252 (4.02)	0.174 (2.37)
High patenting by 1850									0.071 (1.90)	0.056 (1.49)			0.082 (1.75)	0.033 (0.68)
Northern New England		0.012 (0.17)	-0.002 (-0.04)					-0.081 (-1.92)	-0.069 (-1.63)	-0.047 (-1.09)		-0.078 (-1.45)	-0.57 (-1.05)	-0.025 (-0.46)
Southern New England		-0.062 (-0.98)	-0.043 (-0.66)		0.209 (2.99)	0.161 (2.28)		0.044 (0.94)	0.003 (-0.07)	0.002 (0.05)		0.131 (2.37)	0.067 (1.18)	0.025 (0.41)
New York		0.034 (0.66)	0.035 (0.67)					-0.078 (-1.46)	-0.096 (-1.80)	-0.093 (-1.76)		0.092 (1.40)	0.049 (0.74)	0.055 (0.82)
Urban			-0.060 (-1.06)			0.078 (2.12)				0.018 (0.47)				0.074 (1.43)

	1820			1832			1850				1860			
Major urban center										0.102				0.014
										(1.54)				(0.18)
Medium size			0.074			0.178				0.217				0.159
			(1.22)			(3.86)				(4.88)				(2.89)
Large size			0.020			0.149				0.199				0.200
			(0.26)			(3.12)				(3.53)				(3.28)
R^2	0.12	0.12	0.13	0.07	0.09	0.14	0.06	0.07	0.09	0.13	0.03	0.05	0.07	0.10
N	433	433	433	465	465	465	667	667	667	667	566	566	566	566

Sources: These regressions were estimated over all of the observations in the respective data sets that satisfied the criteria underlying the "B" set of productivity estimates reported in Sokoloff (1986). The dependent variable is the logarithm of total factor productivity, where output is measured as value added, and the procedures and parameter estimates used in its calculation are described in that same paper. A set of dummy variables for industry was also included as independent variables in these regressions, but their coefficients are not reported here. The estimates of patents per capita by county are drawn from Sokoloff (1988).

Notes: For 1820, 1832, 1850, and 1860, the patent rates pertain to the years 1812–22, 1822–30, 1843–46, and 1843–46, respectively. Hence, the 1860 regressions rely on a quite dated estimate of patenting activity. The actual estimate of the patent rate was augmented by 0.1, so that a logarithm could be taken for counties with patenting rates of zero. The dummy variables for high patenting signify when counties achieved sustained high rates of patenting, with an annual rate of forty per million residents serving as the threshold. Those that did so by 1820 were flagged by the first dummy. Those that did so by 1843–46, but not by 1820, were flagged by the second. Urban firms were located in counties with cities of 10,000 or more or in counties adjacent to others with cities of 25,000 or more. Firms in a major urban center were located in counties with a city that had attained a population of 50,000 by 1850. The dummies for urban and major urban center are not exclusive. Firms of medium size had six to fifteen employees; large firms had more than fifteen employees. In the 1820, 1850, and 1860 regressions, the constant pertains to a small paper mill in a rural county of Pennsylvania, Delaware, or New Jersey. Because the 1832 regressions could only be run over New England firms, the constant pertains to a northern New England paper mill. t-statistics are reported within parentheses below the respective coefficients.

many patented inventions proved to be of little use, the finding is unlikely to be picking up a causal relationship between productivity and patented inventions per se. Instead, the association is probably due to the joint conditions that patenting rates were representative of all of a population's efforts to increase the value of output obtained per unit of input, and that productivity was causally related to the rates of inventive activity in this broad sense—inclusive of innovation, adoption of superior techniques developed elsewhere, and invention. In principle, one might argue that both productivity and patenting rates were higher in some districts for reasons other than invention and innovation leading to increases in efficiency. For example, skeptics could offer the caveat that in counties with a higher level of education or degree of commercialization, productivity and patenting might both be enhanced, but unrelated to each other. When one critically examines the alternative interpretations, however, few prove satisfactory. Some fail to persuade because they fit less well with evidence that increases in productivity were sensitive to market conditions and were achieved through incremental or organizational change. Others do so because they fundamentally reduce to the same basic idea—that is, greater competition led to higher productivity by ensuring that only those firms able to stay on the cutting edge of technology survived.

Of course the ultimate persuasion is the richness of the evidence. Beyond robustness, there are several other reasons for believing that the statistical association between productivity and patenting is actually picking up the effect of higher rates of invention or innovation on productivity. First, the regression coefficients imply that the geographic differentials in productivity accounted for by patenting were of quite plausible magnitudes. For example, given the observed variation in patenting rates, the coefficients from the 1820 equations suggest that differences in patenting would lead firms from rural counties in southern New England to be about 9 percent more productive than their rural counterparts in either northern New England or Pennsylvania after controlling for other variables. The size of this effect is thus economically significant, conceivable given the less than perfectly integrated product markets of that era, and roughly equivalent to the geographic differentials reported in table 8.2

Another reason to believe that the regression results reflect a genuine relationship between productivity and inventive activity is that the coefficients on the patenting rate are simply more stable and consistently significant than those on other proxies for background characteristics that might be correlated with measured productivity. Moreover, as seen in equations (4) through (6), the same qualitative results hold when the observations are restricted to estab-

14. The questionnaires used by McLane Report enumerators to survey firms in New England and the Middle Atlantic were not consistent in their treatments of several variables. Since the two groups of observations cannot be pooled for analysis of productivity, the 1832 regressions were estimated over the New England firms alone. Since nearly all of the Middle Atlantic firms come from western Pennsylvania, and there is little variation in patenting rates across the covered coun-

lishments in a particular region like New England.[14] Although variables for subregion, firm size, urbanization, and access to transportation are correlated with patenting, and typically depress the latter's statistical significance when appearing in the same regressions, this perhaps crude measure of inventive activity outperforms them in accounting for cross-sectional variation in productivity.

If there is any ambiguity in the evidence, it is with the regressions estimated over the 1850 and 1860 data. When the only independent variables are industry dummies and the logarithm of the local patenting rate in 1843–46 (the latest years for which it can be calculated), the results are qualitatively the same as in the earlier years. But the size of the coefficient on and the statistical significance of the patenting rate decrease with the addition of dummies for subregion, urbanization, and firm size. The diminished explanatory power and statistical significance may be due to the greater error in measurement from the use of dated patenting rates.[15] Especially with multicollinearity between subregion and patenting, the additional noise in the measure might lead the subregional dummies to serve as better proxies for inventive activity and pick up more of the explanatory power and statistical significance.

Two other approaches for getting at the relationship between productivity and patenting in these later years were tried. In the first, as continuous variables state-level patenting rates computed from aggregate data for 1840–49 and 1850–59 were included in lieu of the dummies for subregion and found to be positive and statistically significant in both 1850 and 1860. In the other, reported in table 8.4, dummy variables for the local county having achieved sustained high rates of patenting by 1820 or 1850 were included as the proxies for inventive activity.[16] These capture an interesting pattern in the data. Firms in counties that had achieved high patenting by 1820 stand out as being much more productive than their counterparts after controlling for other characteristics. This effect is large overall (about 17 percent in 1860 by equation [14]), pronounced in the rural counties of southern New England, and consistent with the hypothesized relationship between productivity and patenting. The same areas that led in patenting at 1820 (such as around Boston or along the Connecticut River valley; see Sokoloff 1988) also were at the forefront of the rapid surge of the late 1840s and the 1850s (see figure 8.1). Although a fine

---

ties, it is not surprising that regressions over only these observations yield an insignificant coefficient on the patenting rate variable.

15. The sample of patents employed to compute the county patenting rates does not extend beyond 1846. Accordingly, the latest interval for which the country rates can be computed is 1843–46. These figures are of course dated estimates of patenting rates in 1850 and 1860 and, as the figures in note 3 suggest, likely to be systematically biased as well as to contain random measurement error. Both should lead the coefficient on the current patenting rate to be biased toward zero.

16. These dummies pertain to a county achieving an annual patenting rate of more than forty per million residents and maintaining or increasing it for an indefinite period—by either 1820 or between 1820 and 1850, respectively.

breakdown by county is not yet available for these later years, the point can be illustrated with state data. In each of the two decades, Connecticut and Massachusetts had the highest patenting per capita in the country, nearly twice that of New York and three times that of Pennsylvania.[17]

Taken together, the cross-sectional regressions provide substantial evidence that increases in the commitment of resources to inventive activity or innovation, as reflected in higher patenting rates, raised productivity. In doing so, they support the view that technological change was stimulated by the expansion of markets and that this aspect of early growth helps to explain how the process became self-sustaining. They also reinforce the case established above, that much of the initial advance in manufacturing productivity was realized through improvements in organization and other changes in practice that did not require breakthroughs in technical knowledge and were perhaps easier to generate as a result. They do not, however, reject the influence of supply-side factors on the course of technical change. It remains clear that the effects of a specific change in market conditions on the inputs devoted to inventive activity or on successful invention depend on a range of circumstances including the state of technology, as well as the industrial composition, the endowments of the population, and the supply of capital to entrepreneurs in the respective locality. Since demand-side conditions grew more uniformly distributed by the end of the antebellum period, the persistence of large location-specific effects in patenting and productivity suggest that supply-side factors were important and slow to change.

The significance of both demand- and supply-side conditions on the processes generating technical change is supported by the pooled cross-section regressions presented in table 8.5. Total factor productivity again serves as the dependent variable, with the independent variables including the previous set of dummies for industry, subregion, urbanization, and firm size, as well as the patenting rate in the local county, dummies for the year of the observation and for the achievement in the local county of a high patenting rate by 1820, and interaction terms. Equations (1) and (2) control for changes in industrial and regional composition in finding that productivity grew rapidly between 1820 and 1860, especially during the 1820s and 1850s. The results are consistent with the hypothesis that demand-side conditions contributed to this progress, because the estimated coefficients on patents per capita in the local county are

17. From the 1840s to the 1850s, the patenting rates rose in southern New England from 82.1 to 249.6; in New York from 63.7 to 166.0; in Pennsylvania from 38.5 to 95.8; in northern New England from 24.5 to 75.0; and in southern Middle Atlantic from 45.5 to 100.3. Connecticut and Massachusetts raised their rates from 83.1 to 253.1 and from 92.0 to 274.1, respectively. It is clear that southern New England experienced a marked increase in its relative patenting rates between the 1840s and the 1850s. Since the change was both substantial and to some degree a reversion to an earlier pattern of great dominance in patenting by southern New England outside of metropolitan centers, it is plausible that the dummies relating to past records of patenting are better representations of the patterns of patenting in 1850 and 1860 than the 1843–46 rates are. See U.S. Patent Office (1891).

Table 8.5   **Pooled Cross-sectional Regressions with Total Factor Productivity as Dependent Variable, 1820–1860**

	(1)	(2)	(3)	(4)
Constant	3.879	3.868	3.879	3.789
	(75.60)	(72.75)	(70.47)	(67.88)
Log (patents per capita)	0.018	0.016		
	(5.02)	(3.78)		
Log (patents per capita) × mechanized industry		−0.014		
		(−1.30)		
Northern New England		−0.073	−0.058	−0.039
		(−2.70)	(−2.14)	(−1.42)
Southern New England		0.049	0.022	0.018
		(1.74)	(0.73)	(0.59)
New York		0.010	−0.003	0.002
		(0.31)	(−0.10)	(0.07)
Urban				0.026
				(1.10)
Major urban center				0.100
				(2.53)
Medium size				0.175
				(6.98)
Large size				0.162
				(5.66)
1832	0.254	0.225	−0.227	−0.104
	(8.55)	(6.72)	(−1.04)	(−0.48)
1850	0.341	0.348	0.319	0.309
	(12.45)	(12.63)	(8.47)	(8.25)
1860	0.529	0.534	0.472	0.460
	(18.86)	(18.95)	(11.91)	(11.70)
Log (patents per capita) × 1820			0.019	0.016
			(2.00)	(1.69)
Log (patents per capita) × 1832			0.125	0.075
			(2.48)	(1.47)
Log (patents per capita) × 1850			−0.002	−0.007
			(−0.27)	(−0.87)
High patenting by 1820			−0.024	−0.130
			(−0.43)	(−2.23)
High patenting by 1820 × 1832			−0.005	0.144
			(−0.06)	(1.91)
High patenting by 1820 × 1850			0.202	0.255
			(2.54)	(3.23)
High patenting by 1820 × 1860			0.288	0.281
			(3.94)	(3.88)
High patenting by 1850 × 1850			0.067	0.069
			(1.47)	(1.53)
High patenting by 1850 × 1860			0.100	0.060
			(2.49)	(1.50)
R^2	0.18	0.19	0.20	0.23
N	2,133	2,133	2,133	2,133

Notes: See the note to table 8.4. The dummy for mechanized industries pertains to cotton textiles, wool textiles, and iron and steel.

positive, highly significant, and similar in magnitude to the point estimates obtained in the cross-sections for 1820, 1850, and 1860.[18] Given the substantial changes in patenting rates over the period, the stability of the coefficient to introducing variation over time in patenting increases confidence that the statistical association is not an artifact. Although only marginally significant, the negative coefficient in equation (2) on the interaction between the current patenting rate and a dummy for mechanized industries highlights the possibility that the patterns of invention and diffusion were quite different for technical change embodied in capital equipment. For example, the weaker association between firm productivity and local patenting activity could be due to such technical change diffusing more rapidly through the sale of the capital equipment, or to its being less responsive to demand-based stimuli.

Dummy variables for firm size, degrees of urbanization, and location in a county that had achieved a high patenting rate by 1820, as well as a number of interactions between year and measures of patenting activity, are added to the specification in equations (3) and (4). Again the qualitative results are essentially the same. Controlling for firm size and urbanization indicates that they account for only a small share of the estimated advance in manufacturing productivity between 1820 and 1860. Most of the increase in total factor productivity was clearly realized through technical change. Even more strongly than in the cross-sectional regressions, there is a shift over time in the relationship between productivity and patenting. The coefficients on the interactions between the year dummies and the patenting rate suggest that productivity was positively and continuously related to patenting in 1820 and 1832. Such interactions yield insignificant coefficients for 1850 and 1860, however. Instead, the terms that interact these years with dummies for counties that achieved high patenting rates by 1820 have large, positive, and significant coefficients. Overall, the general pattern is that the increase of productivity with the record of patenting had become a stepwise function by 1850, whereas it had been continuous earlier on. The step increase is much larger for firms in counties that had achieved sustained high levels of patenting early in the process of growth—by 1820—than for counties that had achieved those levels later.

This shift in the quantitative relationship between productivity and the record of patenting likely reflects some aspect of the course of technical progress in antebellum manufacturing. One hypothesis is that the decline over the period in the explanatory power of patenting activity was due to the slow

18. The regressions provide indirect support to the hypothesis that demand-side factors, working through markets, stimulated technical change. Their direct implication is that manufacturing productivity was higher in counties with higher patenting rates, bolstering the interpretation that the latter reflect rates of inventive activity. Not all influences on patenting rates operate through markets, but given that patenting was responsive to market demand and that the extension of navigable waterways accounts for a significant amount of the growth in patenting in the Northeast over the early nineteenth century (Sokoloff 1988), the finding of the relationship between productivity and patenting seems to sustain the more complex causal path from market stimulus to increase in productivity.

geographic diffusion of invention and other advances in technique. In this view, the dummies pertaining to the timing of the achievement of sustained high levels of patenting have more explanatory power in 1850 and 1860 because they are a better proxy for the local cumulation of several decades of technical change than current patenting activity is. Although not completely implausible, technology would have had to diffuse at a glacial speed to account for, say, why in 1860 productivity was so much higher in firms located in counties that had achieved high patenting rates before 1820. Given the relatively small differentials in productivity between subregions, this interpretation does not seem consistent with the evidence.

Another possibility is that the lack of statistical significance for the patents-per-capita variable in 1850 and 1860 results from having to rely on a dated figure. As discussed above, since 1843–46 is the latest period for which the patent rate is available, the measurement error involved in using it to reflect activity in 1850 or 1860 biases the coefficients toward zero and the standard errors up. Since the group averages they focus on would be less disturbed by this imprecision, the dummy variables could continue to have large and significant estimated effects. Unfortunately for this view, the likelihood that whether a county had achieved a high patenting rate by 1820 is a good indicator of its patenting activity in 1850 or 1860 seems remote, unless there were other factors at work.

Perhaps the most compelling explanation is that the relationship between productivity and patenting evolved with changes in the nature of technical advance and in the processes generating it. From this perspective, there was a tighter relationship between productivity and current patenting rates during the first phase of industrialization, when much of the progress was being realized through incremental alterations in the organization of production. A demand-stimulated increase in the commitment of resources to inventive activity, reflected in higher patenting, could reliably yield an increase in productivity in such a context where the supplies of potential inventors and inventions were relatively elastic.

During the late 1840s and 1850s, however, when technological change in manufacturing consisted largely of the spread of mechanization and was more dependent on technical knowledge and breakthroughs, demand-side stimuli alone may not have been as effective in spurring increases in productivity. As technology grew more complex, success at discovering further improvements required more in terms of technical expertise and other resources, and was increasingly out of the reach of the ordinary man or firm. The distribution across counties of individuals with technical backgrounds, of firms specializing in the production of capital goods embodying technology, and of other supply-side conditions conducive to invention had more and more to do with the geographic pattern of manufacturing productivity, while simple access to broad markets had less. An outstanding example is of course the machine tool industry, which was concentrated in several counties in southern New England

and made technological contributions to a broad range of enterprises through the application of general principles to a variety of specific problems (Rosenberg 1963). Coincidentally or not, the counties in which the industry clustered had been among the early leaders in patenting. Such bunching of industries or resources directed at inventive activity may partially account for why firms in counties that had achieved high patenting rates by 1820 had higher levels of manufacturing productivity in 1850 and 1860.

The notion that, as the principal sources of productivity growth changed, the relative importance of demand- and supply-side factors in accounting for technical change did so as well fits with the observation that southern New England and a few other geographic pockets (mostly urban centers like New York City) continued to lead in both patenting and manufacturing productivity from at least 1820 to 1860. Given that the expansion of the transportation grid had extended low-cost access to broad markets throughout most of the Northeast by 1860, it would be difficult to attribute such durable geographic patterns in patenting to demand alone.[19] Moreover, since all areas were realizing substantial productivity growth over time, southern New England's maintenance of leadership in productivity must have been due to an edge in invention and innovation that allowed its firms to stay ahead of those in other subregions while all were making progress. The straightforward inference is that southern New England and these other centers had or developed endowments or supply-side conditions that helped their firms be more inventive, innovative, and productive.

Whether there was something very special about southern New England prior to the onset of industrialization that prepared it for leadership is unclear. What is clear, however, is that with the same areas providing technological leadership throughout the antebellum period, the two phases of technical change are highly unlikely to have proceeded independently of each other. One phase gave way to the next, with southern New England's initial successes serving to build a comparative advantage for what was to come. This advantage undoubtedly flowed from a variety of factors, including a more developed capital market and a local economy and culture geared toward commerce and rapid change, but much of it probably stemmed from the human capital its ranks of entrepreneurs and workers had acquired in pushing out the technological frontiers during the first few decades of industrialization—in response to expanding markets and opportunities. Local blacksmiths and men trained in textile machine shops evolved into specialized toolmakers and machinists. Many more learned of the potential returns to tinkering and to altering the organization of labor. By the late antebellum period, southern New

---

19. Although it might be possible to explain the very high patenting rates in urban centers like New York, Philadelphia, and Boston as attributable to intense competition characteristic of deep markets, the argument would not seem likely to apply to the high-patenting counties in Connecticut and nonmetropolitan Massachusetts. For a discussion of the extension of low-cost transportation throughout the Northeast by 1860, see Meyer et al. (1917) and Taylor (1951).

Englanders were better endowed and positioned to carry manufacturing technology forward into a more technically demanding era.

8.5 Summary and Conclusions

The record of manufacturing productivity during the antebellum period conforms well with the gradualist path of development envisioned by scholars who share the Smithian perspective on early economic growth. Despite a reliance on traditional labor-intensive production methods before midcentury, a broad range of industries in the Northeast was able to realize substantial progress. Indeed, over the entire period from 1820 to 1860, total factor productivity in manufacturing grew nearly as rapidly as after the Civil War and accounted for virtually all of the increase in labor productivity. Only in the 1850s did a second phase of technological development, characterized by mechanization and major increases in the capital intensity of production, spread beyond textiles to the rest of the sector.

The extraordinary expansion of markets that is characteristic of early industrialization appears to have played a fundamental role in the achievement of these gains and in the elevation of such achievements into a self-sustaining process. Their extension not only yielded improvements in productivity through stimulating the realization of economies of specialization and scale, but also induced individuals and firms to raise their commitments of resources to the search for better techniques and products—making possible a long-term acceleration of growth in productivity and in living standards. This latter impact has long been an issue of debate, but the recent analyses of patterns in patenting provide key evidence for its existence and importance. In particular, the procyclicality of patenting as well as the strong cross-sectional relationship between access to broad markets and patenting rates suggests that the expansion of commerce associated with extensions of the transportation network and increases in income may have been a major factor behind the surges in patenting and in manufacturing productivity of the 1820s and 1830s. Although the underlying value of the resources devoted to the search for technical improvements (or of the discoveries made) may not have varied proportionally with patent counts, the quantitative magnitudes of the changes involved are sufficient to allay reasonable doubts about the qualitative relationships. Moreover, the finding that productivity was significantly higher in areas with higher patenting rates suggests that reservations about inferring variation in inventive activity or innovation from such evidence are less than fully warranted in this context (MacLeod 1988; Mokyr 1990).

Even after the relationship between the extent of markets and investment in inventive activity has been established, there is the question of whether such behavior led to more rapid technical change or productivity growth. Surely this would not always be the case as a general proposition. In circumstances where significant progress is circumscribed by technical obstacles, for example, further investment would not yield advances until a breakthrough in knowledge was achieved. In early industrial America, however, it appears from both industry studies and examination of firm-level data that substantial increases in productivity could be and were realized through incremental changes in the organization of production and in the design of tools or output. These are the sorts of technical changes that could well have been realized continuously in response to investments in inventive activity, and with the participation of a broad cross-section of the population in their discovery and implementation. Indeed, the growth of manufacturing productivity (especially in less capital-intensive industries) and of patenting appear to have spread out together from urban districts after 1820, along with the extension of transportation networks and extensive involvement in inventive activity by individuals with rather ordinary skills and backgrounds. The record of productivity growth is, therefore, quite consistent with the hypothesis that during the initial phase of industrialization "demand-induced" investments in inventive activity yielded technological advances across a wide range of industries.

The newest and perhaps most intriguing evidence presented in this paper is the regressions demonstrating the relationship between firm productivity and local patenting rates. Because the expansion of markets during the first stage of industrialization was a powerful stimulus to patenting, the regressions support the view that this era was one of "demand-induced" technical change in manufacturing. They also indicate the importance of "supply-side" factors, however, and suggest that the latter had become more influential by the 1850s when a "second stage" of progress associated with capital-intensive technologies spread across the sector. The significance of these unidentified "supply-side" factors is revealed in the sustained leadership by the same various southern New England counties and urban centers in patenting and productivity throughout the period from 1820 to 1860. This continuity in leadership is a sign that the series of incremental improvements in production methods associated with Smithian growth did not simply exhaust themselves in a one-time increase in productivity, but rather prepared the ground for the next phase of technically more complex advances. Whether they did so by cumulatively altering the factor endowment in ways conducive to technological change or whether some other forms of local externalities in inventive activity were operating is yet unclear and remains for future research to determine.

References

Atack, Jeremy. 1976. Estimation of Economies of Scale in Nineteenth Century United States Manufac...   the Form of the Production Function. Ph.D. diss., Indiana University, Blo...

————. 1977. Returns to Scale in Antebellum United States Manufacturing. *Explorations in Economic History* 14: 337–59.

————. 1985. Industrial Structure and the Emergence of the Modern Industrial Corporation. *Explorations in Economic History* 22: 29–52.

————. 1987. Economies of Scale and Efficiency Gains in the Rise of the Factory in America, 1820–1900. In *Quantity and Quiddity: Essays in U.S. Economic History,* ed. Peter Kilby. Middletown, CT: Wesleyan University Press.

Atack, Jeremy, and Fred Bateman. 1992. How Long Was the Workday in 1880? *Journal of Economic History* 52: 129–60.

Bateman, Fred, and Thomas Weiss. 1981. *A Deplorable Scarcity: The Failure of Industrialization in the Slave Economy.* Chapel Hill: University of North Carolina Press.

Brady, Dorothy S. 1964. Relative Prices in the Nineteenth Century. *Journal of Economic History* 24: 145–203.

————. 1966. Price Deflators for Final Product Estimates. In *Output, Employment, and Productivity in the United States after 1800,* ed. Dorothy S. Brady. NBER Studies in Income and Wealth, 30. New York: Columbia University Press.

————. 1972. Consumption and the Style of Life. In *American Economic Growth,* ed. Lance E. Davis et al. New York: Harper and Row.

Chandler, Alfred D., Jr. 1977. *The Visible Hand: The Managerial Revolution in American Business.* Cambridge: Harvard University Press.

Cochran, Thomas C., and William Miller. 1961. *The Age of Enterprise: A Social History of Industrial America.* New York: Harper.

Cole, Arthur H. 1926. *The American Wool Manufacture.* 2 vols. Cambridge: Harvard University Press.

Crafts, N. F. R. 1985. *British Economic Growth during the Industrial Revolution.* Oxford: Clarendon Press.

David, Paul A. 1967. The Growth of Real Product in the United States before 1840: New Evidence, Controlled Conjectures. *Journal of Economic History* 27: 151–97.

Davis, Pearce. 1949. *The Development of the American Glass Industry.* Cambridge: Harvard University Press.

Dawley, Alan. 1976. *Class and Community: The Industrial Revolution in Lynn.* Cambridge: Harvard University Press.

Depew, Chauncey M. 1895. *One Hundred Years of American Commerce.* New York: D. O. Haynes.

Doerflinger, Thomas G. 1986. *A Vigorous Spirit of Enterprise: Merchants and Economic Development in Revolutionary Philadelphia.* Williamsburg: University of North Carolina Press.

Faler, Paul G. 1981. *Mechanics and Manufacturers in the Early Industrial Revolution: Lynn, Massachusetts, 1780–1860.* Albany: State University of New York Press.

Fishbein, Meyer H. 1973. *The Censuses of Manufactures, 1810–1890.* Reference Information Paper no. 50. Washington, DC: National Archives and Record Service.

Gallman, Robert E. 1971. The Statistical Approach: Fundamental Concepts as Applied to History. In *Approaches to American Economic History,* ed. George Rogers Taylor and Lucius F. Ellsworth. Charlottesville, VA: Eleutherian Mills–Hagley Foundation.

————. 1975. The Agricultural Sector and the Pace of Economic Growth: U.S. Experience in the Nineteenth Century. In *Essays in Nineteenth Century Economic History,* ed. David C. Klingaman and Richard K. Vedder. Athens: Ohio University Press.

Gilmore, William J. 1989. *Reading Becomes a Necessity of Life: Material and Cultural Life in Rural New England, 1780–1835.* Knoxville: University of Tennessee Press.

Goldin, Claudia, and Kenneth Sokoloff. 1982. Women, Children, and Industrialization in the Early Republic: Evidence from the Manufacturing Censuses. *Journal of Economic History* 42: 741–74.

Goodrich, Carter. 1960. *Government Promotion of American Canals and Railroads, 1800–1890*. New York: Columbia University Press.

Goodrich, Carter, Julius Rubin, Jerome Cranmer, and Harvey Segal. 1961. *Canals and American Economic Development*. New York: Columbia University Press.

Gordon, Robert J. 1990. *The Measurement of Durable Goods Prices*. Chicago: University of Chicago Press.

Greene, Jack P. 1988. *Pursuits of Happiness*. Chapel Hill: University of North Carolina Press.

Griliches, Zvi. 1990. Patent Statistics as Economic Indicators: A Survey. *Journal of Economic Literature* 28: 1661–1707.

Habakkuk, H. J. 1962. *American and British Technology in the Nineteenth Century: The Search for Labour-Saving Inventions*. Cambridge: Cambridge University Press.

Hazard, Blanche E. 1921. *The Organization of the Boot and Shoe Industry in Massachusetts before 1875*. Cambridge: Harvard University Press.

Hirsch, Susan E. 1978. *Roots of the American Working Class: The Industrialization of Crafts in Newark, 1800–1860*. Philadelphia: University of Pennsylvania Press.

Hounshell, David A. 1984. *From the American System to Mass Production, 1800–1932*. Baltimore: Johns Hopkins University Press.

Kendrick, John W. 1961. *Productivity Trends in the United States*. Princeton: Princeton University Press.

Kuznets, Simon. 1952. Current National Income Estimates for the Period prior to 1870. In *Income and Wealth of the United States: Trends and Structures*, ed. Simon Kuznets. Cambridge: Bowes and Bowes.

Landes, David S. 1969. *The Unbound Prometheus*. Cambridge: Cambridge University Press.

Larkin, Jack. 1988. *The Reshaping of Everyday Life, 1790–1840*. New York: Harper and Row.

Lazonick, William, and Thomas Brush. 1985. The "Horndal Effect" in Early U.S. Manufacturing. *Explorations in Economic History* 22: 53–96.

Lindstrom, Diane. 1978. *Economic Development in the Philadelphia Region, 1800–1850*. New York: Columbia University Press.

Machlup, Fritz. 1958. *An Economic Review of the Patent System*. Study of the Committee on the Judiciary, United States Senate. Washington, DC: Government Printing Office.

MacLeod, Christine. 1988. *Inventing the Industrial Revolution: The English Patent System, 1660–1800*. Cambridge: Cambridge University Press.

Marglin, Stephen A. 1974. What Do Bosses Do? The Origins and Function of Hierarchy in Capitalist Production. *Review of Radical Political Economics* 6: 33–60.

Martin, Robert F. 1939. *National Income in the United States, 1790–1938*. New York: National Industrial Conference Board.

Meyer, Balthasar, Caroline E. MacGill, et al. 1917. *History of Transportation in the United States before 1860*. Washington, DC: Carnegie Institution.

Mokyr, Joel. 1977. Demand vs. Supply in the Industrial Revolution. *Explorations in Economic History* 37: 981–1008.

———. 1990. *The Lever of Riches*. Oxford: Oxford University Press.

Paskoff, Paul F. 1983. *Industrial Evolution: Organization, Structure, and Growth of the Pennsylvania Iron Industry, 1750–1860*. Baltimore: Johns Hopkins University Press.

Rosenberg, Nathan. 1963. Technological Change in the Machine Tool Industry, 1840–1910. *Journal of Economic History* 23: 414–43.

————. 1972. Factors Affecting the Diffusion of Technology. *Explorations in Economic History* 10: 3–34.

Rostow, Walt W. 1960. *The Stages of Economic Growth*. Cambridge: Cambridge University Press.

Schmookler, Jacob. 1966. *Invention and Economic Growth*. Cambridge: Harvard University Press.

Smith, Adam. [1776] 1976. *An Inquiry into the Nature and Causes of the Wealth of Nations*. Chicago: University of Chicago Press.

Smith, David C. 1971. *History of Papermaking in the United States, 1691–1969*. New York: Lockwood.

Smith, Merritt Roe. 1977. *Harpers Ferry Armory and the New Technology: The Challenge of Change*. Ithaca, NY: Cornell University Press.

Sokoloff, Kenneth L. 1982. *Industrialization and the Growth of the Manufacturing Sector in the Northeast, 1820–1850*. Ph.D. diss., Harvard University, Cambridge.

————. 1984a. Investment in Fixed and Working Capital during Early Industrialization: Evidence from U.S. Manufacturing Firms. *Journal of Economic History* 44: 545–56.

————. 1984b. Was the Transition from the Artisanal Shop to the Non-mechanized Factory Associated with Gains in Efficiency? Evidence from the U.S. Manufacturing Censuses of 1820 and 1850. *Explorations in Economic History* 21: 351–82.

————. 1986. Productivity Growth in Manufacturing during Early Industrialization: Evidence from the American Northeast, 1820–1860. In *Long-Term Factors in American Economic Growth*, ed. Stanley L. Engerman and Robert E. Gallman. NBER Studies in Income and Wealth, 51. Chicago: University of Chicago Press.

————. 1988. Inventive Activity in Early Industrial America: Evidence from Patent Records, 1790–1846. *Journal of Economic History* 48: 813–50.

Sokoloff, Kenneth L., and David Dollar. 1992. Agricultural Seasonality and the Organization of Manufacturing during Early Industrialization: The Contrast between Britain and the United States. NBER Historical Factors in Long-Run Growth Working Paper, no. 30. Cambridge, MA: National Bureau of Economic Research.

Sokoloff, Kenneth L., and B. Zorina Khan. 1990. The Democratization of Invention during Early Industrialization: Evidence from the United States, 1790–1846. *Journal of Economic History* 50: 363–78.

Sokoloff, Kenneth L., and Georgia C. Villaflor. 1992. The Market for Manufacturing Workers during Early Industrialization: The American Northeast, 1820 to 1860. In *Strategic Factors in Nineteenth Century American Economic History: Essays in Honor of Robert W. Fogel*, ed. Claudia Goldin and Hugh Rockoff. Chicago: University of Chicago Press.

Spivak, Burton. 1979. *Jefferson's English Crisis, 1803–1809: Commerce, Embargo, and the Republican Revolution*. Charlottesville: University of Virginia Press.

Sullivan, Richard J. 1990. The Revolution of Ideas: Widespread Patenting and Invention during the English Industrial Revolution. *Journal of Economic History* 50: 349–62.

Taylor, George Rogers. 1951. *The Transportation Revolution, 1815–1860*. New York: Rinehart.

————. 1964. American Economic Growth before 1840: An Exploratory Essay. *Journal of Economic History* 24: 427–44.

Tchakerian, Viken. 1990. Structure and Performance of Southern and Midwestern Manufacturing, 1850–1860: Evidence from the Manuscript Censuses. Ph.D. diss., University of California, Los Angeles.

Thomson, Ross. 1989. *The Path to Mechanized Shoe Production in the United States*. Chapel Hill: University of North Carolina Press.

Thorp, Willard L. 1926. *Business Annals*. New York: National Bureau of Economic Research.
Tryon, Rolla Milton. [1917] 1966. *Household Manufactures in the United States, 1640–1860*. New York: Augustus M. Kelley.
U.S. Bureau of the Census. 1975. *Historical Statistics of the United States, Colonial Times to 1970*. Washington, DC: Government Printing Office.
U.S. Patent Office. 1891. *Annual Report of the Commissioner of Patents*. Washington, DC: Government Printing Office.
Walsh, Margaret. 1982. *The Rise of the Midwestern Meat Packing Industry*. Lexington: University of Kentucky Press.
Ware, Caroline F. 1931. *The New England Cotton Manufacture: A Study in Industrial Beginnings*. New York: Russell and Russell.
Ware, Norman. [1924] 1959. *The Industrial Worker, 1840–1860*. Gloucester, MA: Peter Smith.
Wilentz, Sean. 1984. *Chants Democratic: New York City and the Rise of the American Working Class*. New York: Oxford University Press.
Wrigley, E. A. 1988. *Continuity, Chance, and Change*. Cambridge: Cambridge University Press.

Comment   Jeremy Atack

Kenneth Sokoloff has been extraordinarily creative in his use of quantitative data pertaining to America's early industrialization. In this paper he attempts to tie together two separate threads of that work. One half, represented by his work on pre-Civil War productivity growth in manufacturing, is developed to its fullest in volume 51 of the NBER Studies in Income and Wealth (Sokoloff 1986). Those estimates are based upon firm-level sample data collected by Sokoloff from the federal census of manufacturing for 1820 (National Archives 1964) and from the 1832 McLane Report, and by Fred Bateman and Thomas Weiss from the 1850 and 1860 censuses of manufacturing.[1] They show that manufacturing in the northeastern United States experienced rapid growth in total factor productivity of 1.3–1.5 percent per year in many industries, with somewhat slower rates at the start of the period and faster rates during the last decade (Sokoloff 1986, 718). This pace of productivity growth compares favorably with estimates for later periods by Kendrick (1961) and Gallman (1986, esp. 189–91 and table 4.6). The second half of the theme—the contribution and impact of mechanical inventions—is represented by his more recent work on patenting activity between 1790 and 1846 (Sokoloff 1988; Sokoloff and Khan 1990). The source for these is a sample being developed by Sokoloff from Ellsworth's (1840) and Burke's (1847) patent indexes giving information about the type of patented invention, the name and loca-

Jeremy Atack is professor of economics at the University of Illinois at Urbana-Champaign and a research associate of the National Bureau of Economic Research. This comment is on the paper as delivered at the conference.

1. For a discussion of the Bateman-Weiss samples for 1850 and 1860, see Bateman and Weiss (1981) or Atack (1985).

tion of the patentee, and the date. These data show a marked relationship between patenting activity and market access as proxied by improvements in transportation and urban concentration.

The marriage between these two important topics, however, is troubled in a number of respects arising both from the very nature of the data and the kind of inferences being drawn as well as from the methodology by which those inferences are made. The eminently reasonable premise underlying the study is that the level of total factor productivity at specific benchmark dates—1820, 1832, 1850, and 1860—is a function of organizational and mechanical improvements made by firms. The role of organizational improvements, represented primarily by the switch from artisanal shop to mill and factory, has been well documented by both of us and is captured in Sokoloff's estimates by the labor force size dummies and use of steam and water power in the regressions (Sokoloff 1984; also Atack 1986). However, beyond a few well-documented cases such as those textile firms whose records are in the Baker Library, we know very little about the technology employed by individual firms other than their use of inanimate power.[2] Nor do we know much about the average level of technology in most industries at any moment of time. Consequently, Sokoloff attempts to proxy the use of new mechanical improvements by the stock of recent patenting activity around each benchmark date.

Unfortunately, as Sokoloff readily acknowledges, the granting of a patent is neither identical to, nor coincident with, the innovation of an economically significant improvement by potential users. Quite when a patent is granted during the interval between invention and innovation is unclear. However, since the purpose of a patent is to assign and secure the property rights in an invention to the inventor, a request for patent protection should follow hard on the heels of the invention itself in order to maximize that protection. Innovation of a proven and truly useful invention is then diffused over an indeterminate number of years as conditions change, complementarities appear, and the invention is improved and perfected. Even so we know virtually nothing about the various time lags in the process, such as between invention and patent application, between patent application and its granting, or between successful patent application and widespread adoption. The Patent Office (and its predecessor's) records *may* contain information on the lag between patent application and its disposition, but we expect that this interval was relatively short, if only because of the terms of the patent legislation. The original patent act of 1790 provided that patents on "any useful art, manufacture, engine, machine or device or any improvement thereon not before known or used" were to be granted after review by a committee of three cabinet members who were empowered to grant a patent "if they shall deem the invention or discov-

---

2. Both the 1820 census and the 1832 McLane Report (and Sokoloff's samples therefrom) contain some references to the use of specific machines, but, presumably, these were insufficient in number or so inadequate in description as to defy classification and categorization.

ery sufficiently useful or important." The flood of claims, however, became so great that the act was soon amended to provide that after 1793 patents could be granted upon the swearing of an oath by the applicant that the invention was original and did not infringe existing patents, the payment of an application fee, and the presentation of drawings and a working model. One might thus argue that the date at which patent protection was granted was within a year or so of invention.

Unfortunately, this is not too useful a case to make. The impact of an invention depends upon its productivity advantage over existing technologies and the endogenous rate of adoption and the proportion of potential users who have adopted at a moment of time. The lag between invention and innovation can be short. Or it can be long. In the well-known table put together by Enos (1962, 307–8), the interval between invention and innovation for thirty-five inventions ranges from a year in the case of Freon refrigerants to seventy-nine years for the fluorescent lamp and averaged about fourteen years. Perhaps a fairer comparison, though, for this purpose is the interval between invention and innovation of industrial machines, such as the steam engine or spinning machine, or industrial processes, such as shell molding or the hydrogenation of fats. Here, the interval is much shorter, ranging from three to eleven years and averaging less than six years (Enos 1962, 307–8).

Whether fourteen years or six, though, these lags are troublesome for Sokoloff's formulation of the model if it is accepted that the date of the patent is within a year or so of the date of invention. The reason is simple: Sokoloff models 1820 total factor productivity, for example, as a function of the patent rate between 1812 and 1822 in the county in which the firm was located after adjusting for population density, proximity to transportation and communications routes, firm size and organization, and industry. Yet, by my argument, patents granted after about 1816 would not have been adopted in time for the 1820 census, and it seems most unlikely that patents after 1819 should have had *any* effect. Despite this, however, the regression coefficients on the logarithm of the county patenting rate between 1812 and 1822 are generally statistically significant and of the "right" sign (that is, positive) in his estimates of the relationship using the 1820 census data. For much the same kind of equation but using data from the McLane Report for 1832, however, the results are not nearly so good. Here, Sokoloff models total factor productivity in 1832 as a function of the patent rate between 1830 and 1836, although by my argument we would expect these to have virtually no impact. The results appear to bear this out. Only one of the four coefficients is statistically significant at the 90 percent level. The others are not statistically significantly different from zero, and one has the "wrong" sign, which implies that total factor productivity declined with increased local patenting activity.

The underlying model for the 1850 and 1860 estimates is somewhat different, and the question of lags becomes mute. In these, Sokoloff models total factor productivity as responsive to past historic high rates of local patenting activity in the 1820s or during the 1830s and early to mid-1840s. The argument is that productivity was higher where inventive activity was endemic and pervasive at an early date. The results generally support this hypothesis, particularly with respect to high and sustained patenting activity by the 1820s. Continued use of the navigable-waterway variable as a proxy for contact with the larger economy, however, is questionable in the age of the steam locomotive. By 1850, the northeastern states had over 5,600 miles of railroad track, compared with less than 2,250 miles of canals (Taylor 1951, 79). Even adding navigable rivers and lakes to the total fails to alter the inescapable conclusion that the railroad had become the principal avenue of commercial intercourse within the region.

There are, however, even more fundamental and philosophical questions raised by Sokoloff's use of patent data as a proxy for technological innovation. First, implicit in the use of these data is the assumption that all useful inventions received patent protection and that all patented devices were useful. Yet there is ample evidence that neither was, nor is, the case. Only those inventions patented before 1793 and after 1836 were required to prove novelty and usefulness. The vagueness of the patenting process following the 1793 revision and the growing problem of overlapping patent claims led to protracted court cases and the denial of patent protection to many deserving inventions. A case in point is Oliver Evans's patent on the high-pressure steam engine— an invention of the first order of importance—which was eventually disallowed after innumerable and lengthy battles with the government and those who Evans felt infringed upon his patent.[3] Similarly, the principles of Evans's automated grist-milling process were to find widespread application in other industries but were not protected by the terms of the patent.[4] Second, even where usefulness and novelty were amply demonstrated and a secure patent obtained, innovation was less than certain. For example, it took years for millers to adopt Evans's automated grist-milling process, especially farther west, where he eventually offered his machinery free to any miller willing to serve as his agent in an effort to stimulate sales (Evans 1816). Third, not all patents were of equal economic significance, but they are counted as such in Sokoloff's models. Fourth, much productivity growth doubtless originated through mechanisms such as learning-by-doing that were not patentable and are only very imperfectly captured by the dummy variables for firms with "medium" and "large" labor forces that serve as proxies for the opportunities for mechanization and the division of labor.

Given these kinds of considerations, I do not find it too surprising that pat-

---

3. See, for example, Evans's spirited defense in Evans (1805).
4. Evans (1795), which was continually republished and updated in new editions as late as 1860.

enting appears to have only a very small and marginal impact upon total factor productivity. Indeed, the only surprise is that this slender relationship appears to hold under a variety of different specifications.

There is, however, one specification that I wish had been shown—and one that is certainly more in keeping with the theme of this conference on living standards. I would have preferred that Sokoloff look at the impact of patenting (much of which was in labor-saving technologies) upon labor productivity rather than upon total factor productivity. Given the wage-productivity nexus, this would have provided a much more direct route to at least one important determinant of living standards. The counterargument is that the benefits of total factor productivity ultimately accrue to society as a whole and to individual members depending upon their ownership of specific assets and factors. More pragmatically, however, the decision probably reflects Sokoloff's ill-ease with anomalies in these estimates reported in Sokoloff (1986, esp. 683–97).

I also perceive some other problems with Sokoloff's regression estimates. One is the question of reverse causation; that is to say, poor total factor productivity leads to a search for mechanical improvements, some of which are patentable. More important, though, the dependent variable in each of Sokoloff's regressions, total factor productivity, is unobserved. Instead, Sokoloff estimates it from a hypothetical composite Cobb-Douglas production function. There is, of course, a considerable literature debating the existence, meaning, and interpretation of aggregate production functions (e.g., Fisher 1969), but rather than enter into that debate, let me focus upon more immediate concerns here.

As Abramowitz (1956) has made clear, total factor productivity is the residual output unexplained by the factor inputs. Based upon regression estimates, however, it represents much more; namely it becomes the repository for whatever least-squares errors there are from sources such as misspecification or errors in variables. Misspecification, for example, may arise from the estimation of a single production function across all industries, the imposition of Euler's theorem, or the assumption of unit elasticity of substitution between labor and capital and homotheticity implicit in the Cobb-Douglas form. Of these, I think the first is the most troubling. The substitution of labor productivity estimates that are directly observable would have resolved these questions, and the resultant estimates must contain less "noise" than the estimates of total factor productivity that are used. It would not, however, resolve the question of errors in variables that creep into the data in many ways. For example, at the 1850 and 1860 censuses, firms were to report the average number of male and female employees per month. Even assuming that these were accurately known, since not all firms employed both, Sokoloff must aggregate these into a bundle of equivalent labor. In addition, it is strongly suspected that many if not most smaller firms, particularly sole proprietorships and partnerships, made no allowance for managerial or entrepreneurial labor.

Thus, Sokoloff estimates the labor input as the male employees, plus one-half of the child and female employees, plus one to account for the possible omission of entrepreneurial labor.

My point is not to criticize these decisions—they are ones that I have also faced and made—but rather to point out that the dependent variable, total factor productivity, that Sokoloff seeks to explain in these regressions contains a great deal of noise. Sokoloff tries to finesse some of this noise by truncating the data sets to exclude unusually productive or unproductive firms. In 1820, the bottom 21 percent and the top 3 percent were excluded.[5] The proportions for other years are not reported. One inevitably wonders, though, how sensitive the regression results are to these cutoffs.

The bottom line for me is that, while I am convinced that inventive activity is at least partially market-driven, that innovation is a major source of productivity growth, and that total factor productivity growth was the dominant factor behind labor productivity growth, it is not because of the *empirical* results presented here. Rather I am persuaded by the preponderance of qualitative evidence and the tightly woven theoretical arguments that Sokoloff so cogently presents here and elsewhere.

References

Abramowitz, Moses. 1956. Resource and Output Trends in the United States since 1870. *American Economic Review* 46: 5–23.

Atack, Jeremy. 1985. *The Estimation of Economies of Scale in Nineteenth Century United States Manufacturing*. New York: Garland Publishing.

———. Economies of Scale and Efficiency Gains in the Rise of the Factory in America, 1820–1900. In *Quantity and Quiddity: Essays in Honor of Stanley L. Lebergott*, ed. Peter Kilby. Middletown, Conn.: Wesleyan University Press.

Bateman, Fred, and Thomas Weiss. 1981. *A Deplorable Scarcity: The Failure of Industrialization in the Slave Economy*. Chapel Hill: University of North Carolina Press.

Burke, Edmund. 1847. *List of Patents for Inventions and Designs Issued by the United States from 1790 to 1847*. Washington, D.C.: U.S. Patent Office.

Ellsworth, Henry L. 1840. *A Digest of Patents Issued by the United States from 1790 to January 1, 1839*. Washington, D.C.: U.S. Patent Office.

Enos, John. 1962. Invention and Innovation in the Petroleum Refining Industry. In *The Rate and Direction of Inventive Activity*. Princeton: Princeton University Press.

Evans, Oliver. 1795. *The Young Mill-Wright and Miller's Guide*. Philadelphia: author.

———. 1805. *Abortion of the Young Steam Engineer's Guide*. Philadelphia: Fry and Kammerer.

———. 1816. *Oliver Evans to His Counsel, Who Are Engaged in Defence of His Patent Rights*. Philadelphia.

Fisher, Franklin M. 1969. Existence of Aggregate Production Functions. *Econometrica* 37: 533–77.

Gallman, Robert E. 1986. The U.S. Capital Stock in the Nineteenth Century. In *Long-Term Factors in American Economic Growth*, ed. Stanley L. Engerman and Robert

---

5. These figures do not include those observations that were dropped because of missing data.

E. Gallman, 165–213. NBER Studies in Income and Wealth, 51. Chicago: University of Chicago Press.

Kendrick, John W. 1961. *Productivity Trends in the United States.* Princeton: Princeton University Press.

Sokoloff, Kenneth L. 1984. Was the Transition from the Artisanal Shop to the Non-mechanized Factory Associated with Gains in Efficiency? Evidence from the U.S. Manufacturing Censuses of 1820 and 1850. *Explorations in Economic History* 21: 351–82.

———. 1986. Productivity Growth in Manufacturing during Early Industrialization: Evidence from the American Northeast, 1820–1860. In *Long-Term Factors in American Economic Growth,* ed. Stanley L. Engerman and Robert E. Gallman, 679–736. NBER Studies in Income and Wealth, 51. Chicago: University of Chicago Press.

———. 1988. Inventive Activity in Early Industrial America: Evidence from Patent Records, 1790–1846. *Journal of Economic History* 48: 813–50.

Sokoloff, Kenneth L., and B. Zorina Khan. 1990. The Democratization of Invention during Early Industrialization: Evidence from the United States, 1790–1846. *Journal of Economic History* 50: 363–78.

Taylor, George R. 1951. *The Transportation Revolution.* New York: Holt, Rinehart and Winston.

U.S. Congress. House. 1833. Documents Relative to the Manufactures in the United States. 22d Cong., 1st sess., H. Doc. 308.

Contributors

Jeremy Atack
Department of Economics
Box 18
University of Illinois
1407 West Gregory Drive
Urbana, IL 61801

Stanley L. Engerman
Department of Economics
Harkness Hall
University of Rochester
Rochester, NY 14627

Robert E. Gallman
Department of Economics
CB#3305
Gardner Hall 017A
University of North Carolina
Chapel Hill, NC 27599–3305

Claudia Goldin
Department of Economics
Littauer Center 316
Harvard University
Cambridge, MA 02138

Gloria L. Main
Department of History
Campus Box 234
University of Colorado
Boulder, CO 80309–0234

Robert A. Margo
109 Calhoun
Department of Economics
Vanderbilt University
Nashville, TN 37235

Clayne L. Pope
Department of Economics
154 Faculty Office Building
Brigham Young University
Provo, UT 84602

Winifred B. Rothenberg
Department of Economics
Tufts University
Medford, MA 02155

Carole Shammas
Department of History
University of California
Riverside, CA 92521

Kenneth L. Sokoloff
Department of Economics
University of California
405 Hilgard Avenue
Los Angeles, CA 90024–1477

Lee Soltow
Copeland Hall
Ohio University
Athens, OH 45701

Richard H. Steckel
Department of Economics
410 Arps Hall
Ohio State University
1945 North High Street
Columbus, OH 43210–1172

John Joseph Wallis
Department of Economics
3105 Tydings Hall
University of Maryland
College Park, MD 20742

Lorena S. Walsh
Research Department
Colonial Williamsburg Foundation
Post Office Box C
Williamsburg, VA 23187

Thomas Weiss
Department of Economics
Summerfield Hall
University of Kansas
Lawrence, KS 66045

Jeffrey G. Williamson
Department of Economics
Littauer Center 216
Harvard University
Cambridge, MA 02138

Author Index

Abbott, Edith, 176, 177n6, 188
Abel, Marjorie, 61n68
Abramovitz, Moses, 87, 313, 382
Ackerknecht, Erwin H., 14n11, 297
Adams, Donald R., Jr., 106, 108, 173n1, 175, 176n4, 177, 178, 179, 183n11, 185, 191, 239, 244, 340, 342
Adams, Henry, 19, 30
Adams, T. M., 179, 188
Adelman, Irma, 270
Aitchison, J., 136, 140n12, 146t, 151n17, 168n2
Aldrich, Nelson W., 176
Amsterdam, 139t
Anderson, Ralph V., 326
Angel, Lawrence J., 291
Armelagos, George J., 297
Arnow, H. S., 224, 236, 238, 240
Atack, J., 240, 325, 348, 355n5, 358, 362, 378n1, 379
Austen, R. A., 239

Bailyn, Bernard, 140, 141, 143
Baines, M. J., 275
Bairoch, Paul, 193n17
Ball, Duane E., 340
Baron, William R., 335
Barsky, Robert, 196
Bateman, Fred, 43t, 54, 111, 240, 325, 341, 348, 362n12, 378
Baumol, William, 212, 213
Baxter, J., 148, 149t, 151n16
Beales, Ross W., 326n33

Belden, L. C., 235, 250n18
Belluscio, L. J., 237
Benes, P., 236n10
Bennett, M. K., 268
Berg, Alan D., 277
Berry, Thomas S., 179, 180
Bidwell, Percy W., 318n14, 322, 323n23, 339
Bilson, Geoffrey, 14n11
Bishir, Catherine W., 104n11
Blackman, S. A. B., 212, 213
Blackmar, B., 227, 228
Blackmar, Elizabeth, 180, 219
Blodget, Samuel, 25n20, 84, 101, 102, 103, 109
Blumin, S. M., 228
Bode, Carl, 19n1, 36
Boserup, Ester, 219, 341
Bowen, J. V., 220, 240, 243, 244, 246, 251
Boyd, Mark F., 14n11
Brady, Dorothy S., 86, 103–6, 109, 111, 180, 188, 189, 349
Brainerd, Carol, 40t, 41t, 54n53
Bridges, A. E., 243, 248, 250, 251
Brinkman, Henk Jan, 279n14, 282
Brooke, John L., 331n44
Brown, Charlotte V., 104n11
Brown, G. J., 236, 243, 250
Brown, J. A. C., 136, 140n12, 146t, 151n17, 168n2
Brown, M., III, 241, 243
Brush, Thomas, 348, 359
Bryan, L., 234

Subject Index